MERCHANTS, MONEY AND POWER

The Portland Establishment
1843-1913

E. KIMBARK MacCOLL
WITH HARRY H. STEIN

The Georgian Press
1988

Library of Congress Cataloging-in-Publication Data

MacColl, E. Kimbark.
    Merchants, money and power: the Portland establishment,
    1843-1913/E. Kimbark MacColl with Harry H. Stein.
        p. cm.
    Bibliography: p.501
    Includes index.
    ISBN 0-9603408-3-1: $29.95. ISBN 0-9603408-4-X (pbk.): $19.95
        1. Portland (Or.)—Economic conditions. 2. Portland (Or.)—
    Politics and government. 3. Community leadership—Oregon—
    Portland—History. 4. Merchants—Oregon—Portland—History.
    5. Bankers—Oregon—Portland—History. 6. Politicians—Oregon—
    Portland—History. 7. Wealth—Oregon—Portland—History.
    I. Stein, Harry H., 1938-   . II. Title.
    HC108.P87M295 1938   88-24653
    330.9795'49—dc19   CIP

To Leeanne

my enthusiastic and supportive partner,
who has happily endured an exhausting ordeal

CONTENTS

v

LIST OF ILLUSTRATIONS

All photographs are at the Oregon Historical Society and are listed by their negative numbers unless otherwise stated. Page location in book follows.

ACKNOWLEDGMENTS

In the research and writing of this book, and in the selection of the photographs, I have received the indispensable assistance of my associate, Harry H. Stein. He not only helped me develop the theme of the book, but kept me on track as I was tempted by peripheral areas. As chief editor and collaborator, he was a continual source of ideas, suggestions and specific historical knowledge. What started out five years ago as a re-write of *The Shaping of a City* (1976) became a new work, focused on the growth of community power in early Portland. Major attention was paid to individual behavior and actions rather than to urban physical development. Throughout this arduous enterprise. I received the invaluable aid and understanding of my family, especially that of my wife Leeanne.

It would not have been possible to create this work without Arthur L. Throckmorton's seminal *Oregon Argonauts* (1961). Throckmorton's untimely death over 25 years ago removed one of Oregon's most promising economic historians. To Malcolm Clark, Jr., I am deeply indebted for his encouragement, insight and scholarship. His two-volume edited Diary of Judge Matthew P. Deady, *Pharisee Among Philistines* (1975) was crucial to the development of a narrative in which personal relationships played such an important role. Both works were published by the Oregon Historical Society.

Two friends, among may others who helped, especially deserve my sincere thanks. Retired Professor Dorothy O. Johansen, a former Reed College colleague, made available numerous unpublished materials on Simeon G. Reed. And David C. Duniway, the retired State Archivist of Oregon, offered many suggestions on early Oregon history, in which his family played a notable role.

My deep appreciation is also extended to the staffs of the Portland Archives and Record Center, Bush House and the Oregon Historical Society library, manuscripts room and photographic department. Similar assistance from other generous individuals and staff members of other libraries was gratefully recognized in *The Shaping of a City*. I also wish to thank Henry L. Pittock, II, and Susan Wilson Gallagher for releasing significant materials from their family records, and Philip Wiecking of the Great Northwest Bookstore for use of the James Steel Papers.

Finally, I want to acknowledge the skill and dedication of my computer typist, Mary Dozark, my copy editor, Philippa Brunsman, and my book designer, Corinna Campbell, three dedicated professionals.

INTRODUCTION

This book is an account of how wealth was created, managed and used in Portland, Oregon, from its 1843 settlement to the inception of commission government in 1913. It recounts the history of individuals and institutions, of close family, business and political networks, and of the evolution of a Portland Establishment whose power was based largely on its private wealth. It also details the Establishment's impact upon the growth of Portland as a major urban center on the Pacific Coast. Individuals — their lives and political, economic and social transactions — are central to the story.

Some of the questions and approaches were influenced by the historical work of Sam B. Warner, Jr., Samuel P. Hays, Carl V. Harris, Frederic Cople Jaher, David C. Hammack, and Paul G. Merriam. Who constituted the Establishment? How did it rise to prominence and replenish and maintain its preeminence? How did it organize and utilize the institutions of government, the economy and culture to manifest or strengthen its power? What were the ingredients, limits and distribution of that power?[1]

What influences did it exert on local and state politics, and what did it obtain from that process? How did members of the Establishment think and behave as members of a self-conscious elite? What were their relations with one another, individually and as families, and, to a lesser extent, with those not in the elite? These are questons which still preoccupy us today as we try to understand the nature of community power and the connection between political institutions and economic and social forces.

Portland fits into a pattern of urban growth in the nineteenth-century United States wherein the merchant-turned-entrepreneur dominated towns and regions beyond. It was a society devoted to enterprise, one defined largely in terms of money. Oregon's ample resources were exploited by those who arrived early and came afterwards — and by investors and managers elsewhere. As Henry Steele Commager once wrote:

> Here was a vast continent to be settled, limitless resources to be exploited, infinite wealth to be created, and it was private enterprise, not government, that was assigned the gratifying and exhilerating task...The successful businessman was both the model and the hero...A grateful public—and an expectant one—placed the businessman in posts of dignity and honor, and called loudly for all institutions, but particularly the institution of government, to adopt business standards.[2]

It was assumed that private enterprise could do anything better than government, and was therefore to be preferred. Further, it was assumed that nineteenth-century government should be kept to a minimum, except where it could help business perform its beneficent functions. The immense power of business was usually thrown on the side of maintaining the status quo, especially in politics and relations between capital and labor. Society's well-being was judged in terms of business, and increasingly of business growth. On a smaller scale, Portland's experience paralleled that of Boston's from 1870 to 1900, where, as Sam B. Warner, Jr., observed, "individual capitalists" were basic to city life.[3]

In Portland power was exercised predominately by white men who possessed "wealth, social standing and ability." As David C. Hammack has shown elsewhere, such men constituted in time "a patrician class capable of civilizing and absorbing the newly rich and of gaining the deferential support of the masses."[4]

Between 1843 and 1913, the Portland Establishment exhibited great stability and continuity. It withstood challenges to its economic and political control. Its central figures were hard working, shrewd and long-lived, and their leadership long-endured. Through opportune marriages, it built intertwined family networks locally and, to a lesser extent, with elite families elsewhere.

Portland developed a regime of "first families" almost from its beginnings and more than a generation before Seattle. During its first five decades, according to Paul G. Merriam, Portland also developed "a class conscious, stratified society whose leaders sought to copy old rather than create new societal patterns."[5]

By the 1890s, Portland had become a benevolent plutocracy, dominated especially by the intermarried Corbett, Failing, Ladd, and Couch-Lewis families. Together they controlled over 21 corporations, including banks and insurance companies, and partly owned at least 18 others. They also held extensive real-estate investments in what has become downtown Portland and in the nearby suburban countryside.

Long before then, contemporaries acknowledged and generally accepted the Establishment's great political power in Portland and throughout the state. As increasing challenges to its authority arose, the Establishment persisted in holding on to its political and economic power well into the twentieth century. This book attempts to examine the nature of that power and the forces underlying its remarkable durability. Many of the values and traditions of thought and behavior, firmly implanted by 1900, still exert a strong influence on present-day actions.

1

FOUNDATIONS

William S. Ladd Arrives

The Pacific mail steamer *S.S. Columbia*, six days outbound from San Francisco for Portland, eased over the dangerous bar into the Columbia River. In early April, 1851, this was its second voyage in a new coastal trade between California and the Oregon Territory. It bore William Sargent Ladd and 199 other passengers 112 miles to the small village that was the most important trading settlement in the region sprawling from the California border to Canada and from the Pacific Ocean to the Rocky Mountains.

In late afternoon on April 8, the *S.S. Columbia* turned southward from the Columbia into the north-flowing Willamette River. The small sternwheeler fought the current 12 miles upstream to Daniel Lownsdale's primitive dock. Passengers gazed through rain at a half-mile Portland tract hewed out of a dark, massy forest stretching to the river's edge. Giant firs sprinkled with lighter-toned cottonwoods and alders abutted the shoreline.

To the newcomers, the forest seemed neither awesome, beautiful nor threatening. No Indians emerged from it to bar their way anywhere on the west side of the Cascade Mountains hidden to the east. Forests to them meant exploitable resources and free or at least cheap land, roughly accessible for farms and towns. The Oregon Country represented unlimited possibilities for development and personal enhancement. They saw tiny hamlets nestled in the fertile Willamette Valley, between the Coast and Cascade ranges, competing for residents and trade. Settlement was quickened in the early 1850s as Pacific Northwest commerce burgeoned. From 12,000 territorial residents in 1850, the population would grow to 52,000 by 1860, a year after Oregon statehood.[1]

The 24-year-old William S. Ladd, destined to become a major business and political leader in the territory, believed that Oregon afforded him great opportunity. Short on cash but long on ambition, he had quit as a railroad agent in Sanbornton Bridge (later Tilton), New Hampshire, to journey westward. Ladd chose the sea route over the arduous Oregon Trail, first stopping to weigh his chances of success in Gold Rush San Francisco. He planned to wrest a $20,000 fortune from commerce and then return rich and respected to New England. In Portland, he came ashore with a small consignment of liquor, a character reference from his Congregational minister, a hole in his shoe, and cash to survive for two weeks.[2]

1

Why Oregon?

Single men like Ladd from the Northeast or abroad favored settling on the urban, rather than the farming, frontier in the Willamette Valley. Its villages were to be disproportionately peopled with young unmarried men. Of the 821 Portlanders counted in the December, 1850, U.S. Census, three-quarters were native-born, and 102 came from just two states: New York and Massachusetts. About half of the resident population had arrived in 1850; most were younger than 30. They were spurred by developments unleashed by the California Gold Rush, and by impending congressional legislation to grant free land to white settlers of the Oregon Territory. The first issue of the *Weekly Oregonian* on December 4, 1850, boosted Portland's population to 1,500, counting transients and Indians ignored by the census-takers. By 1851, more people lived in Portland than in the territorial capital of Oregon City 12 miles upriver.[3]

Some 40 years earlier, Meriwether Lewis and William Clark had reported the wonders of the Oregon Country. Explorers, trappers and missionaries spread accounts of the vast area. Hall J. Kelley's influential writings in the 1830s urged American colonization of the Oregon Country over settling in the Floridas, New Orleans or Texas. During 1838 and 1839, the returned Methodist missionary the Reverend Jason Lee lectured throughout the East and Middle West, extolling the natural wonders and economic opportunities of Oregon. In 1840, Methodists founded Salem, the future state capital. Narrators rhapsodized over the verdant Willamette Valley, in which Salem, Oregon City and Portland lay, as a "Garden of Eden."[4]

New England merchant-capitalists became interested in the Columbia River in the late 1830s. Crucial to Portland's future were the activities of Cushing & Company of Newburyport, Massachusetts. John N. Cushing had become the "most wealthy and highly respected foreign merchant in China" before his return home in 1833. He followed the path of his uncle, the Bostonian Thomas H. Perkins, who had amassed one of the earliest fortunes in the China trade. An enterprising and shrewd trader, Cushing made one of the first voyages around the Horn to the Sandwich Islands (Hawaii) and the Columbia River. Through his son Caleb, a member of the Massachusetts congressional delegation, Cushing urged the federal government to take possession of the jointly occupied country by establishing a settlement on the Columbia. To help promote the cause, and his own interests as well, Cushing hired 28-year-old Captain John H. Couch of Newburyport to sail the company brig *Maryland* around the Horn, up the Columbia to the Willamette and up the Willamette to The Falls, the Oregon City site in 1840. Couch repeated the voyage twice on the Cushing brig *Chenamus*, built "expressly for the North West coast," before settling in as an Oregon City merchant and filing a 640-acre personal claim adjacent to the Portland townsite.[5]

Cushing's efforts reflected the increasing involvement of New England and New York capital interests in the Pacific maritime frontier once they were assured that its growing market area would mitigate their risks. The Pacific Mail Steamship Company, whose *Columbia* brought Ladd and others to Portland, was controlled by the highly prominent New York merchant-shippers William H. Aspinwall and

William E. Howland. Ships under contract to New York and New England mercantile firms called increasingly at the mouth of the Columbia and ventured up the Columbia and Willamette to Portland. Under sail, the river voyage alone could require two weeks or longer. The introduction of steam power in 1849 and 1850 lessened the entire trip between San Francisco and Portland to a week. Interest grew rapidly in the Oregon Country once it came under the American flag in 1846. Whether by sail, steam or overland passage on the Oregon Trail, increasing numbers of hopeful migrants made their way to the remote land.[6]

Eloquent newspaper accounts by Samuel R. Thurston, first territorial delegate to Congress in 1849, stirred Ladd to consider migrating. Two men's stories set him on the way. From former schoolmate Charles E. Tilton, he learned of tremendous profits made from selling merchandise in Gold Rush San Francisco. Then a storekeeper named Carr returned to Sanbornton Bridge in January, 1851, with $10,000 in profits from reselling $3,500 worth of San Francisco goods in Portland. California's gold and its furious commercial market had wildly inflated Oregon prices. And California, in turn, was desperate for Oregon wheat, flour, fresh produce, and lumber.[7]

Ladd probably joined most pioneer Oregonians of the early 1850s in trusting individual narrations of first-hand experience over those of outsiders, conveyed through books or the press. Tilton's account and Carr's reported profits dazzled him; as a railroad agent he earned less than $400 annually. Born in Holland, Vermont, one of 10 children of a country doctor, Ladd had supported himself since the age of 16, including a stint at school teaching. Attracted by Oregon, he corresponded with Tilton in San Francisco and arranged to secure a consignment of merchandise that might launch him on the road to riches in the new territory. Savings barely paid his ocean fare in February, 1851. He travelled via the Isthmus of Panama to California.[8]

Pioneers arriving in the Willamette Valley during the 1840s and '50s rarely revealed what caused them to emigrate, except through Ladd's sort of hindsight. The patriotic might recall that before 1846 they wanted to increase the tiny American population to help hold the Oregon Country for the United States. Many a white pioneer sought immigration to a place with few blacks, or away, some futilely hoped, from the economic depressions and floods that scoured the Mississippi and Missouri valleys. Pioneers variously associated the Willamette Valley with improving health, and escaping debts or finding the means to pay them.[9]

"I never saw so fine a population as I saw in Oregon most of the time I was there [from 1843 to 1848]." To Peter H. Burnett, first governor of California, the Oregonians

were all honest, because there was nothing to steal; they were all sober, because there was no liquor to drink; there were no misers, because there was no money to hoard; and they were all industrious, because it was work or starve.[10]

Most Oregon settlers were plain, respectable, reasonably well educated white people of moderate circumstances. The typical immigrant seemed far more a home seeker and builder than an explorer, gold seeker or land speculator. Land speculation, however, did consume the attention of countless new residents. Burnett and his partner, Morton M. McCarver, caught land fever soon after their arrival. In 1844, they hopefully laid out Linnton, which Portland incorporated in 1915. Like founders of a dozen towns along the Willamette, they became rabid speculators, but were only marginally successful. "Our town speculation was a small loss to us, the receipts from the sale of lots not being equal to the expenses," Burnett wrote on quitting Linnton after less than a year. Had he chosen to develop the clearing that became Portland seven miles upriver, he might have tarried longer.[11]

The promise of free land lured thousands to the Willamette Valley during the mid-1840s as the region changed from a fur-trading to a farming frontier. Many immigrants were powerfully moved by existing or impending federal policies to award free land to those settling American territory. The prominent Oregon trailblazer Jesse Applegate believed that newcomers mainly sought farm land. Essentially "nomads," they had "no sort of use for towns except to raise hell in them."[12]

Oregon's new residents gratefully named Linn County, Linn City (West Linn) and Linnton for Missouri Senator Lewis F. Linn, the leading congressional sponsor of land bills prior to his death in 1843. Congress, however, enacted no legislation either to provide liberal land grants or to regularize Oregon townsite and farmland transactions until passage of Samuel Thurston's Oregon Donation Land Act in 1850, some six months before Ladd came to Portland.[13]

The San Francisco Hub

William S. Ladd and some 80,000 others arrived in California during the 18 months after the 1848 gold discovery. To a New England villager, a San Francisco "gone wild with the touch of gold" likely came as both a shock and an entrepreneurial attraction. In less than five years, San Francisco had undergone an explosive growth from 200 to nearly 40,000 people. Violent crime was rampant, and around-the-clock brothels, gambling houses and saloons outnumbered other establishments three to one. An observer in 1851 noted that "Everything there bore evidence of newness, and the greater part of the city presented a makeshift and temporary appearance." Four fires had destroyed the city's core since December, 1849.[14]

Immense, if uncertain, windfall profits awaited the survivors, primarily real-estate speculators. Their lots shot up in value from $15 to $40,000 in five years. Commercial establishments were particularly devastated by the fires. Rare was the tradesman who did not suffer damage to either his store or warehouse. Those lucky few who did survive unscathed realized huge profits. Wild economic swings during the early 1850s added to their travails; merchant turnover was high. Only a minority of merchants elected to remain in San Francisco throughout the decade, but those who did achieved substantial gain and translated their new wealth into positions of political and social authority.[15]

When Ladd arrived, San Francisco was becoming the major trading and financial hub of the Pacific Coast. One heavy spoke of the wheel attached to Oregon, where farmers and merchants found the San Francisco market an especially attractive but sometimes risky connection. Eastern Seaboard trading interests and San Francisco merchants showed little concern over how their competition affected Oregon sellers and buyers as the Oregonians strove to maximize their own profits. The various relationships of supply to demand were chronically unstable. In March of 1851, for example, Ladd encountered an overstocked San Francisco market, and realized that its goods could be sold profitably in Oregon. He witnessed what his friend Carr had reported. Although some shipments to Oregon came directly from New York, the bulk of the eastern merchandise was being unloaded in San Francisco and trans-shipped north to Portland.[16]

Why not form a business partnership? Ladd asked Charles Tilton. Using Tilton's funds and ample family resources in the East, they would work the Oregon market from San Francisco. Rather than act as commission merchants, they would sell directly to the growing Oregon market. Refusing to run the risk, Tilton advised Ladd to continue his journey alone, with a small shipment of Tilton's liquor. Ladd, in other words, came to Portland envisioning himself as playing an important role in developing a regular, profitable New York-San Francisco-Portland trade. Having seen the value of liquor in San Francisco, he could solace himself with the notion that an advantageous sale of Tilton's consignment would help him launch his career on the Willamette.[17]

"Gold," Ladd preferred to remember, "that can be picked up from the ground, cannot continue to be of much value, while good farming land is a sure basis of progress and prosperity." He cherished values similar to those of his celebrated New Hampshire neighbor, Daniel Webster, who believed that "Farmers . . . are the founders of human civilization." Ladd felt that the products and needs of a fertile Willamette Valley would provide a solid basis for true commercial riches. In fact, gold discoveries proved the valley's major economic stimulus.[18]

Willamette Land Speculation

Town speculators still guided Portland's destiny when Ladd came west. Although the city had been incorporated by the provisional legislature on January 23, 1851, elective city government had yet to convene. Its earliest promoters had sought modest profits from selling undeveloped town blocks and lots to newcomers. Their successors entertained grander expectations, including various commercial and transportation schemes, designed to enhance townsite economic growth. Land was the key commodity, to be made quickly saleable. In time-honored American fashion, the founders had located an empty space — in the Indian-free Willamette Valley, claimed and mapped it and staked out streets, blocks and lots. Erecting cabins and lean-tos in the clearing, this newest American community declared itself open for business as another outpost in the nation's fast-growing market economy.

Land speculators, real-estate promoters and other profit-minded newcomers did everything possible to manipulate the Portland market of the 1840s and early 1850s. They conducted themselves within land-speculation traditions hoary since colonial times: either preempt and hold unclaimed land without cost or acquire it cheaply; develop small portions of the holdings and attract buyers who might also purchase adjacent undeveloped property; and, for towns, quickly convert empty land into some sort of urban use for profitable ends. Rarely would town builders consider how their plans and machinations might transcend personal gain for long-term community benefit. In Portland, as elsewhere, town founders could be charged with many things, but seldom with being naive or simon-pure souls. As Lewis Mumford has aptly concluded, the American city

> from the beginning of the nineteenth century on, was treated not as a public institution, but a private commercial venture to be carved up in any fashion that might increase the turnover and further the rise in land values.[19]

Portland had originated as a rest stop for traders and Indians at a clearing on the west bank of the Willamette between Oregon City and the Hudson Bay Company's Fort Vancouver on the Columbia. Asa Lovejoy, a 35-year-old Massachusetts-born lawyer, recognized the townsite worth of The Clearing after a lanky Tennessee drifter, William Overton, pointed it out in mid-November of 1843. Returning to Oregon City from Fort Vancouver, Lovejoy had offered the sick Overton a ride in his big canoe. Approaching The Clearing, Overton grew sicker and suggested they go ashore. Lovejoy could then examine "the best claim . . . around here." As Lovejoy later recalled, "It took my eye. I had no idea of laying out a town there, but when I saw this, I said: 'Very well, sir, I will take it.'"[20]

The two divided ownership of 640 acres, Lovejoy paying a 25 cent fee to record the one-square-mile claim with the provisional government established by American settlers the previous May. In July, 1843, the legislature had allowed any head of a white family to claim 640 free acres and record the claim. Title to the Oregon Country was itself unsettled, and so too for years were most Oregon land and townsite transactions, claims, sales, resales, and the like. Legality of claims and town-lot titles was never assured during Portland's first decade, and many titles remained clouded until the 1870s.

The settlers designed and grasped slim provisional laws to secure, hold and transfer claims, and portions of claims, before Oregon became a territory and Congress enacted the Donation Land Law. They realized that provisional legislation and titles might be rejected, modified or supplanted by Congress, federal land officials, courts, or a territorial legislature. But they hoped for — and many fully expected — congressional confirmation of first-claimants' rights to have and hold 640-acre tracts free, subject to a claimant survey and issuance of a federal patent. Town-lot holders who had purchased from the claimants expected the latter to make good *their* titles once federal land patents were issued. So Oregon settlers filed and jumped claims, made promises and agreements, registered and reregistered deeds while hopefully awaiting their future gains, if not bonanzas.

In 1847, Simpson S. White, a member of the provisional legislature, accurately predicted some of the trouble ahead. Newcomers would "find the same disposition for speculation in land claims that you may have found in some of the new territory of the Mississippi Valley." Beware of fraudulent agents for allegedly absent claim owners, he cautioned publicly. Beware also of those selling lots in all the major Oregon townsites. Certificates, deeds and acknowledgments were not being issued to lot buyers, nor any public record kept of the lot transactions, as required by provisional law. Selling, abandoning and altering unrecognized land claims were common practices.[21]

After Portland became part of a federal territory in 1848, its block, lot and claim filings still remained presumptive transactions. The Oregon Donation Land Act of September 27, 1850, eventually led to the issuance of 7,437 patents covering about 2.5 million acres of Oregon land. One section of the law distressed those who had concluded property transactions before its enactment: it voided any sales by the original claimants *before* the federal land office had issued them patents. Hundreds of lawsuits were filed in subsequent years, most of them decided in favor of the original claimants on largely commonsensical and practical grounds. Such anomalies became "a fruitful source of Litigation," according to attorney David Logan, a future mayor of Portland. Some of the disputes had more serious consequences. As Logan noted in January, 1851: "There have been some fine cases of homicide in the last eight months originating from disputes about Land claims [in the territory]."[22]

One of the more interesting consequences of the law resulted from its recognition — unusual for the time — of women, permitting them to hold their claims in their own right. As Dorothy Johansen has noted: "This did not assure their independence but it did assure any woman of barely marriageable age a husband," even though only a small number of women would have qualified. The great majority of women traversing the overland trail were already married. Until 1849, women accounted for only 15 to 20 percent of these travelers.[23]

Land-claim disputes lay in the dim future when Overton and Lovejoy, staking their claim, made tomahawk slashes on trees in the clearing. Overton built a shingle mill in a lean-to on the south part of the claim; his shingles were transported for sale in Oregon City. Chronically ill and repeatedly washed out by floods, he soon decided to forsake the valley for the warmer Southwest, where he would disappear. He sold his half-interest to Francis W. Pettygrove, a 32-year-old Oregon City merchant and business partner of Asa Lovejoy. Overton received $50 in trade goods but had to pay Lovejoy about $60 for improvements the latter had helped make on their joint property.[24]

Founding of Portland

Maine-born Francis Pettygrove was rapidly becoming the Oregon Country's leading entrepreneur between 1843 and 1845. Backed by the New York firm of Alfred Benson & Company, Pettygrove established well-provisioned stores both on his new Portland property and in Oregon City in partnership with George Abernethy. (Abernethy became Oregon's first elected provisional governor in 1845.) Pettygrove also acquired a granary and boat landing at Champoeg, where the provisional government was organized in May, 1843. Neither Pettygrove nor Lovejoy likely understood the potential worth of their claim, as future actions revealed. The site did need a name, however, so in 1844 they tossed a coin. Pettygrove's choice of Portland, after the principal seaport of his native Maine, won over Lovejoy's Boston.[25]

Together, they proved insufficiently ambitious or assertive to exploit Portland more than minimally. As business associates, they continued to live in Oregon City, where Lovejoy enjoyed a thriving law practice. The two men might not even have platted part of their site except for the strong encouragement of Captain John H. Couch, a Pettygrove competitor in Oregon City. Lovejoy had attended a meeting in Pettygrove's store with Couch and several other merchants. John Minto remembered that they considered "the question of the best point on the lower Willamette for [oceanic] shipping to lie." They decided that the deepest water for ample anchorage and turning space was downriver, "opposite the Overton claim." Three voyages since 1840 had convinced Couch of its superiority to Oregon City's site, located too close to a falls and subject to shifting river depths.[26]

When Couch and his Newburyport associates found in 1845 that they could no longer compete profitably against the Hudson Bay Company's dominance of the Hawaiian trade, Cushing & Company withdrew the *Chenamus* and abandoned the Oregon market. Couch elected to remain in Oregon City and file claim on 640 acres immediately north of the Lovejoy-Pettygrove tract. With no immediate intention of clearing his land, Couch bided his time and minded his store, awaiting the day when the local river commerce would expand into a thriving national and international trade. Experience and historical knowledge convinced him that cities inevitably grew in such areas as the Willamette Valley. As Earl Pomeroy has noted, Pacific Coast cities like Portland developed because "distance required them and geography invited them" and because settlers wanted and needed their services.[27]

During the winter of 1845, Lovejoy and Pettygrove began to clear the center of their forested tract near the present foot of Washington Street. With funds earned selling wheat in Honolulu, Pettygrove hired carpenter John Waymire to build a double log cabin to serve as store and warehouse. Mosquitoes and fleas almost drove Waymire from his labor. The two proprietors then hired itinerant surveyor Thomas A. Brown to survey and plat the uninviting site. Stakes outlined streets, blocks and lots both in The Clearing and among the trees. Brown also surveyed 11 1/2 miles of roadway to connect the townsite to the agriculturally promising Tualatin Plains. Portland was now open for business.[28]

Their plan called for the rectangular grid and lot system widely adopted in nineteenth-century America. A gridiron was "easy to survey and simple to understand," observed John Reps. It offered "all settlers apparently equal locations for homes and businesses within its standardized structure." The gridiron also proved the cheapest way to prepare land for market.[29]

Portland's earliest, precedent-setting grid comprised sixteen 200-foot square blocks, each with eight lots 50 feet wide by 100 feet deep. No space was reserved for alleys. North-south streets were 80 feet wide; cross streets, 60. The grid dimensions were the scantiest of all major Pacific Coast cities surveyed and platted by the late 1840s; on average most streets were 20 feet wider than Portland's. Block and street dimensions adequate to a largely forested 1845 village would impose severe restrictions after the gridiron was duplicated and extended. As one pundit later declared, the early proprietors "pinched the city up along streets too narrow for anything but camel traffic."[30]

Although the arrangement of eight narrow lots on small blocks created more valuable corner lots within each platted section, squeezing out higher land-sale profits was not necessarily the proprietors' primary motive. The time and cost of clearing dense fir stands, employing timber-fallers from Oregon City, more likely determined a design of short, narrow streets. Lovejoy and Pettygrove were probably no greedier than their contemporaries among California town speculators. They laid out a small village with enough lots to yield profits subsequent developers would have considered unduly meager. Even when Pettygrove's ambitions swelled after acquiring a new co-proprietor later in 1845, he continued to devote himself far more to commerce than to real-estate speculation.

Late in 1845, Asa Lovejoy decided his future lay in Oregon City rather than in the unprepossessing townsite. For $1,215 on November 1, 1845, he sold to Benjamin Stark his half-interest in the claim plus half-interest in a cattle herd jointly owned with Pettygrove. The cattle were worth thrice the value of the land. Lovejoy maintained a business association with Pettygrove in Oregon City; he became its mayor in 1845 and later held numerous territorial offices. For more than a decade, he absented himself from the convoluted twists and turns of Portland land deals. On rare occasions, Lovejoy's legal talents were needed in Portland, as during a futile intercession to protect Stark's properties.[31]

Benjamin Stark, a 23-year-old New Orleans native sailing out of New London and New York, acted as supercargo on Captain Nathaniel Crosby's *Toulon*. He was thus the agent in charge of a cargo of goods shipped by Benson & Company to Pettygrove's new warehouse in Portland. Like other young eastern merchants and countinghouse clerks, Stark legitimately used a supercargo arrangement with a respected firm to profit from the sale of goods upon arrival in port. His share of the Portland gains was invested in the Lovejoy property in 1845 as pure speculation. He expressed no intention of remaining in Portland to develop a townsite. To Stark, seaborne commerce afforded short-term profits superior to what Portland might offer.[32]

The immediate result of Stark's association with Pettygrove was a trading partnership that involved Captain Crosby and the *Toulon*. With Stark as supercargo, Crosby engineered a profitable triangular trade in lumber, wheat, salt-fish, and general merchandise between San Francisco, Honolulu and Portland. Part of the goods arriving in Portland was destined for Pettygrove's warehouse, which, as a retail store, was "the first business operation at Portland." Pettygrove shipped the remainder to his Oregon City store, in direct competition with Captain Couch's emporium. Deprived of Cushing's *Chenamus*, Couch found himself without regular transport at low rates. Refusing to pay ruinously high charges to shippers like Crosby, he finally quit and returned to Newburyport in 1847.[33]

Prolonged absences made Stark rely on the wily Pettygrove, who was playing the dominant role in Portland's early development. Pettygrove moved home and business headquarters into his log store at the foot of Washington Street, where he also constructed Portland's first wharf. In short order he built Portland's first frame house; Captain Crosby's Cape Cod-style cottage and others soon followed. During Stark's periodic visits to Portland aboard the *Toulon*, he joined Pettygrove in organizing several additional business ventures. They realized that if Portland was to flourish, it had to become commercially prosperous. Their business ties blossomed into close friendship. On September 30, 1846, the first male white child born in Portland was named Benjamin Stark Pettygrove.[34]

Among their earliest development projects was the construction of a primitive wagon road along the east side of the river to Oregon City. They carved an even less passable wagon track through the West Hills to the Tualatin Valley, following the line of Brown's survey. Access to the abundant regional produce was essential for Portland to become a major trading center. To exploit fully their cattle investment, Pettygrove built a slaughterhouse on the south river bank near present-day Lincoln Street and sold hides to tanner Daniel Lownsdale, who had filed claim just west of the townsite at about the time Stark first landed in Portland. He opened the first tannery on the Pacific Coast.[35]

Like other Portland proprietors throughout the 1840s — and like most of its merchants then and afterwards — Pettygrove and Stark equated personal and town prosperity. As fiercely competitive merchant-traders, they advanced both themselves and Portland especially at the expense of rival towns. Following long-customary practices, they manipulated and controlled markets, buying cheap and selling dear. They added a second ship, the *Mariposa*, expressly to monopolize trade between Hawaii and Oregon. By refusing to import goods for competitors, except at exorbitant rates, they damaged rival merchants like Couch in Oregon City. Additionally, they raised the price of imported salt in an effort to gain control of the salmon trade. Pettygrove also cornered the local salt market through his Portland store, ruining the Hudson's Bay Company competition. These hard-bitten gentlemen would cripple anyone threatening their profits.[36]

The key to Pettygrove's profits, and to the triangle trade generally, was the strong California demand for Oregon lumber. As the *Oregon Spectator* observed, the lumber shipments at least showed that "'there is something to ship from Oregon.'" The lumber trade did not result from any plan or foresight but from necessity. In Thomas Cox's words: "Doing business in the Northwest virtually necessitated dealing in lumber, . . . exporting it was both feasible and profitable." By late 1849, when the effects of the California Gold Rush fully affected Portland, several local fortunes were reaped from Oregon lumber[37]

Impact of the Gold Rush

During the autumn of 1847, approximately 3,000 pioneers crossed the plains to the Oregon Territory, spurred by the conclusion of the Oregon boundary treaty with Great Britain. Most settled in the Willamette Valley, many first passing through Portland. The town's population began to threaten Oregon City's supremacy. While Pettygrove thrived during the onrush, his seafaring partner Benjamin Stark grew restless, anxious to return to his home in New London. John Couch in Oregon City likewise entertained a desire to return home after a three-year absence from his family. Although he had suffered at the hands of such monopoly-seeking competitors as Crosby and Stark, Couch joined them on the *Toulon* for the long voyage back to New England by way of Manila.

Like opposing lawyers in a bitter trial, the frontier merchants were fierce competitors and almost merciless in their dealings. But, once the battle was over, they usually buried their business differences in good fellowship. Within two years, Stark and Couch even became business partners and intimate friends, closely bound by the ties of Freemasonry. Subsequent events revealed that Stark and Pettygrove probably had fallen out with one another and this prompted the hasty Stark departure. Pettygrove remained behind and assumed full authority as sole proprietor. Among 100 or so hardy residents, he languished through the severe winter of 1847 and wet spring of 1848 before news of the Gold Rush reached Portland by ship on July 31, 1848.[38]

The discovery of gold in the California Sierras profoundly affected Oregon. The lure of quick money proved infinitely tempting and almost emptied the Willamette Valley of able-bodied men. Even Captain Newell, who bore the startling report, turned a fast mercantile dollar. Before making a public announcement, Newell nearly cleaned out the local supply of shovels, picks, milk pans and other provisions vital to gold-fevered California, filling his small schooner to the gunwales.[39]

Within a month, at about the time Congress granted Oregon territorial status, Pettygrove himself grew restless. He envisioned greater financial gains in California and only continuing family illness if he remained in Portland. As a merchant, he had done well over the previous three years. Because of his near-monopolistic hold on the market, he had outperformed his competitors to become "the principal commercial man in the country," according to one observer. During an upturn in California trade in 1847, he had sold produce and lumber in San Francisco at more than double his cost. Years later, Pettygrove bragged that he obtained "a large majority of the trade of the upper country" during his stay in Oregon. As a resident proprietor, he simply possessed power and financial leverage unavailable to other merchants. By the autumn of 1848, he was one of the wealthiest residents of the territory, perhaps second only to the pre-eminent Dr. John McLoughlin, who had retired to Oregon City in 1845 from his post at Fort Vancouver. Merchandising and commerce provided most of Pettygrove's fortune; property holdings and real-estate transactions, the remainder.[40]

Pettygrove foresaw little immediate growth ahead for local trade and townsite. That fall, business ground almost to a halt, and a "general lethargy," said future Mayor S. J. McCormick, hung "like a mist over every enterprise that required labor for its completion." By year's end, few men — one account listed only three — remained in Portland; women and children ran the stores and commission houses.[41]

Pettygrove began liquidating assets on September 22, 1848. Largely ignoring Stark's interest, he sold the entire 640-acre Portland townsite claim to tanner Daniel Lownsdale for $5,000 worth of leather. He excluded 64 lots already sold and reserved one double-block section for himself and another for Stark. Pettygrove probably shipped the leather to San Francisco for resale at immense profit. In the spring of 1849, he disposed of his remaining properties and departed with his family for California. During the previous six years, he had multiplied the sale of $15,000 worth of consigned goods into $75,000 of capital. In today's values, his fortune approached $2 million, excluding downtown properties. Alone, he turned a neat 10,000 percent profit from selling the 640-acre claim.[42]

Proprietors Wheel and Deal

Portland's original founders were now superseded. Daniel Lownsdale had control of Portland's destiny — or believed he had. Although Lownsdale and his future proprietary partners never became wealthy from their Portland investments, they provided the initiative, imagination, perseverance and energy, tempered by avarice, to launch their embryonic city toward becoming a prosperous commercial center.

Rampant land promotion and speculation, through the buying and selling of lots in which the proprietors — past, present and future — were deeply entangled, generated two decades of litigation over property titles. What the proprietors did to whom in the few years before Ladd arrived deserves detailed examination. A variety of legal and ethical issues emerged from these dealings, which strongly influenced Portland's early commercial development and the formation of its first elite. The proprietors, like many of the merchants who followed them, were primarily entrepreneurs. They were anxious to make as much money as quickly as possible by any means short of armed robbery. As with Pettygrove and Stark, the newer proprietors equated their own prosperity with that of Portland.

The discovery of gold in California was the catalyst for Portland's success. It sealed the fate of such Willamette towns as Oregon City and Linnton, and the newer Milwaukie and St. Helens, both founded in 1847. Because of a superior location, with deep water and ample docking space, within a year Portland became the Oregon center for the California trade. Everything that went in and out of the city paid its share of tribute. From an average of five vessels a month during the first half of 1849, over twenty at one time were sighted toward the end of the year.[43]

Lownsdale appeared admirably qualified to seize on these developments. An educated, well-travelled Kentuckian of means, the 42-year-old widower with three children had been operating a prosperous tannery for three years. He had paid the highest wages in the area, $10 a day; customers came from throughout the Northwest. Sale of the tannery and his Donation claim to former Ohioan Amos N. King strengthened Lownsdale's ability to develop the adjacent Portland site and his other businesses.[44]

Lownsdale quickly resurveyed the town, adding over 100 new blocks and 19 partial ones. He then sold lots without regard to shared property rights that he and seller Pettygrove undoubtedly knew the absent Stark retained. Lownsdale and the two proprietary partners he subsequently acquired behaved as if Stark had abandoned the claim, and with it any portion of net profits. If caught, Lownsdale and Pettygrove would be claim jumpers.[45]

Lownsdale amply knew that Stark had abandoned nothing. The signed instrument of sale and purchase with Pettygrove, on September 22, 1848, excluded from the transaction a two-block section called "Benjamin Stark's block." Yet, the proprietors' title actually filed in Oregon City described them as alone owning all

640 acres. Stark outsmarted them, however. In late 1845, he had quietly filed his claim to 320 acres in the Recorder's Office at Oregon City. As he later testified, "I never gave up my interest."[46]

Lownsdale subdivided the valuable waterfront area, left open by his predecessors, for future commercial development. Lovejoy later testified that he and Pettygrove had earlier agreed to reserve the levee for general public use, providing ship captains, farmers and shippers a landing without paying docking or wharfage fees to Lownsdale or anyone else. Pettygrove swore to the contrary about the levee in an 1870 court deposition. Of course, no town government existed in 1848 to which any owner might convey property for public use. And it was the slippery Pettygrove, not the former proprietor Lovejoy, who made the sale to Lownsdale in 1848.[47]

Stark later swore that fellow proprietor Pettygrove planned in 1845 to amend the original Brown survey map, to include a two-section (four-block) reserve as their interchangeable property. In Stark's absence, Pettygrove instead amended the map to keep a two-block northern section for Stark and an adjacent southern two-block section, on which his store rested, for himself. Lownsdale's 1848 resurvey subsequently eliminated even this two-block Stark reserve, probably because Pettygrove had already sold lots from it. Stark's valuable portion included much of the land containing Portland's earliest homes and businesses.[48]

Significantly, Lownsdale left a triangular spot blank on his 1848 survey map. It ran west from what became Fourth Street and north from the future Stark Street to Couch's boundary. Lownsdale probably hoped that Stark would not return to press his rightful interest. If he did, an unplotted and undesignated portion of the townsite was reserved for him as insurance. In the meantime, Lownsdale felt he could not afford to wait for Stark's possible reappearance. Pressure to sell lots and the need for operating funds overcame what few principles Lownsdale may have had. But if the improbable occurred, Lownsdale correctly assumed that he could negotiate a financial settlement with Stark.[49]

Lownsdale also would have known, given Portland's size, that Stark could not have abandoned his claim without anyone realizing it. So important a secret could never have been kept in Portland in 1848. "This was a small village. I think each one knew pretty much everyone else's business," future co-proprietor Stephen Coffin later testified. Coffin was intimate with devious local land deals, some of which personally involved him. The Maine-born contractor-promoter had arrived in the area during 1847 and had done business with both Pettygrove and Lownsdale. On March 30, 1849, the 42-year-old Coffin paid Lownsdale $6,000 for half-interest — he and Lownsdale publicly insisted — in the undivided 640-acre Portland claim. Lownsdale reaped a mere 240 percent profit in this transaction minus his already considerable investment in townsite development.[50]

Lownsdale's worst fears were realized by Captain John Couch's unexpected arrival during the summer of 1849, bearing Stark's commission to act as his Portland agent. His surprise return to Oregon was prompted by news of the gold discovery's reaching him in Massachusetts the previous summer. He had written Stark, recently returned to Connecticut, to secure a ship for immediate passage to San Francisco. Stark made all the arrangements, including the purchase of a cargo of lumber and other vital goods. Using his half of the Portland townsite claim as his major equity, he had just entered into partnership with Sherman Brothers of New York for the purpose of shipping merchandise to California. They expected to capitalize on the gold boom. Handling Couch's valuable cargo would be the first of Stark's profitable ventures as commission merchant-shipper in the New York-California trade. Departing from the East Coast in January, 1849, Couch and his brother-in-law, Captain George H. Flanders, headed under full sail via Cape Horn for San Francisco. They arrived in early June and promptly sold their entire cargo at exorbitant profit.[51]

Other men — Orville C. Pratt for one — responded to the lure of windfall profits in the California boom market. The first associate justice of the Oregon territorial court, but paid only $2,000 per year, Pratt felt justified in supplementing income with trade. It was a not uncommon practice for officeholders. One account relates that he met Francis Pettygrove just before the merchant's departure from Portland in the spring of 1849. Boarding Pettygrove's ship, Pratt offered to buy his California-bound lumber for $20 per thousand board feet, an immediate 100 percent profit for Pettygrove. The merchant thought him crazy but readily accepted payment. Accompanying the shipment to San Francisco, Pratt rejected the first offer of $250 per thousand and sold it for $400. Pratt, characterized by Malcolm Clark as "slippery as a greased eel," estimated making some $40,000 on the venture. It was one of several similar deals that generated, Pratt proudly noted, "an ample fortune."[52]

Benjamin Stark and Captain Couch

Stark had preceded Couch and Flanders to California and established two subsidiary commission firms: Stark & Company of San Francisco and Couch & Company of Portland. Couch already had decided to enlarge his interests in and near Portland rather than resettle in Oregon City. Operating out of Portland, Couch and Flanders planned to direct the marine-shipping component of the expanding Stark empire. Together with the Shermans and Stark, they offered wholesale, retail, shipping, credit and banking services stretching from New York to San Francisco and Portland.[53]

Had Sherman Brothers not suddenly gone bankrupt, the Stark-Couch partnership would have been the largest enterprise of its type in Oregon. Stark barely salvaged title to his Portland claim from the Sherman collapse. His property's potential value became desperately important if he was to seize his share of riches from the unexpected events in California and the burgeoning Oregon trade. Stark's efforts to protect his Portland assets were so obsessive that he became, in Malcolm Clark's judgment, "as indefatigable a pursuer of the dollar as might be found west of the Mississippi."[54]

To this end, Captain Couch had been negotiating futilely in Portland during most of August, 1849, until Stark joined him from San Francisco. Stark asserted his rights and claimed his rewards from a Portland thronging with new settlers and rich ex-miners. The complexities of the title and claim situation became all too clear to him. Lownsdale argued that Coffin, through a trust agreement, had legal control of the tract. As Coffin apparently was absent, the frustrated Stark empowered Couch to attempt a settlement. Before returning to San Francisco, Stark additionally retained James W. Nesmith and Asa Lovejoy to begin legal action if Couch was unsuccessful "concerning my undivided half" of the claim.[55]

By chance or design, the elusive Coffin had left for San Francisco just before Stark's arrival in Portland. "He procured a suite of rooms in the best hotel . . . and remained there for several weeks," according to pioneer Milwaukie resident Samuel L. Campbell, who had dealt in person with Coffin. Closely observing all Oregon-bound ships and their sailing dates, Coffin visited with the captains after ingratiating himself by the offer of a "good cigar" or a "refreshing drink" at a bar. According to Campbell, Coffin glowingly boosted the virtues of the Portland townsite. He told the captains: "If you will speak a good word to your passengers on the way up . . . [to Portland], we will donate you a lot.'" He had unsuccessfully offered similar incentives to Campbell and others, to entice them to move their homes and businesses from Milwaukie to Portland.[56]

Coffin's prolonged absence delayed resolution of Stark's claim. In mid-December, 1849, Stark's interests were further complicated by Lownsdale and Coffin's recruitment of a third partner, William W. Chapman, a 41-year-old Virginia attorney and ex-Iowa Territory legislator. Chapman agreed to purchase a third undivided interest in the claim, minus identified lots already sold. He would pay the astronomic price of $26,666 — with $3,300 down and the remainder in three quarterly installments — and perform free legal service for the partnership. The entire claim was to be listed in Lownsdale's name under a new trust agreement. None of the documents mentioned Ben Stark. Chapman's assumption that he had bought an equal third share of the Portland townsite proved painfully in error four months later. Meanwhile, Lownsdale and Coffin pumped their handsome profit back into their Townsite Promotion Company and into other ventures that were draining out cash faster than it came in. Chapman's acquisition was the sixth major proprietorial deal since Overton and Lovejoy had sighted The Clearing six years earlier.[57]

Captain Couch had begun developing his claim in the autumn of 1849. He started work on the first covered wharf and erected an adjacent warehouse to store ship-borne goods. His enthusiasm, advice and facilities attracted the other seafarers who would help make Portland the dominant territorial transportation center for both cargoes and passengers.

As aspiring Portland shipping and mercantile leaders watched a larger-than-ever farming population disperse through the Willamette Valley, they treated it as their hinterland — as belonging to their port village, not some other riverfront rival. With local sawmills and flour mills operating at capacity, and new ones planned, even larger market expansion seemed timely. Captain Couch's dispatch of the brig *Emma Preston* to China in early 1850 symbolized this development. The first trading vessel to sail between Portland and Hong Kong carried locally produced lumber, wheat and flour.[58]

The Willamette Valley was prospering in the early 1850s when William S. Ladd landed. Wages kept pace with price increases. Laborers earned between $2 and

$5 a day, but those with gold often refused to work. Some ex-miners had as much as $40,000 in gold dust or nuggets to serve their ambitions and desires. Portland did what it could to slake both thirsts. By 1853, the village would grow again to, and then surpass, its pre-Gold Rush population, a trend that Ladd had not only hoped for but predicted when he chose to do business in Portland.

In this booming, buying market, Stark's probable legal challenge threatened to block future land sales needed by the three partners. In January, 1850, Lownsdale travelled to San Francisco to negotiate with Stark. He left Chapman in charge with power of attorney, an action he later regretted. Just why it required nearly three months for Stark and Lownsdale to settle their respective claims was never revealed. During that critical period, Chapman and Coffin managed to conclude several lot sales that were to engender much of the future litigation. Chapman assigned crucial waterfront block number 81 to himself and immediately sold all its lots. A problem soon arose when the proprietors discovered that block 81 was in Stark's divided claim, through his new agreement with Lownsdale.[59]

The Lownsdale-Stark agreement of March 1, 1850, ordained the first lasting physical division of the one-square-mile Portland claim. Stark took 48 acres north of a line that became Stark Street. Largely undeveloped, except for a strip along Front and First streets, it contained some of Portland's most valuable commercial and residential properties. It likely was worth at least as much as the remaining acres Lownsdale, Coffin and Chapman jointly owned south of the line. Unhappily for Chapman, the townsite division shrank his supposed one-third interest by about 10 percent. Stark received $3,000 for previously sold lots in his newly divided claim. Proceeds of sales on his property by others after March 1 were also to be paid Stark. The deal represented an impressive return for an ex-supercargo who had done little to enhance the value of a speculative land investment originally costing him about $390. Ironically, he could have thanked the devious Lownsdale, Coffin and Chapman for taking repeated advantage of his absence during Portland's first urban boom.[60]

When Lownsdale returned to Portland in mid-April, Chapman and Coffin refused to ratify the terms. Only Couch's negotiating skills persuaded them to accept the settlement. It contained one key proviso: block 81, previously sold by Chapman, was excluded from Stark's divided interest. Not until December, 1860, when the federal land patents were issued under the Donation Land Act of 1850, was it revealed that the wily Stark had included block 81 in his land-grant claim filed immediately after the passage of the Donation Act and only six months after his agreement with Lownsdale. This and similar unethical transactions prompted years of litigation. The most complex and lengthy series of cases, discussed later, involved Stark and the brothers L. M. and A. M. Starr, prominent merchants and future politicians and bankers. In good faith, they had bought portions of block 81 from Chapman during the winter of 1850 while Lownsdale was negotiating with Stark in San Francisco. Stark's efforts to evict the Starrs led to the litigation.[61]

The proprietorship agreement of April 1850 restored limited harmony among the townsite developers — a condition that lasted for nearly two years. Benjamin Stark was now one of Portland's richest property holders. During the summer of 1850, he "was the only man in Portland . . . who polished his boots and wore a beaver hat." So attired, he "darted carefully about on logs and brush in order to escape the mud and water" in a swampy area while he and Couch settled on the boundary between their claims. That year, the dapper Stark was admitted to legal practice in Oregon, an attainment that likely helped him hold and expand his property during subsequent litigation.[62]

Couch, too, was busy. Before developing his property back from the river, he surveyed and partially platted his claim. Half of it he sold to brother-in-law George H. Flanders for $28,000. He placed his grid on an angle with the Portland plat, squaring it with a bend in the river. "With a clumsiness that seems almost willful," John Reps has observed, "Couch platted his streets without any regard for proper connections to those already in existence." When Portland incorporated in January, 1851, the city boundary drew in 154 acres of Couch's Addition, considerably inflating its value. Portland's boundaries remained virtually unchanged for 30 years.[63]

Couch's plat preserved a strip of five narrow blocks for public parks. The idea for this unique feature originated with Daniel Lownsdale, who had incorporated a similar provision in his 1848 survey. Along the thickly forested western edge of the townsite, Lownsdale preserved a strip of 11 narrow blocks for public use. For Lownsdale, this action represented an unusual degree of vision and generosity at a time when he could afford to be generous. Benjamin Stark inexplicably refused to convey his two narrow blocks, which would have connected the Lownsdale and Couch strips, later known as the Park Blocks. The tightfisted Stark may have felt ill-rewarded by his share of the real estate. A more likely reason for his refusal may have been financial exigency despite his reputed wealth. From the day that he took possession of his truncated claim, Stark borrowed heavily from friends to finance various commercial and realty ventures; he soon became overextended.[64]

The New Merchants

William S. Ladd had arrived in Portland three months after the town's incorporation, when its immediate destiny lay in the hands of the five largest property owners: Lownsdale, Coffin, Chapman, Couch, and Stark. While a local judge described Portland as "a small and beautiful village," the proprietors more likely presided, in Terence O'Donnell's words, over "a raw, disheveled place, gangling and awkward in the spurt of its first growth." The *Weekly Oregonian* boasted of its "most home-like aspect." The arriving Ladd would have seen a half-mile-long tract "literally hewed out of the forest." Some 120 one-story, roughly constructed, box-like buildings, many painted white, straggled from the river front inland about 500 feet amid several older log structures.[65]

Ashore on April 8, 1851, Ladd would have seen ship masts bobbing over Couch's covered wharf, the largest and highest-charging on the river. Other vessels tied up at the smaller dock by the foot of Washington Street or anchored offshore. A largely vacant riverbank and levee, despoiled by storage of supplies and trash, was posted with No Trespassing signs. The proprietor, Lownsdale, had excluded public access to the levee and was being sued over his private use of it.

In the cool, damp spring, a dark haze of smoke from wood-burning stoves rose above Portland. Mud and dust were ubiquitous. Unevenly sawed stumps challenged passage along the few main streets as well as on the potholed cart tracks optimistically called side streets. A "stranger would have to look very close to find" the side streets running back from the river, one visitor wrote in 1852. Bear and cougar awaited venturers into what became Sixth Street.[66]

Upon disembarking, Ladd had repaired to one of the nearby Front Street saloons for refreshment and the latest news. Colburn Barrell, its bartender-owner, furnished him a free drink and a new pair of shoes. Barrell later remembered liking him immediately. A 26-year-old ex-shipwright from Boston, Barrell became one of Ladd's first and best wholesale liquor customers. The next day, Ladd rented space in a small store at 42 Front Street and immediately dispatched a confident order to Tilton for more liquor.[67]

He opened for business in a river port bustling with activity. With the economy no longer fueled by the lust for gold, land hunger and town building were now its motivating forces. The proprietors were busily clearing fir trees from lots platted on the future Second and Third streets. Over 6,000 feet a day of lumber was being noisily ground out at the Abrams and Reed Mill, the first steam sawmill on the West Coast. At the foot of present-day Jefferson Street, the mill was in full production; its whistle pierced all the way to Fort Vancouver. Another steam sawmill and a steam-powered flour mill opened later in the year.[68]

Ladd soon interested himself not only in these happenings but also in the village's few cultural and social opportunities. The latter revolved for respectable folk about the Methodist Church, an embryonic Congregational Church, the private Portland Academy and Female Seminary, and a Masonic lodge in which Benjamin Stark, Daniel Lownsdale and John Couch figured prominently. Ladd probably sensed "an incipient urban spirit at work," to use Paul G. Merriam's words, or at least welcomed urban progress. Cooperative action had established a newspaper, public meeting hall and city government. A privately financed plank road was being planned to traverse the West Hills to the Tualatin Plains.[69]

Ladd would have quickly noticed the six to eight saloons and retail liquor outlets, one saloon having just received its first billiard table. As one pundit later commented, by mid-1851 the "forces of Satan" were fully committed to "the titanic struggle for the Soul of Portland." Participants in this endless contest included "enterprising" Indian maidens who sold the settlers and seamen "professional services" — Portland's first experience with organized vice. Indian families, some of whose women married settlers, inhabited wigwams on the edge of the village. They lived on "beggary," one observer wrote, and overindulged in the local spirits, "blue ruin." Within a few years, their encampments would disappear from an expanding Portland built on commerce, competition and white supremacy.[70]

To rival towns in the early 1850s, Portland was the derided "Stumptown." The friendly ex-steamer Captain John C. Ainsworth remembered "more stumps than houses." A contemporary recalled, "The settlers squatted hard and struggled mightily" in Portland "against the environment of the fir trees." The victor was uncertain at the time of Ladd's arrival. Stumps from fallen firs lay scattered dangerously about Front and First streets. Property owners only begrudgingly dug them out. To lessen night-time collisions, they were thoughtfully whitewashed.[71]

Some preferred calling the village "Mudtown." Ladd came to a Portland drying out after a second winter of heavy snow. Humans and animals, carts and wagons slogged through a sludge of mud and water. The few crude wooden sidewalks sagged under heavy use. Nails and boards tore at women's long skirts. Sidewalks often disappeared during spring floods that plagued downtown Portland for over 50 years. Census enumerator Daniel O'Neil had warned in 1850 that locating Portland on a floodplain was historically inappropriate. Its appeal "should be only to ship captains, not city builders." But residents ignored or denigrated such critical advice. Yield an inch or slacken town building efforts now, self-chosen leaders reasoned, and Oregon City or some newer upstart might regain supremacy over trade and commerce, immigrant interest and real-estate values.[72]

The village, far quieter than San Francisco, still had a certain colorful bustle, particularly along Front Street. Ship and river-boat crews, drunk or sober, mixed with townsfolk, farmers and transients. Ex-miners, disgruntled or rich from the California diggings, swaggered along Front Street. Most villagers lived in the six boarding houses and in homes scattered along First and Second streets, as well as on side streets. Those of the newly arrived who were short of funds had a choice of several crude cabins for temporary lodging or hoisted tents on the outskirts. The more fortunate crossed the townsite for the California House, one of five hotels recently opened. It rested atop Andrew Skidmore's store adjacent to Couch's Addition on First. Skidmore's New York-trained cook, Peter Loudine, received $150 a month — high even in the settled states. A night's lodging there cost $2.50, about a laborer's daily wage in 1851. Prices for everything were inflated that year; businesses were charging what the traffic would bear.[73]

Portland counted 30-odd retail establishments, mainly general stores, when Ladd began selling liquor. Most were one- or two-person operations. Henry W. Corbett, who arrived a month before Ladd, awaited a stock of dry goods, millinery, groceries, drugs, medicine, and powder shot for his store at Front and Oak streets. Pillow and Drew sold watches and clocks; Thomas Pritchard, coffee, spices, candies, baskets, and dried apples. Vaughn's was a hardware store, and Terwilliger's a blacksmithery. Zachariah C. Norton offered brandy, whiskey and wine. Baker and Clark, appropriately, baked for the village, Davis dispensed drugs, and the Starr brothers manufactured stoves and tinware. Occupying a lonely spot on the south waterfront, the town's sole butcher-slaughterhouse retailed meat products and sold hides to Amos King's tannery high on the hill.[74]

Ladd's initial expectations proved premature, as early trade was disappointing. "Things looked pretty blue," he later recalled. In the last two weeks of April, he grossed only $41.40, barely covering expenses. When a city supervisor tried to collect the property tax, Ladd was hard pressed for the money. One of the first ordinance enacted by city council had been a road-improvement levy, considered an important step on the path to civilization. If Ladd could not pay the $6, he could in traditional American fashion dig up and remove two stumps in front of his shop. After he became rich and powerful, he allowed that the two or three nights and mornings of hard work brought the easiest $6 he ever earned. Only the naive would have believed him.[75]

By early May, Ladd's fortunes had markedly improved. He executed a major sale of gin to Colburn Barrell. California House proprietor Skidmore and Captain Ainsworth of the steamer *Lot Whitcomb* became important customers. Innovative and a limited risk-taker, Ladd toured valley farms to add eggs, chickens and other produce to his liquor stock. He made a quick, chance killing of $250 as a commission merchant selling the consignment of supercargo W. D. Gookin, who had known both Tilton and Ladd's father in New Hampshire. Onto his shelves went shaving soap, tobacco, paper, farm tools, blasting powder, and other items. When revenues exceeded $1,000 in August, 1851, William Ladd smelled success after only five months in Portland.[76]

The young, ambitious trader decided to strike out on his own, without any backing from Tilton, although the San Francisco commission merchant remained his major supplier of liquor, Ladd's most profitable merchandise. Locally, he bought from a variety of wholesale firms, including Henry W. Corbett & Company; Allen & Lewis, run by Cicero H. Lewis; and J. Failing & Company, comprising 44-year-old Josiah Failing, oldest and most experienced of the new merchant group, and his young sons Henry and John Failing. Sailing from New York City, Corbett, Lewis and the Failing family had all arrived during the spring of 1851, Corbett in March, and the Failings and Lewis on the same steamer in June. They brought with them or had shipped ahead huge allotments of goods provided by New York commission houses for which they served as resident Portland agents or partners. They all rented or built shops along Front Street, some of them living in or atop their stores.[77]

Within 10 years, this group of dedicated Front Street merchants and their families would dominate the economic, political and social life of Portland. All became warm and lasting friends with Ladd, the former teacher and railroad agent, first among equals. Close-knit, they trusted and respected one another as business people without losing their sharp competitiveness. With Benjamin Stark and John H. Couch, who became Lewis's father-in-law, they formed Portland's earliest Establishment, one of merchant-entrepreneurs. It had dynastic overtones.

A

GENERAL CIRCULAR

TO ALL

PERSONS OF GOOD CHARACTER,

WHO WISH TO EMIGRATE

TO THE

OREGON TERRITORY,

EMBRACING SOME ACCOUNT OF THE CHARACTER AND
ADVANTAGES OF THE COUNTRY; THE RIGHT
AND THE MEANS AND OPERATIONS BY
WHICH IT IS TO BE SETTLED;—

AND

ALL NECESSARY DIRECTIONS FOR BECOMING

AN EMIGRANT.

Hall J. Kelley, General Agent.

BY ORDER OF THE AMERICAN SOCIETY FOR ENCOURAGING

the SETTLEMENT of the OREGON TERRITORY.

INSTITUTED IN BOSTON, A.D. 1829.

CHARLESTOWN:
PRINTED BY WILLIAM W. WHEILDON.
R. P. & C. WILLIAMS—BOSTON.
1831.

1.1 Hall Kelley 1831 Oregon Emigrant Guide title page

1.3 Asa L. Lovejoy (1808-1882)

1.2 Capt. John H. Couch (1811-1870) and Caroline Flanders Couch (1833-1917)

1.5 Benjamin Stark (1822-1898) in the 1860s

1.4 Stephen Coffin (1807-1882) as a general, 1863-1866

1.6 An elderly Francis Pettygrove (1812-1887)

1.7 Francis Pettygrove's store in 1844-1845 probably was the first cabin inside the
original town boundaries (now S.W. Front and Washington)

1.8 Front Street, 1852 south from Alder Street, with Benjamin Stark (top hat) and Brig "Henry" at riverbank

1.10 Daniel H. Lownsdale (1803-1862)

1.9 An elderly William W. Chapman (1808-1892)

2

FRONT STREET TAKES POWER: THE 1850S

Sojourners

"We came out on a sort of adventure, not knowing whether we would stay or not," Henry Failing remembered. Josiah Failing and his sons Henry and John intended in 1851 to stay a few years — maybe fewer, should circumstances dictate. They would make their fortune and leave Portland, "a cool looking sort of place," Henry mused.[1]

Many of the 60-odd merchants along Front Street came as sojourners during the early 1850s. A mobile lot, numbers of them departed within five years, some returning to settle permanently in Portland. These aspiring frontier traders had reasons for caution. Most lacked the important eastern backing the Failings and a few others enjoyed. With smaller stocks than the Failings' three-year supply, little or no credit and unreliable sources and shipping arrangements, they were in a weaker position to withstand the swings of the economy during this era and the great perils facing merchants in the Far West. Engaging in trade was a highly risky business throughout mid- and late-nineteenth-century America. Ladd had only his small consignment of liquor and a hope that Tilton would refill the order before receiving any payment.

New Yorkers Lucius Allen and Alfred De Witt, preceding Ladd and the Failings by a year, operated a general store for "a miserable month" in Portland, then abandoned it. Allen and his boyhood friend, Cicero H. Lewis, reopened the store on a different basis in 1851. Both left town in 1852, only to return in 1853 to run the Front Street store under still another arrangement. Henry W. Corbett also quit his Portland store in 1852 after only 17 months, then returned to Portland from New York in 1853. Simeon G. Reed began clerking with Ladd in 1855 after running a general store for two years 40 miles down river at Rainier. He stayed, and four years later became Ladd's partner.[2]

Philip Wasserman and other Bavarian Jews opened small general-merchandise stores early in the 1850s along Front Street. The druggist Louis Blumauer managed in 1853 to build Portland's second brick building, following Ladd's example — brick being a visible symbol of stability and success. Many Jewish merchants like

Wasserman and Blumauer worked initially in California mountain towns and San Francisco mercantile houses before winding their way north to Oregon, often stopping en route, like Reed, to work in country stores.[3]

A higher percentage of Portland's earliest merchants were more successful than their San Francisco counterparts. The California boom town was more susceptible than Portland to the abrupt market swings of the early and mid-1850s. Bank and business failures were common because California's greater opportunities carried equally heavy risks. According to one study, only a tenth of San Francisco's white merchants present in 1849 remained in business by 1855, and even the largest merchant houses were only moderately successful. In Portland during the 1850s, nearly 20 percent of the Front Street merchant houses were reaping substantial rewards. Henry W. Corbett & Company was one.[4]

Henry W. Corbett

Within 14 months of opening for business, Corbett grossed over $83,000 in sales, splitting $20,000 in profits with his New York supplier, Williams, Bradford & Company. A key to Corbett's success, like that of Lewis and the Failings, was the backing of an established New York merchandising house. He had been its trusted employee for nearly eight years. New York, the new "money center of the United States," paid little attention to the West Coast before the 1848 California gold strike. Before 1850, the Oregon Territory attracted few merchants. Affluent eastern dry-goods houses were unwilling to gamble a large portion of their working capital on an Oregon experiment. Collections on the sale of goods in Portland could take from six months to a year. Only after being reasonably assured of a money supply — largely California gold dust — and a growing market area, especially for Oregon produce in California, did eastern capital risk serious involvement with cash-strapped frontier merchants. Two factors strongly influenced their decision: reports that dry goods could be sold in Portland at 100 percent markup over New York costs; and gold dust, the standard West Coast remittance to New York suppliers, could bring a higher price in New York, some $3 per ounce over the Portland cost, thus providing additional profits to eastern merchant-capitalists.[5]

Corbett's arrangement with Williams, Bradford & Company, similar to one between Josiah Failing and his backer, New York merchant-shipper-capitalist C. W. Thomas, provided the aspiring Portland merchant with a consignment of dry goods worth nearly $25,000. Both parties viewed the Oregon venture as a temporary, speculative enterprise, to last no more than three years. Regardless of the duration, Corbett was obligated to repay his backer by August 1, 1851. He had four months either to do it or return home a failure. Each party enjoyed an equal share of the profits, with Corbett responsible for both the goods and operation of the business in Portland.

The 24-year-old native of Westboro, Massachusetts, motivated by many of the reasons that impelled William S. Ladd to emigrate to Oregon, arrived at Portland by ship on March 7, 1851. He rented a small building on the corner of Front and Oak streets for $125 per month and awaited his cargo. During the interim of over a month, Corbett, like Ladd, travelled the back country and river valleys, sizing up the market. Oregon was ripe: "The countryside was still inadequately supplied to meet the heavy demands for consumer goods that had prevailed during the preceding three years." He opened on April 28, 1851, advertising "the largest and most complete assortment of goods ever offered in this market." Customers immediately flocked from all over the region to his initial stock of shoes, nails, coffee, sugar, tobacco, brooms and silk goods. Business was conducted at the street level, with stored merchandise and living quarters on the second floor. At night, he pulled up the ladder after him.[6]

By the end of May, Corbett's sales totalled $15,300. By August 1, he barely met his repayment contract — $25,000 equaled gross sales for four months. Fulfilling this crucial obligation left him almost profitless, but he had met the challenge by hard work, by "grinding away," as Henry Failing remembered. Then, a brisk trade in the fall of 1851 and spring of 1852 nearly tripled his earlier sales. Competition increased as other merchants arrived and more ships with eastern cargoes put into port. Corbett's particular assortment of dry goods, replenished with merchandise bought in San Francisco, proved immensely profitable and much more resistant to price fluctuations than the local commodity market. Netting $20,000 in profits on $83,000 in sales within 14 months, Corbett realized that a reckoning was at hand.[7]

Facing a downturn in the California market, he was advised by his New York supplier to close and return to New York. Departing in July, 1852, he left his store operation to employees Finley and Robert McLaren. He continued to buy and ship goods from New York on his own authority. He suspected that Portland's future was healthier than most New York commission houses realized. During the six months before his departure, he had witnessed an unexpected phenomenon: a tide of immigration pouring into the city from all parts of the West. In the words of one observer, "Men of many trades and occupations . . . seem to be overcrowding the place. They are pushing in by land and sea." As fellow merchant C. H. Lewis later remembered, the immigration of 1852 brought "a better class of people." It also forced changes in billing and payment procedures, at least for Corbett.[8]

The astute trader clearly perceived that the great influx of potential customers, combined with a dwindling supply of gold dust, would require him to grant credit, a practice not favored by Williams, Bradford, whose strong preference was for cash sales and purchases. Nationally, most importing and exporting rested upon credit. Cash was seldom paid, despite the efforts of merchants like Williams, Bradford & Company. "Almost everything rested on deferred payments of thirty, sixty, or ninety days." A disposition to grant his customers credit and a sense of Oregon's growing commercial needs whetted Corbett's appetite for high Portland profits despite uncertainties in the San Francisco market.[9]

Corbett remained in New York less than a year, marrying Carolyn Jagger of Albany and resuming employment with Williams, Bradford, with whom he split his $20,000 profits. He also established himself as an independent buyer. He purchased for his Portland store (renamed Corbett & McLarens), and for other merchants whom he successfully persuaded to bypass the huge markups and expenses of the San Francisco market in favor of direct shipments from New York.

By the spring of 1853, the Corbetts were convinced that Portland, not New York City, offered the best opportunity for raising both family and fortune. Purchasing sections of a house to be erected on an earlier acquired block, they arrived in Portland unexpectedly in midsummer with the house to follow.[10]

Arriving during a severe downturn in an oversupplied California market (which deflated Oregon revenues), Corbett and his partners thrived. Even though theirs was the first Front Street store to close on Sundays, they still prospered. They bought quality goods at the lowest prices, paying cash. With money tight, they were obliged to grant their customers from 30 to 60 days' credit to meet competition. For extended periods, they charged from 1½ to 3 percent per month, well exceeding the legal interest rate of 10 percent per annum. Dissolving his partnership with the McLarens in June, 1854, Corbett expanded into farm equipment. This specialty alone cleared profits of from 50 to 80 percent a year. By 1860, his assets totalled $50,763, second only to those of William S. Ladd and merchant-real-estate speculator Thomas J. Holmes, both listing assets of more than $70,000 in 1860.[11]

Josiah Failing and Sons

Of the three large Oregon firms purchasing most of their merchandise in New York (Oregon City's George Abernethy, Corbett, and Failing), J. Failing & Company was unique in that it was dominated by its New York partner. C. W. Thomas, of Hunt, Thomas & Company, supplied the Failings' funds for 60 percent of the profits. Exercising tight control, he attempted to manage the business from New York. To surmount the myriad problems of West Coast merchants purchasing in the East, Thomas required from the Failings every detail that might affect the market six to nine months in advance of Portland sale. Thomas in turn sent valuable market news, as when he warned Failing during the spring of 1853 that San Francisco was importing enormous quantities of New York merchandise, some of which might be dumped at lower cost on the Portland market.[12]

Like Corbett, the Failings were involved in a high-risk business in which timing was crucial. Knowing when to order, in what quantity and from whom, differentiated profit from loss. That the Failings survived and eventually amassed a small fortune, although at a slower pace than Corbett, was due to the cautious, methodical and tireless efforts of 44-year-old Josiah Failing and his precocious 17-year-old son, Henry. Josiah, who became "dean of Portland's early business community," was of advanced age for a novice frontier merchant. After 25 years in various occupations, including a stint as New York City superintendent of carts, he possessed much more experience than any competitor he would face, but not experience as a merchant. He had lots to learn and relied heavily on Henry, who had worked since the age of 12 for a leading New York dry-goods house.[13]

Strongly influenced by letters from early Baptist missionaries, Josiah Failing had been fascinated by the Oregon Country for nearly 20 years. With his limited income and six children, he recognized that Portland in 1851 offered him a fresh start in life. His was an uncertain opportunity at best, made less promising by a five-month wait for his supplies. Locating at the corner of Front and Oak streets, diagonally from H. W. Corbett & Company, Failing opened for business in October, 1851, with a miscellaneous stock of goods largely for farmers and farm communities. The Failings never advertised, as their sales were made principally to country storekeepers. Except for a limited retail trade with farmers, they were wholesalers. All remittances to Thomas in New York were in gold dust, transactions that produced additional income for Thomas but at cost to the region. According to Throckmorton, the "gold that might have been used for greater development of the territory was exported in sizeable quantities" by the merchants.[14]

In January, 1853, the firm suffered severely when three shiploads of its New York goods, worth $28,000, were wrecked when inbound on the Columbia River bar. Thomas's $56,000 worth of replacements arrived too late for the normally profitable spring selling. Recoup the loss, Thomas advised, by cornering the Portland nail market. If the Failings bought all the nails in San Francisco and Portland, the 100 percent profit at resale "would not be a bad hit." Such monopolistic practices, or at least attempts, were fairly common. William S. Ladd had cornered the Portland turpentine market in the previous year.[15]

Josiah Failing felt pained by such brutal practices, considered normal requirements of successful business by his merchant friends. He spent decreasing periods of time in the store. According to Henry, his father's "aspirations were less material" than his own. He turned increasingly toward his earlier civic, educational and religious interests. Elected mayor in April, 1853, following four months on the city council, Josiah yielded effective operation of the business to 19-year-old Henry.[16]

From 1853 until the firm reorganized six years later when Thomas withdrew from active participation, J. Failing & Company steadily expanded its sales, except when credit dried up during the western financial panic of 1854. Selling large quantities of imported ironware increased its business volume beyond that of Corbett's. But its profits were less because of a 60-40 split with Thomas until 1859. Corbett could accumulate capital faster than Josiah and Henry Failing, whose combined net worth in 1860 neared $40,000. Congenial but only partial competitors, the two merchant houses were bound more closely together by Henry Failing's marriage in 1858 to Emily Corbett, Henry's younger sister. The tie cemented a family relationship that influenced Portland's history for over a half-century.[17]

Cicero H. Lewis

Cicero H. Lewis, who had known Henry Corbett in the eastern dry-goods trade, was another of the New York merchants who immigrated in 1851. He arrived on the same steamer as the Failings, accompanied by his boyhood friend, Lucius H. Allen. Expecting to stay no more than five years, the 24-year-old New Jersey native had been hired to manage a local wholesale supply house for New York merchant John De Witt, who first visited Portland briefly in 1849 after establishing a branch store in San Francisco. Allen, De Witt's son-in-law, opened a Portland branch the following year but abandoned it after a "miserable" month. Unwilling to accept defeat, John De Witt searched for the right man to run a Portland operation. He chose Lucius's friend Lewis, someone with 11 years of working experience, four of them in a large New York dry-goods house. Shortly after his arrival, Lewis met William S. Ladd, "clerking for Mr. Gookin." From that day forward, the two merchants developed a lifelong friendship.[18]

Allen departed for San Francisco, leaving Lewis to await the arrival in August of a $20,000 stock of goods. Customers, scattered throughout the Willamette Valley, came "on horseback with sacks of gold dust," and sent "ox teams to haul away" their supplies. When business dropped off in early 1852, and the farmers' gold dust payment gave way to credit purchases, Lewis was directed to return to New York, a summons similar to that received previously by Henry Corbett. John De Witt wrote Lewis that "prospects for Portland business were so unfortunate that they would sell the store and close up." Allen had already left the coast for the East, so Lewis wound up the business and started for New York in August, one month after Corbett's departure. Stopping in San Francisco, he accepted a job for $100 a month and was nearly fired for refusing to bargain over prices.[19]

In December, 1852, Lucius Allen arrived in San Francisco with a load of new merchandise and convinced Lewis to join him in returning to Portland, where they would operate their own firm, independent of New York. Opening for business on August 1, 1853, in a rented store at Front and "B" (Burnside) streets, Allen and Lewis offered a mixed stock of dry goods and groceries "adapted for agricultural people." They also carried items that appealed to Indian families, especially beads and blankets. After 12 months of business, they had grossed over $75,000. A prosperous future seemed assured.[20]

Negatively associating price bargaining with "Jewish traders" encountered in San Francisco, Lewis prided himself on offering one "fair price," overcharging none and treating all customers fairly. He boasted that early in his Portland career he had sold a ton of sugar to a Corvallis merchant. When a competing Corvallis storekeeper later bought a similar amount at a reduced price, Lewis credited the first merchant for the unsold portion at the lower price. Such practices helped build strong customer loyalty. Other customer services rendered to miners and farmers included free storage of gold in Lewis's large safe.[21]

The major factor in establishing and maintaining formal ties with customers was the provision of credit. Customers in whom Lewis had confidence were granted unlimited credit and not overcharged for it. When he was first in Portland, he noted that the farmers spent only part of their gold. After he reopened in 1853, "the farmers came to town and spent all of their gold." During the 1854 panic, practically all of his business was done on credit. A decade later, annual sales of $800,000 rested almost entirely on "the long credit," a matter of deep concern to the meticulous merchant, who could not accurately determine his profits until the money was received.[22]

Successful merchandising in a pioneer economy like Portland's was exacting and time consuming. Books had to be kept methodically and profits figured closely. "Merchants measured their personal success" in San Francisco, according to Decker, "by the black ink in their account books." So, too, in Portland. Having avoided two notorious mercantile dangers — overpaying and overstocking goods — Lewis liked to believe that his success derived from intelligence, hard work and honest dealing, unrelated to the substantial backing of his partner Lucius Allen.

Although Allen and Lewis operated independently of New York, Allen possessed ample resources on which to draw as needed.

By the end of the decade, Allen became a silent partner, living in San Francisco, where Lewis purchased most of his supplies. Following a national trend of the period, Allen and Lewis began to specialize in wholesale groceries. Like credit, specialization tied the retailer even closer to the wholesaler. The Failings and Corbett also specialized and grew, and in time, according to Lewis, the three concerns stopped competing with each other. As business specialization increased, wholesale concentration likewise increased in Portland as elsewhere. Allen and Lewis became one of the leading West Coast wholesale grocery firms by 1880.[23]

Lewis was a worrier, cautious, conservative and work-driven. "I could amuse myself no other way" than by work, he admitted. He tirelessly attended to details, sternly supervised employees to do only as directed and seldom wished them good morning. Marrying 19-year-old Clementine Couch, daughter of Captain John H. Couch, Lewis in 1859 launched another career as a family man. While fellow merchants usually lunched together, Lewis walked home to eat, his sole recreational exercise. He rarely went out in the evening and took no pleasure trips. Leisure time was spent with his wife and 11 children, born over a stretch of 23 years.[24]

William S. Ladd & Company

Prosperity came quickly to William S. Ladd after a slow start. Although profits from Charles E. Tilton's liquor consignments formed the base of his operating capital, his fees as commission agent for W. D. Gookin produced even higher returns. Risking no personal capital, he kept all profits. In both cases he was extremely fortunate: family ties and friendships proved essential in establishing the mutual trust that allowed him to function as his own boss.

The Gookin arrangement carried several benefits. Apart from lucrative commissions, Ladd earned a monthly wage of $75. He lived rent-free in a house Gookin leased (next to Benjamin Stark's office), in which Gookin's merchandise was stored. From his small store at 42 Front Street, Ladd sold his own line of liquors and groceries in addition to Gookin's wares. In June, 1852, he bought the remainder of Gookin's stock and rented the home-warehouse. In it he also stored the remainder of Allen and Lewis's stock, purchased before Lewis's departure for San Francisco. After 13 months in Portland, Ladd had netted $3,000. It was time to expand the business.[25]

In July, 1852, Ladd persuaded Tilton, rich from the China trade and other enterprises, to become his silent partner. A. E. Tilton, Charles's brother, would buy and ship New England merchandise Ladd ordered at considerable savings over San Francisco prices. In August, W. S. Ladd & Co. opened, advertising "Jockey Club Home Gin," groceries, oils, door sashes, and rope. (In later accounts, Ladd never mentioned his early liquor trade.) Although the partnership lasted only three years, Tilton became a frequent Portland visitor and Ladd's closest lifetime friend. Ladd's marriage in 1854 to Tilton's first cousin, Caroline Ames Elliott of New Hampshire, further cemented a relationship that soon took a decided upward turn.[26]

Southern Oregon gold strikes proved a bonanza for Ladd and other merchants in 1852 and 1853. "The miners cleaned the whole county right out of everything," paying in gold dust, Ladd gleefully recalled. The strikes quickened the territorial economy and further benefited Portland. Wells Fargo opened a Portland office in October, 1852, connecting it by stage to the gold camps. Prices soared. "Everything eatable is on the rise," reported Episcopal clergyman the Reverend St. M. Fackler. Flour became scarce in 1853, particularly in valley towns to the south. Ladd and other merchants began importing Chilean flour. This was Ladd's first large-scale experience with the wheat and flour trade. It initiated a lifelong interest that made him one of the West's leading flour millers.[27]

The clever merchant missed few bets. Receiving word from Tilton that turpentine was in short supply in San Francisco, where it was selling for $6 to $8 a gallon, Ladd dispatched a supply by return ship to California. Opening his store early the next morning to service farmers, he received word at four o'clock that the ship had wrecked on the Columbia Bar. As each supplier opened for business, he quietly bought all the turpentine available, including Henry Corbett's stock, paying less than $2 a gallon. Shipped without incident to San Francisco, the scarce fluid reportedly sold for $10 a gallon — a 500 percent profit.[28]

The gold strike also put Ladd heavily into gold-dust transactions with San Francisco and New York banks. In 1854, he found himself extending credit along with other Portland merchants, making loans, receiving deposits and generally functioning as a banker to customers. Never a borrower himself, he loaned money to customers at 1 percent per month, probably standard for the period. If not repaid promptly and fully, Ladd took goods in exchange, or in later years, a piece of property. Appointed trustee of the Portland Milling Company, which failed after the 1854 panic, he received his first lesson in bankruptcy procedures. Selling the company's property, settling debtor accounts and paying creditors, like his own lending to customers, stimulated an increasing interest in private banking. In 1859, the Portland merchant and his San Francisco associate would form the Ladd & Tilton Bank, destined to become Portland's leading and most profitable financial institution.[29]

By 1855, the 29-year-old William S. Ladd clearly was Portland's leading citizen. He had erected its first brick structure during the summer of 1853. Located at 163 Front Street, and costing $7,500, the well-built store symbolized his quick rise to affluence and prominence. Elected to the city council in 1853, chosen mayor in 1854 and re-elected to the council in 1856, Ladd was as involved in politics as in his growing business responsibilities. Such time-consuming commitments called for help in running the store. Brothers John Wesley and Marshall arrived from New Hampshire, and Simeon G. Reed moved from Rainier, where he had opened a general store in 1853.[30]

Simeon G. Reed

Simeon G. Reed, who began clerking for W. S. Ladd & Company in September, 1855, was born to a prosperous Abbington, Massachusetts, family in 1830. Graduating from school at 13, he spent nine years in Boston and Quincy, in a variety of jobs and apprenticeships in shoemaking, flour and grain sales and dry-goods merchandising. At 20, he married 18-year-old Amanda Wood, a member of a prominent Quincy family and distant cousin of John Quincy Adams.[31]

In the spring of 1852, Reed took a cargo of grain and merchandise to Sacramento, California, where he opened a tent store. Three profitable buying trips to the Columbia Basin convinced him that Oregon was "a good country to grow up in." Late in 1852, he set up shop in Rainier, 40 miles down the Columbia from Portland. A trip to Ladd's store to buy merchandise inaugurated a friendship that eventually led to close business and social relations. In fact, Amanda, whom Reed had not seen for two years, accompanied the future Mrs. Ladd from New England to San Francisco, where the Ladds were married in October, 1854.[32]

Reed's fortuitous decision to join Ladd in Portland launched a career that would carry him to the pinnacle of Portland's business and social Establishment. Portland appeared particularly promising because the two men already had become good friends, business in Rainier seemed inauspicious, and the ever-present threat of Indian raids in the area disturbed the young married couple.

The most likely compelling reason for Reed's move was his belief that Portland by 1855 had become the mercantile center of Oregon — Oregon's emporium. Two years earlier, he had witnessed the removal of a major obstacle to Portland's economic growth when the Pacific Mail Steamship Company abandoned a fruitless attempt to make St. Helens, halfway between Portland and Rainier, its Oregon terminus. A near-unanimous boycott by Portland's merchants, with the timely assistance of the little San Francisco steamer *Peytona*, forced the crucial withdrawal in favor of Portland.[33]

Oregon's Emporium

Portland's business people, led by Front Street merchant-capitalists, transformed the township into Oregon's principal trading place by the mid-1850s. By making it Oregon's emporium, they were the key group in changing Portland from a tiny village into a small, thriving city. They surpassed their Oregon competitors in fostering urban trade and commerce and in using mercantile profits to finance new, growth-oriented enterprises. Whether aided, impeded or ignored by distant business interests, the major Portland merchants managed to overcome, outlast or turn to their favor regional geographic uncertainties, economic fluctuations and natural disasters. By the mid-1850s, this handful of men had acquired the local economic and political power held in 1850 by the proprietors. Magnified by fresh recruits, their tremendous influence on Portland and Oregon endured for several decades.

Portland was in the long line of settlements that had been urbanizing the American West since Independence. Eastern merchants led in the building of western cities like Pittsburgh, Cincinnati, Lexington, Louisville, and St. Louis. And the cities they built attracted other easterners as well as Europeans accustomed to the varied opportunities of city life. "The opportunity to accumulate instant fortunes was . . . the generator for the migration to the city," Peter Decker demonstrated for

San Francisco. Not every Oregon settlement sprang directly from commerce. Salem had roots in a Methodist mission. Linnton, McMinnville and Albany originated largely from the schemes of land speculators and townsite promoters. Surviving Oregon towns usually had seized and retained important commercial and trade advantages.[34]

Portland, like still-ruder places in the territory, was basically an agricultural marketing and shipping center before 1860. Town and countryside thrived only in combination, merchants liked to say. Portland required the produce, timber and wheat of the Tualatin and Willamette valleys. Valley farmers and merchants needed the worldly goods and services that Portland furnished. Portland merchants like Ladd, Lewis, Corbett, and the Failings quickly recognized the importance of establishing commercial supply lines to the hinterland from their Portland stores. One merchant, John Wilson, reached beyond them into the Willamette Valley by opening a branch store in Albany. Chief clerk for Allen & Lewis in 1854, the 29-year-old Irishman was one of the few early merchants who achieved moderate success without the backing of friends or relatives.

Wilson had immigrated to Oregon in January, 1850, after two years with the U.S. Army in California and an unsuccessful visit to the gold fields. A chance meeting with Benjamin Stark in San Francisco encouraged him to book passage to Astoria on Captain George H. Flanders's ship. Travelling up the Columbia by canoe, he landed in the St. Helens-Milton area, where he secured employment, initially at a small lumber mill and then at a local retail store. Life there was "very dull," Wilson recalled. "If I remained there all my life I would not be better off than the wealthiest of the neighbors . . . . Poverty was their wealth . . . . I concluded to go to Portland and cast my lot there."[35]

Arriving in Portland during the summer of 1853, the future founder of the Olds & King department store and major donor to the Portland Public Library found "things . . . very dull here also." He lived mainly on savings before C. H. Lewis hired him in 1854. During the interim, he worked for Raleigh's dry-goods store and handled bookkeeping and collections for T. J. Dryer's *Weekly Oregonian*.

Wilson's big opportunity came in the spring of 1856. He purchased the business of Robert and Finley McLaren, Henry W. Corbett's former partners, for $1,500 in cash and a $6,000 note. Although selling dry goods and groceries, he engaged mostly in trading Willamette Valley produce from as far away as the Umpqua River. Farm wagons from the south came up Scholls Ferry Road, laden with bacon, butter and eggs for his Front Street store. He slept on its second floor, keeping an "old iron club" handy against thieves.

In 1857, Wilson formed a three-way partnership, which "conducted a prosperous general merchandise business." L. H. Wakefield bought goods in San Francisco and John Connor ran the Albany store. The following year, Wilson moved his Portland store to a new brick building on First Street, the earliest commercial establishment west of Front. In 1870, he would occupy the first store on Third Street, eventually called Wilson & Olds.[36]

Front Street merchants like John Wilson realized only too well that their future prosperity was restricted by limited domestic trade alternatives and a weak foreign commerce. Settlers, travelers, buyers and sellers reached Portland with difficulty or not at all, depending on weather, road conditions, farming demands, and competition from other places. Stumps in streets, choking dust or thick sludge frustrated everybody. With a determination bordering on frenzy, the merchants improved and exploited road and river facilities in widening arcs.

Local mercantile and trading interests worked diligently to increase their access to, and control over, steamboats to assure Portland market supremacy in the Pacific Northwest. Like several growth-oriented ship and steamboat captains, these merchants reckoned Portland would never become a thriving emporium without efficient river transportation and easy access to the hinterland. "Nothing," Richard Wade noted, "accelerated the rise of the [earlier] Western cities so much as the introduction of the steamboat." Portlanders heavily invested in steam vessels and cooperated in or opposed one another's transportation ventures. A handful of them began to build great fortunes.[37]

Captain Ainsworth and Friends

Lot Whitcomb, an entrepreneur in Milwaukie, launched the first steamboat built on the Willamette River on Christmas Day, 1850. Named for its owner, the sleek, 160-foot steam side-wheeler set a new record of 10 hours between Astoria and Milwaukie, seven miles south of Portland. The 28-year-old John C. Ainsworth was captain and 27-year-old Jacob Kamm its chief engineer. They had set course to becoming the foremost figures in Willamette and Columbia river transportation.

Born in Keokuk, Iowa, in 1822 and raised from infancy in Warren County, Ohio, Ainsworth had been clerking in a small-town store when the 1837 depression struck. It left a lasting impression. "The financial crash that carried everything before it," he remembered, "made a slaughter of nerely [sic] all the Southern banks." He could have added many midwestern ones as well.[38]

Ainsworth returned to Iowa after the depression, first as a partner in a small general store and later as a wholesaler-retailer in the Keokuk region where the Mississippi and Des Moines rivers joined. Seeking excitement after his young wife's death, he boldly took command of a small Mississippi River steamboat, learning on the river how to be a captain. Suffused with "glowing accounts of the new Eldorado," Ainsworth mortgaged his property in early 1850, scraped together $900 in cash and headed for Sacramento, California, where the county clerk, who had worked for him in Iowa, made him assistant county clerk. Three months later, while in California on a business trip, Lot Whitcomb met and hired Ainsworth at $300 a month to command his new $75,000 vessel then under construction. Swiss-born Jacob Kamm, with 10 years' experience in steam engines, largely in the New Orleans area, commanded $400 monthly.[39]

Relations between crew and owner strained, then worsened when Whitcomb did not pay them. Other steamboats were appearing on the Columbia and Willamette rivers — 11 by October, 1851, effectively reducing anticipated revenues. The aggressive entrance of the Pacific Mail Steamship Company in March, 1851, doomed the cash-short *Lot Whitcomb*. PacMail, as it would be called, afflicted Portland merchants and proprietors as it attempted to monopolize the San Francisco trade and dictate shipping points, an effort that culminated with the

Peytona episode in 1854.[40]

Oregon City interests acquired the *Lot Whitcomb* in June, 1851, Ainsworth and Kamm becoming minority owners in lieu of unpaid salaries. Its resale to California buyers in the summer of 1854 realized Ainsworth $4,000 and Kamm probably more, providing them sufficient funds to begin their long partnership as steamboat operators. With major backing from Abernethy and Clark Company of Oregon City, Ainsworth and Kamm built the Pacific Northwest's first stern-wheeler, the *Jennie Clark*. The two young steamboat veterans employed the formula used by Portland's most successful merchants: establish a reputation of honest and skillful management, seek all or most financing from wealthy investors, and receive a share of the profits. Ainsworth assuredly benefited from his second marriage in 1850 to the daughter of Judge S. S. White of Oregon City, wealthy Donation Land Claim owner and investor in the *Lot Whitcomb*. According to one account, Ainsworth and his bride lived in "an impressive mansion," built on Judge White's claim, where they resided from 1851 to 1859.[41]

Designed primarily to cater to Portland and Oregon City merchant-shippers, the *Jennie Clark* made money from its first day. A new outbreak of Indian troubles on the upper Columbia, coupled with the continuing Rogue River Indian conflict, placed the ship in constant demand. Portland, to Abernethy and Clark's unhappiness, became the major supply center for army shipments. Renewed mining activities in southern Oregon and northeastern Washington Territory also added to the profits of the young steamboat operators.[42]

The year 1858 proved a turning point in Ainsworth's career. William S. Ladd joined with Abernethy, Clark and others, including Ainsworth and Kamm, to finance a larger sternwheeler, the *Carrie Ladd*. Named to honor Mrs. Ladd and to recognize her husband's major financial stake in the new venture, it was Ladd's first sizable investment in river transportation. Within four years, Ladd would join Ainsworth, Kamm and other investors in the immensely profitable Oregon Steam Navigation Company.[43]

Captain Richard Hoyt, Herman C. Leonard, John Green, and The Dalles resident Robert (R. R.) Thompson were also active in early Portland steamboat promotion and shipping, as were Benjamin Stark and Simeon G. Reed, Ladd's new partner. All but Hoyt, who died in 1862, played increasingly prominent roles in Portland's business and civic life, due partly to their involvement in river transportation. Twelve out of 20 of Portland's richest families in 1870 were heavy investors in shipping and related enterprises.[44]

Captain Richard Hoyt, a native of New Hampshire, arrived on the Oregon coast in the late 1840s. Unlike fellow "blue-water" captains John H. Couch and Z. C. Norton, who turned merchants and Donation Land Claim owners, Hoyt remained at the helm of his ships and steamboats throughout the 1850s. He acquired the first mail contracts for the Willamette and Columbia rivers. His wharf boat at the foot of Stark Street was the first Portland dock designed for river steamboats, and Captain Ainsworth's *Lot Whitcomb* was its best customer. Hoyt also provided the first regular towboat service, much in demand by ocean-going windjammers beating upriver on the Columbia. His riskiest venture was the Columbia River Navigation Company, organized in 1858 with Simeon Reed and Benjamin Stark.

John Ainsworth incorporated it into the Oregon Steam Navigation Company in 1860.[45]

The Inseparable Leonard and Green

Two close friends, Herman C. Leonard and John Green, pursued the more usual Portland path to riches: merchandising and ocean and river shipping. They had known one another in the New York mercantile world before going separately to California in late 1849. Like most others who initially prospered on Portland's Front Street, they were well financed or at least well connected to eastern capital upon arriving in 1852.

Leonard, a 23-year-old New York native, had an older brother, William B. Leonard, associated with prominent dry-goods houses and a major cotton-brokerage firm. The 30-year-old Green, also a New York native, amassed sufficient capital to establish a general-merchandise house in San Francisco. On a trip Green made to Oregon to sell sugar, Leonard recalled, he saw the territory as a more fertile field than California for them both. As partners, they established a general store in Astoria in February, 1850. Leonard furnished it with a large merchandise consignment from his brother in New York, to be sold on commission mainly to Indians. Then, like John Wilson and Simeon Reed afterwards, they soon concluded on removing to Portland, "the city of the future."[46]

When their younger brothers, Washington Irving Leonard and Henry D. Green, arrived, they took over the Astoria business and the partners moved upriver in May, 1852. Operating beside Couch and Flanders's wharf, they assured their initial success by becoming agents for the Pacific Mail Steamship Company. Leonard travelled to purchase merchandise and direct the operations of their new bark, *Metropolis*. Green ran the local commission business and steamship agency. Becoming politically active, he served on the city council in 1855.[47]

Their bark carried lumber and produce south and general freight north until the San Francisco market slumped in 1853. As Throckmorton noted, "The overstocked San Francisco market was the dominating influence governing business in the Far West," lasting well into 1854 and leading to the panic of that year. Leonard and Green then entered the fierce Hawaiian trade, exchanging lumber for sugar. Leonard related one story that suggests something of the era's merchandising techniques.[48]

Receiving word in mid-1854 that the lumber trade was falling off in Honolulu, Leonard sailed immediately for San Francisco to catch a ship to that port, arriving 10 days in advance of the *Metropolis*, which followed directly from Portland with a load of lumber and produce. He quietly discovered that the Honolulu wholesale lumber dealers were conspiring to force the Portland merchant-shippers to sell their lumber for half its worth and then divide the profits among themselves. Leonard swiftly leased a fenced lot and vacant warehouse to store his cargo. The *Metropolis*'s lumber was quickly sold at slightly below market prices to eager retailers and builders. From his huge profit, Leonard won the respect of local merchants and money for a second ship, the brig *Orient*.[49]

The partners next challenged the China trade. In October, 1855, Leonard sailed to Hong Kong as supercargo on the *Metropolis*, escorting a load of lumber, ship spars, salmon, and 300 barrels of flour "manufactured at Doctor John McLaughlin's [sic] mill at Oregon City." Leonard remembered, "I disposed of the cargo to excellent advantage." A profitable Asian trade in 1855-56, which included sailings to Japan and Siberia, allowed Leonard and Green to bypass the West Coast depression of 1854-55. Although market adaptability was a key to their success, like most fellow merchant-capitalists, a good share of luck entered their fortunes. Their third ship, the brig *Orbit*, following service in the Canadian and China trade, sank with all hands in a Yellow Sea typhoon two weeks after Leonard sold it. Shipwreck was a fate — from storms, rocks and sandbars — that Oregon merchants and crews knew all too well. It could destroy a Front Streeter's dreams, then be turned to quick advantage by cornering a market or risking men, ships and goods on another voyage.[50]

Leonard and Green followed Front Street ways by innovatively investing their merchant and shipping profits. They founded the Portland Gas Light Company in January, 1859, the third of its type on the West Coast, manufacturing gas from Vancouver Island coal they imported. Politically shrewd, they quickly secured a perpetual, non-compensatory franchise from the territorial legislature one month before a new state constitution would prohibit perpetual franchises. (The first gas was turned on in late 1859; the first gas lights on June 1, 1860.) In 1862, Leonard and Green formed the Portland Water Company out of the Pioneer Water Works, purchased for $5,400. They capitalized each utility at $50,000. In February, 1865, Leonard joined the brothers Henry and John Green in organizing the Oregon Iron Company in nearby Oswego. William S. Ladd, Henry Failing and Addison M. Starr were additional investors.[51]

Herman C. Leonard and the Green brothers built fortunes from these enterprises, although the iron company ultimately failed. Their merchant friends Henry W. Corbett, Henry Failing and William S. Ladd amassed even greater wealth from banking. Profits from the early mercantile and shipping trade financed them all. In the 1870 census (which John Green missed), Henry Green ranked fourth and Herman Leonard seventh in total assets among Portland's wealthiest residents. All six men were in the first rank of the urban Establishment.[52]

Keys to Success

By the late 1850s, the most prosperous merchants and shippers in Portland had revealed themselves a shrewd, energetic, innovative, and lucky lot. Importantly, they proved to be highly flexible business people. They understood that nineteenth-century trade and commerce, especially in the Far West, required vigorous participation in risky and competitive enterprise. To survive in the fluctuating economy of the period, they continually had to reexamine their business methods and objectives. Flexibility was crucial, whether in credit extension or in market competition.

Another key to their success was Portland's location. Merchants like Reed, Wilson, Leonard, and the Greens, in company with steamboat operators like Captain Ainsworth, wisely recognized Portland's potential. At the confluence of two great rivers, and at the head of the verdant Willamette Valley, Portland lay practically at the mouth of the vast Columbia River basin, awaiting exploitation.

Portland's mercantile-capitalists believed themselves part of a fast-growing American economy, and they wanted their share of the growth. They knew that transportation improvements, especially more and better roads, steamboats and even railroads, would hasten Portland's rise to Northwest market supremacy. They also knew themselves highly subjected to outside forces, including an uncertain San Francisco trade, an increased agricultural output in California, and California-backed development of large timber operations on Puget Sound. Adjusting in part to these challenges, Portland's traders and merchants first established a stable trade pattern involving New York, San Francisco and Portland. It became more clearly defined in the late 1850s and remained essentially unchanged for 30 years.

What saved Oregon and Portland merchants from the extremes of the California market was the discovery of gold in southern Oregon in December, 1851 — the first of several unpredictable but fortunate events for the region's farmers, merchants and shippers. That they were prepared to take maximum advantage of such unforeseen opportunities boded well for Oregon's future. Likewise, they seized upon another stimulus to the Oregon economy: increased federal military spending to combat Indians. Gold rushes, federal spending and sustained agricultural production placed Oregon's economy on a plateau for the remainder of the decade. And Portland's Front Street merchants and shippers took more than their fair share of the profits.

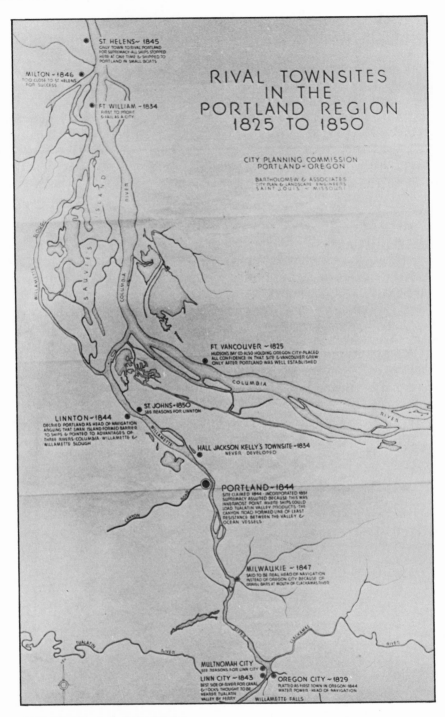

2.1 Rival Townsites in the Portland Region

2.2 The "Lot Whitcomb"

2.4 Cicero H. Lewis (1826-1897)

2.3 William S. Ladd (1826-1893) c. 1873

2.6 Henry Failing (1834-1898)

2.5 Josiah Failing (1806-1877)

2.8 Simeon G. Reed (1830-1895)

2.7 Henry W. Corbett (1827-1903)

2.9 John Wilson (1826-1900) and Rose Bartholomew Wilson (1840-1859)

2.10 1854 Portland, looking southwest from today's Front and Washington

2.11 Couch & Co. and Allen & De Witt Co., Front St. north of Ankeny, 1850

3

PROPRIETORS AND PROMOTERS

Shipping Ventures

The heavily indebted proprietors Daniel H. Lownsdale and Stephen Coffin had recruited attorney William W. Chapman as their partner in the Townsite Promotion Company in December, 1849. Chapman's promised $26,666, for a third interest in the claim, was needed by Coffin to help finance construction of a steamer to provide regular passenger, mail and freight service between San Francisco and Portland. The proprietors knew that the destiny they presumed for their community lay in ready access to both the Portland hinterland and national markets. Potential lot buyers, they also knew, would require more docks, hotels and other facilities. To compete successfully against neighboring river towns, they wanted a local newspaper as a promotional tool. Gambling all their resources on risky enterprises, they seemed unworried about their lack of experience in mounting such schemes, especially those involving transportation services. They proved not only unlucky but often foolish as they forged ahead on their costly projects.

Coffin & Company, organized in late December, 1849, contracted with the Westervelt & Mackey yard of New York, better known for the quantity than the quality of its product, to build a shallow-draft side-wheel steamer called the *S.S. Columbia*. As costs mounted, Coffin secured additional investors, but in mid-1850 he was forced to sell the nearly completed ship to the Pacific Mail Steamship Company of New York. The *Columbia*, arriving in San Francisco in March, 1851, would amply fulfill expectations, but not to the direct profit of Coffin and his partners. It made 102 trips in five years between Oregon and California, carrying 80,000 tons of freight and 10,000 passengers. Ladd, Corbett, Lewis, and the Failings made their initial voyages on it.[1]

Salvaging less than $20,000 from the forced sale of the *Columbia*, Coffin and Chapman travelled to San Francisco in the late summer of 1850 to seek a replacement ship and recruit a newspaper editor. Failing in their primary quest, they successfully enlisted Thomas Jefferson Dryer, a 42-year-old New Yorker of diverse journalistic background who wanted to start his own newspaper. Described variously as "a powerful orator and 'a pungent writer,'" Dryer was, in Malcolm Clark's words, "a Temperance lecturer when seized by sobriety and, despite his name, a dedicated Whig." He looked "as sharp as a steel trap," the *Oregon Spectator* remarked from Oregon City. The new weekly was to be a Whig paper, despite the fact that two of its sponsors, Lownsdale and Chapman, were Democrats (Chapman became a Whig in 1852). Coffin, an avowed Whig and later a prominent Republican, was the most politically active of the three proprietors. Although Chapman reportedly suggested the name "Oregonian," Coffin set the political tone of the new journal. Beyond being given a ticket to Portland and a log shack to house his paper, and promised a salary, Dryer was on his own. He ran the paper as his personal fief, taking orders from no one.[2]

The *Weekly Oregonian*, using Dryer's old hand press and worn type, appeared on December 4, 1850, with free copies distributed throughout the Willamette Valley. The first edition noted the surprise arrival three days earlier of the little side wheeler *S.S. Gold Hunter* from San Francisco. Advertised for sale, the steamer could be bought for $60,000, representing the majority interests of its San Francisco shareholders. Chapman promptly organized a joint-stock company to raise the required $21,000 down payment. The proprietors invested nearly $18,000 from the *Columbia* sale; the remainder came from two investors who secured the jobs as captain and purser. The balance of $39,000 was accepted "in the form of a personal note signed jointly by Lownsdale, Coffin and Chapman."[3]

The *Gold Hunter* provided Portland with three months of more dependable service to San Francisco than had existed previously. PacMail's *S.S. Carolina* had initiated limited steamship service to Portland in June, 1850, but after three trips had abandoned it for Fort Vancouver and Astoria, due to low water on the Willamette. Until the arrival of the shallow-draft *Columbia*, no steamer larger than the *Gold Hunter* could be assured safe passage to Portland throughout the year. And even with this advantage, the *Gold Hunter* lost money. It was too small to carry a profitable freight load, and its passenger complement was rarely filled, despite agent W.W. Chapman's energetic promotion.[4]

The *Gold Hunter's* fate was sealed in San Francisco during the second week of March, 1851, when its ownership changed hands. The captain and purser sold their shares to the minority stockholders, giving the San Franciscans majority control. Captain T. A. Hall of Milwaukie and Purser A. P. Dennison of Portland were accused in Oregon of duplicitous behavior — most likely a specious charge framed by the desperate proprietors. Both men enjoyed good reputations. Dennison was a respected merchant and later served several terms on the city council. The most plausible explanation for their action was threat of foreclosure: the proprietors' inability to meet their note payments due to operational losses.

Upon assuming control of the *Gold Hunter*, the San Francisco stockholders sold the ship to another group of San Francisco investors. The discounted sale price wiped out Coffin, Chapman and Lownsdale's entire investment. Coffin felt especially hard pressed. In the fall of 1851, he approached Philip A. Marquam, a new Front Street commission merchant known to have money. Marquam, later a prominent attorney and judge, gave Coffin a short-term $500 loan at a usurious 5 percent monthly interest. Unable to repay it, Coffin deeded Marquam a block of land. Coffin was in such dire straits that he was forced to exchange or sell many lots at bargain ɔrices in order to meet his losses. Some of the transactions were not recorded, as Marquam discovered. The forgetful — if not slippery — Coffin had already sold part ɔf Marquam's new block to Chapman. Coffin was forced to pay Chapman $800 to regain control of the property conveyed to Marquam, and thus lost $300 on the loan ɔlus a block of eight potentially valuable lots.[5]

The ostensible purpose of the *Gold Hunter* sale was to clear old ship debts allegedly undisclosed to its Portland buyers. The new owners were likely associated with PacMail interests. Coincident with the *Gold Hunter*'s sale, PacMail inaugurated ts *Columbia* service to Portland, free of any scheduled competition. For whatever he reason, the proprietors' catastrophic loss came at a vulnerable moment. Their credit was already stretched, as they were promoting a new scheme to build a plank oad to the Tualatin Valley.[6]

The Great Plank Road

"A base swindle," charged John Waymire at the Constitutional Convention in September, 1857. The pioneer Portland dock builder and business leader referred to he plank road, begun in August, 1851. To be planked for the first six miles over the hills, the road was planned as an all-weather thoroughfare from Portland to Lafayette in Yamhill County, the principal trading center of the Tualatin Plains. Daniel Lownsdale had surveyed the route in 1849 over the present-day Canyon Road.[7]

In the fall of 1850, while searching for a ship, Coffin had joined Lownsdale in seeking a legislative charter for the plank road. Chapman was simultaneously promoting the construction of a railroad over the same route. The three proprietors were seemingly working at cross-purposes. In December, 1850, the *Oregonian* reported that Chapman had drafted articles of association for the Portland & Valley Railroad Company capitalized at $500,000; according to Chapman, nearly $400,000 was "already taken." Chapman noted that "foreign capital would be acceptable" but that he favored "local capital." Readers would have been skeptical of his typical Chapman ploy. The "blatherskite" proprietor spoke wishfully: $400,000 in private capital would not have been available in Oregon in 1850. No money was ever collected; the railroad scheme remained a dream in Chapman's mind.[8]

The plank-road effort moved ahead after the territorial legislature chartered the Portland and Valley Plank Road Company in January, 1851, immediately following Portland's incorporation. The legislative action represented a typical territorial public-works project: authorized but given little or no direction by the legislature, largely or entirely left to private initiative, and consequently underfunded because of insufficient capital in Oregon localities. Usually, it was a formula for failure. To pay or the toll road, stock subscriptions were peddled throughout the Willamette Valley. *Oregonian* editor Dryer, subscribing $500, hailed the project as deserving "particular notice. It allures the settler to redeem lands hitherto desolate, and benefits he farmer in carrying his products to markets." Portland's merchants and proprietors expected increased valley trade as their benefit; few anticipated any stock dividends.[9]

Subscriptions began the same week the proprietors unknowingly lost their investment in the *Gold Hunter*. Coffin and Chapman each pledged $3,000 and Lownsdale $2,000. Richard Perkins (a merchant) promised $2,000; Peter Guild (a farmer) Benjamin Stark and captains Flanders and Norton came in for $1,000 apiece. The newly arrived merchant Henry W. Corbett pledged $200; Captain Couch, $100. O the $35,100 ultimately subscribed, some pledges were later withdrawn and some never paid in full. Coffin, Chapman and Lownsdale were probably the major de faulters.[10]

Oregon Statesman Publisher Asahel Bush insinuated that Coffin met his first 25 percent assessment from $5,000 in public funds granted the plank-road project which Territorial Secretary Edward Hamilton funneled through Coffin in mid-1851 Bush implied that Coffin had personally misappropriated $1,000 for personal and speculative reasons, an accusation that Coffin vehemently denied. Bush, an ardent Democrat, suspected the motives of the equally ardent Whigs, Coffin and Hamil ton. Undaunted, Coffin secured the contract to prepare and lay the planks, sawed at Abrams and Reed's mill, which he and his son-in-law Reed owned.[11]

Coffin's partner Lownsdale presided briefly over the road company's board of directors until giving way to Colonel William M. King, who became paid project manager. King was chairman of the Salem meeting of the Oregon House of Repre sentatives in 1851 which incorporated Portland and chartered the plank road. He became House speaker in 1852. Lownsdale and King had been deeply involved in property sales and exchanges for over a year — transactions that were to benefit King personally. Ardent Democrats, promoters and real-estate speculators, both were businessmen of questionable competence and integrity.[12]

Portland wildly celebrated the laying of the first plank on September 27, 1851. Diners had barbecued pork (one account noted a roasted ox) spread upon the newly laid planks. Encouraged by copious amounts of liquor and patriotic oratory, the throng celebrated a road that heralded Portland's supremacy over Oregon City and St. Helens. Colonel King aimed to finish the first 10 miles by November 1.[13]

Such was not to be. Proceeding up the canyon, 80 workers hacked a path through the forest and steep terrain. Winter rains came early, turning the rutted dirt path into bottomless mud. By November 1, only $2,905 in pledges had been col lected to pay more than $11,000 in expenses. Work halted after fewer than three miles of construction. By the spring of 1852, with over $14,000 expended and $6,026 collected, the pledges were demanded. Scandal erupted, new directors were chosen, and King was replaced; he had been gone much of the time on legisla tive business. Investigations revealed loose and even fraudulent management, espe cially in handling accounts.

Work languished for nearly three years until Supreme Court Justice Cyrus Olney ordered delinquent pledges paid up to 80 percent of their subscriptions. Eight months later, in December, 1855, with eight unpaid workers still owed $3,348 in back wages, Justice Olney ordered remaining subscriptions paid in full and dis patched county sheriffs to find the delinquent stockholders. This judicial action provoked John Waymire to lament later, "'They got honest, responsible men to subscribe and they made them pay to the last dollar'" for an unfinished job poorly done.[14]

On January 25, 1856, the territorial legislature chartered a new company to finish the road. Portland's emerging merchant leaders — men like William S. Ladd, Josiah

Failing and A. M. Starr — raised $75,000 in additional subscriptions for the Portland and Tualatin Plains Plank Road Company and completed the project by the end of the year. Although still "almost inaccessible" from Portland "and most difficult of passage or travel when reached," as Harvey W. Scott recalled, the Canyon toll road at last opened for business. Portland's Front Street merchants had achieved their goal. The road symbolized their recently acquired power and influence.[15]

The Parting

In early 1852, the Surveyor General's Office at Oregon City ordered the proprietors to partition the Portland townsite by designating which parcels each owned. No joint title could be issued. A division would legalize prior sales and protect the buyers. The proprietors' agreement of March 10, 1852, required fulfillment of all sales contracts and an exchange of lots between them to assure equal shares. Those lots sold by Francis Pettygrove were assigned to Lownsdale's section by an escrow contract. Because of potential liability from litigation, the proprietors had to assume a staggering $300,000 fidelity bond. Challenged repeatedly, the partition agreement was finally upheld 19 years later by U.S. Circuit Court Judge Lorenzo Sawyer in *Lamb v. Davenport*, and confirmed by the U.S. Supreme Court in 1873.[16]

None of the proprietors liked the townsite partition. Lownsdale maintained that "neither Coffin nor Chapman has, or ever had, any right to set up claim as claimant to any part of the Portland claim, unless they could do this in shape of town lots." Once the patent was issued to him, Lownsdale, as the only rightful claim holder, promised to convey titles. Coffin grudgingly accepted the terms. Chapman complained bitterly, as his was the least desirable slice of the division and worth less than he felt his investment merited.[17]

Aware that partition might be ordered, Chapman had earlier initiated inquiry into the legality of the Portland townsite claim. In attempting to gain access to some records, he confronted the judicial arrogance of territorial Supreme Court Justice Orville E. Pratt, whom he openly disliked. Appearing before Pratt in November, 1851, on a land-title case in which he suspected the judge to have an undeclared interest, Chapman was found in contempt of court for use of abusive language. Pratt sentenced him to 20 days' imprisonment and disbarred him from legal practice. Offering to "slit Pratt's throat," Chapman was arrested by the sheriff, only to be forcibly released by friends present in the Hillsboro courtroom. Chased back to Portland, he was rearrested and then released on a writ of error granted by Pratt's colleague, Chief Justice Thomas Nelson. The full court then reversed Pratt's decision. The Pratt confrontation was merely one of numerous crises that Chapman had to endure. In subsequent months he faced additional litigation over property titles and personal debts. Although enjoying "the best practice in the Territory," according to his law partner David Logan, Chapman began to seek opportunities elsewhere.[18]

The proprietorial relationship was further severely strained by accumulated indebtedness from the *Gold Hunter* venture and other transactions. In early 1852, the proprietors suffered a $14,000 adverse judgment relating to the *Gold Hunter*. Through appeals and cross-suits, the matter was not settled until 1856, if then. In August, 1856, Lownsdale disclaimed sole responsibility for the ship debts. He charged that his two former partners had "funds in their hands to a greater amount than all the indebtedness of said *Gold Hunter* owner." Unpaid loans, extended to Coffin and Chapman in 1850 and 1851 to help them pay "their proportion of debts" owed to various individuals, embittered Lownsdale even further. Believing that his former partners had stuck him with many of their obligations, he filed suit in 1855, accusing Coffin and Chapman of "faithless promises."[19]

"We became enemies," Coffin later testified of the former proprietors' bitter conflict within a year of their partition agreement. He and Chapman discovered that Lownsdale had secretly amended his partition escrow agreement on file with the General Land Office to embrace the whole claim. Although rejected, the amendment delayed title certification, much to the two ex-proprietors' annoyance. In justifying his action to assume the entire claim himself, Lownsdale accused Chapman and Coffin of "not complying with the first escrow agreement." Enmity increased as the cash short Lownsdale desperately pressed for repayment of the earlier loans. His widespread debts extended even to the *Weekly Oregonian*, which was also short on coin as subscribers and advertisers rarely paid their accounts promptly.[20]

According to one report of August, 1853, Lownsdale could or would not pay the *Oregonian* an advertising bill. During an argument over the matter in Ladd's store Editor T. J. Dryer challenged Lownsdale to "settle with him at the back part of town with from a *Walking cane to a twelve pounder*." Assuming it was a bluff, Lownsdale jestingly offered to meet him on the common at 4:00 p.m. with rifles at 30 paces. Upon arrival at the appointed hour, Dryer "trembled like an aspen leaf and drawled out 'that's nearly hell' and 'sloped', and that was the last of the duel." The duelists were probably inebriated. Both men, known as hard drinkers, were suspended from their Masonic lodges some months later.[21]

Drunk or sober, the warring ex-proprietors continued to do business with one another, particularly if one of the parties needed money. Even as Lownsdale bitterly denounced Coffin and Chapman in an 1855 letter to the *Oregon Statesman*, he sold Chapman several parcels, including his half-interest in what became the Plaza Blocks. In Bush's paper, Lownsdale charged that Chapman and Coffin had "filched out of the pockers of . . . third persons for lots and blocks which was [sic] never paid for by them." Chapman, he said, was "squirming and shuffling" to avoid long-standing obligations.[22]

Chapman and Coffin easily felt justified in ignoring Lownsdale, who had sold many unrecorded lots from sections later assigned their claims. They believed they had been cheated and never fully compensated by the partition. No doubt all three proprietors were equally guilty of shoddy transactions. They became deeply enmeshed in frenzied land sales to cover their debts. Chapman abandoned Portland in 1853 for Fort Umpqua, where he purchased the Hudson's Bay Company's commercial properties. He returned only in 1861, after receiving title certification to his Portland claim.[23]

The Property Holders React

Public outcry over the lengthy property disputes forced Portland's tiny official dom to take action. In late January, 1855, City Attorney William H. Farrar supported a bill in the Oregon House to indemnify Portland against any damages resulting from these title disputes. A recent public meeting, he said, signed a memorial to Congress seeking specific inclusion of Portland within the terms of the Townsite Act of 1844, which Congress extended to Oregon in 1854. Because of uncertainty over the city's status, the Portlanders wanted congressional confirmation that would expressly exclude the city from provisions of the Donation Land Act of 1850. The appealing feature of the Townsite Act was its provision to place in public trust all undeveloped land up to 320 acres. Many Portlanders, including the Starr brothers, who had bought property before 1854, contended all along that the Townsite Act had in fact already been extended to Portland by the Territorial Government Act of 1848. While the Townsite Act would not have prevented abusive speculation, many felt that it would have provided quicker and more direct title certification to purchasers than did the Donation Act.[24]

Farrar complained in behalf of those "who have paid enormous sums for their lots and could have no titles given them." The future mayor contended that

the conflicting of the pretended proprietors render all attempts on the part of the lot holders to obtain titles perfectly futile . . . . These gentlemen proprietors could not give satisfactory titles, for the very good reason that they themselves knew not which or where their property lay [before March 10, 1852].

The proprietors had made "a perfect 'hoch poch'" out of title certification, "leaving the citizens in uncertainty and doubt."[25]

When Congress failed to respond, the city council enacted an ordinance to "enter certain tracts containing 306 acres in a compact form" under the land-trust provision of the Townsite Act. This maneuver of February 1, 1858, directly threatened Coffin's and Chapman's claims, as much of their undeveloped property lay within these tracts. Adding to the confusion, the General Land Office issued title certificates in October, 1860, to Chapman, Coffin and Lownsdale, in the mistaken belief that the lands had indeed been brought under the terms of the Townsite Act by the Territorial Government Act of 1848.[26]

The applicability of the Townsite Act to Portland's land-claim controversies received mention in nearly every court challenge until the U.S. Supreme Court finally resolved the issue in *Stark v. Starr* (1876). Lewis M. Starr, who had bought out his brother, maintained that his rights to block 81 were protected by the Townsite Act, which gave "final right of determination" to the City of Portland and not to Donation Act claimant Benjamin Stark. The Supreme Court surprised many Portlanders, including District Judge Matthew P. Deady and possibly Starr, by upholding Starr's rights to block 81 while reaffirming the supremacy of the Donation Act. According to the court, the Townsite Act was not extended to Portland until 1854. In essence, the court decided that the Starr brothers had bought their property in good faith and improved it, whereas Stark had broken trust with his fellow proprietors by failing to recognize Starr's prior rights when he filed for the entire claim under the Donation Act of September, 1850. Deady, who had upheld both the Donation Act's supremacy and Stark's claim in earlier district court cases, must have been considerably shaken by the Supreme Court's adoption of the doctrine of "equitable title" (fairness) as opposed to his adherence to one of "legal title" (formalism).[27]

Had Chapman, Coffin and Lownsdale acted more cautiously and systematically by recording all title changes and property lines more precisely, as did some neighboring Donation claimants, much of the subsequent litigation might have been prevented. But once they started frantically buying and selling lots to one another and reselling to eager purchasers who repeated the practice, there was no legal way to prevent court challenges. The U.S. Circuit and Supreme courts wisely confirmed most of the earliest (pre-partition) sales and titles, recognizing a form of "squatter's rights" to assure just treatment for the parties concerned.

A Mixed Record

Daniel Lownsdale emerged the poorest of the three townsite proprietors. Although listing $30,000 in real-estate assets in 1860, he was actually insolvent. In September, 1856, he had assigned all his property to Charles M. Carter and Carter's brother-in-law, Joseph S. Smith , as assignees in trust for his creditors. After he died intestate in 1862, his heirs were forced to sell whatever they could to satisfy creditor demands.[28]

Most Portland notables of the period experienced at least one painful encounter with Lownsdale's shoddy practices. In May, 1861, the year before Lownsdale's death, Judge Deady himself sought to purchase as a home site two lots on Alder Street between Seventh (Broadway) and Park. He required a conveyance from Lownsdale, who had sold the lots to the then-owner. Lownsdale swore that the lots lay entirely within his half of the claim. In 1865, when it was determined that the west 20 feet of the corner lot belonged to Lownsdale's late wife Nancy's estate (she also died intestate), Deady learned that he owed Nancy Lownsdale's heirs $353, a sum he initially refused to pay. Ironically, Deady became the victim of a property search initiated by Nancy's heirs, who had brought suit in *his* court to assert their title to parcels Daniel Lownsdale and other proprietors had sold.[29]

That Deady found himself a possible beneficiary in the Lownsdale heirs' litigation must have increased whatever pain he already felt. On general principles, he "could not have enjoyed deciding these cases," in James Mooney's judgment. "They were . . . among the most factually complex and legally unclear of his entire career." Federal Judge Lorenzo Sawyer characterized the "very subtle cases" as "*sui generis*; or like nothing else in the world." For Deady, even a hint of conflict of interest challenged his sense of judicial ethics. While generally supportive of "the common law principles favoring the heirs," his peripheral involvement in these matters undoubtedly strengthened his inclination to favor the heirs. When he later met the $458 debt and interest, he filed claim for recovery against Daniel Lownsdale's estate, settling for an unrecorded amount. Like most of Lownsdale's creditors, Deady probably received less than he sought.[30]

One of Lownsdale's more notorious deals involved conveying two blocks that had been reserved for public use. Both have played a significant role in Portland's history. On April 1, 1858, the insolvent ex-proprietor sold five blocks for $3,800 to his attorney, Lansing Stout, Multnomah County judge and law partner of William H

Farrar. Two weeks later, Stout deeded half of each block to City Recorder Alonzo Leland for $1,900. Of the five parcels, block 132 had been reserved for a public market and block 172 for a federal customs house.

Upon learning of the transaction, *Oregonian* Editor Thomas J. Dryer denounced the deal as "an attempt to steal public property." The city filed suit and retrieved both blocks for the public domain. The market later became the site of the Civic Auditorium, and the customs house the site of the Pioneer Courthouse. In his defense, Lownsdale argued until his death that he alone held rights to the Portland townsite and could dispose of any property he wished. Selling the publicly dedicated lot 132 had invaded Chapman's claim. The remaining three blocks lay in his late wife Nancy's claim, which he unsuccessfully sought to regain after her death.[31]

William W. Chapman (who preferred the title of colonel from his brief service in the Rogue River Indian Wars), returned to Portland in the fall of 1861 after four years as Oregon's surveyor-general. Practicing law quietly for 30 years, he enjoyed a life of comfort but not wealth. Thus, he and Mrs. Chapman required $6,250 for their seven South Park and two Plaza Block donations to the city in 1871, when their assets were listed at $24,000.[32]

Stephen Coffin, who liked to be called "General" from his Civil War militia service, emerged financially strongest from the partnership. The 1860 census listed his Portland real-estate assets at $130,000, a major portion of which comprised way-overvalued property leased for the state penitentiary. The story of this property's conversion to prison use reveals not only typical proprietor shiftiness but also how land and politics so often were entangled.

In June, 1851, nine months before townsite partition, Daniel Lownsdale sold William M. King the usable portion of block 107, on which the territory planned to build part of its new penitentiary. The same wily politician-promoter who mismanaged the Plank Road venture, King was Democratic chairman of the Oregon House faction meeting in Salem and was instrumental in Portland's selection for the prison. "Distinguished by an illuminated nose and a conniving nature," as described by Malcolm Clark, King became chairman of the penitentiary commission charged with constructing the facility. In February, 1854, with little progress to show for the commission's efforts, the *Oregonian* questioned how the prison "property was purchased," as well as King's paying himself $5 a day as commission chairman and another $5 a day for simultaneously filling a commission vacancy.[33]

The legislature that February removed King from the penitentiary commission. Congratulating the "so-called Democratic Party" for dumping him, the *Oregonian*'s Dryer declared, "King has a way of his own in doing things which no sensible or business man could well adopt." The legislature replaced King with Portland merchant William S. Ladd. As in the Plank Road fiasco, Portland's merchants were being called to the rescue. Dryer saluted Ladd, elected mayor in April, as a "man of sterling integrity and acknowledged business qualifications" despite Democratic "political tenets."[34]

Only after receiving his divided share in 1852 had Coffin discovered that his block 106 had been leased by Lownsdale to the territory, which required both his and King's block 107 for the prison. Coffin later complained, "The penitentiary was erected without my permission and against my repeated and solemn protests made to the legislature and penitentiary commission." Refusing to sell his block to the state in 1862, Coffin awaited the prison's removal to Salem some 20 years later.[35]

Alone of the ex-proprietors, Coffin flourished in a Portland of mercantile capitalism. As an active promoter, merchant and politician, he had come to dominate the triumvirate before partition. The first mass meeting of Portland citizens protesting PacMail's contemplated depot removal to St. Helens had chosen him chairman in February, 1852. In 1856, he and his Donation Land claim neighbor, Finice Caruthers, founded the Pioneer Water Works, later sold to merchants Leonard and Green. A recognized commercial and financial leader, Coffin helped found Oregon's Republican Party in 1856 and was elected to the city council in 1857 and again in 1862-63.[36]

In 1862, he was also an organizer and first president of the People's Transportation Company. Headquartered in Salem, PTC vessels controlled upper Willamette River transportation for nearly a decade. Also in 1862, Coffin built the first sawmill in the Pine Belt of eastern Oregon, near LaGrande. Five years later he assumed a large interest in the Oregon Iron Works in northwest Portland. In 1868, he became a major Oregon Central Railroad investor. Several of these ventures lost him a small fortune but still left him with comfortable resources. Rare for the early Portland elite — and for him — in 1871, for a token city payment of $2,500, General and Mrs. Coffin donated valuable land to the public: seven park blocks and several acres for a public levee at the foot of Jefferson Street. Coffin spent his last years quietly on a farm in Dayton, Oregon, dying in near-obscurity in 1882.[37]

Portland's Quiet Neighbors

Donation Land claimants adjacent to and across from the Portland townsite had the chance of wealth, if and when widespread dreams of transforming the village into a prosperous commercial center became true. Several of these men and women took advantage of Portland's proximity and contributed to the town's growth and comfort. Portions of Captain Couch's claim were incorporated in 1851. Other claimants platted and sold lots and larger parcels, which were eventually incorporated into Portland. Some claimants entered transportation, utility and realty ventures in competition or partnership with Portlanders. But by choice or lack of opportunity, neighboring claimants participated little or not at all in the kinds of frenetic land dealings engineered by Portland's proprietors.

Stephen Coffin's neighbor and Pioneer Water Works partner, Finice Caruthers, arrived in 1847 with his mother, Mrs. Elizabeth Caruthers-Thomas. She filed a Donation Land claim in 1850 under her married name, Thomas, but generally used her maiden name, Caruthers, as did her son. Their lives were shrouded in mystery, especially Elizabeth's brief marriage to Joe Thomas in Tennessee. The separated mother and son wound their way overland to Oregon. Believing Joe dead, Elizabeth passed herself off as a widow. Filing under her maiden name caused the General Land Office to question her claim. Finice took the north half of the 640 acres (from today's Southwest Lincoln to Gibbs streets), and Elizabeth the south half to its border with James Terwilliger's claim (near today's Bancroft Street).[38]

Described as a "loner," the bachelor Finice proved a willing and industrious partner for Coffin's ambitious water project. The two diverted the water of Caruthers

Creek (in what became Marquam Gulch) into a primitive network of fir log pipes serving the lower parts of the town. Coffin provided the plan and money; Caruthers, the water and most of the labor. A typical Coffin venture, it was innovative and unprofitable. Barely meeting their costs, the two men sold the enterprise in 1859 to Milwaukie lumber-mill owner Robert Pentland, who resold to Leonard and Green in 1862.[39]

Before his death in 1860 (his mother had died in 1857), Finice laid out some 20 acres as Caruthers Addition to Portland. In the absence of a will or apparent heirs, the $30,000 estate was placed in the hands of a court-appointed administrator, who laid out a second addition and sold the property. Oregon sought title on grounds of a faulty original claim. After much litigation, the state lost and 265 or more acres were sold under suspicious circumstances.[40]

New York native James Terwilliger filed a claim in 1846, immediately south of the Caruthers property. Within the Portland townsite, he also bought four lots from Francis Pettygrove and built a blacksmith shop and the second log house, near First and Southwest Yamhill streets, where he resided before joining the California Gold Rush in 1848. Returning in 1849 with a modest supply of gold dust, he and his family settled on his wooded claim, which he filed under the Donation Act. Reporting property assets of $10,000 in 1860, he farmed his land, ran a small tannery and regularly visited his Portland holdings.[41]

Although Lownsdale died owing Terwilliger a 10-year-old debt of $100 plus 10 percent interest, the latter evidenced no hard feelings toward his late friend when he testified before the Oregon Supreme Court in 1873. In fact, the quiet, retiring farmer expressed no complaints whatsoever against any of the former proprietors whom he knew well. In his later years, Terwilliger platted his claim and began methodically selling off the land, unaffected by speculative pressures until the mid-1880s.[42]

Across the river from Terwilliger and Caruthers, Maine-born Gideon Tibbetts filed a Donation Land claim for 640 acres south of the present-day Southeast Division Street. A 30-year-old farmer, Tibbetts left Iowa for Corvallis in 1847, moving to the Portland area in 1849. On 40 acres of bottom land he raised hay, which he sold for $20 a ton. He developed extensive apple and pear orchards and built and operated the first flour mill on the east side of the Willamette.[43]

Some time late in 1850, Tibbetts unwittingly formed a partnership with Stephen Coffin, providing funds for Coffin to invest in Portland properties. They simultaneously launched a canoe ferry, which operated until Tibbetts's northern neighbor, James B. Stephens, forced suspension of service by court injunction. In August, 1851, with Coffin suffering severe financial stress, the firm of Tibbetts & Coffin dissolved in bitterness when Tibbetts filed suit for recovery of his Portland investment. Knowing how reckless Coffin could be with other people's money, one can assume that he used Tibbetts's funds to meet obligations unrelated to their joint venture. An angry Tibbetts publicly warned readers of the *Oregon Statesman* not to buy land from Coffin.[44]

As interest developed, Tibbetts sold parcels of his claim at $10 to $50 per acre. He also sold property to Stephens, who bought his flour mill. Tibbetts later laid out the town of Brooklyn and platted his Addition to Stephen's East Portland after incorporation in 1871. One term in the Oregon legislature satisfied his political ambition.[45]

James B. Stephens preceded his neighbor Tibbetts by three years, arriving in Oregon City where he opened a small barrel business. In 1845, he acquired a 640-acre tract directly across from the Portland townsite. After returning from the California gold fields with moderate wealth, the 44-year-old Virginian filed under the Donation Act of 1850 and proceeded to lay out a townsite, which he platted in 1861 and incorporated as East Portland in 1871.[46]

No less enterprising than Tibbetts, Stephens had built a rough wagon road to Oregon City with Francis Pettygrove before the latter's departure for California. In the early 1850s, he formed two profitable businesses: the first regional cider mill and the first regular Willamette River ferry service. A mule-powered ferry gave way to horsepower in January, 1852, when Stephens received a legislative charter for the Stark Street ferry, which monopolized cross-river traffic for many years. All challengers were successfully thwarted, on occasion by use of a shotgun. Stephens readily sold non-waterfront land in whatever amounts desired for whatever he could obtain, but interest in it was minimal during the 1850s. As in Tibbetts's case, much of the waterfront property lay in an active flood plain, marshy and gouged by creeks.[47]

Stephens played an active role in regional economic development through numerous dealings with Portland proprietors, merchants and fellow Donation Claim holders. One ambitious but unprofitable venture involved his neighbor James Terwilliger. Together, they harvested a shipload of timber from Stephens's tract, squared the logs and sent them to California, only to discover that the San Francisco market had collapsed. Another costly enterprise was the Pacific Telegraph Company, organized in 1854 by Portland merchants under the leadership of William S. Ladd and George W. Vaughn. Seeking a more secure investment, Stephens acquired a potentially valuable waterfront block between Main and Salmon from Daniel Lownsdale for $2,000. The canny Stephens paid $400 and promised the remaining $1,600 upon conveyance of title from Lownsdale (received in 1860). Lownsdale died owing Stephens $300 at 2½ percent monthly interest, loaned to the desperate ex-proprietor a year before his death. In 1869 Stephens's East Portland waterfront property soared in value as the East-Side Oregon Central Railroad reached Salem, connecting the two cities. By 1871, when East Portland boasted a population of 200, Stephens's real-estate assets exceeded $100,000, much of which he lost upon collapse of his East Portland Savings and Loan Bank following the panic of 1873.[48]

The Balance Sheet: Stark and Couch

Of all the Donation Land claimants in the Portland area during the 1850s, Benjamin Stark, the supercargo-turned-lawyer, ranked first in assessed real estate at $55,800 in 1859. His wealth was largely on paper. He grew increasingly in debt through the decade until his credit became severely restricted. To finance various promotions, including new commercial buildings and river vessels, he borrowed heavily from such friends as *Oregon Statesman* Publisher Asahel Bush. The newsman's lawyer warned the Salem Democratic leader in 1858 to secure any Stark loan with real estate, "but not without having the title examined for he is damned slippery."[49]

Stark lacked a merchant's temperament. As a risk taker, he was basically a speculator who had been lucky, at least until 1860. A born optimist, the vain Stark had repeatedly convinced himself that the next deal would pay off. As Judge Matthew P. Deady observed, "I don't know about Stark's funds. If *airs* were *eagles*, he could pay off the national debt and have something left."[50]

Captain John H. Couch, Stark's former partner, held less valuable real estate than Stark in 1859 because most of his larger holdings were undeveloped. But Couch was already a more important figure in Portland. As a middle-aged ship captain and sometime merchant, he had become immensely respected in the tiny village. He and his brother-in-law, Captain George H. Flanders, shared a Donation Land claim and platted and developed it slowly. Couch's significance stemmed primarily from the superior location of his claim, its subsequent commercial value and its early partial incorporation into Portland (in 1851).

Personal commitment, unostentatious values and integrity were his distinguishing characteristics, uncommon among frontier merchants and land promoters. A quiet and thoughtful person, Couch appeared less aggressively acquisitive than his merchant peers. He did not share the speculative fervor of Chapman, Coffin, Lownsdale and Stark; to him, borrowing money was a cardinal sin. Like Stephens, Tibbetts and Terwilliger, he adhered to simple frontier ways, enjoying the challenge more than the material rewards — which were far from meager. For over 10 years, the Couch family inhabited a modest house on a 13-acre tract along the west shore of a lake (near the present Union Station). From its porch, the captain was often observed fishing or shooting at ducks. Whereas Corbett and Ladd erected large new houses in the mid-1870s, the more comfortable home that Couch built several years before his death, five blocks south of the lake, was small and ordinary by their standards.

Before he was 46 in 1857, Couch had founded Portland's first Masonic lodge, served most of two terms on the city council, built wharves and warehouses on his claim, and served as inspector of hulls, port warden and member of the Columbia River Pilot Commission. Until his sudden death at 59, in 1870, from typhoid pneumonia, he worked hard upon his large wharf.

Couch was almost the last of the unpretentious among Portland's early elite. On the day of his funeral, all activity ceased. Businesses, banks and offices closed to honor him. His personal estate was appraised at $127,600. The 1870 U.S. census listed Couch-Flanders family assets at nearly $200,000, a sizeable fortune for the time.[51]

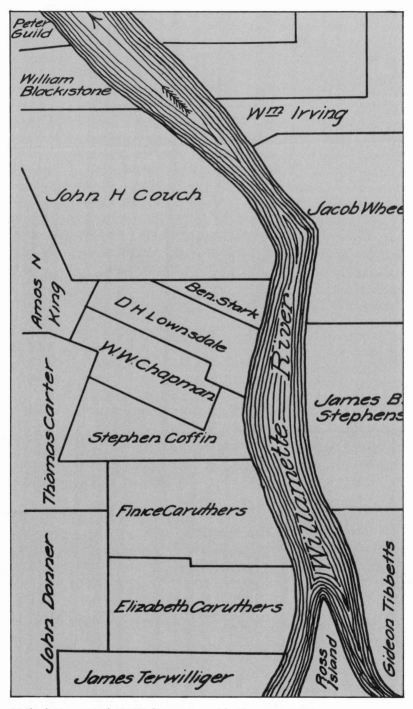

3.1 The division on March 10, 1852, between Lownsdale, Chapman and Coffin
after dividing with Stark on March 3

3.3 Thomas J. Dryer (1803-1879)

3.2 Asahel Bush (1824-1913) in 1850

3.4 An elderly James B. Stephens (1806-1880)

3.5 An elderly James A. Terwilliger (1809-1892)

3.6 The Old Plank Road, segment c. 1890s (today's Canyon Road)

4
LOCAL POLITICAL POWER
STRUCTURE: THE 1850S

Framing Local Politics

For mid-nineteenth-century Oregonians, politics was a major occupation. "Politics was a trough in which the slop of spoils flowed," observes Terence O'Donnell. "It was the crowding at this trough which accounts for the rough and tumble" of Oregon and Portland politics in the decade of the 1850s, a discordant period in which Portland's Front Street merchants seized local political control from the three townsite proprietors. Josiah Failing's election as mayor in April, 1853, marked the transition.[1]

Although achieving political dominance after 1852, Portland merchants were unable to unite politically during the remainder of the decade. Harmony no more reigned in Portland than in such other frontier communities as Oregon City and Salem. Political factions, comprising cliques and personalities, manipulated local and territorial politics. Political contention, inflamed by highly partisan newspapers, grew increasingly strident during the turbulent pre-Civil War years. National and territorial issues — particularly slavery extension, statehood and territorial capital location — occupied the front pages of the *Weekly Oregonian*. Thomas Dryer's pungent editorials championed territorial Whiggism while Asahel Bush's *Oregon Statesman*, which moved from Oregon City to Salem in 1853, similarly expressed the views of the more dominant Democratic partisans. Among Portland voters, however, local issues and personalities generated most interest, stimulating a near-frenzied activity at municipal-election times but subsiding into apathy once local contests ended.[2]

Local government, generally weak and ineffective, was merely one facet of the broader Oregon political scene. Still, it was used as an important mechanism for Portland merchants in shaping local events to maximize their potential business gains. At first, merchants like William S. Ladd usually sought local office. After establishing their political power, they handed the reins to others who would do their bidding. They recognized the distinction between office holding and power holding; that one did not need to hold office to influence political events.[3]

Merchant Josiah Failing served on the city council in 1852 and became mayor in April, 1853. Merchants John H. Couch and William S. Ladd joined Failing as councilmen, with Ladd succeeding Failing as mayor in April, 1854. That same spring, Ladd helped organize Washington County Democrats, six months before Multnomah County was carved from it. Throughout the period and later, Ladd kept Bush apprised of potential anti-Bush Democrats active in legislative and city contests. In 1856, Ladd served his last term on the council. Three years later, he secured election to the Multnomah County Commission, an effort that allowed him and his new Ladd & Tilton Bank to extend their political influence east of the Willamette River.[4]

Like most leading Portland merchants in the 1850s, Ladd was a Democrat, a pragmatic States' righter who supported the party of Andrew Jackson for its "cordiality" toward wealth, to use Rush Welter's term. Democrats favored egalitarian success and a capitalism freed from the paternalistic, pro-tariff nationalism of the Whigs — "property-in-use" as opposed to "property-in-possession." Even Josiah Failing, a staunch ex-New York Whig, voted the Oregon Democratic ticket until joining the new Republican Party in 1859. As Robert Johannsen has observed, merchant Whigs like Failing "differed but little from the Democrats" in antebellum Portland. Only a scattering of Portland diehards — attorneys David Logan and Amory Holbrook, proprietor Stephen Coffin and the *Oregonian's* Thomas Dryer among them — remained true to the Whig cause. In early 1853, as the national party was disintegrating, a local Whig Party was finally organized as a last-ditch effort to counter growing Democratic popularity.[5]

Holding local office in Oregon of the 1850s was hardly perceived as public service. Primarily, it provided access to community power and assured that government, however, weak, would encourage and support private enterprise. Public and private spheres of interest were believed to be inextricably intertwined. "The good society," as Welter has noted, "was one in which every man was left alone to exploit his economic opportunities as best he could." As opposed to the Whigs, who viewed government as an active partner, Democrats of the Ladd and Bush persuasion believed in a passive government, one that would encourage private development generally by leaving it alone.[6]

To them, the primary responsibilities of local government were twofold: to provide the basic legal order and maintain adequate health standards for minimum taxes. Ladd and his peers prized a self-government that advanced general prosperity without excessive restraint on personal liberty. The city — like the territory — was a place for private money making. And government, while necessary for public safety, was potentially, in Welter's words, "a hostile force." Ambivalent about public authority, Portland merchant leaders mistrusted the very institution they helped create and ran. Territorially bestowed city charters confirmed such fears. Portland was constitutionally the child of the territorial legislature. Charters severely limited local governments like frontier Portland's, assigning them only minimal powers. Thus, as national and regional currents swept the struggling western towns, the towns were rarely masters of their own political fates.[7]

Earliest Governments

Portland's incorporation in January, 1851, marked the ending of nearly all proprietorial direction of town political life. Merchants dominated the eight city councils from 1851 through 1857. (Two councils were elected in 1852.) The percentage of merchant membership ranged from a high of 100 in 1851 to a low of 55 in 1855, with the average at 70. Beginning in 1858, the number of merchants on the council dropped rapidly, until there were only 11 percent in 1859. Except in 1862, merchants never again constituted a majority of the city council.

For the 10 city councils between 1852 and 1860, turnover averaged 88 percent. For that same period, 79 men held 87 council seats; 19 were re-elected, but only nine consecutively. Ten left office prematurely: eight by resignation, one by expulsion and one by disqualification. Council instability peaked in 1857, with seven early departures from nine posts. Replacements barely warmed their seats before eight new councilmen were chosen in April, 1858. And an entirely new council replaced them the following year.[8]

MAYORS OF PORTLAND, 1851-1860		
YEARS	MAYOR	OCCUPATION
1851-2	Hugh D. O'Bryant	Carpenter
1852	A. C. Bonnell	Lumber-mill owner, accountant
1852 (Nov.)	S. B. Marye	Attorney, W. W. Chapman's son-in-law
1853	Josiah Failing	Merchant, general
1854	William S. Ladd	Merchant, general
1855	George W. Vaughn	Merchant, hardware
1856	James A. O'Neil	Merchant, manager of Wells Fargo office
1857	James A. O'Neil	
1858	Addison M. Starr	Merchant, tinsmith
1859	Stephen J. McCormick	Merchant, printer
1860	G. Collier Robbins	Merchant, jeweler

The huge turnover in political offices reflected, to Kenneth N. Owens, a "highly personal form of politics that can best be described as chaotic factionalism." By the end of the decade, this "disorderly style of politics" in western territories was replaced by "a more stable and enduring organizational pattern," that of Democrats against Republicans. A new city charter in 1862, establishing two-year council terms, further stabilized Portland government. Merchants pressed for these steadying changes to cope with new economic challenges in the 1860s. Before then, mercantile leaders appeared indifferent to the political turbulence and high council turnover, so long as town commercial life flourished and their own interests were heeded.[9]

Merchant dominance before 1858 never assured competent government. It more often produced non-government. Mayors performed such ceremonial duties as cutting ribbons and signing ordinances and payrolls. Tumultuous city council sessions became endlessly embroiled in bickering. From 1851 to 1854, Portland underwent three legislatively approved city charter revisions, but only to change minor procedures. William S. Ladd's election as mayor in March, 1854, inaugurated an effort to make city government more cost-efficient in providing basic services.

Three months passed after incorporation before city government unsteadily came into being. On April 7, 1851, 140 voters chose a mayor, recorder and five councilmen, all part-time officials. An earlier election in March had bestowed the mayor's office on Thomas Dryer, who declined. Hugh D. O'Bryant, a popular 38-year-old Georgia Democrat, had little notion of the task awaiting him. Previous experience as an Indian fighter and carpenter ill prepared the rough-hewn, uneducated frontiersman to manage even the simplest of governments. O'Bryant's one notable contribution to Portland history was to found the city's first public library, a second-floor rented room on Front Street supplied with books, newspapers and magazines that he and others donated.[10]

Councilman Thomas Robinson rented the council an unheated shack for a considerable $30 per month. For their initial meeting, Councilman George Barnes kindly sold the city fathers $29.95 worth of candles and candlesticks. Lacking funds for a stove and unwilling to endure the rigors of winter, council members forsook their regular early-evening weekly meetings between mid-November and mid-March. With the exception of appointed city officials — the marshal-health officer, the tax assessor, and the constable — no one conducted any formal government business during winter months for three years.[11]

Early sessions pitted frontier ways against the formalities assumed beneficial to a civilized place. The mayor had to stand when addressing council, and councilmen had to speak from assigned seats. These procedures were usually forgotten during heated debate and the ensuing confusion. Unpaid councilmen feared the added constraint of a $5 fine for absence at roll call.

Earliest ordinances dealt with health, street improvement and discharging firearms. Councils repeatedly legislated against gambling, drunken disturbance, riotous behavior, and "fast and furious driving through the streets." Fines of $5 to $25 and even jail sentences faced the guilty, but there was neither local court nor jail. The accused were transported with difficulty to Hillsboro, the Washington County seat. (Portland became the seat for Multnomah County in December, 1854.) When local voters rejected a jail-tax levy in June, 1851, city merchants raised $1,200 privately and constructed a 25-by-16-foot log jail near Front and Stark streets.[12]

The financing of fire protection, dear to the merchant heart, faced more difficult hurdles. Until 1853, the town had to rely on a bucket brigade organized by Thomas Dryer. Voters strongly approved the council's levying a tax for purchase of a pump engine and hose, but Mayor O'Bryant refused to execute the mandate. The obstinate O'Bryant wrote the council prior to leaving office in April, 1852:

In answer to your Resolution inquiring to know of me disposition I have mad [sic] of the duplicates levying [sic] a tax to collect and raise a fund to purchase a ingine [sic] and hoes [sic] for use of the City, I will say for your information that they are in my desk without my signature.[13]

Perplexed and frustrated by their government's apparent inability to meet the city's most basic needs, over 200 Portlanders, including the merchant leadership, petitioned the territorial legislature for a new city charter. As enacted in January, 1853, and overwhelmingly approved by the voters, the new instrument divided

Portland into two electoral districts, granted veto power to the mayor, increased the council size from five to nine, provided for an elected marshal, and more sharply defined and expanded the city's police powers, as in making the operation of "bawdy houses" a crime. Enthusiasm for the new charter, embodying hopes for more effective municipal governance, induced Josiah Failing to run for mayor in April, 1853. The dean of Front Street merchants was so consumed by business concerns, including the recent loss of an entire shipment on the Columbia River bar, that he proved barely more effective than his three predecessors. And personal discord still divided the enlarged 1853 council. Thwarted in his effort to convince the council to undertake much-needed street improvements, Mayor Failing had to make them around his store at his own expense. Other merchants, including Henry W. Corbett, did likewise.[14]

During the fall of 1853, the city government came under increasing editorial attack from the *Oregonian*. Thomas Dryer charged council malfeasance for failing "to improve the streets and sidewalks . . . . The city council and surgeons of this city ought to enter into partnership. Breaking bones and setting them will prove a profitable business." An earlier editorial castigated the government for its failure to enforce law and order. "Our city of late," Dryer remonstrated, "has been the scene of disgraceful midnight rows and bacchanalian revelry, disgusting to every sober mind, by a group of vagabonds hanging around the low groggeries in the day time and destroying property at night." As one not known for sobriety, the *Oregonian* editor was apparently offended by *public* drunkenness and property destruction.[15]

Partisan municipal politics, two years in the making, emerged full-blown with Democrat William S. Ladd's election as mayor in March, 1854. Although the national Whig Party had crumbled, the local party continued to field candidates under the forceful prodding of Thomas Dryer and David Logan. A minority of prominent merchants and large property owners, like Henry W. Corbett and Stephen Coffin, maintained their traditional Whig loyalties until the birth of the national Republican Party in 1856. Dryer infinitely preferred a Whig mayor to the Democrat Ladd, even after badgering previous Whig councilmen for inaction and dereliction of duty. "Be prepared for mongrel tickets," he warned a Whig rally. To his chagrin, voters on March 17 chose an all-Democratic slate. They also approved the city's third charter, which empowered the mayor to participate in council discussions, a change advocated by Ladd before the legislature. Dryer foresaw ruination — "sin, sorrow and death" — under Democratic dominance.[16]

The new government made sweeping changes under the new charter. To a later city archivist, "the city of Portland experienced a re-birth." All previous ordinances and resolutions were ignored. New ordinances, starting with a new number one, wiped out "all which had gone before in Portland's existence." The earliest council minutes would have been destroyed had not Volume I been less than half used. Their preservation reflected Ladd's characteristic frugality. The merchant mayor's habits of thrift were legendary. He would reply to a letter by writing between its lines and then mailing it back. He would also slice open envelopes and use the opened inner side for letter paper. As mayor, he applied his yardstick of frugality to all city expenditures. By force of personality, he was the first Portland mayor to exert strong influence on city government. Even though he faced a discordant council, he used his newly granted power in council deliberations to win more skirmishes than he lost.[17]

William S. Ladd was also instrumental in the formation of Multnomah County halfway through his term as mayor. Responding to the vocal demands of Portland merchants, the territorial legislature created the 16th Oregon county on December 22, 1854. Portland lawyers and tradesmen had found it costly and inconvenient to journey 15 miles to Hillsboro, in Washington County, to conduct court business. They clamored that a new county seat would properly recognize the territory's largest town.

The first board of county commissioners, elected in early January, 1855, comprised east county resident Emsley R. Scott, Sauvie Island landowner James F. Bybee, and Portland resident George W. Vaughn. Hardware merchant Vaughn, a native of New Jersey, came to Portland in 1850 and quickly established an aggressive and successful business. Three years younger than Josiah Failing, he was a senior member of the merchant establishment. With Ladd, he strongly supported the formation of Multnomah County and was a popular choice to assume Portland's mayorship in April, 1855, when Ladd declined re-election.

A flamboyant promoter, Mayor Vaughn ran weekly ads publicizing his hardware business. An advertisement of June, 1855, issued under the threat of Indian raids, proclaimed to a somewhat frightened public, "We are still alive and well, still on Front Street." Following Ladd's example, Vaughn invested his mercantile profits in a three-story brick building and extensive real estate. By 1859, he was listed as the third-wealthiest property owner in Multnomah County, with real estate worth $44,000. In 1865, he built the city's largest flour mill. Increased real-estate assets of $500,000 in 1870 won Vaughn top ranking as a local property owner. In 1873, fire and recession all but wiped him out. Retiring into obscurity, he died four years later at age 68.[18]

Local Issues and Political Factions

Discord, mixing personalities and politics, increased during the last five city governments of the 1850s. While gold discoveries in the Rogue River area and on the upper Columbia during 1855-56 stimulated intense business activity in Portland, the threat of Indian attacks created near-paranoia, which inflamed existing political factionalism. The influx of miners into the gold fields aroused Indian resentment; outbreaks of fighting led to full-scale wars. Over strong objections from some members, the city council hired guards to prevent Indians from burning the city's wooden buildings.[19]

Mayor George W. Vaughn felt particularly alarmed in October, 1855, by rumors of murdered settlers near Fort Vancouver. He and four other merchants persuaded Governor George L. Curry to provide arms and ammunition for local volunteers then gathering in Portland. Locally owned horses were commandeered from merchants like Henry W. Corbett; other merchants like Stephen Coffin personally underwrote additional equipment costs for companies of untrained recruits. Even Daniel Lownsdale responded. Unable to provide funds, he volunteered as an assistant quartermaster for six months. For Portland and its environs, the threat proved unfounded. A small band of Yakimas penetrated no closer than 40 miles form the city.[20]

From cessation of the Indian threat through the end of 1861, the city council fought repeatedly over ownership of the city levee and regulation of alcohol sales. Both issues, like most others of the time, became entangled in personal quarrels. The most prominent dispute involved the outspoken Democratic merchants Thomas J. Holmes and Shubrick Norris and two-term mayor James A. O'Neil. Although the mayor was a nominal Whig, partisan politics were irrelevant in these instances.

The Holmes-Norris feud was the most extreme example of political infighting during the decade. It began while grocer Norris served on the first city council in 1851. Over the next six years, the English-born Holmes, a politically ambitious and increasingly successful shoe merchant, grabbed appointive and elective offices. Some he held concurrently, like those of street commissioner, city collector and city marshal. During his third council term in 1854, Norris attacked Holmes's moonlighting and forced him to resign all other positions to retain the lucrative elected marshal's job. In the process, Norris created a bitter enemy.

Holmes gained revenge in 1857 after finally securing a long-sought city council post: he blocked Norris's confirmation as replacement for Captain John H. Couch, who had resigned for personal reasons. This episode was part of the most horrendous council session in Portland history. One councilman was even expelled — a unique event. All others but Holmes resigned, including Simeon Reed, whose business demanded his full attention. Eight ballots were required to elect Stephen Coffin over Daniel H. Lownsdale for one of the vacancies. His brief tenure ended with the 1859 Democratic landslide. The discouraged Norris never again sought public office.[21]

Holmes had similarly been assailing Mayor James A. O'Neil, who, at 57, was one of Portland's senior public figures. Since arriving in Oregon in 1834, the New York-born O'Neil had engaged in various commercial enterprises and served as a Yamhill County judge. Appointed first manager of the Wells Fargo Portland office, the nominal Whig was too cautious for the feisty Holmes. O'Neil twice blocked Holmes's efforts to remove him from office for being absent from the city for more than 30 days without council consent. O'Neil further angered Holmes in 1857 by opposing the councilman's successful effort to move the city hall (a second-floor office on Front Street) to a site that happened to be closer to Holmes's residence. The ever-confident and apparently popular Holmes served on the council through 1858, and again in 1862 and 1863. Succeeding Henry Failing as mayor in November, 1866, the wealthy merchant died in office in June, 1867, leaving an estate of at least $100,000.[22]

The Alcohol Problem

Public regulation of alcohol sales embittered local politics during the 1850s because it intimately affected most Portland men. The first regulatory ordinance in April, 1854, ineffectually controlled what Charles Tracy and others have described as "the busy barrooms and drinking shops." Widespread public protests against "'outrages on common decency,'" followed. "Portland's major crime problem throughout

1856 appears to have been related to the sale of alcohol," Tracy concludes. A more punitive measure in January, 1857, merely fueled bar and patron complaints that license costs and high fines hurt business. The debate, as Tracy observes, reflected "the age-old conflict between commerce and morality," a battle usually won in Portland by commerce.[23]

Leading Portlanders knew the attractions of alcohol. While Thomas Dryer periodically raved against public drunkenness in his editorials, he was removed as master of Willamette Lodge No. 2 of the Masonic Order for intemperance, having "been previously suspended in a sister jurisdiction." Grand Master Benjamin Stark suspended Daniel H. Lownsdale, Colonel William M. King and others for similar cause. Previous Grand Master Captain John C. Ainsworth despaired that "intemperance [has been] allowed to stalk into our sanctum sanctorum and disagreements and discords" had flourished. The lodge accepted a rule in early 1857 suspending Masonic sellers of liquor "for producing drunkenness."[24]

Masonic discord likely contributed to the stridency of city council liquor debates in the chaotic spring of 1857. Captain John H. Couch and Simeon G. Reed were ardent Masons, as were Thomas J. Holmes and council President Charles Hutchins, himself once briefly suspended from Willamette Lodge for intemperance. When Couch and Reed resigned, ostensibly for personal and business reasons, their replacements included the suspended Mason, William M. King. The new councilmen, a mixture of Whig-Republicans and Democrats, publicly backed the saloon interests.

Partisan politics played a role in the liquor debate. Both King and Holmes were outspoken Democratic Party leaders, but their zeal for unimpeded free enterprise, heartily embracing commercial profit, was also shared by Whig-Republican businessmen like Stephen Coffin. None of the pro-liquor councilmen seemed constrained by the moral issue when private profits were involved. Thus Holmes and King encountered only minor opposition when they forced repeal of the more objectionable sections of the liquor ordinance of January, 1857, leaving few limits on alcohol sales. Under Democratic leadership, the saloon interests regained their authority and maintained council dominance for nearly a decade.[25]

The electorate further stabilized saloon power when it choose Democrat Addison M. Starr as mayor in April, 1858. Tin merchants and stove manufacturers, the Starr brothers also operated Portland's first distillery. In April, 1859, A. M. Starr was elected sheriff; he appointed his brother, L. M., his deputy. The same voters chose James H. Lappeus as city marshal. A staunch Democrat and co-owner of the popular Oro Fino Saloon, he was also known as a man of firm character, with considerable organizational skills useful to commercial interests, especially the liquor trade. Although he would be accused of unprofessional conduct on numerous occasions, he remained generally popular. Defeated in 1862, he was re-elected in 1868 and won appointment as Portland's first police chief in 1870, serving "until removal for cause in July, 1877."[26]

The Public Levee

No issue facing early city councils held longer-term importance for Portland history than determining the ownership of the Willamette River levee. Portlanders generally recognized that levee development, public or private, was essential to a river-dependent city. But as the controversy evolved in subsequent decades, the real question became which *private* parties should control development rights to the increasingly valuable river front property.

From the 1850s until legal determination of ownership in 1861, the city vacillated in its effort to preserve the levee against private claims. Changing council membership crucially affected the outcome. Until his death, attorney Asa Lovejoy repeatedly maintained that he and his fellow proprietor, Francis Pettygrove, meant to preserve the levee for public use, an allegation Pettygrove later denied. No written evidence existed to support Lovejoy's contention. The subsequent proprietor-promoters Lownsdale, Coffin and Chapman opposed public ownership of the riverfront once Captain Couch had built on his own property a profitable covered dock and warehouse. Designed like those in New England river and seaport towns, Couch's dock proved far better for ships than moorage along the open-ground levee running south from Stark's Addition.[27]

Pettygrove erected the first building on the levee, a small warehouse next to his wharf at the foot of Washington Street. Both structures came into Daniel Lownsdale's possession upon purchase of the township. When Lownsdale placed a small building on the levee north of Pettygrove's wharf, he precipitated the first court challenge. The Reverend Josiah L. Parrish, a Methodist missionary who served as Indian agent from 1849 to 1854, sued in July, 1850, to keep the levee for free public use. Meanwhile the Starrs were constructing a riverfront tin shop on the contested block 81 in Stark's Addition, and A. P. Dennison of *Gold Hunter* fame was building a store just over the townsite boundary. Parrish sought an injunction to preserve a riverfront view from his Front Street property. Obviously more concerned about private view than public use, Parrish had paid Pettygrove a premium price for his property in 1849. Supporting Lovejoy, Parrish claimed that Pettygrove had dedicated the levee to the public.[28]

It took three years for Parrish's case to wind its way to the territorial supreme court. During the interim, the city council, in Harvey Scott's opinion, "acted in a manner peculiar and contradictory. They either forgot for a time that they had any rights to protect and secure for the city, or deemed these of little importance." An 80 percent turnover in council membership discouraged a consistent policy. In the meantime, Lownsdale was selling lots along the river to anyone meeting his price. One sold to hardware merchant George W. Vaughn in 1851 was the subject of a dispute between Vaughn and the council in subsequent years.[29]

On April 29, 1852, six weeks after the townsite division, an entirely new council adopted the Brady map as an "authoritative diagram of the city." On Lownsdale's instructions, Brady had copied the 1850 Short survey in which "the land on the river bank east of [Front] . . . street was laid off in lots and block," implying private ownership of the levee. In its naivete (a charitable characterization) the council wanted an official map, and "because the Brady map was most convenient they declared it to be the correct plat of Portland." The action was taken by informal resolution, not by ordinance, and so never entered official city or county records.[30]

Emboldened by council approval of the Brady plan, Lownsdale attempted to build additional wharves along the levee. Two incidents in 1853 slowed but did not stop him: election of an entirely new and enlarged city council in April, and, six months later, the territorial supreme court decision in the Parrish case. The new council and eight subsequent ones opposed all attempts by Lownsdale and others at private levee development but failed to repudiate the Brady map until January, 1857. The Ladd administration's 1854 abrogation of previous council actions likely removed any felt need for official retraction.

Speaking for the supreme court, Justice Cyrus Olney strongly endorsed Parrish's position. After reviewing the testimony, Olney concluded that the proprietors had recognized the public right "until, 'after much importunity from some who had an itching palm for this attractive property, they yielded to the desire and hope of reclaiming the tempting prize.'" The following term, Chief Justice George H. Williams "emphatically" denied a rehearing request. "Public levees are almost as necessary in such towns as public streets." Newly appointed Justice Matthew P. Deady dissented without opinion.[31]

The issue was far from settled. Affected property owners Lownsdale and Vaughn launched an appeal, which did not reach the U.S. Supreme Court until 1857. They also continued to make use of their levee property in defiance of the new council Ordinance 51, of June 7, 1856, requiring removal of "all obstructions," including lumber stored in crude shacks on top of the levee. Fearing a city loss in the nation's highest court, in January, 1857, the council replaced the Brady map with the 1845 Brown map, and sought voter approval of a special tax to pay its heavy litigation costs. Hailing the map decision, voters rejected the tax levy. Opinion apparently prevailed against engaging a high-priced Washington lawyer to protect rights that voters believed the city already possessed. Councilman Thomas J. Holmes, a leading advocate of public-levee rights, raised funds to argue the case in 1858.[32]

In October, 1858, the council further resolved to halt improvement on the levee. When the city street commissioner sought enforcement through court order in January, 1859, George W. Vaughn defiantly began construction of a wharf between Alder and Morrison streets, claiming his property-owner's rights. The council angrily charged the former mayor with "aggressions on the public levee." Under the leadership of a new councilman, Henry W. Corbett, Vaughn and others were ordered to "cease trespassing on 'Public Property.'" In the absence of any enforcement, the wharf was completed.[33]

The issue reappeared in mid-March, 1860, when Vaughn began a building to enclose his wharf. On March 22, the council ordered Marshal J. H. Lappeus to remove it within 24 hours. The next day, defying the marshal, Vaughn employed a large gang and hastily completed the building. That afternoon, the mayor, the marshal and assistants started removal preparations. They were arrested by Sheriff Starr on a warrant from the city recorder. Following a hearing, which apparently justified their intentions, Mayor S. J. McCormick, assisted by "a large body of citizens," tore down the building. The *Oregonian* reported that "it was almost a riot . . . lots of excitement but no violence." Its harshly critical editorial accused the mayor and council (all Democrats but one) of being "a body of small men, . . . party hacks and selfish officeseekers, . . . indifferent to the real interests of the city." Attorney William H. Farrar, who was elected mayor in 1862, joined Alonzo Leland in printing a pamphlet that accused McCormick of fanning up "a flame of vengeance," arousing "passion and the mobocratic spirit of our community."[34]

Publisher Stephen J. McCormick, one of the only two mayors in Portland's history to engage personally in the physical destruction of private property, victoriously retired from office in April, 1860. The same election returned six incumbents to office. A jeweler and East Portland property owner, G. Collier Robbins, whom Henry Failing would later castigate for financial incompetence, became mayor. Within weeks, the U.S. Supreme Court dismissed the Lownsdale-Vaughn appeal for lack of jurisdiction and returned it to the Portland federal district court presided over by Judge Matthew P. Deady. The thwarted appellants, remembering Deady's 1854 Parrish dissent while serving on the territorial supreme court, optimistically expected vindication, as did other would-be developers.

Stephen Coffin, for one, wished to build a wharf on his section of the levee south of Madison Street. Like other riverfront property owners, he was enjoying Portland's booming economy during the summer and fall of 1860. Trade and river commerce was expanding rapidly, stimulated by the new Oregon Steam Navigation Company. Development pressure increased, but the council refused to budge. Newly elected councilman and council President Captain John C. Ainsworth induced a new resolution to "remove and prevent obstructions on the levee." But such acts were mooted by federal issuance on October 17, 1860, of Coffin's and Lownsdale's Donation Land Act certificates, granting them titles to the levee.[35]

Ainsworth's role in the levee controversy merits attention. His Oregon Steam Navigation Company already owned a full block of riverfront property in Stark's Addition. Threat of competition rather than support for a public levee per se may well have prompted his council stand. By blocking private wharf construction south of Stark's Addition, the OSN would protect itself from competing river transportation companies in need of Portland dock space. It was no coincidence that Ainsworth, who had been in Portland less than a year, successfully won a council seat and its presidency just as he was organizing the OSN, which would monopolize river transportation within two years.

Although Daniel Lownsdale's federal patent would not be issued until 1865, three years after his death, his rights and those of his heirs appeared secure. His son J. P. O. Lownsdale promptly began constructing his own wharf, only to have his crew arrested. He filed suit in Judge Deady's court and proceeded with the work. The resulting chaos, coupled with a change in public opinion that seemed to favor private levee development, influenced the city elections of April, 1861. Seven of the nine incumbents were replaced. The two leaders of the council revolt were prominent, pro-development Democrats: commission merchant John McCraken, elected council president and veteran promoter William M. King of Plank Road notoriety. By two votes in June, 1861, one overriding Mayor John Breck's veto, the city council formally opened the gates to private levee development.[36]

Judge Deady's two decisions of December 5, 1861, and January 11, 1862, in favor of J. P. O. Lownsdale and George Vaughn were probably predictable. Deady ruled that "the city failed to sustain its burden of proof. Evidence of a dedication to the public needed to be 'clear and cogent.'" He noted that the Portland city council, by adopting the Brady map in 1852, "'deliberately recognized and adopted' his map as correct, and twice — in 1854 and 1858 — it taxed those fractional [waterfront] blocks as private property.'" As Ralph James Mooney has observed, "Deady's most influential contemporaries, even those who thought the decision unfortunate, tended to blame others." The city had "'already decided the case against itself,'" Jesse Applegate wrote Deady, "'by approving Short's map and survey [incorporated into the Brady map].'" Deady concluded that there was no provision in federal law authorizing the city to hold property in trust for the public prior to 1854. Portland had only one recourse: to buy the land.[37]

William S. Ladd, who likely supported John McCraken and the other pro-development forces, did not appear surprised by his friend's second opinion. Writing to Democratic U.S. Senator James W. Nesmith, he commented, "In a change today, Judge Deady decided the levee Case in deciding it gave it to the claimants and against the City. No doubt he will have innumerable suits for damages for moving houses . . . by the City. Vaughn claims 20,000 for damages. Carter & Capt. Smith have similar claims." Vaughn sued for $17,275 and won only $1,000 in 1863.[38]

The resolution of levee ownership in favor of private property rights, decided on narrow, legalistic grounds, was consistent with prevailing norms of local American land-use law in the mid-nineteenth century. Governmentally — and judicially — there was little real distinction between private and public matters. City government became the arena, as Michael Frisch has concluded about Springfield, Massachusetts, where such "overlapping and conflicting private purposes were adjusted." The structure of city government was not as important as the people who served in it.[39]

Pressured by private economic forces, Portland factional alignments often shifted rapidly, dictated by personalities and cliques of leaders. Thomas J. Holmes and William M. King, allied in the liquor-control fight, split in 1858 over the levee issue. By 1861, Holmes might have switched his position from public to private ownership after recognizing the growing pro-development feelings in the Democratic Party and among voters. His re-election to the council in 1862 supports this thesis. The presence of King and Holmes on the council symbolized and accentuated mounting political partisanship at the local level in the late 1850s and early 1860s. As on the national scene, local, territorial and then statewide factionalism, while always comprising a degree of intra-party discord, increasingly pitted Republicans against Democrats.

Merchants Confront Partisanship

The council elected in April, 1859, dramatically revealed that merchants were no longer the dominant members of Portland city councils. Among the nine posts, merchants occupied only two. Merchant membership in 1859 had fallen to a low of 11 percent from a previous nine-year average of 64 percent. A trend toward decreased merchant participation began in mid-1857, when merchant-councilmen were forced by financial panic in the East to turn their attention to the uncertainties affecting their firms. It was also the year of highest council instability.

Merchants did not withdraw in 1859 from direct exercise of political power in Portland. They retained their hold on the elected mayor and city treasurer posts. Voters chose merchant Henry W. Corbett, a rising figure in the new Republican Party, to manage city finances in April, 1858, a year after his defeat for mayor — his first political campaign. In October, 1858, Corbett was elected by the council to fill the remaining six-month term of a resigned member. Commission merchant John McCraken, allied with the Democrats' ruling Salem Clique and a close friend of William S. Ladd, succeeded Corbett as treasurer in 1859. McCraken simultaneously held the patronage job of U.S. Marshal. (Holding two or more offices in the same or different jurisdictions was common in the territories.)

The 1859 council was significant on other accounts. The "unwashed and unconquerable Democracy" had won a great victory, lamented Dryer of the *Oregonian*. All its members, except one, were now Democrats. The Democrats had happily ridden into Portland office on a wave of approval for winning Oregon statehood two months earlier. Erasmus Shattuck, David Logan's law partner and a future Oregon Supreme Court justice, was the sole Republican councilman. Defeated was a citizens' ticket that included such important merchants, landowners and ship captains as Henry Failing, Stephen Coffin and Alexander Ankeny. In their places sat men of different occupations: a physician, a steamboat captain, the penitentiary superintendent, a builder, and a house painter. Party affiliation, rather than economic position, seemed to be counting more heavily in the selection of Portland city councils.[40]

The greater diversity of occupations on the 1859 council also reflected an 1858 charter change dividing Portland into three wards, as well as changes under way in the town since the 1840s. Men popular in the wards — not necessarily merchants with city-wide reputation and influence — were more easily chosen because of the three smaller electoral districts. Perhaps more significantly, the population had nearly tripled in the previous nine years. And the economy and jobs were more diverse in 1859 than in 1851. As David Johnson has observed, Portland demographic changes reflected the "fate of the Jacksonian generation in the Far West." According to Richard Hofstadter,

> The typical American . . . was eager for advancement in the democratic game of competition — the master mechanic who aspired to open his own shop, . . . the lawyer who hoped to be a judge, the local politician who wanted to go to congress, the grocer who would be a merchant.[41]

Dryer and old-line Whig-Republicans like Logan and Coffin, largely attorneys and merchants, never quite accepted the changed complexion of Portland society. But the Whig-Republican merchants did not abandon their political interests even though they may not have fully understood the subtle change in their relation to the offices through which they wielded authority. Merchants Henry W. Corbett and young Henry Failing both hitched their political futures to the rising Republican Party, Corbett aiming for the U.S. Senate and Failing for the office of Portland mayor. Both men represented a "remarkably persistent class of merchants" who powered Portland's growth, but at a slower and steadier rate than San Francisco's. More than in ante-bellum San Francisco and even New York, Portland merchants of both parties would maintain their political pre-eminence by holding many key offices throughout most of the 1860s. They would share the mayor's office with leading attorneys and a socially prominent physician.[42]

The last election of the 1850s produced a new breed of merchant-mayor far better educated than the general run of frontier political leaders. A professed Jeffersonian Democrat and printer by trade, Stephen J. McCormick had opened the Franklin Book Store in 1851, the town's first bookshop. In March, 1853, he began publishing the short-lived semi-weekly *Portland Commercial*, "to foster the commercial interests of our thriving territory." He achieved prominence and popularity as one of 60 delegates to the state Constitutional Convention in 1857.

Following the demise of his paper — Portland business life was still too small-scale and underfinanced to support a commercial journal — McCormick proceeded to publish a monthly magazine and, in 1863, Portland's first city directory. In a sense, he was Portland's first public-relations expert for business. During his eventful one-year term as mayor, he pressed the city to advance its legitimate businesses, to establish a police force and to replace its "untenantable" jail with a more secure and humane prison. Unsuccessful over the police and the prison he achieved a partial if short-lived victory by his last official act, maintaining public ownership of the levee by personally directing the destruction of George Vaughn's covered wharf.[43]

Although McCormick advocated government encouragement of private business, he did not consider private ownership of the city's riverfront a legitimate business function. Being the life-blood of the city, the river should be accessible to every citizen. Such views expressed his Jeffersonian conviction that a city should be an egalitarian society, where everyone would have a fair shot at improving his material condition. Subsequent events reversed McCormick's policy, as private developers assumed ownership of the city's riverfront. As in Philadelphia and other eastern cities a hundred years earlier, America's "enduring tradition of privatism" became firmly established in Portland. As Sam Bass Warner, Jr., observed:

> The tradition of privatism has meant that the local politics of American cities have depended for their actors, and for a good deal of their subject matter, on the changing focus of men's private economic activities.[44]

For Portland's public levee, the changing focus occurred in June, 1861.

4.1 "First Five Mayors of Portland"

4.3 Lewis M. Starr (1824-?)

4.2 David Logan (1824-1879)

4.5 An elderly Stephen J. McCormick (1829-1891)

4.4 Addison M. Starr (1828-1892)

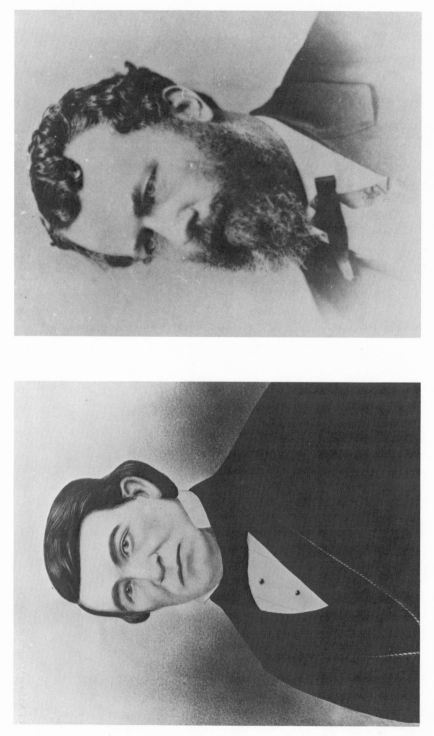

4.7 Matthew P. Deady (1824-1893), c. 1869-1870

4.6 James A. O'Neill (1800-1874)

4.8 Kuchel & Dressel lithograph of Portland in 1858

4.9 Oak to Ash Street, 1858 (1 to r) City Hotel, Benjamin Stark office, W.S. Ladd residence, Captain Molthrop residence, Benjamin Stark residence, unknown

5

TERRITORIAL POLITICS AND EARLY STATEHOOD: 1848-1864

The Portland-Salem-Washington Nexus

National politics broadly influenced Oregon local and territorial politics during the 1850s, especially after Democratic Franklin Pierce's elevation to the presidency in March, 1853. Territorial status introduced Oregon to the politics of federal patronage. Presidential appointments exercised a strong influence on the territorial power structure and even control over it, with consequent impact on Portland's business and political establishments.

The key person in the Portland-Salem-Washington nexus was General Joseph Lane, a Mexican War veteran known as "Joe" to friend and foe alike. Born in North Carolina, he was appointed Oregon's first territorial governor by Democratic President James K. Polk late in 1848. His selection forged a direct link between Oregon and national Democrats, one which was reinforced by Samuel R. Thurston's election in 1849 as territorial delegate to Congress. Lane's succession to that office upon Thurston's sudden death in 1851 gave the popular general primary responsibility for nominating patronage appointees and obtaining federal funds for roads and other internal improvements. Lane's arrival in Oregon in March, 1849, inaugurated a 30-year period in which Democrats increasingly dominated Oregon politics except in the years 1862-1870. And from the party's territorial organization in 1852 until mid-1860, Asahel Bush, reinforced by Lane's Washington connections, drove the party machine.[1]

At the regional end of the nexus was the growing Ladd-Bush relationship. It began in 1852, when Bush bought supplies from Ladd's store, and burgeoned into a business partnership in 1869, with the Ladd & Bush Bank of Salem. Of more than mutual economic benefit, the friendship played an integral role in strengthening the Democratic party network, despite Ladd's later assertion that he always voted for "the best man regardless [of party]." By 1854, with merchant Ladd as Portland mayor and editor Bush as leader of the "Salem Clique" (the party's dominant fac-

tion), the territory's largest city was effectively connected to the territorial capita
and, through Joe Lane, the nation's capital. In general agreement on such majo
issues as the state capital's location, statehood, and the extension of slavery, Lad
and Bush held one overriding concern: the preservation, strength and unity of th
Democratic party, the source of their political power and generator of large eco
nomic rewards to the party faithful.[2]

Inheritors of the Jacksonian tradition, which linked the fortunes of the Demo
cratic party to "the ambitions of the small capitalist," Ladd, Bush, Lane, and thei
friends sought concrete gains from political involvement: unrestricted governmen
aid for commerce and trade; personal investment possibilities; lucrative govern
ment appointments and contracts; and the prestige and authority of office. Th
right territorial alliances made them and their friends judges and marshals, postmas
ters, Indian agents and land-office registrars, governors and congressional delegate
and, later, U.S. senators and representatives. Their supporters and positions helpe
them found and maintain business enterprises. Their influence in the legislatur
and courts protected their status and assets. Like their fellows throughout ante
bellum America, they manipulated place and position to personal, town and part
advantage without bothersome moral qualms or public inquiries. To these Demo
crats and their opponents, political and economic life — government and busines
— were interdependent. "Indeed," as Gene M. Gressley has concluded, "the eco
nomic mix of private and public enterprise had been with the westerner since h
crossed the Mississippi."[3]

Joe Lane's Reward: The Island Mills

Lane wasted little time after his arrival in Oregon City before engaging in
scheme to make himself rich. At stake were the Island Mills on Government Island i
the Willamette River, near Oregon City. Comprising three sawmills and two grist
mills, the properties had been obtained surreptitiously by wealthy Oregon City
merchant and former Provisional Governor George Abernethy in collaboration
with Samuel R. Thurston, at the time an attorney in Oregon City. They had de
frauded the former Hudson's Bay Company Chief Factor John McLoughlin of hi
rightful 1846 claim, which included the mill properties. Deeding the island to Lane
month after the governor reached Oregon, Abernethy then sold a 50 percent inter
est in the Island Mills to the recently arrived first territorial chief justice, William I
Bryant, an old friend of Lane's from Indiana. By Malcolm Clark's determination, th
reported price of $35,000 was "a sum so far beyond the judge's available means . .
that only a small part was rendered in cash and the remainder in what lawyers ca
'other valuable consideration.'" With Bryant safely obligated, Abernethy littl
feared any McLoughlin suit for claim recovery in Bryant's court.[4]

Bryant's briefly held "investment" amounted to a holding operation financed b
Abernethy as a favor to Lane. Before Bryant's hasty departure from Oregon in Novem
ber, 1849, Joe Lane and his son coincidentally arranged to purchase Bryant's half
interest in the Island Mills. Joining the Lanes as purchaser of the other half-interes
was future Portland business leader (and major Oregon Steam Navigation Compan
investor) Robert R. Thompson, recently returned from the California gold field

with a modest fortune. For their share, the Lanes paid $20,000 down and obtained a $30,000 mortgage from Abernethy, using their Indiana farm as collateral. Thompson apparently paid his share in gold and may have loaned Lane some of his down payment. Whatever the financial arrangements, Lane unquestionably put himself under obligation to Thompson. The Lane-Thompson financial partnership cemented a political alliance that would exert strong influence on the Democratic party and reward Thompson with numerous economic benefits, including appointment as Indian Agent at Fort Dalles in 1854. Lane dreamed of a "fortune" that would support his family for many years.[5]

Disaster struck during the Christmas season of 1849, when a massive flood swept down the Willamette Valley. By midwinter in 1850, before the mills could be rebuilt, lumber prices had declined 70 percent. By mid-1851, after Lane had gone to Washington as territorial delegate, the family lost most of its investment; Lane's share reverted to mortgage-holder Abernethy. Thompson, with sufficient funds to weather the loss, decided nevertheless to liquidate his investment, using his proceeds to buy a large flock of sheep for transport to Oregon. In early 1852, he sold his interest in the Island Mills to English-born John McCraken, an Oregon City settler who had arrived from Stockton, California, in 1850.[6]

Within two years, flood swept away McCraken's warehouse, rendering him insolvent. Unable to repay Thompson, the future Portland merchant leader and councilman, a devout Democrat, apparently endeared himself to Thompson and Bush politically. The Salem Clique (so named by detractors like the *Oregonian*'s Dryer) helped its own. Thompson and Bush arranged for McCraken's election as clerk of the territorial House of Representatives, a key insider position. McCraken repaid the favor by facilitating Bush's receipt of the territorial printing contract. This succulent fruit more than fed the hunger of printing the *Oregon Statesman*. "Territorial government" in the West, as Kenneth Owens observes, "was fundamentally concerned with the allocation of political power and the rewards of power in control over public policy."[7]

Whether Whig or Democrat, aspiring, successful Oregon insiders of the 1850s like John McCraken bound themselves through political patronage into sometimes shifting pacts of reciprocal loyalty and benefits. Rewarding the party faithful was the first commandment. "I believe the bestowal of public patronage is and ought to be partisan," McCraken wrote his chief, Asahel Bush, in October, 1855. "Why should not that be the case where men every way as well qualified for the position can be found among our friends?" McCraken's greater reward came from Democratic President James Buchanan, through their mutual friend Lane, in 1857: appointment as U.S. marshal, with headquarters in Portland. The post conferred considerable personal prestige within the merchant community and among voters, who elected McCraken to the city council in April, 1861, where he was named council president.[8]

Asahel Bush and the Salem Clique

A native of Westfield, Massachusetts, Asahel Bush arrived at Oregon City in September, 1850, with the financial backing of Territorial Delegate Samuel R. Thurston. "Aggressive, calculating and relentless," Bush was selected by Thurston to build a territorial Democratic organization and be its chief spokesman "through the pages of a party journal." In short order, Bush and his *Oregon Statesman*, published initially in March, 1851, mobilized the Democratic rank and file and forged the party machine that controlled Oregon politics for nearly a decade.[9]

To help sell subscriptions to the *Statesman*, Bush sought out influential political friends who would travel the valley. His most effective circulation agent was Matthew P. Deady, an 1849 pioneer from Maryland. Attorney Deady, a member of the territorial legislature, introduced Bush to James W. Nesmith and Joe Lane. The three men quickly became close friends.

The congressional vacancy created by Thurston's death in April, 1851, worried Bush. Fearful of splitting a party that was still not unified, he backed neither Deady nor Lane, the two most obvious candidates. When Deady and Thompson supported Lane, Bush was free to unify the party behind the general. Bush and Lane never forgot these favorable withdrawals. Lane's friend, President Franklin Pierce, appointed Deady to the territorial supreme court in 1853.

Robert R. Thompson's influence was equally important to Deady's future and Bush's efforts to strengthen the party. In August, 1852, after selling his Island Mills interest earlier in the year, Thompson joined Lane at the Democratic Convention in Baltimore, where both played roles in Pierce's nomination. The Democrat's November victory secured the national power base of Bush's Oregon Democratic party. Patronage rewards began flowing in 1853, as Thompson had predicted after the convention: "We are looking forward . . . to the election of Pearce [sic] and King as did the prophets of old to the coming of the Messiah." After the 1852 election, Lane promised, "'Things will be put right in Oregon, early next March.'" The hungry in Salem were impatient, as Deady derisively observed: "Political adventurers are floating around the capital like crows over a fresh carcass."[10]

Bush moved the *Oregon Statesman* to Salem in June, 1953, a year after the town's designation by Congress as the territorial capital. The shift culminated a bitter struggle against the Whigs' two-year attempt to keep the capital in Oregon City. Being in Salem would allow Bush to consolidate and maintain control over territorial politics, and strengthen his faction of the Democratic party.

Partisan factions had fractured the 1851 legislative session. A large majority of both houses, including most Democrats, sat in Salem, while the Whig-appointed governor, John P. Gaines, a legislative minority and two Whig-appointed supreme court justices sat in Oregon City. Led by Portland's William M. King, the Salem legislators awarded the two most lucrative plums: the capital to Salem and the penitentiary to Portland.

The capital-location controversy, not settled until 1864, launched "an avalanche of newspaper articles on each side of the question. Virtually every issue of both the *Oregonian* and the *Statesman* devoted some part of its space to the location question." Merchants and their attorneys were meanwhile discomfited by endless delays in lawsuits for payment. The constantly shifting courts prevented the territorial supreme court from functioning effectively. Attorney William W. Chapman's bitter clash with supreme court Associate Justice Orville C. Pratt at Hillsboro in November, 1851, reflected Whig frustration with the court's sole Democrat. The charges against the Whig Chapman were dropped when the two Whig supreme court justices overruled Pratt from Oregon City. Portland merchant leaders like William S. Ladd were pleased by Salem's designation; they mainly credited Lane and Bush for the action.[11]

The months following President Pierce's inauguration were happy times for editor Bush and his clique as the political rewards were distributed. The first four patronage appointments went to clique faithful Matthew P. Deady, James W. Nesmith, Benjamin F. Harding, and George L. Curry. But Deady's installation on the territorial supreme court was delayed for six months when his commission bore the name Mordecai Paul Deady. To Lane's embarrassment, he had taken Deady's first name from a derisive *Oregonian* article. (Deady used only his initials or last name in correspondence.) "'How the hell Lane made Such a botch of it is surprising to me,'" Deady angrily exclaimed to Bush. Dryer and the Whigs gloated over the temporary misfortune.[12]

These appointments underscored the role of political patronage in political and public advancement. Deady rose to the position of U.S. district Judge in Portland in 1859. Harding, named U.S. attorney and then territorial secretary of state, succeeded U.S. Senator Benjamin Stark in 1862. Nesmith was made U.S. marshal and then superintendent of Indian affairs before moving to the U.S. Senate in 1861. George L. Curry was named territorial secretary of state, acting governor and then governor from 1854 to 1859. Other members of the clique included Salem businessman Lafayette Grover, Oregon's first elected U.S. representative, and then its governor and U.S. senator. Grover had strong Portland ties through his marriage to Elizabeth Carter, daughter of wealthy landowner Thomas J. Carter. Another Salemite with Portland roots was attorney Reuben P. Boise. A Bush friend from Massachusetts, he received appointment to the territorial supreme court in 1858. Elected to the Oregon supreme court in 1859, he served on and off the state bench for over 30 years.

Not to be forgotten, Robert R. Thompson, an unofficial member of the Salem Clique, received a substantial reward in late 1853 when President Pierce appointed him Indian agent for the eastern Oregon Territory. He had just arrived at Umatilla after driving 1,400 sheep across the plains with the help of 12 hired men. Moving family, sheep and agency office to Fort Dalles, he "took up a Donation Land claim" with grateful thanks to the "liberality of the government."[13]

Thompson raised sheep, traded cattle, sold feed, and studied the Upper Columbia River as a major trade artery. He associated himself with Orlando Humason and John A. Sims in their portage between The Dalles and Celilo and threw himself into the transportation business. The partners built "Kinker" boats to navigate the rapids and employed Indian gangs to pull them up river. As business improved, new and larger craft were built, including schooners and sloops, for service eastward above The Dalles. When the resident quartermaster at nearby Fort Lee needed transport for government supplies to fight the Indians, Thompson used his official position and private vessels to win the immensely profitable contract. Too busy becoming a river czar, he resigned as Indian agent in 1856. Government subsidies underwrote his next venture: constructing the first sternwheel steamboat for the Upper Columbia. Within 10 years, he would be a major owner of the Oregon Steam Navigation Company and one of Portland's wealthiest residents.[14]

Whigs Organize

Reacting to Bush's enormous success and Lane's overwhelming re-election in June, 1853, Thomas Dryer endorsed immediate organization of an Oregon Whig Party. "Conceding the realities" of Bush's operation, "the *Oregonian* did an abrupt about-face." Until June, 1853, Whigs had insisted that parties "were unnecessary" and "harmful [to] . . . the best interests of Oregon." It was now a matter of Whig life or death. Dryer endorsed a platform of federally sponsored internal improvements, including construction of a railroad to the Pacific. Like the Democrats, the editor was vague about local issues. (Robert Wiebe notes that as the national Whig Party was disintegrating by mid-1853, local Whigs, with little to lose, grew more aggressive and transformed "their electioneering rhetoric into full-fledged organization.")[15]

"The Sewer man [Dryer] is in favor of organizing the Whig party," responded an equally vitriolic Asahel Bush.

> Greely [sic], of the New York Tribune, says that the Whig party is dead in the states. But, like all animals of the reptile order, it dies in the extremities last; and him of the Sewer is the last agonizing knot of the tail.[16]

The Whigs managed to send David Logan from Washington County to the territorial legislature for one term in 1854, even as the newly formed Portland Democrats under William S. Ladd swept local offices in 1854 and again in 1855. To Logan in November, 1855, "The Whig Party [was] dead." Logan entered a nearly decade-long political eclipse after Judge Deady, writing under a pseudonym in Portland's new *Democratic Standard*, charged that a drunken Logan had publicly raped an Indian woman on a Jacksonville, Oregon, street. Badly damaged, Logan fought the lurid account for years. He barely lost election as the Republican party's first congressional candidate from Portland five years later. In 1863, espousing the Union cause, he won election as Portland mayor.[17]

Deady's vehicle against Logan and other Whigs was a weekly conducted by Daniel Lownsdale's friend Alonzo Leland between 1854 and 1859. Active in local politics, the future city recorder Leland attacked such Whigs as Logan and Dryer and selected figures in the Salem Clique, particularly Bush. Although Deady disdained the Leland-King-Lownsdale faction of the Democratic Party, its *Standard* was the only local medium available to fight the *Oregonian*. The paper also hammered the new Native American, or Know-Nothing party. In the East, the Know-Nothings were anti-Catholic and anti-immigrant. In an Oregon Territory with few Catholics and little anti-foreign sentiment, the party largely opposed the growing power of the Salem Clique. Frustrated Whigs like Stephen Coffin, his son-in-law Cyrus Reed and former U.S. Attorney for Oregon Amory Holbrook assumed its Portland leadership.

Lane, facing re-election as territorial delegate in 1855, worriedly invited Whigs and "honest well-meaning Know-Nothings" to support Democrats at the polls, a tactic that Bush severely criticized. Months earlier, Nathaniel Lane had warned his father that the Know-Nothings might carry the entire territory. "I do think the democratic party in Oregon is made of the poorest hackneyed rotten hearted set of Office Seeking Sons of Bitches I ever knew," said the Democrat who would be elected territorial treasurer in 1855. Ladd more confidently reported on Portland opinion as the election of June, 1855, neared. Critical of Lane's pandering to the "evil" upstarts, Ladd assured an apprehensive Bush that the Democrats had nothing to fear from a bunch of "disaffected" voters. The election results proved him correct: the Know-Nothings died along with the Whigs.[18]

Statehood and Slavery

The move toward Oregon statehood occurred in the "midst of the national tangle that followed the Dred Scott decision" in March, 1857. The U.S. Supreme Court ruling that Congress had no power to exclude slavery from territories like Oregon posed a serious dilemma for Oregon Democrats who expected to control the new state government. Excepting Matthew P. Deady, Joe Lane and Benjamin Stark, no prominent Democrats favored slavery. In fact, few Oregonians favored any extension of slavery into the territories, but those who did were all Democrats. The bitter controversy increasingly fragmented the Democratic party and simultaneously stimulated growth of the Oregon Republican party, which ran its first state ticket in 1858.[19]

During the spring of 1857, Lane and Bush began diverging openly on questions of patronage and federal appropriations. Publicly they ignored the slavery issue, as Lane quietly but reluctantly deferred to Bush on the matter. Lane respected Bush's warning that his openly advocating slavery might create an anti-slavery wing of the party and splinter Democratic power in Oregon. Anti-slavery victories among Democrats would surely enrage Lane's large following of Southern transplants. Leading Portland merchants like William S. Ladd also had to face political reality. Despite differences with Lane, who was seeking re-election in March, 1857, he was their only hope of keeping the Democratic Party united. They saw no option but to support their party's leader. As Ladd wrote Bush, Lane "is the choice of every business man in town of my acquaintance."[20]

By the opening of their Constitutional Convention in August, 1857, white Oregonians held clear positions on slavery extension and the rights of free Negroes. For Deady, chosen presiding officer, the question was a legal one, as ordained by the *Dred Scott* decision. For supreme court Chief Justice George H. Williams, it was one of economics. In the *Oregon Statesman*, he warned that Oregon should "keep as clear as possible of negroes," slave or free. Slave labor was both involuntary and lazy, while free black people would degrade the labor market. Although agreeing with Williams, Bush feared more the political consequences of slavery, calling it "an impossible institution for Oregon." Expressing views largely shared by his friend Ladd and widely accepted by westerners, Bush wrote that "the African is destined to be the servant and subordinate of the superior white race." No Democratic figure considered slavery immoral.[21]

At the convention, David Johnson notes, "The delegates' discussion of slavery and the rights of people of color had a timeless quality." Slavery was "anathema" to most delegates, and so, too, "the idea of racial equality." The convention overwhelmingly outlawed slavery and by a greater majority excluded free Negroes. Following Justice Williams's entreaty, delegates consecrated Oregon "to the use of the white man." Delegate Thomas Dryer wished further to "'exclude negroes, China-men, Kanakas and even Indians. The association of those races with the white was the demoralization of the latter.'" A 60 percent Democratic delegation steered Ore-gon on "a middle course," according to Robert Johannsen, "to avoid the extremes of both North and South." The convention essentially adhered to the popular sover-eignty doctrine.[22]

Of much greater interest than slavery to Portland merchants was the conven-tion's handling of economic issues. The delegates generally feared public debt and distrusted corporations and banks of issue. Accordingly, the delegates supported "rigid debt limitations upon the state and local governments," many of which still prevail. As Gordon B. Dodds notes, "No government was permitted to become a stockholder or lend credit to a corporation." Such general mistrust of corporate practices was rooted in the territory's agricultural ethos. As Deady said, "'We have an agricultural community, and the domestic virtues incident to an agricultural people; and there is where you look for the true and solid wealth and happiness of a people.'"[23]

Corporations and banks, in Deady's view, were "devices intended to swindle creditors by limiting individual liability." Portland delegate John Waymire agreed:

> Let us bring this thing right home and apply it to things we have seen. We have here a plank road. How was that got up? . . . They got honest, responsible men to subscribe, and they made them pay to the last dollar. And who had benefited by this plank road? Nobody but these fancy stock gentlemen who never paid anything. The road was a humbug and a curse and . . . a base swindle.[24]

Delegates were also aware of experiences in other parts of the country where legislatures granted corporate charters out of favoritism and corruption and spawned monopolies at public expense. With much reference, as David Johnson notes, to "history, honesty, virtue and social degredation," the delegates compro-mised upon a simple clause that permitted limited-liability corporations. Corpora-tions could be formed only under *general* laws, not by "special" legislative acts. But banks of issue they totally prohibited. "Banks of *deposit*," they agreed, "were neces-sities in any progressive community. But . . . banks of issue with their power to create money out of thin air were a sure source of misery and ruin."[25]

The state Constitution was ratified in November, 1857, by a popular referendum of 7,195 to 3,215. Not surprisingly, the convention vote two months earlier had car-ried by an even larger margin, 35 to 10, with 15 absent. The six-man Portland delega-tion (10 percent of the convention), was proportionately overweighted. (Portland had but 5 percent of the state's 1860 population.) Two of its six delegates were mer-chants: small-businessman and craftsman John Waymire and bookseller-publisher Stephen J. McCormick. Three of the four-delegate Salem Clique subsequently lived and worked in Portland and became prominent members of the city's Establish-ment: Matthew P. Deady, Reuben P. Boise and LaFayette Grover.

Judge Deady exercised a predominant influence on the shape and content of the state Constitution. Not only did he prove to be "an astonishingly even-handed" presiding officer, as Malcolm Clark noted, but he wrote more of the document than any other delegate, "though it cannot be said he was responsible for it all." While pro-slavery in sympathy, he accepted as the majority will the doctrine of popular sovereignty endorsed by Ladd and Bush. His accomplishment received a surprising endorsement from Joe Lane not that Lane had much choice. As Lane wrote in the *Statesman* from Washington,

> I am much pleased to learn that our Constitution has been ratified by the people, but am sorry to find that there are some still harping over the slavery question. It has been settled by a vote of the people, and with their decision all should be satisfied. Our motto was, in the late canvass, and in our platform, and it is the true principle of the Kansas-Nebraska bill, 'leave it to the people.'[26]

Oregonians clearly intended to preserve the white man's democracy long advocated by most northern Democrats. Serious debate over this and other constitutional provisions delayed congressional approval until February 14, 1859, when Oregon finally gained statehood. In recognition of his 10-year struggle to attain this goal, Joe Lane achieved his long-sought ambition: legislative election as Oregon's first U.S. senator, if only for a two-year term.

Coalition Politics: Edward D. Baker

Over the next 15 months, as Lane and Bush diverged sharply on federal policy toward slavery, the Republicans continued organizing locally and searching for a strong U.S. senatorial candidate. At the party's state convention in April, 1859, the name of San Francisco attorney Edward D. Baker surfaced among top party leaders. Through Baker's close friend, Yamhill County resident Dr. Anson G. Henry (Abraham Lincoln's former physician), word had been received that Baker might be interested in moving to Oregon. A political activist, Henry believed that Baker could win a seat in the U.S. Senate once Oregon gained statehood. Baker was regarded as one of the most eloquent and dynamic speakers in northern California. A veteran Whig, an intimate friend of Abraham Lincoln and an experienced Illinois legislator and congressman, Baker yearned for a U.S. Senate seat despite enjoying a lucrative five-year legal practice in San Francisco. Republican chances in heavily Democratic California looked slim.[27]

Dryer became Baker's staunchest supporter at the state convention in April, 1859. Acknowledging the irrelevance of the Whig movement, Dryer threw the *Oregonian* behind the growing Republican party. Horrified by the city elections that were almost solidly Democratic earlier in the month, he assailed the "simple-minded democracy .... The great unwashed." His worst fury was directed at Lane's popularity and his control over federal patronage.[28]

While popular with Portland voters, Lane experienced increasing difficulty with Asahel Bush and the Salem Clique. As supporters of Stephen Douglas nationally, they were deeply offended by Lane's ambition for national office (on a pro-slavery plank) against Douglas. Bush's worst fears were being realized: the Democratic party was being splintered by Lane and Douglas Democrats. The Oregon showdown would occur at the special legislative elections in June, 1860.

Sensing a great opportunity for the Republican party, Dryer and David Logan went to San Francisco in late September, 1859, to ask Baker to move to Oregon and campaign for Republican candidates. Having just suffered defeat for the U.S. Senate in California, Baker was ripe for the challenge. He knew Logan, whose father had been a law partner of his and Lincoln's in Springfield, Illinois. With his friend Lincoln preparing to run for the Republican presidential nomination in 1860, Baker's presence in Oregon would energize the new party. And Dryer hoped that Baker's popularity would also win him one of the two U.S. Senate seats to be chosen in September, 1860.

Baker made his initial trip to Oregon in December, 1859, and returned to settle in Salem in February, 1860. On both voyages north he was accompanied by Dryer, whose activities were carefully monitored by the *Statesman*. Baker went right to work, speaking throughout the state and drawing increasingly large crowds. Within weeks, Bush and the Salem Clique decided to replace Lane with James W. Nesmith at the party's April convention, convened to nominate candidates for the first state legislature. At the opposing Republican convention, Baker advised the delegates not to nominate a ticket, in the hope that some Douglas Democrats might form a coalition with the Republicans. These, he predicted, would hold the balance in the U.S. senatorial elections. T. W. Davenport recalled Baker as saying, "'The Douglas men are at heart with us and we shall need their help . . . . The old Democratic barrel is falling to pieces and why should we who need some of their staves hoop them together?'" Baker's strategy aimed at widening the split between the "Bushites" and the "Beetle Heads," Bush's epithet for Lane and his supporters.

The special elections of June 5, 1860, doomed Lane's senatorial career. Of the 50 legislators elected (15 senators and 35 representatives), 19 were Lane Democrats, 18 were supporters of Stephen Douglas and 13 were Republicans. As Baker predicted, the Republicans would hold the balance of power when the first state legislature met in September, 1860.[29]

An agreement was apparently struck in mid-June to elect a coalition ticket with Nesmith and Baker on the same senatorial ballot. Along with Dryer, Logan (a candidate for Congress), Stephen Coffin, and Bush, Portland merchant leaders likely played key roles in the coalition strategy. Henry W. Corbett was serving his second year as chairman of the Republican state central committee, and his good friend William S. Ladd, a Bush ally, was a leader of the Douglas Democrats. None wished to repeat the deadlocked session of May, 1859, when the last territorial legislature rejected Delazon Smith's senatorial re-election bid. By failing to choose a replacement, it left Oregon with only one U.S. senator, Joe Lane, after March 3, 1859. By terms of the agreement, Nesmith would succeed to Lane's long term and Baker to the short term formerly held by Smith. Realizing that his chances for re-election to the Senate were slim, Joe Lane, in late June, 1860, secured the vice-presidential nomination on the Southern Democratic ticket headed by his friend Vice-President John C. Breckinridge, of Kentucky.[30]

The first state legislature met in Salem on September 10, 1860, with the election of two U.S. senators as its foremost business. Sensing a coalition agreement, Lane's followers "vacated their seats," according to George H. Williams, who was also a candidate. They "took to the woods": in a barn five miles outside Salem, returning two weeks later after being threatened with arrest. The legislators then struggled through 14 ballots until Nesmith and Baker gained majority approval on October 2.

The following day, Bush justified his anti-Lane stance and support of Baker in the *Oregon Statesman*:

> In voting for Colonel Baker, we were influenced, to some extent, by his well-known position upon the question of Slavery in the Territories — a position different but little from that of our own party . . . . Aside from partisan politics, we are satisfied that Colonel Baker will prove a wise, able and prudent Senator, . . . which is more than can be said with truth of our Senators hitherto [Lane and Smith].[31]

Lane's political ambition and pro-slavery stance had deeply divided the Oregon Democratic party and ruptured the power of the Salem Clique. For seven years, the clique had essentially maintained a one-party system, based on control of federal patronage and an absence of effective non-Democratic opposition. The decision to import Baker to Oregon invigorated the Republican rank and file and enhanced the influence of party leaders like Portland merchants Henry W. Corbett and Henry Failing.

Corbett's defeat in the 1857 mayoralty race inspired him to seek higher office. His taste for local office diminished during a temporary seven-month service on the city council in 1858-59, after which he built a state power base within the new Republican party through chairing the state central committee. (Failing succeeded to the post late in 1862.) That year, Corbett organized a state Union party, a supposedly non-partisan coalition of Republicans and "War Democrats," much like the coalition that elected Baker and Nesmith. Supporting his efforts were prominent Portland-area Democrats like William S. Ladd, George H. Williams, Simeon G. Reed, Asa Lovejoy, and A. M. Starr, and Reuben Boise from Salem. As Bush had feared, Republicans dominated the Union party and through it gained the governorship from 1862 to 1870, and Oregon's lone congressional seat from 1863 to 1869. All ran as Republicans, as did Portland mayors William H. Farrar in 1862 and David Logan in 1863.[32]

Lincoln's election on November 6, 1860, marked the end of one-party rule in Oregon. With Baker the first Republican senator elected from the Pacific Coast, and Lincoln in the White House, patronage would begin flowing to Oregon Republicans in the spring of 1861. By what Lincoln called "the narrowest in political bookkeeping," the Illinois attorney barely won Oregon's three electoral votes. Lane's popularity in Southern Oregon nearly carried the election for the Breckinridge-Lane ticket. No party commanded a majority in Oregon. The Douglas Democrats amassed only 23 percent of the vote. But the combined Lincoln-Douglas plebiscite revealed strong Union sentiment among Oregon voters, especially those in the northern and eastern regions of the state.[33]

Dryer became ecstatic over Lincoln's victory. On November 10, 1860, he wrote in his final editorial before leaving the paper:

> The State of Oregon has gone for Lincoln for President — crushing out the influence of Joe Lane and all his banded office-holders and their hangers-on — all their insolence — all their tyranny . . . . Oregon, in her virgin pride and beauty [has been] rescued from the spoilers.[34]

Republican spoilers now hungered for revenge. Dryer and Logan, among others, wasted no time seeking their own patronage rewards. On April 1, 1860, Dryer had mortgaged the *Oregonian*, its office and equipment to his printer, Henry L. Pittock, for accumulated debts of nearly $5,000. He remained on the masthead as editor until November 24. Unemployed and heavily in debt to others than Pittock, Dryer viewed Lincoln's election as his salvation, especially with Baker pressing his cause. Selected to carry Oregon's three electoral votes to Washington, Dryer arrived in mid-January, 1861, and remained in the capital for a month. Early in April, 1861, President Lincoln appointed him commissioner to the Sandwich Islands (Hawaii).[35]

David Logan was not as fortunate. Twice defeated for Congress, the ever-ambitious Logan complained to Lincoln that Senator Baker (with whom he had never been congenial) had ignored his request for a federal district judgeship in Southern California. The President did not like criticism of his close friend Baker. Lincoln remarked that he "would not appoint David Logan to any office. But he would willingly appoint his father [and ex-law partner, Judge Stephen Logan of Illinois] to almost any office he wanted." David Logan had to content himself with running for Portland mayor in April, 1863.[36]

End of an Era

Oregon's passionate expression of pro-Union sentiment devastated the returning Lane in late April of 1861. He haplessly travelled on the steamer that bore news of the outbreak of the Civil War. Widely considered a secessionist ringleader, he was shocked to discover his low popularity. None "would handle his luggage at dockside." Four months earlier, he had further damaged his reputation by refusing to introduce the popular Edward D. Baker to fellow members of the U.S. Senate, violating a long standing senatorial tradition for incumbents.[37]

In Portland, old merchant friends like Ladd avoided Lane, but "the Deadys . . . . had him to supper." Although welcomed with a reception at Corvallis, "where Southern sentiment was strong," he saw himself hanged in effigy in Dallas. After driving a team and wagon south to his home in Douglas County, he "retired to a small cabin on the banks of the Umpqua near his daughter. His sole companion was a Negro boy."[38]

Senator Baker, in contrast, seemed an ascending star in Oregon and national Republican politics. But as a heralded veteran of the Mexican War, he was excited and challenged by the chance to serve in the Union Army. He rejected a brigadier general's stars for a regimental colonelship (which allowed him to remain in the Senate). Two months after assuming his seat, Baker, the first congressional incumbent to serve in any war, fell at Ball's Bluff, Virginia. He was immortalized as a Union hero despite evidence that his own rashness caused his death.[39]

Oregon's Democratic governor, John Whiteaker, created a public outcry — especially among the party faithful — by choosing a fellow Southern sympathizer, Portland legislator Benjamin Stark, as Baker's replacement. Although opposed to secession, Stark was invidiously labeled a "Copperhead." A public storm swept from Portland to Washington and delayed his seating in the Senate. Replacing the heroic Baker with a slavery advocate repelled northern Republican senators. Neither Bush nor Ladd liked Stark's politics or character, but they expected a reasonable working relationship with him. Both had done business with him, and Ladd would continue as custodian of his Portland assets for many years.[40]

Stark enjoyed little support within the 1862 legislature, which chose House Speaker Benjamin F. Harding to complete Baker's term. No longer an effective voice in public life, Stark passed into Oregon political oblivion. He and his family moved permanently to his boyhood town of New London, Connecticut. He would return periodically to Portland to consult with Ladd and examine properties retained with every deployable financial trick. Within 10 years, Stark would enjoy a rich retirement.

Harding's selection was a last-gasp victory for Bush's Salem Clique. Single-party politics gave way to coalition politics, with factions battling over federal appropriations and patronage. Despite the presence of clique members Nesmith and Harding in the U.S. Senate, with Republican mayors in Portland and a Republican President in Washington, the old Portland-Salem-Washington Democratic nexus was dead. Confronting reality, Ladd, Boise, Williams, and others joined the Republican-dominated Union party in 1864, although Ladd resumed his Democratic party affiliation after the Civil War. The Portland attorney Williams personified how coalition politics transformed many Democrats into Republicans via effective Union party organization. Formerly a prominent Democratic leader and territorial supreme court chief justice, he blamed the Salem Clique, with whom he had never been close, for denying him a senatorial bid in 1860. He became a Republican, and as such won legislative election to the U.S. Senate in 1864. He thus reversed his loss to Baker while avenging himself on the clique. The ambitious Williams sallied forth into a lengthy public career of questionable distinction, concluding with the Portland mayorship in 1902.[41]

In 1866, a legislature full of Republicans chose their wealthy party leader, Portland merchant Henry W. Corbett, to replace clique veteran James W. Nesmith in the Senate. Until 1869, Republicans would hold all major state and federal offices in Oregon, with their control increasingly centered in, and exercised through, Portland. After the Civil War, however, they could only yearn for the great party unity Bush had achieved in the Democratic organization of the 1850s.

5.2 James W. Nesmith (1820-1885)

5.1 Joseph Lane (1801-1881)

5.4 Robert R. Thompson (1820-1908), c. 1846

5.3 John McCraken (1826-1915)

5.5 Edward D. Baker (1811-1861), c. 1860

6

INGREDIENTS OF POWER

Wealth: Essence of Community Power

The essence of Portland's merchant power was its concentrated wealth, which accumulated rapidly during the mid-1850s. Prosperity returned in the spring of 1855 as the vital California market started recovering from the end of its gold rush. Indian wars beginning in the late summer of 1855 further stimulated the economy, despite hardship to some merchants. As noted earlier, Mayor George W. Vaughn's hardware store was "thriving" on Front Street, even as the city perceived itself threatened by Indian attack.

While enjoying brisk trade, Portland's larger-volume merchants bitterly objected to federal government purchase and delayed-payment policies. To equip its 3,500 volunteers, the army purchased immense supplies in Oregon, including requisitioned horses and mules. Oregon merchants reluctantly honored over $3 million in federal scrip for these supplies. Six years later, Congress began a repayment process that required over 30 years to complete. Much as the merchants had feared, most were reimbursed with depreciated paper money.[1]

Josiah Failing's New York partner, C. W. Thomas, had refused to allow Failing & Company to sell goods for scrip, which Thomas treated as credit that might require years for collection, if then. Failing was forced to buy for his own account from San Francisco. He accepted scrip only for "readily merchantable" items and charged the army 3 percent interest a month. Henry W. Corbett doubled his wholesale prices for goods he sold the troops and charged 2 percent interest a month. He correctly figured that he would be lucky to recoup 50 cents on the dollar. Some Oregonians' claims for requisitioned animals — later known as the "lost horse claims," of which Corbett originally held two — were not fully settled until the mid-1880s. As U.S. senator in 1871, Corbett unsuccessfully prodded Congress to expedite repayment procedures. For the big merchants, such matters were but minor inconveniences. Corbett, Failing, Ladd, and C. H. Lewis extracted large profits from the Indian Wars. In 1855 Corbett netted a lofty return of $14,000 on sales of $44,500.[2]

By the end of 1855, 17 Portlanders had taxable assets of at least $10,000; 14 of them were merchants. Most of these young men had amassed their considerable fortunes — worth at least 20 times those amounts in current values — in less than five years. Their profits came largely from groceries, liquor, dry goods, and real-estate speculation.[3]

Booming Years: 1857-1859

The years 1857-59 enriched Portland's Front Street. In January, 1857, David Logan predicted for Oregon "a better prospect, than ever before, for the speedy growth . . . in wealth." His spirits had markedly improved over the previous year, when he characterized Oregon as "a land of mountains, mongrels, half-breeds, . . . and grasshoppers." Fellow-Whig and future Republican colleague Henry W. Corbett experienced his most prosperous year to date. He owned a store, a residence and two blocks of property, giving him a net worth of $50,763 in 1857. Over the next two years, as he assumed command of the territorial Republican party, his profits exceeded $14,000 a year and rose higher after he began selling McCormick combines. Like most other successful Portland merchants, he reinvested the profits in his business while maintaining a modestly comfortable way of life.[4]

Settlement in eastern Oregon and Washington Territory, closely linked to Portland's early economic growth, was blocked until the Indian troubles ended in 1857. Gold discovery in the upper Fraser River region of eastern Washington and British Columbia in 1858 energized the Portland economy. Belgian resident Jean-Nicolas Perlot saw "more than 20,000 emigrants" passing through Portland, and Dr. Carl Freisach thought Portland citizens "in the greatest state of excitement." Although the gold rush lasted only four or five months, it doubled Portland's population to 2,917 between 1855 and 1860. It also stimulated much new construction. Thirteen brick buildings went up in the period 1856-58, including Corbett's two-story emporium and Ladd's second-story addition to his store (later housing his private bank). Each project cost approximately $10,000.[5]

Ladd apparently enjoyed greater prosperity than Corbett. He shared Corbett's advantage of a sole proprietorship, having purchased C. E. Tilton's interest in the store in mid-1855. Along Front Street, the Failings had to split their profits with C. W. Thomas until 1861. While they did more business than Corbett or Ladd, they netted less. But because the three merchant houses specialized in dry goods, hardware or liquor, their prices were more stable and their supplies generally more dependable than those of Front Street merchants who handled produce and agricultural commodities.[6]

The larger-volume merchants, including Abernethy, Clark & Company of Oregon City, remained dependent on the non-perishable goods sent around the Horn, despite the opening of the new cross-Panama railroad in 1855. Orders and payment drafts often required 40 days to reach New York, where most purchases were made. Shipments needed up to six months to reach Portland. In an attempt to expedite shipping and tighten its costs, especially the San Francisco transshipment charges on New York merchandise, Ladd decided early in 1856 to become his own shipper. In partnership with Wakeman Dimon & Company of New York City, he ordered construction of a "clipper barque" expressly for the Portland trade. The *C. E. Tilton* arrived in Portland on June 8, 1857, in a record 116 days. The cargo — also a record load for a direct New York shipment — was half-consigned to J. Failing & Company. Ladd sold his interest the next year, when he decided that investing in river transportation would yield even higher profits than shipping his own New York merchandise.[7]

Trade and commerce expanded impressively. In the boom year of 1857, Oregon exports worth $3.2 million reached a new height. Flour, the key economic index for the Oregon economy at the time, together with pork products, lumber and lesser commodities, went to San Francisco. (Foreign trade, however, remained minimal, with only an occasional ship like Leonard and Green's *Metropolis* venturing to Asia.) Portland was the chief collection point for Oregon commodities, primarily from the Willamette River Valley. River traffic increased between the upper valley and Portland and between Fort Dalles and Portland, the main route in 1858 for miners and supplies into the Fraser River. To seize the river's opportunities, Ladd joined Ainsworth, Kamm and Abernethy in building the *Carrie Ladd*, as noted earlier. Launched at Oregon City in 1858, the commodious *Carrie Ladd* reigned over the Willamette and Columbia rivers for the next several years.[8]

Ladd restlessly pondered fresh ventures. He foresaw the need for a private merchant bank to provide local working capital for new enterprises. Surplus capital, concentrated in the hands of a private banker, would also bring stability to the average merchant who was continually at the mercy of a fluctuating credit system. Most merchandising and commerce, including importing and exporting, rested upon a credit basis. Cash was seldom paid, despite the efforts of certain merchants to do only a cash business. A Portland merchant was obliged to give customers 30 to 90 days of credit. If the merchant had ample resources, he could simply hold his draft for the three months and receive full payment. If, however, he wanted immediate payment for other obligations, he could discount the draft directly at a private bank by selling it for 90 to 95 percent of value. The bank could wait up to 90 days for its 5 to 10 percent profit. As Robert Albion has concluded of New York merchant bankers, they "made it possible to keep things going, with capital available, during that period of lag in payments." Fees and interest were "part of the reward which bankers obtained for their services; the remainder of the reward lay in their power to grant or withhold credit." That power also counteracted a merchant's tendency to overtrade. By requiring payment when due, a conservative private banker forced the merchant to buy no more than he thought he could sell.[9]

Convinced that Portland needed a private bank (the 1857 Oregon Constitution prohibited only state-chartered banks), Ladd wrote C. E. Tilton to arouse his interest. He asked his former business partner (first cousin of his wife, Caroline)to join him in the enterprising venture. If Tilton agreed, Ladd would sell his mercantile business to his brothers and Simeon G. Reed. Receiving an ambivalent response, Ladd elected to take his family to New Hampshire in the spring of 1858. They would visit friends and relatives and Ladd would attempt to persuade Tilton, who had returned to his family home the previous year, ,to invest in the bank.[10]

The Ladd family travelled to San Francisco and then visited a planter uncle near New Orleans. Ladd knew that he "liked the planter's life," but lacked the money to buy and operate a plantation. (Years later, he and Reed approximated the life of enlightened gentlemen farmers, after jointly acquiring thousands of farming acres in the Willamette and Tualatin valleys.) Travelling on to St. Louis and Chicago, Ladd encountered his old trading partner Gookin. In New Hampshire, Ladd received a hero's welcome as the local boy who had made good only seven years after leaving home.[11]

Satisfied by Ladd's argument that the West offered the greatest opportunities, Tilton agreed to re-establish their partnership (ended three years earlier) with a private bank in Portland the following year. Relieved by the decision, Ladd readied the family's return to Oregon. On the way south through Concord, the Ladds ordered the plans of a house much admired by Mrs. Ladd. Finished by Christmas of 1860, the home occupied one of three blocks of timbered property bought previously "way out" on Sixth Street, between Jefferson and Clay. Fourteen years later, the Ladds enlarged it and added formal gardens and a coachman's house.[12]

The Ladd & Tilton Bank

Ladd launched his new financial venture during an era of tremendous expansion in American private banking. Private banks jumped in number from 298 in 1853 to 1,108 in 1860. Highly successful merchants like Ladd were their main instigators, emulating the wealthy Philadelphia merchant Stephen Girard, who had founded his private bank in 1810. Boston, New York and Philadelphia merchants controlled most of the available cash in ante-bellum America and customarily handled most of the early financial and credit transactions. Philadelphia's Bank of North America (1781), Boston's Massachusetts Bank (1784) and the Bank of New York (1784) were originally financed by mercantile profits. The switch from merchant to banker was a familiar transition to Ladd. As a merchant, he was accustomed to acting informally as a banker to customers — granting them loans, extending them interest-bearing credit. His fellow merchant C. H. Lewis stored customers' gold in his safe and furnished advances on future purchases (a form of working capital) to small Portland manufacturers and suppliers. But these merchant loans constituted a limited, inflexible system that severely restricted commercial growth.[13]

By temperament and experience, Ladd and his fellow merchant-capitalists were inclined to keep their capital resources moving by investing in new financial enterprises. In isolated Portland, Ladd understood the need for locally generated working capital. San Francisco banks had been promoting Portland enterprise, but on their own terms and in accordance with fluctuations in the California market. Ladd envisioned a similar promotional role for the "Banking House of Ladd & Tilton." His friends and fellow merchants Henry W. Corbett and Henry Failing would follow suit in 1869 by purchasing the First National Bank, also started by merchants.

A form of traditional banking had been introduced to Portland by the arrival of the large new express companies — Adams in 1851 and Wells Fargo in 1852. Mainly transporters of gold to San Francisco, they also acted as exchange dealers, buying drafts on discount. Conditions were changing in 1858, however. Ladd envisioned a new role for banking in which a gradual switch from credit to cash transactions would eliminate "the merchant's role as a credit consultant and guarantor of payment." He could not predict how the Civil War would affect Oregon business and banking, but proved to be fully prepared. According to Porter and Livesay, "The use of cash and the re-establishment of a national currency reduced the prewar blizzard of commercial paper to a manageable trickle." And as a logical consequence of the banker's involvement in financing manufacturing, "The private banker replaced the merchant as consultant."[14]

In 1880, the Oregon Supreme Court would rule that the Constitution precluded state banks from issuing paper money, but permitted them to perform savings, loan and exchange functions. Until this clarification, Oregon incorporated no state banks. Ladd & Tilton largely monopolized the profitable Portland banking field from June 1, 1859, until the First National Bank opened in 1866. As late as 1872, Oregon had only five banks: three in Portland and one each in Albany and Salem, the Salem bank being owned by Ladd and Bush.[15]

Ladd delayed the bank's opening for six months, until June 1, 1859, probably because the Fraser River mining boom collapsed almost immediately, resulting in a brief recession. He reported on March 23, 1859, that "money is tight" here and "business is very dull." The produce trade with California had dropped precariously, and small shippers were in trouble. Benjamin Stark's Columbia River Steam Navigation Company, among others, fell heavily into debt. Farmers needed credit extension. Both Corbett and Failing, who had assumed active management of the Portland store, began to deny credit to some customers.[16]

The short-lived recession of 1859 may have been a boon to Ladd's banking plans. No one else in Portland had sufficient cash to grant short-term loans to merchants and farmers. The bank opened with $50,000 in capital and recorded $10,000 in deposits within the first month. After three weeks of business, Ladd enthusiastically reported, "Our remittances to San Francisco will be about fifty to sixty thousand dollars per month." With the discount fee at 10 percent, these transactions alone were worth nearly $6,000 a month, and additional profits resulted from exchanges on New York banks. Short-term loans paid Ladd & Tilton interest of 1 1/2 to 5 percent a month; favored customers were charged a maximum of 2 1/2 percent.[17]

As Ladd apparently provided the greater share of the capital, he received a proportionately greater return than Tilton, who was living in San Francisco again. From the first, Ladd was the active manager of the bank's business in Portland. He often signed for the bank rather than himself. In correspondence with customers, he pretended that the bank was a separate entity. The fiction fitted his growing aloofness, and distanced the bank from customers who were his social acquaintances and friends. While courteous, Ladd often appeared austere and demanding to customers. The future judge and prominent real-estate investor Phillip A. Marquam recalled having had "severely hard experiences with Ladd the banker" in 1859; Ladd was a "stickler on notes," and charged him a "high interest" of 5 percent.[18]

Considering Ladd's meteoric eight-year rise, his contemporaries could expect him to succeed as a banker. After six months, deposits totalled $49,981. Two years later, they had increased to $113,344. The first bank on the Pacific Coast north of San Francisco did so well that Ladd's uncle, Stephen Mead of New London, Connecticut, entered into partnership, increasing the capital stock to $150,000. Within two and a half years Ladd & Tilton was a veritable money machine, the most powerful financial institution in Portland.[19]

Like other western regional banks, Ladd & Tilton provided an "urban-oriented economic service," as Michael P. Conzen has noted. "Cities were efficient points" for concentrating funds. The bank indispensably advanced Portland's growth and industrialization by providing working capital to many non-mercantile enterprises, especially manufacturing. In 1860, Portland had over 50 industrial establishments, mostly small processing plants and small workshops. Sawmills and flour mills, the oldest and most productive local industries, had the highest capitalizations. The Portland Milling Company was the largest, at $20,000. Mainly through the bank, Ladd involved himself in many of these enterprises as an incorporator, stockholder or financial agent. By 1860, he was extending his transportation interests beyond the Willamette to the Columbia. His investment in the *Carrie Ladd* linked him to Captain John C. Ainsworth. Bank loans to Columbia River portage operators involved him with the venturesome Robert R. Thompson, and, through Thompson and Ainsworth, with the Oregon Steam Navigation Company as it opened up the country east of the Cascades. In tying Portland directly to these various activities and to correspondent banks in San Francisco and New York, Ladd & Tilton helped break down the city's insularity. Achievement of statehood in 1859 reinforced the trend that was further advanced in 1883 by the arrival of transcontinental rail service.[20]

Voluntary Associations

The predominant commercial spirit of early Portland suffused the town's many volunteer organizations. Voluntary activities manifested the American tradition of "privatism," which Sam Bass Warner, Jr., argues "is . . . the most important element of our culture for understanding the development of cities." In Portland, voluntary organizations afforded Front Street another channel for social control and another means of extending its power. Traditional in purpose, Portland's volunteerism displayed the same "conspicuous and ingrained conservatism . . . [as] western banking practice." A mercantile and political leader like William S. Ladd moved to the apex of community authority and social prestige through involvement in major voluntary organizations of which he helped to establish several. Henry W. Corbett, C. H. Lewis, Henry Failing and John McCraken played similar roles. As Samuel P. Hays has observed, merchant and financial leaders "became the dominant elements of the community, and their role in associational activities was related . . . to their desire and capacity to shape and influence the social order." McCraken, for example, promoted the organization in October, 1859, of the Portland Philharmonic Society, modeled on New York's venerable music association.[21]

Portland merchants had come to Oregon in the early 1850s with clearly defined social aspirations. In May, 1852, Clementine Couch wrote an eastern friend: "Portland is continually increasing in size. Three years ago when father came here, there were only two decent houses and no ladies. Now, both houses and ladies are almost numberless. Very good society, three or four churches . . . ." Those who stayed, like Captain Couch, and Cicero H. Lewis (whom Clementine later married), hoped to emulate and even improve upon the world they had previously known. They were not political, economic or social innovators, but created new lives for their families within familiar social surroundings. As Bray Hammond describes the process,

> They used friendly and honored place names, set up conventional structures, read Plutarch, Milton, and the Bible; and while they laughed at the effete manners of the East and of the Old World, they never ceased to worry lest they appear ridiculous without them.[22]

Church Life and Freemasonry

The future Mrs. Cicero H. Lewis witnessed how social life for many centered around families and church, a characteristic of early western towns. Six established churches and several informally organized congregations were active in Portland by 1855. Early denominations included the Methodists (1850), Congregationalists (1851), Episcopalians (1851), Catholics (1852), Presbyterians (1854), Baptists (1855), and Jews (1858). The predominant Protestants tended toward informality in their services and facilities. Methodist minister the Reverend James H. Wilbur constructed a crude house of worship with his own hands. Congregationalist Horace Lyman did likewise with the assistance of 10 parishioners. Attached to posts, the First Congregational Church flooring was none too firm. On one occasion, noisy pigs rooting under the shaky supports pushed aside a loose board and "joined the congregation." At a nearby parish, the preacher exhorted his flock to bring their children to church but leave their dogs at home.[23]

At Trinity Episcopal Church, the first of its denomination to organize on the West Coast, worship and atmosphere were more formal than in other Protestant churches. Services were initially held at various locations. With money and land donated by Benjamin Stark, Trinity built its first permanent home at Second and Oak streets in 1854. Destined to become Portland's most socially prestigious church, its membership included names prominent by 1860: Dryer, Norris, Stark, Deady, McCraken, Flanders, Couch, and three Couch sons-in-law, C. H. Lewis, Dr. R. B. Wilson and Dr. Rodney Glisan. Trinity exhibited its early regard for wealth when its young families vied over furnishing the most magnificent upholstery for their pews.[24]

Despite such airs, increasingly embraced by the better-known churches, through most of the 1850s Portland congregations welcomed white believers without regard to social, political or financial standing. As in Portland itself, something of an egalitarian democracy reigned in all parishes, even if the more outstanding community figures favored one or two Protestant denominations over others. Ardent Baptist Josiah Failing and his family were instrumental in founding the First Baptist Church. Corbett and Ladd attended and supported the First Presbyterian Church. Captain John H. Couch, a nominal Congregationalist, preferred a Masonic dedication. Masonic affiliation did not preclude membership in a Protestant church, despite a Congregational minister's reported boast that there were "no Masons in his congregation." Trinity Church's vestry included four zealous Masons: Dryer, Lewis, Flanders, and Stark. The Reverend P. B. Chamberlain's attack on secret societies so outraged his congregation that it dropped to 10 members by the late 1850s.[25]

Masonic membership thrived in Portland among white, non-Catholic males who preferred exclusively male company. Early Masonry was not unlike the private gentlemen's clubs of later years. On July 17, 1850, Willamette Lodge No. 2 held its initial meeting on the upper floor of Captain Couch's warehouse on North Front Street. Led by Benjamin Stark, the secret fraternal order dedicated itself to benevolence and charity. It drew many of Portland's early business and civic luminaries including Couch, Dryer, Flanders, Lewis, Lownsdale, T. J. Holmes, W. M. King, H. D. O'Bryant, G. L. Story, and John Logan. Within a year, 116 men belonged to Masonic lodges in Portland, and in Oregon City (where the first lodge had been established in 1846). John C. Ainsworth and Robert R. Thompson had joined the latter upon their arrival in 1850, and with Simeon G. Reed they later transferred their memberships to Portland. While living in Oregon City in 1854, Ainsworth became grand master of Oregon Masonry.[26]

The Masons, Methodists and Baptists shared at least one major concern: the drinking problem. As Harvey Scott remembered, "Portland . . . was a place where drinking was carried to a most ruinous extreme." The Masons struggled for several years before expelling alcoholics and liquor dealers from membership. From the beginning, Methodists and Baptists banned alcohol from their lively parish activities. They organized the first of Portland's temperance crusades in March, 1851, an action that led to the initial city ordinance against public drunkenness. In the face of sporadic enforcement, Josiah Failing subsequently formed a Multnomah County chapter of The Sons of Temperance in 1856, one of over 5,000 such groups in the nation. Gaining wide support among Baptist and Methodist churches, especially in the Midwest and the South, the American temperance movement of the 1850s recruited few staunch members in the Northwest outside of Portland. The Oregon Territory, despite its claimed New England heritage of Puritan roots, failed to follow Maine's lead as one of 13 states passing prohibition laws. New England, excepting Maine, and westerners professing a New England heritage were generally unsupportive of temperance.[27]

Portland's New England Heritage

In 1853, the Sons of New England inaugurated a banquet open to any Portlander claiming New England family ties and a fortunate few "chosen from the outside." Eleven years before President Lincoln proclaimed an official Thanksgiving Day, they gathered to honor "the landing of Pilgrim Fathers on Plymouth Rock." Held annually a week before Christmas, the New England dinner became the leading social event of early Portland. As with other associational activities, it satisfied a need of a transplanted population to legitimize itself through traditional ceremonies and nostalgic links to the past. Portlanders related their New England attachment — heritage, as they called it — to the city's founding by New England traders. The celebrated coin toss by Asa Lovejoy and Francis Pettygrove, and the later enshrinement of the large copper penny, symbolized that heritage for future generations.[28]

Many of early Portland's leading merchants and shippers qualified for the prestigious invitation. Either through birthplace, lineage or marriage, they all had
bonafide ties to at least one New England state. The borders were stretched to
include some like the Failings from upper New York. Henry Failing's marriage to
Henry W. Corbett's sister Emily in 1858 authenticated his New England connection. Benjamin Stark, while southern-born and lacking, to some contemporaries,
a genuine New England character, qualified by virtue of his New London child-
hood. Without a direct link, aspiring Portland society weighed a proper Yankee
outlook and temperament more heavily than place of birth, lineage or marriage.

Visitors often commented on the New England heritage or "flavor of the town."
To a Boston *Journal* writer,

> 'Oregon has peculiar attractions . . . to New England folks. It is more New England
> than any of the states on the coast . . . . The people are mainly from New England.
> The social status is Eastern. The industry, the thrift, the briskness of business all
> remind one of Maine.'[29]

In reality, New Englanders constituted less than 25 percent of Portland's population in the 1850s and less than 5 percent in 1860. Because the town's social and
financial leaders had strong New England ties, many — both then and later —
presumed its New England character. There were certain similarities in the landscape and the way of life and in business behavior. Still, Portlanders have always
overdramatized the heritage claim throughout the city's history. References to the
city's "New England conscience" and "moralistic politics," stemming from its
"New England heritage," ill fitted Portland before 1900. Portland experienced few
outbursts of "moralistic politics" until well into the twentieth century. *Oregonian*
Editor Harvey W. Scott's claim that "there was a high moral tone in the early days"
was largely wishful thinking, unless he meant Henry W. Corbett's Sunday store
closure and Josiah Failing's disdain of cutthroat merchandising. From early on,
Portlanders — and Oregonians — inflated their professed pioneering New England virtues to the point where myth became reality.[30]

School and Community

The school usually followed the church in early New England. The reverse
happened in Portland, where the first school opened in a log cabin during the fall
of 1847. Like most pioneer schools, it was private and short-lived, lasting three
months. Parents of children under 12 paid $10 per child for the term. Julia Carter,
daughter of wealthy landowner Thomas J. Carter, opened the second school in
the spring of 1848. It, too, closed after one term.[31]

The Reverend Horace Lyman, a Massachusetts-born Congregational minister,
raised $2,000 in private subscriptions and won limited funding from the territo-
rial legislature to open a tuition-paying school in December, 1849. It was the first
joint private-public educational institution on the Pacific Coast. Stephen Coffin
and Daniel Lownsdale sold the school its First and Oak Street site for $300. Lowns-
dale then reneged on a $400 pledge to the construction fund, and the endeavor
fell victim to the California Gold Rush migration. Serving as a schoolhouse for

only three months under the tutelage of several teachers, the building became successively a church, a courthouse and a public meeting house.[32]

Opening a well financed private school and Portland's free public school were educational watersheds in 1851 — a crucial year for the city's economic and political future. The city had been incorporated, merchants had arrived in full force, and the Plank Road was under construction. On land adjacent to its entrance, donated by the proprietors to the Methodist Church, the Reverend C. S. Kingsley opened the Portland Academy and Female Seminary in the fall. Having begged and borrowed $5,000, he recruited the newly arrived William S. Ladd as trustee-treasurer. Kingsley's prospects looked brighter than those of his predecessors.[33]

Three months later, Portland citizens organized their first public school district. John T. Outhouse, a 20-year-old Canadian, received $100 a month as sole teacher. To help support his wife, he worked on the docks and removed stumps until a better offer took the couple to Polk County the following year. A second school house opened in November, 1852, after voters passed a district tax of $1,600. Within nine months, both free schools closed when funds were exhausted, ending an experiment that by practical standards was probably destined to fail. Considering the conditions of frontier life, with large numbers of unmarried males holding little or no interest in schools, sustained public tax support for free education met stiff voter resistance.[34]

Even some married voters with children opposed allocating scarce tax dollars for public education. Dryer, a trustee of the Portland Academy, fumed against spending $1,000 "'for pedagogueing some dozen or two of children.'" To Stark, it was a matter of priorities. Before a citizens' gathering, he argued against levying school taxes. He supposedly declared,

> I am by no means against education, and I do not deny the need for a school. Our greatest need at this time is for a jail. The taxpayers can't afford both a jailhouse and a schoolhouse, and since we seem to have in our midst more scoundrels than scholars, I say we must opt for the jail.[35]

Stark's reasoning prevailed, and Portland languished for over two years without free education. His argument reflected the feelings of many residents, including some of the larger property owners, that tax-supported, free public education was an ill-affordable luxury. Stark and Dryer, being closely identified with the tuition-paying Portland Academy and Female Seminary, may also have feared public school competition.

Fortunately for Portland, its wealthy merchant leadership exhibited more vision than Stark and Dryer. In early December, 1854, a "call" went out to voters, signed by Henry W. Corbett, Josiah Failing, Mayor William S. Ladd, and others who were persuaded to support free public education as essential to a growing city. Nine months were consumed in raising funds and private subscriptions and securing passage of a school tax to reopen Horace Lyman's old schoolhouse. The directors hired Sylvester Pennoyer, a 24-year-old New Yorker and recent Harvard Law School graduate, as teacher. Despite his obvious talents, the school closed after six months when operating funds expired. Pennoyer became a teacher and educational administrator in newly organized Multnomah County until he chose a more rewarding career in lumber. He invested wisely in Portland real-estate, and was elected governor in 1887 and mayor in 1896.[36]

Under the energetic leadership of merchant Josiah Failing, Portland reorganized its school district, raised public funds and private subscriptions, and bought a city block for $1,000. The new Central School opened in the winter of 1858 on the present site of Pioneer Courthouse Square. Nine years' service on the school board earned for Failing the sobriquet "Father of Portland public schools." His tireless voluntary efforts in behalf of free education set a pattern of service for younger members of Portland's social establishment. Ladd joined Failing on the school board for three years (1865-1867) and served another term 10 years later. Captain John C. Ainsworth devoted four years to the school board in the mid-1870s.[37]

Fire Brigades

Great civic necessity and concern prompted organization of voluntary fire brigades. Portland's wooden structures were unusually prone to spontaneous combustion. A month after city incorporation, Dryer and 36 other stalwarts organized the informal Pioneer Fire Company No. 1. It acted only as a bucket brigade because Mayor Hugh O'Bryant had overridden voter approval and refused to purchase pumping equipment. Disastrous fires like the $25,000 loss at the Jefferson Street sawmill could not be contained. Until Willamette Engine Company No. 1 formed in August, 1853, Portland lacked an official fire service. Equipped with buckets and ladders (the first pumper did not arrive until 1856) Willamette Engine attracted the social elite, especially among merchants with buildings and stock to protect. William S. Ladd, Cicero H. Lewis, David W. Burnside, George H. Williams, Walter F. Burrell, Alonzo Leland, and Henry and Josiah Failing transformed it into an important social institution. On November 17, 1853, Willamette Engine launched Portland's first social season with a ball at the waterfront Columbia Hotel.[38]

"Northsiders" from Couch's Addition were not to be outdone or left unprotected outside the original town boundary. The fast-spreading city needed two companies, especially after fire leveled a second sawmill on North Front Street. The eager citizens established Vigilance Hook & Ladder Company No. 1 in the fall of 1853. Dryer, anxious for the public limelight and prestige (when he was not inebriated), became its chief warden despite his south-side residence. The honor barely compensated him for not being chosen to lead Willamette Engine No. 1. Obtaining the first brick firehouse, Willamette Engine retained the higher prestige. Like its competitors, it increasingly became a male social club resembling a college fraternity. When the young druggist Stephen Skidmore joined Portland's third company, Multnomah No. 2, in 1857, his biographer said Skidmore "had 'arrived' socially"; that "he was considered a jolly and companionable young man." By 1860, when the volunteer Portland Fire Department was officially mandated by the legislature, membership in the various companies remained selective with acceptance based on social standing.[39]

Early Social Leadership

Trinity Church, Portland Academy and Willamette Engine No. 1 manifested the early urban Far West tendency to "copy old rather than create new societal patterns," in Paul Merriam's phrase. In modeling their local private academy-seminary on eastern schools, the more affluent helped create a wealth-based, class-conscious society. Although their social origins were egalitarian rather than elitist, Portlanders clung to and studied traditional institutional forms and practices that deferred to riches and admired success. Individual success was deemed rooted in the wide-open opportunity to make money: the right to compete on equal terms, at least for white males, and a felt prerogative to increase individual wealth without too fine a regard for scruples.[40]

Portland's small size and isolated location encouraged successful merchants, shippers and bankers to advance socially. Successful upward mobility for them depended more upon acquiring status in the community than upon being entrepreneurial innovators. Innovation, in fact, rarely marked local enterprise or social activity in early Portland. Henry Failing described the assiduous Cicero H. Lewis as "a master of the trade, ...[but] no genius for new enterprise." Control, continuity, stability, hard work, and opportune marriages created a structure that long perpetuated the Portland elite's power and social prominence, which spread the ethic of personal responsibility. Like Lewis, men were largely thought to be what they themselves had created.[41]

Portland soon became a place of tightly knit "first families," and these connections fundamentally shaped both business and social commitments. Kinship cemented the emerging social class network as Failings, Corbetts and Ladds intermarried and the Couch and Lewis families extended into clans. Henry Failing's marriage to Henry W. Corbett's sister, and his later business and banking partnership with Corbett firmly established the pattern of intermarriages and kinship economic alliances.

Proper Bostonians might dismiss Portland's pretensions as a social and cultural outpost before the Civil War. Scores of parties, dances and informal musical and theatrical entertainments demonstrated the young town's increasing acceptance of urban values. Still, "Theatrical amusements never ranked high," remembered the observant Matthew P. Deady. Most shows were "low grade minstrels and vulgar comedy." In their new, larger and costlier homes by the late 1850s, the affluent popularized afternoon women's luncheon receptions and bachelor soirees. The socially active Green and Leonard brothers hosted "chafing dish suppers" in their comfortable quarters near the site of their future gasworks.[42]

Mrs. Henry W. Corbett's "wishbone party" highlighted the 1857 social calendar. As described by one attendee, each lady was given a chicken wishbone, after which she selected a gentleman partner. Together, the pair made a wish and broke the bone. The hostess provided cards with little verses of sentiment, which were read aloud to the embarrassment of several readers. As the chronicler later remembered: "Mrs. Corbett knew how to entertain" in her large residence (considered by the envious as "highly pretentious"). She was popular with all ages, known for her vivaciousness and pleasant disposition — a fitting wife for one of Portland's leading merchants and aspiring Republican U.S. senatorial candidates. Her garden wedding reception for the Henry Failings in 1858, the major social event of the decade, symbolized the dominance of Portland's emerging elite family trees, fertilized by rapidly accumulating wealth.[43]

Henry L. Pittock

A young English-born printer, two years Henry Failing's junior, knew the importance of financial success for gaining community stature and influence in a youthful Portland. When 24-year-old Henry L. Pittock assumed control of the *Weekly Oregonian* from Thomas J. Dryer on April 1, 1860, something of the old order of rugged frontier political journalism passed from the scene. In contrast to the emotional, intemperate, political sniper Dryer, who fired through a partisan paper, the quiet, methodical, industrious Pittock treated the newspaper primarily as a business to be run efficiently for handsome profit. Like his commercial and banking friends, he became a merchant — a highly successful merchant of the press.[44]

Pittock had covered wide ground since leaving his Pittsburgh home in April, 1853. From sleeping on a shelf below the front counter of the *Oregonian*'s print shop, where it was so cold that he had to pour boiling water over the composing stones to melt the ice, he had advanced to partnership with Dryer three years after his arrival in Portland. Two months later, in January, 1857, he made his first real-estate investments. For $74.79, he purchased three wooded blocks on Tenth and Eleventh streets, between Morrison and Taylor. He understood the indispensability of private investments to building a personal fortune. Over the next 10 years, he bought additional property and erected Oregon's first paper mill at Oregon City.[45]

As the new publisher, Pittock sensed that Portland readers wanted more information about what as happening. He determined to make the *Oregonian* a "'NEWSpaper.'" If the journal remained a weekly, he believed that "it would ultimately fail." People, he felt, wanted their news reported as close to the event as possible, and wanted increased local news coverage. "He had the choice of quitting or going daily. He decided to take the plunge." He went to San Francisco in December, 1860, and ordered a new press. He also arranged for national and international news to be sent by telegraph to Redding, California (later to Yreka), thence by stagecoach to Jacksonville, Oregon, and by pony express to Portland.

When the first *Daily Oregonian* appeared on February 4, 1861, Portlanders received their most current printed news from Henry Pittock. Within six weeks, after the outbreak of the Civil War, the paper's financial success seemed assured.[46]

Pittock continued publishing the weekly along with the daily. His first daily editorial contrasted sharply with those of his predecessor, Dryer. We "will be influenced by Republicanism," he assured readers, but not at the expense of truth. The *Daily Oregonian* "will desire not wantingly to injure the feelings of its political opponents." Along with a more balanced editorial tone, Pittock's daily introduced a new feature on page two. "The City," a full-length column, contained news of current city events and matters of local concern. During its first months, the column covered the jail, fire-company competition, the insane, Chinese pros titution, the need for a city attorney, flour shipments, a boat regatta, musica groups, city-budget details, the need for an open-air market, Oswego iron mines and street and drainage matters.[47]

By informing readers on current issues, and thereby encouraging them to set their own political agendas, Pittock and his *Oregonian* acquired an increasing degree of community power equal to, if not greater than, that exercised by Port land's leading bankers and merchants.

6.1 Mr. and Mrs. Henry W. Corbett's home, brought around the Horn, 1852

6.2 Trinity Church, September 21, 1854

6.3 The *Oregonian* Building beside Thomas J. Dryer's home, c. 1854

6.4 The original Central School, built 1857-1858

6.5 Ladd & Tilton Bank, 1859

6.6 First choir of First Congregational Church, Summer of 1857 (l to r) Back row: H.L. Hoyt, Thos. A. Savier, E.S. Penfield, J.B. Wyatt, Henry Law, Harley Sarah Abrams; Front Row: Helen Burton, Mrs. A.E. Chamberlain, Mrs. Hiram S. Pine, Mrs. A.R. Shipley; Elizabeth A. Failing, Mrs. Alonzo Leland

6.7 Multnomah Engine Company No. 2 (?), July 9, 1858 (l to r) Charles Henry Hill, Ansel C. Briggs, Joseph Buchtel, Augustus C. Ripley, John W. Pailing, William V. Sheneer, Thomas Brooks Trevitt and Ella Varicycle on hose carriage

6.8 Leading Portland businessmen, c. 1857–58 (l to r) Top: L.M. Starr or C.H. Lewis; Henry Failing, possibly Addison M. Starr, possibly Simeon Reed, possibly Edward Failing, unknown, possibly John McCraken; Bottom: unknown, possibly J.K. Gill, Henry W. Corbett, William S. Ladd, possibly Matthew P. Deady

7

THE CONSOLIDATION OF POWER: 1860-1870

Thompson Opens the Upper Columbia

At Fort Dalles, Robert R. Thompson was positioned to take advantage of federal supply needs after troubles with the Indians intensified in 1855. He had built a fleet of bateaux and sailboats to carry merchandise from the mouth of the Deschutes River up the Columbia to Fort Walla Walla, Washington Territory. To accelerate operations in 1857, he constructed the stern-wheel steamer *Venture* in partnership with New York native Lawrence W. Coe, part owner of a Donation Land claim near Hood River. Designed to run between the Upper Cascades and the Celilo Falls at Fort Dalles, the *Venture* made a trial run in 1858 under Coe's command. The ship's engines failed; it was swept over the Cascades and onto a submerged sandbar.[1]

Undaunted, Thompson towed the boat to Portland for repairs. He accepted the offer of his friend Captain John C. Ainsworth and merchant-shipper John Green to purchase a half-interest in the stern-wheeler, renamed the *Umatilla*. Unwilling to risk returning the vessel to the Upper Cascades, the owners dispatched it to Victoria, where it performed profitably. The Thompson-Ainsworth transaction established a close 40-year business association. It was Thompson who "sold Ainsworth on the upper river," where both would become wealthy. Thompson later took credit for their good fortune when he boastfully wrote: "I went up and opened up that whole country."[2]

Although advised strongly by many of his Portland friends not to build and run ships on the Upper Columbia, Thompson persevered in his vision that the real future lay upriver. Not wishing to repeat his earlier mistake, he built his next boat east of Celilo, at the mouth of the Deschutes. It was appropriately named the *Colonel Wright*, after the army colonel who commanded the forces in eastern Washington. With his usual aversion to borrowing funds, Thompson and his minority partner, Coe, underwrote the costs themselves and were immediately rewarded. The government paid well for their services — $80 a ton by sail and $100 by steamer. Beginning in the summer of 1858, the *Colonel Wright* earned a fortune transporting supplies to the military and to miners. Gold had been discovered in the upper Fraser River country of eastern Washington and British Columbia. Although short-lived, the mini-gold rush was a taste of what would follow in 1860, when gold was discovered in the Idaho Territory. Twenty thousand new immigrants were to come by sea and 10,000 by land in search of quick riches.[3]

Birth of the Oregon Steam Navigation Company

"The financial wonder of its day and age," Ainsworth's associate Jacob Kamm labeled the Oregon Steam Navigation Company. "One of the most valuable properties of its kind in the United States," Thompson, another OSN founder, gleefully remembered. As the source of most of Portland's earliest fortunes, the OSN played a crucial — if not dominant — role in Oregon's explosive economic growth during the 1860s. Its genesis is unclear. Both Ainsworth and Simeon G. Reed later claimed responsibility for its origin, although Ainsworth also credited Thompson for his contributions. All agreed that events during the spring of 1859 — a time of economic stagnation in the Columbia-Willamette Valley — called for drastic action. River transportation seemed to them chaotic and wasteful. They wanted "one large combination" to provide "proper management," more control and protection, and better service than in the past.[4]

In 1859 Ainsworth and Thompson had organized the Union Transportation Company, combining the services of Ainsworth's *Carrie Ladd* and *Jennie Clark* with those of Thompson and Coe's *Colonel Wright* and *Umatilla*, of which Ainsworth was part owner. He aimed to compete head-on with the aggressive Columbia River Steam Navigation Company, founded in 1857 by Portlanders Richard Hoyt, Reed and Benjamin Stark. Although Thompson and Coe were making "big money," their profits were threatened by the rising competition and costs of portaging freight around two obstructions in the Columbia, the Cascade Falls below Hood River and the Celilo rapids above Fort Dalles. Ainsworth and Thompson needed complete portage control to fulfill their plans for a transportation system that would monopolize the Columbia River trade from Astoria to Idaho. While Thompson held part ownership of the Celilo portage, others owned the two Cascade portages.[5]

Deferring portage acquisition until sufficient funds were accumulated, Ainsworth, Reed and Thompson moved to consolidate existing steamboat interests into one corporation. Their model was the Sacramento River's California Steam Navigation Company, with which Ainsworth was thoroughly familiar. They organized the OSN in May, 1860, and incorporated it on December 19, that year, by act of the Washington Territorial Legislature. (The new state of Oregon did not pass its first incorporation law until 1862.) The OSN issued 542 shares of stock at $500 par value. Thompson received 120 shares, the largest number. The Ladd & Tilton Bank, for its majority interest in the *Carrie Ladd*, received 80. The other major shareholders were Coe (60), Kamm (57), Ainsworth (40), Reed (26) and Stark (19). Eight others held the remaining 140 shares.[6]

Ainsworth, with approximately 7 percent of the stock, became president by virtue of his experience and reputation as an efficient operator. Thompson, with 22 percent, chose an unofficial role because of his other interests, and received a director's fee of $1,000 per month. In later years, he enjoyed telling friends how he had initially shocked the other investors, except for Ainsworth, who recognized his true worth. As the key figure in the group, Thompson exacted his tribute. In addition to the largest number of shares, he received $20,000 in gold, which he channeled into Portland real estate and other non-maritime ventures worth over $500,000 in 1884.[7]

Ainsworth was just the sort of tough steamboat operator to cooperate with the rough-hewn Thompson in attempting the domination of Columbia River traffic. As Dorothy Johansen has noted, the two devout Masons "thought and acted as one person" in forming the policy of the OSN. Ainsworth had moved from Oregon City in 1859 to a newly built mansion on Portland's Pine Street. Thompson came the following year, and built an adjacent townhouse. Corporate headquarters were soon established nearby on a double waterfront block between Pine and Ankeny streets. Although not involved in day-to-day decisions, Thompson was crucial to Ainsworth. When asked his advice, Ainsworth later remembered, Thompson would jot down some item "with stubby pencil and retire quietly. A day or so later, he would say, 'I think that you had better do so and so.' He was always right!"[8]

One reason for the two men's success was their ability to respond to, and even predict, the regional economic forces. They concentrated on one activity they thoroughly understood and knew they could administer efficiently. The diversity of their backgrounds and experiences proved beneficial. Thompson was a self-made man, and was almost alone among Portland's early elite in first making much of his money outside the Willamette Valley. California gold, added to ranching and shipping in The Dalles, created his initial fortune. Although Ainsworth had started with modest sources, he had close banking friends in San Francisco like William C. Ralston, who generously advanced him money. His second marriage was to the daughter of wealthy Oregon City Judge S. S. White.[9]

Idaho Gold and Reincorporation

Even before the formation of the Oregon Steam Navigation Company, Thompson became convinced that Oregon's future economic growth was tied to the Upper Columbia. His mining experience led him to suspect the possibility of gold deposits to the east of Portland, and he may well have been one of the first to hear reports in the spring of 1860 that gold had been discovered in Idaho. When the rush ensued in the spring of 1861, the OSN was prepared to cash in on the biggest boom yet in the Oregon country. Belgian landscape gardener Jean-Nicolas Perlot watched "more than 20,000 emigrants" pass through Portland from April to June that year.[10]

OSN steamboats carried most Idaho bullion downriver under consignment to Wells Fargo's Portland office, whence it was shipped to San Francisco. From a low of $4,700 in February, 1861, the average payload of gold dust climbed to $400,000 a month by June. Gold discoveries in eastern Oregon and Washington the same year increased the pace. Upriver freight traffic was even more profitable than downriver gold shipments. Molasses costing 70 cents a gallon in Portland retailed in Boise, in the Idaho Territory, for $6 a gallon. The OSN received an average 8 percent on retail price, while the remainder was pocketed by Boise merchants. Between 1861 and 1864, the OSN carried over 100,000 passengers, many from California. "Portland has taken a lurch forward since you left," Judge Matthew P. Deady reported to Senator Benjamin Stark in October, 1862. "I suppose the business has doubled. The immigration is pouring in here mighty thick, and from here spreading out through the country . . . Every night the streets are alive with music dance houses and other flash amusements."[11]

In addition to freight and passengers, lucrative government mail and army supply contracts filled OSN's coffers. The frenzied shipping activity created an immediate need for more boats. Foregoing a 20 percent dividend in June, 1861, company directors, in traditional Portland merchant-banker caution, reinvested profits back into the company. They increased its capitalization from $271,000 to $690,000 and issued a four-for-one stock split. In succeeding months, they paid two dividends of 2½ percent and further increased capital stock by 40 percent to $966,000. Before the end of 1861 they paid three more dividends. In one year, OSN investors had received $240 for each original $500 stock share. To Ainsworth, "Our success was beyond our most sanguine expectations."[12]

OSN's prosperity roused envy among small competitors with ties to the Washington Territory. Ainsworth proposed buying them out, an action requiring a charter change to allow increased capitalization. When the Washington Territorial Legislature imposed restrictions, the OSN reincorporated under Oregon's newly enacted state incorporation law — which it had strongly supported. As an Oregon corporation after October 18, 1862, the expanded OSN was capitalized at $2 million — 4,000 shares issued at $500 par value. The 10 largest shareholders were:

Bradford & Co. (N.Y.)	758 shares	T.W. Lyles	210 shares
R.R. Thompson	672 shares	J.C. Ainsworth	188 shares
Harrison Olmstead	558 shares	A.H. Barker	160 shares
Jacob Kamm	354 shares	S.G. Reed	128 shares
L.W. Coe	336 shares	Ladd & Tilton	94 shares

William S. Ladd, in addition to his bank's holdings, controlled 88 shares through his brother J. Wesley Ladd, Reed's partner in Ladd, Reed & Company. Reed also held an additional 40 shares for others. The remaining 414 shares were split among 11 minor stockholders. Daniel F. Bradford, of New York and Massachusetts, received the largest number of shares, for three steamboats added to the OSN fleet. His partner, Harrison Olmstead, received the third-highest amount.[13]

Thompson's shareholdings were reduced when he sold his portage interest to the OSN for cash. The remaining portages were to trouble Ainsworth for two more years. Bradford owned the Washington portage at the Cascades, while Olmstead and Joseph Ruckle owned the Oregon portage. Although part owners of the OSN, each retained his share of portage ownership and received a percentage of user fees paid by the company. Portage fees amounted to one-half of the freight charges from Portland to The Dalles.[14]

A Monopoly Under Fire

By January, 1863, the Oregon Steam Navigation Company was a de facto monopoly, dominating the Columbia's trade and passenger traffic from its mouth at Astoria to Lewiston, Idaho, by way of the Snake River. Over the next six months it faced "the most formidable opposition of its history," according to Arthur Throckmorton. In December, 1862, concerned Salem business interests had incorporated the People's Transportation Company, which absorbed the assets of Stephen Coffin's People's Line, organized in 1857 to serve Willamette Valley farmers and merchants. Capitalized at $2 million by Coffin, Edward N. Cooke and Asa and David McCully, the PTC aimed to challenge the OSN on both the Willamette and lower Columbia rivers. The Dalles merchants, feeling victimized by the OSN's high rates, were threatening to buy directly in San Francisco at Portland's expense. In challenging the OSN monopoly, the *Oregonian* editorialized, the PTC would actually benefit Portland, especially its "merchants and trades." After thwarting rivals on the Willamette, the PTC turned to the lower Columbia in January, 1863, to compete with the OSN for The Dalles trade.[15]

Portland merchants, also chafing under the OSN's high rate schedule, joined battle in early January, 1863. Led by Henry W. Corbett and Captain Alexander P. Ankeny, they formed the Merchants' Transportation Company. The resulting rate war, which reduced per-ton shipping costs by 80 percent, split Portland's merchant elite into two camps. Achieving a limited victory on the Willamette and lower Columbia, the MTC profitably sent one of its two steamers, the *Spray*, to the upper river on the Lewiston route. The other boat competed on the lower Columbia until Ainsworth drove it out of business by identifying its illegal Canadian registry for the U.S. Customs. Reduced to one vessel and lacking assured access to Columbia portages, the MTC sued for peace. The OSN bought the line for a token sum in mid-1863. Corbett withdrew forever from the transportation business, except for a later investment in overland stages to California. Ankeny, a merchant-meatpacker, was to become an original investor in Portland's First National Bank and eventually engaged in Puget Sound and Alaska shipping.[16]

By June of 1863, as the MTC folded operations, the PTC boats on the lower Columbia forced an OSN compromise proposed by Ladd. As financial agent to both companies, Ladd & Tilton had nothing to gain by a prolonged conflict. The OSN agreed to quit the Willamette and the PTC to abandon the Columbia. Within days, freight rates from Portland to Lewiston jumped nearly 400 percent to pre-competition levels. The PTC profitably monopolized the Willamette Trade; it was acquired in 1871 by California stagecoach owner Ben Holladay for $200,000. The OSN-PTC agreement was a classic, though legal, pool arrangement favored by such contemporary would-be monopolists as Cornelius Vanderbilt and John D. Rockefeller. By dividing the territory into exclusive areas — staying off one another's rivers — the companies blocked potential competition by absorbing losses and then raised rates as high as the traffic would bear.[17]

A golden stream poured into OSN's coffers during the latter half of 1863. A monopoly on the Columbia and Snake rivers, the OSN earned $1.3 million by the end of the year. It paid off all Ladd & Tilton Bank loans on its boats. Never again would the company need to borrow capital or operating funds. It added five luxurious and well-appointed boats in 1863-64, as the mining boom continued. "Thousands of men are rushing on to new mines east of the Cascades and Blue range of Mountains," reported Episcopal missionary Bishop Thomas F. Scott. They came "from every direction in this state; and every steamer from California brings on hundreds more." Prospectors carrying 50-pound sacks of gold were common sights on OSN vessels returning to Portland.[18]

To accommodate the throngs of passengers and their baggage, the OSN constructed a large new Portland dock in 1864. Costing $39,000, it measured 250 feet long by 160 feet wide, with two decks to handle normal river levels and annual spring floods. In 1865, it built twin two-story, cast-iron-fronted office and storage buildings next to the docks. A central third story was added in 1870. Along with these costly improvements, the OSN strung its own telegraph lines from Portland to The Dalles and beyond. New company warehouses lined the route to Lewiston. A growing fleet of 18 steamboats, 12 of them large and luxurious stern-wheelers, proclaimed their suzerainty over the "Empire of the Columbia."[19]

The Power Struggle

The company's prosperity created serious internal management problems and differences among shareholders over portage ownership and profit distribution. Splitting with the other board directors, Ainsworth, Thompson and Kamm wanted the company to buy those portages not under OSN ownership, using funds that might otherwise be paid stockholders. Ainsworth and Thompson secretly negotiated with the portage owners, playing off one against the other. They succeeded in buying up all portage interests but Bradford's and Ruckel's. They convinced the devious Ruckel, Bradford's agent, to sell out on terms disadvantageous to Bradford, who was then in the East. Feeling tricked by Ainsworth, Bradford returned to Portland and called for a vote of no confidence at the annual meeting in November, 1864. Owing Ladd & Tilton a sizeable debt, portage owners Bradford, Ruckel and Olmstead prevailed first on banker Ladd and then on Simeon Reed (neither of whom had paid close attention to company operations) to join with them and other minority stockholders in ousting Ainsworth as president. Ruckel became figurehead president, with Reed as vice-president and general manager. The board then declared a 4 percent dividend. With unbounded energy, Reed enthusiastically immersed himself in the demanding and complicated operation of an expanding shipping empire.[20]

Over the following months, Ainsworth kept an eye on company affairs while concentrating on other investments, particularly mining properties. Thompson initially reacted to Ainsworth's removal with discouragement. He even contemplated emigrating to California. But closer involvement with Reed bred growing respect for the general manager's skills. Reed soon realized the folly of Ainsworth's ouster and informed both Thompson and Ainsworth of Ruckel's apparent deception. When Daniel Bradford and John Wesley Ladd also reached similar conclusions, Ainsworth regained the presidency with Reed remaining as vice-president and general manager. Reed's total involvement in the OSN and Ladd's desire to move to New York led the two merchants to sell Ladd, Reed & Company to new owners in 1865.[21]

Crucial Years

Four years after the Oregon Steam Navigation Company's formation, Captain Ainsworth began to question its strategic goals in the light of impending developments in western transportation. By early 1865, changing demands for facilities, new overland wagon routes, and threatening railroad competition required, in Dorothy Johansen's opinion, "an imperialistic policy" if the OSN were to survive. The Union Pacific had been chartered in 1862. The Central Pacific, using California money, began construction in 1863, and the Northern Pacific received its charter in July 1864. Ainsworth asked: How would the OSN be affected by such developments? Could the OSN link itself to a railroad? Could it supply construction crews? As a first answer, he suggested to Thompson and Reed that the OSN should expand to secure its control of the Idaho trade and extend its service to Montana. Such a policy, which would compete successfully against railroad intrusion, would require the OSN to offer the best transportation facilities possible to serve those regions.[22]

While the three men believed that Portland was an important commercial and trading center, they knew that compared with San Francisco it was a village. West Coast commercial life centered in San Francisco. Once the bay city gained direct rail service to the east, San Francisco was sure to enhance its stature at Portland's expense. (In 1865, it already dominated the coastal trade.) Ben Holladay had taken control of the California Steam Navigation Company, which had earlier absorbed the Pacific Mail Steamship Company, Portland's old nemesis. Without competition, PacMail had allowed its equipment to deteriorate. Coastal service had become slow and dangerous. "Some of these rotten carcasses of ships are so frail that the very rats long ago instinctively quit them," the *Oregonian* thundered in May, 1865. Reed and Ainsworth decided the OSN must build its own first-rate coastal steamer for the San Francisco-Portland run. They proceeded secretly, lest Holladay were to dispatch CSN steamers to challenge OSN's control of the Columbia.[23]

Reed and Thompson, embracing Ainsworth's strategic goals, won the support of the Ladd brothers for their more expansive policy. They devised a scheme for providing Daniel Bradford with only the barest information; the other stockholders were to be kept in ignorance. Bradford (in New York) and most of the other shareholders were opposed to any expansion plans that would deprive them of their rich stock dividends. As far as Bradford knew, the ship would be built in New York and financed by A.E. and C.E. Tilton. The insiders failed to inform him that the $400,000 to build and outfit the ship was a loan, to be repaid from retained stockholder dividends. To conceal OSN's ownership, title was registered in the names of Bradford, A.E. Tilton, John Wesley Ladd, and William S. Ladd.[24]

The decision to build the *S.S. Oregonian* forged a new and firm alliance between the "big four" — William S. Ladd, John C. Ainsworth, Simeon G. Reed, and Robert R. Thompson. Never as close to his colleagues as they were to each other,

Ladd remained aloof, formal, even austere. But his involvement in the OSN's future was crucial. As their banker, he would handle the many complex financial details, and no matter would be more complex than the disposition of their new ship.[25]

By April, 1866, when the *S.S. Oregonian* was launched, conditions on the Pacific Coast had changed. Holladay and his CSN, learning of the ship's construction, added new vessels to the Portland run and sharply reduced his rates in anticipation of the competition. Bradford and his associates, unhappy with their decreased dividends, not only feared that a rate war would decimate the *S.S. Oregonian*'s potential revenues but also suspected that stockholder dividends were being diverted to pay for the ship. When Bradford proposed to sell the *S.S. Oregonian* in New York and distribute the proceeds to shareholders, Ainsworth and his friends became infuriated. Only one option seemed feasible to the OSN leadership — as long as they blithely ignored ethical and legal questions. They agreed to eliminate the other owners and consolidate management and ownership in fewer hands. Four thousand shares of stock, held by 33 owners, posed an unworkable arrangement. The company's future survival depended on its ability to react quickly when challenged by competitive market forces like the Holladay interests of California.[26]

What followed was unique in the annals of Portland business. The Big Four used what Wall Street later called a squeeze play. They first floated rumors that the company faced ruinous competition. No balance sheets or profit- and-loss statements were issued to dispute their gloomy predictions. They then created a "blind pool"to buy up company stock as dire economic forecasts depleted its value. Lastly, they arranged to send the *S.S. Oregonian* to San Francisco, tie it up, and make no announcement of its future disposition. They thereby froze this major asset on the company's books, effectively reducing the OSN's net worth.[27]

Through his friend William C. Ralston, president of the Bank of California, Ainsworth selected a friend of Ralston, the wealthy San Francisco capitalist Alvinza Hayward, to act as front for the "blind pool" designed to buy up the outstanding OSN stock. C.E. Tilton and Ralston provided the funds to acquire OSN stock in Hayward's name while William S. Ladd, as agent, actually purchased most of the shares. Ainsworth later denied his involvement in these machinations, although a surviving letter, clearly marked with the words "private, to be destroyed," revealed his key role in the legally questionable transactions.[28]

Beginning in December, 1866, after the *S.S. Oregonian*'s arrival in San Francisco, discreetly issued press releases revealed that "a Mr. A. Hayward of California" was attempting to buy control of the OSN. Ainsworth, Reed and Thompson set the market by reportedly selling their shares at discounted prices. Ladd acted his part by deliberately breaching his banker's fiduciary role. In a letter encouraging Benjamin Stark to sell his shares (which Ladd held as agent), he told his client that OSN stock was selling at "75% to 80% of par value." The canny Stark, expecting a higher price, became suspicious. He refused to sell, even though he had been advised six months earlier that Ladd & Tilton would loan him no more money because of insufficient funds on deposit. Selling his OSN stock would have increased his liquidity, thus qualifying him for additional loans.[29]

Over the next nine months, additional reports of stock sales, intermixed with gloomy profit predictions, greatly increased stockholder confusion and concern. When stockholders complained to Thompson and Ladd about the discounted price of their shares, they were assured that the price was fair, given the company's bleak future. Thompson strongly believed that stockholders had no justifiable grounds for complaint: their original investment had increased tenfold in six years. Worry turned frenzied in the spring of 1867, when the eastern stockholders, including Bradford, learned that the Ladds had sold to Hayward at 75 percent of par value. Little did they realize that Ladd had merely sold his shares to himself as corporate agent. In a rush to bail out before the price dropped even lower, the remaining stockholders, including many Ladd & Tilton customers (but excluding Stark), quickly liquidated their holdings.[30]

Jacob Kamm, the second-largest stockholder after Thompson, resigned as OSN's chief engineer in June, 1865, and sold his shares in late December, 1866. He must have known what was secretly transpiring during the fall of 1866 as he expanded his shareholdings by 15 percent. His decision to sell out may well have been prompted by strong disapproval of the increasingly deceitful tactics pursued by his former associates.

Concurrent with Kamm's stock disposal, the Big Four sold the *S.S. Oregonian* to Ben Holladay for nearly $360,000, including a $50,000 note "extorted" from Holladay, to be repaid only if Holladay kept his promise not to use the ship on the Portland-San Francisco run. Although the OSN lost $100,000 on the transaction, the owners more than recouped the shortfall. They had paid for the *S.S. Oregonian* out of retained dividends rightfully belonging to the disfranchised shareholders — whose pain was aggravated when the company declared its largest dividend (37 percent) on December 31, 1867. The four surviving owners — Ainsworth, Ladd, Reed and Thompson — realized greater windfall profits than they had dreamt of. Some of their local friends — Asahel Bush, Henry W. Corbett, Henry Failing, and Addison M. Starr — who owned from 35 to 50 shares apiece must have felt victimized, but their reactions were not revealed. Seven other minor stockholders did react angrily by filing suit in Judge Matthew P. Deady's court in 1871.[31]

Charges of Fraud

Four years after the Big Four's consolidation of control of the Oregon Steam Navigation Company, seven former minor stockholders individually filed suit to recover $131,774 in damages. They charged Ainsworth, Ladd, Reed, and Thompson with "fraudulent conduct." They sought compensation equal to the dividends they would have received from an honest sale of the *S.S. Oregonian*. Handling the *Oregonian* cases for four years placed Judge Matthew P. Deady in a most uncomfortable position. A social friend of the defendants, he had close ties to Ladd, or was as close as anyone could get to Ladd. On several occasions, Ladd proffered him money — a cash advance or gift, not a loan — to help him build a new home on his Alder Street property. In declining the offers, which he never seemed to consider bribes, Deady was governed by the proprieties of his office. As he noted in his diary in February, 1872, "I would like to take the money, but I am afraid that if I do decide these *Oregonian* cases against the OSN people, that he (Ladd) could not help feeling ugly about it."[32]

"We acted properly, legally and legitimately," Captain Ainsworth insisted in an autobiographical diary prepared for his children. He blamed Ben Holladay for the lawsuits. By 1871, Holladay had become a resident of Portland, where he made many bitter enemies among the city's Establishment. Ainsworth branded him "a most unscrupulous man." The company's leadership had merely acted to thwart Holladay and consolidate management. Minority stockholders "more than received their due . . . They were made rich by the OSN" and had "no grounds for complaint." Complainants, indeed, only sued after they saw how well the company did after 1867. The fact that John H. Mitchell, Holladay's attorney, filed the suits made Ainsworth angrier. Mitchell, considered by Portland's Establishment an unprincipled rogue, was a rising star in the Republican Party.[33]

Ainsworth was further angered by the $35,000 out-of-court settlement that William S. Ladd arranged to prevent public trial of the cases. Ainsworth thought that Ladd primarily feared jeopardizing his image of a trustworthy fiduciary. Ainsworth obviously knew that the banker had been acting as both buyer of the pooled stock and agent for many minority stockholders like Stark, whose interests he was supposed to protect. Ainsworth, Reed and Thompson wanted to fight the charges. The $35,000 compromise to save their "friends" (Ladd, Ralston and Hayward) made them suffer "in purse and reputation," Ainsworth remembered. He grudgingly paid his share of the damages, something in excess of $9,000.[34]

Some 20 years later, Deady heard that Thompson's California home had burned with a loss of "about $300,000," including all personal effects. "Considering that he got this out of the 'Oregonian steal,'" he mused, "the old proverb applies — 'What comes under the devil's belly goes over his back'." Deady seemed convinced that fraud had been perpetrated. The compromise spared him a painful decision.[35]

Reed Woos Congress and the Northern Pacific

In the winter of 1866, as the *S.S. Oregonian* underwent construction, company officers sent Simeon Reed to Washington, D.C., to gain federal assistance. The Oregon Steam Navigation Company had been encountering increased competition from new steamship companies freely chartered by a Washington Territorial Legislature responding to public indignation over the OSN's "ruthless . . . practices," to quote Oscar O. Winther. Reed and Ainsworth viewed these hostile actions as "unwarranted interference with free business enterprise." The two entrepreneurs conveniently disregarded the fact that the OSN had received its initial charter by similar tactics. Like most monopolists, they wanted governmental protection to safeguard their vested interests against upstart competitors. The OSN needed some legal assurance, as Reed recalled, allowing it to "grow up with the business of the country." Reed's assignment was to lobby congressional passage of two bills to prohibit territories like Washington, and later Idaho, from enacting legislation harmful to existing corporations.[36]

Arriving on the East Coast in March, 1866, Reed succeeded in enlisting sufficient congressional support for the two enactments in 1867. He became friendly
with a number of important congressmen, including House Speaker Schuyler
Colfax, whom he had met in Portland the previous summer. Colfax in turn introduced him to major railroad lobbyists. Nearly everyone seemed to have heard of
the OSN, pleasing Reed because "they put it down as among the big institutions of
the country." He found Washington to be a world apart from Portland. As he wrote
Ainsworth, "'I have learnt *one thing*, viz- That business is done very different here
from what 'tis with us.'" Reed found national politics overly slow and tedious. Still,
his genial, socially affable nature made him an ideal company contact with eastern capitalists, especially railroad men and their bankers. He planned to visit important investors in Philadelphia and New York, and in Boston, the nation's postwar center of investment capital.[37]

In New York, Reed met John Wesley Ladd and Daniel F. Bradford. He witnessed
the launching of the *S.S. Oregonian* in April and tried to convince a doubting
Bradford of the wisdom of sending the ship to San Francisco. He found himself
immersed "in the excitement of the moneymaking craze and in the whirl of luxurious living. He saw all around him men who had, within a short time, become
wealthy through fortunate stock deals." With Ladd and Bradford, he visited such
splashy resorts as Saratoga Springs. Eastern "glitter and wealth," especially thoroughbred racing, awed the Portlander. It was a far cry from the provincial environment he knew in Oregon.[38]

Soon enough, Reed conceived grand designs for the OSN, more extensive than
those previously developed with Ainsworth and Thompson. To Ainsworth, he
exclaimed,

I am satisfied with the O.S.N. Co., but our business has been managed very different
from what such things are managed here, but there is an old saying 'that its (sic) never
too late to learn' and we are *now* in a position to make all the money we could
reasonably ask.

Recapitalize the company at $5 million and consolidate ownership, he advised. To
him, personal aggrandizement and corporate need were synonymous. They became the overriding motives for the OSN's subsequent actions, initially provoked
by Bradford's demand to sell the *S.S. Oregonian* in New York. The move toward
consolidation and recapitalization began almost immediately after Reed's return
to Portland.[39]

A corollary purpose of his eastern trip was to explore close ties to a major
railroad. Eastern contacts and his awareness of planned western transportation
developments convinced him that "the days of the supremacy of steamboat navigation on inland waters were numbered." Consolidating ownership and increasing its size and capitalization as soon as possible would make the company a valuable prize for railroad acquisition. For two months, he worked "*early* and *late*
endeavoring to forward the interests" of the OSN "both directly and in connection with" the Northern Pacific Railroad, to which he hoped to sell out. The OSN
already had indirect ties to the Northern Pacific. Ainsworth had been one of its

many incorporators in July, 1864, along with fellow Portlanders Henry W. Corbett and Henry Failing. As a matter of policy, new railroads generally sought as incorporators key business leaders from those parts of the country they expected to serve.[40]

Reed exuded great confidence before heading for Boston, home of the Northern Pacific's initial investors. "My strong points," he assured Ainsworth, "will be with New England Capitalists or men who expect to go down into their pockets." He wanted to persuade the railroad to start construction on the upper Columbia-Lake Pend Oreille route as soon as possible; the rails would connect with OSN steamers beginning service the following year. He found Northern Pacific pockets shallower than expected. In fact, the Boston promoters had been trying for two years to raise additional construction capital from Philadelphia investment banker Jay Cooke, who had turned them down on two occasions.[41]

Reed then travelled to Philadelphia to meet Cooke, whose investment firm had become the nation's largest, from wartime underwriting of U.S. Government bonds. Cooke seemed only mildly interested in backing the Northern Pacific, which was then in the earliest stages of building a line between Lake Superior and Puget Sound, with a branch to Portland via the Columbia River. He told Reed he would probably examine the properties, but it would take him at least three years to reach a decision. The 36-year-old Reed was suitably impressed by Cooke. Investment bankers of his stature were "at the apex of upper-class authority and social prestige" after the Civil War. Sam Bass Warner, Jr., describes Cooke as "confident of himself and his ultimate success and fascinated with the business of making money."[42]

Reed apparently did not understand that Cooke was more opportunistic and greedy than Boston investors of his acquaintance more accustomed to long-term profits. What made the Northern Pacific potentially attractive to him was a huge land grant of nearly 47 million acres, contingent on actual construction. While the valuable land asset would facilitate construction bond sales, Cooke was more interested in land sales than in building and operating a profitable railroad. Lack of foresight was "his great defect," in Glenn Chesney Quiett's estimation. "Cooke's schemes were based on the delusive idea that the pendulum of trade and finance always swings upward. He did not make provision for the inevitable downward swing." Reed judged Cooke solely on his public record and was smitten by the banker's contagious enthusiasm. Even without a commitment from Cooke, Reed returned West optimistically predicting that a future deal might be struck between the OSN and the Northern Pacific Railroad.[43]

The Railroad to California

Reed's strategy of selling the Oregon Steam Navigation Company to the Northern Pacific hit a snag after his return to Portland. Californians appeared ready to follow up earlier surveys with a railroad from Marysville, California, to Jacksonville. The Oregon & California Railroad, according to rumors, planned to secure huge federal land grants available to construct a California-Southern Oregon route. The first step in qualifying for the bounty was Oregon legislative approval of the route. The second requirement stipulated completion of the first 20 miles of operational track within two years of the railroad's incorporation. Reed and his OSN associates became deeply worried. They feared not only competition for the OSN, but loss of OSN control if a rail line were built by Californians.

Incorporation of the California & Oregon Railroad on September 3, 1866 — superseding the O&C incorporated in 1865 — panicked OSN executives. One incorporator, C. Temple Emmet, was a close friend of Ben Holladay, who was in the process of selling his vast Overland Mail Company to Wells Fargo for $2.3 million. Holladay had been contemplating the move for over a year, as he foresaw a limited future for the stagecoach business. Like Reed, who held similar views about river steamboats, Holladay had the "railroad itch."[44]

Joseph Gaston, the ambitious 33-year-old editor of the *Jacksonville Sentinel*, prodded the OSN leaders to build their own railroad between Portland and the California border. This decision, coupled with hopes for an ultimate OSN merger with the Northern Pacific, provided additional incentives for Ainsworth, Ladd, Reed, and Thompson to eliminate the other OSN stockholders.

The Struggle to Build a Railroad

The competition to build a railroad between Portland and California was part of the broader effort "to weld national transportation objectives with private investment." Bribery, scandals, delays, and mismanagement plagued both Oregon and national rail building. Public incentives invited private, high-risk speculation on a grand scale. Fortunes were made by some while many investors, particularly in railroad bonds, were to suffer grievously.[45]

Joseph Gaston announced Portland's entry into the high-stakes rail-building competition when he incorporated the Oregon Central Railroad on October 6, 1866. Legislative approval followed four days later. The Oregon Steam Navigation Company quadrumvirate of Ainsworth, Ladd, Reed, and Thompson was among its incorporators. They did not realize that Salem interests, led by the governor and the secretary of state, would soon back another Oregon Central Railroad. The Portlanders had planned their route down the west side of the Willamette River to Corvallis, bypassing the state capital. Former railroad surveyor (and incorporator of the California & Oregon Railroad in September, 1866) Simon G. Elliott claimed that Gaston's incorporation was improper and filed his Oregon Central Railroad incorporation papers on April 22, 1867. Now there were two Oregon Central Railroads: Gaston's, holding the legislative franchise, known as the "West Side Company," and Elliott's, backed by worried Salem interests, known as the "East Side Company."[46]

The day after Elliott incorporated his railroad, John C. Ainsworth noted that "Portland is duller than I ever saw it before at this season of the year." Interest in the west-side railroad was certainly dull. While a number of Portland's most substantial merchants and bankers had already invested $500 apiece — a total of $50,000 would be raised from the initial promotion — the available funds were a mere token of those required to build 20 miles of railroad by October, 1868.[47]

Elliott meanwhile gathered investors from both sides of the Willamette. East-siders included James B. Stephens, the East Portland founder; Dr. J.C. Hawthorne, operator of the Oregon Hospital for the Insane; Lot Whitcomb of Milwaukie; and Asa L. Lovejoy of Oregon City. West-siders included Bernard Goldsmith and Philip Wasserman, prominent merchants and future Portland mayors, who believed that an East Portland-to-California railroad would economically benefit Willamette Valley farmers and Portland grain brokers. They believed that the east-side rail-road would provide a quicker and cheaper connection to California. Planning to make unincorporated East Portland his northern terminus, Elliott issued millions in mostly worthless stocks and bonds and signed a contract with a bogus con-struction company he established. Flourishing these official-looking documents, he offered to sell out to the west Portland group. Distrusting him, Gaston and the OSN leadership rejected the chance to control both east- and west-side lines. This refusal inadvertently permitted Holladay to acquire the east-side railroad's corpo-rate shell 15 months later.[48]

Over the next five months, while the OSN leadership completed the stock pool and prepared to sell the *S.S. Oregonian* to Holladay in San Francisco, Simeon Reed became an active promoter of the west-side rail project. He felt it wise to keep Oregon's congressional delegation informed of the increasingly tangled skein of events. To senators George H. Williams, and Henry W. Corbett (one of the compa-ny's original incorporators), he proclaimed,

> This enterprise (the West Side road) I would further, not that I have any faith in the Road being built through to California, which in my judgment is of doubtful policy for Oregon, but because I think a Road from Portland, up the Willamette Valley would greatly benefit Portland, at the same time benefit the State. Again I take this ground that whether either of these roads are built up the valley immediately or not, it is only a question of time (and not far distant either) when *some* Road will be built, and in the meantime neither the State or Portland is loosing (sic) much on the score of the Road not being built at once, further there is no danger of California tap[p]ing us except by this route, and in the meantime we retain to ourselves what we have al-ways had until such time as the Road is built up the Valley — then Portland & the State will reap the benefits and *not* the State of California and her Rail Road Capitalists.[49]

The day Reed wrote Corbett and Williams (December 9, 1867), he and 34 friends organized a "SocialClub," its chronicler wrote, "where they could frater-nize for mutual enjoyment and relaxation, and to provide a meeting place for discussing their own and Portland's destiny." The Arlington Club (its name was chartered in 1881) was to become the social headquarters of Portland's male elite. In addition to Reed, its founders included John Green, Lewis M. Starr, C.H. Lewis, Henry Failing, John McCraken, Alex P. Ankeny, R.R. Thompson, the Ladd & Tilton Bank (for W.S. Ladd), John C. Ainsworth, Henry D. Green, and Thomas J. Carter. While they were discouraged from promoting business deals, the members would have been hard put not to discuss two items of great civic concern: the restructuring of the OSN, which culminated that month, and the future of the west-side Oregon Central Railroad, whose incorporators included 20 of the 34 club members. Portland's destiny was intimately tied to both corporations. Four months later, their Oregon Central broke ground south of Marquam Gulch, and Portland's big rail push was under way.[50]

Ben Holladay

It was probably unrealistic to expect Ben Holladay (and his California money) not to compete with Portland's business establishment. Once in possession of the *S.S. Oregonian* in early 1868, he showed increasing interest in Oregon affairs. As operator of weekly steamboats into Portland, he received timely economic reports and details of railroad activity from his agents. When a distressed shareholder of the east-side Oregon Central visited his San Francisco office in July 1868, he eagerly purchased a sizeable block of heavily discounted company stock. He foresaw the promise of greater profits at Portland's end of the line rather than California's. Hoping to clean up $3 million, he moved his headquarters to Portland within a month.[51]

Ever since the two companies had begun a widely publicized construction race that April, progress had been slow on both sides of the Willamette. Gaston's operation crawled 10 miles through difficult terrain and suspended work for lack of funds in June, 1868. By the end of August, when Holladay arrived, Elliott was in a similar predicament. The former stagecoach mogul moved quickly to seize active control of the east-side company. He arranged to finance more construction through purchase of the railroad's heavily discounted bonds, and recruited such prominent non-Portlanders as Asa Lovejoy, Asahel Bush and Governor George L. Woods as directors. Being an experienced speculator, Holladay valued the services of a shrewd lawyer. He hired Portland's first city attorney, John H. Mitchell, an ambitious knave ready for any task at the right price. After replacing the ineffectual Simon Elliott, he approached the legislature to transfer the land-grant franchise from the west-side to the east-side Oregon Central line.[52]

Holladay, though aware that the Oregon Steam Navigation Company group would fail to meet its two-year construction deadline that October, left nothing to chance. Expecting stiff opposition from Gaston and Ainsworth, he introduced the Oregon legislature to the big-time bribery practiced in other states. According to Glenn Chesney Quiett's account,

> Royal entertainment was provided for the legislators, and it was said that money was freely used otherwise to influence their decision. Holladay and a band of his henchmen kept open house in Salem, entertaining in such grandeur as the Oregon legislators had never seen and seeking to influence the press of the state as well as the lawmakers. He also entertained certain chosen spirits on one of his river-boats turned into a yacht, on which, it was said, the decks were damp with champagne.[53]

A worried Gaston reported to Ainsworth, "The Holladay crowd are here (in Salem) in strong force and are taking a very good plan — getting one man at a time." Gaston nevertheless felt that "all the farmers are with us on general principles of common honesty." Within six weeks, pliant lawmakers transferred the franchise to the east-side Oregon Central and granted it a two-year construction extension. Holladay later boasted of spending $35,000 to "influence" the legislature. A dejected Gaston wrote Ainsworth, "Our road must be built . . . . I have no money but I have the determination."[54]

Ainsworth and Reed immediately borrowed $5,000 from the Ladd & Tilton Bank to help restart construction of the west-side line. Still owing Stephen Coffin $2,500 for two trestle bridges, they were perilously short of rail iron. Reed then formed his own construction company but never adequately funded it. He figured the costs at $30,000 a mile — much more than the OSN and its Portland backers were prepared to spend in late 1868, when the OSN was completing its costly extension into British Columbia, Montana and Idaho. By mid-1869, the west-side Oregon Central, out of funds, stopped construction.[55]

The former stagecoach king from California was defeating the very Portland business interests that disdained and maligned him. Wherever he went, the 49-year-old native Kentuckian generated controversy. In action, speech and appearance, Holladay presented a marked contrast to Portland's merchant-financial elite. Upon first meeting, he impressed strangers as a gentleman, overdressed in the latest fashions and bejewelled with diamond rings and studs. He always wore a "flashy" heavy gold-linked watch chain and sported a cane with a long handle "of the richest polished quartz." Warm and generous when he wished, he could be haughty and dictatorial, especially when striving to gain the best bargains. To his former attorney, John Doniphan, he had the Napoleon-like bearing "of one born to command" and was a man for whom the end justified the means. Not unlike his OSN competitors in this respect, Holladay was a person businessmen feared to alienate.[56]

Immediately upon his arrival in Portland, he made his operational base in East Portland, the site of his railroad terminus. He bought several hundred acres of land and declared that the city of the future would be on the east side. He boasted that "the grass would soon be growing on Front Street," and that he would "make a rat-hole out of West-side Portland." By Quiett's account, "He thus antagonized in a single breath the rich men of the city, all of whom owned west-side property, and their antagonism never abated."[57]

Little bothered by the opinions of others, Holladay drove his railway project at breakneck speed. He completed the first 20 miles of the east-side line the day before Christmas, 1869. On March 12, 1870, for legal reasons, he changed the corporate name to the Oregon and California Railroad, transferring all of its former holdings to a new entity capitalized at $5 million, "not one cent of which was ever paid in," according to Malcolm Clark. Holladay then issued $10.9 million in bonds guaranteed by the lands he expected to receive from the federal government. Aided by Milton S. Latham, president of the London and San Francisco Bank and a former California governor and U.S. senator, Holladay inveigled leading German banking houses to purchase $6.4 million of the bonds, with English and American investors taking the rest. Rated high risk, the bonds sold at 60 percent of face value. This discount "saddled the company with insupportable interest payments," concluded Clark. William S. Ladd correctly predicted that Holladay would eventually hang himself financially.[58]

But Holladay was far from through in the spring of 1870. Proving that he was "an apt student in the rough-and-ready school of railroad promotion," he rallied his forces for an assault on Congress to gain an extension of his land grant, the long-term security required to guarantee the railroad bonds. Ainsworth was angry over this action, which he blamed on Oregon's Senator George H. Williams, and implied privately that Williams had received financial incentives. On the initiative of Senator Henry W. Corbett, the west-side Oregon Central, closed down for lack of funds, received its first congressional land grant on May 4, 1870. But the action came too late to save the railroad.[59]

Jay Cooke and the Northern Pacific

In mid-spring of 1870, Jay Cooke telegraphed Captain Ainsworth to send to New York a delegation from the Oregon Steam Navigation Company that was authorized to act. Since agreeing to finance the Northern Pacific late in 1869, after Congress had approved adding Portland to the NP's main line, Cooke had watched the navigation company's profitable expansion. Between May, 1866 and June, 1870, OSN earnings exceeded $1 million. Total earnings, including the sale price of the *S.S. Oregonian*, exceeded $1.5 million. The Big Four had reaped a 900 percent return on their original investment in less than 10 years.[60]

Cooke's summons came at a crucial time for Ainsworth, Reed and Thompson. The west-side Oregon Central Railroad was a losing cause into which they were reluctant to pour any more OSN funds. With the prospect of a continental railroad reaching Portland, the wisest and most profitable course was to merge with Cooke and forget Holladay. Ladd joined his colleagues in a fateful decision: they agreed quietly to sell the railroad to Holladay once negotiations with Cooke were concluded.

As reported by Thompson, he and Ainsworth went to New York in May 1870. They were ushered into the "fancy" New York offices of the Northern Pacific Railroad, where Cooke kept them waiting — an act of rudeness to "frontier people." Angered, Thompson walked out and had to be "hunted up" by the railroad directors. Both groups haggled over the terms of sale without reaching an agreement. Cooke then made his first appearance and invited the Oregonians overnight to his Philadelphia estate. After a pleasant dinner marked by "generalities" — Cooke's way of "sizing them up" — they moved to the library, where they made "a deal."[61]

Cooke agreed to buy 75 percent of the OSN stock for $3,750,000. He would purchase it for the benefit of the Northern Pacific Railroad but retain it in his personal possession for the time being. The OSN owners were to receive one-half ($1,875,000) in cash and the other half in NP bonds paying 7.3 percent interest. The transaction would remain secret until November, 1872 — the main reason Cooke would keep the OSN stock in his personal estate. Before returning to Portland, Ainsworth agreed to be Cooke's construction manager once the Northern Pacific started laying track north from Kalama, Washington, later in the fall. Cooke planned to run the main line down the Columbia River to Portland. Passengers would be ferried to Kalama and transported by rail to either Seattle or Tacoma, the line's Pacific Northwest terminus. (Tacoma would not be chosen as terminus until July, 1873.)[62]

Holladay Blackmails Portland

After Ainsworth and Thompson returned to Portland, the Oregon Steam Navigation Company owners and their railroad-building friends sold the stalled west-side Oregon Central Railroad to Ben Holladay on July 2,1870. Rumors of the impending sale had floated through Portland since Ainsworth and Thompson had left for New York. The *Oregonian* editorially condemned William S. Ladd and the OSN leaders for yielding to Holladay. "The Democratic capitalist" and his friends had lacked "pluck" by refusing to buy Elliott's east-side Oregon Central three years earlier. By defending west-side (that is, exclusively Portland) interests, they left the field to Holladay. They were "too limited in their ideas of the wants and growth of the Oregon country," charged Editor Harvey Scott. "They could lend money at from one to three percent a month, take mortgages and swallow up property; but they were afraid to take hold of a land grant for a railroad when it was offered them . . . . When somebody else has taken hold of it, they cry out 'monopoly.'" Had Scott known of the secret sale of the OSN to Cooke's Northern Pacific, he might have tempered his opinion of Portland's major capitalists — men who knew the enormous costs of building a railroad, which they could not meet without eastern or European capital. Ladd, who strongly favored selling out to Holladay, correctly predicted that the arrogant speculator would break himself by acquiring "'more unproductive property than he has capital enough to carry.'"[63]

For $1, Holladay assumed the debts and promised to pay the long-suffering creditors of the west-side Oregon Central. Once in possession of its properties, he failed to restart construction. His energies and money went into the Oregon & California line, which began regular service to Salem at the end of September, 1870. Portland would only get rail service with a $100,000 subsidy, Holladay told its angry citizens in December, and threatened to bypass Portland as a terminus for his California line. In short, he offered Portlanders standard monopolistic fare. To add insult to injury, he made no effort to repay the railroad's creditors.[64]

What Holladay called his "proposal" was really a blackmail threat. Fearing dire economic consequences for the city's future growth, citizens organized a series of meetings in the city council chamber between December 16,1870, and January 7, 1871. By the February 11th deadline, the full sum of $100,000 had been raised, assuring the completion of a 20-mile stretch of track to Hillsboro and Forest Grove. The major subscriptions accurately reflected the asset ranking of Portland's wealthiest citizens, with the exception of George Flanders, who topped the list at $5,000. Ladd gave $3,500, followed by C.H. Lewis, Ainsworth, Thompson, and Reed at $2,500 each. Henry W. Corbett and Jacob Kamm each subscribed $2,000. In garnering an average contribution of $500, the organizing committee had derived a formula "to get from a citizen four percent of his tax assessment, . . . exempting widows, non-residents and 'possibly a few who never help the public good,'" to cite Arlington Club minutes. Club members prided themselves on their leading role in the successful effort.[65]

Ainsworth, Ladd, Reed, and Thompson viewed Holladay as a dangerous nuisance whose demands had to be met for the good of Portland. Their sizeable contributions to the railroad subsidy fund were a mere fraction of what each received from Jay Cooke. They could logically contend that the deal with Cooke, in the long run, would benefit Portland far more than the merger of two uncertain Oregon-to-California railroads. The OSN sale certainly proved more rewarding to them personally. And for the OSN, of which they collectively still owned nearly 25 percent, Cooke's investment was a bonanza.

The OSN Pays Off

The Oregon Steam Navigation Company-Northern Pacific tie allowed another major expansion of the OSN's fleet, with three new luxurious stern-wheelers and a fourth two years later. It also extended Portland's national influence while solidifying its position as the center of the region's banking, trading and transportation network. Even before control shifted to the NP, the OSN had become Portland's most successful and powerful corporate enterprise. For the next 30 years, through its successor, the Oregon Railway and Navigation Company, it would retain its premier position in the region's economic and political life.[66]

Reported OSN corporate income of $201,283 for 1869 far exceeded that of any other Portland firm. The OSN paid 15 percent of the Multnomah County tax levied that year. Among various income-producing categories in the county, the steamboat operators, as a group, showed the highest published incomes (incomplete figures at best). Ladd, Thompson and Ainsworth actually received additional OSN income, and Reed most of his income, from a reported dividend payout of $255,333 sent to William S. Ladd as agent. (Most of the OSN stock shares were still held in the pool established in 1867, and Ladd was agent for the pool.) Much of Ladd's reported income of $42,554 probably came from Ladd & Tilton Bank profits generated by the region's booming economy.[67]

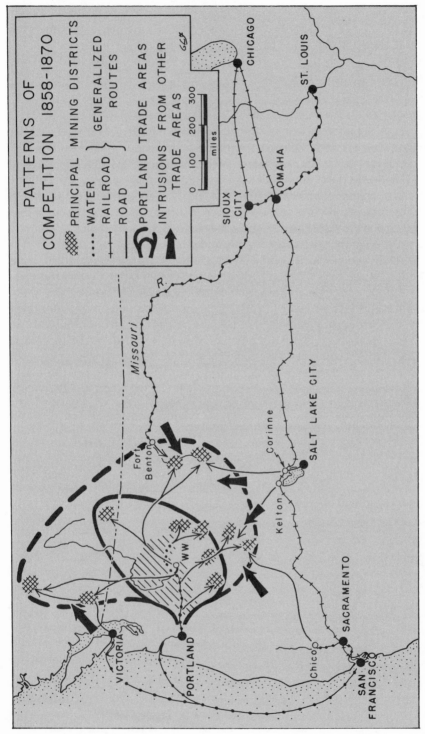

7.1 "Patterns of Competition, 1858-1870" map

7.2 "S.S. Oregonian," launched April , 1867

7.3 First spike for Oregon Central Railroad, East Portland, October 28, 1869

7.4 Jacob Kamm (1823-1912) in 1850

7.5 Capt. John C. Ainsworth (1822-1893) in 1850   7.6 Ben Holladay (1819-1887)

8

THE MERCHANT INVESTORS: THE 1860s

The Prosperous 1860s

T he 1870 Census offered dramatic evidence of Portlanders' personal wealth, much of it earned during the decade of the 1860s. Excluding his real-estate assets, William S. Ladd led the list with $400,000 from banking, the Oregon Steam Navigation Company and related enterprises. Others included:

INVESTORS	ASSETS	MAJOR SOURCES OF WEALTH
Henry Green	$287,000	Water, gas, mercantile, shipping
J. Teal, Sr.	236,000	Mining, shipping, wheat
H.C. Leonard	169,000	Water, gas, mercantile, shipping
H.W. Corbett	105,000	Mercantile, banking
G.W. Vaughn	100,000	Mercantile, manufacturing
R.R. Thompson	100,000	OSN*
H.F. Failing	100,000	Mercantile, banking
B. Goldsmith	100,000	Mercantile, banking, shipping, wheat
L.M. Starr	65,000	Manufacturing, banking
J. Kamm	60,000	OSN, shipping
J.C. Ainsworth	50,000	OSN*
S.G. Reed	50,000	OSN*

* Northern Pacific sale profit not included.

In all, 18 Portlanders and their families reported total assets, including real estate, of $100,000 or more. Merchant Cicero H. Lewis, who missed the census, would have been included among the wealthiest. His reported 1869 income led all others, at $48,014. After less than 20 years in Oregon, 19 Portlanders and their families had become multimillionaires by current values.[1]

Commerce and Finance

Eastern Oregon and Idaho gold, the major generator of OSN profits during the 1860s, brought similar and permanent benefits to Portland's commercial and financial life. Earlier gold rushes had briefly stimulated the local economy. Serving "as a place of passage for the mass of emigrants," the town still attracted many a gold seeker permanently, as Jean-Nicolas Perlot observed. Like hundreds of others, he decided to stay and "establish" himself in Portland. In September, 1862, he reasoned that

> If they [the miners] extracted the gold of these fabulous mines without me, a good part of it came back to me by indirect route. In fact, the more they would produce, the greater the chance Portland had of prospering and growing, for its situation was such that it ought to profit especially from the increase in wealth and in population which resulted for the country.[2]

Grain was the second major generator of Portland's prosperity. In the 1850s the price of flour had become the key index of regional economic growth. Flour sent mainly to California continued as the leading export throughout the 1860s. Its estimated value shot up tenfold in the decade from about $100,000 to over $1 million. Wheat gradually rose from fifth place in 1867 to become Portland's leading export staple in 1874. Most of it went to Liverpool, in England. "Portland was nothing but a warehouse," Perlot noted,

> a sort of terminus where outside commerce came to deposit the merchandise which was distributed throughout the country, and where, on the other hand, there flowed the products of Oregon to be exchanged against this merchandise: it was this double movement of commerce which made the importance of the place and gave it so much animation.[3]

This commerce and its attendant services created Portland's high level of personal wealth recorded in the 1870 Census. As Judge Matthew P. Deady commented, the town's real importance and prosperity rested not upon "the uncertain foundations" of gold discovery, but on the farms, which held 80 percent of the state's 100,000 residents. "Portland is the mart of the Willamet valley, and such it ever has been and will be." It might be "comparatively a provincial place,"said a boosterish Deady, "but it will be worth more dollars per head than either London or New York."[4]

To service its flourishing commerce and growing population, Portland recorded 89 different commercial, trade and professional specialties in 1863 — a large number for a town of 3,000. Retail liquor outlets (42) and dry-goods and general-merchandise stores (37) constituted nearly half of the 169 specialties. Five wholesale-liquor dealers, led by Ladd, Reed & Company, and three hardware stores numbered among the most profitable concerns. The two agricultural-implement and machinery dealers, Knapp, Burrell & Company and H.W. Corbett & Company, prospered equally.[5]

Portland had only one bank in 1863, but Ladd & Tilton was central to its commercial and industrial growth. (Wells Fargo limited its banking functions mainly to shippers.) Ladd involved his bank in practically every new enterprise as incorporator, banker or promoter-investor. After Oregon passed an incorporation law in October 1862, he became an incorporator of seven new ventures, including the previously established OSN and the west-side Oregon Central Railroad.[6]

The bulk of Ladd & Tilton's assets, in the early years, came from a loan portfolio that grew steadily in proportion to rising deposits. Until the appearance of the Bank of British Columbia in early 1865 and the opening of the First National Bank on May 7, 1866, Ladd & Tilton enjoyed a near-monopoly of commercial loans, which usually bore 2 percent interest per month — the bank's most profitable revenue source. The OSN, the bank's largest depositor, placed increasingly large sums with Ladd & Tilton; by 1869 over $200,000 of OSN funds were on the bank's ledger. Ladd & Tilton was thus able to increase its capitalization in seven years from $50,000 to $400,000. When Ladd's uncle, Stephen Mead of New London, Connecticut, increased his investment by $100,000 in 1869, the bank's capitalization stood at $600,000. It was an astonishing 12-fold increase in the bank's first 10 years.[7]

Ladd increasingly treated the bank — organized as a partnership — much like a single proprietorship, and bank profits as his own, according to his son: "'The money in the bank he had made . . . was his.'" Ladd, unlike his peers Ainsworth, Corbett, Failing, Lewis, and Thompson, could be "an adventurous trader and speculator," according to his son's biographer. Ladd's readiness to invest in new ventures and make risky commercial loans unquestionably advanced Portland's economic growth at typically handsome profits to himself. To his son, he showed imagination and a "shrewd understanding of the strengths and frailties of other men." When an enterprise languished he cut his losses quickly; overdue loan and mortgage payments received "somewhat ruthless" treatment.[8]

Indeed, most of the vast real-estate holdings Ladd had accumulated as a banker came from forfeited mortgages and defaulted loans. Woe befell those like Colburn Barrell who were not Ladd's equals or friends! It was former saloonkeeper Barrell who had replaced Ladd's shoes and given him his first drink when the unknown New Englander landed at Portland in 1851. He was one of Ladd's first wholesale-liquor customers. Farming on the east side of the Willamette late in the 1860s, the cash-short former customer borrowed $3,800 from Ladd & Tilton, using his last 13 acres as collateral. A loan Barrell assumed to be a mortgage was recorded as a demand note and called a year later. After years of litigation, Barrell and his crippled wife were removed from their home, which was burned to prepare for the new Tilton's Addition.[9]

Successful merchant customers enjoyed happier treatment from banker Ladd. Henry Failing, who had assumed active management of the family business in 1859, was a favorite. The careful 27-year-old merchant abjured the mine trade in early 1861; holding a dim view of gold-seeking speculators. But with returning miners bragging of daily $1,000 finds, Failing, like many other cautious Portland merchants, changed course to meet their immense spring orders. This was to cause him trouble.

New York-ordered merchandise was cheaper than supplies from California, but required six to nine months for delivery. San Francisco suppliers of mining tools charged monopoly prices. The Idaho-bound miners and Boise traders who consti-tuted much of Failing's trade from 1862 to 1865 required long-term credit. With a huge business volume resting heavily on credit, his cash reserves fell dangerously. Though the Failings' sales volume had always been larger than Henry W. Corbett's, they had divided their profits with C.W. Thomas in New York before 1859, and thus lacked Corbett's accumulated cash reserves. Thomas maintained a sizeable cash investment in the firm until Failing bought him out in 1863. Thomas's earlier withdrawal of $40,000, in violation of their partnership terms, had seriously jeop-ardized J. Failing & Company. Henry Failing turned increasingly to Ladd & Tilton for short-term loans to tide him over. Ladd, as he commonly did with close friends, charged Failing little or no interest.[10]

Impact of the Civil War

The Civil War, which, according to Gordon B. Dodds, "touched Oregon per-haps the lightest of all states in terms of blood and treasure," affected Portland merchants in at least one important way. They tried to finance operations by doing business for cash rather than by their traditional granting of long-term credit, as with Idaho miners. In 1862 Congress enacted the Legal Tender Act, mak-ing paper money (greenbacks) the basic federal currency. Huge amounts of green-backs, issued to help defray increasing war costs and unsupported by gold re-serves, ignited an immediate inflation in the Union. Upon first issue, they traded in Portland at 50 cents for one dollar in gold. Oregon and California merchants and bankers were reluctant to accept greenbacks, despite official exhortations that their evasion was unpatriotic. Banker Ladd feared loaning in gold and being re-paid in depreciated paper. Merchants like Failing, Corbett and Lewis feared depre-ciated greenbacks for merchandise bought with gold.[11]

In January, 1863, Portland and San Francisco merchants jointly agreed to accept only gold. While disapproving of greenbacks, both groups figured a legal way to beat the system by profiting from currency exchanges. Judge Deady told Ben-jamin Stark:

> The San Francisco dealers control the price of everything on this coast that comes from the East. They buy it in New York for paper, and sell here for an advance on gold, besides the premium. No wonder they are in favor of gold currency here and paper where they buy.

Larger Portland merchants like Failing, paying in greenbacks, increased their New York purchases. Failing's overstocked inventory was then sold off gradually, in accordance with market demands, with most contracts payable in gold. Mean-while, responding to merchant-banker pressure in October, 1864, the Oregon leg-islature reinforced the double standard with a law requiring sole payment in gold for all contract obligations. William S. Ladd strongly supported the effort. Citing the impersonal third party, he wrote Deady that such a law would help Ladd & Tilton Bank "much to secure them in return for what they may loan out. To loan gold and be paid in greenbacks is to (sic) much of a losing game for them. Their pile is not sufficiently large to stand it long."[12]

Ladd had already enforced similar gold requirements on outstanding loans. Former Senator Benjamin Stark, retired to Connecticut with a bank debt of $11,000, complained bitterly to agent Ladd: "To be paying interest on such notes in gold, and the principal too, is willfully giving the lie to our daily prayer, 'lead us not into temptation.'" He assured Ladd, "I must and will pay off." He ordered Ladd to sell properties to liquidate his debt. Ladd's failure to comply with Stark's wishes ultimately benefited both parties. Ladd & Tilton profited from letting the loan interest accumulate and be added to the principle, while Stark profited by the inflated value of his real-estate collateral, which far exceeded his loan total of $17,609 in 1875. He finally paid it in 1880.[13]

As the war continued, Failing and other merchants accumulated large gold reserves through currency exchanges. With the Confederate surrender in April, 1865, many others besides Failing suffered severe losses as gold values plummeted. By July, 1865, Failing was $50,000 in debt to Ladd & Tilton, payable in gold. He continued to borrow from all sources, including Multnomah County, from which, using his influence as mayor, he borrowed an additional $20,000 at an unusually low 10 percent per annum.[14]

Henry W. Corbett experienced many of his brother-in-law Henry Failing's problems. However, he could more rapidly accumulate and expand his resources. He, too, purchased most of his merchandise in New York. Banking much of his money there, he became less involved than Failing in speculative currency dealings. As a merchant, says Throckmorton, Corbett seemed shrewder and more venturesome than Failing. In 1863, Corbett gained a competitive edge in gold-pan sales, until then a San Francisco monopoly. He had the pans copied and manufactured in the East and packed in square boxes, surrounded by other goods, to escape notice when the shipments passed through San Francisco. He predicted the rising prices of 1864, laying in a heavy stock the previous fall to anticipate future mining demand. Failing feared taking "the risk of wintering a large stock of goods and of waiting until they were sold in the mining country. Corbett's stock was twice the size of Failing's in the fall of 1863." Corbett's cash reserves were also much larger than Failing's. In 1862 he began to fulfill a banking function by loaning money well below the Ladd & Tilton rate to customers. He later made small loans to Failing, a major competitor, and "offered to endorse Failing's notes in the East to help . . . meet his obligations."[15]

In line with national trends promoting specialization during the Civil War, Corbett and Failing began concentrating on non-competitive items. Corbett moved heavily into farm machinery and Failing increasingly stocked iron products. As warm friends and relations, they grew nearly inseparable in business and politics during the 1860s. Edward Failing, Henry's younger brother, went to work for Corbett in 1861. The following year, Henry succeeded Corbett as chairman of the Republican State Central Committee. They worked together successfully in promoting each other for office in 1864, Failing for mayor and Corbett for Multnomah County commissioner. Serving only one year in county government (until he served again from 1884 to 1887), Corbett increased his political visibility in preparation for his 1866 campaign for the U.S. Senate. In 1869, the duo bought control of Portland's First National Bank and in 1870 combined their mercantile firms. Both moves increased their wealth and ensured Corbett-Failing family power for the next two generations.[16]

The First National Bank

The First National Bank of Portland symbolized those energetically entrepreneurial times. Organized on July 4, 1865, but not opened until May, 1866, the bank was the brainchild of Addison M. and Lewis M. Starr (known respectively as A.M. and L.M.). The brothers arrived in Portland early in 1850, with large stocks from a New York-based mining company for whom A.M. had worked. They opened the first stove and tin works and built the region's first distillery, both of which were on the waterfront block 80 of Stark's Addition and subject to later litigation.[17]

The Starr brothers were active Democrats. A.M. served on the city council in 1854 and 1864-65. He was elected mayor in April, 1858, and served as county sheriff from 1858 to 1862. L.M. served one term on the council in 1856 and as deputy sheriff under his brother. Neither was hesitant to draw a pistol, as Sheriff A.M. Starr did when confronting a lynch mob during the winter of 1862.[18]

L.M. sold out to his brother and in 1864 went to New York, where a bank president advised him to return to Portland to establish Oregon's first national bank. The new National Banking Act had just authorized the comptroller of the currency to charter national banks, some of which were to be federal depositories. The Starrs drew in three other investors, men of diverse background and interests: Captain Alexander P. Ankeny, Henry W. Eddy and Philip Wasserman. Ankeny, described by his biographer as a man of "dynamic energy" who gave "constant attention to all aspects of his busy life," owned the Northwest's largest hog slaughterhouse and packing plant and five butcher shops in Portland. Earlier, he had been part-owner with Henry W. Corbett of the Merchants' Transportation Company. Eddy owned extensive east-side fruit orchards in association with the Luelling family. Bavarian-born Philip Wasserman, a successful tobacconist, had investments in numerous local enterprises; he would be elected mayor in 1871.[19]

The bank's opening was delayed for eight months, pending receipt of its federal currency issue of $100,000. Meanwhile Ankeny, pursuing other interests, sold his stock to an associate, Asa Harker. An apparently restless Wasserman dealt his shares to his fellow Bavarian and close friend Bernard Goldsmith, a wealthy merchant who would precede Wasserman as mayor in 1869. In November, 1865, A.M. Starr relinquished the presidency to his brother before moving to New York.[20]

With greenbacks traded at 79 cents on opening day and gold quoted at $1.26, L.M. Starr had to act quickly to attract more gold to offset the drain from the discounted greenbacks. He worked for four months to secure government deposits, which arrived only as the bank faced liquidation. In September, 1866, the First National became the official Pacific Northwest depository, especially for U.S. Army posts. But private deposits were meager. Most of the more than $30 million of Oregon gold produced in 1866, passed through Portland to the benefit of Wells Fargo. The bank's first large private deposit came from the Oregon Steam Navigation Company in January, 1867 — $10,447 in coin. Ladd & Tilton's largest depositor most likely decided that it would be good business and politically wise to promote competition by ensuring the First National's survival. By the end of the first year of business, bank loans totalled $29,385. Compared with Ladd & Tilton, it was a slow beginning. After three years of Starr management, deposits reached an encouraging $354,759 (80 percent in government funds), but loans totalled only $75,492.[21]

On August 11, 1869, Henry W. Corbett and Henry Failing bought control of the First National Bank for an undisclosed sum. Corbett (who had bought Henry W. Eddy's shares in March, 1867) held 500 shares, Henry Failing 250, and his father, Josiah 50. They immediately increased the bank's capitalization from $100,000 to $250,000. Failing assumed the presidency as Corbett was serving in the U.S. Senate. Other stockholders included William S. Ladd's partner, C.E. Tilton, and the bank's young cashier, James A. Steel.[22]

Steel, of whom more will be heard later, made himself a key First National Bank figure as its day-to-day manager. He had arrived in Portland from Ohio in 1862, at the age of 28. Having some experience of merchandising, he worked for Henry Pittock's brother, the grocer Robert Pittock, before becoming a bookkeeper at the new Oregon City Woolen Mills. His marriage to Ladd's sister, Mary, brought him into banking, albeit with a Ladd & Tilton competitor. The Steels lived with the Ladds until they could afford their own home.[23]

An older friend of Steel, L.M. Starr, chose the young bookkeeper as the bank's first cashier. In 1867, the two formed an outside business partnership with Morton M. McCarver, the co-founder of nearby Linnton and, a veteran real-estate speculator and recent eastern Oregon mining promoter. The three men bought and sold "lost horse claims" from the 1855-56 Indian Wars, and in another speculative venture founded Tacoma, Washington. Steel's Tacoma "Adventure," originally called Commencement Bay, was a 54-acre share of the townsite platted by McCarver. Fearing that they would be accused by Portlanders of promoting a rival town, Starr and Steel kept their involvement secret by removing their names from promotional literature and maps. Unfortunately for the trio, the tract became practically worthless in 1873 after the Northern Pacific Railroad chose as its Pacific Northwest terminus a site one mile northeast of McCarver's. Other investments, particularly in Portland real-estate, proved more rewarding to the clever banker-speculator. By 1870 Steel had already amassed gross assets of $46,584, with liabilities and debts totalling $36,486. Borrowing $13,000 at 6 percent per annum from his employer, Henry W. Corbett, Steel bought a city block and erected a home near the Ladds'. Within eight years, aided by business, social and family ties, James Steel was a rising star in Portland's young urban Establishment.[24]

Industrial and Related Investments

The commercial, consumer-oriented economy of Portland flourished during the Civil War. Local industrial growth was uneven and remained so until the 1880s. The town had some 50 small industrial establishments in 1860, the largest being flour and sawmills. The Portland Milling Company, a sawmill, had a mere $20,000 capitalization and employed 14 workers. Smaller still were the processing plants, factories, foundries, and shops.[25]

Excluding some brief activity in iron and paper manufacturing, woolen manufacturing was the only regional industry besides flour milling to increase its growth. "The Civil War," Gordon Dodds has noted, created "a demand for the production of wool and for the manufacture of woolens." All six operated outside Portland; the largest was the Willamette Woolen Manufacturing Company of Salem. Founded in 1856, the company developed strong Portland ties through a major investor, Joseph S. Smith, Oregon Democratic congressman (1869-71), and the son-in-law of wealthy Portland pioneer Thomas J. Carter. The Oregon City Woolen Mills (1865), the former employer of James A. Steel, developed even closer Portland ties. Its Polish-immigrant founders, the brothers Isaac and Ralph Jacobs, had become rich from the California gold fields and a thriving Oregon City mercantile business. They moved to Portland, where they later built twin Renaissance Revival mansions along the Park Blocks. William S. Ladd was banker to both woolen concerns.[26]

The real money from wool came from the export of the raw clip. In 1862, Oregon's first direct wool shipment to the East dispatched 100,000 pounds to Boston, the great national wool center. By 1867, wool was second only to flour in export value. The Dalles was fast becoming the largest primary wool market in the world. The Oregon Steam Navigation Company extracted immense profits from the growing wool, wheat and flour trade.[27]

The same elements dragged against industrial growth as against Oregon trade and commerce. Opportunities in the Northwest were much less diversified than those available to San Franciscans. Overdependence on rivers (and the Oregon Steam Navigation Company monopoly) and the late development of transcontinental rail service impeded growth. Portland's own population was too sparse to support other than a limited market, and the region lacked sufficient investment capital to launch larger, more capital-intensive industries.[28]

High transportation costs (OSN rates were 10 times those on the Missouri River) and restricted communication with California, the Midwest and the East kept Portland on the margin of information and production. Stages needed seven to 12 days to reach Portland from Sacramento and four to six days to travel from Yreka, in 1861 the northern California terminus of a new transcontinental telegraph line through Sacramento. As with ships and railroads, Portland's business leaders knew there must be an active local role if they were to have quicker and more direct communication with their primary markets. It was Ladd, Reed and Corbett who incorporated the Oregon Telegraph Company in 1862, capitalized at $75,000, to connect Portland with Yreka. Ladd became president, Reed the secretary, and Corbett the treasurer. John McCraken became superintendent and Asa Lovejoy a director. Construction proceeded quickly and the line opened with much fanfare on March 5, 1864. The *Oregonian* published an extra edition with news only 20 hours old from New York. Three days later, Mayor David Logan exchanged greetings with the mayor of Portland, Maine. Direct telegraph communication with the San Francisco and New York markets, as planned, greatly benefitted such Portland merchants as Corbett, Failing and Lewis. Daily price quotations now directed their orders.[29]

Improved mail service was equally essential to Portland's expanding commercial life. Local postal receipts increased from $3,609 to $14,535 during the 1860s. A threatened Post Office cancellation of daily overland mail service from Sacramento aroused Portland's business interests in September, 1865. Only mail carried by unreliable steamers would have remained. Steamer delivery schedules were nonexistent, and freight from San Francisco took precedence over mail sacks. Oregon's congressional pressure forced renewal of the mail contract with the California Stage Company, which then sold the Oregon route to San Francisco investors. When the contract came up for annual renewal in June, 1866, Corbett underbid the San Francisco syndicate and renamed the company the Oregon Stage Company. He shifted headquarters to Portland, putting his older brother Elijah in charge. Henry Corbett probably sought the contract more for its commercial value to merchants like himself than for its investment value. He underbid an operator who was already losing money, even as rail service to California loomed within the foreseeable future. Investors understood that overland stages were doomed except for short connections to out-of-the-way areas.[30]

"Corbett gave his new line a good send-off," according to Oscar Winther. "Many reorganizations were made," including personnel changes, colored placards and handbills. He received wide praise from business associates and passengers. One account in the *Sacramento Daily Union* described Corbett as a man "'of energy, tact, thrift, and abundance of prudent judgment.'" A traveler extolled the line's organization, hostlers and stock: "'There was but little . . . that could be complained of except bad bridges . . . .'" Winter rains in 1867 damaged more than bridges. Floods and slides along the route caused numerous accidents, making daily mail service impossible. Additional difficulties arose when Corbett discovered that as a recently elected U.S. senator he was prohibited from signing a mail contract with the federal government. A Senate resolution in March, 1867, released him from the restriction, but still the Post Office Department withheld approval. Its mail-contract award to a San Francisco operator in August, 1867, effectively terminated the Oregon Stage line's major business.[31]

Local merchant promoters fared little better with their Portland and Milwaukie Macadamized Road Company, capitalized at $55,650 in 1863. Conceived as a toll road, it was to connect Portland with Taylor's Ferry, which crossed the Willamette River to Milwaukie. Included among its 33 stockholders were many of Portland's top financial and mercantile leaders, led by the Starr brothers, who invested nearly $3,000. Other major shareholders included Ladd, H.C. Leonard, John Green, Robert R. Thompson, Reed, Cicero H. Lewis, Corbett, Henry Failing, Bernard Goldsmith, and Joseph Teal.

From its opening in 1864, the toll road ran a continual deficit. Ladd's report to stockholders in April, 1865, noted a cash deficit of $14,567. Ladd & Tilton purchased $10,300 of the company's indebtedness, and the officers, led by President L.M. Starr, assessed stockholders $14,770. Enticing additional investment, the company proposed extending the road south into what later became Riverwood, where several stockholders owned property. The future highway to Oswego finally turned a small profit in 1870, and nine years later Multnomah County purchased its portion of it for $5,000, a fraction of its cost. Public funds were rarely spent on outlying roads in late-nineteenth-century Oregon, especially those serving strictly private interests.[32]

The costliest failure, apart from the Oregon Central Railroad, was the Oregon Iron Company. Capitalized at $500,000, the venture was incorporated in February,

1865, by Ladd and the Green brothers, owners of the profitable Portland Gas Light Company and Portland Water Company. Stockholders included Henry Failing, A.M. Starr and H.C. Leonard. Ladd, the largest investor and chief creditor through Ladd & Tilton, became president, with Leonard vice-president and Henry Green secretary.[33]

The existence of iron ore in the Tualatin Valley, immediately southwest of Portland, had been known for over 20 years. In 1861 a bed of rich ore was reported on the west bank of the Willamette River, near the village of Oswego. Demand for iron products was increasing, and the two Portland foundries, Oregon Iron Works and Willamette Iron Works, wanted to manufacture pig iron locally if a blast furnace could be constructed. Investors Henry and John Green and their associate H.C. Leonard, who had bought Ladd's 30-year city water franchise in 1862, particularly needed large amounts of cast-iron water pipes, which were otherwise supplied expensively from New York. In the summer of 1866, Ladd, John McCraken and Judge Matthew Deady dreamed of Oswego as a future West Coast Pittsburgh. Unfortunately for the local investors, they badly underestimated costs. Scottish pig iron purchased in San Francisco sold in Portland for $4.96 less per gross ton than the Oswego iron. The Pacific Coast's first pig-iron blast furnace could not produce on a scale to compete with imported pig iron. Legal problems over Oswego water rights doomed the enterprise. It closed in April, 1869, after only 19 months of production. The disputed body of water was appropriately named Sucker Creek.[34]

The Oregon Iron Company stockholders probably *were* suckers, too easily deceived by the prospects of pig-iron manufacturing. Like many of their moneyed friends, they were convinced that their business successes made them excellent judges of nearly every promising industrial activity. Until the end of the Civil War, particularly during 1864, mining-related activity seemed specially alluring to most of Portland's leading investors.

Captain John C. Ainsworth invested in six mines (three in partnership with Robert R. Thompson) during his year's absence from the OSN presidency; he added another mine in 1865. All proved to be losers. He ruefully warned his children, "Never invest in mining stocks." The *Oregonian* advised similar caution after the formation of the Board of Stockbrokers in March, 1864. The editor's concern that Portland's earliest stock exchange represented "the first step towards introduction of the mining stock mania so prevalent in California" went unheeded. The board initially listed the stocks of the OSN and the Union Mining Company of the North Santiam area. Thompson, the board's president, McCraken, its secretary, and directors Henry Green, Ainsworth and Lloyd Brooke were characterized as "high toned" social and business personages. These promoters gained certain advantages through public stock listings. Risks were spread, prices could be manipulated upwards (or downwards, as with the OSN in 1866), and original investors could recoup their capital more rapidly through public sales.[35]

Most leading Portland businessmen tended to invest in mines near home, as in the North Santiam district, where Ladd, Reed and John Green established the Oregon Gold and Silver Mining Company in July, 1864. They generally refrained from direct investment or stock purchase in remoter mining operations, fearing that their effective control would diminish with distance. Indeed, they rarely invested in any enterprise that did not permit them some official authority (as officers or directors). On the whole, Portland's wealthier investors invested in nearby mines and farm lands and in city real estate, businesses and transportation. With some notable exceptions, they drew a regular 12 to 17 percent profit through their local banks.[36]

The ever-cautious merchants Henry Failing and C.H. Lewis frowned on mining investments during and after the Civil War. Failing "thought there were entirely too many men with 'Quartz on the Brain' sponsoring wildcat mining schemes." In 1865, he refused a letter of support for former Portland jeweler and Mayor G. Collier Robbins, who had accompanied Morton M. McCarver (future Starr and Steel partner) to New York in search of venture capital. Failing wrote his New York business associate John Hatt that Robbins "'failed here a few years ago. He was generally reputed as rich and made a bad failure . . . He is a passionate, violent tempered man, and has no control over his tongue. He owes a large amount of money here.'" Failing had changed his opinion of the Republican Robbins, whom he had supported over the Democrat Robert R. Thompson in the 1860 mayor's race. Having achieved some success, Robbins was boosting the Owyhee quartz mining district of eastern Oregon. In early 1866, OSN stockholder Harrison Olmstead wrote Ladd that there were still "'about 1000 Oregonians and Idahoins'" in New York "'looking after the Almighty Dollar.'"[37]

Mining investments may have been derided by some cautious merchants, but none disdained pursuit of the "Almighty Dollar." In February, 1865, Portland's "high toned" entrepreneurs threw themselves into currency trading as a well understood and respected commercial activity. The new telegraph kept Portland dealers and brokers abreast of current market conditions in San Francisco, Chicago and New York. When gold dollar trading reached its peak of $2 in greenbacks that month, they transformed the Board of Stockbrokers into the Portland Stock and Exchange Board. Reflecting their strong confidence in gold during the waning months of the Civil War, even Failing and Lewis played the currency market. The 12-member Stock and Exchange Board included many of Portland's financial elite: Failing, McCraken, Ladd, Ainsworth, Henry Green, S.B. Parrish, Reed, Lewis, Thompson, Dr. J.H. Chapman, A.M. Starr, and Goldsmith. Two years later, all but Starr and Goldsmith would be Arlington Club founders. Starr had left Portland and Goldsmith was barred because he was a Jew.[38]

Though he was excluded from membership of the Arlington Club, Goldsmith, who was Portland's eighth-wealthiest resident in 1870, commanded wide public respect. His term as mayor (1869-71) was one of the more successful in Portland history. He justifiably boasted that "I have been identified with almost everything that has been going on in this town since I came here." From an affluent family, he had made money from a decade of California and Southern Oregon merchandising before arriving in Portland in 1861 at age 33. As a jeweler and assayer, he had to be interested in the gold currency market, which he played with consummate skill in 1865 and 1866 before founding a dry-goods firm with several of his seven brothers. It soon became a major supplier of frontier troops. Subsequent investments in Wasco County cattle and Willamette Valley wheat production drew him into transportation and the grain trade.[39]

Trade Liberates Portland

Bernard Goldsmith's entry into the wheat trade signaled a growing awareness among Portland merchants and their bankers that "wheat was the most valuable and most marketable commodity then produced in Oregon." It might be the instrument for Oregon's independence from California if it could be shipped directly to Liverpool (bypassing San Francisco) to help meet growing British demand in the late 1860s. Before 1869, Portland's almost wholly coastal export commerce was dominated by the California market. California's development of its own wheat production meanwhile cut into Portland's wheat exports by 40 percent in 1867.[40]

Portland commission merchant John McCraken apparently initiated Portland's first wheat shipment to Liverpool. His chartered *Helen Angier* left port on April 29, 1869, carrying $31,000 of McCraken & Merrill Company wheat. Closely associated with Ladd, McCraken easily secured Ladd & Tilton financing for its Willamette Valley wheat purchases. Goldsmith later claimed co-responsibility for the inaugural shipment. "Whether that claim is accurate," Scott Cline has noted, "does not change the fact that he [Goldsmith] was involved in the early direct trade with Liverpool." Others increasingly duplicated these transactions in following years. During 1870-71, when $399,519 worth of wheat was shipped to Great Britain, two of the principal Portland shippers were wholesale grocers Allen & Lewis, and Corbitt & Macleay, a recent entrant to Portland's commercial life. (Co-founder Donald Macleay, who expanded into fish packing and other enterprises, became one of Portland's leading business and banking figures within 30 years.) A generator of many fortunes after the 1860s, wheat exported from Portland in 1871 alone represented 57 percent of the value of Oregon's port exports.[41]

Dangerous obstacles to ocean-going vessels, especially Portland-region river bars at Swan Island and at the mouth of the Willamette, hindered faster expansion of the export trade before 1869. Deep-drafted ships grounded on the shoals almost daily. Downriver towns received the larger vessels at Portland's expense. Goldsmith built grain warehouses at the Astoria bar for wheat shipped down the Columbia on barks and barges.[42]

The earliest organized effort to improve restrictive channel conditions had been undertaken in September, 1864, with the formation of the Portland River Channel Improvement Committee. Chaired by Josiah Failing, the committee included H.C. Leonard, Alexander P. Ankeny, John Green, Corbett, Ladd, Lewis, and David W. Burnside. Charged with raising a voluntary fund from interested private sources (no public funds were then available), the blue-ribbon committee procured $9,200 from 60 Portland businessmen and firms (the Oregon Steam Navigation Company gave $1,000) toward purchase of $42,000 in dredging equipment. The City of Portland, led by Mayor Henry Failing, supplied the difference. An 1866 congressional appropriation launched the Corps of Engineers on a three-year, 17-foot channel-dredging project using Portland's equipment, loaned without charge.[43]

A second obstacle affecting Oregon's export trade until after the Civil War was the lack of ocean-going (as opposed to coastal) vessels, even those that could negotiate the bars. Until the six-vessel Mercer Line opened the first direct service to New York in 1868, ocean commerce depended almost entirely on a few British ships. Charter rates consequently remained high.[44]

As Portlanders tried to develop the wheat trade, they encountered a further obstacle: the old OSN-People's Transportation Company exclusive-markets agreement. The PTC's monopoly of Willamette River commerce, exercised through its ownership of the key Oregon City portage, greatly inflated what Portland brokers had to pay Willamette Valley grain growers. Goldsmith, himself a grower, helped organize the Willamette Falls Canal and Locks Company in 1868 to bypass the Oregon City portage. Joseph Teal, Sr., one of Oregon's wealthiest residents; Orlando Humason, an OSN organizer and former Cascades portage owner; James K. Kelly, future U.S. senator (1871-77); and David P. Thompson, Oregon City Woolen Company manager and future Portland mayor, served with Goldsmith as directors. Capitalized at $450,000 the company expected a major legislative subsidy for the project. But Ben Holladay, operating from a steamboat tied up at Salem, employed the same tricks to thwart the canal and locks company that he used to transfer the franchise to the east-side Oregon Central Railroad. Randall V. Mills later wrote that "he succeeded in staving off the construction of the locks . . . by keeping firmly restricted the funds voted." Appropriating only a token subsidy in 1868, the legislature increased the amount by $200,000 in 1870. The two-year delay allowed Holladay time to complete his railroad to Salem and then to buy out the PTC in 1871. The purchase gave the much-feared and disliked tycoon virtual control of transportation enterprises in the Willamette Valley.[45]

Never profitable to the founders, the costly canal and locks paid off handsomely to wheat farmers and Portland grain brokers and commission merchants who had warmly celebrated their opening on January 1, 1873. Freight rates between upper and lower Willamette River towns immediately plunged 50 percent. But Goldsmith and Teal were still challenged by Holladay's dominance of Willamette River traffic. In 1873, they and Jacob Kamm invested in the Willamette River Transportation Company, founded in 1870 by Captain Joseph Kellogg, former PTC ship captain and boat builder. They built the *Governor Grover*, the largest boat to go up river to Harrisburg, and the large *Willamette Chief*, designed to carry wheat from the Willamette's headwaters to Astoria. Within a year, they broke Holladay's monopoly just as he became financially embarrassed.[46]

But the wheat farmers and Portland merchants won only temporary relief. By 1875, the Willamette Falls Canal and Lock Company was heavily in debt as it faced increasing OSN pressure. According to Dorothy Johansen, Ainsworth sent two specially built boats to the locks, where they demanded passage upon threat of legal action. "The boats of the Oregon Steam Navigation Company worked with Holladay's company and their combined strength forced the Willamette Company to capitulate." In its last 90 days, the canal and lock company lost "almost $100,000." Early in 1876, control of the transportation and lock companies passed to the OSN monopoly, with Ainsworth as president and Reed as vice-president of the newly formed Willamette Transportation and Locks Company. Goldsmith and his partners lost $225,000 on the transaction.[47]

William S. Ladd Goes to Salem

William S. Ladd, believing that the Oregon economy would grow apace with its increasing exports and imports, shrewdly decided early in 1868 to expand Ladd & Tilton into a regional bank. Salem seemed the natural choice for its first branch. It was the state capital and the center of regional wheat farming. Ladd did not guess that Salem would have a rail link to Portland within two years.

He turned to his long-time friend and fellow Democrat Asahel Bush. With cash on hand from a recent sale of the *Oregon Statesman*, Bush seemed a likely investment partner. Probably early in the spring of 1868, he agreed to a partnership with Ladd & Tilton holding half-interest. How much of the $50,000 capitalization Ladd eventually underwrote was not recorded. The name Ladd & Bush Bank was chosen, writes an historian of state banking, "because it would more closely identify the institution with the Salem community" and Bush's long-standing local prominence.[48]

Observers may have been astonished that two such hard-headed, fiercely independent personalities expected a harmonious partnership. Each had a weakness for his own opinion. Still, correspondence before the bank opening on March 29, 1869, was full of thoughtful give-and-take. Neither attempted to impose his wishes on the other. Bush made no pretense of being a banker (he became a highly successful one), but he knew he was an efficient manager. Ladd's judgment would be sought on the important matters, and Ladd would make the final decisions.[49]

Ladd built new Portland headquarters while planning the thrust into Salem. The three-story Ladd & Tilton Bank opened on January 12, 1869. It was a handsome addition to the richly decorated cast-iron architecture with which Portland businessmen were proclaiming their own — and the town's — substance. In Salem, the Ladd & Bush Bank, designed and constructed by the same architect and craftsmen to resemble a sixteenth-century Venetian library, was almost identical to the Portland bank. Opening day of March 29, 1869, brought brisk business to the Salem bank. Deposits totalled $1,450, bills receivable $3,832 and interest collected $221. Ladd & Bush was off to an encouraging start.[50]

The opening of Ladd's two new bank buildings and the purchase of the First National Bank by Henry W. Corbett and Henry Failing marked the conclusion of an era dominated largely by local merchants. As Arthur Throckmorton has observed, "The advent of railroad building and the rise of foreign commerce in 1869 so altered the old system as to mark the end of a distinct period of pioneering." In two years, Oregon's exports had more than doubled, while imports nearly tripled. Oregon "changed from a pioneer subsistence farming area to a surplus producing area," according to Dorothy Hirsch. "Oregon farmers were producing wheat in quantities too large to be taken up entirely by the San Francisco market."[51]

A tenfold increase in wheat export values from 1868 to 1871 supports Hirsch's contention that 1870 was "the beginning of a new era, the post-pioneer era of Oregon." New patterns of trade and transportation, resulting from the explosive growth of wheat and flour exports, loosened San Francisco's hold on Oregon's economy. Portland shippers, brokers, merchants, and bankers, who serviced the

city's productive hinterland, profited immensely. As Portland's population doubled from 1867 to 1877, its banks were able to generate badly needed surplus
capital for further commercial and industrial expansion.[52]

8.1 Oregon Iron Works smelting furnace and workers, Oswego, Oregon, 1867

8.2 Bernard Goldsmith (1832-1901)

8.3 An elderly Herman C. Leonard (1823-1916)

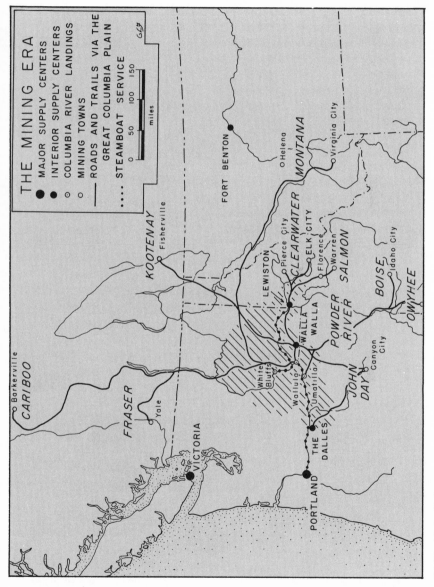

8.4 "The Mining Era" map

Are constantly receiving by direct importation from the Eastern States, large and desirable additions to their already EXTENSIVE STOCK, which being one of THE LARGEST ON THE PACIFIC COAST, laid in, and constantly recruited at the East, we are enabled to offer goods in our line at as FAVORABLE RATES as can be obtained in San Francisco. We would direct public attention to this FACT, as an examination of Stock and prices will prove.

8.5 Smith & Davis advertisement

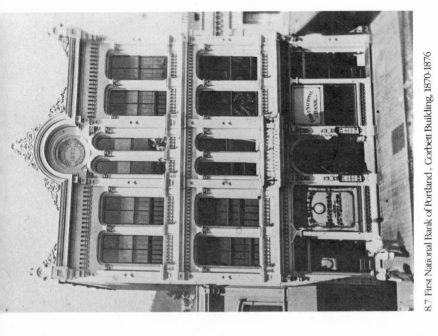

8.7 First National Bank of Portland, Corbett Building, 1870-1876

8.6 Overland Mail Route poster

8.8 1867 partial panorama of Portland

9

Money and City Politics: 1860-1875

Wealth and Public Office

Of Portland's 30 wealthiest men in 1870, 10 held at least one public office from 1853 through 1859, and 17 at least one public office from 1860 through 1877. Their direct political involvement peaked with Henry Failing's second mayoralty (1873-75) and Robert R. Thompson's last council term 1874-75).

Henry W. Corbett achieved his long-sought goal of election to the U.S. Senate in October, 1866, after 16 bitter legislative ballots. In Judge Matthew P. Deady's estimation, former mayor and councilman William S. Ladd could have won the governorship in 1878 had his health permitted. Instead, he contributed nearly a decade of school board service, as did Captain John C. Ainsworth. Corbett, 12 years after his senatorial re-election defeat, returned to the Board of Multnomah County Commissioners for two terms (1884-87). In the interim, he struggled for Republican party control against the insurgent Holladay-Mitchell faction. To the admiring Deady, Corbett was "'a Radical in thought and Conservative in action, a man of strong convictions, but temperate and moderate in speech and conduct.'"[1]

In the earlier years, men of property were expected to run for political office. Such public participation involved far more than an effort to protect property rights and aid business growth. As office holders, Failing, Corbett, Ladd and their peers — men of reasonable honesty, some imagination, and considerable business courage — exhibited a high degree of civic pride and an equal amount of ego. They enjoyed being recognized as town leaders and good citizens. But their civic concern often faded when confronted with conflicting political or business interests. In Portland, as throughout America, according to David C. Hammack, merchant leaders of the 1850s and early 1860s had "urged the introduction" of basic municipal services, "but then failed to provide leadership for maintaining, improving and expanding them in the 1870s," especially when faced with the need for increased taxes.[2]

An acerbic Judge Deady exaggerated when he wrote Senator James W. Nesmith in 1865 that "Portland has prospered pretty well in spite of the *fools* who lead in

her affairs." The issue was far more complicated than Deady implied. In the mid
1860s Portland's political leadership was fragmented by partisan politics that
rested on complex community relationships, not the least of which were eco
nomic. It was also divided between a weak mayor's office and an increasingly
aggressive city council that was dominated by special interests. In addition, the
leadership may well have reflected the older merchants' struggle to grapple with
the growth of new industry, larger businesses and more powerful financial and
transportation interests they did not control.[3]

Growth and Demographic Change

Deady's concern about leadership reflected his frustration and even confusion
over Portland's direction. In five years the population had doubled, from nearly
3,000 in 1860 to over 6,000 in 1865. It would redouble by 1876. Gone was the
quiet, peaceful village, the intimate club comprising a handful of city fathers who
could express the community's purpose — *their* purpose — through their control
of a limited government. Politics became a full-time occupation for an increasing
number of office holders as the community grew larger, more diverse and ever
more complex. Portland's growth rate of nearly 300 percent surpassed that of the
state as a whole, a trend that would continue over the following two decades.

The town's foreign-born inhabitants increased at a similar rate through the
1870s, making Portland one of the most heterogeneous in the Far West. By 1870,
nearly a third of its total population was foreign-born and approximately half had
at least one foreign-born parent. This may partially explain why Portland's early
political leadership was drawn disproportionately from New England and the
Middle Atlantic regions. By the late 1860s, the Germans (one-third of whom were
Jews), who constituted the largest European group, became the first of the foreign-
born to achieve successful careers in both business and politics. The wealthy
German-Jewish merchants Bernard Goldsmith and Philip Wasserman served consecutively as mayor (1869-1873), preceding Henry Failing in his second term.[4]

Despite their obvious business talents and personal commitment to Portland,
the merchant mayors failed to understand the significant changes rapidly envel-
oping their city. Few of Portland's elite comprehended that the society they were
helping to create imposed social and environmental costs of growing magnitude,
as in the quality of municipal services. Some like the future railroad tycoon Henry
Villard, seemed infatuated on his visit in 1874 by the town's magnificent setting,
by "the three snow-clad giants of Mt. Hood, Mt. St. Helens and Mt. Adams clearly
visible in their mighty splendor." Likewise, Oregon pioneer Jesse Applegate, after
his daily walks through Portland in the fall of 1869, emphasized the "good taste
displayed in the selection and arrangement of the trees, shrubs and other orna-
ments." He ignored the unsanitary streets. His friends in the Portland Establishment, anxious to avoid higher taxes for new services, also ignored the mounting
problems of public health, security and conveniences. Few in the West seemed to
care about such conditions, Lawrence H. Larsen concluded. "The same kind of
commercial considerations that superseded aesthetic factors in the Northeast,
Midwest, and South prevailed west of the ninety-fifty meridian."[5]

One who did care was Deady. Peering below Portland's splendrous heights, he envisioned converting "municipal government into a practical 'Cooperative Union,' for the purpose of supplying the community" with all the necessary services such as "water, gas and telegraphs," provided such an institution "could be found or constituted with the requisite sense and integrity." The antics of city government both annoyed and amused him. An honest man of good judgment, he offered a public vision for Portland that was shared by few of his business and banking friends. In his voluminous writings he implied that the best political leadership, whether for city, state or country, required more than a merchant's experience of a counting-house mentality.[6]

Mayor Henry Failing

Merchant Henry Failing shared many of Deady's concerns about Portland's political future. He, too, was annoyed by the petty squabbles and factionalism afflicting city government, especially during Mayor David Logan's administration (1863-64). Influenced by the success of the Union party (in which he had played a major role) in uniting Democrats and Republicans behind the Civil War effort, Failing proposed his version of Deady's "Cooperative Union." In 1864 he launched a municipal non-partisan movement and offered himself as candidate for mayor, presumably receiving strong support from his brother-in-law and political mentor Henry W. Corbett, who had preceded him as state Republican party chairman.

Failing's campaign platform called for a restructuring of city government, with staggered three-year council terms and a two-year mayor's term. Failing recommended that city offices be redefined to meet the needs of the exploding population and particularly advocated the use of a trained accountant as city auditor. Increasing services while keeping taxes low became the overriding goal for his administration; business-like efficiency was his standard.

Failing's non-partisan stance proved popular and he was overwhelmingly elected mayor in April, 1864. His Citizens party swept the city council races, producing a 100 percent turnover. Among the nine new members were several who were prominent in Portland's Establishment: John McCraken, A.M. Starr, and James W. Cook, a socially active young merchant who would be succeeded in 1865 by Oregon Steam Navigation Company executive Robert R. Thompson. Also elected to the council in 1864 were the U.S marshal and the manager of the U.S. assessor's office. Entering public office for the first time, Joseph N. Dolph succeeded his partner John H. Mitchell as appointed city attorney. Both then and often later, the city attorney's office provided a launching pad for politically ambitious young lawyers. Dolph soon became U.S. district attorney, then state senator and two-term Republican U.S. senator (1883-95). He also served for over 20 years as chief counsel to the OSN.

As mayor, Failing gave priority to planting trees and paving streets, measures designed to improve the city's physical and commercial environment. The old-growth fir had been cut as far west as the Park Blocks, leaving the landscape nearly bare. The dirt streets were a menace to humans and beasts, raising swirling dust that severely irritated the eye in summer; in winter, especially during rainy peri-

ods and floods, the manure ground down by wagon wheels created virtual cess
pools. An organizer of the Portland and Milwaukie Macadamized Road Compan
in 1863, Failing might have gained personally as well as politically by promotin
the paving of city thoroughfares. Street cleaning remained a private responsibil
ity, however, as the city sprinkled the streets only weekly.

Failing's major accomplishment, a new city charter drafted by Deady, gaine
council approval and legislative confirmation in October, 1864. Its restructurin
made councilmen serve for three years on staggered terms and the mayor for two
The mayor's authority was strengthened by a grant of veto power requiring a two
thirds council override.[7]

The increasing costs of police protection, and the desire to centralize enforce
ment procedures under council authority, led to another charter revision in 1864
The city marshal was to be elected by council rather than by public vote, and wa
removable at any time for just cause. Fees payable to the marshal were restricte
solely to his enforcement of municipal laws. This constraint, imposed on an al
ready poorly paid constabulary, created "serious law enforcement problems dur
ing the next several years," according to Charles Tracy.[8]

In his annual message of June, 1866, Failing complained about the costs o
police protection, the "unprofitable . . . business of maintaining law and order.
For the previous six months, costs had run to about $3,000 "*in excess of the reve
nue from fines for violations of City Ordinances.*" Unwittingly, the mayor ha
been primarily responsible for the cost increases when he appointed two part
salaried deputy marshals in November, 1864. A significant increase in crime ha
forced the action. But when police service costs doubled over the next two years
well in excess of the fines collected to pay for them, Failing was in a quandary
Adamantly opposed to tax increases, he believed that government could be run a
a private business by increasing cost-effective management or reducing services
Like many of his merchant friends, he failed to realize that, with salaries and othe
compensation already low, recruiting reliable and honest peace officers was al
most impossible. Though the council ignored Failing's advice to reduce polic
expenses, it did increase general revenues by raising liquor-license bonds to $500
Liquor licenses and bonds provided 50 percent of city revenues.[9]

Failing resigned on November 15, 1866, for personal reasons — most likel
financial problems when the sharp decline in gold prices effected his busines
adversely. He could look back with some satisfaction on his two and a half years ir
office, particularly on the improvements in the city's appearance. As the *Orego
nian* had observed three months earlier, "Men of capital . . . have full confidenc
in the continued progress of the city."[10]

The costs of police protection continued to plague Failing's successors, the firs
of whom was Thomas J. Holmes, a wealthy merchant, former councilman an
veteran city marshal elected as mayor by the council. Holmes's annual message t
the city council in January, 1867, decried "'extravagant and useless [police] ex
pense.'" Speaking for many in the business community, he recommended fiv
ways to lower expenditures as part of a broader program to reduce excessive cit
governmental costs: private boarding for prisoners; using convict labor; discharg
ing one deputy while reducing compensation of the other; and either closing o

heavily taxing "Chinese bawdy houses." Until two months before his sudden death on June 18, 1867, one day after his re-election, Holmes and the council remained dead-locked over police expenditures. Repeated council votes to increase police services were vetoed by the mayor and sustained by the council. In April, 1867, the council finally prevailed, with the "establishment of a completely salaried force" of a marshal and two deputies. For a city of 8,300 people, three police officers were inadequate, but the seeds of Portland's first professional police department had been planted.[11]

The German Mayors: Goldsmith and Wasserman

Of growing concern to Portland's city government in the 1860s and '70s was the increasing number of Chinese immigrants, who formed an embryonic primitive Chinatown around First and Washington streets. By 1875, they constituted Portland's largest foreign-born ethnic group, surpassing the Germans. During the peak of Ben Holladay's railroad construction recruitment in 1868, the *Oregonian* noted: "Two hundred Chinese landed last week. They are now as thick as rats." Numerous attempts were made to discourage permanent residency. In 1863 and 1865, the city council had imposed prejudicial taxes on Chinese washhouses. The Multnomah County Circuit Court ruled the first ordinance unconstitutional and Mayor Failing vetoed the second as discriminatory. In 1868, the Oregon legislature passed a bill to tax and regulate Chinese workmen and prevent their employment upon public works. Introduced by Multnomah County Representative William W. Chapman, one of Portland's former proprietors, it was promptly vetoed by Governor George L. Woods.[12]

In July, 1869, newly elected Mayor Bernard Goldsmith ordered the city marshal to quarantine Chinese passengers on an arriving ship suspected of carrying smallpox. In the absence of state laws or health officers, handling such matters became a police responsibility. Four additional policemen were hired to sequester the Chinese. The police also had to deal with Chinese prostitution, referred to by Mayor Holmes in 1867. Much to the horror of the city's Establishment, clearly identified Chinese bawdy houses "had become a fixture on Second, between Morrison and Alder," according to Tracy. Neither Goldsmith nor Wasserman was interested in cracking down on such places, but an increasing incidence of disorderly conduct forced their hands. Throughout the 1870s, the arrest of Chinese prostitutes was many times that of their less obvious but just as numerous non-Chinese counterparts.[13]

While disdaining the Chinese, Portlanders relied on their cheap labor to perform distasteful manual tasks. The volunteer fire department could not have functioned effectively without the Chinese who worked the pumpers. As long as the Chinese performed jobs commonly considered "women's work," they were not regarded as competing with caucasian labor. But when they were hired as common laborers for street building and repair, resistance mounted. In June, 1873, Mayor Wasserman vetoed a council ordinance prohibiting Chinese laborers from being employed on city contracts, arguing that such acts conflicted with federal law and treaties.[14]

William Toll, in his study of Portland Jews, has noted that Wasserman

> could have agreed with the majority of the city council and sustained their discriminatory ordinance. That he did not demonstrates some willingness to protect the civil rights of an unpopular people in a spirit of social stewardship.

The views of mayors Failing, Goldsmith and Wasserman reflected those of the merchants in the upper stratum, who generally defended the employment of low wage Chinese labor. In Toll's opinion, their defense of the Chinese was "an assertion of their right to uphold civic order rather than . . . [an] expression of any special regard for an ethnic minority." Indeed, Portland business leaders faced a serious dilemma: while they needed to enforce city laws in order to defuse anti-Chinese agitation, they were more dependent on the Chinese work force than they cared to admit openly. Low wages paid to subservient labor directly benefited both private enterprise and under-funded public services.[15]

The actions of Portland's merchant mayors in the 1870s displayed some sympathy for the Chinese. Wealthy and socially secure, these men exhibited, in Toll's words, a "more paternalistic treatment of . . . [Portland's] Chinese than that found in most other West Coast cities." Goldsmith and Wasserman, as "offspring of a stigmatized people," might also have appreciated, more than most of their gentile colleagues, the civil-rights dimension of the Chinese problem. However, their feelings were not shared by a number of small, less secure Jewish shopkeepers who joined the anti-Chinese agitation of the late 1870s and early 1880s.[16]

As mayors, Bernard Goldsmith (1869-71) and Philip Wasserman (1871-73) epitomized the best of the merchant group. Neither had held previous elective political office, and Goldsmith even apologized to the city council for his inexperience. But he wasted no time facing the Chinese problem and the need for expanded police service. He spent over a year trying to convince the council that the "police force . . . [was] too small to be throughly efficient." In the interim, he hired special policemen with funds previously allocated for salary increases to other city officials. Compromise ordinances, which he signed on September 10 and 12, 1870, established Portland's first police department. But the outcome was short-lived. On October 21, 1870, Democratic Governor Lafayette Grover approved a new city charter amendment, enacted by the Democratic-controlled legislature, giving complete authority over the Portland police to the governor through his appointed Board of Police Commissioners. Henceforth, Portland's Republican mayor and council were restricted to the sole power of payment for services. Mayor Goldsmith, who would return to the Democratic ranks in 1875, suddenly confronted the increased political partisanship and factionalism that would roil local and state governments in subsequent years. By temperament and experience, he was unprepared for the change.[17]

The governor, who had close ties to Portland through his wife, Elizabeth Carter, and the Democratic legislators had been reacting to the Republican strong-arm tactics employed by Ben Holladay and John H. Mitchell in the previous legislature. In Salem, they feared that the Holladay-Mitchell Republicans would gain control of Portland's city council, and thus of its police department. The police commission amendment had been introduced by Portland state Senator Lansing Stout, a close friend of Deady, Asahel Bush and former Salem Clique member Lafayette Grover. Mayors Goldsmith and Wasserman were their unwitting victims. As Charles Tracy has noted, "The traditional difference between the political responsibilities and objectives of . . . [municipal and state] government were to cause continual . . . disruptions in the orderly development of Portland's police." In July, 1872, Mayor Wasserman expressed concern to the still predominantly Republican council that the police force had been used "for political purposes." At least he had the satisfaction of opening the city's newly constructed Police Building three weeks later. But, as Tracy comments, "Ironically, the first prisoner to be booked in the new city jail . . . on charge of abduction . . . was arrested by a private citizen rather than a police officer." The three-story structure, in Terence O'Donnell's opinion, looked "like a town house in Louis Napoleon's Paris."[18]

Goldsmith's and Wasserman's major contributions were in raising funds and acquiring land for municipal parks. Early in his term, Goldsmith began working tirelessly to settle ownership of the Plaza and Park blocks in favor of the city. A strong believer in public parks, he had the foresight to look beyond the boundaries of the small city of 8,000, surrounded by forests, hills and the Willamette River. Portland was growing rapidly; within a generation, little nearby land would be available except at prohibitive prices. With council support, Goldsmith acted quickly to secure both the Plaza and the remaining Park blocks.

The Plaza and Park Blocks

The Plaza Blocks, between Third and Fourth, and Salmon and Madison, were originally dedicated to the city by Daniel Lownsdale and William W. Chapman in 1852, but Portland had received title to neither. The two open squares were bisected by the north-south dividing line between Lownsdale's and Chapman's claims. For unexplained reasons, by 1870 Chapman legally owned both blocks 53 and 54, including the eastern halves formerly owned by Lownsdale. With encouragement from Mayor Goldsmith, on September 13, 1870, Chapman informed the council that he and his wife would transfer title to the two Plaza Blocks and seven Park Blocks for $7,000. After brief negotiation, the Chapmans accepted a reduced price for immediate cash payment. A check for $6,250 was dispatched on September 22, and the city received title the following day. Mayor Wasserman negotiated a similar purchase with General and Mrs. Stephen Coffin in July, 1871. Their seven Park Blocks, and title to the 400-foot public levee, were deeded to the city for $2,500. The price difference reflected the greater value of the Chapman properties, two downtown blocks and seven closer-in park blocks, bordering property facing development.[19]

While negotiating with the Chapmans, Goldsmith had asked the council to investigate purchasing from Nancy Lownsdale's estate the six remaining South Park Blocks that Daniel Lownsdale had originally reserved to the city. Included within her half of her husband's Donation claim, the blocks had never been legally dedicated before her death in April, 1854. In the absence of a will, her property was equally divided among her heirs, whose rights were confirmed by Judge Erasmus D. Shattuck in August, 1865.

The city council committee on streets and public parks reported to Goldsmith that only four of the six blocks were for sale, between Stark and Yamhill streets. The other two (one of which would one day include the Arlington Club) were in the process of development. At an asking price of $6,000 per block, for a total of $24,000 (twice what the city offered), the amount proved too high to gain council approval. Attention then turned to acquiring available property in the west hills. A deal was struck to purchase from Mr. and Mrs. Amos N. King 40.78 acres at $800 per acre, for a total cost of $32,624.[20]

With the transfer of the King deed on February 20, 1871, Portland acquired the nucleus of what became City Park, a tract containing essentially 145 acres dedicated to public use. Subsequently renamed Washington Park, it linked 11 other park areas into a greenbelt of over 4,500 acres. Some criticized the purchase as wasteful. Rumors later spread that Amos King had made money out of the transaction above the public sale price. According to one report, a deal was arranged by veteran councilman Luzerne Besser, chairman of the council committee on streets and public parks. Working with private developers, Besser allegedly convinced the Lownsdale heirs that they would make more money by selling to developers than to the city. By doubling their price, they would discourage city interest. For selling his property to the city, King supposedly received an interest in the four-block tract. While no proof ever surfaced supporting the charges, Besser was indicted for bribery 12 years later on a similar deal.[21]

Regardless of the pressures and possible chicanery, the decision to forego the Lownsdale blocks and acquire the King tract was in retrospect the wiser choice, considering that public funds to purchase both tracts were unavailable. Public apathy toward parks was so widespread that Mayor Wasserman cancelled a special park-fund levy election in December, 1871, for fear of its defeat. By abandoning the Lownsdale blocks to private developers, Portland forfeited a major amenity, which would have provided a valuable public resource as the downtown expanded. Loss of the six small park blocks, along with two other blocks for which Stark had made the outrageous demand of $138,000, effectively destroyed the purpose of Daniel Lownsdale's original town plan. In contrast, the generous Captain John H. Couch had deeded the five North Park Blocks to the city free of charge on January 25, 1865, 10 days after receipt of their federal patent.[22]

The Mitchell-Holladay Era

Bernard Goldsmith discovered through bitter experience that "Municipal government . . . rested on a system of broker politics, of bargaining and dealing," as Jon C. Teaford has observed about 1870 America. Both Mitchell and Holladay used this system to their own advantage. While a litigious, economically swelling Portland probably needed rough-and-tumble lawyers in the 1860s and '70s, the city received more than it expected in the person of John H. Mitchell.[23]

Born John Mitchell Hipple in 1835, the young Pennsylvania native attended a local university, taught school and studied law. In 1857, he was forced to marry a

15-year-old student whom he had seduced. After admittance to the Pennsylvania bar, he deserted his wife and two of his children, leaving them penniless, and headed to California. Accompanying him on his flight were his eldest daughter and a young school teacher with whom he was having an affair. In July, 1860, he abandoned the woman, changed his name to John Hipple Mitchell, and travelled to Portland with his daughter.[24]

As an arriviste, Mitchell had, in the opinion of journalist Burton J. Hendrick, the

personal graces that count for everything in a small community — good looks, amiability, personal force, and a certain dash and aggressiveness that passed for intellectual brilliancy.

His ability to engender confidence in new acquaintances undoubtedly influenced his selection as city attorney. More importantly for his future, the same talent led to partnership with a young New York attorney named Joseph N. Dolph, who arrived in Portland in 1862. Specializing in land litigation and railroad right-of-way cases, Dolph and Mitchell soon became the leading railroad law firm in the state. While launching his professional and political careers, Mitchell entered into a bigamous marriage with a young local woman whom he increasingly disliked; nevertheless she bore him six children. By 1871 he was in love with his wife's sister and maintained an open affair with her for many years.[25]

Mitchell first achieved statewide Republican prominence with his election to the state senate in 1862. Chosen senate president in 1864, he spent two years promoting himself as Oregon's 1866 candidate for the U.S. Senate seat held by Democrat James W. Nesmith. The election of 1866, won by Henry W. Corbett on the 16th ballot, was, in Walter C. Woodward's judgment, "the first of a long series of political intrigues and imbroglios which have been associated with the history of the Republican Party in Oregon . . . . The man round whom the fierce political warfare . . . was long to rage [was] . . . John H. Mitchell." Mitchell's political ambitions strained his relationship with Dolph especially after Holladay retained him as his personal lawyer and adviser. That they were two of a kind was revealed in a remark attributed to Mitchell: "'Ben Holladay's politics are my politics and what Ben Holladay wants I want.'" Whether or not he made the statement, it accurately reflected his political ethics.[26]

While ambition and infidelity increasingly marked Mitchell's career, it was greed that drove it. His role in the Caruthers affair was, like most of his actions, well camouflaged from public scrutiny. In 1868, after the State of Oregon lost its U.S. Supreme Court appeal to declare the original Caruthers Donation Land claim faulty, "the vultures settled," wrote Eugene E. Snyder. They began seeking title to the remaining 265-90 acres (adjacent to a growing Portland) left by Fenice Caruthers, who died intestate and without apparent heirs.[27]

In 1869 Mitchell and some promoter friends sought their own heir in the form of a long-lost Joe Thomas, Elizabeth Caruthers's former husband and Fenice's father. In St. Louis they found a man who answered to the name, bribed him and brought him to Portland to testify and confirm his relationship. The schemers paid him an additional $8,000 and had him deed away his property rights. In 1870 they formed the South Portland Real Estate Association out of the old Caruthers Land Company and collected all contested deed claims in return for share interests worth nearly $275,000. More than $40,000 worth went to bona fide contestants, while the Mitchell group apparently took $150,000 worth; Mitchell grabbed a $10,000 share. The rest went to legal fees and related expenses. Even the highly respected Mayor Goldsmith received a $20,000 share. In 1873 Joe Thomas was exposed as John C. Nixon, but nobody tried to unscramble the transactions. Too many powerful interests were involved.[28]

While Mitchell was plundering the Caruthers estate, he joined Holladay in promoting U.S. Senator George H. Williams's re-election in 1870. Despite huge sums spent on legislators' votes, the Republican Williams lost to Democrat James K. Kelly, Asa Lovejoy's partner. In Malcolm Clark's opinion, "the 'Chief of the Mercenary Brigade,'" the group that raised and paid out the bribes, "was probably John H. Mitchell, but any number of Oregon politicians were sufficiently mercenary to qualify for the title." Mitchell's equally soiled but successful elimination of Henry W. Corbett from the 1872 U.S. Senate race not only ended his partnership with Dolph but generated a lifelong enmity that Corbett refused to soften.[29]

The Holladay empire looked invincible in 1872 when it challenged the Corbett-Failing leadership of the Republican party. The arrogance of propertied power knew no limits in the May 1872 city primary. As Judge Deady lamented: "Money and employment on the Railways, steamships and boats prevails over all other arguments and considerations with non-taxpaying voters." Ned Wicks, owner of the American Exchange saloon, later recalled how he was summoned to meet Holladay in April, 1872: "When I went to his office he had his feet on the table and was tipped back in a big office chair" smoking a cigar. Holladay told Wicks that he was prepared to spend what it took to make a traditionally Democratic ward "go Republican." Holladay "furnished me with a sack of $2.50 gold pieces. I kept pretty busy till election day," moving from one hotel and lodging house to another. "On election day I served as paymaster . . . . We carried the old Modoc ward — the Democratic stronghold — and for the first time in its history it went Republican." Holladay reportedly spent $20,000 to re-elect three city councilmen and insure John H. Mitchell's legislative defeat of Corbett for the U.S. Senate.[30]

Corbett gained partial revenge for his 1872 loss through a special congressional election in 1873. In a rare breaking of party ranks, he refused to endorse the Mitchell-Holladay candidate. His weapon was the *Oregonian*, which he had bought in October, 1872, from a financially strapped Henry Pittock. Corbett's editor, city Councilman William Lair Hill, accused the Mitchell-Holladay candidate of running on a "'bigamy platform.'" Printing a lengthy expose of Mitchell's private life, the *Oregonian* stopped short of endorsing Democrat James W. Nesmith, whom Corbett had defeated for the U.S. Senate in 1866. But its personal attacks on Mitchell affected the election's outcome. While losing Multnomah County, where the *Oregonian* estimated that one-fourth of the votes cast were illegal, Nesmith won general statewide support for Oregon's lone congressional seat, achieving a victory that Corbett must privately have relished. After Holladay's power crumbled in 1877, Corbett resold control of the paper to Pittock.[31]

Like Holladay, Mitchell seemed immune to criticism. He thrived on it, turning accusations of bigamy and chicanery into personal popularity referendums. Deady's admonishment to him in April, 1872, that "he had too much 'business' in his politics," fell on deaf ears. Mitchell had learned early that mixing business with politics was highly rewarding. In less than 12 years, the young, penniless lawyer had managed to accumulate assets of $50,000 and enter the U.S. Senate. Although defeated for re-election in 1878 by Democrat James H. Slater of Eastern Oregon (Holladay's money had run out), he recaptured the seat in 1884 and served two consecutive terms.[32]

Henry Failing Challenges Ben Holladay

In the six-and-a-half-year period between Henry Failing's two administrations, Ben Holladay's presence and power permeated Portland's economic and political life. As his Oregon and California Railroad pushed southward in 1871, Holladay organized four additional corporations: the Portland Dock and Warehouse Company, with facilities on both sides of the Willamette River; the Oregon Transfer Company, for handling local transportation of passengers and freight; the Oregon Steamship Company, with service to California; and a real-estate domain comprising large East Portland holdings. With his associate George W. Weidler, he also built the first horse-drawn streetcar in 1872, along First from Glisan to Sherman streets.

To extend his political influence, Holladay started a newspaper in 1872. He acquired an entire printing plant in San Francisco and shipped it to Portland. The *Bulletin* became his mouthpiece and provided severe competition to the *Oregonian*. The *Bulletin*'s debut led Henry W. Corbett to buy the controlling interest in the *Oregonian*, whose editor, Harvey W. Scott, had been eulogizing Holladay. Fired by Corbett, Scott became associate editor of the *Bulletin* for two years, until Holladay lost his fortune and the paper went bankrupt. According to Malcolm Clark, *Bulletin* editor James O'Meara once declared that "Scott had an affinity for men with money and was fascinated by them." Holladay apparently squandered $200,000 on the ill-fated venture.[33]

Holladay's well-financed challenge to Portland's Republican Establishment in 1872 led to the re-creation of a Citizens party in the municipal election of 1873. To Corbett and Failing, the municipal crisis was a civil war, not unlike the one the Union had faced. To combat the Holladay-Mitchell forces, civic-minded men of both parties were encouraged to support a strong non-partisan ticket. The city council, while heavily Republican, was almost evenly split between the Holladay-Mitchell and Corbett factions. City government authority was further fractured by the state's assumption of city police power in 1870. Reflecting Democratic dominance at the state level, the Portland Police Commission comprised three stalwart Democrats, led by Absalom B. Hallock, a leading architect-builder with 11 years of city council service since 1857. To Henry Failing, the Commission was another partisan threat to local authority that further destabilized city government. In agreeing to run again for mayor by heading a citizens' ticket, he charged the Democratic state leadership with mandating a costly police system over which Portland exercised no control but which it had to finance.

The municipal election of June, 1873, revealed an unexpected split in Portland's Establishment when merchant John McCraken, a close associate of William S. Ladd and the shipping community, filed as the Democratic mayor candidate against Failing. The *Oregonian* charged that McCraken was being used by the Holladay Republicans to draw votes from Failing, the popular favorite. In a surprise editorial written by Corbett's editor, city Councilman William Lair Hill, the paper declared: "If there is one man in Portland pre-eminent for neglecting every duty of a public nature which he undertakes to perform, that man is Colonel John McCraken." In the same edition, the *Oregonian* labeled the Holladay-Mitchell group "the ring" that did not have enough courage to run its own brand of Republican.[34]

Failing's victory, by only 40 votes out of 2,036 cast, confirmed a resurging partisan split within Portland's business Establishment. Regardless of Holladay's personal standing, his accomplishments were admired by many Portlanders, especially Democrats, who favored more aggressive economic development and an expansion of city services to match the demands of the fast-growing region. McCraken, Goldsmith, and, one suspects, Ladd held to a broader view of city growth than Failing's. Not without serving their own interests (Goldsmith and McCraken were allied in the wheat trade), they were forever willing to risk and spend both public and private monies to promote a development that generated revenues to fund additional police, fire and water services. Failing's Republican vision was limited to a merchant-banker's traditional espousal of low taxes, minimal costs and affordable services. His were popular positions, especially among Republican city councilmen. They feared alienating taxpayers who disregarded publicly expressed concerns that the private water system was inadequate, the fire department underequipped and the old wooden sidewalks a perennial fire hazard.[35]

Mayors Goldsmith and Wasserman had been apprehensive that the private municipal water system was inadequate for a major fire. Goldsmith had argued in his 1870 annual message that "wooden buildings should no longer be allowed in the central business district." Two years later, Wasserman had recommended that "a special election of taxpayers be held to determine how a municipal waterworks should be financed." No action followed either request. A four-block fire in December, 1872 (the city's worst to date), did not prompt immediate steps to defend against worse outbreaks. But Failing hardly addressed the issue during his campaign, appearing preoccupied with the high cost of police services and their control by a state-appointed agency. In his inaugural message he suggested ways to increase police fees and lessen prisoner costs, as had Mayor Holmes six years earlier. A bitterly divided council seemed unreceptive. Even among his five supporters (four councilmen were pro-Holladay), Failing could neither induce nor expect unanimity.[36]

The Great Fire

Disaster struck early in the morning of August 2, 1873. Propelled by exploding sidewalks, a fire destroyed 22 blocks along and near the waterfront from Taylor to Morrison streets. The fire of December, 1872, had destroyed only a few blocks around Morrison and Front streets. Not rebuilt, they created a fortuitous firebreak that prevented loss of the entire waterfront. The performance of the volunteer fire department, while heroic, left much to be desired. Operations were directed by elected unit chiefs, not by experienced professionals. Bedlam resulted, as Deady had noted after the fire in December, 1872: "The firemen worked hard and exposed themselves heroically to fire and danger, but done little if any good for want of intelligent control and direction." The holocaust of 1873 confirmed Deady's prior criticism: "The fire department lacked a head or it [the fire] might have been supressed in the morning."[37]

The causes of both fires were never officially determined. According to Deady, city leaders fastened blame upon anti-Chinese activists, the December fire having started in the rear of a Chinese laundry. Ironically, the Chinese filled a crucial role for the fire companies as they were expected to do most of the heavy work, especially the pumping. To Deady, they "were cruelly used and abused by the Fenian Guards," his contemptuous title for an Irish brigade of the Oregon Militia. Witnesses described how the Chinese were forced to walk over live coals in their thin slippers under the pretense of moving hoses and working the pumpers.[38]

The total loss, less insurance, amounted to $927,625. Properties damaged or lost numbered 179. The largest loss was suffered by former Mayor George W. Vaughn, whose destroyed grist mill, worth $150,000, carried only $6,000 in insurance. Merchant Aaron Meier, founder of what later became Portland's largest department store, lost $60,000 with insurance coverage of $18,000. Former county Commissioner Judge Philip Marquam was particularly distressed; his office was burned out twice. Mayor Failing's response to the emergency received mixed reviews. Few criticized his organizational talents and tireless efforts in providing shelter and food for the victims. But he was roundly condemned, especially by Holladay's *Bulletin*, for declining all offers of financial assistance from outside sources. Donating $10,000 himself, Failing called on the "rich men of Portland" to "dig down . . . and contribute." His rejection of proposals that the city should reimburse fire victims also drew *Bulletin* criticism, especially in the fall when the Panic of 1873 affected Oregon. Failing felt strongly that reimbursement "would have amounted to a tax on those whose property had not been destroyed or who had insurance." As Eugene Snyder has noted, "'The Ring' fanned up this dissatisfaction, whispering that Banker Failing was cruelly indifferent."[39]

The only immediate official reaction to the catastrophe was the purchase of a loud, 4,000-pound bell, to inspire a faster volunteer response to the next fire. No steps were taken to build water mains once the city focused on a speedy reconstruction that would restore normal business operations. Mayors Goldsmith and Wasserman, pointing to inadequate wooden street cisterns which emptied after two hours of pumping, had sought legislative enactment of a $1 million bond issue to finance a municipally owned and extended water system. But Portland legislators, reluctant to raise the city debt — and ultimately its taxes — blocked approval in Salem. Mayor Failing had neither the inclination nor the time to reopen the issue.

Portland also lost the opportunity to replan the destroyed area by widening the streets and enlarging the blocks to provide better access for commerce and transportation. To merchant-banker Failing and his divided council, such suggestions, coming from only a few, were too ambitious, too costly and too time-consuming. As for the waterfront property owners, they saw the destruction as an excellent opportunity to build larger, covered docks and more elaborate commercial buildings along the levee. Banker William S. Ladd also found gold in the ashes. He proposed the formation of a large furniture-manufacturing company from the remaining assets and skills of the small furniture dealers and manufacturers ruined by the fire. The resulting Oregon Furniture Manufacturing Company opened on April 1, 1874. With Ladd as major financier, the company soon became the leading furniture manufacturer in the Pacific Northwest.[40]

Failing on Crime Prevention

The fire necessitated adding 35 special police officers who were successful "in protecting most of the property of the fire victims from being stolen," according to Charles Tracy. The additional expense, however, concerned a mayor and city council already convinced that the regular force of 19 was too large. A council-appointed special committee recommended limiting the force to 10 policemen, one chief and one captain. The Board of Police Commissioners rejected council arguments as unrealistic and unfair. Criticizing suggestions that the force be reduced by discharging six night policemen, the board asserted that

> all citizens are entitled to equal protection for their lives and property . . . — that the property of the laborer, residing upon Eighth Street, is entitled to our care and protection as well as the storehouse of the merchant located on Front street.[41]

By recommending that police patrols be eliminated west of Fifth Street, the council had tried to protect the bulk of commercial property and the homes of Portland's wealthiest citizens from the cutback. (The mayor and his brother-in-law Henry W. Corbett lived on adjoining blocks along Fifth Street.) The board also challenged the council's assertion that crime had abated in recent years. Arrest totals for 1873 were about double the number of any year before 1871. Questioning the board's figures, the council refused to pay the March, 1874, salary claims of the police commissioners. But a violent temperance march on downtown saloons, resulting in wide public disorders, caused the council to reverse its position in June and to approve payment for a larger force. An unhappy Mayor Failing signed the ordinance while criticizing the council action.[42]

The city election of June, 1874, strengthened Failing's council support. Elijah Corbett, Henry's brother and an independent Democrat, and Deady's brother-in-law, attorney John Catlin, a moderate Republican, defeated two Holladay "hard-shell" Republicans. This transformation led the Board of Police Commissioners, with a nudge from Governor Grover, to acquiesce in the new council's determination to maintain a 12-officer limit. Failing, with nearly unanimous council backing, prodded the legislature in October, 1874, to return police control to the city. With Holladay's influence apparently diminished, Grover reversed himself and told the legislature that the mayor should be the "responsible head of the police system of the city." The legislature voted to empower the council to determine the size of the police force, and its pay. The Board of Police Commissioners was made appointive by mayor and council on January 1, 1875, and elective for three-year terms beginning with the June, 1875, city elections.[43]

Pleased with his record, Failing decided to seek re-election in June, 1875. But he underestimated the still-powerful influence of Ben Holladay despite the fact that his financial empire was crumbling. Failing's opponent, Dr. James A. Chapman, a registered Democrat and a former mayor (1867-68), had been close to the saloon interests while serving as Holladay's physician. An Arlington Club member, Chapman was a founder of the Progress Club, Portland's first booster organization. As reported by *The West Shore*, it was composed of 100 "prominent merchants, bankers and professional men" who favored more aggressive economic development.[44]

Holladay's *Bulletin* harshly criticized Failing's remiss leadership after the fire and his unconcern for those who had suffered. The saloon interests blamed him for their recent troubles with the temperance movement. And Failing undoubtedly lost votes on election day for signing a council ordinance to close the bars while the polls were open. The bitter contest ended with his defeat by six votes.[45]

Failing's overthrow enabled him to resume full-time responsibility as president of the First National Bank. He could also enjoy the spacious new 15-room home into which he and his family had moved in the spring of 1875. Under his watchful eye, it had taken two years to design and build. He had wanted all the latest technical contrivances, including speaking tubes and a complicated burglar-alarm system that cost over $140. After much discussion with his architect, he had decided that a good fence and an alert "little terrier dog" were equally effective deterrents to crime, and certainly much cheaper. While not opposed to spending money, merchant-banker Failing always held out for the best bargain, whether in private or public life.[46]

9.1 John H. Mitchell (1836-1905), c. 1870

9.2 Philip Wasserman (1827-1895)

9.3 George H. Williams (1823-1910), c. 1865-1871

9.4 Joseph N. Dolph (1835-1897)

9.5 Artist's rendition of Temperance reformers versus Burnside denizens, c. 1870s

9.6 Multnomah Company No. 2, 1866

9.7 Fire-damaged area in 1873: marked on 1870 map

10

WEALTH, PROPERTY AND SOCIETY: THE 1870s

Earned Wealth

B y 1870, Portlanders were idealizing their small city as a New England town, "prosperous, healthy and moral," village-like and full of mercantile energy. That it was reportedly one of the richest cities of its size in the United States gave it a certain national status. Americans increasingly defined their society in terms of money; wealth was the standard that measured social progress.[1]

To successful merchant and banker William S. Ladd, the pursuit of wealth was more important than its possession, although he accumulated riches eagerly. When elderly, he would distinguish between enterprise and inherited wealth: "I have no respect for puffed up aristocracy . . . . I have no respect for any aristocracy of wealth exclusively." Still, he knew he was a prominent figure in an urban elite, a local aristocracy that derived most of its authority from wealth. But it was earned wealth, and to the nineteenth-century elites that was an important distinction.[2]

The founding of the Social Club (later the Arlington Club) in December, 1867, symbolized Portland's growing society based on riches and its attendant social stratification, and reflected the gradual passage of local economic, political and social power into the hands of a privileged few. The club's 35 founders were largely self-made men, although many of them received their initial Portland backing from family or former business associates elsewhere. Eight of the city's highest reported incomes in 1869, ranging between $11,600 and $48,000, were earned by club members. Of the 21 reported Portland incomes over $9,000, 12 came from this self-styled exclusive "company of men." Members with lesser incomes were socially and politically connected, or were associated with the more prestigious businesses or banks. They included a prominent judge, an early supporter of the Portland Library Association, three city councilmen, and Mayor James A. Chapman. Reported income did not necessarily reflect wealth, however. While Arlington Club members Henry and John Green and their associate Herman C. Leonard, owners of the gas and water companies, listed joint incomes in 1870 of only $20,000, their combined assets exceeded $500,000. Of the 16 Portland men (and in some cases their families) with total assets exceeding $100,000 in 1870, 11 were Arlington Club members.[3]

Urban social stratification, as represented by the Arlington Club, typically accompanied the development of America's cumulative-growth cities (those not based on a covenant or a religious sect). Cumulative-growth cities like Portland and most others in the West grew largely in response to the speculative market. "The philosophy of speculation, of treating land like a commodity to be put in handy packages for quick sale, or regarding townsite promotion as a means of raising ready cash," was the dominant attitude of western town builders, according to John Reps. As Simeon G. Reed observed in May, 1871: "Now we do know the values of Real Estate and if we put our money into that we can manage and control it." Reed and his friends John C. Ainsworth, Robert R. Thompson, William S. Ladd, and Henry W. Corbett invested heavily in downtown real estate during 1870 and 1871. Corbett was already the largest non-corporate downtown investor by 1870, with 12 large parcels of land and at least nine buildings of various sizes.[4]

Growth and Property Values

During the decade of the 1870s, Portland experienced a commercial boom. It was propelled by the explosive growth in population from 8,293 residents to 20,931. "Every steamer brings from 300 to 500 passengers, besides what comes by land," Reed noted in May, 1871. "As a consequence Portland is improving rapidly and the country filling up. Real Estate is very active . . . . We certainly have the *Garden spot* of the Pacific Coast." By year's end, assessed values of Portland property reached $10,156,000, an increase of $3,250,000 in 12 months. The total would climb to $18 million by 1878. According to Judge Deady, true cash value was probably double the assessed value. Much taxable property was omitted from the assessment rolls, with the rest not assessed at more than half its market value.[5]

The largest increase in property values was in Couch's Addition, where Reed reported annual advances "from 50% to 100%." Nine parcels appraised at $2,900 in 1869 sold for $62,000 in 1871-72. The bulk of Captain John H. Couch's net estate, greatly undervalued at $127,678, was in property, over half of it unimproved. At the final accounting in 1872, it included an undivided interest (shared with Couch's brother-in-law George H. Flanders) in 380 unplatted acres appraised at $30,000 and 14 unsold blocks appraised at $52,556. The total market value would have exceeded $200,000. In 22 years, Couch's 640-acre Donation Land claim had appreciated from practically nothing to nearly $330,000 in market value, excluding what he had previously deeded to his wife and children and to Flanders. The basis of the family's enduring fortune was well established.[6]

In 1873, *Samuel's Directory of Portland and East Portland* confidently proclaimed that "there is probably no class of businessmen in any city in the United States, with a population of 12,000 that has so many firms of solid wealth." By 1878, R. G. Dun & Company reported 10 firms with assets worth from $100,000 to over $1 million. Manifesting its created wealth and its attendant social prominence, Portland's commercial and financial elite erected over 20 major downtown buildings between 1869 and 1879 (see accompanying chart). Like successful business people elsewhere, they usually named the buildings for themselves as if reminding present and future generations of their achievements. Six of Portland's richest men dominated the building boom. Four of them — Alex P. Ankeny, Henry W. Corbett, Henry Failing, and Reed — were active in the Arlington Club. A seventh, Ladd, had erected a newer, more imposing Ladd & Tilton Bank in 1868.[7]

PARTIAL LIST — MAJOR COMMERCIAL BUILDINGS
CONSTRUCTED 1869-1879

YEAR	NAME	BLOCK SIZE	OWNER(S)	APPROX. VALUE
1869	Glisan Block	1/4	R. Gilsan	$30,000
	Ankeny Block	1/2	A.P. Ankeny	50,000
	Lewis & Flanders Block	1/2	C.H. Lewis, G. Flanders	50,000
1870	Corbett Bldg. (1st N. Bank)	1/8	H.W. Corbett	40,000
1871	Dekum's Block	1/4	F. Dekum	70,000
1872	Smith's Block	1/2	J.S. & W.K. Smith	50,000
	New Market Block (1872-75)	3/4	A.P. Ankeny	100,000
	Pittock's Block (Oregonian)	1/8	H.L. Pittock	25,000
1873	Strowbridge Blk. (addition, 1876)	1/3	J.A. Strowbridge	30,000
1874	Corbett Bldg.	1/8	H.W. Corbett	25,000
1875	Dekum & Reed Blk. (addition, 1880's)	3/4	F. Dekum S.G. Reed	250,000
	Strowbridge Bldg.	1/8	J.A. Strowbridge	25,000
	McCraken Block (with dock)	1/3	J. McCraken	50,000
1876	No major construction — bad flood			
1877	J.S. Smith (1 of 3 bldgs. attached, 1877-79)	1/2	J.S. Smith	75,000
	Weinhard Block	1/4	H. Weinhard	50,000
1878	Cosmopolitan Blk. (additions, 1881)	7/8	S.G. Reed H. Failing	100,000
1879	Central Block	1/4	J.W. Cook	50,000
	C.E. Smith Bldg.	1/8	C.E. Smith	30,000
	Union Block	2/3	H.W. Corbett H. Failing	90,000

Portland's two other richest men, Joseph S. Smith and Frank Dekum, similarly affirmed the connection between earned wealth and civic standing with their new buildings. Smith was a pioneer in the Oregon and Washington territories, and a Salem resident until his election to Congress in 1868. The son-in-law of wealthy Donation Land claimant Thomas Carter, he moved to Portland in 1871, where he practiced law and engaged in real-estate development with his brother William K. Smith. The Smith brothers had assumed control of Salem's Willamette Woolen Mills in 1860, an investment that proved highly profitable, especially during the Civil War. In 1868, Joseph Smith reported Salem's highest income, of $10,784. The following year his brother William, an Arlington Club founder who lived alternately in Portland and Salem, reported Salem's highest income, of $26,471.[8]

With minimal resources, the Bavarian-born Frank Dekum opened Portland's first fruit and confectionery shop on Front Street in 1853, after arriving from the California and Idaho mines. With his partner, Frederick Bickel, a friend from St. Louis (where they had both learned the confectionery trade), he gradually developed the largest wholesale fresh-fruit business in the Northwest. Joining the frenzied real-estate speculations of the early 1860s, he amassed large holdings and in 1871 put up the first of several buildings to bear his name. In 1875, he joined Reed in erecting the city's most expensive building. Its opening symbolized Dekum's position in the top stratum of Portland's business community. He later became a major investor in banks and street railways.[9]

Portland's urban capitalists used their business and real-estate profits to construct these new, highly ornate masonry and cast-iron edifices. To some extent each new building reflected its owner's ego and claim of success, as one who had been free to exploit his economic opportunities. To visiting London attorney Wallis Nash, however, such efforts were pretentious. In Nash's opinion, the "chief ornament and pride of the city" was Judge Matthew P. Deady's "Public Library," located "in spacious rooms over Messrs. Ladd & Tilton's Bank, . . . [not] the ambitious but faulty structures in wood, stone and iron on which most of the citizens glori[fied] themselves." As Nash sardonically commented in 1882:

> To one who has seen real cities . . . [Portland] is but a little place; but some of its twenty-one or twenty-two thousand inhabitants raise claims to greatness and even supremacy that make it difficult to suppress a smile.[10]

Characterizing Portland as "juvenile but audacious," Nash opined that Portland's business leaders relied on what they called "the concentration of capital" to pull them through. As "toll-gate" operators, they levied "tribute" on all who passed through. They also locked up most of the city's valuable riverfront property. In the dozen years following the 1873 fire, 24 separate wharf permits were awarded to private interests by council action, creating a veritable wall 15 blocks in length. Public access to the river was totally blocked except south of Jefferson Street. Property owners who built along the riverbank of Front Street included Reed, Failing, Henry L. Pittock, the brothers James W. and Vincent Cook, Elijah and Henry W. Corbett, Joseph N. and Cyrus A. Dolph, and the Smith brothers. The Oregon Steam Navigation Company, the waterfront's largest property owner, built its central three-story addition in 1870.[11]

Living in Style

In the early 1870s, Portland's more successful merchants, shippers and profes-sionals began trading their first small, white New England-style frame houses for larger and more elaborate ones, called "mansions" in local parlance. Like their owners' commercial edifices, the new houses were outward and visible signs of success. Like Henry Failing's, they tended to be imposing, three-story, 12-to-15-room residences on entire city blocks that were worth almost as much as the houses. Opulently furnished, they had expansive gardens and meticulously groomed lawns.

The extravagant mansions of the new rich in San Francisco or Chicago or along the East Coast dwarfed them, but not for want of trying. Portland's first families crammed their homes with ostentatious marble fireplaces, heavy mahogany pieces, statuary, gilt-edged mirrors, crystal chandeliers, and oriental carpets. They draped their dark, fabric-covered downstairs walls with animal trophies, "the stuffed heads attest[ing]. . . devotion to (and success in) sport." Like most respect-able homes — not just those of the rich — they incorporated the prevalent "fash-ion for clutter," as Mary Cable has noted. "It was expensiveness that distinguished millionaire's clutter from clerk's clutter." For those unable or unwilling to buy the best, more was always better. To a dismayed Judge Deady — privately envious of his friends and supposed social equals, and their larger homes — money defined the character of Portland society.[12]

Captain Ainsworth built the first of the new houses in 1859 before moving from his substantial estate in Oregon City. Twenty-two years later, the Ainsworth resi-dence on Second and Pine streets became the first home of the Arlington Club after the Ainsworths moved to California.

Oregon Steam Navigation Company executive Simeon Reed built the second new, imposing residence, surrounded by an expansive lawn, in 1868-69. In the south side of the city, the house was topped by a stylish mansard roof, recently introduced to the Northwest. While it was still being built, Ladd thought it would be "the best in the city," and when it was finished, John Wesley Ladd praised Reed for "the finest house in Oregon." Inevitably, Deady was sarcastic. "They [the Reeds] have made a small fortune and are about to enjoy it as well as could be expected for people [who] have no children and not much intellectual culture."[13]

As if competing with their friend Reed, Jacob Kamm, Failing, Corbett, and Ladd followed suit over the next five years. Failing was sufficiently impressed with Reed's house to retain its architect, Henry Cleaveland of San Francisco. Sty-listically, both houses had similarities: bay windows, porches, towers, and man-sard roofs. Corbett's home, on the adjoining block south of Failing's, was designed in the popular "Villa" style. Using another San Francisco-trained architect, Ladd chose the "Stick" style, combining elements of the Queen Anne, long popular on the East Coast. With its elaborately high tower, Ladd's spacious estate, on two and a half city blocks, attracted wide attention. Its formal gardens included an "arbo-retum of rare plants and manicured beds of annuals grown in the sizeable conserv-atory."[14]

Cicero Lewis and his wife waited until 1880 to begin construction of a house large enough to accommodate their 11 children. The basic floor plan followed that of Failing's, which Lewis greatly admired. According to Richard Marlitt, the "exterior [was] an interesting version of the bracketed stick style at its best." Erected on a double-size block given Clementine Couch Lewis by her father, the home's location, between Northwest 19th and 20th streets, represented a significant residential shift from downtown, which was undergoing increased commercial development. The South Park Blocks similarly became a new higher-income and socially prestigious residential area in the 1880s. The Lewis house sported wide lawns, a stable, a greenhouse, and a long, sweeping driveway bordered by carefully placed trees and flowering bushes. In 1873, retired OSN executive Jacob Kamm located his 10-acre estate at the western outskirts, along 14th Street. Moved six blocks to the west in 1950, it is the only surviving mansion of nineteenth-century Portland. "Alone among the Northwest mansarded houses" of the period, writes W. K. Huntington, it was "correct in spirit and proportion to its European prototypes."[15]

Portland's elite families followed America's wealthy to Europe in the 1870s and 1880s, returning with artworks to grace or clutter their mansions. The Reeds had "little taste or training and certainly no helpful advice," according to Johansen and Gates, and "spent $20,000 for objects of dubious quality," including "scores of second-rate Munich oils of tediously sentimental themes and dull brownish tones." The Ladds and Corbetts "were more fortunately endowed and brought back to Portland fine pieces of Oriental art and popular but good examples of contemporary European schools." Failing returned from Europe in 1880 laden with several large arts works costing over $10,000 apiece, and a pair of candelabras worth $550.[16]

Pastimes of the Establishment

Enjoyable pastimes took many forms among Portland's urban Establishment in the 1870s. Farming and horse and stock breeding, if not the most popular enterprises, were certainly the most expensive. Gentlemen's farms afforded an escape from the city, or were used as rural spreads to train trotters. Ainsworth invited Alvinza Hayward, his San Francisco ally in the OSN blind pool, to "come to Oregon for the 'summer sports'" in 1868, writing of "'trotting matches with private teams nearly every evening.'"[17]

Reed (who became Portland's most celebrated gentleman horseman) and Ladd were the grandest gentlemen farmers in the area. In May, 1871, Reed bought over 7,000 acres of improved Willamette Valley farmland for $17.50 an acre. By July, he had paid $122,610 for 14 farms covering 8,023 acres. Ladd became his partner in this expansive enterprise, although the extent of the banker's involvement was never recorded. None of the jointly owned properties incorporated as the Ladd and Reed Farms, remained in Ladd's estate after his death in 1893. A farm manager believed that the two men "superintended farm affairs in alternate five year periods," with Ladd assuming his responsibility in 1877.[18]

Although Reed loved raising pure-blooded horses, stock and sheep, he did not like country life. While he may not have known good art, he knew good animals and equipage. With his coffers overflowing from the sale of the OSN to Jay Cooke, he happily paid for show-place farms and showy results. Ladd remained his tight-fisted self when he assumed management, ordering old harnesses to be mended with wire and other frugal makeshifts. In February, 1877, he complained to Reed that the farms were "a regular sinking fund losing over $2,000 a month." Winning national fame as a stockbreeder ultimately lost Reed a small fortune. With Ladd's apparent consent, he planted alfalfa and other ungrowable crops and imported Scottish Highland cattle that were unable to survive in western Oregon. Only with trotting and racing horses was he able to break even financially. He did spend $20,000 of his own money, but failed to breed a winner of the English Derby. He later lamented: "'My experience thus far has been that Horse Racing is a very expensive luxury without much fun in it either for me.'"[19]

Late in life, many members of Portland's leading families were asked to write a memoir of themselves for Hubert Bancroft's volumes on early Oregon. Ladd remembered only the happier and more positive side of his extensive farm investments, which he viewed primarily "as a relaxation." Never mentioning Reed, he recalled their Broad Meads farm in the Tualatin Valley, with "the finest herd of shorthorn cattle on the Pacific Coast." But he failed to note that the fame paid no bills. He derived greatest joy from his two solely owned farms on the east side of the Willamette: Hazel Farm, of 462 acres, which later became Laurelhurst, and Crystal Springs Farm, of 500 acres, which was later developed as Eastmoreland, the home of Reed College. The practical Ladd disdained show and racing animals. He preferred raising thoroughbred Clydesdales and breeding Guernsey and Jersey dairy herds, all in demand and all able to survive profitably.[20]

Social Entertainment

In the 1870s, Portland's self-confident elite led and happily joined the increasing number of institutions, clubs and societies devoted to dance, music, drama, and literature. After the Civil War, Deady glumly reported that "theatrical amusements never ranked high in Portland, and now are at a very low ebb." Several years later, Frances Fuller Victor noted some improvement. "Public amusements are only tolerably well supported." By 1875, however, Captain Ankeny had opened the New Market Theater, "the finest architectural achievement yet seen in the city," according to architectural historian William John Hawkins. The leading (and many not-so-leading) families flocked to the 800-seat auditorium and stage on the two upper floors of the New Market building. The luxuriously appointed theater — and the city's increasing prosperity — at last enabled Portland to attract better entertainment.[21]

The New Market Block was far more costly in building time and money (over $100,000) than Ankeny had anticipated. He followed the national fashion of incorporating culture and commerce in the same building. The block contained north and south wings for retail shops and business offices, while the central section housed a public produce market on the ground floor and the newly organized Portland Board of Trade on the mezzanine. Spirited buying and selling suffused Portland's entry into America's cultural mainstream.

Portland's elite, if often copying the ways of larger and more socially elegant cities, led the way in local entertainments and fashions, that were marked by Victorian social graces and behavior. Fancy-dress parties and balls became frequent events. Deady noted a particularly memorable "Home Ball" in January, 1876, "a sort of Presbyterian-Unitarian charity" organized by Mrs. Henry Corbett. Sixteen costumed couples danced the minuet, with Mrs. Robert R. Thompson appearing as "Lady Washington." Musical pastimes included brass-band concerts on the Plaza Blocks one or two afternoons a week. "All the youth, beauty and fashion of Portland [came] out for a promenade," Mrs. Victor reported. However, the energetic younger ones preferred the city's popular roller-skating rink.[22]

Portland's most fashionable recreation was "driving fast horses" south on Macadam Road, along the Willamette River to the White House and its adjacent Riverside Race Course. Operated by the colorful "White House Bob," the roadhouse increasingly catered to all forms of pleasure. In later years, the White House gained an "aristocratically shady" reputation until it was bought by Herman C. Leonard in 1886, moved across the street and renamed the Riverside Hotel.[23]

Organizations and Associations

Portland in the 1870s possessed most of the traditional white-male organizations found throughout America. Elite men, in general, kept to the Masonic Order (equipped with a new $60,000 hall in 1872) and to three other associations, rather than favoring more recent and, to some, more plebeian institutions like the Odd Fellows. Jewish fellowship became centered in the B'nai B'rith Oregon Lodge 65, founded in 1866. (A second one was founded in 1879.) "Just as the Masons accepted men of most religious faiths — including Jews — so the B'nai B'rith accepted Jews of all synagogues," William Toll has observed, noting:

> The gentile fraternal lodges (like the Arlington Club) in most communities contained a select mercantile and professional subgroup which helped formalize a local elite; but, because the German Jews were almost entirely within that subgroup, the B'nai B'rith, at least in its early stage, did not serve a socially selective function within the ethnic enclave. Instead, it integrated young men rather than formalizing social boundaries.[24]

In 1874, wives of young B'nai B'rith members organized the Hebrew Ladies Benevolent Society "'to administer relief to the poor, the needy, the sick, and to prepare the dead for interment.'" Initially under the direction of men, the society's leadership passed to the women with Mrs. Bernard Goldsmith's presidency in 1884. She later drew strong praise from Deady as "'an excellent woman, an admirable women. She is a woman of a great deal more than ordinary ability.'"[25]

The founding in 1879 of Portland's Concordia Club, in which Bernard Goldsmith later figured prominently, signified the emergence of a Jewish elite. Initially, its membership comprised younger clerks and owners of small businesses. Until the 1880s, according to Toll, the older, wealthier Jewish merchants "met gentile merchants as equals in Masonic lodges, partisan politics and business partnerships." As a Jewish counterpart to the Arlington Club and an outgrowth of Congregation Beth Israel, Concordia attracted younger prominent merchants like Ben Selling, Louis Fleischner, Emil Frank, Edward Ehrman, and others with south German family ties.[26]

Non-religious fraternal bonds — whether they were through a club or another association — did not appeal to Deady, even though he might have joined the Arlington Club if he could have afforded the cost. In his diary, he enjoyed deriding secret societies like the Masons, whose membership included such friends as John McCraken, Ainsworth, Flanders, Lewis, Reed, and Thompson. "There are some things," he wrote sarcastically, "about these pseudo Knights, their titles, pretensions and dress that make one smile." He characterized their ceremonies as "Masonic Mummeries," and "Pagan," in contrast to the traditionally proper rites of the Episcopal Church.[27]

The First Unitarian Society, organized in 1866, probably drew similar ridicule from Deady because Unitarians rejected the Holy Trinity, a fundamental Episcopal tenet. By commitment and tradition, the Unitarians applied their liberal theology to such problems as poverty, alcoholism, prostitution, and prison conditions. Under the leadership of their first pastor, Thomas Lamb Eliot of St. Louis, they were instrumental in awakening the upper echelon of Portland society to such human afflictions. Among the earliest church trustees were several Portland leaders: Thomas Frazar, Judge Erasmus D. Shattuck, Thompson, James W. Cook, Ankeny, and Reed. Thompson initiated monthly collections for the poor, the first of which underwrote a Thanksgiving dinner for the inmates of the county jail. During the 1870s, Reed led the church's building fund.[28]

Unitarians were active in establishing the Ladies' Relief Society in 1867, the first organized effort to coordinate numerous city-wide women's charitable causes. Within four years, the society decided to create a Children's Home for orphans and children abandoned by mothers unable to provide them proper care. It would also temporarily shelter destitute pregnant women. As with similar organizations in other small cities, society volunteers came from families of local entrepreneurs.[29]

Ladies' Relief Society members recruited Ladd to preside over its board of trustees. Ainsworth, Failing, David C. Lewis (son of Cicero Lewis), and the Reverend Thomas Lamb Eliot became fellow trustees. In 1872, the Home (as it was popularly known) moved from Couch's Addition to Southwest Corbett Street, where it remained for 37 years. Enjoying the highest social standing among Portland's volunteer institutions, it proved an abiding success and became the predecessor of the Parry Center. Corbett, a new trustee, donated $10,000 to the building fund in 1884, and bequeathed $50,000 to the Home from his estate 20 years later.[30]

The Ladies' Relief Society, the Women's Temperance Prayer League, the Hebrew Ladies Benevolent Society, and other similar organizations encouraged charitably inclined women, who could not participate directly in government, to broaden their efforts and concerns. Aided in many cases by their husbands or other local leaders, they interested themselves in economic and social conditions that the town fathers resolutely ignored or insisted were not public responsibilities. Voluntary associations channelled their efforts into numerous social concerns related to vice, liquor, drugs, prisons, education, and woman suffrage.[31]

Thomas Lamb Eliot and Abigail Scott Duniway

Thomas Lamb Eliot came from a prominent family of clergymen and educators. His father, the Boston Unitarian missionary William Greenleaf Eliot, had founded Washington University in St. Louis. A cousin, Charles William Eliot, launched his illustrious 40-year career as president of Harvard University in 1869. Within a decade of his arrival in Portland in 1867, Thomas Lamb Eliot became the city's most influential religious figure.

He wasted little time reaching out to the community. On the second Sunday of each month, he made the radical move of holding services at the County Farm, at the Insane Asylum in East Portland, or at the County Jail, where he discovered frightful conditions. Dorothea Dix's visit to Portland in the summer of 1869 had triggered his interest in penology and led to his regular prison visits and services. The famous educator, social reformer and Civil War superintendent of nurses had "insisted that Eliot escort her on an inspection trip . . . to the jail." An aroused Eliot afterwards mobilized numerous women volunteers from his Unitarian congregation into a long battle against what he called Portland's "'open sore,' a 'fearful blunder in public morality' . . . a 'black hole of Calcutta,' and a 'corporate idiocy.'" As Eliot's biographer, John F. Scheck, has commented, such criticisms "fell mostly upon deaf or indifferent ears."[32]

When Abigail Scott Duniway and her family moved to Portland in 1871, Thomas Lamb Eliot was the first and only minister to call at their house. Her reputation as an outspoken advocate of woman suffrage had preceded her, and Eliot was anxious to meet her. Duniway and Eliot became good friends and co-workers in most of the era's political and social reform movements. United in their goals, they often differed in their methods. *Oregonian* Editor Harvey W. Scott's sister was skeptical of religiously inspired moral crusades because they made little long-term impact on public and private apathy. Even though Abigail Duniway strongly admired Eliot's forthrightness, she could never bring herself to join the church even though she attended regularly when in town. To her, the ballot, not religion, was the only sure way to bring about social justice, especially for women whose economic and legal serfdom she found intolerable. With many of Portland's clergy dubious about woman suffrage, Eliot's outspoken support of Duniway's efforts made him and his church suspect in the eyes of Portland's social elite.

While Eliot refrained from personal attacks, Duniway thrived on them when provoked. Much to her brother's dismay, the first edition of her *New Northwest* weekly paper assailed Mrs. Henry W. Corbett and some friends for signing an anti-suffrage "remonstrance" to Congress in the winter of 1871. Wrote Duniway the following May:

> The wife of our worthy Senator . . . imagines that she is capable of dictating to the toiling women of America concerning what they shall and what they shall not do . . . . Does she . . . toil for half wages at double work over the wash-tub or in the kitchen . . .?

She chided the women's fear that suffrage would oppress Portland's ladies by disrupting their marriages.[33]

According to one report, Scott "'held his breath, then whistled out'"when he read the editorial in Duniway's office. He knew that the *Oregonian* would soon be mostly owned by Senator Corbett and that he would be writing for it. (Scott did not suspect that he would be fired for supporting Ben Holladay.) "'Mr. Corbett has made a great contribution to Portland business and politics. You have an ad for his business on page one. Mrs. Corbett and her friends are social leaders. You should be more discreet.'"[34]

Discretion was not one of Abigail Duniway's strong points. In the same issue of *New Northwest*, she charged Portland's city government with "'notorious laxity'" for not enforcing anti-prostitution laws, claiming that it enforced laws against "wandering cows" more strictly than against "bawdy houses." She urged women to prevent their "'sons and daughters'" from "'being snared by the sirens of sin.'" Sympathizing with prostitutes, she cited them "as victims of the double standard which judged women much more harshly than men."[35]

Duniway never aspired to inclusion in Portland's social Establishment; she thoroughly enjoyed challenging it. But her personal assaults on its leaders helped to define the Establishment's structure and character. As an influential force for change, she acquired power through her writing and her abilities in the way that Eliot did through his pulpit and community endeavors. When she spoke out, she attracted attention and even quiet support from the likes of Ladd and Joseph N. Dolph, both of whom rescued the *New Northwest* from financial disaster through interest-free loans. Dolph and his former partner, John H. Mitchell, remained her strongest financial backers among the Portland Establishment. When the national woman suffrage leader Susan B. Anthony visited Portland in June, 1871, her travel expenses from California were paid by Mitchell's close ally, Ben Holladay. However radical her pronouncements in the minds of Portland's conservatives, Abigail Duniway remained a staunch Republican, like her brother Harvey Scott. In fact, she constantly "associated liquor and prostitution with Democratic politics."[36]

Duniway and Eliot both actively supported the Portland Temperance Crusade of 1874, but for different reasons. Duniway disdained the women crusaders as "upper class" and religious snobs. She also ridiculed two young anti-suffrage ministers from the East who were Crusade organizers. However, she happily welcomed "any excitement, any fanaticism," that would "arouse in women the desire to have an *actual existence:* the desire to be a concrete number in the sum-total of humanity." She saw the Temperance Crusade as the beginning of the Oregon women's movement for greater rights and status.[37]

Eliot's aversion to alcohol reflected the strong influence of his father, a national temperance leader among Unitarians. Refusing to use sacramental wine in the communion service, he substituted grape juice. But, as Scheck has noted, "Eliot's chief objections to alcohol were social rather than sacramental." Drunkenness remained almost epidemic in the 1870s, as earlier in Portland's history, when, according to Scott, "drinking was carried to a most ruinous extreme." Reports varied as to the exact number of saloons, but Police Chief James Lappeus (himself a saloon owner) listed 71 liquor outlets in January, 1876 — one for every 200 Portlanders. Portland was a wide-open saloon town, with such well-known establishments as the Oro Fino (where Eliot occasionally held Sunday services), the Liva, the Oreflame and the Webfoot. The most notorious saloons lined Yamhill Street's "Court of Death." Editor Scott called them "deadfalls without exception; poisonous dens from whence little gusts of viciousness puffed into the streets, pushing before them cargoed demi-reps."[38]

The Portland Temperance Crusade was launched in March, 1874, when 12 determined Women's Temperance Prayer League members descended upon Walter Moffett's popular saloon. Thus began a month-long battle known locally as "The War on the Webfoot Saloon." A stunned Moffett insisted that he ran a respectable shop and always gave customers full measure. Law-abiding and generally peaceful, the former city council member was, moreover, a quite substantial citizen, with assets exceeding $50,000 in 1870, before the 1873 fire destroyed all his saloons except the Webfoot. Near-violent confrontations with the fearless women merely turned anguish to anger.[39]

After their arrest for disturbing the peace, and the judge's dismissal of the complaint, the women returned a week later and attracted a large crowd. Fights erupted between customers and male temperance sympathizers. According to Malcolm Clark, "guns and knives were drawn, chairs were thrown about, glass was smashed," before the police restored order. The next day, 21 women returned and were arrested for disorderly behavior. Former Governor Addison Gibbs ably defended the six crusaders actually brought to trial. Jury foreman Robert R. Thompson, leading contributor to and trustee of the First Unitarian Church, was even more uncomfortable than his peers. His young new minister, Thomas Lamb Eliot, had personally urged the women to action. Finding them guilty, the jury recommended mercy. The defendants rejected the verdict by demanding justice. They refused to pay the $5 fine and were sentenced to 24 hours in the new city prison. Police Chief Lappeus opposed their spending the night in custody. They were released and ordered home late in the evening without an escort, a degrading experience. Although they had lost the battle, the war had just begun.[40]

The crusader ranks grew, together with increased attacks on the saloon trade, urged on by local clergy under Eliot's leadership. Duniway became actively involved after the Temperance League published the explosive *Voter's Book of Remembrance*, which linked the liquor and brothel trades as one evil. In her *New Northwest*, she proclaimed hopefully: "We saw that your failure [to close the saloons] . . . would open your eyes to the power of the ballot." Aroused voters had just elected three new councilmen, including the Independent Democrat Robert R. Thompson, who swung the council temporarily against the saloon interests.[41]

Public School Trials

Eliot's immersion in the temperance movement coincided with his election as Multnomah County superintendent of schools (1872-76), a part-time position that did not conflict with his pastoral responsibilities. His willingness to undertake the task reflected his civic commitment and the priority that Portland's first families gave to public education. Apart from business and politics, public education elicited the greatest interest of local leaders who dominated the school boards from 1855 to 1878. Six of the 24 members during that period served 38 of the 72 annual erms. Josiah Failing served 10 years; Judge Erasmus D. Shattuck, eight; Ladd, even; Ainsworth, six; Thomas J. Holmes, four; and Asa Lovejoy, three. Also drawn o the school board from the upper social ranks were Joseph N. Dolph, who erved three years, and former Mayor James A. Chapman and Dr. Rodney Glisan, who each served one term. As in Chicago after 1870, according to Frederic Cople aher, "Premier entrepreneurs and their offspring served mostly in park commis- ionerships [of which Portland had none until 1900]and on the board of education . . . These positions were marginal to the preservation of group power."[42]

A majority of Portland's school board directors actually enrolled their own children in private schools, where classes were smaller and religious instruction was often available. (Many of the same children were later sent to prestigious eastern boarding schools.) Ladd, Lovejoy, Josiah Failing, and Shattuck, among other school board directors, were also trustees of one or more private schools in Portland. Some of them, including Ladd and Dolph, had briefly been teachers in the East. They firmly believed an educated citizenry essential to a community's economic growth and social stability.

As tax-conscious business leaders, the school directors wanted public educa- tion conducted in a businesslike manner, though they were constrained by tax- payers who neglected the school system and other municipal services (with the possible exception of the police). In the late 1860s, annual school budgets approxi- mated $10,000 — an average cost of $10 per student. Teachers in the first through sixth grades, confronting class sizes of from 24 to 88 pupils, received an average pay of $650 a year. All such expenditures were thoroughly scrutinized by the thrifty Ladd, whose fellow director Ainsworth recalled his disapproval in May, 1874, of the school district's paying for students' ink, pens and penholders. Ladd remembered how earlier Portland students made their own ink by boiling oak bark and bringing it to school in animal horns. Ainsworth informed the banker that the school now bought its ink in large wholesale batches. The quality was better, and the supply more assured. But it was hard to convince a man who sliced open envelopes and used the inner sides for letter paper.[43]

Possibly the most vexing issue for the directors during the 1860s and '70s was the enrollment of black students, then commonly known as "coloreds." Board members were not about to oppose the prevailing anti-black feeling in Multno- mah County. When they were forced to act, and to establish a "colored"school, they ran the newly segregated system as cheaply as possible.

Until challenged in 1867 by Maryland-born shoemaker William Brown, who was one of the fewer than 200 black residents in Portland, the city's 16 black children had been denied the public education guaranteed all children by legisla- tion. When the school board members refused to hear Brown, he secured legal aid from a sympathetic student of law who forced the directors to recognize his children's rightful claim. But the directors still resisted on grounds of cost. "'If we admit them,'" they argued, "'then next year we will have no money to run the schools'" Directors Ladd, Shattuck and Josiah Failing seemed afraid to provoke the taxpayers' reactions.[44]

Negotiations ensued, and a public meeting on March 23, 1867, resolved that the district should commit $800 for a separate "colored" school. Refusing the compromise, black parents began court action while again unsuccessfully attempting to enroll their children. Ladd later recalled advising them: "Do not go to the law. The prejudice against you here is very strong. It won't do to call in the police to protect your children." But if black parents accepted a separate elementary school, and if their children "by dilligence prepare[d] themselves for the higher departments," they would "fit themselves for promotion [and] . . . slip into the upper grades, and then nobody . . . [would] dare object." On July 19, 1867, Judge Shattuck, one of the three school board directors, refused in circuit court to order the admittance of Brown's children. (None challenged his lack of impartiality.) The appellants conceded to the compromise, and the one-teacher so-called Colored School opened in the fall of 1867. The district rented the building from Judge Shattuck for $60 a term.[45]

The Colored School discontinued operation at the end of the 1872 school year, when local voters approved admitting black children to the three district elementary schools. Of the 1,048 students enrolled in December, 1873, 30 were black and were spread evenly among 21 classes. Few, if any, black children went beyond the sixth grade in the ensuing years. In his later account, Ladd glossed over the basic issues of schooling for blacks. He remembered himself as a "real democrat," whose "democracy did not influence him to go contrary to his convictions of humanity and justice."[46]

Culture and Cash: The Library Association

Banker Ladd and Judge Shattuck enjoyed greater harmony when they were helping to establish a subscription library in Portland. The rented reading room into which Hugh O'Bryant, the town's illiterate but well-meaning first mayor, had stuffed used books and magazines had closed in 1856 for lack of funds. Portland was left with only the small Athenian Library Association, organized in 1862 by attorney Julius Caesar Moreland and closed to public use.

From colonial times, library movements had been private endeavors, inspired and financed by wealthy citizens. Believing libraries to be essential ingredients of urban culture, affluent merchants and prominent attorneys had generally taken the initiative. Many of the large private libraries, like New York City's Astor and Lenox collections, provided the foundations for future municipal public libraries, as occurred in Portland with the addition of the John Wilson collection in 1900. Like most new cities, Portland resorted to subscription as the only way to fund and build a library available to a paying public.[47]

Late in 1863, Wilson's partner, the merchant Leland H. Wakefield, began a house-to-house canvass to raise funds for a reading room and library. Ladd was the first to subscribe. On January 12, 1864, Ladd, Shattuck, Wakefield, Lewis, Henry Failing, Judge Deady, Henry W. Corbett, and other subscribers met to form the Mercantile Library Association. Deady, who probably suggested the name change to the less restrictive Library Association of Portland, was elected president of the temporary organization. At the time, none wanted a tax-supported free public library. The founders also proclaimed that "the library should forever be kept free of politics." Membership initiation fees were set at $5 and annual dues at $12.[48]

By March, 1864, 153 members had subscribed $2,500. The first permanent officers elected were: Ladd, president; attorney William Strong, vice-president; Bernard Goldsmith, treasurer; City Clerk William S. Caldwell, recording secretary; and Henry Failing, corresponding secretary. Rooms were rented on the second floor of Stark's Building at 66 First Street, and Harvey Scott was appointed part-time librarian, a post he would hold for 15 months before becoming editor of the *Oregonian*. Within one year, 600 of 1,400 volumes ordered from New York had arrived, by 1878, the collection surpassed 8,700, requiring the library's removal to more spacious quarters above the Ladd & Tilton Bank.[49]

Dreaming of a free public library, Deady, who served as president from 1874-1893, devoted much of his non-judicial time to raising building funds until two years before his death in 1893. He conceived the idea, modelled on eastern practices, of selling life memberships for $200 and perpetual memberships, which could be bequeathed, for $250. (Those fees still apply.) To Deady, it was "hard" and "disagreeable" work, "like pulling teeth," to squeeze money and pledges from nearly everyone he encountered, even Ben Holladay. Facing unusual resistance from those "closefisted narrow visioned millionaires" in January, 1888, Deady confided in his diary: "The rich men of Portland will never do much for it until they die, and maybe not then."[50]

Deady's judgment, colored by frustration, may seem over-harsh, but he did prophesy correctly that Portland's rich would never do much for the library before they died. The first major bequest — $5,000 — came in 1883 from the estate of a druggist, Stephen Skidmore, who was intensely interested in cultural and civic affairs. The second major bequest — $6,250 — came in 1886 from the estate of attorney Morris Fechheimer, a young friend of Deady. Of a total of over $300,000 in major gifts to the building, maintenance and debt-reduction funds, received through 1904, estate bequests amounted to $173,700. The largest — $127,500 — came in 1889 from the residuary estate of Miss Ella M. Smith, daughter of pioneer Captain Benjamin F. Smith. The Failing family gave $67,300, nearly half of it received before Henry Failing's death in 1898. The Henry Corbett family followed with $32,000. Simeon and Amanda Reed gave $20,000, and the Cicero Lewis family, $17,000. Businessman and former U.S. Marshal Edward S. Kearney, and his wife, close friends of Deady, gave $11,000. Ladd bequeathed $20,000 in 1893. Former merchant John Wilson's 8,000-volume bequest in 1900 was valued at $20,711. (He also bequeathed $2,500 in gold for an endowment.)[51]

It took 27 years of dedicated effort to raise $156,000, enough to construct a solid, stone, two-story library for 20,000 volumes. Opened in 1891, it filled a prominent place in Portland's expanding cultural life. With a few exceptions, the same small group that supported most of the more enlightened causes, like public schools, parks and private welfare agencies, gave the largest sums to the library. As Ladd commented in 1889, the library "kept its doors open . . . for many years without resources or aid save the faith and true friendship of comparatively a few persons."[52]

By 1890, when Corbett and Failing made their first large gifts, Portland's wealthiest citizens had already built their large homes and commercial buildings. The library became a symbol of their expanding urban culture as they perceived and shaped it. Blending wealth with culture was, after all, a long-standing American tradition. And it was Henry Failing's belated example and leadership, following upon Deady's strenuous efforts, that provided the major force for the library's financial growth. In contrast to most of his close friends, Failing continued his learning throughout his life, reading widely in literature, science and the arts. He had begun work in a New York mercantile firm at the age of 12, and believed in the strong classical education denied him in his early schooling. President of the Portland Library Association after Deady, and of the University of Oregon Board of Regents, he developed an emotional and intellectual commitment to learning that was transmitted to his family. As with other similar efforts, strong family and social relationships, bound closely by business and property ties, provided the underlying financial support of the library by future generations of Portland's Establishment.

10.1 Some of Portland's elite women and friends, c. 1864: (Standing) Mrs. Henry
Law, Mrs. Charles Hodge, Mrs. Henry Failing, Mrs. G. Collier Robbins, Mrs.
(J.L.?) Hallet, Mrs. Cicero H. Lewis. (Seated) Mrs. (A.L.?) Woodworth, Mrs.
R.B. Wilson, Mrs. Thomas Robertson, Mrs. William S. Ogden, Mrs. Henry W.
Corbett, Mrs. Bradford

10.2 Ladd & Tilton Bank, 1868

10.4 Joseph S. Smith (1824-1884)

10.3 Frank Dekum (1829-1894)

10.5 Interior of Simeon Reed home, built 1868-1869

10.6 Jacob Kamm home, built 1872-1873

10.7 William S. Ladd home, built 1874-1875

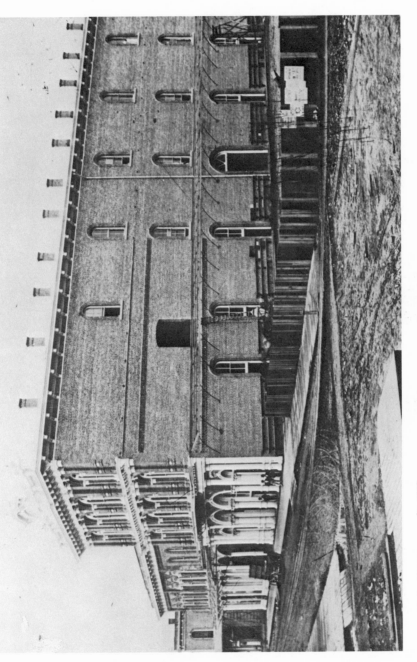

10.8 New Market Theater, opened in 1872

10.9 The Children's Home, c. 1895

10.10 The Rev. Thomas Lamb Eliot (1844-1936)

10.11 Abigail Scott Duniway (1835-1915) with her *New Northwest,* first issued in May, 1871

10.12 Crowd outside the new city jail when it held convicted Temperance Women Crusade participants, 1874

10.13 The Park Blocks (right), 1878, after eight of its blocks were sold and built upon. The tower is on the Ladd School, now the site of the Portland Art Museum

11

HENRY VILLARD CHALLENGES PORTLAND:1872-1885

The OSN Steams Ahead

During the 1870s, Portland continued to strengthen itself as the center of Pacific Northwest banking, trade and water-borne transportation. Pursuing traditional lines of commerce and finance was the preferred course of action for most of the city's business leaders. Remembering the failure of the Oregon Iron Company in 1869, they eschewed the risks of investing in new manufacturing ventures except those designed to meet local consumer needs. "Portland remained, as it began, primarily a commercial city," as one historian has put it.[1]

As the state's population nearly doubled in the 1870s, from 90,923 to 174,763, the fortunes of the region's leading commercial enterprise, the Oregon Steam Navigation Company, grew proportionately. Greater demand for its service came from eastern Oregon, which attracted more settlers than the Willamette Valley because of its greater opportunities for wheat growing and stock raising. Using proceeds from the company's sale to Jay Cooke, the OSN added four new ships between 1870 and 1873. These acquisions increased the company's strategic control of the region's gateways. Charging all the traffic would bear, the OSN incurred the wrath of nearly every agricultural producer in eastern Oregon.

In August, 1870, the Baker City *Bedrock Democrat* blasted the OSN as "'a positive curse to Eastern Oregon, Idaho and Washington Territories . . . . Ainsworth, Reed and Ladd were each and all poorer than skimmed milk before they embarked on this enterprise.'" The *Democrat* called them "'codfish aristocrats, . . . sordid and grasping,'" adding that they were filled with "'overreaching avarice . . . .'"

About all they had to do was to stand, at each end of the route, and shovel the gold dust into their coffers with a scoop-shovel. It is no wonder that they are now living in princely style, in palatial mansions, or making the tour of Europe; or that they give $500 a year for a cushioned pew in one of the churches of Portland.[2]

205

The *Walla Walla Union* condemned the OSN as "'the most soulless and little hearted set of monopolists that ever cursed a country.'" The company's chief officers, Simeon Reed and John Ainsworth, paid little heed to such editorial attacks, especially from back-country papers. But Reed was sensitive to local caricatures. On one occasion, when J.W. Hayes was working for the telegraph company, a wire came for "S. Greed." He figured the recipient must be S.G. Reed, the error being that of a new operator. When Reed saw the wire, "he blew up."[3]

As general manager of the OSN's operations, Reed was responsible for most of the company's expansion during the 1870s. With a sharp eye for detail, he controlled costs tightly. In September, 1868, examining the dining-room expenses for each ship, he had commended his food supervisor for reducing the losses on four boats by 30 percent. According to the *Oregonian*, it was the company's policy "'to keep all their boats in the best possible running trim. No sooner does one of the steamers show the least sign of want of repair than it is ordered to the boneyard . . . for an overhauling and another . . . boat takes the place.'" The company expended $1,897,467 on purchases and construction between 1872 and 1879.[4]

The same efficiency and concern for quality that marked Reed's management of the OSN were evident in all aspects of his life. He was "a kind of industrial enlightenment figure," according to Barnett Singer, "always on the lookout for new equipment and techniques, providing the cost factor was not prohibitive." As in his farm operations and cattle purchases, he sought out "'the best,'" whether for new elevator equipment for one of his buildings or for his cigars and business suits. From his New York tailor, he once requested a suit "'of fashionable cut and material suitable for Fall and Winter wear.'" From his New York tobacconist, he ordered "2,000 'assorted' cigars." His supplier added another 3,000, noting that "'theprices [were] as low'" as those sold "to the largest jobbers." To assuage his love of hunting, "he procured the finest of guns and dogs."[5]

In bearing, style of life and curiosity, Reed was admirably qualified to be the OSN's front man in national and regional affairs. His outgoing personality and self-confidence allowed him to move easily in "the political and business world — whether that of provincial Portland, New York, or the nation's capital," Dorothy Johansen has observed. He particularly enjoyed the limelight in Washington, D.C., where he met important politicians like Congressman Thaddeus Stevens and Vice-President Schuyler Colfax, both ardent railway expansionists. On one occasion, he was invited to lunch with President Ulysses S. Grant, whom he had known in 1853 when Grant was stationed at Fort Vancouver.[6]

After joining the board of the Northern Pacific Railroad, Reed received a letter from William M. King stressing the political possibilities of his new position: "'The supreme control of the great Enterprise . . . properly Manipulated will Enable you to dictate the politics of your North West.'" Colonel King, former Speaker of the Oregon House and a long-time fellow Mason, spoke from experience as Portland's foremost political manipulator of the 1850s. Reed was no manipulator, but he was a cleverly practiced lobbyist and wire-puller whenever the OSN's interests were at stake. He likely arranged in 1871 for William S. Ladd's partner C.E. Tilton to pay a judge in Washington, D.C., $1,200 of OSN funds to persuade President Grant to veto a congressional bill introduced by Oregon Senator George H. Williams on behalf of Ben Holladay. To Reed, a nominal Republican by 1871, politics was the servant of economic interests; partisan political loyalties were essentially meaningless. According to Johansen, "it was said that at political rallies he marched in the torch-light processions down one street with his party and up another street with his Democratic friends and business associates."[7]

The profit-driven strategy of the OSN leadership rewarded its stockholders handsomely. Even during the depression year of 1873-74, Ainsworth, Reed, Robert R. Thompson and William S. Ladd received a total of $300,000 in OSN dividends. Cost containment, luxurious passenger service and monopolistic freight rates created and sustained the veritable cash machine that was bitterly resented by the eastern Oregon merchants and farmers. As The Dalles *Weekly Mountaineer* commented in September, 1873: "'We do not believe there is any place in the United States where freights are as high for water transportation, as on the Columbia River route.'" The rate from Portland to The Dalles (80 miles), "$15 a ton, was the same rate as that charged for a ton of freight from New York, or from China, to Portland," according to Johansen.[8]

The panic of 1873 barely affected OSN operations. While the nation suffered for five years, the Northwest recovered quickly. Being industrially underdeveloped, the region escaped major economic disruptions. OSN ship owners Ainsworth, Reed and Thompson made ever larger fortunes as the domestic wool and foreign wheat trades continued unabated.

The Arrival of Henry Villard

The panic of May, 1873, triggered by the refusal of German and Austrian banks to purchase additional American rail bonds, precipitated the collapse of the powerful banking firm of Jay Cooke & Company in September. The ensuing national depression also brought about Ben Holladay's doom when he was unable to obtain further funds.

Between 1870 and 1872, German investors had unwittingly bought $10.95 million of 7 percent bonds issued on Holladay's Oregon & California Railroad by the London & San Francisco Bank. Holladay defaulted on interest payments in October, 1872, and over the next 18 months. While English investors who had bought additional bonds were initially protected, German bond-holders received nothing. After a second default in October, 1873, following the panic, the Germans dispatched a trusted representative to find out what had happened.[9]

The arrival in New York of the 38-year-old Bavarian-born Henry Villard in the spring of 1874 "marked the entry into American railroad affairs" of one who, in Glenn Chesney Quiett's judgment, "became the king-pin of transportation in the Northwest," linking the destiny of the Holladay and Northern Pacific rail systems with that of Portland's Oregon Steam Navigation Company. Villard's "meteoric flight across the financial skies was the sensation of two continents." What Holladay and Cooke had begun would be completed and enhanced by the shrewd, energetic and magnetic former newsman.[10]

The highly experienced emissary was the friend of many international bankers and American political leaders. Renowned as the *New York Tribune*'s Washington correspondent during the Civil War, Villard had achieved further prominence by marrying the abolitionist editor William Lloyd Garrison's daughter Helen. Whether in the United States or abroad in subsequent years, Villard kept abreast of Oregon's affairs either in person or through his agents. In the Pacific Northwest, he eventually won support from Portland's business leadership, including OSN stockholders Ainsworth, Ladd, Reed, and Robert R. Thompson, who at first were wary of the forceful young German.

The OSN Bonanza

By mid-1874, the OSN leaders had much more on their collective minds than Holladay's growing financial troubles or Villard's impending arrival. The panic had exposed President Jay Cooke's Northern Pacific as "a house of cards," in Albro Martin's judgment. Expenditures had run totally out of control as Cooke, an absentee manager, desperately tried to continue the railroad's construction in the Washington Territory. In mid-1873 he had unsuccessfully solicited additional funds from his western capitalist associates Reed, and Ainsworth, who was manager of the Northern Pacific's western division. But Portland investors remained their cautious selves. The recent Credit Mobilier scandal, involving Union Pacific Railroad construction funds, had cooled their interest. And Reed's discovery that Northern Pacific bonds were selling at a marked discount revealed that Cooke was in serious trouble.[11]

Cooke had wired Ainsworth in June, 1873, that no more than $30,000 remained to complete some 30 miles of track in Washington between Kalama and Tacoma, the recently chosen western terminus of the Northern Pacific. Portlanders' dreams of a transcontinental rail link looked bleak. When the Northern Pacific entered receivership in September, 1873, upon failure of the House of Cooke, mainline construction ceased. Ainsworth immediately organized a new company, consisting of himself, Reed and Thompson, to finish the job by the federal charter deadline. Ignoring Northern Pacific orders (from the railroad's new president, George Cass) to build only a temporary line to Tacoma, the partners contributed $76,000 of their own money to complete the line as planned. (Ainsworth forced the crews onward while Reed and Thompson supervised the hurried delivery of iron and other supplies. They drove the last spike on December 16, 1873, only 24 hours before the deadline.[12]

Reed and Ainsworth were motivated far more by financial self-interest than by their corporate directoral responsibilities. Their Northern Pacific bonds, received in exchange for half their OSN stock in 1870, had already dropped to 10 cents on the dollar. Any hope of recouping their losses lay in making the railroad profitable. Although the shrewd Thompson had sold his bonds two years earlier, he felt obligated to support his partners in the most strenuous three-month effort any of them ever undertook. While the Kalama-to-Tacoma segment of the mainline was only a fraction of the overall system, it was crucial to the federal charter requirements, and thus releasing further federal subsidies.[13]

In the spring of 1874, fortune intervened for the three Portlanders and their associate William S. Ladd. Their OSN stock, which had been sold to Cooke in

1870, had never been turned over to the Northern Pacific; it became part of Cooke's bankrupt estate in the hands of the financier's creditors. Cooke's trustees and creditors were not informed of the stock's true market value. Eastern financial markets were unaware that during the depression year of 1873-74 the OSN had experienced one of its more profitable periods. As part payment to the creditors, the trustees placed Cooke's OSN stock on public sale at a marked discount. Ainsworth, Reed, Thompson, and Ladd quietly repurchased their former stock from the trustees, who were only too willing to sell for an average of 20 cents on the dollar. It took them nearly five years to regain full control of the company. No one knew better than they the true value of their bonanza, but Villard was soon to find out.[14]

Villard Seals Holladay's Fate

Henry Villard journeyed to New York City in April, 1874, with two assignments: to execute a plan devised by the Frankfurt bondholders' committee and Ben Holladay's creditors; and to act as receiver for the Kansas Pacific Railroad, which had likewise defaulted on interest payments owed another group of Frankfurt bondholders.

Unlike those in most American financial institutions, German investors and bankers rejected foreclosure in favor of a longer-term course of keeping enterprises in operation. Villard carried a contract with four basic provisions: that Holladay place his corporate properties in trust to prevent their sale or transfer to another party or their use as collateral; that he draw no more than $6,000 in annual salary; that he first pay off the interest and principal on the still-profitable Oregon Steamship Company; and that he next begin to reduce the indebtedness of the Oregon & California and Oregon Central railroads.[15]

Villard met Holladay in New York and presented him with the contract, which Holladay wanted more time to consider before signing. Agreeing to meet soon in Portland, Villard secretly left on an inspection trip to San Francisco, and to Roseburg, the southern terminus of the Oregon & California Railroad. He found many doubtful ventures, misspent funds, and an unaccounted Holladay expenditure of $250,000 to "make Oregon a Republican state." Stories of Holladay's opulent and riotous living reinforced Villard's resolve to make him accept the contract terms.[16]

When the two men resumed negotiations in Portland, Holladay reluctantly signed the contract. Villard then returned to Germany, leaving his assistant Richard Koehler in Portland to monitor Holladay's behavior. In his report to the German bondholders' committee, Villard couched whatever doubts he may have had about Holladay within a broader context of Oregon's promising railroad prospects. His enthusiastic impressions of the state obviously colored his judgment. Overawed by Oregon's beauty, and the Willamette Valley's fertility, he assured the bondholders' committee that the Oregon & California Railroad could become profitable if the committee would organize an immigration program to promote the region's attractions. He also recommended a southern extension of the westside Oregon Central Railroad, and costly service improvements for the Oregon Steamship Company.[17]

Reports in 1874 and 1875 that Holladay was violating his contract in numerous ways, defaulting again on interest payments, and even trying to sell the O&C property to Collis P. Huntington of the Central Pacific Railroad, galvanized the German bondholders to assume control of Holladay's three major corporations. For an annual payment of $18,000, they would acquire all his corporate stock, and for an additional $200,000, they would purchase the Portland Dock and Warehouse Company. Holladay reluctantly acceded on February 29, 1876, and by August was finished as a large-scale operator anywhere. A reputed $2 million in Portland real estate, as well as Holladay's New York estate and many personal assets went to pay his creditors. His Oregon Real Estate Company, which had developed parts of Holladay's Addition in East Portland, was gradually liquidated. The sale of its final portions in April, 1888, to satisfy $330,000 of estate debts a year after his death, prompted Judge Deady to conclude: "It has been a long chase on the creditors part but I suppose the game is bagged at last."[18]

Holladay's and Cooke's failures halted major railroad construction in Oregon for several years. A worried Portland Board of Trade (organized in 1874) approached the Central Pacific's Huntington in April, 1876, for a Portland transcontinental connection, linking Roseburg and Winnemucca, Nevada. However, Huntington's reply to Board of Trade members William S. Ladd, Henry Failing, Bernard Goldsmith and John McCraken was not encouraging. He expressed interest but stated that "the Oregon constitution for[bade] the creation of any state debt beyond a certain trifling sum." The state, he said, would have to sell $25 million in bonds and guarantee whatever private investments were secured. Annual interest payments could run to $210,000. Huntington saw little chance of Oregon's providing direct public subsidies for railroad construction, and there was insufficient private capital in the state to undertake such a venture and ensure its profitable operation. Population density was too thin to support a railroad financed by local funds.[19]

Villard was well aware of these realities when he returned to Germany during the winter of 1875-76. Some thought had already been given to the role that he and his German backers might play in raising the necessary capital to make Portland the western terminus for a transcontinental railroad. Thus he became deeply disturbed some months later to learn of the Board of Trade's inquiry to Huntington. He criticized the Portland business leaders "for not consulting" him on their desire to connect to the Central Pacific, a project that appeared dead in any case. Villard politely reminded his friends that European interests had "contributed largely to the prosperity of Oregon."[20]

Portland's business leaders would not have known that Villard had already been given new responsibilities by the time they approached Huntington. After his return to Germany, the Frankfurt bondholders had been so pleased with his conduct of their affairs that they appointed him managing director of their Oregon properties. In effect, Villard became presidents of the Oregon & California and Oregon Central railroads and of the Oregon Steamship Company. Still vague in his plans, he pondered securing capital from Boston and New York financiers, and to this end, established headquarters in the heart of New York's financial district. The summer of 1876 marked Villard's transition from "bondholders' representative to entrepreneur."[21]

Villard Eyes the OSN

By September, 1876, when Villard returned to Portland from New York, he had developed a plan for using Ainsworth's thriving monopoly to buy out the German bondholders and put himself in control of their Oregon enterprises. The key to the scheme was the Union Pacific Railroad, a majority of whose stock was in the hands of New York financier Jay Gould, America's most notorious and detested speculator. Villard approached Ainsworth about OSN participation with the UP in building a rail line between Portland and Salt Lake City — Ogden, along a route already surveyed by the UP (a project long advocated by former Portland proprietor William W. Chapman). The line would follow the Columbia River as the easiest and cheapest route to tidewater. While Reed favored the idea, Ainsworth was skeptical, largely because of his well-founded mistrust of Jay Gould.[22]

No further approaches were made to the OSN over the next 18 months while Villard first negotiated with Gould on the UP's purchase of the Kansas Pacific Railroad, whose German bondholders he also represented. By early 1878, Gould met Villard's price, enabling the German financier to concentrate his attention on the Pacific Northwest. Villard's success in outmaneuvering the crafty speculator — considered a major victory in New York's financial markets — enhanced his national reputation and increased his ambition to become the dominant leader in Northwest transportation.[23]

In May, 1878, Villard proposed to Ainsworth that they merge the old Holladay properties with the OSN to form a giant transportation monopoly. He and his New York backers had devised a complicated financial plan offering payment of $1 million in cash and $2 million in newly issued stock. Neither Ainsworth nor Reed favored the scheme, primarily because the offer was too low. Both men also saw the proposal as nothing more than an attempt by Villard to use OSN profits to buy out the Frankfurt bondholders, and feared that Villard was adopting Holladay's strategy of using a profitable shipping company to finance and control a railroad. Villard failed to understand that he needed the OSN more than the OSN needed him.[24]

Nothing further transpired for nearly a year, as the OSN continued to generate increased profits while adding more ships to the fleet. During the interval, when the OSN attained the height of its power, Villard and Gould created a loose working relationship by forming the Oregon Construction and Improvement Company to build a rail line from Ogden to Portland. They soon realized that control of the "grand monopoly of the Columbia, the Oregon Steam Navigation Company," was essential for gaining direct access to Portland.[25]

The Oregon Railway & Navigation Company

Villard made a new proposal at a second meeting with Ainsworth in May, 1879. The shrewd Ainsworth handled the negotiations alone with a Villard whom he considered unduly arrogant. Thompson had moved to California, Reed was in Europe and Ladd was not consulted. Villard's bid was still too low for Ainsworth, who then took him on a tour of the properties which were appraised at $3.3

million. Greatly impressed, Villard met Ainsworth's price of $5 million, representing the company's full capital value. For each $100 share, OSN stockholders would receive $50 in cash (totalling $2 million), $20 in bonds, and $30 in stock of the new enterprise, which Villard planned to call the Oregon Railway and Navigation Company.[26]

Ainsworth still needed the confirming votes of other OSN stockholders. From New York, Reed, after failing to reawaken Northern Pacific interest in Portland as a major terminus (and thus encouraging a higher offer than Villard's), wired his consent on May 23. Also from New York, C.E. Tilton, the fifth-largest stockholder, wired his enthusiastic acceptance: "'We must make some money out of this for we may not get another so good a thing.'" Ladd agreed with Tilton, but Thompson initially balked. Although trusting his friend's judgment, he urged Ainsworth to demand more than $2 million in cash. Undissuaded by Thompson, Ainsworth signed the sale contract. The major stockholders were handsomely rewarded. Ainsworth, Ladd, Reed, Tilton, and Thompson each netted between $800,000 and $1 million (at current values, approximately $10 million to $13 million). Jacob Kamm, George Weidler (Holladay's former associate), and other Portland stockholders, who had purchased some of Cooke's shares, received lesser amounts. The OSN properties were formally transferred to the OR&N on April 1, 1880.[27]

Of the $6 million in new stock, Villard issued approximately 60 percent to himself, 30 percent to the OSN stockholders, and 10 percent to such Portland investors as Henry Failing, Cicero H. Lewis, David P. Thompson, and Henry W. Corbett, who became resident directors with Ainsworth, Ladd and Reed. The $2 million in cash to former OSN stockholders came as a loan from the Farmers Loan & Trust Company of New York, with Villard's new OR&N stock as collateral. Villard successfully sold the first issue of OR&N bonds through a London syndicate. Bond proceeds went for initial OR&N railroad construction and for paying off the long-suffering Holladay bondholders. With their elimination late in 1880, Villard gained full control of Holladay's former railroad and shipping properties. As Ainsworth had anticipated, he used the substantial OR&N profits to service his debts.[28]

Ainsworth at first agreed to manage the OR&N for an indefinite period, but soon became disturbed by Villard's authoritarian manner of making decisions without consulting management or local directors. He also worried over the increase in Villard's expenditures and his commitment to rapid rail expansion. Ainsworth resigned early in 1880 and moved to his new home in Alameda, California. (The Arlington Club leased his Portland home for $150 a month.) He also resigned his OR&N directorship and sold his stock, which had nearly doubled in value within a year. Reed, who succeeded Ainsworth, experienced similar apprehension and resigned in September the same year. His unhappiness stemmed largely from restlessness. Used to setting his own course, even under Ainsworth's official authority, he apparently yearned to explore a new entrepreneurial challenge. With a fortune of more than $1 million, he dreamed of resurrecting the Oregon Iron Company in Oswego, south of Portland. But his first venture was more prosaic: he spent $40,000 on building eight residences on a full city block near his home.[29]

On gaining control of the OR&N, Villard intended to complete the Oregon & California Railroad to the California border and to construct a rail line from Portland to Huntington, Oregon, along the south side of the Columbia River. Originally he counted on splitting the cost with Gould, but the latter pulled out in July, 1879, under pressure from the Central Pacific, whose rail line connected San Francisco to the UP at Ogden. With his construction funds curtailed, Villard directed all available resources (much to Ainsworth's and Reed's dismay) toward building the OR&N rail line eastward out of Portland; work on the O&C was halted. (No further action would be taken on the California line until 1884.) At Huntington, the OR&N would connect with the UP's Oregon Shortline, under construction from the railroad's main line at Granger, Wyoming. Villard expected to provide Portland its first transcontinental rail service by 1884.[30]

Portland's Expanding Economy

The Portland that Henry Villard planned to make his West Coast terminus experienced significant demographic and economic growth during the period 1877-1881. The city's population increased by nearly 40 percent, to reach 20,931. Commercial wealth grew at a similar pace: six enterprises were estimated by R. Dun & Company to be worth at least $1 million in 1878. Joining Allen & Lewis, Corbett & Failing, Ladd & Tilton, and the OSN were three relatively new out-of-state concerns: E. Martin & Company, San Francisco wholesale liquor dealers; Walter Brothers, San Francisco wholesale carpet merchants; and Balfour Guthrie & Company, a giant British grain dealer. Two San Francisco-based firms occupied Dun's $500,000-to-$750,000 category: A.P. Hotaling, wholesale liquor dealers; and Neustadter Brothers, wholesale men's clothiers. Four Portland-based companies were in its $300,000-to-$500,000 range: the merchants Corbitt & Macleay and L. Goldsmith, Oregon City Woolen Mills, and Northrup & Thompson Hardware. Five firms were rated at between $150,000 and $300,000. The most prominent were agricultural-equipment wholesalers Knapp & Burrell, and wholesale dry goods merchants Fleischner & Mayer. Included among the 10 businesses in the &75,000-to-$150,000 category were Dekum & Bickel, grain dealer John McCraken & Company and William Ladd's Oregon Furniture Manufacturing Company. With two or three exceptions, Portland's wealth was largely commercial.[31]

Liquor and wheat had proved to be among the more profitable generators of personal income, one from regional consumption and the other from foreign demand. In 1878, over 60 saloons served a population estimated at 16,000 (one per 266 people). As previously noted, two of the 10 liquor wholesalers, the San Francisco-based Martin and Hotaling companies, were among Portland's wealthiest commercial firms. In 1880, the city derived 34 percent of its general-fund income from liquor license fees and bonds.[32]

The arrival in Portland of Balfour Guthrie in 1877 accelerated the profits of the wheat export trade, which had already enhanced the fortunes of Allen & Lewis, Corbitt & Macleay and John McCraken. (Wheat exports doubled in value between 1876 and 1880.) Balfour Guthrie's local managing director, Walter J. Burns benefited accordingly. Inquiring of George Weidler what steps he should take to assure his future happiness and success in his new home, the Scotsman was advised: join Trinity Episcopal Church and marry a Couch. He did both, became a charter member of the Arlington Club and prospered abundantly.[33]

Burns was one of several Scots coming to Portland in the 1870s whose varied entrepreneurial talents stimulated Portland's economic growth. James B. Montgomery, a civil engineer, arrived in the Northwest in 1871 to work on the Northern Pacific roadbed running from Kalama to the Puget Sound. After settling in Pittsburgh, Pennsylvania, in 1869, he had met Jay Cooke and had helped raise $800,000 for Cooke's Northern Pacific Railroad venture. Cooke then sent him to Portland to help Ainsworth complete the rail line before the federal charter deadline. After a year spent designing bridges for the O&C railroad, in 1874, Montgomery joined a fellow Scot, William Reid, in purchasing the Albina townsite. North of East Portland and close to the waterfront on a bend in the Willamette River, the Albina tract had been platted by former U.S. Senator (and U.S. Attorney General, 1871-75) George H. Williams and Englishman Edwin Russell, manager of the Bank of British Columbia's Portland branch. When Russell, the majority owner, went bankrupt and fled mysteriously to San Francisco, Montgomery and Reid acquired the property, using Scottish capital at Reid's disposal, and promptly began developing homesites. Both men, who became charter members of the Arlington Club, later sold key riverfront property to the railroads.[34]

Glasgow-born William Reid initiated Scottish investment in Oregon. From his arrival in the spring of 1874 (after having served as U.S. vice-consul in Dundee), the well-connected Reid took Portland's business community by storm. A solid recommendation from Donald Macleay to John C. Ainsworth launched his career. From Dundee, Macleay wrote: "Mr. Reid represents an extensive company of capitalists in Scotland who are looking to our new country for an outlet of capital which we so much need." In a 10-year period, Reid attracted over $6 million of Scottish capital for investment in Northwest farming, commercial and residential property. As a first step, he organized the Portland Board of Trade, with William S. Ladd as president and himself as secretary. Within five years, he had established the Oregon, Washington Trust Investment Company; the Oregon, Washington Savings Bank; the Dundee Mortgage Company; and the Scotch Bank. To stimulate business, Reid ran provocative newspaper ads, asking readers:

DO YOU WANT TO BORROW MONEY, either to buy more land for yourselves or your sons, to build new houses and barns, to clear off brush land or otherwise improve your farms, to change your present mortgage and get a new one, or FOR ANY OTHER PURPOSE? IF YOU DO — write WILLIAM REID, PORTLAND, OREGON.

By 1890, over 10 major Scottish institutions were thriving throughout the state. As Scottish investor Robin Angus noted, the Scots sought "international diversification . . . . Diversification for opportunity, to increase wealth . . . . Scottish greed [was] . . . profitable greed."[35]

During the 1878 legislative session, Reid's influence led to the passage of a law authorizing foreign corporations to build railroads in Oregon. In February, 1880, he joined Macleay, Montgomery and Portland attorney and investor Ellis Hughes in forming the Oregon Railway Company to purchase the properties of the Willamette Valley Railroad, Joseph Gaston's former narrow-gauge line, running from Sheridan to Dayton in Yamhill County. Backed by $150,000 secured by Montgomery from Dundee (Scotland) capitalists, Reid and his associates reorganized their new venture by incorporating the Oregonian Railway Ltd. They intended to build a railroad from Dayton to Dundee (Oregon) and on to Portland as the first segment of a planned Willamette Valley line. It was appropriated, over Reid's strong protest, by Villard's OR&N in 1881.[36]

Among the early Scottish merchants and financiers, none succeeded better than Donald Macleay, whose firm amassed assets of over $300,000 in less than 12 years after his arrival in 1866. Starting as grocery and liquor merchants, Corbitt & Macleay soon became one of the largest Portland firms to export wheat to England. With the growth of salmon canneries along the Columbia (by 1874 there were 13 operating on the Oregon side), Macleay became a major salmon packer and shipper. In 1876, taking advantage of the coolie trade from Hong Kong to Portland, the firm began supplying Hong Kong with spars, ship planking and provisions. The partners bought and dispatched their own bark regularly for several years. Macleay's association with Reid involved him in railroads, which, while less profitable than some of his other ventures, led to an economic alliance with Villard and the OR&N.[37]

Macleay's shipping enterprise may have influenced his friend and fellow Arlington Club member Ainsworth to enter the Hong Kong trade. (Years later, Ainsworth's bank would merge with Macleay's U.S. National Bank.) The ink on the OR&N sale contract was barely dry when Ainsworth purchased two barks. Two years later, while living in California, he added a full-rigged ship. All three were operated out of Portland under the direction of his son George, and dispatched to Hong Kong and Australia. According to Thomas R. Cox, "Ainsworth was the largest single investor" in the Far East lumber trade by 1880. "Well received" in Hong Kong, the lumber was produced at Weidler's Willamette Steam Mills Lumbering and Manufacturing Company, adjacent to the OR&N's Ainsworth Dock in Couch's Addition. Weidler (Holladay's former associate and an agent for Villard's Oregon Steamship Company) owned Portland's largest and most profitable lumber mill at the time. Ainsworth also profited handsomely from the plant's output. According to Cox, "from an investment of $40,000 in the two barks, Ainsworth earned a profit on the first voyage of $9,810, . . . a rate being earned by few others in the seventies and eighties." In addition to his own vessels, Ainsworth chartered others to meet the Chinese and Australian demand for Oregon products.[38]

With a decline in the Far East lumber market following the passage of the Chinese Exclusion Act in 1882, Ainsworth had terminated most of his shipping operations by 1885. As Cox noted: "From the first to last, John Ainsworth's participation in the Pacific lumber trade stood outside the mainstream of the business. He was an entrepreneur seeking return on an investment in merchant vessels," a commerce he knew well. As he had with the OSN, Ainsworth sought to ship the most profitable cargoes he could find.[39]

Ainsworth lived in California until his death in 1893, but remained active in Portland business and financial affairs. Apart from shipping, he invested his OSN profits in Portland real estate and banking, but not in manufacturing or industry. At the end of his life, he owned 14 different parcels of property, from full blocks to quarter blocks. He wisely gave the management of his local interests to Lester Leander Hawkins, better known as L.L. The Ohio-born, University of California educated civil engineer became prominently involved in banking and electric power development and won national recognition as a founder of Portland's extensive park system.[40]

In 1883, Hawkins established the private banking firm of Ainsworth & Company, which was reorganized in 1885 as the Ainsworth National Bank. It was housed in the Ainsworth Block on Third and Pine streets, next to Ainsworth's former home leased to the Arlington Club. Two years in design and construction, the 1883 building "was one of the best ever to be constructed in Portland," in architectural historian William John Hawkins's judgment. Costing $100,000, its entrance was "among the grandest . . . to be found in the city."[41]

David P. Thompson's Portland

Mayor David P. Thompson, whose 1879-82 term of office paralleled the OR&N's formation and rapid expansion under Villard, had much in common with Captain John C. Ainsworth. Twelve years younger than his fellow Ohioan, Thompson had similar motives and values. Devout Masons, both men shared interests in shipping, mining, real estate, and banking, and both knew how to turn a profit. While listing himself as a "speculator" in the 1878 City Directory, Thompson was a cautious risk-taker. Like Ainsworth, he controlled his varied entrepreneurial ventures directly, accumulating the highest percentages he could exact. And finally, both men's lives were influenced by Robert R. Thompson (no relation to David). It was Robert who in 1853, had recruited the 19-year-old David to join him in driving his Merino sheep overland to Oregon.[42]

Robert R. Thompson introduced his young protege to John McCraken in Oregon City. McCraken employed him as a wood chopper at the Island Mills, where he became a willing worker for the Democratic party. Commending him to Territorial Governor George L. Curry in February, 1859, Territorial Surveyor-General L.F. Cartee called David Thompson "*a good democrat, a good man.*" Curry helped Thompson gain a patronage job as deputy U.S. surveyor for Oregon, Washington and Idaho. He returned to Oregon City during the Civil War to work for the Oregon City Woolen Manufacturing Company. In 1866 he was appointed manager of the woolen mill and won election to the state senate from Clackamas County as a Unionist. In the senate, he played a crucial role in securing legislative funding for Bernard Goldsmith's Willamette Falls Canal and Locks Company, of which he became a director. As a staunch Grant Republican in 1874, Thompson was appointed governor of the Idaho Territory. Afterwards, he moved to Portland and won election in 1878 to the Oregon House from Multnomah County.[43]

As with others, David Thompson's career showed how public office-holding could be profitable. It may have been this trait of mingling business with politics that led Judge Deady to question his honesty in 1871. The matter concerned an Oregon City Land Office bond receivership that Thompson had guaranteed for

$40,000 and which required Deady's approval. "I've no doubt," Deady wrote, "that he [Thompson] is worth three times the sum, but I have my doubts about what amount could be collected off him. He would hide his assets." Nine years later while mayor, he was accused in city council of falsifying his 1879 county assessor's return by not listing his purchase of the New Market Theater from Alexander Ankeny. The charge was not pursued when Thompson claimed that he took final possession of the property on January 5, 1881. The title records reveal that he bought 80 percent of block 33 (containing the theater) for $50,000 on August 8, 1879, and assumed an $80,000 mortgage. On January 5, 1880, he bought the remaining 20 percent for $16,666.[44]

Through the first half of his mayorship, Thompson appeared content to see Portland follow its traditional development pattern of slow, controlled commercial growth. He made good personal use of his prominence. With the railroad contractor J.W. Brazee, he organized Portland's first savings bank in 1880. Their fellow investors and directors included Frank Dekum, William K. Smith, and Cyrus A. Dolph, the brother and law partner of Joseph N. Dolph. Within 10 years, the Portland Savings Bank accumulated "paid-up capital of $125,000 with a surplus and undivided profits of $120,000." In addition to his purchase of the New Market Theater, Thompson organized a syndicate to buy 288 acres of the Irving Estate in East Portland, using savings bank funds to finance homesites. In 1881, he and the two Dolphs bought the famous block 80 in Stark's Addition from the Starr brothers, who had left Portland. On it, they designed and built Portland's largest building to that date, "one of the most expensive buildings ever constructed in the city," according to William John Hawkins. Costing well over $200,000, the Starr Block contained two large dock levels and four floors for commercial use, topped by a 140-foot tower. Within a few years of its opening in 1882, Corbitt & Macleay became the major tenants.[45]

As mayor, Thompson adhered to the traditional cautiousness of earlier merchant-banker mayors like Henry Failing. As a large property owner, he continually urged the "strictest economy in the financial management of the city . . . with the lowest tax levies." He supported borrowing funds from New York banks rather than raising taxes to amortize bonded indebtedness. He opposed the city's selling or leasing Coffin's public levee to William Reid's Oregonian Railway for depot use. He also opposed a new city charter, passed by the legislature in the fall of 1880, which strengthened the mayor's office and streamlined city administration in an effort to make the city council less divisive.[46]

It was this mode of thinking and action that provoked Villard's lieutenant, Thomas Oaks, to charge in December, 1880:

There has been a lamentable lack of enterprise here [in Portland]. A large number of persons have made a great deal of money and live in fine houses, but they have shown so little public spirit, it is not difficult to guess their money has been made almost exclusively in trade without competition, and that with the infusion of new blood they will give way to another class.[47]

Villard and Oaks were challenging Portland's business and financial leaders to wake up and recognize that the city's economic destiny was now entangled in a vast national network of high finance over which they could not hope to exercise their accustomed local control. Undoubtedly, only a handful of Portland residents could expect to participate in the speculative aspects of transcontinental railroad financing. While Ainsworth and some friends continued to doubt the wisdom of Villard's goals and methods, the city's leaders were being pressured to support his high-flying venture if they hoped to maintain their pre-eminent roles in Portland's future economic development. One who readily responded to the challenge was the ambitious 30-year-old railroad attorney Joseph Simon, a recent partner in the firm of Dolph, Mallory and Bellinger, which had drafted the OSN sale agreement with Villard. Simon had two overriding commitments: his railroad clients and the Republican party.[48]

The German-born attorney, son of a Jewish retail merchant, rose swiftly in a spectacular Oregon career. Admitted to the bar at 21 after studying law with Dolph & Mitchell, Simon established a reputation for thoroughness, tactical facility, and complete loyalty to client and party. Elected to the city council in 1877 at age 22, he achieved immediate recognition for his organizational talents, even serving as acting mayor while council president. During his three-year council term, he always espoused the interests of his railroad clients, especially William Reid and Henry Villard. More importantly for his future, he began to build a Portland power base for the state Republican party. Elected state central committee secretary in 1878, he moved up to state chairman in 1880 while winning election to the state senate, a position he was to hold for 11 years.[49]

Simon wasted little time securing legislative passage of two bills directly affecting Portland. The first measure gave the Oregonian Railway all rights granted by the State of Oregon to Coffin's public levee. Vetoed by Democratic Governor William W. Thayer, the measure was repassed over strong objections from Mayor Thompson and the council. The city filed suit with the Oregon Supreme Court, which invalidated the act in March, 1881. Simon's second bill amended the city charter (as previously described), again over vehement objections from mayor and council.[50]

Frustrated by city hall opposition and Thompson's party independence, Simon unexpectedly challenged the mayor's re-election bid in June, 1881, while not jeopardizing his own senate incumbency. Nominated by an ad hoc Republican city convention, he ostensibly based his campaign on the need for more aggressive city leadership in promoting Portland as a major railroad center. Although Mayor Thompson had proclaimed five months earlier that Portland would soon be "the great Railroad Center of the Northwest," his continued opposition to railroad acquisition of the public levee provoked Simon's real motive for challenging Thompson. He wanted to gain personal control of the state Republican party. As Thayer had at least one more year to serve as governor, capturing the Portland mayorship seemed an essential step toward reaching his goal.[51]

The Republicans had gained control of the legislature in 1880. They were to dominate the senate for 77 years and the house for 55. The prominent Portland merchant Solomon Hirsch, a partner in Fleischner & Mayer, served as senate president in 1880; and the future governor Zenas F. Moody, the state's leading wool exporter from The Dalles, was Speaker of the House. Simon's longer-range goal was to replace Oregon's Democratic U.S. representative and two U.S. senators. By 1881, he was already promoting his partner, OR&N attorney Joseph N. Dolph, to succeed Senator Lafayette Grover in 1883. No friend of John H. Mitchell, Simon would try almost any tactic to prevent the former senator's re-election.[52]

The mayor's race of June, 20, 1881, proved ill-advised — one of the few mistakes Simon ever made. The *Oregonian* flayed him for putting his own political interests ahead of the city's. Running as an independent Republican, Thompson received the backing of a citizens' committee headed by Frank Dekum and George J. Ainsworth. The *Oregonian* editorialized that Thompson would promote "the great business and commercial interests of the City," and that his candidacy represented the "People over Party." Two days before the election, the *Oregonian* accused Simon of "stealing the levee."[53]

Surprising the older Republicans, Simon won an apparent victory by nine votes, but his triumph was short-lived. Charging gross corruption and bribery, the *Oregonian* and Mayor Thompson demanded a recount. According to the paper, Thompson got two-thirds of the Republican vote and Simon carried the Democratic wards. Two days later a tally error was discovered, giving Thompson a surprising one-vote margin for re-election. Refusing to concede defeat, Simon marched into city hall on July 6 demanding to be sworn in. During a frenzied session, council members voted to keep Thompson in office pending further investigation. On August 3, when the official recount showed a tie vote, the council decreed that neither candidate was elected and that Thompson should remain in office "until a successor" was "duly elected." Contesting the decision, Simon filed suit in the state supreme court, which upheld the council's action in December, 1881. Thompson remained as mayor until the next municipal election while Simon retained his senate office.[54]

Simon played no direct role in the campaign of June, 1882, when Thompson sought re-election. Running for the first three-year mayor's term (as mandated by the recent charter change), Thompson lost to former Mayor James A. Chapman. The results saddened but did not surprise the *Oregonian*, which charged that Chapman was "elected chiefly by the non-taxpaying voters of both parties, led by the machine managers of both." Although Simon was not mentioned as a machine manager, his influence on the outcome was implied.[55]

Chapman had fallen on hard times, even dropping his Arlington Club membership. He badly needed the recently approved mayor's salary of $1,500. When he was accused of bribery in the fall of 1883, few city hall watchers were surprised. He acknowledged signing a contract on May 16, 1882, with former councilman Luzerne Besser to appoint him superintendent of streets upon "receipt of '1,000 in gold coin.'" Chapman was also to receive $1,000 annually. Disgraced politically and impeached by the council, he was not tried or removed from office, as he had neither received the money nor made the appointment. He did confess, however, that Besser and his friends had "spent some money" to pay "election expenses." To a reporter he volunteered: "You know that such bargains are made before every election . . . . Presidents of the United States do it too." Six months after leaving office, Chapman was killed when thrown from his buggy by a hanging telephone wire. At final accounting, his estate was $500 in debt.[56]

As for the defeated Thompson, he knew where his future economic interests could best be served. Already a director of the OR&N, and a sizeable stockholder, he became a corporate vice-president and president of its construction subsidiary, the Oregon Construction Company. Two years later, he was elected vice-president of the Arlington Club. In subsequent years, he developed the Irvington tract, invested in numerous banks and other enterprises, and served on the school board. He ran unsuccessfully against Governor Sylvester Pennoyer in 1890 and served as U.S. minister to Turkey in 1892-93. Today he is popularly remembered as the donor in 1900 of the "Thompson Elk" statue on Southwest Main Street.[57]

Villard's Historic Gamble

In late December, 1880, Henry Villard learned that the Northern Pacific intended to duplicate facilities to the West Coast: one line over the Cascades to Tacoma; the other down the Washington bank of the Columbia to Portland, to compete with his OR&N-Union Pacific line. Competition would hurt his ability to raise funds, and might drive down the value of OR&N stock, then at its high of $200 a share. Fortunately, his New York financiers no more favored competition than he. As bankers also for the Northern Pacific, Drexel, Morgan & Company suggested a merger of the OR&N and NP to provide common control and reduce costly duplication. However, neither was willing to play a secondary role. Realizing that the OR&N would be at Gould's mercy once it was connected to the Union Pacific, Villard sought control of the NP. If he connected *it* to the OR&N, Portland would gain a transcontinental railroad more quickly and he would obtain the largest federal land grants so far awarded to a railroad — as many as 10 million acres. His reputation would soar in the world's financial markets.[58]

With Drexel, Morgan's blessing, Villard organized a "blind pool" of 53 wealthy investors, including the Chicago tycoon George Pullman and Portland's Simeon G. Reed. Each eagerly subscribed between $200,000 and $900,000 to an undisclosed project; Wall Street speculators exhibited more than $25 million of confidence in Henry Villard. In Maury Klein's judgment, it was "one of the boldest schemes ever devised." Villard secretly purchased Northern Pacific stock until, by early March, 1881, he had acquired control and, to the joy of his investor pool, publicized the venture. Having accumulated much more stock than he needed, and having driven up the price by 30 percent, Villard unloaded $8 million in NP common stock at a handsome profit to both himself and the pool. His own investment of $900,000 had grown to $1.2 million in less than three months. Reed's $200,000 investment was worth $270,000.[59]

Villard's holdings and his reputation enabled him to set up the blind pool and reap the profits without soliciting underwriting from established financial houses. His success indicated that if huge inter-regional rail networks were to be financed and constructed, the rail barons required close alliances with large investment banking firms. Among the nineteenth-century railroad leaders, in Thomas Cochran's opinion, "the roles that Villard played extremely well were those of a mobilizer of capital resources for pioneer investments, and effective public relations for the development of an area." Gifts totalling $57,000 to the University of Oregon's building fund, secured by Judge Deady, won him many admirers. And his Northern Pacific Immigration Bureaus heavily publicized Portland and Oregon throughout the United States and Europe.[60]

Villard left little to chance. Having secured his northern and eastern flanks, he moved to cut off potential competitors to the south. In mid-1879, through attorney Joseph N. Dolph, Villard had offered Reid's predecessor, Joseph Gaston, $10,000 for the Dayton, Sheridan narrow-gauge line. Gaston's refusal only delayed the inevitable. By the spring of 1881, with over 163 miles of road completed and Portland only 28 miles away, Reid's Oregonian Railway posed a real threat. Villard turned directly to its Scottish owners. In James B. Montgomery, he found a willing agent to do his bidding. Betraying Reid, Montgomery travelled to Scotland in May, 1881, to persuade the temporarily cash-strapped Dundee bankers to cut their losses by leasing their properties to the OR&N. Reid was instructed to terminate all further building; no more Dundee money would be forthcoming. Montgomery had convinced the Scots that Reid was financially reckless and unheeding of advice. Despite some truth to these claims, Montgomery's motives were questioned by many, including John C. Ainsworth, who noted that his former associate Montgomery was "not to be trusted."[61]

Reid was greatly angered. Late in 1881, he severed his Scottish ties. Villard had played "a thieving game," he later asserted. Reid warned his former colleagues that Villard had no intention of completing the line; that he would remove the iron rails and use them on his main road to California. All Villard was interested in, he said, was suppressing competition. As it later turned out, Reid was right. But in the fall of 1881, Villard's word was magic. In addition to David P. Thompson, skeptics and former opponents like Ellis Hughes and Donald Macleay happily joined the Villard bandwagon. Most of Portland's business Establishment now believed that the city's future growth was in Villard's hands.[62]

The Portland Board of Trade treated the flamboyant financier exuberantly when he addressed it on October 22 that year. The previous month, the OR&N had received a perpetual, non-compensatory franchise from East Portland and Multnomah County for a single track up Sullivan's Gulch to the Columbia River. Construction was proceeding at both ends of the OR&N right-of-way. The alternate Cascade route to Tacoma had been abandoned. The main NP line would go to Wallula Junction, Washington Territory, at the confluence of the Snake and Columbia rivers, where the trains would be ferried to the Oregon side and then proceed to Portland over the OR&N tracks. By October, only about 700 miles of transcontinental track remained to be laid.[63]

To the enthusiastic audience, Villard announced his great plans for Portland: a freight terminal and shop facilities in Albina, a passenger terminal west of the river and a large hotel downtown. Fifteen months earlier, he had introduced to Portland the Edison system of electric dynamos and incandescent lamps, installed on the new Oregon Steamship Company's *Columbia*. Shortly thereafter, he installed an electric plant on the OR&N's large Ainsworth Dock. Such innovative achievements and grandiose plans evoked the *Oregonian's* highest commendation: "Mr.

Villard has organized and combined interests, which . . . form the most stupendous scheme yet undertaken on the American continent." Although overstated, Villard's accomplishments were certainly unique in the Pacific Northwest. Within two years, he had assembled a $60 million empire that would put Portland on the national map. Included among the vast properties acquired by 1881 was the OR&N's purchase of the five-steamer Puget Sound Navigation Company from the Starr brothers. (Former Portlanders A.M. and L.M. Starr took their $600,000 in cash and settled happily in Oakland, California, near John Ainsworth and Robert R. Thompson.) A profitable facsimile of the OSN, the PSN stood to benefit from Tacoma's future Northern Pacific terminus.[64]

Villard also received praise from local investors for another of his promotional schemes, The Oregon & Transcontinental Company, incorporated in the spring of 1881 as a holding company to control both the OR&N and the Northern Pacific. Pioneered by the Pennsylvania Company (owner of the Pennsylvania Railroad) in 1870, holding companies were not a common Wall Street practice at the time. OR&N and NP shareholders were offered the opportunity to exchange their stock for the new Oregon & Transcontinental shares. Great profits were promised as eager investors bought $12 million of the new issue. Within two months of Villard's visit, $30 million worth went on the market. Besides the two transportation companies, the Transcontinental owned and operated construction and contracting firms that were working hastily to complete both lines. (David P. Thompson became directly involved in the OR&N portion.) The company's charter also authorized it to build, purchase and own docks, union depots, hotels, steamboats — anything to service transportation needs. Villard who considered the giant enterprise to be the "'cornerstone' of his whole financial and corporate edifice," won even wider acclaim on Wall Street.[65]

Among Portland's older Establishment, William S. Ladd, for one, seemed pleased by what had transpired. To Judge Matthew P. Deady he wrote:

> Since you left matters have moved along much the same. Tho, if anything, business is better this fall than ever heretofor. Real estate has been, since Mr. Villard's friendly visit, booming. Particularly in the Couch Lake and river frontage as far as Swan Island. I hear that Dr. Wilson [a Couch son-in-law] now holds his 300 foot frontage for $500 per front foot, $150,000 — not yet sold, however.

Couch Lake was rumored to be Villard's preferred site for his union depot. Within two years, it would be filled in, and adjacent riverfront property rose sharply in value.[66]

Villard did not by any means enjoy universal acclaim. One of his directors and large investors in the "blind pool," Boston financier William C. Endicott, Jr., considered the Transcontinental "a very speculative concern." In California, Ainsworth was even more disturbed:

> Mr. Villard today with his numerous wealthy followers stands in a very critical condition before the business world. [He] has been . . . praised by leading press of the country. He has been entertained by boards of trades and communities and legislatures and has acquitted himself well in his speeches and presentations of his plans,

but I observe that he never prepares for, nor anticipates disaster or disappointment but presumes always on a greater increase of business than the growth of the
country will warrant. I cannot but think he will meet with heavy reverses and ruin
many of his confiding friends . . . . I have said this to warn my children against the
dazzle of rapidly accumulated wealth.[67]

Oregon Iron & Steel and the Fall of Villard

Three months after Ainsworth penned his deep concern and prophetic warning about Villard's financing schemes, Simeon Reed incorporated the Oregon Iron
& Steel Company. Even before his resignation from the OR&N, Reed had dreamed
of this exciting new venture. In stark contrast to his former partner Ainsworth,
Reed admired Villard's financial operations. Of the former OSN quadrumvirate,
only Reed seemed dazzled by rapidly accumulating wealth — or at least by the
possibility of quickly increasing his own wealth. With Villard's encouragement,
he saw great potential for a new large Oregon industry that would attract wide
investor support. While giving little attention to the broader iron market, Reed
hoped that a refinanced and enlarged iron mill could help meet Villard's extensive
need for iron rails. By June, 1881, he had already invested $86,000 in the project.[68]

When Villard organized his "blind pool" earlier in the year, both parties apparently struck a deal. Reed agreed to invest $200,000 in the pool if Villard would do
likewise in a newly organized Oregon Iron & Steel Company. Villard also agreed to
interest some friends and work the New York financial markets. By the time of the
company's official incorporation in April, 1882, capitalized at $3 million, over $1.8
million had been raised by the sale of stocks and bonds. Reed had invested over
$300,000; Villard's close friend Darius Ogden Mills, a New York and California
financier, had invested $150,000. Reed also involved William S. Ladd and his son
William M. Ladd as incorporators and bankers through Ladd & Tilton, which also
bonded the property. The Ladds each subscribed to 150 shares. Expecting to invest well over $1 million in the expanded iron plant, the company spent an addi-
tional $500,000 to buy 24,000 acres of timbered land, reported to contain rich
iron deposits, nearly half of it in the Iron Mountain — Oswego region south of
Portland.[69]

The announcement of Villard's participation in Reed's Oregon Iron and Steel
Company venture made the financier even more conspicuous locally. He further
enhanced his reputation by incorporating the Northern Pacific Terminal Company, capitalized at $5 million. The OR&N held 40 percent, while a number of
Portland business leaders held the rest, including Ladd, Henry Corbett, and Henry
Failing, who became president. Portland's Establishment thus held a major stake
in the railroad's future. To demonstrate their "appreciation" in June, 1882, the
city's leading businesses and financiers sent Villard a "beautiful" painting by an
Oregon artist, Edward Erpy. Expressing their "high regard and esteem" for "opening to commerce the great inland empire" were:

Corbett Failing Company	George H. Flanders
Henry W. Corbett	Fleischner Mayer Company
Henry Failing	Honeyman Hardware
William S. Ladd	Corbitt & Macleay
C.H. Lewis	Robert R. Thompson
Oregon Furniture Company	E.J. Northrup
George J. Ainsworth	S.G. Skidmore
Goldsmith & Lowenberg	C.H. Prescott
J.K. Gill	Woodward & Clark

The prosperous San Francisco-based wholesale liquor firms of Hotaling and Martin also added their appreciation.[70]

Within five months, ominous reports revealed that Oregon Iron and Steel's indebtedness had reached $516,000, forcing Reed to sell a quarter of his stock to Darius Mills. Villard found himself facing similar difficulties as construction expenditures went far over estimates. Both men suffered sharp securities losses as OR&N stock depreciated 25 percent, while Northern Pacific was off by half. The onset of a three-year recession aggravated their problems. As Ainsworth had predicted, Villard was an over-optimistic business forecaster. Neither he nor Reed had any practical experience in the industries they were attempting to build and operate. Both underestimated the dimensions and costs of their projects and unrealistically inflated market possibilities.[71]

In the spring of 1883, after nine years as a major player in the volatile American economy, Villard was in serious trouble. He was determined to complete the Portland line by September, and just as determined to polish his reputation or at least to hide the growing exasperation of his predicament. While gladly accepting the appreciation of Portland's business leadership, he unquestionably would have preferred increased financial support from local investors. As his executive Thomas Oaks complained to the OR&N's general manager C.H. Prescott: "'Notwithstanding the lavish expenditure of money that has greatly benefited Portland, we do not get the slightest encouragement from her representative men in an undertaking they alone should carry through.'" Despite this disappointment and a shortage of cash, Villard fulfilled his $50,000 pledge (made through Judge Deady) to the University of Oregon for what was to become Villard Hall. Like Ladd and Reed, Deady believed that Villard was a victim of circumstances. As the judge observed in April, 1883: "He is evidently a strong, deep man and I think an upright one — at least compared with other Railway Kings and speculators of the U.S."[72]

Character and motives aside, some of Villard's Transcontinental directors had lost faith in his management. As the company's stock slid precipitously, they covered their losses by short-selling 20,000 shares of their stock. They realized all too painfully that Villard had watered the value of the securities by issuing additional shares to halt the construction drain on the company's treasury. Angered by their

.ctions, Villard wrote his friend and attorney Joseph N. Dolph, recently elected J.S. Senator from Oregon, that suspending construction was unthinkable: it would trigger a catastrophe by further depressing Northern Pacific stock. "'The very existence of the O&T Co. depends on the success of the Northern Pacific .tock,'" he insisted. He refused to alter plans to fill four trains with dignitaries and transport them from New York to Portland at Northern Pacific's expense. Invited were diplomats, German and English bankers, governors, congressmen, former President Ulysses S. Grant, and three British jurists, including the famed Lord ames Bryce. Sitting Bull and 2,000 war-painted Crow Indians were mobilized to observe the driving of the last railroad spike at Gold Creek, Montana, on September 8, 1883.[73]

When Villard and his 300 guests steamed into East Portland on September 11, 1883, few were aware that his empire was beginning to crumble. It was a Portland holiday, "The greatest display ever witnessed in this city," headlined the *Oregonian*. "A new destiny is upon us." A gigantic commercial pageant lasted into the night. "'We are now incorporated with the rest of the world,'" proclaimed Board of Trade President Donald Macleay. For Portland, "the day of long credits" was past.[74]

For Villard and Reed, the celebration was short-lived. Reed especially, must have understood the message that Ladd sent him on January 17, 1884:

> Reed what a fearful shrinkage in Villard's stocks no telling where it will end & poor Villard I pitty him. A sorry termination of a business Manns career. How uncertain these large enterprises unless you have the Money in hand to successfully develope & Cary out the work . . . .[75]

Within four months of this triumph, Villard was forced to relinquish the presidencies of the OR&N, the Oregon & Transcontinental, and Northern Pacific. Wall Street continued to exercise a firm hand over Portland's quest for Northwest predominance. Banker J.P. Morgan counseled a take-over of Villard's properties and headed the committee to choose Villard's successor as president of the Northern Pacific. Unlike Villard, Robert Harris "was strictly a railroad career man," a management specialist "fully responsive to the investment bankers," according to Villard's biographer. Villard's closest advisers had declared him insolvent and formed a syndicate that acquired all his Oregon companies except the Oregon & California Railroad.[76]

Ladd must have approved these actions. Once the Northern Pacific and OR&N paid off, he wrote Reed in January, 1884, it would

> make money matters easier for a few people . . . . All of us who have held on to V.[illard] securities have suffered fearfully in the shrinkages O R N Co 90 today. Would not be surprised if shall declin much more . . . . No use Crying for spilled Milk What do you think? Are all going down to Nothing? What a difference to me if I had sold my O R N Co stock in the 150 or 60s but too late to say nothing of O T stock all gone all gone — Well we must live and learn if we only would profit by our experiences which we seldom do — At least I have not in this instance . . . .[77]

After resigning his three presidencies, Villard transferred his cash and securities to the syndicate and left to recover in Europe. Reed was left to salvage the Oregon Iron & Steel Company as its affairs went from bad to worse. Earlier in 1884, he had learned that its Ladd & Tilton account was overdrawn by $100,000. The plant manager had needed $2,000 immediately "'to pay Chinamen wood choppers . . or hell [would] be to pay.'" Reed was forced to sell some of his OR&N and Northern Pacific stock at a heavy discount. By the time of Villard's departure, his Transcontinental stock was practically worthless.[78]

Over the next two years, Reed faced increasing troubles resulting from two lawsuits filed by his former plant manager, who also held a large block of OIS stock. After both were overturned on appeal and dismissed, he was hit by a third suit filed by New York financier Elijah Smith acting president of the O&T, which controlled Villard's shares. Smith had formed a voting trust aimed at squeezing Reed out of the company's management. Smith won the backing of William S. and William M. Ladd, who had previously supported Reed as co-defendants in the first two suits. Feeling betrayed by the Ladds, whom he accused of duplicity and blackmail, Reed resigned as OIS president in June, 1886, with losses exceeding $500,000.[78]

A New Era

For Portland, many of whose investors had collectively lost between $2 million and $3 million from Villard's failure, the major consequence of his departure was the free hand given local management of OR&N affairs. Under Henry Failing's direction, the Northern Pacific Terminal Company was to become one of the city's most influential institutions and one of its largest property owners. Old-guard business leaders like William S. Ladd, forced to retain their original OR&N stock, actually increased their power as the railroad industry prospered. A model for future giant corporations, the railroad industry became Portland's first employer of a large labor force. This development was to have significant city-wide political consequences as the Oregon Railway & Navigation Company achieved corporate dominance throughout the region. On July 1, 1885, Captain John Gates, veteran construction engineer for the OSN and OR&N, succeeded James A. Chapman as mayor.[79]

11.1 Henry Villard (1835-1900) and railroad associates

11.2 Donald Macleay (1834-1897)

11.3 George W. Weidler (1837-1908)

11.4 OR & N ferry landing used for Portland, 1883-1888

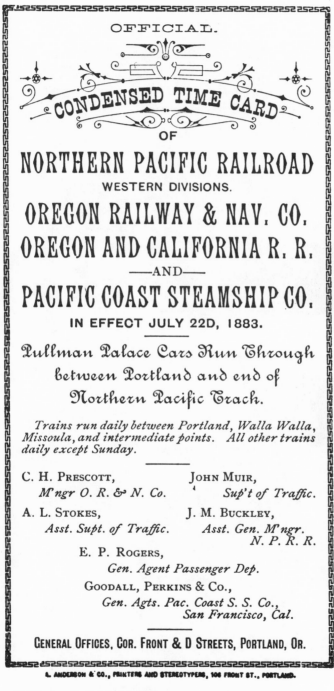

OFFICIAL.

CONDENSED TIME CARD

OF

NORTHERN PACIFIC RAILROAD
WESTERN DIVISIONS.
OREGON RAILWAY & NAV. CO.
OREGON AND CALIFORNIA R. R.
—AND—
PACIFIC COAST STEAMSHIP CO.

IN EFFECT JULY 22D, 1883.

Pullman Palace Cars Run Through
between Portland and end of
Northern Pacific Track.

Trains run daily between Portland, Walla Walla,
Missoula, and intermediate points. All other trains
daily except Sunday.

C. H. Prescott,   John Muir,
M'ngr O. R. & N. Co.   *Sup't of Traffic.*

A. L. Stokes,   J. M. Buckley,
Asst. Supt. of Traffic.   *Asst. Gen. M'ngr.*
                             N. P. R. R.
E. P. Rogers,
Gen. Agent Passenger Dep.
Goodall, Perkins & Co.,
Gen. Agts. Pac. Coast S. S. Co.,
San Francisco, Cal.

GENERAL OFFICES, COR. FRONT & D STREETS, PORTLAND, OR.

L. ANDERSON & CO., PRINTERS AND STEREOTYPERS, 106 FRONT ST., PORTLAND.

11.5 Northern Pacific Schedule, 1883

11.6 Mines and Works of the Oregon Iron and Steel Co. at Oswego, Oregon

Mayor Thompson —

Committee of Arrangements

—— O F ——

✦ GRANT RECEPTION ✦

Portland, October 11, 1879.

Dear Sir :

The steamer *"City of Salem,"* with the Reception Committee, will leave Pacific wharf at 9:30 a. m. on Tuesday next, *for Vancouver* to escort Gen. Grant from thence to Portland.

As the steamer cannot hold all persons invited to the procession, and ill-feelings might arise if some persons were invited and others not, this Committee deem it necessary to state that none but the General Committee of Twenty-four, their Ladies, and the Military Officers and Ladies, and Press Reporters are intended to go on board the " City of Salem" from Portland to Vancouver.

Yours respectfully,

John McCraken,
Chairman Com. of Arrangements.

NOTE.— Your carriage in procession is No. *1* ....in which along with you will be... *General Grant, Governor Mayor & General Howard* —

.... Look out for them.

At Procession - Tuesday - Dress suit
At Reception - Wednesday Full dress suit

11.7 Committee of Arrangements, 1879

11.9 William Reid (1841-1914)

11.8 James B. Montgomery (1832-1900)

11.10 Corbitt & MacLeay, Front Street

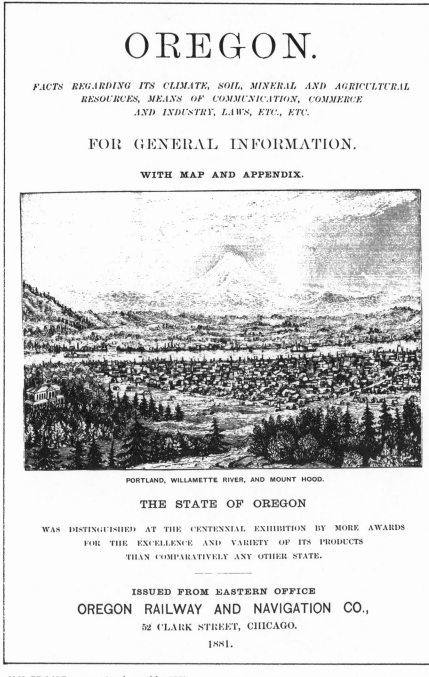

OREGON.

*FACTS REGARDING ITS CLIMATE, SOIL, MINERAL AND AGRICULTURAL
RESOURCES, MEANS OF COMMUNICATION, COMMERCE
AND INDUSTRY, LAWS, ETC., ETC.*

FOR GENERAL INFORMATION.

WITH MAP AND APPENDIX.

PORTLAND, WILLAMETTE RIVER, AND MOUNT HOOD.

THE STATE OF OREGON

WAS DISTINGUISHED AT THE CENTENNIAL EXHIBITION BY MORE AWARDS
FOR THE EXCELLENCE AND VARIETY OF ITS PRODUCTS
THAN COMPARATIVELY ANY OTHER STATE.

———————

ISSUED FROM EASTERN OFFICE

OREGON RAILWAY AND NAVIGATION CO.,

52 CLARK STREET, CHICAGO.

1881.

11.11 OR & N Co. promotional pamphlet, 1881

12

TESTING THE ESTABLISHMENT: 1880-1887

Good Times: 1880-1883

A pervasive optimism marked Portland's economic life in 1883 as costly railroad construction poured money into local coffers. Northern Pacific Railroad promotional efforts helped stimulate a 70 percent increase in the city's population between 1880 and 1883. Commercial construction boomed, with 19 major buildings erected during the three-year period, eight of them in 1883 alone. Investing between $40,000 and $200,000 each were familiar Establishment figures, who included John Ainsworth, William Ladd, David Thompson, Cyrus and Joseph Dolph, Cicero Lewis, Henry Failing, Henry Corbett, James and Vincent Cook, Frederick Bickel, J. Frank Watson, and Ferdinand Smith. It was the age of cast-iron architecture, which gave Portland commercial life a distinctive refinement.[1]

A similar quality of extended to new residences along West Park Avenue on the Park Blocks, near Montgomery Street. Marion Ross portrayed it as a boulevard of formal mansions built in the Italianate style. Ralph and Isaac Jacobs, owners of the Oregon City Woolen Mills, built twin houses next to each other, one of which was later occupied by Cyrus Dolph. Residential development also extended west beyond Jacob Kamm's property and northwest to the exclusive Nineteenth Street compound of the Couch-Lewis clan. As Harvey Scott observed, it was "a region . . . forever dedicated to dwellings of wealth and beauty."[2]

Adjacent to City Park, at the top of "B" (Burnside) Street, Henry Green, an owner of the water and gas companies, built his plush Cedar Hill estate, "the gayest home in Portland." On a tract of five acres, the house was almost submerged in trees, its large hothouses filled with exotic plants. Every day Mrs. Green could be seen

driving out in her Victoria, behind her cockaded coachman and bobtailed horses, silver jingling on the bridles and a carriage robe made from the peacock green neck feathers of mallard ducks, bound with seal skin and spread over the back of the seat.[3]

The Northwest of November, 1885, listed 21 millionaires in Portland: "In all essentials of a high civilization the city is as far advanced as the old cities of New England and New York of like size that have enjoyed more than a century of growth." On private residences generally, the *West Shore* commented:

> Portland leads all the cities of the coast in the number of elegant and costly dwellings as compared to her total population . . . . In the matter of perennially green grass and ever blooming flowers, the people of Portland possess an advantage over their friends in the east. The services of the lawn mower are in constant demand, for the rains of winter and the ever-ready garden hose of summer keep the lawns fresh and beautiful the entire year . . . . The beautiful lawns and profusion of choice and carefully cultivated flowers speak more loudly of the culture and refinement of the people than do palatial residences. Flowers are the property of rich and poor alike.[4]

Crucial to the region's prosperity was the enormous expansion of foreign trading in wheat between 1881 and 1882 — up 170 percent from the previous year. Commission merchants Corbitt & Macleay, John McCraken and Everding & Farrell enlarged their docks at the rear of their stores along Front Street. The increase in wheat exports reflected a shifting of the center of production from the Willamette Valley to Eastern Oregon as the railroad brought new migrations of farmers from the upper Midwest. To take advantage of such developments, which also spurred demands for domestic flour, William Ladd incorporated the Portland Flouring Mills in 1883, an outgrowth of his smaller Albina Flour Mills. It soon became the largest milling operation in the Northwest, guided and directed by his protege, Theodore B. Wilcox. Discovered by Asahel Bush while visiting his home town of Westfield, Massachusetts, in 1877, the 21-year-old bank clerk went to work for Ladd & Tilton and became Ladd's administrative assistant in the early 1880s. Wilcox joined the Arlington Club in 1886, and became a commanding figure in Portland business, financial and social circles.[5]

Ladd was instrumental in the formation of several other businesses in the early 1880s: the Oregon Artificial Stone Company, the Oregon Paving & Contracting Company, and the Oregon Pottery Company. All three became major recipients of street-paving and waterpipe contracts awarded by the city. The secretary of the firms was the banker James Steel, Ladd's brother-in-law, who was to play an increasing important role in Portland's business and politics.

By 1883, approximately 400 men, out of a work force of nearly 5,000 employed in manufacturing, were engaged in foundry and machine work, much of it stimulated by the production of rail track and cast-iron building ornamentation. In descending order of size, the largest were Smith & Watson, Willamette Iron Works, City Foundry, and Union Iron Mills. Simeon Reed's giant Oregon Iron and Steel Company, south of Portland at Oswego, employed over 300 workers. Several of the foundry owners were active, then or later, in city politics. City Foundry's William B. Honeyman served on the city council from 1880 to 1884, and as council president for two years. J. Frank Watson, co-owner of Smith & Watson, had served during 1879-80 and would return to the council in 1891-92. Both were active members of the Arlington Club.[6]

Excluding lumber products, which were second to wheat and flour in foreign exports, foundry and machine work constituted the largest Portland industry in 1883-84, producing primarily for the metropolitan market. Although Portland made "impressive gains in the expansion of manufacturing during the 1880s," according to Paul Merriam, it was "largely of the type oriented to the local consumer [including government] rather than that oriented toward extra-regional markets." As long as the city's business leaders could protect their commanding geographic position and make good money from commerce and traditional small industry, they were disinclined "to invest heavily in new, untried ventures," some of which might have served broader regional markets. It was this kind of caution that had provoked Thomas Oaks's complaint in February, 1883. Echoing a similar note seven years later, Harvey Scott observed that Portland industry "had no aim to reach out to something distant and world wide."[7]

Simeon Reed proved the exception among Portland's industrial leaders of the late nineteenth century. In manufacturing a traditional product — iron — he planned for distant markets, and when he bought northern Idaho's Bunker Hill and Sullivan silver mine in 1887, his aim extended worldwide. The iron and silver ventures, ill timed and ill managed, required extensive eastern capital. In both, Reed assumed unusually large risks for a Portland investor — the kind admired by Oaks, Henry Villard and their New York bankers. Unfortunately, like Villard, Reed was at least partially a victim of uncontrollable circumstances. The depression of 1884 caught him unprepared, and monopolistic railroad rates (similar to those the OSN had imposed on its shipping customers) helped generate heavy losses in silver in 1892. (Twenty years after Reed sold the mine at a heavy loss that year, it became immensely profitable as one of the largest lead-silver mines in the world.)[8]

Bad Times: 1884-1885

The depression of 1884 was "scarcely typical," according to Samuel Reznick. "It was a depression without an initial or introductory panic." As Horace White noted in the *Nation*, "'The decline in stocks [especially railroad securities] has been gradual, and there has been no collapse of credit, yet we are having all the other effects of a crisis in full measure.'" Nationally, through 1886, "business activity fell by almost a fourth." Two other developments particularly affected the Northwest: a nearly 50 percent drop in foreign immigration between 1882 and 1885, and worldwide overproduction in wheat. "In consequence," the 1885 *City Directory* declared, "our great agricultural staple, was brought down to a lower price than has been known for one hundred years." For the year 1882-83, wheat exports from Portland dropped a devastating 56 percent.[9]

Heavy declines in the grain trade, added to shareholder losses in Villard's Transcontinental stock, caused local lenders to call in their loans, while an Oregon mortgage tax law encouraged outside capital to withdraw from local investment. A combination of such causes prompted a falling off in business. "That in turn," reported the *City Directory*, "has produced a general croaking, which of itself has done more to cause a general depression than all the other causes combined." The cessation of railroad work, the stoppage of construction on Villard's Portland Ho-

tel, and a 50 percent reduction in major commercial building created serious unemployment problems for foundry workers and the approximately 2,000 workers
engaged in the building trades, who constituted about 40 percent of the industrial
work force.[10]

In December, 1884, the *Oregonian*, while noting "a presence of hard times,"
with "hundreds of idle men . . . without work," reported that business generally
was "pretty good." Despite the depressed wheat market, the harbor presented "a
businesslike appearance," with ships going up and down river daily. "Merchants
have plenty of customers, although they do not buy as extensively as in the days of
the Villard boom." Meier & Frank, soon to become the city's largest general store,
prepared to move into its first two-story building on First Street.[11]

Anti-Chinese Agitation and Union Labor

The completion of the Northern Pacific Railroad in 1883 and the termination of
work on the Oregon & California line in 1884 released thousands of laborers,
many of whom were Chinese. They flocked to Portland. Immediately, cheap Chinese labor flooded markets previously filled by Caucasians. The collapse of the
building boom released hundreds more workers to compete for scarce jobs. Confrontation between Caucasian and Oriental seemed inevitable, considering the
long-standing efforts to exclude Chinese immigrants, legislate their social habits
and segregate their domiciles. In 1879, U.S. Senator James H. Slater, an Oregon
Democrat had introduced a bill to restrict Chinese working rights. The same year,
merchant-Mayor W.S. Newberry had advocated excluding Chinese from contracted city public works. By 1884, when the resident Chinese population exceeded approximately 4,000 (the city's largest foreign-born group), opposition
grew increasingly militant. As Carlos A. Schwantes has noted, the anti-Chinese
crusade "is significant because it resulted in the [Northwest] region's first major
outburst of industrial violence." Much of the opposition in Portland was led by
recent Irish immigrant labor, anxious to emphasize its "American patriotism by
casting aspersions on the Oriental population," according to Merriam.[12]

The Chinese question stimulated a heated debate at a Board of Trade meeting in
late December, 1884. President Donald Macleay had appointed a committee to
formulate a new city charter. Included were David P. Thompson, Bernard Goldsmith, Henry Failing, Judge Matthew P. Deady, banker Richard L. Durham, and
attorneys John Catlin, Julius C. Moreland and Sylvester Pennoyer. Calling the Chinese "'nuisances,'" the Harvard-educated Pennoyer, an avid Democrat and champion of labor, demanded insertion of a charter provision "to prescribe limits in
which the Chinese may be domiciled." Agreeing that the Chinese had caused
labor problems, Deady vigorously opposed the action. Goldsmith, backing
Deady, observed that such a provision could not be enforced legally. Deady and
Goldsmith won unanimous endorsement of their position with the exception of
Pennoyer, who became the state's most outspoken opponent of Chinese residency.[13]

The leader of the Pacific Northwest anti-Chinese crusade was 38-year-old carpenter Daniel Cronin. He landed in Seattle during the summer of 1885 to organize

a territorial chapter of the Knights of Labor, which had been founded in Philadelphia in 1869. Cronin adroitly used the growing power of the Knights (whose national membership approximated 500,000 in 1885) to seize the leadership of the Chinese expulsion movement. He was helped by Mayor R. Jacob Weisbach of Tacoma, whom Harvey Scott, in the *Oregonian*, labeled a "'German Communist.'"[14]

Cronin arrived in Portland in late January, 1886, nearly three months after leading the removal of over 300 Chinese from Tacoma. (Most of them were shipped to Portland by train.) Local Knights of Labor eagerly welcomed him with a large mass meeting at the New Market Theater on January 27. Cronin and others called upon Portland business and labor to "rid the country of the heathen Chinese," and to join in "the greatest victory ever known in Oregon." Portland attorney John Caples, the principal speaker, called for boycotts of businesses and banks that refused to join the crusade. He warned: "We may be able to shake even the First National Bank on its foundations." To cheers from the packed audience, Cronin recounted his experience "in ousting 'Chinamen'" from Tacoma. In three months, he declared, there will "not be a working Chinaman in Portland."[15]

On February 7 and 8, rioters at Seattle drove some 400 Chinese to the waterfront, where they were loaded aboard ships. The violence was so severe that Washington's territorial governor declared martial law. Two days later, International Workingmen's Association leader B.G. Haskell of San Francisco landed in Portland and staged several boisterous anti-Chinese assemblies. Apprehensive that Seattle's experience might be repeated in Portland, especially after Haskell publicly warned the Chinese to leave the city within 40 days, Mayor John Gates doubled the police force and swore in 300 armed citizens, including 75 Grand Army of the Republic war veterans.[16]

On the night of February 22, 1886, a thousand men and boys marched through the streets of Portland in a torchlight parade to the Plaza Blocks. Armed men shipped 160 Chinese employees of the Oregon City Woolen Mills to Portland, where they were displayed before the mob. The *Oregonian* likened the crusade to the anti-Negro riots in New York in 1863. "It is the base instinct of race hatred," thundered editor Scott. The *Oregonian* counseled calmness. "They cannot be expelled by force. . . . If they cannot find work, they will go." The leading extraditors were arrested and brought before Deady's court, but the violence continued. That very night 30 armed "whites" broke up a camp of Chinese workers in Albina; they reportedly were "cutting wood for Judge Deady." Early in the morning of March 4, according to the *Oregonian*, 100 to 200 Chinese were "driven by 50 masked men" from East Portland and Mount Tabor into Portland's Chinatown, a 35-block area between Front and Third, and Ash and Salmon streets. From the floor of the U.S. Senate, John H. Mitchell vigorously supported the expulsions.[17]

Portland officialdom reacted slowly. Not until March 13, two days after a raid on Chinese farmers at Guild's Lake, did Mayor Gates convene "a meeting of the law and order forces." By Malcolm Clark's account, "it was a ludicrous fiasco." While former mayors Henry Failing and Bernard Goldsmith and others joined Gates to plot strategy at the county courthouse, the anti-Chinese throng packed an adjacent room and elected Sylvester Pennoyer as chairman. Over the next two weeks, as sporadic outbursts continued, the militia arrived and federal indictments were returned against those who had led the raids. As the events were recounted by merchant Ben Selling, who later became one of Oregon's most prominent figures: "The better class of citizens deprecate this and here in Portland have enrolled about 200 deputy sheriffs. I am one and have done patrol duty two nights." Editor Scott, who was on the deputized force, was reported to have shot a hole through his coat tail and "singed that part of his anatomy immediately beneath, when a pistol he was carrying in his hip pocket accidentally fired."[18]

According to Malcolm Clark, "the violence was never actually brought under control. It simply wore itself out." Many Chinese left Portland, some to seek refuge in San Francisco. Their departure left a void in the work force not easily filled by Caucasian labor. In the *Oregonian*'s opinion, "the Chinese performed with fidelity our hardest and lowest kinds of labor."They were instrumental in starting many industries "that would otherwise have remained underdeveloped." The Oregon City Woolen Mills, for example, claimed that until Chinese workers were employed it had sent its cloth to San Francisco for manufacturing into clothing because of an insufficient supply of skilled white labor. To Abigail Duniway, and to her former Democratic enemy Pennoyer, the use of cheap coolie labor, however industrious and skilled, was pure exploitation. Chinese and female white workers received from 50 to 60 percent less on average than white male workers in the woolen mills.[19]

For all its viciousness, the anti-Chinese crusade did call attention to workers' grievances. But it split the labor movement in Portland, where many workers were more conservative than their Washington brethren, most of whom were recent arrivals, lured by Northern Pacific advertisements proclaiming "a guarantee of success to any laborer willing to work." By 1886, Portland had more than 10 trade unions, whose skilled workers joined the newly formed American Federation of Labor. As Schwantes has noted, they "put down roots in the community, enrolled their children in public schools, and planted roses around their bungalows." Most rejected the radicalism of the Knights, which was converted to Populism in the 1890s. As for migratory and seasonal workers, nearly all remained outside the mainstream of organized labor.[20]

While the bulk of Portland's trade unionists opposed violence against the Chinese, they still favored their removal. Thus, when Pennoyer ran for governor in 1886, he received wide support from workers of all persuasions. At a Portland campaign rally in early May, 1886, he "brought cheering workers to their feet . . . . 'Today,'" he warned, "'the great producing and laboring classes of our state are being ground down between the upper and nether millstones of corporate power and cheap servile labor.'" If this were to continue, he predicted, "'the Willamette Valley will be the home only of rich capitalists and Chinese serfs.'" In Umatilla County, future Governor Walter M. Pierce heard Pennoyer's familiar refrain: "'The Mongolian must go!'"[21]

The anti-Chinese crusade and Pennoyer's harsh pro-labor rhetoric belatedly galvanized Portland's cautious establishment into limited action. Its power and authority were being tested. Once organized, it "clearly meant business," in Malcolm Clark's judgment. Most of the city's commercial and professional leaders would have agreed with Deady when he called Pennoyer an "intelligent, virtuous fanatic . . ., a dangerous depository of power." Although many, like Deady, Failing and Goldsmith, were sympathetic to the plight of the Chinese, their major concern was to maintain political order against attacks on private property and established social and economic interests. Again like Deady, most of them had employed and exploited Chinese immigrants as industrial or manual laborers and domestic servants. In Ralph James Mooney's opinion, Deady's support of Chinese rights, by opposing "'mob rule'" and "'demagoguery,'" was "fundamentally aristocratic in nature." The concerns of a Failing and a Goldsmith, on the other hand, more broadly reflected the merchant's "rational response to social conditions," as Digby Baltzell portrayed reactions of Boston merchants to similar threats.[22]

The Charitable Impulse

Charity represented one rational response to social conditions. Portland leaders feared that tumult and poverty, generated by the racial and labor strife accompanying the depression of the mid-1880s, threatened the established order. Encouraged by religious leaders like Thomas Lamb Eliot, who injected a higher moral sense and human sympathy into the urgency, efforts were launched to reform the poor and improve the quality of relief. The resulting charitable "impulse," as Frederic Cople Jaher observed, "generally involved wealth, power, civic pride, *noblesse oblige*, the need for recognition, and the desire of political-economic elites to strengthen their authority."[23]

In 1885, fourteen years after the founding of the Children's Home, the Boys and Girls Aid Society of Oregon was established "to improve conditions of homeless, neglected or abused children." William S. Ladd, Henry W. Corbett and the Ainsworth Bank gave it major support. One of the society's sponsors was the Reverend Eliot's First Unitarian Church through its Christian Union. Organized in 1876, the Union administered the church's charitable funds and conducted its philanthropic work. Among the more active Unitarians were Simeon G. Reed, Judge Charles B. Bellinger, Walter F. Burrell, James W. Cook, David P. Thompson, and Robert R. Thompson before he departed to live in California. All were members of the Arlington Club. Other prominent Portland Unitarians included Henry L. Pittock, Judge Erasmus D. Shattuck, Martin Winch, and Alfred F. Sears, Jr.[24]

While the Unitarian husbands raised money, their wives became actively involved in delivering social services. The Christian Union in 1887 sponsored a gathering of over 100 women to found the Portland Women's Union for the purpose of assisting "young working girls." They agreed to "'establish a hotel for self-supporting young women, coming strangers to Portland . . . to provide counsel and assistance when necessary, to minister to their well-being and happiness." According to one account, "its founders would dispense benevolence, not charity; safety, not reformation." Another report noted that: "'Without the Union, those of limited means would be obliged oftentimes to take cheap quarters in undesirable locations, amid pernicious surroundings.'" Two years later, the Ladies Union Relief Society of Albina incorporated the Patton Home for the Friendless, to "provide assistance, food, clothing, fuel and other necessities to the afflicted."

Matthew Patton, a wealthy pioneer with extensive property on Portland Heights and in Albina, donated a block of land on which the society built its first home. Until well into the present century, social welfare organizations like the Boys and Girls Aid Society, the Women's Union and the Patton Home remained private efforts, supported by the churches and the older and more secure rich.[25]

Conservative Growth

After assuming office in July, 1885, Mayor John Gates observed that Portland still faced "hard times . . . . Corporations and individuals alike are exercising every endeavor towards retrenchment and economy in business as well as in private matters." But within five months, Board of Trade President Donald Macleay noted increasing construction and retail activity. A reviving economy during the first half of 1886, and more plentiful jobs, defused the anti-Chinese crusade. Pennoyer's election as governor in June represented a vindication for those who had struggled to preserve those jobs. As Malcolm Clark noted, "Men found work more rewarding than tormenting an inoffensive people."[26]

In Portland, the center of retail trade was moving west, away from the river and the costly damage of spring floods. The Portland Savings Bank opened its four-story, $75,000 building in 1885 in the center of Chinatown on Second Street, and Henry Corbett had located his 1884 four-story Cambridge Block, which also cost $75,000, to its west between Third and Fourth. In 1886, Reed built Portland's first five-story structure, the Abington Building. Situated on Third Street and costing $95,000, it was considered, according to Hawkins, the city's finest. Perhaps the most lauded opening of early 1886, however, was the new Turkish & Russian Bath, to the north of Chinatown at Second and Ash streets, cited by the *Oregonian* as "a step nearest to Godliness."[27]

Banking expanded rapidly during the mid-1880s as money became plentiful throughout the state and local real estate flourished in anticipation of renewed railroad construction on the Oregon and California line. In 1882, Portland's First National was the state's only national bank; by 1886, the number had risen to 18. Except for savings banks, no failures resulted from the 1884 depression. Major banks, like the Ainsworth, and First National, and the private Ladd & Tilton and Ladd & Bush, operated conservatively. They maintained a "high capitalization to liability ratio," following John C. Ainsworth's advice to his children, to "be conservative . . . with slow, healthy and natural accumulation." The Scottish group, led by Donald Macleay's Oregon & Washington Mortgage Bank of Scotland, observed similar practices. But after the legislature had removed the short-lived mortgage tax, the Scots became more aggressive in meeting the needs of the population influx, especially those of wheat farmers. According to Merriam, "The major shares of loans on wheat harvests of the Inland Empire came from Portland institutions" until 1900.[28]

Banks operated under little state supervision. The Oregon legislature had fixed the legal rate of interest at 8 percent in 1880, "but lenders were permitted to ask slightly higher rates under special agreement," according to bank historian Claude Singer. With capital scarce until 1886, the pressure of demand kept the price of credit high. As the railroads drew Portland closer to the national markets, however, the flood of immigrants brought in new capital, and the city's manufacturing firms came to life. Two new national banks were founded especially to take advantage of the capital inflow: the Commercial, and the Merchants. Both involved leading members of Portland's business and professional Establishment, including a younger generation led by James Steel and Richard L. Durham.[29]

James Steel, William S. Ladd's brother-in-law, had left the employ of the First National Bank in 1882 to enter business on his own. In less than 20 years, he had accumulated gross assets of $148,556, including real-estate investments of $72,069. Optimistic about his future, he formed the Willamette Savings Bank in 1883 while helping to found the Oregon Pottery and Oregon Paving & Contracting companies under Ladd's direction. But additional investments of $52,516 in the Oregon Construction Company and Villard's Oregon & Transcontinental Company proved disastrous in 1884. With a loss in gross assets of nearly $30,000 in 1885, Steel was forced to merge his Willamette Savings Bank into the new Merchants National Bank, of which he became a major stockholder and, later, president. Other major stockholders were Julius Loewenberg, a wealthy mine and real-estate promoter and a former Willamette Savings Bank investor, and J. Frank Watson.[30]

Durham, close in age and interest to Steel, was named vice-president of the Commercial National Bank upon its opening in 1886. Son of the founder of Oswego, attorney Durham became active in Republican politics under Joe Simon's direction, first as a deputy county clerk and then as a deputy city auditor. While in public office, he invested heavily in Albina real estate. Directors of the Commercial included Frank Dekum, David P. Thompson, John McCraken, George H. Williams, and Cyrus A. Dolph, Simon's law partner and also a board member of the First National Bank. They also ran the Portland Savings Bank in the same building.[31]

An obviously fertile field for investment in the mid-1880s was that of fire and marine insurance. It took considerable capital to open an insurance business, even though the local firms were usually agents for large national and foreign insurance companies. Not surprisingly, Portland's first home-based fire insurance company, Oregon Fire & Marine, was established under the aegis of Henry W. Corbett and William S. Ladd in 1883. Within two years, Loewenberg, McCraken and Frank M. Warren, a wealthy salmon packer in the Alaskan trade, organized the Northwest Fire & Marine Insurance Company. Not to be outdone, the Commercial National Bank interests founded the Columbia Fire & Marine Insurance Company, of which Dekum and Durham were the chief executives.[32]

The Portland Establishment, closely connected by marriage, corporate directorships and political preference, was thus firmly in control of the city's major commercial and financial institutions by 1886. (The Corbett and Ladd families had been officially united in 1879 when Henry J. Corbett married Helen Kendell Ladd.) Most Establishment families were also socially united through church affiliation and Arlington Club membership, with the exception of Jews and a few like Steel and Dekum who held other interests. Politically, nearly all were loyal Republicans, including former Democrats Ladd and McCraken.

The Political Power Structure: 1885-1886

The lines of political authority were complex. Portland attorney Joseph Simon was clearly the most powerful individual in Oregon's politics from 1880 to 1910, but he was not "The Boss,"as his detractors claimed. Although Republican state chairman (1880-86), state senator (1880-91 and 1895-98) and partner of the Dolph brothers, he never commanded loyalty from all segments of the party, particularly downstate. He had to barter and bargain to achieve his goals. As Jon C. Teaford has noted about urban party organizations generally: "'Broker' better describes the role of the major party leaders" like Simon. He operated from a solid base of support as corporate secretary for both the OR&N and the Northern Pacific Terminal Company. An intense, ambitious "wheeler-dealer" of great personal charm, he dedicated his life to business, law and politics. In common with the Portland Establishment, he never separated his private and his public interests.[33]

Simon continually struggled to exercise control over the state and local political machinery of a party that was splintered into various factions until 1905. When he was elected mayor of Portland in 1909, the *Oregon Journal* naively observed, "Probably no state in the union . . . ever witnessed party strife so malignant or so deadly." Apart from personal enmities and competing egos, the party was split between big-city Republicans and the rural, or downstate, members. There was also a growing animosity between the Republicans on the city council and those in the legislature, the councilmen jealously guarding their prerogatives in the face of legislative encroachment on what the council considered to be municipal matters. Through the smoke of political battle, however, no matter how many skirmishes were fought, the major transportation corporations and banks, somewhat aloofly, maintained their dominance over the city's economic life.[34]

The bitterest struggle in Portland municipal politics at the time involved the Mitchell and Simon factions. John H. Mitchell sought to return to the U.S. Senate in 1885, but the regular winter legislative session adjourned after 69 ballots without electing anyone. Simon had promoted the candidacy of the wealthy Portland merchant and senate President Solomon Hirsch, who lost in a tie vote. (Hirsch had failed to vote for himself.) He then proposed his friend and ally, former Senator Henry W. Corbett. The downstate Republicans rejected Corbett, citing his corporate and national banking interests and his attachment to the Simon "Ring." A special fall session of the legislature, with the support of over half of the Democrats, returned Mitchell to the U.S. Senate by one vote. Back in office, he presented an increased threat to the Corbett-Simon faction in Portland.

The Simon forces controlled the offices of district attorney and mayor, while Mitchell's allies occupied the offices of police judge and city attorney. The nine-member, three-ward city council usually supported the Corbett-Simon economic interests, but was jealous of Simon's political power in the legislature. The 1885 council comprised Sylvester Farrell, a wealthy pioneer fish canner and grain merchant; Jacob Fliedner, a prosperous German-born realtor; C.M. Forbes, a downtown real-estate investor and furniture-store owner; A.F. Sears, Jr., a prominent young lawyer, who became an assistant district attorney the following year; Frank Hacheny, a German-born wholesale grocer, who became city treasurer for 10 years; and W.H. Andrus, a hotel owner. From the North End, which was fast earning a reputation for its transients and its raucus behavior, came a wholesale liquor dealer and two ship craftsmen affiliated with enterprises relating to the OR&N. District Attorney John Gearin, a future Simon partner, was the only Arlington Club member in city government and one of few Democrats in the club.

During the special session of 1885, after Mitchell's re-election, Simon moved to isolate his power and gain tighter control over Portland municipal government. With relative ease, he secured passage of two major pieces of legislation. One created the new Board of Police Commissioners; the other, the Portland Water Committee, also known as the Water Board.

The Board of Police Commissioners was given absolute authority over Portland's Police Department. Appointed by the governor, it was to comprise three civic-minded patriots who would donate their valuable time to serve staggered terms, their successors to be elected by Portland voters. Governor Zenas Moody, a wealthy eastern Oregon wool shipper and former Mitchell supporter, named Simon and two Simon confederates, Byron P. Cardwell and Jonathan Bourne, Jr. Recognizing the stakes involved, Moody could, in Deady's estimation, "be relied on to do anything which the exigencies of party politics" might demand. Cardwell, recently retired from 21 years of loyal service as the local collector of internal revenue, was equally committed to serving Simon's interests.[35]

Bourne, a 30-year-old native of New Bedford, Massachusetts, was climbing the business-political ladder rapidly after only seven years' residence in Oregon. The son of a prosperous textile manufacturer and the owner of a fleet of whaling ships, he had dropped out of Harvard University in his senior year to sail to the Far East. Shipwrecked, he made his way to Portland via Hong Kong and decided to remain. According to one account, during his first days in the city, he "hired a cab, and drove up and down Washington Street and Morrison Street, accompanied by the leading lady of a travelling show, and with an ice bucket filled with champaign bottles sitting in front of them in the cab. They drank publicly at intervals. Such was Bourne's introduction to Portland."[36]

Within three years, Bourne became a charter member of the Arlington Club and was elected to a three-year term as club treasurer in 1883. He read law and gained admittance to the bar in 1881, but practiced only briefly before deciding "to follow the family tradition of accumulating wealth." In partnership with Charles E. Ladd, William S. Ladd's second son, he invested in numerous silver mining properties, capitalized at over $8.5 million. He became so heavily committed to the free coinage of silver at the 16 to 1 ratio with gold — to create a genuine bimetallic currency — that he supported Mitchell over Corbett for the U.S. Senate in 1885. He believed that Mitchell's silver position was closer to his own, while Corbett, along with most Portland bankers, favored the gold standard.[37]

Bourne represented a new breed of businessman-politician beginning to emerge — more aggressive, wealthier and more speculative financially, and more impatient than the older generation. According to former Congressman A.M. Lafferty, "most everyone liked him. He dressed well. He always had money, remittances from Bourne Mills. He entertained much at best eating places and was a charming host." He also proved to be ruthless in business and politics, success in the former whetting his appetite for the latter. His staunch loyalty to Simon in the Oregon House during the two hectic sessions of 1885 (excepting the Mitchell vote) made the police board one of the most influential public agencies in the city and an instrument of personal political ambitions. However, before the decade ended, the police department would be in shambles.[38]

The Water Committee

The creation of the Water Committee, which had the power to acquire and operate a municipal water system, was the most constructive political move in Simon's long career. Like most American cities after the Civil War, Portland had outgrown its traditional water sources. "As domestic water sources dried up or became polluted," Stuart Galishoff has noted, "cities were compelled to develop public water supplies by bringing in water by gravity from mountain streams or, more commonly, by pumping it from nearby rivers and lakes." Portland had increasingly pumped from the Willamette, but citizens feared that population growth and industrialization would eventually pollute the river. There was also an obvious need for an up-to-date distribution system, deemed too costly for a privately operated company. Over half the 3,000 public water supplies built in the United States between 1860 and 1896 were municipally owned.[39]

Simon's bill nominated 15 of the city's most prominent business and civic leaders — the cream of the Portland Establishment — to serve as committee members. They included Cicero H. Lewis, Mayor John Gates, William S. Ladd, Henry Failing, Henry W. Corbett, Simeon G. Reed, Frank Dekum, Julius Loewenberg, Richard B. Knapp, and William K. Smith. Initially, there was widespread local opposition to its formation. The city council reacted negatively, especially to those individuals chosen. By a 6-to-1 vote, the council labeled them an "Oligarchy of 15."[40]

The council complained that the committee members lacked responsibility to taxpayers; that there was no limit on their terms; and that their primary qualification was "simply to be moneyed." By a further vote of 7-0, the council petitioned the county's legislative delegation to restore the waterworks as a function of city government. Turning a deaf ear under Simon's prodding, the legislature enacted the charter amendment on November 25, 1885.[41]

Meeting on December 8, the Committee elected Failing as president and Lewis as treasurer. Although Failing would be the official leader for 12 years, Ladd dominated the committee until his death in 1893. To accommodate his disability (Ladd was paralyzed from the waist down after 1877), the meetings were always held in his office at the Ladd & Tilton Bank, which advanced $20,000 to "get the program going." The Water Committee was initially authorized to sell $700,000 in bonds to finance the expanded system, but a small group of Portland residents challenged its constitutional authority. The state supreme court's decision in November, 1886, upholding the city charter amendment, permitted the committee to purchase existing waterworks and accept bids for equipment and construction. It bought the Green and Leonard properties for $478,000 — about 70 percent of the Portland Water Company asking price. With little discussion, it paid $150,000 for the

Crystal Springs Water Company (in Southeast Portland), financed by Ladd & Tilton. A possible Ladd conflict of interest was neither perceived nor addressed.[42]

As high bidder, Ladd & Tilton purchased $200,000 of the authorized tax-free water bonds, with the First National Bank buying $170,000 worth. While Ladd and Failing had met their expected obligations and assumed some risks, they had also placed their banks in positions of financial control. Conflicts of interest were bound to develop over the funding of future water needs. Such concerns may have influenced Simeon Reed's objections to the committee's decision to use Bull Run Lake as the city's new water source. Reed was not impressed by a professional report claiming that Bull Run water would provide Portland with the purest water of any city in the world except for one in Scotland.

In early January, 1887, when the committee voted 12-1 to acquire the mountain lake, Reed was still smarting from Ladd's "duplicity," which had forced him from the Oregon Iron & Steel presidency the previous June. However, he based his recorded opposition on the projected cost of $500,000, which would require additional bonding capacity. He rightly counseled that the existing supply was as good as that of Bull Run. Furthermore, he favored cheap water rates and no increase in costs to the ratepayers. The tax-free bond interest would have to be met by either a special tax on all residents or a combination of tax and increased rates. Although he did not mention it, he knew that Ladd & Tilton would be the major beneficiary.[43]

From its first meeting, the Water Committee found itself continually embroiled in discussions over residential water rates, projected at $1.50 per month for a family of six persons or less. Herman C. Leonard, of the former water company, joined Reed in protest. Leonard told the committee that while Ladd could afford $5 a month, a poor man could not afford $1.50 when his take-home pay was only $2 a day. On March 2, 1887, the committee submitted to public pressure and set the rate at 75 cents per month. Reed seemed satisfied. Portland would have the second-lowest rates in the nation, only slightly more than those in Niagara Falls, New York.[44]

Within six months Reed was even happier, when the committee awarded an $84,872 contract to the Oregon Iron & Steel Company for 1,997 tons of water pipe. In attempting to patch up their differences, Ladd and Reed must have struck a deal. Whatever concerns Reed may have had about Ladd's conflicts of interest quickly dissolved. They both had heavy financial commitments to salvage. After lengthy negotiations, Reed returned as president and Oregon Iron & Steel received the pipe contract. Ladd & Tilton agreed to advance the company $100,000 and Reed took $150,000 of stock. The future looked brighter as the company expanded its facilities and built a new, 160-foot chimney. After three years of no production, the smelter was fired up in October, 1888. The future also looked brighter for Oregon Paving and Contracting. The company, in which Ladd and his brother-in-law Steel were the controlling investors, received a Bull Run contract for forest clearing and road building in east Multnomah County.[45]

Several months later, in early 1889, the Water Committee purchased approximately four square miles of property within the Bull Run watershed. Most of the remaining land within the watershed was owned by the federal government. Unfortunately for the committee, Governor Pennoyer vetoed a legislative bill that granted the extended $500,000 bonding capacity. Deady, who had drafted the bill for Failing and the committee, was thoroughly put out: "In view of his impracticable, cranky nature and conduct he ought to be called Sylpester Annoyer," he wrote. The governor then vetoed a second bond authorization bill for similar reasons: he opposed the tax-free provisions that would benefit the banks and wealthy investors who bought the bonds. (The prevailing tax rate was a minuscule .5 mills per dollar of assessed valuation unless specifically exempt.) Finally, in 1891, with needs and costs increasing, the legislature authorized a $2.5 million bond issue that *was* subject to taxation. Pennoyer quickly approved it, enabling the Water Committee to go to work on the Bull Run water line. At a January, 1895 celebration honoring the arrival of the first Bull Run water in the city, the governor tasted the water and allowed that it had neither the body nor flavor of the Willamette.[46]

Through its first decade of operation, the Water Committee had provided efficient and economical service. Failing's estimates of annual revenues and expenses always turned out to be accurate. The committee enjoyed a freedom to operate that encouraged a long-term view that a political council government, open to partisan and personal strife, might not have provided. But it was clearly an elite oligarchy, enmeshed in conflicts of interest. The bankers, wealthy investors and contractors, including some committee members themselves, benefited accordingly. In foregoing tax-free bond interest, the committee secured the city's obligation to back any bonded indebtedness. The city and the state thus "took a calculated gamble" in support of private entrepreneurship. The investment paid off handsomely for all concerned, including the public.[47]

The Southern Pacific and The Union Pacific

Railroad politics largely dominated legislative and city council sessions during the mid-to-late 1880s. As Martin Shafter noted, railroad influence detracted from strong party unity in Oregon. "The railroads enjoyed allies and exercised influence in both parties" at all levels, as evidenced by Mitchell's garnering of over half the votes of the legislative Democrats in 1885. Showing an interest in the abandoned Oregon & California Railroad, the Southern Pacific had secretly placed Mitchell on its payroll. Spreading money about liberally, in the Ben Holladay tradition, the Southern Pacific and other railroads conditioned local and state politicians, farmers and businessmen, to reconcile their self-interests with railroad interests at the expense of party unity. According to Paul Kleppner, the resulting weak party structure, more often found in the Far West, accounted for "the high levels of volatility that marred the region's election outcomes" and its legislative and municipal actions.[48]

One who knew how to play the volatile game of railroad politics was William Reid, who found himself a free agent in January, 1885. At the supposed urging of downstate farmers, he reincorporated his former Oregonian Railway as the Portland & Willamette Valley Railroad. Its numerous incorporators included many familiar names and some new to the Establishment: W.S. Ladd, C.H. Lewis, S.G.

Reed, R.B. Knapp, H.C. Leonard, Aaron Meier, and Van B. DeLashmutt, a wealthy real-estate owner who would succeed John Gates as mayor in 1888. To gain railroad entrance to Portland, Reid had a new depot-site bill introduced into the legislature, containing essentially the same grant provisions as the unconstitutional 1880 law. After a stiff fight, he won.[49]

The climate of opinion had changed in Portland. Ladd and Reed, for example, now wanted rail service for their Oregon Iron & Steel Company. A belated legal test to preserve Portland's only remaining public levee was denied. Reversing a position taken five years earlier, the courts held that the grant to the railroad was not inconsistent with the land's use as a public levee. They argued that, the dedication having been made in favor of the public, the state rather than the city was the actual beneficiary. The city council, also reversing its position under pressure, granted a right-of-way franchise in South Portland on June 17, 1887. The Dundee-to-Portland connection was completed in July, and the depot opened a year later.[50]

The whole episode was one gigantic sleight of hand. Unbeknown to the public, most of the funds for the Portland & Willamette Valley Railroad, according to Harvey Scott's account, "were supplied by Collis P. Huntington," president of the Southern Pacific. The company was capitalized at $150,000 in stock and $400,000 in bonds. The fact that Simeon Reed invested in the enterprise would indicate that at least he, Ladd and William Reid were well informed on Southern Pacific involvement. The OR&N hierarchy must also have known and given tacit support. In late 1885, the OR&N had apparently begun preliminary negotiations with the Southern Pacific for leasing of its southbound trackage and rights of way, including that of the Oregon Central (West Side) Railroad. The OR&N had suffered a 40 percent drop in net earnings in 1885 as a result of Villard's bankruptcy and the depression of 1884. The Southern Pacific knew that the OR&N was badly in need of increased revenues, and was anxious to gain a foothold in western Oregon. Meeting Reid's financial exigencies would provide just the opportunity. The Southern Pacific would also be given added leverage in its negotiations with the OR&N.[51]

Joseph Simon faced a dilemma in the 1885 session. Five years earlier, he had sponsored the public levee's acquisition. Sensing (or perhaps knowing) Mitchell's involvement with the Southern Pacific, and well aware that pro-Mitchell legislators were supporting Reid's bill, he resolved to lead the opposition (which must have dismayed his fellow OR&N directors). As corporate secretary, he was probably cognizant of Southern Pacific's intentions. He tried every possible parliamentary maneuver to defeat the measure. Only he and state Senator H.B. Miller from Josephine County in southern Oregon voted against it. Miller sensed a phony deal when he stated publicly that the Portland & Willamette Valley Railroad was "not a bona fide enterprise."[52]

On April 11, 1887 (retroactive to January of that year), the OR&N leased most of its North Portland and Columbia River Division trackage and railroad real estate, including the Albina yards, to the Union Pacific Railroad. The Union Pacific had been running trains into East Portland since December, 1884, having completed its Oregon Shortline track from Granger, Wyoming, to Huntington, Oregon, in 1882. There it connected with a branch of the OR&N, which in turn connected to the main OR&N line used by the Northern Pacific.

In May, 1887, the Southern Pacific's control of the Portland & Willamette Valley Railroad was revealed in a public announcement that the Pacific Improvement Company was the real owner. The officers of this enterprise were the "big four" of the Southern Pacific: Collis P. Huntington, Charles Crocker, Leland Stanford, and Mark Hopkins. In July, after much negotiation, the OR&N's Oregon and California (held in trust for Villard) and Oregon Central properties were leased to the Southern Pacific, which subsequently bought them. Richard Koehler, Villard's Oregon agent and a charter member of the Arlington Club, became resident manager of the Southern Pacific's Oregon railroad operations. Under Koehler, the Southern Pacific completed the Oregon & California rail line from Ashland to the California border. The first through train from San Francisco arrived in East Portland on December 19, 1887.[53]

The OR&N still survived as a corporation. When its stock continued to decline through 1887, its directors became concerned about the leasing arrangements with the Union Pacific. Villard, after regaining his health and reassuming the presidency of the Northern Pacific in September, 1887, favored a joint leasing of the OR&N properties to both the Union Pacific and the Northern Pacific. The Boston and Portland OR&N directors bitterly opposed such an arrangement, considering that competition between the Union Pacific and Northern Pacific would grant Portland more favorable shipping rates which they demanded. In March, 1888, a delegation that included Lewis, Failing, and *Oregonian* Editor Harvey Scott, went to New York to consult Villard. Eventually, the Union Pacific withdrew from the joint lease arrangement and in 1889 bought control of its leased OR&N properties through purchase of Villard's Oregon & Transcontinental railroad holdings.[54]

Outside Control

Portland's experience with the Union Pacific and Southern Pacific clearly showed that, in the late nineteenth century, the railroads, controlled by powerful outside monied interests, had become "the most important institutions in the economics of the western states." As *Fortune Magazine* later observed, referring to the Southern Pacific's "big four":

> The simple theme that the quartet evolved was that riches should be distributed to all, though not necessarily in equal measure. The legislators should make a profit for passing laws, and the state . . . should make a profit for having a railroad, and the town should make a profit for the same reason, and the railroad should make a profit (in the form of subsidies as well as traffic) from the state and the towns.[55]

The Portland Establishment was well aware of these realities. If it could not fight the railroads, it joined them, and drew whatever profits it could from the arrangement. The sale of the OR&N railroad properties to the Union Pacific netted handsome rewards to those like Corbett and Failing who kept their OR&N stock and converted it to Union Pacific stock. In 1911, long after their deaths, the OR&N name was changed to the Oregon, Washington Railway and Navigation Company. The OR&N remained a major stockholder in the Northern Pacific Terminal Company, sharing ownership with the Northern Pacific Railroad and later, James J. Hill's Great Northern Railroad.

The national railroads brought tangible benefits to Portland. They ended the region's isolation and opened a period of full economic development. Industrial employment increased rapidly as large service yards and bridges across the Willamette were built. Of particular benefit to Portland's real-estate developers was the opening up of southwestern suburban districts. The Southern Pacific's Portland & Willamette Valley line provided 14 trips daily between Portland and Oswego, with half a dozen intermediate stops. As the *West Shore* accurately predicted in December, 1888: "In a few years this route will be the main reliance of thousands of suburban residents employed or doing business in the city of Portland."[56]

The Establishment, led by the intermarried Ladd, Corbett and Failing families, was quick to take advantage of such developments by accumulating huge property holdings with easy access to the rail line. The railroad's presence also stimulated the growth of electrified street railways, in which Portland's leading bankers, merchants and politicians became major investors. There was even more money to be made as the surviving Establishment welcomed new members to its fold.

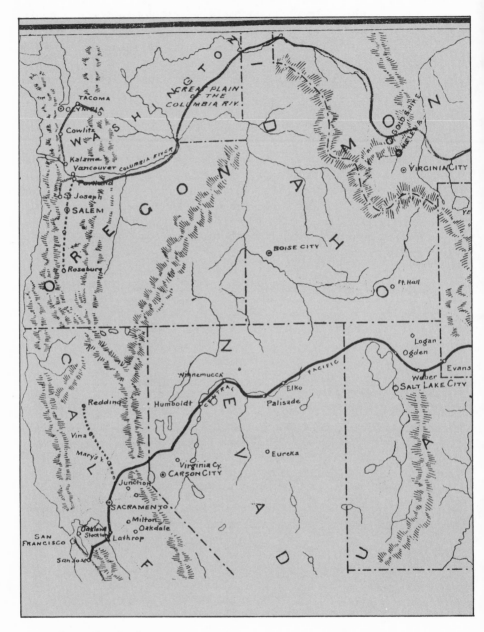

12.1 Northern Pacific Railroad, 1883

12.2 Cleveland Rockwell's water color of the 1885 Portland waterfront

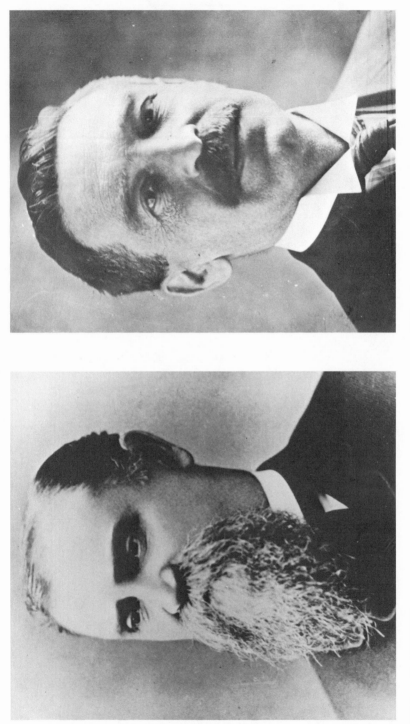

12.4 Joseph Simon (1855-1940)

12.3 James Steel (1835-1913)

12.6 Chinatown, 1890, Second St. south from Washington

12.5 Jonathan Bourne, Jr. (1855-1935)

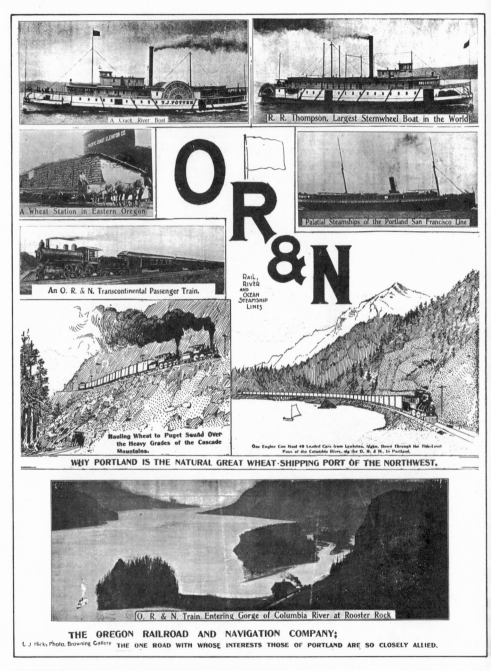

A Crack River Boat

R. R. Thompson, Largest Sternwheel Boat in the World

A Wheat Station in Eastern Oregon

Palatial Steamships of the Portland San Francisco Line

An O. R. & N. Transcontinental Passenger Train.

RAIL, RIVER AND OCEAN STEAMSHIP LINES

Hauling Wheat to Puget Sound Over the Heavy Grades of the Cascade Mountains.

One Engine Can Haul 40 Loaded Cars from Lewiston, Idaho, Down Through the Tide-Level Pass of the Columbia River, via the O. R. & N. to Portland.

WHY PORTLAND IS THE NATURAL GREAT WHEAT-SHIPPING PORT OF THE NORTHWEST.

O. R. & N. Train Entering Gorge of Columbia River at Rooster Rock

THE OREGON RAILROAD AND NAVIGATION COMPANY;

L J Hicks Photo, Browning Gallery THE ONE ROAD WITH WHOSE INTERESTS THOSE OF PORTLAND ARE SO CLOSELY ALLIED.

12.7 OR & N page

12.8 Nth and Davis Streets, looking east, 1888

12.9 "Portland Flouring Mills, Albina, Org."

12.10 Gov. Sylvester Pennoyer (?) watches first Bull Run water arrive at City Park reservoir, 1895

12.11 Second Street, north of Yamhill

13

BANKERS, POLITICIANS AND UTILITIES: 1887-1892

Growth and Mass Transit: The Early Years

Ten transit companies spread their tracks over the streets of Portland and East Portland between April, 1888, and December, 1891. Transit growth accompanied the city's exploding population, which doubled to nearly 41,000 between 1880 and 1887. The East Portland railroad terminals and the $500,000 Albina railroad yards, employing more than a thousand workers, quickly made the east side of the Willamette River a minor urban area itself, with a population of approximately 10,000 by 1887. The east side also received the population overflow from an increasingly congested west side, situated as it was on a narrow shelf and hemmed in on three sides by hills.[1]

The pattern of mass transit that developed on both sides of the river was, in Randall V. Mills's judgement, "the product of the combined forces of geography, mechanical advancement, competition, and real estate development." Portland's bankers, merchants and politicians immersed themselves in what became an increasingly costly and contentious enterprise. From its inception in 1871, when Ben Holladay built the Portland Street Railway's single horsecar line along First Street, transit was a major local political issue, under the sole authority of city government. Councilmen and mayors, often investors themselves, continually debated the franchise provisions, routes and fares.[2]

In a turbulent three-year period leading to Portland's consolidation with East Portland and Albina in 1891, public transit service became subordinate to the interests of politicians, utility operators and land speculators. Business and political leaders in Portland were pursuing a course of action considered normal in most of America's developing urban centers during the latter years of the nineteenth century. In the words of Lewis Mumford,

The extension of the speculative gridiron and the public transportation system were the two main activities that gave dominance to capitalist forms in the growing cities. Thus the city . . . was treated not as a public institution, but a private commercial venture to be carved up in any fashion that might increase the turnover and further the rise in land values.[3]

259

Holladay's decision to build Portland's first street railway on the west side, in
stead of on the east side where he owned extensive property, indicated his astute
judgment that a profitable transit system required a higher level of population
density than that of East Portland in 1871. A street railway on the west side at least
gave the area the metropolitan appearance — a sure sign of progress — essential to
his grandiose plans for the region. It also gave him financial leverage in dealing
with the city's government and business leaders. While not satisfying the need for
mass transit, "it still served," according to Mills, "as a kind of civic window-
dressing and prideful display."[4]

For over a decade, the Portland Street Railway Company held a monopoly on
Portland's transit business, largely because there was insufficient traffic to warrant competition. During the boom of 1882, in anticipation of the arrival of the
Northern Pacific Railroad in 1883, two more horsecar lines were built: the Multnomah Street Railway and the Transcontinental Street Railway. Partially backed by
prominent business leaders James W. Cook and George Weidler (who was also a
part owner of the Portland Street Railway), the Multnomah line was largely financed by engineer-promoter D. E. Budd and Woodson A. Scoggin, a burgeoning
local capitalist and member of the 1882 city council that awarded the franchise.[5]

Within weeks, the Multnomah Street Railway was challenged by the newly
formed Transcontinental Street Railway Company, which received the Third
Street franchise eagerly sought by the Multnomah line. The Transcontinental's
backers and incorporators included William S. Ladd, Henry W. and Elijah Corbett,
and Lauritz Therkelsen. In December, 1882, they had key friends on the city council. William H. Adams worked for the Oregon Furniture Manufacturing Company
financed by Ladd & Tilton, and Donald MacKay was Therkelsen's partner in the
prosperous North Pacific Lumber Company, financed by the First National Bank.
As with later transit companies, bank resources exerted the greatest influence in
gaining council approval.

The Transcontinental's president and general manager from its founding until
September, 1891, was 47-year-old Tyler Woodward, a native of Hartland, Vermont.
After attending Kimball Union Academy and teaching school, he emigrated to
California in 1860. For 10 years he lived in frontier gold-mining communities in
California, Idaho and Montana, doing everything from mining to running a trad-
ing post for Portland merchant Leland H. Wakefield. Then, with $30,000 in gold
strapped to his saddle, he rode into Portland, where he invested in real estate and
served briefly on the Multnomah County Commission (1876-77). He then went to
Walla Walla to supervise railroad construction.[6]

In 1882, Elijah Corbett drew him back to Portland to build and manage the
Transcontinental system. Four years later, as the company grew rapidly after surviving the ill effects of the 1884 depression, Woodward won election to the city
council, on which he was to serve for six years as its dominant member. From
December, 1888, to December, 1889, the council awarded four separate franchises
to the Transcontinental system, which by then had laid 10 miles of track that
extended to the city limits in all directions. In each case Woodward voted in favor
of the ordinance, and on two occasions he signed the ordinances while serving as
acting mayor in his capacity as elected council president. The 30-year franchises

required no payment for the use of city streets, only for car license fees of $50 per year for a two-horse model, and $25 for a one-horse rig. Protecting his corporate interests, he always voted against franchise awards to competing lines.[7]

George B. Markle, Jr., Impresses Portland

One competitor who gave Woodward a run for his money was a brash, 30-year-old, recently arrived from Hazleton, Pennsylvania. George B. Markle, Jr., came to Portland in 1887 with solid social credentials and access to an extensive fortune. His banker father, a director of the Lehigh Railroad and the founder of the Jeddo-Highland Coal Company, one of the largest independent anthracite mining operations in the East, was an early associate of Thomas Edison in building the first two central-station coal-fired electric power plants in the United States. After graduating from Lafayette College and gaining eight years' experience with various family businesses, George, Jr. traveled through seven western states and decided to settle permanently in Portland. According to his nephew, Alvan Markle, Jr., the city offered George the best inducement to better his fortune by investing his sizeable resources in several new enterprises, of which street railways, mining and banking seemed the most promising.[8]

In 1887, Portland was experiencing its biggest boom to date, ended only by the depression of 1893. The Lombard Investment Company, a national investors' service, published a glowing but exaggerated statement of Portland's economic health. Citing a total of 100 millionaires and invested capital of $50 million, it also reported that several million dollars had been invested in eastern Oregon and Idaho mines since 1884. This led to the organization of the Portland Stock Exchange, which coincided with Markle's arrival. Markle joined 24 other investors as charter members of the exchange under the leadership of Jonathan Bourne, Jr. Two members of the group were Tyler Woodward and Van B. DeLashmutt, a merchant-banker and real-estate investor who would be elected mayor in April, 1888.[9]

The opening of the Morrison Street Bridge in April, 1887 (the largest bridge west of the Mississippi), and the incorporation of the Willamette Bridge Railway the same month, attracted Markle's attention. He could see the transit potential in connecting the west side with the fast-growing east side. He also noted the electric lights along First and Third streets, provided by the U.S. Electric Lighting and Power Company, under contract with the City of Portland since March, 1885. Formed in March, 1884, by the Ainsworth Bank's president, Lester Leander Hawkins, businessman George Weidler, engineer P. F. Morey, and attorney Fred V. Holman, the company generated its power by coal-fired steam engines, a process familiar to Markle through his father's association with Edison. He could envision the probability of electrically propelled streetcars, a technique that in 1887 was generally considered experimental and rather suspect.[10]

To succeed in Portland, Markle needed to make the proper friends. An enthusiastic man, he found just the vehicle: a campaign to resurrect the construction of the Portland Hotel, the foundations of which had lain exposed for over two years. "Villard's ruins," as they were called, into which the railroad magnate had pumped

$125,000, were an "eyesore and a public nuisance." Within months, Markle had succeeded in persuading 150 of Portland's leading citizens to subscribe a total of $525,000. William S. Ladd invested $100,000; Henry W. Corbett, $80,000; Henry Failing, $50,000; Cicero H. Lewis, $25,000; Simeon G. Reed, $20,000; and Van B. DeLashmutt, $20,000. For his part, Markle subscribed to 15 shares of the 100 par value common stock. Corbett, who subsequently invested a total of $200,000, was elected president of the Portland Hotel Company; attorney Cyrus A. Dolph, vice-president; and Henry Failing, treasurer.[11]

Markle was now in with the right crowd, and he had proven his ability. His efforts led to a close friendship with DeLashmutt. In the 46 years since his birth in a small Iowa town, the latter had enjoyed extraordinary financial success. According to a later account in the *Oregonian*, he was a man of "unusual personal attractiveness which led to wide acquaintances and great popularity." Originally a printer by trade, he entered the wholesale grocery business soon after arriving in Portland. He also entered the real-estate market by purchasing and platting acreage on which was to be built part of the future town of Beaverton. Near Hillsboro, he developed Witch Hazel Farm and horse track, which became the "sporting center" of the state. As an avid horse breeder, he began a long association with Simeon G. Reed.[12]

Politically, DeLashmutt was an aspiring power player in 1887. His wife's cousin was Penumbra Kelly, U.S. marshal and sheriff of Multnomah County from 1888 to 1894. Kelly had married a daughter of the wealthy and politically active Judge Philip Marquam. In February, 1888, in a mutually beneficial partnership, DeLashmutt teamed up with Markle to buy control of the Multnomah Street Railway Company and merge it with the Portland Traction Company, which he had incorporated in August, 1887, with a capital stock of $500,000. The two men needed the Multnomah franchise to gain street access for a proposed 10 miles of railway track. Markle was elected president and DeLashmutt vice-president. Three months later, the popular ex-grocery merchant was elected mayor by the city council to succeed John Gates, who had died in office. In June, 1888, he won popular election to a regular three-year term. As mayor, he promoted and signed four franchise ordinances in behalf of the Multnomah Street Railway operation, all with the same fee schedule.

In 1888, DeLashmutt and Markle organized the Oregon National Bank by absorbing the Metropolitan Savings Bank, which DeLashmutt, Judge Erasmus D. Shattuck, *Oregonian* Editor Harvey W. Scott, and outgoing Governor William W. Thayer had formed in 1882. They also created the Northwest Loan & Trust Company to finance real-estate transactions. DeLashmutt presided over the former while Markle assumed direction of the latter, with both banks housed in Markle's building.

For anyone starting a bank, the readiest source of large deposits was that of public tax revenues. Thus it was not surprising that Sheriff Kelly deposited the school tax funds with the Markle-controlled banks. Mayor DeLashmutt made sure that the city also deposited its funds with the Markle banks. H. C. Monnastes, city treasurer until 1890, was a long-time mining investor associate of the mayor. The new city treasurer in 1890, former city councilman Frank Hacheny, was equally close to the mayor. He had bought DeLashmutt's wholesale grocery business in 1882. As any banker knew, public funds attracted private deposits. Soon the Markle banks had sufficient assets to launch an aggressive campaign to promote commercial loans for investment in real estate and traction properties. In August, 1888, DeLashmutt boasted that he "probably own[ed] more houses than any man in Portland."[13]

In the spring of 1888, Markle gained admission to the Arlington Club; he also became a local celebrity. His mother and two sisters were visiting him in Portland when they received word that his father was desperately ill in Hazleton. He hired a two-car special train and headed east with his family at breakneck speed: "Tables and chairs were piled in a heap as the cars swayed and bounced over the rails." In 63 hours the Markles were in Chicago, the fastest trip recorded until then and only five hours slower than the streamliner schedule 60 years later. Costing Markle $2,000, the venture enhanced his reputation as a colorful man of action. Not long after the trip, his father died, and the young Markle's already substantial wealth was increased by an inheritance. He used the money to build up his bank resources and street-railway properties, and to purchase several hundred acres of Portland real estate.[14]

His eyes lit upon a handsome brick mansion under construction in early 1889 on Southwest Hawthorne Terrace, on the heights above Portland. It belonged to lawyer-realtor J. Carroll McCaffrey, a transplanted Philadelphian who was secretary and manager of the Portland Building and Loan Association. McCaffrey and Preston C. Smith, who were active Arlington Club members, were largely responsible for promoting both the new Cable Railway and the residential development of Portland Heights, which was regarded as the playground of the wealthy. McCaffrey was strapped for cash. The Cable Railway Company, incorporated in July, 1887, had encountered unexpected costs that delayed its opening for another year. He happily sold Markle the unfinished house for $20,334 (including an $8,000 mortgage), and 10 additional acres for $2,700. In late May, Markle moved in and in June married a considerably younger woman, Kate Goodwin, the daughter of an army lieutenant stationed at Vancouver (Washington) Barracks. The wedding was reported to be the greatest social event of the season in Vancouver, where Markle had already purchased several parcels of land. He took his bride to the largest and most prominent home on the Portland skyline, to begin their married life in the grand style that he had sought since his arrival in Portland.[15]

Markle's star shone more brightly in 1890, when he was appointed to the Public Improvement Standing Committee of the Board of Trade, which was merged into the newly incorporated Portland Chamber of Commerce on April 7. On that same day, the Portland Hotel opened its eight floors, 326 bedrooms and extensive dining facilities to an eager public. For three decades it was to play a leading role in the social and business life of the city. Well over a million dollars had been spent on construction and furnishings. Its imposing and lively presence boosted civic pride and confidence in the city's future growth. Its designers, former Bostonians Ion Lewis and William M. Whidden (trained by the McKim, Mead & White firm), were active Arlington Club members and generally recognized as Portland's Establishment architectural partnership.[16]

Markle was already involved in several other projects that reflected *his* confi
dence in the city's future. With Frank Dekum, he had been responsible in 1888 fo
promoting the construction of the North Pacific Industrial Association Expositior
Building (at Southwest Burnside and 18th). He had personally bought the land anc
assumed a $62,000 mortgage with the Scottish American Investment Trust Com
pany Ltd. of Edinburgh. Erected at a cost of $150,000, the building opened ir
September, 1889, and was an immediate success as a trade exhibition center. It alsc
served as a public auditorium for large gatherings. On the night of May 5, 1891
over 15,000 Oregonians squeezed within its portals to welcome President Ben
jamin Harrison.[17]

In 1890, Markle's enthusiasm persuaded the recast Chamber of Commerce tc
build new headquarters on the north side of Stark Street, between Third and
Fourth. As ground was broken on September 2, he committed the support of both
of his banks, which were to move into prime space at street level. He negotiated
the mortgage with the New York Life Insurance Company, and when the construction costs overran the budget by almost $170,000, Markle personally secured
signed notes covering the excess. Later known as the Commerce Building, it remained the major meeting place of business and political figures for decades.
Besides banks, its eight floors contained offices, saloons, a bowling alley, a billiard
room, an auditorium, and the prestigious Commercial Club. Upon its opening in
September, 1893, wealthy hardware merchant E. J. DeHart was elected president
and banker Richard L. Durham treasurer. Both were active Arlington Club members. In recognition of his untiring efforts, George B. Markle, Jr., was elected
Chamber president. At 34, he had reached the pinnacle of Portland's business
community.[18]

Transit Companies Scramble to Survive

Beginning in 1889, Portland's traction firms, following a national trend, engaged "in a mad scramble to electrify horsecar and cable trackage and build new
lines . . . . To the lasting misfortune of the street railways," in Stanley Mallach's
opinion, "shabby and unwise practices pervaded this rapid growth." The major
promoters often milked their properties by contracting to construction companies they themselves owned. The most questionable practice was overbuilding,
particularly in laying miles of track in thinly populated areas in the expectation of
increasing the value of distant land owned by railway operators and their political
friends. The result of such frantic activity was a massive, confusing series of incorporations, bankruptcies and consolidations. Few of Portland's lines ever turned a
profit, but some adjacent real-estate developments produced appreciable rewards.[19]

Fulton Park, developed by the Southwest Portland Real Estate Company, did
provide reasonable profits to some of its owners within 10 years. These included
Oregonian publisher Henry L. Pittock, James Steel, and his attorney brother,
George, who in 1887 bought 400 acres of land from Judge Philip A. Marquam for
$150,000. They platted 1,000 lots for sale at a uniform price of $400 each, and as an
inducement, held a lottery drawing on November 15, 1888. Every tenth lot in-

cluded a house: 98 were cottages costing $1,000 each; two were more "elegant," costing $5,000 each. As their *West Shore* advertisement proclaimed: "Here is, undoubtedly, the best opportunity the man of small or large means will have to secure a good suburban home on the confines of Portland."[20]

Two months later, the Fulton Park investors incorporated the Metropolitan Railway Company to provide electric streetcar service from Second Street to south of Oswego above the west side of the Willamette River. Major stops included Fulton Park and the Riverview Cemetery, the final resting place for Portland's Establishment families. Capitalized at $200,000, the Metropolitan received financial backing from the Merchants National Bank (of which James Steel was president), and from Henry Pittock's Portland Trust Company, organized in 1887. Some Ladd & Tilton money also went into the venture, as access to the cemetery was essential to its founders, Ladd, Henry W. Corbett and Henry Failing.[21]

Like similar enterprises nationally, transit companies such as the Metropolitan had to build their own costly powerhouses. Moreover, they needed direct access to the city center. James Steel therefore prevailed upon his good friend Markle to sell franchise rights along Second Street held by the Multnomah Street Railway. The installation of the poles and overhead wires caused consternation to some citizens, who complained of their ugliness. With his usual good humor, Henry Pittock replied that the rails, poles and wires were a lot less unsightly than a tired horse pulling a car up a hill. As he implied, the day of Portland's horse-drawn streetcars was drawing to a close.[22]

Launching Portland's second electric line in January, 1890, was no easy task. Equipment problems and collapsing steep banks that temporarily blocked the tracks added to the costs. When the line was finally completed in March, 1891, Metropolitan provided the longest electric streetcar service in Oregon, a distance of six miles from Northwest Second and Glisan streets to the Riverview Cemetery. The Steel brothers, as majority owners, abruptly decided to forego further construction toward Oswego and instead to explore possibilities on the east side of the Willamette. They looked to the Mount Tabor Street Railway Company (incorporated in February, 1890), which had opened the city's third bridge in January, 1891.

The Madison Street Bridge (connecting Madison Street on the west side with Hawthorne Street on the east) was built to provide the Mount Tabor line with direct access to downtown Portland. It had a deserved reputation as a poorly designed structure, incapable of withstanding the heavy jolts of trolley cars. In November, 1891, four months after Portland and East Portland were consolidated, the owners of both the bridge and the rail line informed the Steels that they wanted to sell out quickly and recover their investment. The consolidation charter amendment allowed the city to buy the two existing privately owned bridges by selling bonds. The Free Bridge Committee, established by the council, recommended that the city purchase the Madison Street bridge first, rather than the older Morrison Street span. When the council voted 12-3 to buy the bridge for $142,500, eleven months after its completion, a public outcry ensued.[23]

A deal had obviously been struck between the politically influential bridge and railway owners (who included Sheriff Penumbra Kelly), the Free Bridge Committee (whose treasurer was William M. Ladd) and the Steel brothers. James Steel was Ladd's uncle, and George was the politically powerful Republican Portland postmaster from 1890 to 1894. The controversial ordinance authorizing the bridge purchase also awarded a 30-year franchise to the Mount Tabor Railway Company, which the Steel brothers bought on the day the ordinance was enacted. The franchise fee for bridge use was set at an unusually low figure of $1,200 a year. This was considered by many an over-generous public subsidy for a well-connected private utility, and was roundly assailed for decades. In 1926 the *Oregonian* claimed that "the city got the worst of the bargain." In May, 1892, the Steels bought the electric East Side Railway Company from the former owners of the Mount Tabor Line and merged the two into what became the area's first interurban system, extending to Oregon City.[24]

A second example of the interrelation between mass transit and land speculation was the narrow-gauge Portland & Vancouver Railway, incorporated in April, 1888, by bankers Frank Dekum and Richard L. Durham, who had previously founded the Oregon Land & Investment Company. Like the Steel brothers, they received bank financing from their own institutions, the Commercial National and the Portland Savings banks. David P. Thompson, who was developing the Irvington tract and was a director of both banks, assisted the company in gaining franchises from East Portland, Albina and Multnomah County, despite objections from competitors. The partners planned a steam-powered line from the Stark Street Ferry landing in East Portland, extending north along Union Avenue through Albina to the Columbia River opposite Vancouver, which was to be reached by ferry.[25]

North of central Albina, the countryside was sparsely settled, but the developers who platted Woodlawn in Northeast Portland were confident of their prospects. Accessible land was saleable land. The railway offered "cheap and quick communication between its terminal points," passing through "some of the most desirable suburban property in East Portland and Albina." By early September, new houses were reported to be springing up all along the line.[26]

The major competitor who had opposed the Dekum-Durham franchise award was Charles F. Swigert, manager of the Portland office of the Pacific Bridge Company of San Francisco (owned by his uncle Charles Gorril). In 1888, the 26-year-old Swigert, a native of Bowling Green, Ohio was the driving force behind the Willamette Bridge Railway Company, which had been incorporated a year earlier to run horse-drawn cars over the Morrison Street Bridge. The bridge was the brainchild of William G. Beck, Portland's leading gunsmith and a respected community leader. Beck had originally contracted with Pacific Bridge in 1880, but court litigation had blocked the project. Reincorporated in 1886, the Willamette Iron Bridge Company received public approval to build a toll bridge to East Portland. Simultaneously, it received a franchise to operate streetcars across the bridge. Swigert directed the bridge construction and became one of the incorporators of the railway company that was formed a week after the bridge opened on April 21, 1887.[27]

His fellow directors in both enterprises were Beck, former Congressman Rufus Mallory (a partner in the Dolph-Simon firm), and Homer and James Campbell, relatives of Swigert who were to be associated with him for many years. Swigert's goal was to build an electric system, but for two years he had to content himself with horsedrawn and then steam-powered service, extending through Sunnyside to Mount Tabor. When the Union Pacific, through the Oregon Railway & Navigation Company, began construction of the Steel Bridge in 1887, to provide the railroad with direct access to a west side Portland terminal, Swigert saw an opportunity to build an extensive electric line through Albina to St. Johns. Using Mallory, whose law firm represented the OR&N, he negotiated an exclusive agreement to operate the area's first electric street-railway system, which began service in November, 1889, 16 months after the bridge opened. By extending service to a distant St. Johns, the company's 15 miles of track made it the largest streetcar system on the West Coast. It also opened thousands of acres to land speculation and development.

The economic interests of property owners in Albina and St. Johns influenced legislative approval of city consolidation in 1891. Many of the propertys owners were downtown Portland businessmen and bankers; others were corporations, like William S. Ladd's Portland Flouring Mills and the OR&N, which between them held nearly two miles of waterfront in Albina. As further reinforcements, Mallory's partner, OR&N attorney Joseph Simon, was state senate president in 1891, while James B. Montgomery, a former associate of John C. Ainsworth, William Reid and Henry Villard and a large property owner in Albina, served in the House session that year primarily to promote consolidation. The state senator, whose district included the Albina-St. Johns area, was attorney P. L. Willis, a close friend of Swigert and his partner in the Electric Land Company, which had been established in 1889 to develop and sell property in the Portsmouth district of St. Johns, where much of the land was originally owned by the pioneer Waud, Mock and Caples families. The Electric Land Company evolved into the Portland Guarantee Company for the purpose of developing its University Park tract as the site of the new Portland University.[28]

Founded in 1890 by dissident Methodists who had broken away from Willamette University in Salem, Portland University had a brief life of barely 10 years before it was succeeded by Columbia University, which in turn became the University of Portland in 1922. Senator Willis (who was also secretary of the university's board of trustees and brother-in-law of its first president) and Swigert were instrumental in convincing the trustees to locate on a 71-acre portion of their 600-acre University Park tract, platted by the Guarantee Company along a high bluff overlooking the Willamette River.

According to University of Portland historian James T. Covert, the institution "had no sooner started when rumors of graft and incompetency arose concerning the promotion of the University Park property by the Portland Guarantee Company." Harvey Scott, president of the board of trustees, denied any irregularities, insisting that "the board of trustees had secured the land directly from the original owners and not through real-estate brokers, a point that in 1922, F. S. Akin, former chairman of the guarantee company, seriously questioned." The university had actually purchased the 600-acre tract through a trust agreement with the guarantee company, which had assembled the property and would hold it for the university. The university financed the $300,000 cost from the sale of five-year bonds guaranteed by the company. While the original owners might have been listed as the legal sellers, the guarantee company, as agent, promoter and trustee, received hefty commissions. The university had allowed itself to be used as the vehicle and major attraction for a huge real-estate promotional scheme, designed to benefit both the development and the railway. The close tie between the two also appeared in a display of Portland Guarantee real-estate information at a store adjacent to the railway's University Park station. Serving as a district post office, it was also the university's bookstore.[29]

Electric Power and Railway Consolidation

The generation of electric power in the Portland region began modestly in September, 1880, when George Weidler erected a dynamo at his west bank saw-mill on the Willamette River across from Albina. Weidler was instrumental in organizing the U.S. Electric Lighting and Power Company in 1884. Like other small power plants in the region, built to service electric railway and street lighting needs, the company used steam-generated dynamos. As the area's electric load grew voraciously in 1888-89, it became obvious to the company's president, P. F. Morey, and investors David P. Thompson, William K. Smith and Weidler, that a larger and more efficient generating plant was required. With financing from the Ainsworth National Bank through Hawkins, Morey and Oregon City capitalist E. L. Eastham formed the Willamette Falls Electric Company. They merged U.S. Electric with the Oregon City Electric Company, which controlled the water rights, to use the falls as the source of generating power. When Portland, 14 miles away, received its initial power from the new plant on June 3, 1889, it was the first long-distance commercial transmission of hydroelectric power in the United States.[30]

The consolidation of small power plants into larger entities, of which Willamette Falls Electric was merely the beginning, preceded a similar consolidation of competing electric-railway companies. To First National Bank owners Henry Failing and Henry W. Corbett, who had granted Charles Swigert a full line of credit for his railway expansion, there were too many traction companies, too much competition, growing inefficiency in service, and increasing financial burdens. Under their direction in June, 1891, Swigert, attorney Rufus Mallory and others organized the City and Suburban Railway Company, which merged the Willamette Bridge Railway with Elijah Corbett's and Tyler Woodward's Transcontinental system. Two other railways electrified by Swigert were included: the Waverly-Woodstock line, and the Portland and Fairview line, running to the Columbia River, where Swigert owned property. Incorporated one week after city consolidation and capitalized at $1 million, the new company drew most of its power from two plants that Swigert helped establish: The Albina Light and Water Company (1889) and the Union Power Company (1891). Union Power, financed by the First National Bank, was a joint enterprise of Woodward's Transcontinental and Markle's Multnomah Street Railway. The City and Suburban was enfranchised in December, 1891, with Woodward guiding the ordinance through the council. Economic consolidation was following political consolidation, allowing Portland's business and financial Establishment to extend its control throughout the growing city.[31]

More was involved in this reorganization than the mere combination of five street-railway companies. For the first time, the city's largest bank became a partner in what was to become, 13 years later through further merges, a giant amalgamation of all the street railways into a monopoly, mainly financed by the city's three largest national banks. Henry Failing, representing the First National, became president of the City and Suburban, and Swigert chief engineer and general manager. After several months, Woodward was named president, a post he held for 13 years, while also serving as president of the U.S. National Bank from 1895 to 1902.[32]

The new U.S. National Bank, which was to become a major force in the merging of public transit and electric utility companies in Portland, opened for business in early February, 1891. "Commercial activity had reached such volume that in 1889 local bankers formed a clearing house for the settling of daily balances," according to Claude Singer. In 1891, as the financial center of the Northwest, Portland cleared most payments for Oregon's expanding commodity production. With the state's population growing just as rapidly, and with capital scarce and interest rates high, "to those with money to invest," notes Singer in understatement, "the creation and operation of a bank could bring a worthwhile return."[33]

Merchant-banker Donald Macleay has traditionally been credited with founding the U.S. National Bank, although the bank's largest initial stockholder, a wealthy Denver businessman, G. W. E. Griffith, contested this assertion 40 years later. However, by lending his name and prestige to the bank he headed for four years, Macleay was certainly responsible for its early success. Of the $250,000 in capital stock at $100 par value, Macleay bought only 150 shares, while Griffith subscribed to 1000. Other major stockholders and directors included Jacob Kamm (200), Woodward (50), Mallory (100), hardware merchant James Haseltine (110), and businessman Edward S. Kearney (100). With rented offices in the Kamm Block, the bank flourished through the end of 1891, when deposits and capital stock reached $450,000. Loans totalled more than $350,000, including $20,000 lent to the new Portland University. Lines of credit were granted to several small electric companies. By the end of 1892, with resources reaching $750,000, Griffith was bought out as Macleay and Woodward increased their holdings. When Macleay retired for health reasons in 1895, Woodward succeeded to the presidency. Guided by Mallory, the bank's fortunes were increasingly tied to those of the City and Suburban Railway Company.[34]

1892: More Mergers and Growth

In the spring of 1892, George B. Markle, Jr., James Steel and Richard L. Durham incorporated the Portland Consolidated Street Railway Company. Capitalized at $1 million, the merged transit system combined the Multnomah Street Railway Company, the Portland Traction Company, the Metropolitan Railway Company, and the Portland and Vancouver motor line. Once the different track gauges and motive powers could be synchronized, the company proclaimed that passengers could travel for one fare from the Riverview Cemetery north to the Columbia River terminal.

Markle had spent months planning how to fund this costly scheme. From his banks he would borrow deposits to attract investors, issue stock, float a million-dollar bond issue to repay bank loans, and seek a private assessment from property owners who would benefit from improved service to their businesses and homes. As Martin Winch wrote his uncle Simeon Reed in California, the improvements were designed to hold business on First Street. Markle was offering to lay double track and "put on a first class service" if property owners would agree to a shared assessment of the costs. In Reed's case the amount would be about $1,500; Winch advised him to accept the terms. The beginning of construction on the Burnside Bridge in November, 1892, over which the Consolidated expected to run its Portland-Vancouver line, augured well for the company's future. With stockholder-director Woodson A. Scoggin on the city council, Markle expected no difficulty gaining franchise approval.[35]

He was creating a speculative venture fraught with danger. Not unlike transit systems elsewhere in the 1890s, the Portland Consolidated sold huge amounts of stock to small investors and "a hungry public at large," in the words of Stanley Mallach. When Markle secured a mortgage of $1.5 million from the Mercantile Trust Company of New York, he saddled his company with a long-term burden of fixed charges.[36]

The Portland Cable Railway Company had pursued a similar course. The Ainsworth National Bank, through Hawkins, had advanced an initial loan. Most of the stock in the company, capitalized at $800,000, had been bought by Darius Ogden Mills of New York and San Francisco, the financier whom Simeon Reed and Henry Villard had lured to invest in the Oregon Iron & Steel Company. The bonds were bought by San Francisco's Crocker Bank, which had helped finance that city's cable railway. When Portland's cable railway went bankrupt in August, 1892, it was to take years to salvage the remains. Through involvement in this ill-fated venture, California and eastern financiers became ever more enmeshed in Portland's transit development.

By 1892, the electric street railways and the utilities that powered them had found their place both locally and nationally. The axiom of electric power — that electricity could not be stored and that power plants must be large and expensive — became accepted as a standard for growth. It called for, and even dictated, a power system that could be run only by huge regional monopolies. As such, the Willamette Falls Electric Company was in a dilemma. It found itself growing rapidly, but without sufficient local capital to replace equipment that soon became obsolete. Having built its first Portland substation on the west side of the Willamette at the foot of Montgomery Street, it faced burgeoning demands from the east side. A new and larger substation was needed, which could be financed only by a bigger and more highly capitalized corporation.[37]

To Willamette Falls president Morey, city consolidation in 1891 seemed an essential first step. He ran successfully for the Oregon House and worked tirelessly for legislative passage. He then went east in search of financing and secured the backing of Boston's famed Old Colony Trust Company. On August 6, 1892, Morey,

Henry Failing, Charles Swigert and Fred Holman formed the Portland General Electric Company, capitalized at $4.25 million. Additional investment capital came from the First National Bank and the General Electric Company of Boston. Following a practice that it repeated nationwide, General Electric invested in operating companies that were then strongly encouraged to buy its electrical equipment. Swigert's membership on PGE's board of directors presaged a close working relationship with the City and Suburban Railway Company. Another key director, Holman, was a brilliant, scholarly attorney who mastered the legal technicalities of utility organization. One of the few Democratic members of the Arlington Club, he became Portland's leading utility lawyer and served on the PGE board for years.[38]

Portland Gas and Security Savings & Loan

The year 1892 — a turning point in the fortunes of Portland's electric utility industry — witnessed a similar development, on a smaller scale, at Portland's only gas utility. Like electricity, gas service faced enormously increased demand in the period before and after city consolidation. Founded in January, 1859, by Herman C. Leonard and Henry and John Green, the Portland Gas Light Company had remained at its original location at the foot of Flanders Street in Couch's Addition. Manufacturing its gas from coal, the company enjoyed a perpetual franchise awarded by the legislature before enactment of the state constitution and its exclusion of such grants to corporations. In 1882, the owners incorporated the East Portland Gas Light Company, building a plant on East Second and Ankeny streets. After Henry Green's death in 1885, the owners carried on the gas business until August, 1892, when they received a generous offer to sell the gasworks to a newly formed syndicate headed by the recently arrived young bankers Charles F. Adams and Abbot L. Mills.[39]

The Gas Light Company followed a familiar course of American business consolidation. The sale price for the Leonard and Green properties was supposedly $850,000. The new owners reincorporated their purchase as the Portland Gas Company, and, adhering to normal financing practices, issued $1 million in bonds and $1 million in common stock. Two months later they acquired the stock of the East Portland Gas Light Company, and in the process picked up two more franchises. They connected the two systems with a 10-inch pipeline (the first transmission main laid under the Willamette River), and then dismantled the east-side plant.[40]

Gasco president Charles F. Adams was born in Baltimore in 1862, educated at Phillips Exeter Academy and at Yale, where he majored in civil engineering. Secretary-treasurer Abbot Low Mills was born in Brooklyn, New York, in 1858 and educated at Brooklyn Polytechnic Institute and at Harvard. Both men came west in 1882 in search of new opportunities, Adams to work for the federal land office in Walla Walla, Washington, and Mills to take up farming near Carlton, in Yamhill County in company with a Harvard classmate. Mills split the purchase of 1,000 acres of land at $8 per acre, which he later sold for $40 an acre. In 1885, Mills and Adams were both in Colfax, Washington, near the Idaho border, living in the same rooming house. Mills had forsaken farming for a private banking partnership; Adams had taken a job as cashier with the First National Bank of Colfax, which had been organized by former Portlander Levi Ankeny, with Cicero H. Lewis and Henry Failing as two of the larger stockholders.

Some time in 1889, Mills and Adams decided to expand their opportunities by founding their own bank in Portland. It was reported that they had apparently secured pledges of support from eastern friends and relatives totalling a surprising $5 million. Arriving in the city in late 1889, they discussed their plans with I ᴧvis, Failing and Henry W. Corbett, who told them that $5 million of outside money was too much for two young men to invest in a new banking venture in Portland. The region could not profitably support so vast an undertaking. Furthermore, Portland was not used to such sums, especially when offered by outside investors, free of restrictions and mortgage obligations. Whatever the reasons for their expressed caution, including fear of external control or competition, a more limited venture seemed to offer greater rewards. Mills and Adams agreed to found a locally controlled bank, capitalized at $500,000. They would raise $250,000 initially with $112,500 from the East and $137,500 from local sources. They also agreed that the new bank should concentrate on savings and trust functions as well as offering general banking services.[41]

The Security Savings and Trust Company opened on June 10, 1890, with the stated primary purpose of providing trustee services for individuals, families and estates in the management of residential and commercial real-estate properties. It was to be closely identified with, but separate from, the First National Bank for 24 years, even though the two institutions shared the same building and the same board of directors. Henry W. Corbett served as president, Henry Failing as vice-president, Mills as second vice-president, and Adams as secretary-treasurer. The trust company issued 2,500 shares of stock. Adams and Mills took 10 percent, as did Mills's eastern relatives. Boston investors, Harvard classmates of Mills, purchased 25 percent. Oregon investors Corbett, Lewis, Failing, Cyrus A. Dolph, and Asahel Bush bought the remaining and controlling, 55 percent.[42]

The record is unclear as to how Adams and Mills arranged financing for the purchase of the Portland Gas Light Company two years later. The pattern was probably similar to that followed in the founding of the Security Savings and Trust Company, which played an important role in the Gasco reincorporation. Mills was the key to the financing of both institutions, particularly in attracting eastern money. His cousin, Seth Low, was president of Columbia University and mayor of New York City. An uncle, Abiel Abbot Low, rich from the China trade, had shared in the financing of the first Atlantic cable and in the building of the Chesapeake and Ohio Railroad, while prominent Wall Street financiers William Augustus and Alfred M. White were married to Low's cousins. As for Portland connections, Mills's marriage in 1891 to Evelyn Scott Lewis, daughter of Cicero Lewis, established close personal ties to the city's first families. In that same year, Mills and Adams were admitted to the Arlington Club. Both were destined to play an active part in Portland club and society life.

The experiences of these younger members of Portland's Establishment in the 1890s showed that, although talent and industry were important qualities for seekers of venture capital (to invest in banks, street railways and public utilities), family and political connections, and club and old school ties, proved equally — if not more — valuable in achieving wealth and power.

13.1 Van B. DeLashmutt (1842-1921)

13.2 Madison Street Bridge Line

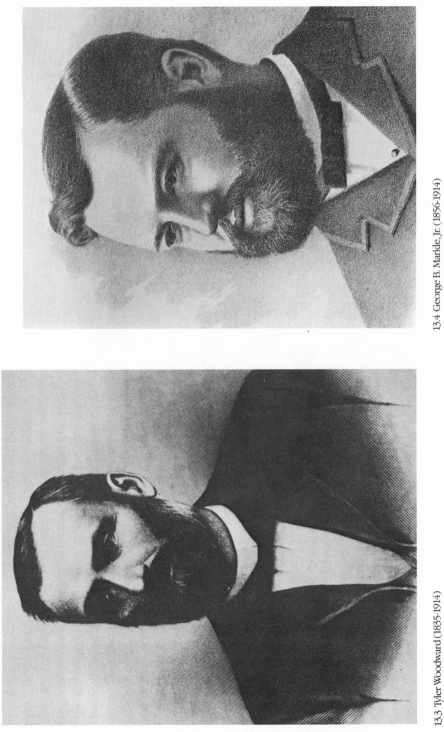

13.4 George B. Markle, Jr. (1856-1914)

13.3 Tyler Woodward (1835-1914)

13.5. The new Steel Bridge, looking south

13.6 The Portland Hotel

13.7 Henry L. Pittock (1835-1919)

13.9 Charles F. Swigert (1862-1935)

13.8 Fulton Park advertisement

13.10 Cable car over Goose Hollow

13.12 Abbot L. Mills (1858-1927)

13.11 Charles F. Adams (1862-1943)

13.13 Portland and surroundings, 1889

13.14 Hall of North Pacific Industrial Exposition

14

CITY GROWTH AND CONSOLIDATION

Causes of Growth

I n the months preceding the consolidation of July 6, 1891, many Portlanders felt their city was poised for greatness. For several years, the consolidation of Portland with East Portland and Albina had increasingly been advocated. When Mayor Van B. DeLashmutt and a citizens' committee found that the first 1890 census was in error by 11,000 and that Portland's west side actually contained nearly 46,000 people, the move for consolidation became almost irresistible. With a land area of only 7.38 square miles, the population density had reached 6,230 to the square mile, an alarmingly high figure for people not accustomed to being crowded together.

The opening of the Morrison Bridge in 1887 and the rapid extension of the street railways (as previously noted) were largely responsible for the explosive east side population growth. The promotional campaigns of the real-estate developers, who had bought up thousands of acres of cheap land, strongly backed consolidation, as did the transit and utility companies. Most of them were connected not only to each other, but to the downtown Portland banks as well.

Through the Ladd & Tilton Bank, William S. Ladd was Portland's largest individual, non-corporate property owner east of the Willamette River. He held over 700 acres within the proposed new city boundary, and an additional 500 acres southeast of the city in Multnomah County (Crystal Springs Farm, later developed as Eastmoreland). He had created his vast holdings out of forfeited mortgages and defaulted loans, seldom letting past friendship govern his strict financial dealings. Considered long-term investments, his larger tracts were used for farming, grazing prize dairy herds, and raising pure-bred cattle, horses, sheep, and hogs. The shrewd and patient banker had correctly assumed that the acreage would eventually be worth millions. His experience illustrates Michael J. Doucet's thesis that "At the root of all urban growth is the land development process — the conversion of rural or vacant land to some sort of urban use." While "people from all walks of life engaged in land speculation, . . . control over the nineteenth-century rural land market . . . rested in the hands of a limited number of powerful individuals and firms."[1]

Ladd's 486-acre Hazle Fern Farm, acquired between 1869 and 1878 through auction, foreclosure and purchase for less than $100 per acre, was valued at over $1,500 per acre in 1893. It was conveniently serviced by the City & Suburban Railway's Sandy Road line. Sold in 1909 to the Laurelhurst Company, it brought about $4,500 per acre. Ladd's substantial holdings along East Hawthorne Avenue were acquired through auction in March, 1878. East Portland's founder James B. Stephens had mortgaged 75 acres to Robert R. Thompson for $40,000, and when Stephens lost much of his money after the panic of 1873, the mortgage was foreclosed and Ladd bought the property for $53,407, or about $700 an acre. He subsequently acquired another 50 acres for what became Ladd's Addition. In 1895, the property was assessed at $2,000 an acre.[2]

It was hardly coincidental that Ladd and his oldest son promoted city acquisition of the Madison Street Bridge as its first public bridge purchase following consolidation. James Steel's Mount Tabor Railway provided direct service to downtown Portland, using Hawthorne Avenue. The Water Committee's decision to lay the main Bull Run pipeline along the addition's southern boundary (now Division Street) further increased the area's value in later years.

East Portland in Trouble

Largely for economic reasons, East Portland's business and political leaders strongly supported consolidation. Ever since Ben Holladay's fortunes had crumbled, they had found themselves increasingly overextended financially. The municipality of almost 10,000 residents had issued $100,000 in sewer and water bonds and was not generating enough tax revenue either to retire them or to pay the interest. The most serious financial problems stemmed from the construction of elevated roadways and streets. The near east side, just back from the river, was dotted with creek beds and marshy swamps, necessitating either land fills or elevated, bridge-like roadways. Many of these thoroughfares were hastily and poorly designed. As the *Sunday Oregonian* noted in 1893:

> The greatest loss entailed on the city was in the construction of the bridge over Sullivan's Gulch...now known as Grand Avenue. A flimsy structure was built there, which the contractors were afraid would fall down before they could get it finished. Property owners declined to pay for it, and the city, after long and expensive litigation, was compelled to pay for the whole structure, the cost being over $6,000.[3]

Portland later experienced a similar fate with an elevated section of East Morrison Street.

The East Portland City Council approved without charge almost every franchise request presented it in the 1870s and '80s, and was so desperate for services that two or more companies were often enfranchised for the same purpose. Downtown interests receiving favorable treatment included the Ladd-controlled Portland Reduction Works, which required a special railroad siding; the Oregon Railway & Navigation Company and the Oregon & California Railroad; the Portland Gas Light Company; and the electric street railways. Several more non-compensatory franchises were granted in the closing days that also witnessed the frantic passage of some hastily drawn legislation to escape Portland's more restrictive ordinances (with the exception of saloon regulation).[4]

For many years, East Portland had an ordinance that required saloons to be closed on Sundays. But by a peculiar wording of the law, only the front doors had to be locked while the back doors could (and did) remain open. As the *Oregonian* reported, "The battle of nearly every election was fought out on this question," which apparently "cut quite a figure in the vote for consolidation." After July 6, 1891, the saloons were thrown wide open on Sundays.[5]

Inconsistency in East Portland's law enforcement — and not just on saloons — had long dismayed Portland attorneys like Joseph Simon, who lost his first case there. As he later recalled: "I took the case of a merchant and after looking into the case thoroughly I didn't see how I could lose it." It was tried before Justice of the Peace Barney Trainer who also ran a hotel and saloon. The decision left Simon speechless. "'After listening to all the evidence produced,'" said the judge, "'I am in some doubt as to the merits of the case, but inasmuch as the defendant is a woman, and moreover as she lives here in East Portland, I'll decide the case in her favor.'" Simon never forgot the experience, which reinforced his efforts, as state senate president in 1890-91, to spearhead consolidation. If nothing else, it was likely to improve the administration of justice across the river.[6]

Albina: The Corporate Town

Albina, with a population of approximately 6,000 in 1891, was one place where Simon could expect consistent justice for his largest client, the Oregon Railway & Navigation Company. Few towns in American history, excluding company-owned and planned communities like Pullman, Illinois, or the Markle family's Hazleton, Pennsylvania, were so dominated by private business interests. Until its incorporation in 1887, it was little more than a privately owned preserve, presided over by corporate lords in downtown Portland. Before the construction of the Oregon Railway & Navigation Company and Union Pacific railway works, it had been controlled by large landowners like former Senator George H. Williams, Bank of British Columbia manager Edwin Russell, Portland attorney William W. Page, and William Reid and James B. Montgomery. The expenditure of several million dollars on the Union Pacific's massive rail center had doubled the town's population in four years and quadrupled its property values. Following its incorporation, and as the Willamette Bridge Railway built its line northward, Albina had vastly expanded its borders to include the village of St. Johns. By 1891, it covered more land area than East and West Portland combined: 13.5 square miles with a population density of only 450 to the square mile.[7]

A year after its incorporation, William M. Killingsworth, a major residential real-estate investor in Albina, revealed to the *Oregonian*: "Albina has been selected as the place to build these industrial enterprises"— selected, as implied, by the Establishment in downtown Portland. This was a major private decision that was to have a long-term impact on the public life of greater Portland. Killingsworth was "bullish on Albina's future."[8]

Harvey Scott, who had invested in the Albina and St. Johns areas, was equally bullish on Albina's future. Writing in early 1890, he noted that two "great buildings . . . demand first attention, and show upon what a great scale the city is now working." He cited William S. Ladd's Portland Flouring Mills and the Pacific Coast Elevator, owned by F. H. Peavy, "a capitalist of Minneapolis. . . . Albina strikes one with the general weight and importance of its operations." As for the remaining business part of the town, Scott expressed less enthusiasm. It was "of rather mean appearance, of cheap temporary structures, small sized and of inferior architecture." The main residence portion, where Killingsworth lived in one of the town's seven mansions, was built high up on the face of the river bluff and contained "many pretty cottages."[9]

Albina's city ordinances from 1887 to 1891 served private economic development without regard to fiscal responsibility. Charles F. Swigert's Willamette Bridge Railway Company gained four franchises, three of them two months before consolidation. The last one, on June 30, 1891, was of 50 years' duration. It constituted a carte blanche for the company: all designated routes were to be extended as the city limits themselves were extended. Starved for funds, Albina's municipal services were rudimentary at best. During the rainy season, "the streets were . . . at times hub-deep with mud, and there were no sidewalks," as one long-time resident recalled.[10]

Responding to the city's needs and their own interests, Swigert, and his partners George W. Bates and Lee Hoffman, organized the Albina Water Company in 1888. It received a franchise to lay water pipes and in 1889 contracted to provide fire hydrants and cisterns. Re-incorporated as the Albina Light and Water Company in 1890, it obtained the franchise to erect electric poles and wires once the power plant was completed. Its primary purpose was to generate power for the Willamette Bridge Railway Company. In 1890 the utility's president was the popular Dan McLaughlan, mayor of Albina since 1888 and also manager of the OR&N railway shops.

The 1891 legislature, prodded by Republicans P. L. Willis and James Montgomery, sanctioned Albina's expansive annexation program and authorized the city to issue $150,000 in improvement bonds. One month before consolidation, the city council, under McLaughlan's direction, rushed through three implementing ordinances with no provision for financing them. These irresponsible measures authorized $40,000 to pay the floating indebtedness and meet the current city expenses; $50,000 for paving streets; and $50,000 for parks. Such actions placed heavy burdens on the taxpayers of East and West Portland, who inherited the obligations. The day before consolidation, the city council approved an exclusive contract with Edgar Quackenbush's Investment Company for lighting the recently developed Piedmont District in North Albina, adjacent to Dekum and Durham's Portland & Vancouver Railway line. The City of Portland later had also to honor this commitment. Quackenbush, a former cashier with the Ladd & Tilton Bank, was well connected to Portland's Establishment.[11]

Mayor McLaughlan, who was to win appointment to the Portland Board of Police Commissioners in 1894 and later serve as Portland police chief, opposed the timing of consolidation in 1891 because he feared that certain properties he owned would decline in value. He correctly foresaw that his local power base, which had produced high profits for a small group of investors and speculators (including himself), would likely be destroyed through the transfer of political control to a new city government, headquartered on the west side of the river. But Bates, Swigert and Hoffman, the chief beneficiaries of McLaughlan's mayorship, saw expanded opportunities through consolidation. They hoped to maintain, if not increase, their city-wide influence. Recognizing that Albina could not support its increased financial load and that it really had no alternative, they fully expected a consolidated Portland to assume precisely those obligations that had subsidized their corporate ventures. And like most Albina residents, they wanted free ferry service and access to Bull Run water.[12]

George Bates was a preeminent example of the younger businessman-politician emerging in the late 1880s. Born in Iowa in 1851, he joined a railroad construction crew at 17, and six years later went to work for Swigert's uncle in the San Francisco office of the Pacific Bridge Company. In 1880 he accompanied Swigert to Portland to supervise local construction projects, including the building of a large dock for Reid and Montgomery on the Albina waterfront, and immediately saw opportunities for himself, especially in freewheeling Albina. He became proprietor of the Portland Box Factory, and in 1883, with Lee Hoffman, formed a company to build covered bridges and bridge piers throughout the Northwest. In 1885, Hoffman and Bates and a relative of Swigert, H. C. Campbell, opened offices in the First National Bank Building, advertising themselves as bridge builders and contractors.[13]

Lee Hoffman, born in Pennsylvania in 1850, had also been sent to Portland by Swigert's uncle to work on the Morrison Street Bridge. His family would play an important role in Portland business and cultural life, especially after his son married into the C. H. Lewis clan. Until his death by accident in 1895, he enjoyed a close personal and business association with Swigert and Bates, much of it in Albina. Together, they built the Albina Light and Water Company and helped construct the electrified St. Johns section of the Willamette Bridge Railway Company. State senator P. L. Willis, their personal attorney, handled such legal and governmental matters as incorporations, land purchases and franchises. In 1892, they sold the lighting division of Albina Light and Water to the Portland General Electric Company for $200,000. Bates used his share of the proceeds to found the Bank of Albina with former Portland Mayor Van B. DeLashmutt. In 1893, Hoffman and Bates received a $467,000 contract to build the first Bull Run pipeline for the Portland Water Committee, which Bates later joined in 1898. Their hope for expanded opportunities and city-wide influence through consolidation became a reality.[14]

For more than 10 years, Hoffman, Bates and Swigert not only exploited available opportunities, but created new ones, especially in the fertile fields of Albina. With attorney Willis, the intrepid entrepreneurs rarely separated their business from politics. Like the pioneer merchants, they well knew that politics provided the means — and usually the power — for achieving business success. In June, 1891, a political consolidation was viewed in just such a light by Portland's business Establishment.

Consolidated Government: 1891-1892

The vote for consolidation produced overwhelming approval. In Portland and Albina, the voter response was three to one in favor; in East Portland it was six to one. Overwhelmingly elected to his first term as mayor was wholesale grocer William S. Mason. Although he was a Republican, Mason ran on the Consolidation Ticket against former Republican Congressman M. C. George, the Corbett-Simon candidate who had close ties to Portland's older Establishment. A native of Virginia, the 59-year-old merchant had come to Portland in 1881 from San Francisco, where he had made a small fortune. In 1885, he formed a partnership with Edward H. Ehrman, a younger member of a prominent San Francisco Jewish family, and in 1891, was elected vice-president of the Portland Chamber of Commerce. According to one account, Mason's victory was hailed as "'the end of municipal misrule and the defeat of bossism, the sack, insolent policemen and hoodlum firemen.'" Presenting a marked contrast to his predecessor, DeLashmutt, Mason's official actions were never tainted with conflicts of interest. Although an officer of William Reid's Portland National Bank, he was not a property investor who sought franchises or laws to enhance his wealth. A public spirited businessman, he was described as "a quiet, thoughtful man, . . . [who] usually made haste slowly."[15]

Consolidation increased Portland's population rank to third among the cities west of Omaha (outranked only by San Francisco and Denver). With nearly 62,000 inhabitants within 26 square miles, Portland's population density declined to a low of 1,946 per square mile. To govern the expanded metropolis, the new charter provided for 16 city council members drawn from eight wards. Elected were three manufacturers and realtors, two merchants, bankers and street-railway investors, an attorney, a contractor, a travel agent, and a carpenter. (Five were incumbents.) Albina sent two prominent residents: realtor John Pittinger and sawmill owner John Parker, both good friends of Bates, Hoffman and Swigert. Banker-manufacturer J. Frank Watson, serving a second non-sequential term, was the only member of the Arlington Club, although elected officers City Attorney William T. Muir and Police Judge Charles H. Carey, both from the Mitchell Republican faction, subsequently became members.[16]

Mayor Mason opened the first meeting of the new city council on July 22, 1891, with a stinging criticism of the "hasty" legislation passed by the former councils of Portland, East Portland and Albina. He reminded his colleagues that the new charter limited municipal debt and expenditures, despite the heavy obligations inherited from the three improvident municipalities. As prescribed, the debt limit could not exceed $150,000 except for four categories of capital improvements (for which no sinking fund was provided): a new city hall, $500,000; water works, $2.5 million (taxable bonds already authorized); parks, $250,000; and free bridge purchases, $500,000. A two-year limit was placed on all non-bonded debts.[17]

Six months before consolidation, Portland's operating funds were so depleted that its fire department had to defer salaries. The city's high floating debt also affected the police force, of which Mason was most critical. It was far too small to perform an adequate job. Ironically, Portland — one of the wealthiest cities per capita in the country — had the smallest police force of any major city in proporion to its size. Although Mason did not make the charge, the blame rested heavily on Portland's banks, real-estate, transit, and railroad corporations, which had always resisted tax increases, even for necessities.[18]

For years the county, which assessed and collected taxes, had kept property assessments as low as 25 percent of true cash value. The three-member board of county commissioners had long been dominated by large real-estate interests, and more recently by corporate attorneys who endeavored to keep property taxes as low as possible. Henry W. Corbett, downtown Portland's largest non-corporate property owner, served on the commission from 1884 to 1887. Corporate attorney John Catlin, Judge Deady's brother-in-law, served from 1886 to 1890. Utility attorney Julius C. Moreland, who was active in Republican politics, secretary of the Willamette Falls Electric Company and principal owner of the Portland Real Estate Company, dominated the county commission from 1891 to 1893, the very years when Portland faced its most serious financial crisis.

Of the more pressing orders of business that faced Mason and the council during the summer of 1891 was one obligation assumed through consolidation: the construction of an East Portland electric-light powerhouse. The East Portland City Council had authorized the sale of $50,000 in bonds for a city light works — four days after the affirmative plebiscite. Over a period of four months, the Portland City Council authorized the expenditure of $40,342 to build and equip the plant. Within 15 months of the plant's completion, the council voted 12-4 to sell the light works to the new Portland General Electric Company for $27,000. Although the company agreed to some reduction of charges for municipal power use, the transaction constituted a generous gift to a private company at the taxpayer's expense. The ordinance was drafted and promoted by veteran Councilman W. A. Scoggin, a director of George Markle's Consolidated Street Railway Company, which held a contract with PGE to supply electricity to the recently enfranchised conglomerate. Mason reluctantly signed the ordinance on March 3, 1893, because he did not want the city in the power business.[19]

Mason Challenges the Police Commissioners

The Board of Police Commissioners, established by the legislature in 1885 through the efforts of Joseph Simon and Jonathan Bourne, Jr., had come under fire before the 1891 mayoral election, when William S. Mason had based much of his campaign on previously leveled charges of political corruption and bribery. Even though the 1891 charter made the three-member police board elective, strong feelings were expressed that this independent agency was still unresponsive to the needs of the city.

In a message to the council on November 11, 1891, Mason declared: "We lack the power to enforce the laws . . . . [We have] . . . no control . . . over the police force of our city . . . . Our police perambulate the streets day and night and we hear of no arrests for the violations," most specifically for gambling and for illegally operated saloons. Ordinances on gambling, said Mason, "are a dead letter on our statute books." Are the police the "protectors, the sharers in the spoils?" he asked. Railroad builder Joseph Gaston thought they were. In December, 1891, he wrote

President Benjamin Harrison (who had visited Portland the previous May), excori
ating Simon, who was a candidate for the U.S. Circuit Court of Appeals. He ac
cused Simon of ruining the police force by making it a political tool. Enforcemen
was lax, officers were receiving bribes, and Simon, as chairman of the police
board, was responsible.[20]

Bourne had been succeeded on the police board in 1888 by George Frank, a
farm-implement merchant who would succeed Mason as mayor. Frank's public life
revealed him as being a man of few principles and extreme rascality, whom
former Senator George H. Williams had the temerity to label publicly "an inferna
scoundrel." During Frank's last year on the board (1891), he secured the appoint
ment of future local Republican party boss Jack Matthews as clerk of the depart
ment. The crafty, shrewd and politically dedicated Matthews had first won ap
pointment from Mayor DeLashmutt as deputy city clerk. He advanced to deputy
city auditor and finally city auditor before receiving the police post. While deputy
auditor in 1889, he was responsible for overseeing the city's street cleaning, and
apparently did a poor job: according to the *Oregonian* in June of that year, Port
land was "the most filthy city in the Northern states." With characters like Simon
Frank and Matthews running the police department, or at least setting policy, the
job of Police Chief C. H. Hunt became increasingly untenable. Hunt complained
to Mason and others that he was "constantly hindered in enforcing the laws by
political influence," and that he could not depend on the officers and men of the
police force to obey his orders.[21]

Establishment Profits From Vice and Liquor

The inability of Hunt and Mason to enforce city vice laws was directly related to
the ownership of properties that harbored such activities. The Ministerial Associ
ation of Portland, principally concerned with prostitution, undertook the first o
several vice probes in late 1892, although its completed report was not published
until the following year. Under the chairmanship of the Reverend George R. Wal
lace of the First Congregational Church, the investigators discovered that many o
the properties devoted to vice (gambling and prostitution) were owned by lead
ing members of the city's Establishment.

Prominent citizens whose property housed such operations included Cyrus A.
Dolph, brother of U.S. Senator Joseph Dolph and Joe Simon's law partner. Dolph
and attorney John A. Caples, a partner of County Judge Julius C. Moreland (former
county commissioner, utility lawyer and real-estate investor), owned a building at
the Northeast corner of Second and Everett streets, that was labeled a "rendez-
vous of thieves and stolen goods." The vice committee found "young girls of 16
years of age . . . consorting with the Negroes, Italians and the lowest elements of
the city." Other wealthy property owners included brewer Henry Weinhard,
Ainsworth Bank Vice-President William K. Smith, former mayor and banker De-
Lashmutt, North Pacific Lumber Company president and water committee member Lauritz Therkelsen, Robert R. Thompson (who was living in California), and
Joe Simon.[22]

The committee also listed a number of liquor outlets and saloons that encouraged activities related to vice. Henry W. Corbett was named as the owner of the
city's largest wholesale liquor store at the corner of Second and Oak streets. Of the
245 saloon properties identified, DeLashmutt and Thompson each owned seven.
Owners of at least three properties included Corbett, Ainsworth, Donald Macleay,
I. W. Cook, and Weinhard. (It was common for brewers to own saloons.)[23]

Of the many gambling locations cited, three were singled out as "the most
notorious": The Brunswick, on Southwest Third, owned by former mayor and
banker David P. Thompson; The Arion, on Southwest Yamhill, half-owned by
Henry W. Corbett; and a dive on West Burnside and Second owned by Frank
Dekum's Portland Savings Bank. More than 50 prominent citizens named were
active in the churches that sponsored the original vice probe.[24]

The flourishing of vice, so disturbing to Mayor Mason and Chief Hunt, could
not be blamed directly on city consolidation. As a large and powerful business,
vice had always existed in most capitalistic societies because it paid high profits.
Its particular ability to thrive in Portland of 1892 — sanctioned by the principal
businessmen of the city — reflected a broader development associated with consolidation. The role and status of the central city, particularly the older sections
along Second and Third streets, was changing. While consolidation was an inte-
grating force politically and economically, it was a decentralizing force socially as
the Establishment separated its residential living pattern from its business life. The
wealthier Establishment families, particularly the older ones, were moving to the
upper Northwest and Southwest sections of the city. Others, like the Simeon G.
Reeds, John C. Ainsworths and Robert R. Thompsons, went to California. The
Arlington Club left the former Ainsworth mansion on Second for a new home on
Southwest Park and Alder streets. Establishment figures retained offices and businesses downtown near the older properties that harbored their profitable investments in vice and related enterprises. Portland's experience confirms Samuel P.
Hays's commentary on late nineteenth and early twentieth century American cit-
ies:

> The urban upper class faced two ways at once; decentralist in residential institu-
> tion, it was integrative in its economic and occupational life. While it sought to
> separate itself from the city in one way, in another it was propelled back into the
> center of urban affairs.

Divorcing its residential and social lives from its business management, the Establishment easily overlooked any personal responsibility for vice activities.[25]

Consolidation and Economic Integration

Economic integration, emerging as a dominant force in cities like Portland during the 1890s, found its principal expression in the "Chambers of Commerce representing the city's most powerful businessmen," according to Hays. Portland's
chamber, which grew out of the Board of Trade, came to play an increasingly
important role in the city's municipal affairs for over 50 years. Its first four presidents were canvas merchant Thomas F. Osborn, George B. Markle, hardware mer-

chant E. J. DeHart, and commission merchant John McCraken. All except Osborr were Arlington Club members.[26]

Of even greater importance to Portland's future economic development wa: the Port of Portland Commission, established by the 1891 legislature. Its primary purpose was to maintain and deepen the shipping channel between Portland and the sea. The existing 17-foot channel barred deep draft vessels from maneuvering in the harbor, especially as the ships and wharfs were forced to the lower reache: of the river by the construction of the three bridges from 1887 to 1891. None of the affected municipalities — Portland, East Portland, Albina or St. Johns — had a sufficient tax base for developing and keeping open an adequate channel. Municipal consolidation provided the political framework within which an integrative state agency with taxing and bonding authority could function effectively.[27]

From its inception, membership on the Port of Portland Commission was considered an honor, reserved for the city's business and community leaders. For 30 years, the appointment power was vested in the legislature, and membership became more politically partisan and less diverse geographically as the west-side Portland Establishment increasingly dominated the commission. Under state Senate President Joseph Simon's direction, the legislature named 15 well-known men, drawn proportionately from the populations of the three consolidated cities. Not surprisingly, William S. Ladd was named as president, with John McCraken as vice-president and James Steel as treasurer. The others were:

From the West Side

Henry Failing, President of the First National Bank, director of the Oregon Railway & Navigation Company, President of the Northern Pacific Terminal Company, and President of the City & Suburban Railway Company.

Ellis G. Hughes, corporate attorney with railroad clients, and a developer of the Irvington tract.

George B. Markle, President of the Oregon National Bank, and owner of numerous street-railway interests.

John Couch Flanders, attorney and partner of former Senator George H. Williams, and a prominent railroad attorney.

Thomas P. Richardson, capitalist.

John E. Lombard, Manager of the Portland Natural Ice Company and a marine surveyor by training.

Edward D. McKee, Manager of the Meyer & Wilson Company, commission merchants and shippers.

From East Portland

Dr. Simeon E. Josephi, secretary of the Port of Portland Commission, and Dean of the University of Oregon Medical College.

Cyrus Buckman, Vice-President of the Citizen's Bank, and a civic activist and school board member.

David Raffety, physician and druggist.

From Albina

William M. Killingsworth, wealthy realtor, and incorporator of Albina in 1887.

John H. Steffen, first mayor of Albina, and owner of the Albina Hotel.

Seven of the commissioners, all from the west side, were Arlington Club members.[28]

From its earliest days, the Port of Portland Commission was torn between divergent railroad and grain-shipping interests. In 1891, according to the U.S. Army Corps of Engineers, "15 million bushels of wheat were shipped to the Pacific Coast" from East of the Cascade Mountains. "The existing rail system not only proved unable to transport the entire crop in a timely fashion, but also charged monopoly rates." Already dominating the legislature in 1891, railroad influence would also dominate the port commission by 1900, much to the detriment of waterborne commerce. Restricted largely to dredging activity, the port exercised no control over the larger private docks, most of which were owned by the railroads. OR&N attorney Joseph Simon played a key role in preserving his client's rights. In such efforts, he won support from younger members of the Portland Establishment like Charles F. Swigert and Charles F. Adams, both of whom would later serve on the port commission.[29]

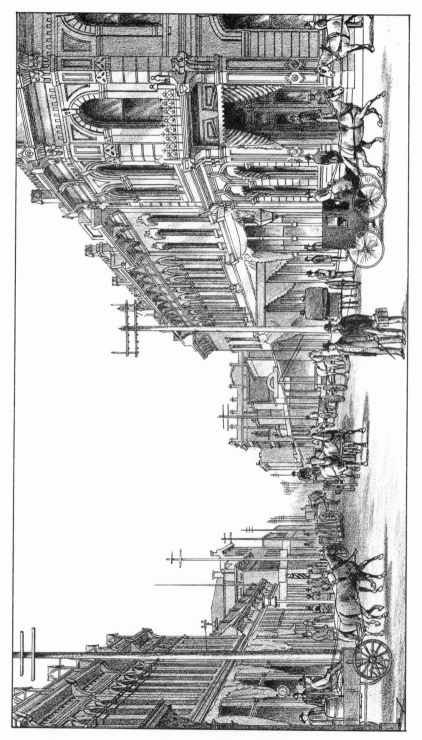

14.1 East Fourth Street, East Portland, 1881

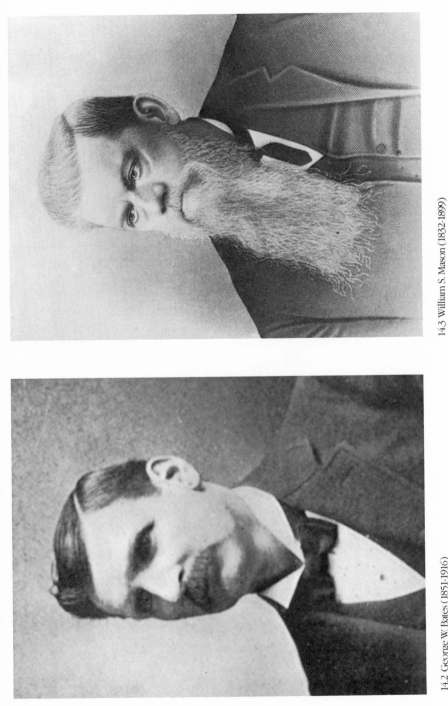

14.3 William S. Mason (1832-1899)

14.2 George W. Bates (1851-1916)

14.4 The Railway Works at Albina

14.5 Portland, c. 1893-1895

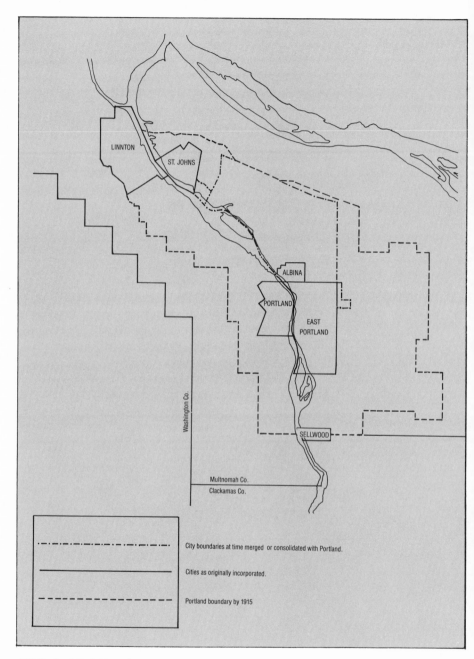

14.6 Portland's Early Expansion

14.7 Morrison Street, east of Second, 1889

14.8 Lee Hoffman (1850-1895)

14.9 An 1889 commentary on the Portland police

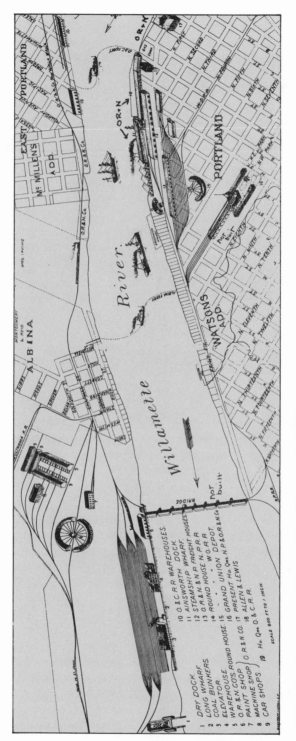

14.10 Location of Various Existing & Proposed Railroad Works in Portland, 1882

15

CHANGING THE GUARD:
1892-1894

"The Four Young Merchants of 1851"

On the evening of March 4, 1892, Henry W. Corbett gave a dinner party at his home to celebrate the 41st anniversary of the arrival in Portland of Henry Failing, Cicero H. Lewis, William S. Ladd, and himself, all of whom had ventured to Portland during the spring of 1851. He had originally planned to hold the event the previous spring, but illness had forced its postponement. Judge Deady, who was among the guests, described the dinner as "elegant, and the wines choice and abundant." Another account reported the "silver service a magnificent one," recently imported from Europe. The high point of the evening was Corbett's after-dinner eulogy, delivered by John McCraken, entitled "The Four Young Merchants of 1851 and the Four Old Merchants of 1891."[1]

Corbett sat at the head of the table, with Lewis on his right, and Deady and then Ladd on his left, with Failing at the opposite end, facing his host. Besides McCraken the other guests (all close friends of Corbett) were Lloyd Brooke, George L. Story, Jacob Kamm, L. Brooks Trevett, Judge Erasmus D. Shattuck, Henry L. Pittock, John Green, George W. Snell, Thomas A. Davis, and Herman C. Leonard. Had John C. Ainsworth, Simeon G. Reed and Robert R. Thompson still resided in Portland, they likely would have been invited. With the exception of Pittock and Shattuck who reached Oregon in 1853, all had preceded "The Four Young Merchants of 1851," (Brooke and Deady arrived in 1849). Eleven of the sixteen were merchants or former merchants; Kamm and Brooke called themselves "capitalists;" two were jurists, and Pittock, a publisher.

It was a gathering of socially prominent members of the Portland Establishment. (Seven belonged to the Arlington Club.) However, their position in society was not entirely based on money. Deady, Shattuck and Pittock, for example, had great influence but little comparative wealth (Pittock made his money late in life). Likewise, McCraken, one of Portland's leading citizens, held assets of under $150,000 in 1893 — not a large sum compared with the assets of Leonard, Green and Kamm, which ranged from $200,000 to over $1 million each.

Three of the guests were Portland's earliest druggists. Story had opened the first pharmacy, in 1851, later selling out to Heitshu and Woodard and entering the paint and oil business. By 1891 he was a realtor and insurance agent, a member of the legislature and a Portland fire commissioner. Davis had opened the city's second pharmacy, which he had likewise sold to Heitshu and Woodard. An early Arlington Club member, he was an active Mason and a successful real-estate investor. Snell was president of Heitshu and Woodard, Portland's largest drugstore, with reported assets of between $150,000 and $300,000 in 1894. Story and Davis lived on Southwest Seventh Street, while Snell had moved to Northwest Eighteenth and Davis, the fashionable section of Couch's Addition developed by C. H. Lewis.[2]

Trevett, the least ambitious of the group, had worked as a hardware clerk for Corbett & Failing and then Honeyman and DeHart. A neighbor of Lewis and a card-playing crony of Failing and Deady, he was bound even more closely to the judge as a fellow vestryman of Trinity Church and through his wife's brother, the California historian-publisher Hubert Howe Bancroft. Deady had edited many of the biographical sketches for Bancroft's *Chronicles of the Builders*.[3]

Brooke, Deady's closest friend, had arrived in 1849 as an employee of the U.S. Army Quartermaster Corps, to which he remained attached for many years. He married the daughter of General Edward Hamilton, the territorial secretary, Benjamin Stark's law partner and later a Multnomah County judge. While in government employ, he engaged in numerous enterprises, including the cattle business, and acquired 631 acres of land south of Portland, in what later became the Riverwood development. Over the years he sold off his acreage to Herman C. Leonard, John McCraken, members of the Ladd and Corbett families, and others of the Portland Establishment who sought property for their country homes. In the city, Brooke lived along Seventh Street, near his friends McCraken, Story and Green.[4]

In his eulogy, Corbett first praised Cicero Lewis, "our great merchant prince." Citing him as the "typical merchant" who had "sought simply to be a merchant after the old style," he conducted "his business in the best manner to the advancement of his own as well as the community." Of William S. Ladd, whose oldest daughter was married to Corbett's surviving son, Corbett asked: "How shall I designate another in his varied pursuits as a merchant? He is not only a merchant, but a merchant-manufacturer, a merchant-miller, and a merchant-ironmonger. He is also a banker, our merchant-banker." To his closest friend and partner, Henry Failing, Corbett directed his highest praise: "The typical banker, not excelled if equalled in our Northwest." He extolled Failing as one "who fits every place and every place fits him. He is master of every situation in which he has been placed." Of himself, Corbett was barely less modest: "He has ever continued a merchant no matter what he was doing. He is your merchant statesman." Henry Pittock, a small man and an avid horseman, was cited as the "Napoleon of the Press," and Judge Deady characterized as "our good and faithful servant."[5]

Reminiscing generally, Corbett reviewed the growth of Portland from a town of 800 to a city of 75,000 in 41 years. "Through Providence we have succeeded beyond our human expectations and advanced in prosperity beyond our most sanguine hopes and anticipations. To persistent zeal, staunch loyalty, through all trials, during these many years, Portland has had their [her merchants] and other backbone at her disposal." Through dark days, "such men have shouldered the burden and carried our interior merchants. ...And now, our labors, so well begun, are nearly done. ...A permanence, prosperity and wealth of this thriving city is secured beyond all peradventure."[6]

While Corbett was premature in this last declaration, he clearly revealed the values and goals that had guided the city's leading merchants in building their community. It was "wealthy, respected, stable and possessed of land." As Doucet has observed, these kinds of people "were the cement that held places together…within every nineteenth century community."[7]

Passing The Torch

Within six years, half of the group would be dead. Ladd died suddenly on January 6, 1893, after one of several strokes that had afflicted him as early as 1875, when he became paralyzed from the waist down. His last public meeting was that of a Water Board subcommittee, which decided to purchase the Mount Tabor reservoir site. Three days before his final attack, he remarked that he wanted to live long enough to see the completion of three projects of special interest: the Riverview Cemetery, the 25-foot Willamette River channel to the sea, and the Bull Run water system.[8]

Although his physical activity had been curtailed, Ladd's mind remained as alert as ever. Despite his austere mien, and an air of dominance, he had a gentleness seldom seen by those outside his family. Charles Erskine Scott Wood, a brilliant and many-talented attorney (called C.E.S. by his friends), described one occasion that brought Ladd to tears. Wood had been largely responsible for selecting the prominent New York sculptor Olin L. Warner to create a drinking fountain for the city, fulfilling a $5,000 bequest of druggist Stephen G. Skidmore, who had died in 1885 at age 44. When the total cost came in at $18,000, Charles Sitton, Henry Failing and Tyler Woodward made up the difference. As Wood recalled the episode during the fountain's unveiling in 1888, Ladd sat in front of him "in his buckboard."

> When I paid tribute to the boy, Steve Skidmore, who in his last hour thought of the city which had received him penniless, and where he made his money, and spoke of the nature that could think of the downtown busy part of the city, the sweaty drivers of trucks and drays, the thirsty horses and thirsty little dogs, I saw tears trickling down Mr. Ladd's face unchecked.[9]

Ladd also had a good sense of humor, as revealed by a story his son Charles told friend Erskine Wood, C.E.S.'s son. Apologizing for its "indelicacy," Wood related the following episode. One morning a "handsome, slightly overdressed" woman, a stranger to Ladd, was ushered into his office. After a pleasant 20-minute conversation, Ladd said to her, "'Madam, I've enjoyed your visit…but what is it you came to see me about? What can I do for you?' " She replied that she wanted $25,000 unsecured and "that he was going to give it to her." She then threatened to tear open her dress, ruffle her hair and scream. "'When your clerks rush in, I'm going to say that you attempted to ravish me.' With that, Mr. Ladd leaned back in his chair and began to laugh. 'Madam,' he said, 'I want to thank you for the first merry moment I have had in this rather dull day. If you can get anybody in this whole town to believe that I have had a hard-on any time in the last 20 years, I'll give you fifty thousand dollars.' "[10]

Ladd left an estate estimated to be worth in excess of $5 million, almost half of it in 4,000 acres of undeveloped land in areas of Portland and Tacoma, Washington. During his lifetime, he had donated well over $500,000 to various charities, and his will established a trust of $450,000, the income to be used for educational and charitable purposes. The Ladd & Tilton Bank, the largest single estate asset, was removed from probate by another trust. Some years before his death, Ladd had constituted his three sons as trustees and partners in the business. As William M. Ladd told Asahel Bush in 1898, they continued to operate the private bank as partners. For some years the Ladd sons had resented Theodore B. Wilcox's influence over their father. Until January 6, 1893, he had functioned as Ladd's executive assistant in both bank and flour-mill operations, with primary responsibility for the latter, the second largest single asset of the estate. Six weeks after William S. Ladd died, grain merchant Peter Kerr noted that "Charlie Ladd [his second son] sits downstairs in the bank now and people say that Wilcox has now no connection with the banking business — only to Flour Mills."[11]

Ladd's death led to one of the more gruesome episodes in Portland's history. In May, 1897, a gardener pruning trees at the Riverview Cemetery noticed a pile of dirt next to the banker's grave. Investigating police officers discovered that robbers had stolen both his body and the headstone that had been dragged down the hill to the Willamette River. Several days of crack detective work turned up four suspects who confessed to the ghoulish deed, which they had committed in the hope of extorting ransom from the Ladd family. The body had been floated downriver in a rowboat for about a mile and buried in the sand at the river's edge. To prevent any reoccurrence, the family built a substantial mausoleum into which Ladd's remains were interred in concrete. The four robbers were dispatched to the state penitentiary for lengthy terms.[12]

Matthew P. Deady died one year after the anniversary dinner. He had gone East in September, 1892, to attend the general convention of the Episcopal Church in Baltimore. After a brief visit to Washington, where he attended a Supreme Court dinner given by Chief Justice Melville W. Fuller, he returned to Portland a "desperately ill" man, having suffered a stroke on the trip. He was barely able to carry on his judicial duties over the next five months, and died on March 24, 1893, from the effects of the stroke and a lingering kidney disease. Nine months later, John C. Ainsworth died in California; Simeon G. Reed followed him within two years. Upon Amanda Reed's death in 1904, the Reed estate, valued at $1.8 million, went to found Reed College, which opened in 1911.[13]

Cicero H. Lewis died in January, 1897, from the effects of a stroke, and Henry Failing succumbed to heart disease a year later. Both left estates worth approximately $1.5 million. Henry Corbett still had 11 active years ahead. Henry Pittock, George Story, Jacob Kamm, Herman Leonard, and John McCraken lived well into their eighties. All faced the depression of 1893, which rocked the Portland Establishment.

The Depression of 1893 and Its Consequences

The year 1893 opened with a flourish within the Portland business community. President George B. Markle assured the annual Chamber of Commerce dinner in January that "this is the most remarkable period in the history of Portland....The city [is] at its highest level of prosperity...[and] lowest level of financial depression." Citing the role of banks, Markle made the interesting comment (in the light of what soon followed) that "public monies need to be protected." The *Pacific Banker & Investor* added two months later that "Oregon is singularly deficient in laws pertaining to banking institutions. In fact it may be said without fear of contradiction that it has no laws at all upon this subject."[14]

By February, ill winds were blowing in from the East Coast, where banking institutions were feeling the effects of the Reading Railroad bankruptcy. The stock market had been falling for three years, since the esteemed London banking house of Baring Brothers had been saved from collapse by the Bank of England. Gold had been rising in value, while the general level of prices, especially for commodities, had been declining. Great Britain, which had enormous investments in American western lands and railroads, began withdrawing capital, much of it in gold, from American markets, depleting the federal government's gold reserve. It had been drained ever since the Sherman Act of 1890 allowed free coinage of silver and required Treasury notes to be backed by gold. The structure of speculative credit cracked. Banks and railroads, including street railways, were seriously affected. Throughout the country, a general tightening of credit was already at hand in April as worried depositors withdrew funds and banks called in loans.[15]

On April 17, 1893, Markle quietly took out a home mortgage loan of $120,000 with the Scottish American Investment Trust Company of Edinburgh. A month later Scotsman Peter Kerr wrote home:

It's very hard to find any safe investment for money nowadays. Things in America are pretty shaky....I think there will be a good deal of trouble in the Eastern States before the year is out....Out in these Western States and in this town in particular I don't apprehend a great deal of trouble. This is a rich town for its size and has been going along in a comfortable conservative way.[16]

Kerr was undoubtedly aware of the "Industrial Black Friday" of May 5 on the New York Stock Exchange, which led to a panic. Somehow, he expected Portland's wealthy bankers and merchants to escape the consequences. Kerr had first visited the city in 1888, with solid family connections to the Macleays and other Scottish investors like William Reid and Robert Livingstone, manager of the Scottish American Investment Trust Company office. A story is told of his first breakfast in Portland at the Arlington Club, where he was served rainbow trout and teal duck. Highly impressed, he vowed to return and live in such a wonderful place. Four years later, the ambitious 30-year-old Scot immigrated, with great expectations. In a letter of December 5, 1892, he observed that there were many Portlanders "who have made large fortunes and some of them are fabulously wealthy. I wish I could find out the way to do it." Within weeks, he formed a commission-grain partnership with William S. Sibson, president of the Arlington Club. By 1894, he was living at the club, and would be elected its president in 1896.[17]

In June, 1893, Kerr's friend William Reid abruptly skipped town after the closure of his Oregon-Washington Mortgage Savings Bank, which left 196 depositors devoid of their savings. In 1898, he returned to Oregon a poor man. He was quoted as saying: "I came to Portland with $10,000, made $200,000 and left with $1." Except for a year as U.S. vice-consul in New Zealand, he spent the remaining 16 years of his life eking out an income from the practice of law and an occasional consulting job for minor railroad-construction projects, renting a cheap inside office in Henry W. Corbett's Worcester Building.[18]

By July, the credit crunch was seriously threatening Markle's and James Steel's railway operations. For over three months, Steel had sought to mortgage the East Side Railway and to sell bonds to raise capital for further expansion. Kerr reported to his uncle on July 18 that "the Electric Car lines" were "finding it hard to float its debt re bonds." The company was faced with creditor seizure and sale of its cars and other stock. According to Kerr, "Donald Macleay has lots of land out there but heretofore has let everybody else do the work and spend the money—for his benefit to a large extent —which we other people interested are getting tired of." Refusing to invest any more money in Steel's operation, Kerr said, "If it isn't good enough for Donald Macleay it isn't good enough for us."[19]

A week later, Kerr noted that even the Ladd & Tilton Bank had curtailed its loans. "Banks failing everywhere and no predicting when it will happen in Portland. ... Of course everybody knows that Ladd & Tilton's, or Failing's bank, is as safe as the bank of England—but no bank, even the bank of England, can stand a run." Commenting on the Portland Establishment, of which he was now a younger member, Kerr observed, "There are lots of very rich people here, but the great part of their money is invested and there is little free cash comparatively speaking. The great source of money supply — the English Interests — has of late not only stopped investing, but is drawing out already invested money—just to have a look at it. ...Money is exceedingly tight now."[20]

The next day, on July 27, Martin Winch wrote his uncle Simeon Reed that "The Northwest Loan & Trust Company and the Oregon National Bank here failed to open this morning. These are controlled by George B. Markle. It of course has created a very uneasy feeling again." The *Oregonian* reported that the deposits were being withdrawn faster than the banks could call in their notes. Sheriff Penumbra Kelly had at least $100,000 of county tax funds on deposit with the Oregon National Bank, while the Port of Portland (of which Markle was a commissioner) had $5,000 on deposit there.[21]

In short order, the First National Bank of East Portland and the Union, Commercial National, and Portland Savings Banks closed. The Ainsworth National Bank closed briefly but was reopened within a month. The First National Bank had a close call. In the early morning hours of July 28, Sigmund Frank and young Max Hirsch secretly wheeled bags of gold coin from the Meier & Frank Company safe through the back door of the bank. The following morning, a smiling Henry W. Corbett redeemed deposits and assured the fretful that there was no need to worry; all deposits were safe. In the following weeks, the First National Bank distributed over $2 million throughout the Northwest and thereby stabilized the banking community.[22]

Writing again to Simeon Reed on August 1, Winch reported: "Friday and Saturday last week were the gloomiest days this place ever saw, and we will feel the effects of it for sometime to come. ...DeLashmutt I guess is in a very bad way financially. Common report has it he is busted, and from the worried hang dog look he has I judge it isn't far out of the way." Two days later, Markle quietly took out a second mortgage on his home and property for $60,000. He then let it be known that he had $46,000 of his own money on deposit in his banks and that this should breed confidence. Given time, he would redeem all deposits as requested.[23]

Markle was in even deeper trouble than his friend Van B. DeLashmutt. He had used depositors' money to purchase the two additional street railways that he had merged into the Consolidated system. The Northwest Loan & Trust Company had loaned the railway $160,000, secured by a mortgage on 40 miles of track, property and stock. With a panic threatening, he began to use public tax funds to pay off depositors. When Sheriff Kelly tried to withdraw school tax deposits, he was told, "No. ... The banks would close." Kelly then compounded his error by depositing $200,000 in additional tax funds with both Markle banks. Unable to sell the million dollars' worth of railway bonds, which had already been negotiated for sale, he was caught short, and the Consolidated Street Railway Company's future was sealed. Markle promised Sheriff Kelly that he would get him his money, hoping he could could raise $300,000 from friends and relatives.[24]

Living up to his reputation among the family as "the world's greatest optimist," Markle returned to Pennsylvania in September. He soon wired his associates that he had the money, whereupon the Oregon National Bank reopened on September 9. When he arrived in Portland, however, he learned to his dismay that the deal had fallen through. The Oregon National closed permanently; the Northwest Loan & Trust never reopened. Neither bank ever occupied its new quarters in the Chamber of Commerce Building, which had opened inauspiciously the same month.[25]

Markle promised Sheriff Kelly $50,000 for the December payroll, but only $5,000 was forthcoming. In all, Kelly had deposited $149,000 in the Oregon National Bank and $169,000 in the Northwest Loan & Trust Company. On December 8, 1893, Markle, his cashier D. F. Sherman and Sheriff Kelly were indicted by the Multnomah County Grand Jury and arrested for fraudulent misuse of public funds. Bail bonds of $20,000 were posted for Markle and Kelly and signed by *Oregonian* editor Harvey W. Scott and David P. Thompson. No further word of this case was ever printed in the local press, nor is there any record of its disposition. The city sued the Oregon National Bank in April, 1894, to recover $5,000 of deposited funds, but there were no assets left to retrieve.[26]

The Unemployed Join Coxey's Army

The depression of 1893 was taking its toll at all levels of society. Everything came to a dead halt. Nationally, over $2.5 billion of railroad capitalization went into receivership by 1898 — "the most massive set of receiverships in American history," according to Alfred D. Chandler, Jr. Seventy-four railroad companies, including the Northern Pacific and Union Pacific, fell into bankruptcy. Over 600 banks and banking institutions folded, including seven in Portland. As Joseph Gaston remembered, "There was a large population of unemployed and penniless men...(who) walked the streets, idle and hungry....There was no work for them to do." The summer of 1893 produced "the hardest days" he had "ever known," recalled banker Charles F. Adams in January, 1932. Conditions were especially severe during the winter of 1893-1894, when Mayor William S. Mason personally donated 400 sacks of flour to the poor. He unsuccessfully sought to convince the Water Board to construct a low service reservoir at Mount Tabor, with unemployed married men given job priority for the project. The Establishment committee did not consider such a rescue operation a proper function for the independently financed municipal water system.[27]

In the early spring of 1894, Jacob S. Coxey, a successful Ohio businessman, organized a national movement of the unemployed known as Coxey's Army. He called on the nation's unemployed to descend on Washington, D.C., to impress upon Congress the severity of their needs. Oregon's Governor Sylvester Pennoyer, a Democrat with populist leanings, joined several western governors in expressing support for Coxey's activities. On April 18, 50 members of the "industrial army" arrived in Portland by freight train from San Francisco; others were to follow. Although they were mostly skilled mechanics, they were called "tramps and beggars" by the *Oregonian's* Harvey W. Scott. Camping in East Portland's Sullivan's Gulch, they received emergency rations from the police and the mayor's office, much to the dismay of Thomas N. Strong of the city's Board of Charities. Expressing the Establishment's reaction, the socially prominent Portland attorney urged city officials to ignore the "army of tramps." Protesting such vilification, the Coxeyites explained to authorities that they were on their way to Washington via Seattle and simply wanted to enlist the unemployed of Portland to join them.[28]

The Great Northern Railroad strike occurred simultaneously with the Coxeyite turbulence, with unorganized trainmen flocking to the new American Railway Union. At an organizational meeting to sign up members for Coxey's campaign, held on the Plaza blocks, a member of the American Railway Union told the men: "'We stand here as a living protest to present conditions. If you remain in the city of Portland nothing awaits you but souphouses and the chain gang. We do not want charity, but we ask for employment.'" The chief recruiting station was on the sidewalk at the northeast corner of Third and Burnside streets.[29]

When Governor Pennoyer failed to convince the Union Pacific to grant them transportation, the buoyant 446 recruits, deprived of further city rations, wound their way to Troutdale, where they seized a Union Pacific freight train and headed east, pursued by U.S. marshals. Caught 120 miles up the Columbia River at Arlington, they were returned to Portland, where 52 of them were lodged in the county jail and the remainder confined to boxcars at the Albina freight yard. Since the Union Pacific Railroad was in federal receivership, custody went to the U.S. District Court, which treated the men more leniently than the county would have. Charges were dismissed, and all non-Oregonians shipped back to California.[30]

The Establishment Suffers

The Establishment was hard hit, but not to the point of starvation. Ironically, the *Oregonian's* owner Henry Pittock found himself cash-short in October, 1893, but he knew where to turn. From his friend George T. Myers, a wealthy fish packer, he requested a loan of $35,000, offering as collateral most of his property (five city lots and over 2,000 acres of unimproved land) and stockholdings, exclusive of the paper and its new building. He planned to secure a $125,000 mortgage on the Oregonian Building and borrow $50,000 from the publishing company. He told Myers that Henry W. Corbett would lend him $75,000 when the situation improved. "He would now," said Pittock, "but the money cannot be found." As Peter Kerr wrote a friend, "The stringency (banks) is indeed very severe, and many names that would surprise you are upon the delinquent board of the Club."[31]

Besides Markle, Delashmutt and Reid, the banker who suffered the heaviest loss was Frank Dekum, who died in 1894, partially from the strain of the depression. With

David P. Thompson's help, he had managed to salvage enough out of the wreckage of the Portland Savings Bank to leave an estate of over $1 million, largely in downtown real estate; his railway holdings had collapsed. Thompson, who had been president of the savings bank from 1880 to 1886, had sold all his bank stocks before his appointment in 1891 as American Minister to Turkey. Upon his return in 1893, he was appointed receiver for the bank. After nine months of work without pay, he reported that $345,000 had been distributed to depositors.[32]

In October, 1910, Acting Governor Jay Bowerman was to charge Thompson, Dekum and Jonathan Bourne, Jr., with fraud. The Portland Savings Bank had been looted, he said, and hundreds made destitute. Like Markle's Northwest Loan & Trust Company, Portland Savings had inflated its assets and had conducted a commercial loan business with savings deposits. It was not a commercial bank, yet it had incurred heavy risks in large commercial loans. Furthermore, it had paid overly generous interest rates on its savings accounts. Five thousand of the 7,000 depositors had $500 or less on deposit. One of the largest accounts was the Port of Portland deposit of $11,500. The bank had reopened in May, 1894, but it closed in October after Dekum's death. Bowerman accused Thompson of reopening the bank just long enough for Thompson to bail out his favored creditors, including the Port of Portland.[33]

Dekum's Commercial National Bank was bought by Wells Fargo of San Francisco in January, 1894, and Richard L. Durham re-emerged as vice-president. When the Portland Savings Bank liquidation was finally settled in 1901, less than 40 percent of depositor's money had been refunded. At least one victim later gained revenge. In 1906, during her term as city health officer, Dr. Esther Pohl Lovejoy, herself a victim of the Portland Savings collapse, "heard a strange tale from an undertaker which supports the theory that justice will be done and virtue triumph in the end." As Lovejoy later recalled the episode,

> The last remains of a wicked capitalist partly responsible for wrecking the Portland Savings Bank fell into the hands of one of the victims who had become stoker at the crematorium. Such an opportunity! Instead of placing the ashes of this bank wrecker reverently in the golden urn provided for the purpose, the long-suffering stoker threw them down the sewer.[34]

The panic and depression illuminated the dishonest and honest alike. Desperation and greed drove men like Markle, DeLashmutt and perhaps even David P. Thompson to engage in fraudulent activities for which they were not, or seldom, called to account. Many innocent people were harmed by trusting them. The Hoffman family placed its fiduciary trust in a friend, attorney P. L. Willis. The former associate of George W. Bates, Charles F. Swigert and Lee Hoffman, would find himself in serious difficulty in 1907, when the Oregon Savings & Trust Company, in which he was deeply involved, closed at great personal loss. Although Willis had put in $400,000 of his own money—his entire savings—to keep the bank operating, he also used other people's funds of which he was custodian. As trustee, he misappropriated a large part of Lee Hoffman's estate. A settlement was finally reached, but at significant loss to Hoffman's widow. Like others, Willis escaped penalty. As with David P. Thompson, he received public praise for his heroic efforts to save the bank.[35]

The ordeal of the panic depressed Henry Failing and Donald Macleay. Martin Winch reported to Simeon Reed in the summer of 1894 that he had found Failing "blue," and thought "it is unfortunate for the town when a man carrying the influence Mr. Failing does holds the views he expresses." Macleay was similarly depressed, although his U.S. Bank weathered the crisis along with the First National, both of which held on long enough to be "fortified by a shipment of gold — $500,000 worth — which arrived by chartered train from San Francisco." According to bank historian Claude Singer, the U.S. Bank had followed a conservative policy of deferring dividend payments and "maintaining the lowest loans-to-deposits ratio of any national bank in Portland." While deposits declined 15 percent over a three-year period, loans and discounts declined 32 percent. Macleay not only loaned the bank large sums of his own money, but took no pay during the same period. Exhausted by the experience, he relinquished the presidency to Tyler Woodward in the spring of 1895. Never regaining his strength, he died at the age of 63 in July, 1897. Failing died at age 64 in November, 1898.[36]

Cicero H. Lewis, known as a generous man who quietly loaned thousands of dollars to friends in need, rescued several members of Portland's Establishment in the post-panic crisis, among them John McCraken, who received $10,088 in May, 1894, and William M. Ladd and his brother Charles E. Ladd, who secured a $20,338 loan in May, 1895. Lewis loaned the financial agent George Good, an old Arlington Club friend and fellow Episcopalian, two sums in 1894 and 1895, totalling $23,918. Brooks Trevett and his wife had borrowed $1,500 two years before the crash. All these obligations, and many more, were outstanding at the time of Lewis's death in January, 1897.[37]

James Steel was ruined by the depression. His Eastside Railway line, in serious financial shape during the fall of 1893, suffered a disastrous wreck on November 1, when the electric car Inez plunged off the Madison Street Bridge on a cold, foggy morning while the span was turned open to permit a ship to pass through. The resultant damage suits occasioned by the death of five passengers broke the company, which was forced into receivership on December 9 that year. By early January, 1894, Steel was wiped out. A year earlier, he had held gross assets of $388,000, with liabilities of $224,000. In January, 1894, his net losses stood at $33,700. The last entry in his cash journal was for $11.50 on April 6, 1894. He withdrew from all investing, and faded into relative obscurity for nearly a decade. He and his brother George operated an insurance agency and continued to manage the East Side Railway for its new owners.[38]

George B. Markle Goes Home

In early January, 1894, Kate Markle, with her young son, George B. Markel III, fled from her home on Portland Heights to her family in Allegheny City, Pennsylvania, where she filed for divorce. Three months later, Markle himself stole out of town, never to be seen in Oregon or heard from again. Among his many debts was one for approximately $140,000, owed to Robert Livingstone's Scottish American Investment Trust Company Ltd. of Edinburgh. The Multnomah County Circuit Court issued a summons for his arrest on March 12, 1895, but the new Sheriff, G. C. Sears, made no real effort to find him. After years of litigation, Markle's home on Hawthorne Terrace was awarded to Livingstone's SAIT Company, which in turn sold it in December, 1904, to the Pittock family. Other Markle ventures experienced a similar fate. His Exposition

Building had defaulted on its mortgage and was sold to local investors for $85,000. The Commerce Building was sold in March, 1906, to the Spokane, Portland & Seattle Railroad for $800,000.[39]

At the age of only 38, George B. Markle, Jr., slipped home to Hazleton, Pennsylvania. However, he was not a defeated man. Over the years he involved himself in a number of family-related enterprises and drew dividends from the immensely profitable coal business. He apparently made no attempt to repay his Portland debts, nor did he ever remarry. He lived what must have been a lonely life and allowed his weight to exceed 300 pounds. He died wealthy in July, 1914, at age 58. Thus ended the career of a most unusual person who, in the span of seven years, made a lasting imprint on the physical shape of Portland. He also had the distinction — held to this day — of being the only incumbent president of the Portland Chamber of Commerce to be indicted and arrested for fraud.

New Blood Transfused into Old

Markle's successor as chamber president was hardware merchant E. J. Dehart, active in the Arlington Club, president of the Commercial Club and a staunch member of the Portland Establishment. He was succeeded in 1895 by the 69-year-old merchant John McCraken, who had also ascended to the presidency of the Port of Portland Commission upon Ladd's death. For the remaining years of the century, McCraken (who would later serve in the Oregon House) and Henry W. Corbett would constitute the leadership of the older Portland Establishment as new blood mixed with old.

The institution that best symbolized this transfusion was the Portland Art Association, organized in 1888 and incorporated in December, 1892. Led by Henry W. Corbett and Henry Failing, the incorporators included William M Ladd, C. E. S. Wood, Winslow B. Ayer, The Reverend Thomas Lamb Eliot, and Dr. Holt C. Wilson (Captain Couch's grandson). In 1893, Corbett initiated the creation of an art museum as part of the association. He placed major responsibility on the younger members, who would later lead the Portland Establishment in making the art association Portland's foremost private cultural institution. He gave Ayer $10,000 to take with him on a trip to Europe, where he could purchase reproductions of classical works of sculpture. The museum opened in 1895 with a modest gallery of plaster casts, located in the new library building.[40]

Moving into the upper ranks of the Establishment were several more second-generation family members, including the younger John C. Ainsworth and his brother-in-law, Samuel Heitshu; Charles E. Ladd; Henry J. Corbett; Roderick Macleay; L. Allen Lewis; Rodney L. Glisan; Joseph N. Teal; Julius Meier; Frederick W. Leadbetter (son-in-law of Henry L. Pittock); and Paul Wessinger (son-in-law of Henry Weinhard, Portland's wealthiest brewer). Other younger men of community prominence included Charles F. Adams, Abbot L. Mills, Peter Kerr, Charles F. Swigert, Charles F. Beebe, John M. Gearin, Henry W. Goode, Ion Lewis, Theodore B. Wilcox, George H. and Richard L. Durham, Max Hirsch, David Solis-Cohen, Charles H. Carey, Ben Selling, and Leo Samuels.

Most of these men would play some political role, but few would run for elective public office unless to protect or advance their business or financial interests. From

1892 until the end of the century, no Arlington Club members would serve in elective city government. A charter change in 1894 established 11 wards with single representation. The city council became the domain of small merchants, tradesmen and corporate agents, rather than managers or owners, and local political power became increasingly fragmented by the continuing warfare between the Mitchell and Simon Republicans.

15.1 Skidmore Fountain and Stephen G. Skidmore (1838-1883)

15.3 United Bank Building, Oregon National Bank, Northwest Loan & Trust Co.

15.2 Peter Kerr (1861-1957)

15.4 Couch clan picnic in City (now Washington) Park, 1889, including (from left): Hamilton Brooke (straw hat), Sanderson Reed, Lee Hawley Hoffman, W. J. Burns, Dr. Holt C. Wilson (with plate), Clementine Wilson, Mrs. George B. Wallace, Dede Page, Phillips Beck, Dr. R. B. Wilson, Virginia Wilson, Mary Pope, Dr. Eaton, Rodney L. Glisan, and Erskine Wood (standing, far right).

15.5 Arlington Club, 1892

16

POLITICAL WARFARE: 1894-1899

Mason's Final Days: The Flood of 1894

Portland's record flood of early June, 1894, presented outgoing Mayor William S. Mason with the most serious challenge of his crisis-ridden term. The city was still experiencing the effects of the severe depression when everything ground to a halt. The flood did, however, prove a godsend to the unemployed, many of whom were hired on a temporary basis to perform the massive clean-up, which consumed the city's emergency funds. Fortunately, the mayor, the city council and other officials had moved six months earlier into the still unfinished new City Hall at Southwest Fourth and Jefferson streets, where they were on higher ground than the old City Hall at Second and Ash streets, which lay in over seven feet of water.

The flood of 1894, the eighth since 1853, peaked when the Willamette River reached 33½ feet over its low-water mark. The floodwaters covered 250 square blocks, reaching to Northwest Tenth and Glisan and Southwest Sixth and Washington streets. Business was virtually at a standstill, all the bridges were open, and 1,500 boats of all sizes and descriptions took to the flooded waters. Train service into Portland had been shut off on May 27. The Union Pacific Railroad suffered severely, with over 100 miles of track washed out and two and half feet of water in its Albina shops. The unfinished Union Station was inundated, and many wharves and warehouses along the riverbank were twisted from their foundations. A hundred or more houses on the east side were destroyed, along with Dekum and Durham's Portland and Vancouver Railway line.[1]

George Bates showed "commendable energy in keeping water out of the boiler room of the Albina Water Company pumping station," reported the *Albina Weekly Courier*. Using Lee Hoffman's expertise, he built a cofferdam of brick and cement around the machinery and heightened the walls as fast as the water rose. The submerged pumps never stopped. The Portland Gas Company suffered a worse fate. The only entire interruption in the company's history occurred when the gasworks were flooded, halting the generators, and its submerged line connecting the east and west sides was washed out. It took several years for Abbot Mills and Charles Adams to recover their losses. They received sizeable loans from the First National Bank and their own Security Savings and Trust Company. Mills even borrowed $10,000 from the C. H. Lewis Estate in 1898 — part of his wife's inheritance.[2]

Downtown merchants frantically erected platforms to hold their stocks; some provided free boat transportation to their stores. According to a later account,

One could step from the elevated sidewalk to a floating saloon and after quenching his thirst he could catch a quick shave on the floating barber shop before entering his favorite retail store by way of the second story.

A prominent businessman and social leader, General Charles F. Beebe, nearly drowned when he fell off one of his Front Street store platforms. Only the lumber companies thrived as they were swamped with emergency orders to furnish materials for the elevated walkways and scaffolding.[3]

Despite the incurred deficit and the strain on municipal services, the city survived without any epidemics, lootings or major fires. The fire department had gone nautical by mounting engines and hoses on 40- to 60-foot barges. The emergency brought out the best traits in Portland's citizens, who responded to the challenge with humor. Even the crime rate (excluding pranks) remained unusually low. But despite the positive public reaction, Mayor Mason and the city government were in a state of shock. As the *Albina Weekly Courier* reported, Portland had suffered "unbelievable damage."[4]

Political Chicanery: James Lotan

If God Almighty should come to this city during…[a] campaign and try to work against the schemes and combinations of practical politicians, he would lose the fight.

So said the prominent realtor, Charles K. Henry, one of several self-proclaimed reformers who leveled charges of corruption at "unprincipled political bosses and vice peddlers" operating in Portland during the latter years of the 1890s. The story of the city's political strife after the flood is not simply an account of the war between bosses and reformers. All bosses were not villains and all reformers were not heroes. The conditions and relationships involved were too complex to fit into any such rigid framework. This account attempts to reconstruct a struggle that consumed the energies of several of Oregon's leading citizens for over a decade. Even though some of the battles took place in Salem, the effects were always keenly felt in Portland.[5]

The chief contestants were Joseph Simon and U.S. Senator John H. Mitchell. Simon's major compatriots were the banker Henry W. Corbett, Multnomah County Circuit Judge Henry McGinn, U.S. Senator Joseph N. Dolph, and Jonathan Bourne, Jr. Bourne had switched his allegiance to Mitchell in 1892 because of the latter's pro-silver stance. After the election of 1896, when Mitchell abandoned his pro-silver position to embrace the predominant "gold wing" of the party, he returned to the Simon-Corbett faction with a vengeance. Mitchell's chief lieutenants were Charles H. Carey, W. F. (Jack) Matthews, Wilson T. Hume, George P. Frank, and James Lotan.[6]

Lotan, a maverick businessman-politician, owned half-interest in the Stark Street ferry. He had fought a futile battle against the city consolidation legislation that authorized public purchase of the Willamette River bridges. He had begun his business career as a shop foreman with the Willamette Iron Works (of which he later became an officer), and had soon enlisted as a Simon protege, performing many minor but distasteful tasks for the political boss. The payoff came in the mid-1880s when he won appointment to a series of federal positions: local inspector of shipping and machinery, inspector of boilers, and finally, in 1892, customs collector, a rich political plum.[7]

Lotan had broken with Simon in 1885 over the question of supporting Mitchell for the U.S. Senate. By 1887, both Mitchell and Lotan were fellow Arlington Club members and close political allies. After Simon left the state senate in 1892, withdrawing temporarily from politics, Lotan wrested control of the state Republican leadership. This gave him extensive influence within the legislature. Because Portland had already exhausted 80 percent of its authorized bonding capacity for free bridge and ferry acquisition, the city was forced to seek a further legislative authorization of $200,000. Lotan made sure that the bill remained buried throughout the 1893 session, and demanded that he and his partner receive $50,000 for their ferry as the price of legislative approval of the extended authorization.

In early December, 1893, Lotan's power base was damaged by his indictment in federal court for smuggling over 4,000 pounds of opium into Portland during the last six months of 1892 while serving as U.S. customs collector. As reported by Dean Collins, "hundreds of thousands of dollars were involved in the ring, with Lotan heading the Portland end of it." The smuggling ships tossed over "five tael cans of opium on floats in the lower harbor," where they were retrieved by Lotan's "gang." Also indicted were Seid Back, the wealthiest and most prominent Chinese merchant in the Northwest, and a dozen lesser-known figures. At the much publicized trial, the future U.S. Senator Charles W. Fulton defended Lotan, while Simon and John Gearin defended others of the accused. The judge was Simon and Gearin's former law partner, Charles B. Bellinger; the jury foreman was Charles E. Ladd, a fellow Arlington clubmate of Lotan, Bellinger and Gearin, and a business associate of Jonathan Bourne, a close friend of Lotan. The jury convicted 10 of the group but deadlocked on Lotan and Back. A retrial was not sought by the government after the unexplained disappearance of the leading witness, the disreputable Nat Blum. Lotan, supported loyally throughout the ordeal by his Establishment and Arlington Club comrades, survived with his reputation more or less intact.[8]

During the 1895 session of the legislature, the re-elected Joe Simon managed to push through the required authorization. Included in the package was a provision to purchase the Stark Street ferry for $40,000. The price of the Morrison Street Bridge was to be $150,000. When these figures were released, public reaction was immediate. Although the bridge had cost $175,000, it had deteriorated badly during its eight years of heavy use by street railway cars. (It was replaced within 10 years, at a cost of $385,383.) Seven months later, in the heat of a vicious political campaign, District Attorney Wilson T. Hume charged "fraud and a steal" in denouncing the Morrison Bridge "deal." He was not referring to the Lotan payoff, but to the amount paid for the bridge itself. A member of the Lotan-Mitchell Republican faction, he was aiming his barbs at the Simon-Corbett faction.[9]

Some years later, the press reported that Henry W. Corbett had a sizeable investment in the old Morrison span. If he did, it would have been through First National Bank loans to Charles F. Swigert and Swigert associates, who controlled both the bridge and the City & Suburban Railway that was enfranchised to use it. (When he died in 1903, Corbett owned $245,000 of City & Suburban stock.) It was similarly reported that Lotan had amassed heavy bank debts, but the bank was not named; its identity can only be surmised. Simon was certainly not doing Lotan a favor. But he wanted the bridge bill approved, and if there were outstanding First National Bank loans to either the bridge company or Lotan, it was worth it to him, as Corbett's attorney, to secure the total legislative package. In any case, within seven months, the old Stark Street ferry was abandoned. Passenger revenues had diminished markedly, and the ferry boat proved mechanically inoperative and generally an unseaworthy piece of junk.[10]

Bribery

Bribery was the accepted practice in Oregon politics, as it was throughout the country during the nation's "rapid urbanization" of the late nineteenth century. Oregon's experience reinforced Lincoln Steffens's argument, in his *Shame of the Cities,* that a corrupt alliance of "machine politicians" and "special interests" were "free to aggrandize themselves, especially through franchise grants, at the expense of the public. Their power lay primarily in their ability to manipulate the political process, by bribery and corruption, for their own ends."[11]

"There was never a time that the [U.S.] Senatorship wasn't up for barter or sale," recalled Henry McGinn. "The Oregon Assembly is a great big political machine in disguise," remembered Clackamas County Republican leader, former senate president and businessman George C. Brownell in 1910. Henry Villard and the Northern Pacific Railroad spent $300,000 on Joseph Dolph's unsuccessful reelection bid in 1895; it offered $50,000 for two votes. Jonathan Bourne admitted that he spent $10,000 of his own money on George McBride's victory in the same election (both were Republicans). McBride was Mitchell's candidate, while Dolph carried the Simon-Corbett colors. National Republican Committee Chairman Senator Mark Hanna of Ohio told Bourne that the Committee had spent $7 million to beat William Jennings Bryan in the presidential election of 1896; $390,000 of that amount in Oregon alone, distributed by the Portland merchant Solomon Hirsch. Circumstantial evidence indicates that Bryan's loss of Oregon by only 2,000 votes was due to a massive vote fraud. Bourne later contended that repeaters accounted for at least 6,000 votes; that "with an honest vote Oregon would have gone for Bryan by 4,000." Honor aside, Establishment prayers had been answered. As Henry W. Corbett had publicly implored before the election, "Give us a safe, conservative and reliable man for president."[12]

Bourne revealed that he had spent $10,000 to stuff ballot boxes for Mitchell's legislative candidates in 1896. He took the responsibility for electing 60 legislators whose campaigns received a total of $225,000 from the Southern Pacific Railroad. The recipients signed pledges to Bourne before accepting their money, and the Southern Pacific had the pledges locked in the corporate safe. To Bourne an honorable man was one he could buy, who would stay bought, and who would maintain his silence. According to future Governor Oswald West,

> The prevailing prices [for political bribery] were ... four thousand for Republicans and three thousand for Democrats—such prices became common knowledge. As a Democrat I always resented this unjust discrimination and when I once asked a political kale purveyor how they justified the discrimination he said 'As a rule the Republicans occupied a higher social scale.'[13]

Both the Simon-Corbett and Mitchell forces resorted to the same ballot-stuffing procedures, which involved the hiring of hobos to "work" in the primaries. Never bothered by the police, they congregated in gangs about the polling places, turning away voters for the opponents and allowing repeaters to vote for their candidates.

Warfare at City Hall Under Mayor Frank

The election of George P. Frank as mayor of Portland in June, 1894, was a political fluke. A successful merchant in agricultural implements, the 42-year-old New York native was an active Chamber of Commerce member and registered Republican, with no known leaning to either the Simon-Corbett or Mitchell factions. He had friends in both camps, each of which expected to dominate his administration. When William S. Mason decided not to seek reelection, Simon and Corbett announced their support of Frank, who was opposed by Democratic lumberman Robert D. Inman. By most accounts, the wealthy and respected Inman should have won. But the flood had diverted interest from the campaign, and Republican bribes, spread discreetly among the unemployed, produced enough bogus votes to ensure Frank's election.[14]

On his first day in office, Frank disavowed a major campaign pledge to divorce the police department from politics. Using a new power, granted by the Lotan-controlled legislature in 1893, he appointed three neophytes to the police commission, to hold office at the mayor's pleasure. They were D. M. McLaughlan, a former mayor of Albina and manager of the Union Pacific Albina Shop; A. L. Maxwell, an official of the Oregon Railway & Navigation Company and an Arlington Club member; and H. Hausman, a wholesale tobacconist. Three months later, on the mayor's orders, the commissioners fired the beleaguered police chief, C. H. Hunt, and replaced him with John Minto, Jr., the son of a prominent Oregon pioneer and member of the Mitchell faction. Allied to Frank and Minto were District Attorney Wilson T. Hume and his assistant, Dan J. Malarkey (whose political star was to rise in future years).[15]

As results of the continuing vice probe leaked out to the community, largely through the *Telegram* (the *Oregonian* gave the story only limited coverage), public pressure forced a reluctant Chief Minto to conduct a few raids, initially on the least important places. "Liverpool Liz" and her Senate saloon were not touched as she was in the North End, where such activities belonged and the police were handsomely paid off. The downtown received official attention because such "lower pleasures" were not deemed dignified for the civic center. Madame Fanshaw's "Mansion of Sin," across from both the Portland Hotel and the Arlington Club, was the "ne plus ultra of Portland's parlor houses," reported Stewart Holbrook. There was "nothing more elegant or refined in Portland," but it was awkwardly located, at least for the Arlington Club. As Dean Collins observed, "these two institutions were not mutually unaware of one another's existence, and some of the social and political history of Portland haunts the ghosts of those buildings" that replaced them. During one raid, 12 of Madame Fanshaw's girls were arrested, but they were exonerated for lack of absolute proof.[16]

Through the winter and early spring of 1895, scores of prostitutes were picked up. Most of them were released. The judges found that lewdness could not be established "beyond a reasonable doubt." All the top madams escaped punishment; only the "negresses and other low types were convicted," the *Oregonian* reported. District Attorney Hume declared that there would be no more indictments. He thereby lost

$17.50 for each indictment, regardless of conviction. Within a year, he had earned $20,000 in fees for all indictments, including those for vice.[17]

Mayor Frank's two-year term was stormy. He fired not only three of his own appointees to the fire board, but four of his own police commissioners. To the latter, he appointed A. B. Croasman, a prominent businessman and Arlington Club member; George Bates, whom he removed after a year; and Bates's associate P. L. Willis, the dishonest executor of the Lee Hoffman estate. On the fire board, he put attorney George H. Durham, also an Arlington Club member. Before he left office in 1896, Frank had replaced almost the entire police force and fire department. He told the wealthy merchant and Fire Commissioner Sylvester Farrell: "I am going to control the politics of this town. ...I have the Police, Street Cleaning, and now the Fire Department in my control. ...Why ain't you my friend, Mr. Farrell?" Farrell resigned before he was fired.[18]

Frank's bluster and crude arrogance stirred up the Portland Establishment. Even Joe Simon and Henry Corbett realized that their original support was a disastrous mistake. Various reform groups were formed, including the Committee of 100 Taxpayers, headed by Corbett. Their targets were organized gambling, which was giving the city a poor reputation, and Mayor Frank's profligate administration, labeled by Corbett "the tax eaters." Coincidentally, the names of many of the Committee of 100 were also on the list of property owners compiled by the ministerial association's continuing investigation of vice and saloons. Skeptics might have concluded that they took the initiative to cleanse their own reputations.[19]

Six months later, coinciding with the demise of the vice investigations, the Central Municipal Reform League was organized. This disparate group included attorney William M. Cake, a Mitchell Republican; James Steel, a Simon-Corbett Republican; T. F. Osborne, a former Chamber of Commerce president; and E. W. Spencer, the former police chief dismissed by Mayor Mason. They all had in common an intense dislike of Mayor Frank. However, little was to result from their efforts, for within months the state's leading Republicans would be fighting daily over "who would control the spoils." The campaign of 1896 was fast approaching.[20]

Facing increased opposition, Frank chose not to seek reelection in June, 1896. (He died two months later.) He had supposedly been promised the U.S. collector of customs job by Senator Mitchell. For two months, he had raised $12,500 by requiring all his appointed city officials to contribute a tenth of their salaries to a legislative lobbying fund. Matthews would take the money to Salem after the legislature convened in January, 1897. Police Chief Minto was to receive appointment as U.S. marshal if Senator Mitchell won reelection.[21]

Narrowly elected chairman of the Republican County Central Committee, Joe Simon succeeded in keeping control of the local party machinery. His slate of state senatorial candidates included Bates, McLaughlan, and Ben Selling, a prominent Portland merchant. The Mitchell forces were led by District Attorney Wilson T. Hume who was also a state senatorial candidate. Besides attacking the Morrison Bridge sale (as previously noted), Hume accused the Trinidad Asphalt Paving Company, a Ladd-Simon firm, of monopolizing the lucrative municipal paving business in Portland. The charges were partially true. By requiring high performance bonds, the council had eliminated most other bidders, who could not match the Ladd financial resources to meet the bond requirements.

The slate of mayoralty candidates further confused the political line-up. David Solis-Cohen, a former police commissioner and prominent attorney, was Simon's regular Republican candidate. Past-president of the Chamber of Commerce General Charles F. Beebe, who had previously been picked as the official Mitchell candidate, ran as an Independent Republican, drawing some Mitchell support. According to Marie Lazenby, it was rumored that "a deal had been made between the Mitchell and Pennoyer managements by which Beebe was sacrificed in the interests of the Mitchell legislative ticket." With the backing of most Mitchell Republicans, including Jonathan Bourne, who was secretary of the state central committee, Sylvester Pennoyer ran as the Democratic-Populist candidate. Winning handily, the former governor (who, like Mitchell, enjoyed wide popularity among working people) severely damaged Simon's local power base. Before repairing it, however, Simon had to concentrate on blocking Mitchell's bid for reelection in the forthcoming legislative session.[22]

Jonathan Bourne and the Hold-Up Session

Bourne played a key role in support of William Jennings Bryan's November campaign against William McKinley, and in this endeavor he was joined by a number of pro-silver Republicans. As reported by Cornelia Marvin Pierce in her diary:

> Jonathan told me that he sent to California for a notorious criminal who supplied repeaters for elections. ...Jonathan agreed to pay transportation and the living costs of repeaters, all of whom should leave the state the day after election. The terms were settled except for the leader. The agreement was fully carried out and the night after the election the leader met Jonathan in the Arlington Club and together they burned in the fireplace the picture of the leader, which had been taken from the police walls by Jonathan. ... It seemed that when he asked the leader what his price would be, he said he wanted just one thing — and that was that his picture should be removed from the Rogue's Gallery in Portland. ... The reason they didn't win was that Corbett employed more men and sent them up and down the river to vote and they voted at outside towns as well as in Portland.[23]

The "notorious" Californian was probably Billy Smith, who worked with Larry Sullivan, a boxer and political fixer and Bourne's chief North End lieutenant. Bourne, who was close to Mayor Pennoyer and knew his way around the police department from his days on the police commission, assumed a surrogate role in police affairs. He was accused by the *Oregonian* of exercising supreme dictation over the department: "His word, backed by that of Mayor Pennoyer, is the law." Thus he had little trouble removing the picture from the department's files.[24]

Shortly after the election of November, 1896, Bourne was horrified to learn from Mitchell that the senator was abandoning his pro-silver friends and planning to embrace the "gold crowd." Bourne warned him, "You are [not] going to be elected." Having won a seat in the Oregon House, with a chance to become speaker, Bourne was in a strong position to carry out his threat. He approached his old friends Simon and Corbett (with whom he had been allied 10 years earlier) with plans to stall the forthcoming session — to prevent it from organizing, if need be — to deny Mitchell reelection. As Bourne later recalled:

> I then hired the best chef in the State of Oregon; sent him to Salem to fix up apartments in the Eldridge Block; things to eat and drink and entertainment. I said to the chef, 'I pay all expenses. I want to take care of all my friends in the lower House who signed pledges with me, the friends of silver.'[25]

Bourne and Simon gained the support of William U'Ren, the future father of the Oregon System's direct legislation and the leader of the state's Populist movement. U'Ren felt betrayed by Mitchell's refusal to honor a pledge to support U'Ren's efforts to enact Initiative and Referendum amendments to the Oregon Constitution.

To an observant George C. Brownell, the Eldridge Block in Salem, (known as "Bourne's Harem,") became "the den of prostitution and evil." Many of the representatives "were kept drunk and intoxicated for days." Although Bourne admitted that the entertainment cost $80,000, he denied that the money bribed anyone. It was enticement, he said. He told his secretary, Anson Prescott, that "he was afraid that if he started to pay, ... [it] might launch sell-outs." He did, however, pay the living expenses "of a majority of the house members for several weeks, entertaining them so royally that they forgot all about their legislative duties." He never revealed the other sources of funding.[26]

It was rumored, but never verified, that U'Ren was the bag man. He supposedly picked up the money from Henry W. Corbett at the First National Bank and took it to Salem for delivery to Bourne. A year later, Corbett denied that he had committed any improprieties. To the *Oregonian,* he declared:

> I had not communicated with or spoken with Mr. Bourne or made any combination with him to hold up the Legislature, and I had no desire to do so. ...I may have done many things that I should not have done and left many things undone that I should have done, but I have never been accused of being a grafter or levying blackmail.

He then went on to say that he had done what he could to defeat Mitchell, "legitimately!" He concluded by citing Mitchell's demand of $20,000 (for his reelection campaign) from the late President Frederick Billings of the Northern Pacific Railroad, confirmed to him personally by Billings.[27]

Oswald West recalled handling deposits of some of the "subsistence" money while a young teller at the Ladd & Bush Bank in Salem. Simon's nephew also informed his friends about the cash that he took from an unidentified source in Portland to his uncle in Salem. Bourne admittedly raised at least $10,000 through blackmail contributions from Portland's Chinese gamblers and North End saloonkeepers.

When the 40 day session ended on March 3, 1897, nothing had been accomplished. Republican Governor William P. Lord, a close associate of Corbett and Simon, then appointed Corbett to the U.S. Senate to succeed Mitchell. Corbett's long standing ambition to return to Washington was thus realized, but his triumph was short-lived. Stories of the hold-up session were circulating through the Capitol. Mitchell had some well-placed friends in Washington, including agents of the Southern Pacific. Collis P. Huntington was not about to lose the railroad's $250,000 investment in Mitchell without a fight. The Senate refused to seat Corbett, who returned to Portland, where he assumed the presidency of the First National Bank after Henry Failing's death. A special legislative session in October, 1898, elected Corbett's ally, Joseph Simon. Corbett, having withdrawn his name in the interests of party harmony, informed Governor Lord that Oregon needed a senator who was "in accord with the sound financial principles of the party."[28]

City Hall in Crisis: 1896-1898

While Simon and Bourne were focusing their attention on the election of November, 1896, Sylvester Pennoyer came charging into office like a myopic bull. Wildly popular with labor, the former governor was generally disdained by the Portland Establishment, and was dubbed "His Eccentricity" by Harvey Scott. His only redeeming quality in the eyes of this elite was his active involvement in Trinity Episcopal Church. The former governor, who had kept President Benjamin Harrison waiting in the rain and told President Grover Cleveland to mind his own business, thought he knew how to run a city after eight years in the statehouse. Impatient, autocratic and scornful of advice, Pennoyer replaced the entire police force in one year, appointed four chiefs in two years, and unpredictably intervened in the daily details of police and fire operations. After only four months of service, he removed the prominent business leader and brewer Paul Wessinger (son-in-law of Henry Weinhard) from the Board of Fire Commissioners over a policy difference. Although he could be an adroit politician on occasion, Pennoyer brooked neither criticism nor opposition.[29]

During the summer of 1897, while Bourne was in Massachusetts for an extended visit, Simon wrote of his concern over Pennoyer, who was making a mess of things. Simon wanted good traditional leadership restored to Portland — through his own efforts, of course. "I am anxious to get control of our city government," he told Bourne. The two men had apparently discussed such a plan the previous winter, relating to the June, 1898, elections. Worried about Mitchell and his previous support "from the railroad companies," Simon declared it necessary to enlist Henry Corbett's services; his money was needed. He was unaware that Corbett, waiting to gain his seat in Washington, had already discouraged Bourne's approaches for money. He had been left with heavy debts after the death in 1895 of his son, Henry J. Corbett, following a prolonged bout with tuberculosis. "I took upon myself quite an amount of his obligations which are not yet liquidated," Corbett explained in a letter to Bourne.[30]

In late December, 1897, Simon again wrote Bourne that it was "absolutely impossible to carry this county in opposition to the *Oregonian*," and predicted that the Mitchell Republicans would join hands with "the Pennoyer outfit." There was need to arouse public sentiment through the *Oregonian*. He continued: "The friends I have and who usually cooperate with me are largely embraced among the business element of the community." Their support would be lost if the *Oregonian* became antagonized. Advising care in handling the Mitchell faction, he obliquely warned Bourne not to break party ranks again. The latter had already shifted his allegiance to the "gold" Republicans. After the onset of the Alaska Gold Rush in July, 1897, he had incorporated three gold-mining companies, capitalized at $5 million. Bourne's economic interests and ambition always took precedence over any consideration of principle.[31]

William S. Mason to the Rescue

The municipal election campaign in the spring of 1898 was overshadowed by the Spanish-American War. The race for mayor was a typically complicated affair. The Mitchell-Carey Republicans and the "Pennoyer outfit" backed former Police Chief John Minto, an old-school machine politician. The Simon Republicans and sound-money (gold) Democrats supported former Mayor William S. Mason, president of the Chamber of Commerce. Bourne was back in town and up to some of his old tricks. In early May he received word from his co-worker Amadee M. Smith, a business associate of Charles F. Swigert, that he had raised $2,700 in Astoria for Bourne to employ during the campaign. "The money will be used in hiring workers and on election day in securing the floating vote." Two weeks later, Smith advised Bourne to channel the funds through Wells Fargo, where it was "least liable to incite suspicion."[32]

Running as a reform candidate, Mason was depicted as "a progressive businessman of positive and well-founded convictions." He sold his interest in the Mason-Ehrman Grocery Company, but maintained his presidency of the Portland National Bank while he prepared for the fight against Minto, Pennoyer, District Attorney Hume, and the North End saloon crowd. The *Oregonian* provided strong support, as Simon had hoped it would: "There is no better, more worthy, more honorable man." The paper lambasted Hume for criticizing Mason. The former mayor's opponents were "the pirates of local politics, ... a gang devoid of principles."[33]

To encourage the "positive vote" for the Chamber of Commerce leader, most larger downtown stores and businesses closed on election day. Mason was overwhelmingly elected, the first and only incumbent chamber president to become mayor in Portland's history. Simon regained some of his former authority, although the independent Mason meant to be nobody's man.

Within 11 days of resuming office in July, 1898, Mason had replaced the entire police department, appointing Simon men to the leadership. Former Police Commissioner D. M. McLaughlan became chief. The three new commissioners were hardware merchant James E. Hunt, attorney David Solis-Cohen, and George W. Bates, who thus held membership on two of the three most powerful and prestigious public commissions in Portland. (He had joined the Water Committee earlier in 1898.) As Mason told the city council on July 6:

> We have a police commission, and chief of the Department composed of some of our best citizens, whose aim it will be to carry out your ordinances, to enforce your edicts and to preserve order and give reputation to our city. ... Some of our current ordinances are practically a dead letter, so far as their enforcement is concerned.[34]

Regular patrolmen returned to North End beats, replacing special officers who were working for their private employers. Chief McLaughlan was ordered to clean up the brothels and close the gambling establishments, including the Chinese games and lotteries. Commission president Hunt ordered police officers to "refrain from collecting any fees from houses of prostitution, gambling houses, or any objectionable class of people." Such attempts were naive in concept and hopeless in execution, as Mason sadly found out. Community resistance was ingrained; too many profitable commercial enterprises were involved.[35]

Compounding the difficulty of enforcement was a shortage of police operating funds in the post-depression years. From 1893 to 1899, county tax assessments had been reduced by almost 50 percent, because county commissioners believed that Multnomah County was paying too high a share of state taxes. The police budget had to be curtailed at the very time that the city's population was surging ahead by 30 percent. To complicate matters further, Mayor Mason died in office on March 29, 1899. Thus the last of Portland's nineteenth-century merchant mayors passed from the scene. It would be nearly 50 years before another merchant won election as mayor.[36]

The city council took almost two months to select Mason's successor. George W. Bates led in six of 13 formal votes, but never by as much as the required majority. Finally, Council President William A. Storey was chosen to complete the remaining 13 months of Mason's term. A woodmill worker by trade, his undistinguished qualities matched those of most of his fellow councilmen. The 11-ward body reflected the dispersed economic and social interests of a fast-growing city—largely middle-class tradesmen, small merchants and manufacturers, and self-employed attorneys. No leading businessmen or Arlington Club members were in evidence. The council's most dynamic member was 30-year-old George L. Baker, assistant manager of the Marquam Grand Theater, who was to play an increasingly important role in city government and be elected to the first of four terms as mayor in 1917. Storey's selection initiated a period of weak, ineffective government that lasted for six years, as economic and demographic forces almost overwhelmed the city and the surrounding metropolitan area.

16.1 June, 1894, flood outside Chamber of Commerce Building

16.2 Fire fighting during June, 1894, flood

16.3 Stark Street ferry, c. 1884-1893

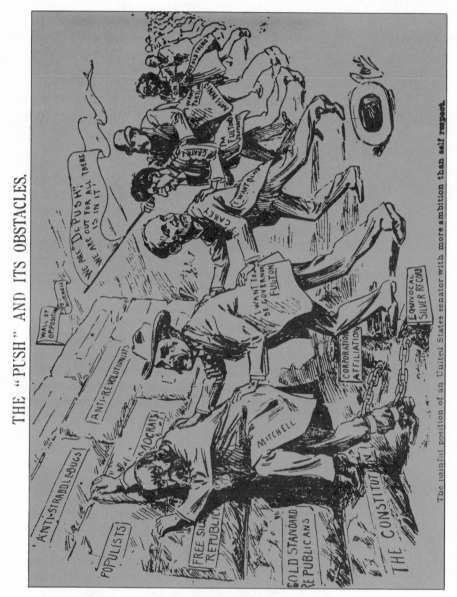

THE "PUSH" AND ITS OBSTACLES.

The painful position of an United States senator with more ambition than self respect.

16.4 *The Oregonian* on Oregon politics, 1897

16.5 Portland Harbor and grain ships, c. 1900

16.6 Portland, looking east toward Mt. Hood from present-day Washington Park, c. 1900

16.7 Police force in front of the city jail, 1885

17

CROSSING THE LINE OF RESPECTABILITY: 1900-1903

Booming Years: 1897-1900

The Alaska Gold Rush, which "burst into headlines" during the summer of 1897, started a local economic boom. According to Charles M. Gates and Dorothy O. Johansen, it inaugurated "a vigorous economic advance that quickly lifted the whole Northwest out of the depression doldrums into which it had fallen during the panic of 1893." Seattle derived the greater financial rewards from the explosive development, but an increased demand for wheat especially benefited Portland's trading economy. In addition, mining and related enterprises created 136 out of the more than 300 new businesses incorporated in Oregon from 1897 to 1899. Their big investors included some familiar names: Ladd, Watson, Flanders, Bourne, McCraken, Ainsworth, Livingstone, Beebe, Mason, Simon, Knapp and Goode.[1]

One fortunate investor, less known to old Portlanders, was German-born Henry Wemme, a tent and awning merchant, who had arrived from the east in 1882. According to a later account, Wemme proudly noted that he "did an immense business in selling tents" to Alaska-bound miners. He spent all of his money and even borrowed to buy canvass and bolts of cotton. He had more tent material "than all the rest of the dealers on the coast put together." When the Klondike fever subsided in 1898, he found himself stuck with a big stock of goods on hand, no market and payments for material coming due. As Wemme recalled his salvation:

> I couldn't borrow any more money and I was headed for the rocks. Just at the particular moment the Maine was sunk. [The Spanish American] War was declared. I landed an order for 16,000 shelter tents. I put a big force at work. The Government gave me an additional order for 16,000 more tents and they gave me an open order for hospital tents, telling me to make all I could. Fleischner & Mayer turned their factory over to me. I had 400 people at work turning out tents. When the Government told me to stop making tents for them, I had used up all my material and instead of going broke I had made a clean-up.[2]

The details of Wemme's birth, early life and marriage were never divulged. The founder of the White Shield Home for wayward girls became a much publicized figure when he introduced the first automobile to Portland in 1899. "My automobile [a Stanley Steamer] was not popular either with horses or their owners," he remembered. "There were more runaways the first year I had it than had occurred in Portland for the twenty preceding years." He also brought the first plane to Portland, and was one of the earliest advocates of a Columbia River Highway. Foreseeing Mount Hood's scenic possibilities, he bought the old Barlow Toll Road for $6,000, and spent $25,000 of his own money on it, and then gave it to the people of Oregon.[3]

Record Growth

Between 1890 and 1900, Portland's growth rate was the third fastest of major American cities. In 1901 its businesses recorded their best year to date. In late 1902 the Title Guarantee and Trust Company, founded by the Ladd family, reported, "Never in the history of Portland has the real estate market been in a more healthy ... and prosperous condition than it is today." The minimal annual return to the average real-estate investor was 18 percent. The real-estate market had rebounded with a vengeance from the depression doldrums. In April, 1897, Peter Kerr had written to his Scottish uncle that,

> Real estate here is dirt cheap. ... This is a very good time to buy anything in or near Portland. It has got so low that there can hardly be any possible loss — while the possibilities of the future are great.[4]

Portland had the largest area of any city on the Pacific Coast. In the three-and-a-half-year period beginning in 1900, more than 25,000 new residents settled in the city and over 10,000 in adjacent metropolitan areas. (Kerr himself later bought hundreds of acres on the Clackamas County line.) More than 5,000 new buildings were constructed, representing an investment of $9 million. Street and sewer improvements alone cost over $600,000. Bank deposits increased 150 percent, while manufacturing more than doubled. In 1901 Portland was the fifth-largest wheat-exporting city, nearly equaling San Francisco and far exceeding Seattle in that capacity. Grain merchants and brokers like Kerr rapidly grew rich, while owners of the numerous lumber, fruit-growing and fish canning enterprises almost matched them in achieving new wealth. The *Financial Redbook of America* in 1903 listed 74 Portlanders with assets of over $300,000 — a sum equal to at least $4 million in 1988 buying power.[5]

The prominent journalist Ray Stannard Baker in January, 1903, found Portland

> a fine old city, a bit, as it might be, of central New York—a square with the post office in the center, tree shaded streets, comfortable homes, and plenty of churches and clubs, the signs of conservatism and solid respectability. And yet no decay.

Baker encountered definite signs of boosterism. "Every citizen," he said, "will give you fifty reasons why it is to be, shortly, the very greatest in the world." Portland's projected growth, extending its speculative gridiron and public transportation system, reflected, in Lewis Mumford's judgment, "the dominance of capitalist forms in the growing cities of the nineteenth century." As Mumford concluded:

> An expanding economy demanded an expanding population; and an expanding population demanded an expanding city. The sky and the horizon were the only limits. On

purely commercial terms numerical growth was synonymous with improvement. The census of population was sufficient to establish a city's cultural rank.[6]

By 1900, Portland business leaders had become apprehensive over Seattle's burgeoning growth — its population was now growing faster than Portland's. The city's long dominance in the Pacific Northwest was being challenged. One way to boost Portland's fortunes was to stage a national exposition to memorialize the Lewis and Clark expedition to Oregon in 1805. Colonel Henry E. Dosch, its major early promoter, had declared in April, 1899, that a national exposition meant "money—lots of money;" it had to "be on a grand scale." Dosch spoke from his experience as Oregon's official ambassador to national expositions at Omaha, Buffalo, Charleston, and New Orleans. "I know that such expositions pay," he declared, "—pay immensely." As Carl Abbott has observed: "The ostensible purpose was to memorialize the great explorers, but impetus and organization came from bankers, brokers, and the Board of Trade." In November, 1899, Albina realtor William M. Killingworth and others had organized the Portland Board of Trade "to bring together men of 'push and progress' who felt uncomfortable in the stodgy Chamber of Commerce."[7]

In February, 1901, Henry W. Corbett, elected president of the Lewis and Clark Centennial Exposition Association, subscribed to the largest block of stock—$30,000 worth. As Joseph Gaston commented, "The very decision to hold the exposition, strengthened every man that put down a dollar for it; and from that very day Portland business, Portland real estate, and Portland's great future commenced to move up." By May, 1901, some 3,000 investors had bought over $417,000 in stock. On the board of directors were Abbot L. Mills; George W. Bates; Charles E. Ladd; John C. Ainsworth; Paul Wessinger; P. L. Willis; Harvey W. Scott; and Henry E. Reed, secretary and director of promotion. More than being simply money raisers and trade and population promoters, such fairs were designed, in the words of Mills and Wessinger, "to celebrate the past and to exploit the future."[8]

Going First Class on a Steerage Ticket

Like many of his Establishment peers, the banker Abbot Mills, who strongly supported efforts to promote Portland, was ambivalent about the city's growth. As Mansel G. Blackford has observed, Portland business leaders "both loved and feared it." They "equated growth with progress, but they were afraid that growth might erode their social influence and physical control over the city. ... Businessmen wanted Portland to grow and expand, but only along lines socially acceptable to themselves."[9]

Mills had additional concerns that he addressed to a state meeting of bankers in November, 1901. Comparing Portland with other cities, he observed that it was spread over too great a geographic area—a condition that was costly. Although well-served with such services as water and light, the city received poor protection from an inadequate police force. While directing criticism at the number of franchise awards, Mills called for increased revenues, particularly a higher property tax assessment percentage, to support needed municipal services. He warned that "one cannot travel first class on a steerage ticket."[10]

City income came from three major sources: property taxes, business licenses and franchises. For over a decade, Portland had received approximately 40 percent of its revenue from property taxes, an amount well below the average for other American cities of comparable size. Speaking as a banker, Mills wanted to increase public revenues so that government would have the means to provide more services and thus play a more vigorous role in promoting economic development. Additional revenues were also needed to pay interest on bond issues (especially for sewers), and thereby maintain the city's high credit standing. Speaking for many downtown merchants (including the bank's customers), whom, he felt, had long borne the heaviest revenue burdens through excessive license fees, Mills challenged the real-estate interests that had kept property taxes unduly low. Representing the City & Suburban Railway Company, Mills was prepared to pay higher property taxes and thus reduce public pressure for higher franchise and license fees. His criticisms of the number of franchise awards most likely reflected his fear of competition. As with the lumber industry, too many competing street railway companies created instability and unbalanced growth that could not be controlled. The process was costly to a corporation that required an efficient operation and a predictable market.[11]

Six months later, Circuit Court Judge Alfred F. Sears, Jr., raised similar concerns as he questioned the city's direction. Where was all the construction and land development leading Portland? "The aggregation of property interests ... confronts us as a menace," he charged. From his own experience, he knew what ailed civic life. For 10 years, the former city council member and assistant district attorney had been the law partner of Henry McGinn and Nate Simon, Joe Simon's brother. His firm had represented many of the street railway interests, including those of the Markle organization. Pointedly, Sears feared "the despotism of the dollar." What was needed was "more of utopia and less of utility, ... more of Plato less of Edison."[12]

He recognized that Portland's government in the early 1900s was dominated by the same interests — real-estate, construction and financial — that were booming and squeezing maximum profits from the system. Accusing these enterprises of starving the city's economy, Sears challenged them to bear their fair share of the costs of basic civic services, which downtown businessmen considered absolutely essential. Until Multnomah County increased the property assessment rate in 1901 from 33 to 50 percent of true market value, assessments had declined while property values increased. He cited the major railroad corporations whose Oregon properties were vastly underassessed compared with their properties in other Pacific Coast states. These big enterprises had left little to chance. The appointed Multnomah County Court clerk (a key position for computing tax assessments) was Frank S. Fields, a Mitchell Republican and the brother of L. R. Fields, general superintendent of the Southern Pacific Railroad in Oregon.

Cases of tax fraud were not uncommon although rarely prosecuted. In 1907, the fledgling *Oregon Journal* reported that the Philip Marquam properties in downtown Portland should have paid a tax of $42,814 in 1900 but instead paid only $15,774. The county had apparently "compromised" at the lower figure, saving the former judge and legislator over $27,000. Marquam's attorney allegedly received a cash fee of $3,000, which was charged off against the tax; half the fee was then paid to the county clerk. The lawyer in question was state Representative J. Thorburn Ross, an ally of Joe Simon, William M. Ladd, George Bates, and Mayor Henry S. Rowe.[13]

Secretary of State Frank I. Dunbar addressed the broader question of tax and assessment practices in his *Biennial Report* of December, 1902. He suggested to his Republican friends in the legislature that they enact a graduated corporation tax, a franchise tax, and a corporate filing fee larger than the then current $5. Oregon counted over 3,000 active corporations in 1902, of which 866 had been incorporated since January, 1901. According to Dunbar, over half of the states had license fees. "The assessment and valuation of the property of express, telephone, telegraph, sleeping or Pullman car, and transportation car companies should receive ... careful investigation...." Such companies, he declared, "do not contribute to the revenues of the state." They wanted to go first class at discounted prices — on steerage tickets.[14]

Portland's corporate establishment pursued similar tactics in promoting the Lewis and Clark Exposition. Corbett, Mills and their friends wanted to go first class at discounted labor costs. In 1902-1903, the exposition association solicited trade unions to buy blocks of exposition stock. For their subscriptions, according to the *Labor Press*, the unions received promises that "all work on the grounds would be done under union conditions with union men." But in April, 1903, after the state legislature had appropriated $500,000 for the fair, the management authorized an open-shop policy, denying that any commitment to the contrary had ever been made to organized labor. "The construction trades reacted to the denial with outrage," according to labor historian Craig Wollner. Their fury increased when the same legislature failed to pass a corporation tax, as recommended by Secretary of State Frank Dunbar. To them, the legislature had willingly appropriated public funds to subsidize an essentially private venture but had refused to tax the very corporations—the railroads and street railways — that would chiefly benefit from the extravaganza.[15]

The angry Building Trades Council, led by the painters' and carpenters' unions, threatened to strike for a minimum wage of $3.50 per day, the standard West Coast rate. But many union members were reluctant to force a confrontation that might cause a strike. Above all, they wanted to participate in the expected economic windfall from the fair, and were fearful of jeopardizing its opening in June, 1905. Aware of the split in union ranks, the exposition management merely embarked on a publicity campaign to quiet union labor opposition. The Portland Establishment had never given much credence to union activity so long as labor was conservative and poorly organized. For the most part, business leaders did not believe unionism a serious threat. As Peter Kerr had comfortably observed a decade earlier, "The American working man...considers himself as good as you. ... He smokes cigars."[16]

Acceptable Pleasures

The Portland Establishment, generally oblivious to the growing costs of public services and the demands of union labor for a minimum wage of $3.50 for a nine-hour day, wanted the best for its fair city, but largely in terms of its members' private lives. The quality of life was judged by private experience; by appearance, politeness, and the surface decoration of tidy neighborhoods, well-manicured lawns and rose gardens; by formal parties, and the close fellowship of intimate club life. If members of the urban Establishment were thriving and happy, the benefits of their good life would undoubtedly seep down to the working classes whose lives would be enriched accordingly.

Portland's Establishment was indeed thriving and happy during the early 1900s. As the *Oregonian's* society editor commented some years later, "The period between 1900 and 1914 found Portland gayer than ever before or since in its history." It was not uncommon to plan a four-hour luncheon for 30 guests, with orchestra music and entertainment. In fact, "There was ample opportunity to satisfy almost any variety of tastes in polite entertainment, as Marie Lazenby has noted. For an evening of culture, one could attend a Musical Club show; for amateur theatricals, the Oregon Road Club presented winter musical dramas; for athletics, the Multnomah Club offered numerous sporting and physical activities.[17]

For Establishment men, shooting and golf and, later, polo became favorite recreations. Intimate shooting groups were available for those who needed to escape from city and family burdens to wilderness-type reserves where men could be men. The Morgan's Shooting Club roster included Abbot Mills; Roderick Macleay; Charles F. Adams; and Dr. Kenneth A. J. MacKenzie, Macleay's father-in-law and Portland's most eminent surgeon.[18]

The most exclusive institution in the Portland area, the Waverly Association, was organized in October, 1899, to raise $15,000 to buy 80 acres of the renowned Lambert farm for the Waverly Golf Club. (The "e" in the suffix was not used at the time.) After three years of play on a nine-hole course (limited to the season and length of grass), laid out on a converted meadow in Southeast Portland, the club wanted a regulation 18-hole course befitting the aspirations, tastes and skills of its members. Located south of the city, near Milwaukie, and sandwiched between the Willamette River and the Eastside Railway line, Waverly attracted the social elite of the *Portland Blue Book*, with a strong Scottish flavor. Mills was elected association president; J. Wesley Ladd, vice-president; architect William M. Whidden, secretary. Charter members of the golf club, organized in 1896 under Robert Livingstone's presidency, included William Mac-Master, William J. Honeyman, Walter J. Burns, Charles F. Swigert, Homer C. Campbell, Roderick Macleay, Walter F. Burrell, John C. Ainsworth, and Peter and Thomas Kerr. At its first annual meeting in May, 1897, the club had 74 male and 23 "lady" members. As distinct from the club, the association was charged with acquiring land. By 1901, it had 160 more acres, part of which was later leased to the Portland Polo Club. Next to the course, the wooded Waverly Heights development attracted some of Portland's Establishment families, who built summer cottages there, many later converted to permanent residences. The entire area became an enclave for Portland's leading white, Anglo-Saxon Protestants. Here they could enjoy mutual fellowship in strictest privacy.[19]

For recreation, the less privileged could sit across from the Portland Hotel on warm summer afternoons and listen to band music wafting from the hotel's parkway area. Others took a leisurely stroll through the Exposition Building, which was usually humming with a variety of activities. Sunday-afternoon band concerts drew throngs to City Park (now part of Washington Park). The Park Zoo was equally popular, although the conditions under which the animals were kept and displayed were abominable by modern standards.[20]

For Portlanders, rich and poor alike, bicycle riding had become a craze by 1900. The United Wheelmen's Association promoted the construction of a riding path from East Portland to the Columbia River. Dealer Fred T. Merrill sold 8,850 bicycles in 1898 alone, making him the largest operator west of the Mississippi. Among other models, he handled the famous Pacemaker which accommodated five riders on its 12-foot, 130-pound frame. According to Merrill, bicycle use began to wane around 1903, when "the favouring women from the North End took to the wheel." They wore bright cycling clothes and "scandalous split skirts," and rode around town ringing their bells. The society girls would have none of it, and their loss of patronage hurt the business.[21]

Less Acceptable Pleasures

During his term on the city council (1900-1905), Fred Merrill represented the Third Ward, from Southwest Washington to Northwest Glisan streets, and became a legendary figure in the North End as he unabashedly defended prostitution and gambling. He believed that such activities should not be outlawed but, rather, should pay their fair share through licenses and taxes. "There has never been a time during my fifty-four years in Portland when a total stranger couldn't find a gambling game or a sporting house," he recalled later. His initial council race in 1900 was "a lark." Never expecting to win, he wanted only to promote his bicycles. In 1903, he ran on a "Keep Portland wide open" ticket.[22]

Recounting his political experience, Merrill claimed: "I never took a cent of money from anyone....I became a sort of fixer for people in trouble." Once, he retrieved "a wild young daughter of a prominent Portland family out of a house of ill-fame." In council, he often voted against corporate or other vested interests when he felt they were self-serving and insufficiently beneficial to the public. On one occasion, he prevented the Standard Oil Company from establishing an oil-storage district on the east side of the river. On another, he prevented Jonathan Bourne's North End crony, Larry Sullivan, from acquiring a 50-year garbage-collection franchise. Representing his working-class constituents (who constituted a majority of his ward), he made no pretense of joining any establishment organization.[23]

His good friend Judge Henry McGinn, on the other hand, was a bona fide member of the Establishment by virtue of his influential friends and his state senate leadership. Early in his career he publicly supported vice and gambling operations, and actively participated in them. He had been a consort of the Madame P. Shong of bordello fame. He loved booze and women and was not afraid to admit it. Still, his voice carried authority in a community that ostensibly disdained such activities. During Mayor Story's brief tenure, McGinn blithely appeared before the Board of Police Commissioners with a petition from a large number of merchants and property owners requesting that it "take into consideration all the various interests involved in determining upon a policy as to control and regulation of saloons and gambling within the city." The board's policy should not be so restrictive as "to become a detriment and injury to the business community."[24]

The police commission was amply receptive. Not only was McGinn Nate Simon's partner, but the board president was Joe Simon's close friend David Solis-Cohen. Commissioner C. N. Rankin worked for the *Oregonian* and Harvey Scott was an intimate associate of McGinn. The third board member, George W. Bates, derived a healthy income from property on Fourth Street that was rented to gamblers. Observing commission policy, the police were tolerant of vice within Portland's "primrose precincts," specifically the block between Second and Third streets on Burnside, known as "the blazing center." According to one account,

> Here were the Erickson, Fritz and Blazier saloons, with the House of All Nations establishment opposite Erickson's on the northeast corner of Second and Burnside. Lights glared, music blared, chips rattled and glasses clinked from dark till the milkman made his rounds.[25]

Witnessing such activities in October, 1902, three years after his arrival at Temple Beth Israel, Rabbi Stephen Wise was appalled to see members of his own congregation playing the slot machines. In frustration he wrote his wife, "Disgustedly I blurted out, 'What's the use of preaching to stone walls?' The rotten, Golden West." Years later, he reflected on his early rabbinate in Portland:

> I came into closer touch with the things out of which grew lawless power of civic corruption. It was the union of gambling and liquor interests plus organized prostitution, which, in collusion with city officials and above all with the police department, poisoned and corroded the life of the city. The hold of these forces upon the city's life was fully known to the acquiescent and rather cynical population, which seemed to take it for granted that organized vice was entitled to no small part in managing the city and its affairs.

As local pundit Dean Collins concluded: "The men who controlled things in those days believed, to paraphrase a later utterance, in 'Open-vice, openly arrived at.' "[26]

Politics As Usual

The administration of Republican Mayor Henry S. Rowe (1900-1902), representing "the men who controlled things," provided a safe government for business. Rowe had long been an employee of the Oregon Railway & Navigation Company, as a steamship agent and then a railroad superintendent. He continued to maintain strong railroad connections and private real-estate interests during his term of office, climaxing his career as general agent for the Chicago, Milwaukee and St. Paul Railroad. Throughout his varied and active life in business and government, he maintained a close working relationship with Joseph Simon and George Bates.

The 11-member city council, all neophytes, was decidedly upper middle class, and Establishment oriented. Among them were four attorneys (two in real-estate development), two realtors, four merchants, and one accountant. The mayor and three of the councilmen were Arlington Club members. The council president was the proper young attorney Rodney L. Glisan, a grandson of Captain Couch and a nephew of Cicero H. Lewis. No innovations or reforms were expected from a group, whose motto was "Business as usual." Councilman William T. Branch, an accountant and former city auditor, reportedly said: "A city officer ... [is in a] delicate position, faced with forcing compliance to ordinances ... [which] makes him many enemies."[27]

As in previous administrations, the city found itself strapped for funds. The police department exhausted its operating revenues two months before the end of the 1900 fiscal year and had to borrow to stay in business. Major downtown thoroughfares were in appalling condition, particularly First Street between Burnside and Madison streets, which was cluttered with railway tracks. The most perplexing headache was the city garbage dump and crematorium. Garbage disposal had always been a costly municipal problem. As the *Oregonian* commented some years earlier: "The old, old question of 'What shall we do with our garbage?' which, like Banquo's ghost, or the smell of a garbage dump, 'will not down,' nor be downed, is … coming to the surface again." In 1900 the dump was beside the crematorium-furnace plant above the depot yards in Northwest Portland. At night, refuse dumped was apt to end up almost anywhere on the unlighted and undermanned premises. In 1903 the city moved the plant to Northwest 25th Street, near Guild's Lake, but, as in the past, it soon proved inadequate for the load, and the operation costs continued to rise.[28]

One of the city's most controversial issues during the winter of 1901-1902 was the purchase by the water committee of the Albina Water Company property. Bates had been the majority stockholder since the company's founding as the Albina Light & Water Company in 1889; minority stockholders included Mayor Rowe and Chief of Police D.M. McLaughlan. In December, 1901, the water company offered to sell its properties for $250,000 cash — $80,000 more than the city engineer's appraisal. Even the lower amount contrasted sharply with the company's assessment record. In 1899 it had been assessed at $11,000, in 1900 at $17,000, and in 1901 at $25,000 — the year in which the rate should have increased to 50 percent of market value. Assuming the property was worth at least three times the county's listed value, the Albina Water Company had grossly underpaid its taxes for over a decade. In addition, the company had never paid a license fee. Friends in high places had paid off handsomely to the owners.[29]

After a series of meetings during December of 1901, the water committee, with Bates absent, voted 7-3 to pay $200,000. Chairman Henry W. Corbett opposed the motion, while the *Oregonian* praised the deal as a "bargain." Harvey Scott, a member of the water committee, had supported his friends Bates and Rowe in demanding the higher amount. In subsequent years, the *Oregon Journal* attacked the city purchase as "a sell-out" to powerful private interests. Eighteen months later, Bates was accused of fraud by his opponents and lost his bid for a seat in the 1902 legislative session.[30]

The Board of Public Works

A new city charter of October, 1898, had authorized the establishment of a board of public works, to be appointed by the mayor. Joe Simon had devised this maneuver during his last term as senate president to bypass a city council that might fall under the control of the Mitchell Republicans, particularly during the ensuing five years when Simon expected to be in Washington as Oregon's junior senator. The board was required to review all city purchases, bids, contracts, and franchise applications before transmission to the council for final approval. Although in most cases the council acted pro forma in accordance with the board's recommendations, it was not obliged to.

Mayor Mason's appointments to the board were drawn exclusively from the Establishment, heavily weighted toward real-estate interests. With Abbot Mills as chairman, the others were Walter F. Burrell, Otto Breyman and William MacMaster, all Arlington and Waverly Club members. Mills remained in office until January, 1903, when the board was replaced by a new agency. Though the board was intended to provide a more efficient and economical purchasing system, it merely facilitated collusive bidding, using standard ploys to circumvent formal requirements. Orders were always distributed to different politically influential dealers with no saving in costs. Everyone got some of the gravy. Reaching the council, with no published agenda, proposals were rushed through without public review.[31]

The city's major purchases were hay, hardware, sawdust, and lumber. The man most often cited as the largest beneficiary of city business was Donald MacKay, veteran state senator, president of the North Pacific Lumber Company, and chairman of the Republican City and County Central Committee off and on for 10 years. A political associate of Simon and Corbett, Arlington Club member MacKay came under attack by the *Democratic Daily Times* for being the major organizer of City Hall graft: "Not a single item enters into the consumption of the two governments [city and county] that has not paid its portion in tribute." The *Times* accused MacKay not only of extorting kickbacks, but of furnishing lumber to the two governments at his own price.[32]

Providing insurance coverage for city properties also lay within the board's jurisdiction, and produced a lucrative income for many insurance agents. Street-paving contracts, enmeshed in politics and influence peddling, were equally rewarding. The Ladd-controlled Trinidad Asphalt Paving Company won the major share of extremely profitable jobs, free of competitive bids. The charter required that the award go to the "lowest *responsible* bidder," with responsibility defined in terms of bonding capacity. No other company could match the resources of the Ladd & Tilton Bank, which guaranteed Trinidad's performance bonds.[33]

During 1901, the Board of Public Works increasingly devoted its time to franchise applications, which divided the business community according to the interests at stake. In September Ellis G. Hughes, a prominent attorney who had drafted the Port of Portland Commission legislation in 1891, remonstrated to the council against awarding a railroad track franchise along North Front Street to George Weidler. According to Hughes, his Arlington clubmate had "no interest in railroads." All Weidler wanted, claimed Hughes, was "a valuable franchise to sell." Hughes asked, "what public interest is there to be served by this franchise?" In his opinion, if the land were privately owned and used for a similar franchised activity, it would be worth $100,000. "I would not be adverse to having a few hundreds of thousands of dollars worth of these franchises myself. ... There is a wide difference between what Mr. Weidler and his associates may desire and what the public interests require." Weidler's chief associate was his attorney, Charles H. Carey, former police judge, member of the Mitchell machine, and in 1901 president of the Weidler lumber operation. Carey was also legal counsel to the Northern Pacific Railroad.[34]

Hughes claimed that the franchise was being sought for the Northern Pacific, which wanted to buy Weidler's mill property, and that Weidler already had a contract for sale with representatives of the railroad. "If the Northern Pacific wants this franchise, why does not that company ask for it in its own name?" inquired Hughes. The attorney who had represented the old Oregonian Railway Company Ltd., later acquired by Southern Pacific, charged that the N.P. "has been the persistent enemy of this city, seizing every opportunity to injure it, by diverting its trade to its own so-called terminal at Tacoma, or of late to Seattle." Hughes concluded with the declaration that "Portland owes the Northern Pacific no favor." His anger with the railroad stemmed from his dislike of Henry Villard, who had squeezed out the Scottish and Oregon investors when he seized control of William Reid's original railroad properties in 1881.[35]

Through a series of ordinances, the franchise was finally endorsed by the council on December 3, 1901. The Board of Public Works had previously approved the award, with chairman Mills in opposition. Mills actually voted against the interests of two close Harvard friends, Northern Pacific director William Endicott, Jr., of Boston, and the railroad's president, Howard Elliott. In later years, when the First National Bank's interest became involved in financial dealings with the N.P., Mills supported the railroad, but no such conditions prevailed in 1901.

Dirty Politics

The intraparty fighting of the latter 1890s continued to afflict the Republicans in the early years of the new century. With Joe Simon in Washington, the Corbett forces relied on state Senator Henry McGinn to prevent John H. Mitchell from gaining his strongly desired reelection to the U.S. Senate, denied him in 1897. Corbett, still politically ambitious at 74, wanted one more attempt. As the legislature opened on January 20, 1901, Jonathan Bourne, assisting McGinn, had 32 signed Corbett pledges in his pocket.

In the early balloting, Corbett held a slight edge over incumbent Senator George W. McBride, a Mitchell ally. With the election still unresolved a month later, George H. Williams replaced McBride as Corbett's chief contender. On the last regular day of the session, Senator George Brownell, reputedly representing the Southern Pacific, nominated Mitchell. After 25 ballots, lasting well into the night, Mitchell was elected, with the aid of 11 Democrats who were rumored to have struck a deal with the Mitchell high command, comprising Charles H. Carey, W.F. (Jack) Matthews and Dan J. Malarkey. Democrats were supposedly promised positions on the Portland police and fire boards and some county offices if they would support Mitchell. Ten years later, Brownell publicly referred to the episode and to Corbett, whose agents, Bourne and McGinn, he said, "bought men and paid them in money and whiskey and other things for their votes." One House member, a parishioner of a leading Portland church, was allegedly given $100 every time he voted for Corbett plus a slug of whiskey in the cloakroom. After Matthews and Carey delivered their promised votes, one observer noted, the "S.P. money beat the Corbett money." Bourne blamed "four traitors" for breaking their pledges, and Corbett blamed the Mitchell machine for having sold the Republican party to the Portland Democrats for a few offices. As Bourne declared, "They sold out the city government to their political enemies."[36]

Strange Alliances: The Election of 1902

The 16 months following the end of the 1901 legislative session produced the most complicated and anomalous series of events in Oregon's tortuous political history. A charter commission, headed by Abbot Mills and including 22 of Portland's most eminent citizens, was drafting a new city charter. For over a year its members argued over provisions to accelerate the governmental process and grant the mayor more authority for which he could be held accountable. The fire and police boards were to be abolished, a civil service board was to be established, and the water committee limited to four members. The Board of Public Works was to be replaced by an Executive Board of 10, whose members could not hold any other public office. Franchises were to be non-exclusive and limited to 25 years, and were to be published before final action was taken by the council. The city would be authorized to acquire existing utility plants by vote of the people and to issue utility bonds if two-thirds of the voters approved. Total bonded indebtedness could never exceed 7 percent of the assessed value of all real and personal property in the city. The city would also be authorized by popular vote to provide for its own light plant, with a maximum expenditure of $300,000.[37]

While these deliberations were being conducted, William S. U'Ren and Jonathan Bourne organized the state-wide People's Power League with the help of numerous farm and labor groups which had been promoting direct legislation since 1886. By the early 1900's, according to Walter Pierce, direct legislation "had lost its earlier Populist stigma." The organizers' purpose was to secure popular approval of an initiative and referendum amendment to the state constitution at the election of June, 1902. Support came from a diverse group of business and professional men, including Harvey Scott, who guaranteed the *Oregonian*'s endorsement. Other Establishment members of the league were Mills, Simon, Mitchell, Charles E. and William M. Ladd, Ben Selling, C. E. S. Wood, and George H. Williams.[38]

The Mitchell-Carey-Malarkey group supported the amendment, knowing that Mitchell was the most popular political figure in Oregon and hoping that the change would end Simon's influence. Personal reasons motivated most of the support of other Republicans — each expected to gain something. Bourne was fed up with the old system, which had cost him a fortune. He also entertained ambitions as a United States senator, and was working for a direct primary system which he knew could be achieved only through the initiative, and not through legislative action. Voters overwhelmingly approved the amendment: 62,024 to 4,668. The "Oregon System" had been launched. Little did the more conservative leaders like Scott realize the nature of the popular revolution they had unleashed.[39]

None of the statewide cooperative spirit carried over to a particularly devious city election in June, 1902. The Mitchell forces meant to harm Simon personally. The *Oregonian* had switched its allegiance to Mitchell. When Simon announced that he would not run for reelection to the U.S. Senate, Scott decided to seek the office and wanted Mitchell's backing. In April, 1902, Scott called the Simon group "a beaten faction...desperately trying to hold on to the shreds, rags and remnants of the political power still in their hands."[40]

The Mitchell machine, with Scott's support, was running a compliant George H. Williams for mayor, while Simon was backing Democratic lumberman Robert Inman. Simon devised a strategy to create the impression that his ticket was independent of machine control, in keeping with the new spirit of popular government sweeping across the state. He depicted Mitchell's ticket as the old type of boss system, antagonistic to popular government. The black-owned *New Age*, smarting over Matthews's decision to exclude blacks from the 1902 Republican county convention, picked up the theme: "Does Jack Matthews own the alleged Republican party of Multnomah County?" The same electorate that approved the initiative and referendum and the new city charter heartily supported the Mitchell slate. Soundly beaten were Simon state senatorial candidates Donald MacKay, J. Thorburn Ross, Sylvester Farrell and George Bates—all members of the Portland Establishment. Abbot Mills lost in his first attempt to seek a House seat. The 79-year-old political warhorse George H. Williams squeezed into the mayor's office by 643 votes out of 13,000 cast. The only major loss suffered by the Republicans was in the closely contested governor's race. George E. Chamberlain, the popular Democratic Multnomah County district attorney ran as a "reform" candidate. He called for municipal control of public utilities, state anti-trust legislation, and programs to benefit organized labor. Above all, he sought to eliminate "machine" politics in Oregon and to protect public rights in the management of state-owned lands.[41]

One positive consequence of this political skirmishing was the founding of the *Oregon Journal*. Established as the *Evening Journal* on March 10, 1902, the paper was bought on July 23 that year by Charles S. Jackson (known as "C.S."), the Virginia-born owner of the *East Oregonian* since 1880. He sold the Pendleton paper and moved to Portland to rescue the struggling sheet, which he renamed the *Oregon Journal*. The list of his Establishment backers included John C. Ainsworth, William M. Ladd, George Bates, Abbot Mills, and Joseph N. Teal, son-in-law of former Mayor David P. Thompson and the paper's attorney. Most of the group were reacting against Harvey Scott's blatant attack on Joe Simon. In future years, the *Journal* would not always support the interests of its major backers. Coming from Southern Democratic roots, Jackson generally endorsed Democratic candidates. Scott never forgave Mills for his early support of the *Journal*.

The Enigmatic Mayor: George H. Williams

George H. Williams, at the time Oregon's most prominent citizen nationally, and reportedly the oldest chief executive of a major American city, was an enigma to many of his Establishment friends. A man of great charm, a charter member of the Arlington Club, and Harvey Scott's closest friend, Williams elicited contrasting appraisals of his ability and character. Judge Matthew Deady had never held a high opinion of his legal talents, and yet he was in partnership with the brilliant C. E. S. Wood for over a decade. (Wood and Williams were on opposite sides of most political issues, an arrangement that gave the firm of Williams, Wood and Linthicum a diverse list of clients.)

For years, Henry W. Corbett thought Williams "wholly insincere, except in one thing, that is his own advancement at all hazard." Corbett never forgave him for "selling himself out to Ben Holladay." His second marriage, to Kate Hughes Ivens (commonly referred to as "Aunt Kate"), provoked social storms in both Washington, D.C. and Portland. According to Malcolm Clark, she "was a curious compound of social elegance, loose language, and un-Victorian behaviour." In Washington, she was considered brash, extravagant and a social climber. Her costly tastes were reflected in the large, excessively ornamented house that the couple built on Northwest Couch, between 18th and 19th streets. Williams continued to live in the grandiose edifice after his wife died in 1894.[42]

When Mayor Williams addressed his first council on July 2, 1902, he commented that the existing charter authorized the council "to prevent and suppress bawdy houses." This was an "unpleasant subject" to Williams, who told the council that it might not be able to suppress "this evil." But, he said,

> ... it is in our power and duty to protect public decency. ... The cribs on streets between the railroad depot and the hotels and elsewhere on our main streets should be suppressed and their inmates compelled to quit their business or to move into more secluded quarters ... .If these people would [only] occupy houses that have an air of respectability.....[43]

As to gambling, the mayor had no "utopian schemes contemplated," but he felt that the existing ordinances should be enforced. He was instructing his police chief (McLaughlan) to check "rumors" of police payoffs. The same words were repeated to the board of police commissioners the next week. He wanted "the removal of the vicious class from the prominent streets of the city." Bates was still president but William M. Ladd, who had inherited his father's mantle, replaced Simon's protege, David Solis-Cohen.[44]

Police payoffs were apparently common within the Chinese community, where opium use was condemned officially but condoned in practice. The opium trade occasionally bred Tong wars, which erupted between the rival secret societies and led to an undetermined number of deaths. Each Tong recruited and trained full-time "hatchet squads," comprising insignificant individuals who would be hard to identify. When a Portland Tong decided to eliminate a member of a rival local Tong, word was sent to its brother society in San Francisco. On a given day, the executioners would slip into town, shoot their target in cold blood and then try to depart south on the next train. If they were caught, as many were, they were sure to be executed.[45]

One younger member of the Portland Establishment, attorney Dan J. Malarkey, made a living by defending the Tongs. A key member of the Mitchell machine, he won election to the Oregon House of Representatives in the landslide of June, 1902. He went on to the state senate, where he became president in 1913 and a leading Progressive Republican. As one of the city's foremost trial lawyers, he devised a sure defense stratagem. Lining up six or eight Chinese who looked—at least to Occidentals —very much alike, he challenged the state's star witnesses to identify the defendant. They invariably failed, and Malarkey won another victory. According to his son, "The Tongs were good pay. As a child, I burst into Father's office one day just as a benign and smiling Chinese was handing over a roll of bills the size of a large grapefruit."[46]

Well aware of such activities in the unrespectable part of the city, Mayor Williams exerted efforts to keep opium use, gambling and prostitution away from the "prominent" areas. If they could not be banished, they could at least be controlled and subject to a system of "periodic fines," and the city treasury would gain sorely needed compensation. Councilman Merrill staunchly supported the mayor's policy, although he preferred more open regulation and less obvious hypocrisy.

Much of Williams's three-year term of office suffered the same police and budgetary problems as those of previous administrations. The police department was operating on a budget of $75,000 which was $23,000 less than the 1893 budget when the city's population was half as large. The 50 patrolmen were paid less than their predecessors in 1889. Not only was the force undermanned, but the jail and station houses were in deplorable conditions. The new civil service code anticipated improved officer quality, but with a base pay scale of only $1,020 a year, first-rate candidates were hard to recruit.

The police continued to bear the brunt of public criticism directed against a wide open Portland. Chief Charles H. Hunt, back in office after eight years, faced charges from the *New Age* that the police were discriminating against Negroes, especially in vice arrests. The Portland Municipal Association, organized in July, 1903, by Thomas N. Strong and Thomas Lamb Eliot, published the first of several broadsides charging that public gambling was "controlled by a trust in league with city government." Brothels and beer halls were flourishing. The city was deriving over $7,000 monthly from fines, or, as the association called them, "pay-offs." The Portland Club, on Southwest Fifth and Alder streets, was reported to have grossed $20,000 in December, 1903, "with marked cards."[47]

During the summer of 1904, the municipal association singled out sailors' boarding houses as centers of violence. The most notorious belonged to the infamous Jim Turk, a political crony of Jonathan Bourne. Turk had a small private bar in the rear of his adjoining saloon, into which he invited prospective crew members needing persuasion to sign onto ships with unsavory reputations. After providing drinks on the house and manifesting his friendship for the sailors, he would spring a trap and the unsuspecting seamen would fall into a chute, to be hustled away at the bottom by two burly thugs, victims of the much-feared "Shanghaiing." Described by Dean Collins as a 225-pound "florid-faced, beef-fed Britisher, with a voice like a foghorn," Turk rid himself of his troublesome son by the same method. Having contracted with a skipper to supply 13 men, and unable to find the remaining member, he chose his son, who, according to one account, was "his most weighty problem."[48]

Billiards With The Boys: Williams's Last Years

The remaining two years of Williams's term were stormy. The city made great material strides in building offices, streets and sewers, but scandals accompanied such developments. A weak political leader, Williams eloquently defended his record, but never faced the issues directly. He disliked contention and preferred to yield to pressure rather than engage in hostilities. Like his predecessors, he believed that the role of local government was largely one of facilitating private development, a stance generally supported by the business leaders. Isolating itself from the serious public problems of an expanding urban community, Portland's Establishment could easily avoid their presence as long as its respectable, parochial, elite society could function to its own satisfaction. The energies and monies that might have gone into meeting the city's growing public needs were instead diverted and invested in private developments and private entertainments such as the 1905 Lewis and Clark Exposition, the Waverly Golf Club, and even billiard tournaments.

A traditional club game, billiards held a special fascination for the skillful mayor. In his later years, according to one account, he steeled himself for the annual match with fellow octogenarian John McCraken. It was a celebrated occasion when "the pioneers of the city gathered to watch the two cronies fight it out."[49]

Despite some long-standing political differences with fellow members of the Establishment, George Williams was affectionately regarded by many like McCraken, who had known him for nearly half-a-century. Williams's former partner and long time political critic C. E. S. Wood, himself a more rebellious member of the Establishment, eulogized him during his 85th birthday dinner at the Arlington Club: "'The counsel of a friend is good, but better than all counsel is sweet Friendship's self, the blossom and the fruit of life.'" Wood's feelings expressed the essence of intimate fellowship — a network of social ties — that bound the Establishment more closely than the impersonal experiences of public life. Such was the Establishment's definition of respectability.[50]

17.1 Ericksons, which boasted having the longest bar in the world

17.2 Freight Handlers Union #334, Portland, 1902, Labor Day Parade

17.3 The Waverly Golf Club

17.4 1899 bicyclists at Mt. Tabor

17.5 Outing club in courtyard of the Portland Hotel

17.7 Charles S. Jackson (1860-1924)

17.6 Harvey W. Scott (1838-1910), October, 1904

17.8 69 N.W. Fourth, including unmarked Chinese gambling house, early in the century

17.9 S.W. Morrison, looking east from Third

18

PRIVATE ENTERPRISE AND PUBLIC INTEREST: 1902-1905

The Exposition Site

On September 12, 1902, amid charges of conflict of interest, the Lewis and Clark Exposition board of directors chose Guild's Lake as the site of their "Great Extravaganza." Despite more than $2.2 million of public funding ($450,000 from Oregon and $1,775,000 from the U.S. Government), Portland's business and political leaders presumed that the fair was a private enterprise, and they acted accordingly. Other sites under consideration included Hawthorne Park in Southeast Portland, favored by Harvey W. Scott, and City Park, favored by Henry W. Corbett. Both men supported the final decision in a unanimous vote.[1]

Forty-six parcels of swampland were involved, covering 406 acres, of which 220 were under water. All the parcels were leased except for one, bought for $6,000. Major landholders, who received property tax exemption during the period of their lease, included the Stephen Mead Estate (administered by the Ladd family), Amanda Reed (widow of Simeon Reed), the T. J. Cottle Estate, and P. L. Willis, a member of the exposition board of directors. Positioned to gain immensely from the site's development was Robert Livingstone's Scottish American Investment Trust Company of Edinburgh, owner of over seven blocks of prime residential property on lower Willamette Heights, adjacent to the grounds. Livingstone was also an exposition director, along with Abbot Mills, who was promoting the interests of the City & Suburban Railway Company, whose rail line ran within a block of the future main gate. Equally interested was the banker John C. Ainsworth, another director, who had recently assumed financial management of the Portland Railway Company, whose tracks could easily be extended to the main gate. Portland Railway had been formed in 1896 to take over the bankrupt Markle system, which was merged with the former Dekum properties in 1900. Ainsworth had been instrumental in gaining additional financing from San Francisco banker William H. Crocker and New York financier Darius Ogden Mills (no relation to Abbot Mills), both of whom had invested in the ill fated Portland Cable Railway.[2]

The Bankers Take Charge

Two months after the selection of the exposition site, the Board of Public Works (to be replaced two months later) faced several franchise decisions that put chairman

Abbot Mills in a potential conflict of interest. Through the First National Bank, he represented the extensive investments of the Corbett, Failing and Lewis families in the City & Suburban Railway Company. (He was to succeed Corbett as bank president within four months.) The new city charter, which was expected to take effect upon legislative approval in January, 1903, contained provisions that might damage future efforts to sell the company to eastern investors — an action that Mills had been contemplating for some time. The fact that he had been chairman of the new city charter commission, which had drafted the revised regulations that were meant to provide greater protection to the public interest, did not deter him from what he felt was his primary obligation: to serve the private interests entrusted to his custody.

His close friend the young John C. Ainsworth, representing the Portland Railway Company, shared similar feelings. Both bankers agreed that immediate action had to be taken to protect their street railway investors. The 32-year-old Ainsworth had just bought majority control of the U.S. National Bank from Tyler Woodward, for $117 per share. As Ainsworth later recalled when Woodward "turned control over to me, he said, 'Ainsworth, you are a young man, and the deposits I am turning over to you are an even One Million Dollars, which is a grave responsibility for any man to assume.' " Merging his bank with the larger U.S. National, Ainsworth elected to drop the family name and take the U.S. National Bank title. With combined resources of $2.3 million, the U.S. National moved into the distinctive Ainsworth Building at Third and Oak streets. Its directors included Roderick Macleay, Rufus Mallory, Governor George E. Chamberlain, a California winery owner and a San Francisco bankers, who were old friends of the Ainsworth family. Within months, Henry L. Pittock, and Winslow B. Ayer, president of the Eastern and Western Lumber Company, joined the board.[3]

While the U.S. Bank was changing ownership, two of the three major street railways that were to combine into the giant Portland Railway Light & Power Company in 1906 received new franchises from the city council after approval by the Board of Public Works. The Portland Railway Company, beginning to show a profit under Ainsworth's direction, received a 30-year exclusive franchise with a schedule of compensation payments to the city that began at $1,500 a year, moving by steps to $5,000 a year after 20 years, and in one jump to $12,000 a year after 25 years. The Oregon Water Power & Railway Company (the survivor of the Steel brother's East Side Railway Company), which in 1902 was under the control of the Portland General Electric Company, was granted a 25-year exclusive franchise, requiring car license fees rather than annual fixed payments.[4]

On January 9, 1903, the city council approved a new 30-year exclusive franchise for Swigert and Corbett's City & Suburban Railway Company, with a schedule of payments that ran in steps from $3,000 to $9,000 a year over a 25-year period, moving to $12,000 a year for the last five years. The City & Suburban had been doing reasonably well. In 1901, the 63-mile system had net earnings of $126,692 on gross earnings of $356,000. It had $2.3 million of indebtedness, with $1.5 million out in stock and $860,000 in bonds. It paid $49,000 to the stockholders and $45,000 to the bondholders.[5]

On January 14, the very day the Board of Public Works received the franchise for its final approval, the legislature was passing the new city charter for the governor's approval. Working faster than Mills had anticipated, the Senate completed action on the House-approved bill. However, it was never transmitted to the governor's office for his signature. Nothing happened for five days, much to the astonishment of legislative observers, who wondered about its disappearance.[6]

As it was later revealed, the franchise was not valid until it had received both final approval by the Board of Public Works and acceptance by the company. Mills feared that the governor might sign the new charter legislation before company acceptance of the franchise had been received. Had this occurred, the new charter would have taken precedence and the City & Suburban Railway, the largest unit of the future monopoly, would have lost its exclusive 30-year franchise, and with it much of its attractiveness to a future buyer. The telephone lines to Salem must have been busy on January 14. W. F. (Jack) Matthews, who had seized control of the local and state Republican party machinery from U.S. Senator Joe Simon, probably used his legislative influence to ensure that someone did not upset the deal. Five days later, the House passed a new charter measure and then passed a motion to strike the first charter bill because of a defective title. The mystery had been cleared up. On the morning of July 23, the Senate unanimously approved the second charter measure and rushed it to Governor Chamberlain for his signature. Portland had its new charter, the City & Suburban its new franchise, and Oregon an example of how business got results in the state capital.[7]

Mills and Ainsworth had faithfully performed their private duties at public expense. The previous year, Ainsworth's Pacific States Telephone and Telegraph Company, the Oregon branch of the California-based utility that later became part of the Bell (AT&T) System, had received two city franchises without paying any compensation other than the cost of providing city government with 39 free phones. In securing such privileges at minimal charge, Portland's corporate leaders acted much like they did in their Lewis & Clark Exposition involvement. In Carl Abbott's judgement, they "made no clear distinction between public and private responsibilities for promoting their city's growth." Mills continued to serve this overlapping public-private role as a member of the new Executive Board, appointed by the mayor to succeed the Board of Public Works. Charged with approving all city expenditures and franchise applications, the 10 members were prominent in Portland's business and professional life. Four belonged to the Arlington Club: attorney Whitney L. Boise, Jr., realtor William MacMaster, merchant Charles F. Beebe, and Mills. The new police commission, a subcommittee of the Executive Board, comprised tobacconist Sig Sichel, Beebe, and Mayor Williams.[8]

Rampant Corruption: The 1903 Legislature

The sleight of hand that guided Portland's charter through the 1903 legislature characterized the entire session. The choice of a U.S. Senator to succeed Joseph Simon (who opted not to run) dominated events "from the very first day," according to newly elected state Senator Walter Pierce of Umatilla County. Candidates included recent Governor Theodore T. Geer, Jonathan Bourne, Jr., Harvey W. Scott, and Charles W. Fulton of Astoria from the Republican ranks, and attorney C. E. S. Wood for the Democrats. The election of June, 1902, had provided for a nonbinding preferential popular vote to guide the legislature. Geer had defeated Wood, as "the people's choice," by a majority of more than 12,000, but the legislature defied the popular will.[9]

Bourne had been the most active Republican contender during the previous six months. After failing to secure Matthews's support, he had approached Abbot Mills, but was turned down. He next sought out Harvey Scott through Henry McGinn. He would support Scott in 1903 if Scott would pledge Bourne all the federal patronage and help elect him (Bourne) as Mitchell's successor in 1907. Scott later denied that he had ever made a deal with Bourne, yet Bourne did support Scott during the balloting after he had dropped his own candidacy. On the 42nd ballot, Scott lost to Charles W. Fulton, a veteran state senator, Simon's successor as senate president and a close political ally of Mitchell. Wood, the only contending Democrat, came in third. As in past sessions when U.S. senators were chosen, much money changed hands. Walter Pierce remembered the "selling, the trading, the corruption was astonishing." State Senator Pierce Mays, a law partner of Portland attorney Charles H. Carey and counsel to the Northern Pacific and Great Northern railroads, told Pierce, "I have 40,000 in the bank. I would give it all to be elected United States Senator, but I do not know how or where to spend it so I shall continue to vote for Charlie Fulton." Bourne spent so much money that he overdrew his bank account in Providence, Rhode Island.[10]

Under Governor Chamberlain's prodding, the legislature did pass some noteworthy bills during the 1903 session despite its failure to enact a corporation tax and to reform county property assessment practices. In addition to the Lewis & Clark appropriation, school fund increases were approved, agricultural experiment stations were authorized, and Oregon's first law regulating child labor was enacted along with one establishing a 10-hour working day for women, later upheld by the U.S. Supreme Court in Muller v. Oregon (1908).[11]

Henry W. Corbett Dies

Henry Winslow Corbett, the most significant and complex of the successful frontier merchants, died on March 31, 1903, five weeks after the legislature had adjourned. Although he had spent little time on exposition business during the previous months, as president he had strongly supported the legislative appropriation of $500,000. Suffering from degenerative heart disease, he refused to follow his doctor's advice to take life easier. Said Dr. A. B. Nichols: "I have never seen a man equal to Mr. Corbett in determination and energy. Responsibility only stimulated him. Work only moved him to greater efforts." Harvey Scott wrote a glowing editorial, emphasizing his "earnestness and tenacity." The *Oregon Journal* cited his "industry, integrity and charity." And the *Oregon Statesman* emblazoned its front page with the headline "Grand Old Man of Oregon Dead". All Board of Trade members closed their businesses for two hours in deference to the funeral at the First Presbyterian Church.[12]

Corbett's life had embodied many seemingly contradictory qualities. He could be kind and generous, and yet tough and unscrupulous. His demeanor — calm, smiling expression, like an understanding father — often disarmed his business and political competitors. He could be ruthless in politics and benevolent in community projects. His will bequeathed more $200,000 to seven institutions. The Children's Home and the Portland Art Museum each received $50,000; the YMCA, $30,000; the Portland Academy and the Presbyterian Board of Home Missions, $25,000 apiece; the Home for Old Ladies, $15,000; and the Boys and Girls Aid Society, $10,000.[13]

Moments of sadness had cut through his personal life. His first wife had died after 13 years of marriage. Hamilton F. Corbett, his youngest son, had died at the age of 25, and his oldest son, Henry J. (the husband of Helen Ladd), had died at 35 in 1895. He was survived by his second wife, 20 years his junior, who lived to be 90, dying in 1936 while still living in the Corbett mansion, where she had for years grazed a cow in the yard. Management of the vast Corbett Estate fell to his oldest grandson, Henry Ladd Corbett, who had to assume his family responsibilities at the age of 22, just before his graduation from Harvard. Later joined by his two younger brothers, Elliott and Hamilton, he was to play an active role in Portland business and political affairs for over 50 years. While Abbot Mills, as president, directed the First National Bank's operations for nearly 25 years, the Corbett boys owned the bank, controlling well over 60 percent of the stock, while the Failing heirs held less than 30 percent.

Henry W. Corbett's estate, valued in excess of $2 million in 1903, included 27 downtown holdings worth $625,395. They would increase in value by over 500 percent within seven years, much of the appreciation being due to the population growth stimulated by the Lewis and Clark Exposition. Corbett's $30,000 investment was returned many times over. His largest single downtown property investment, not included in his personal real-estate holdings, was in $200,000 of Portland Hotel stock —a controlling interest. Of $1.13 million in other securities, the three largest holdings were in the First National Bank ($574,000), the City & Suburban Railway Company ($245,000), and the Union Pacific Railway ($127,000). The frontier merchant had done well.[14]

Planning for the Fair

Upon Corbett's death, Harvey Scott succeeded to the presidency of the exposition's board of directors. After a brief tenure, the mantle of authority passed to the operations chief, Henry W. Goode, president of the Portland General Electric Company. An active member of the Arlington Club, Goode was widely known for his administrative skills, which were largely responsible for the creation of the giant Portland Railway Light & Power Company in 1906, a year before he died prematurely. Apart from his organizational talents, he contributed a 110- by 30-foot electrical sign to the exposition cause. Placed at the summit of Goldsmith's Hill (later Westover Heights), "1905" could be seen for over 30 miles.[15]

Preliminary grading of the Guild's Lake site had started a month before Corbett's death. It was halted in late April for the impending visit of John Olmsted, of Brookline, Massachusetts. The son of Frederick Law Olmsted, who had designed New York's Central Park, John Olmsted carried his own high credentials. Originally invited by Dr. Thomas Lamb Eliot, of the Portland Board of Park Commissioners, to formulate some general plans for Portland's future parks, he actually came on a dual mission. When Corbett and his executive board had heard of Olmsted's availability, they agreed to split his $10,000 fee with the city if he would help design the site plan for the exposition.

The Portland Board of Park Commissioners had been authorized by a legislatively approved city charter amendment in 1900. The enactment crowned years of dedicated effort by Eliot, L. Leander Hawkins and others to create more urban parks and playgrounds. In 1902, Portland owned only 136 acres of park land in 10 locations. Compared with Hartford, Connecticut, a city slightly larger in size and area, which had 15 percent of its land dedicated to public parks, Portland had only 1½ percent. To

Olmsted and the park commissioners, the exposition should embody a noble planning ideal that might serve as a model for the city of the future. They were not
unmindful of the Chicago World Columbian Exposition of 1893, whose chief architect,
Daniel Burnham, proposed a lakefront development that would add a new and
beneficial social dimension to the life of the average Chicagoan by permanently
restoring Lake Michigan's shoreline to the people.[16]

Much to the disappointment of the park commissioners, the Guild's Lake site had
already been chosen by the time of Olmsted's arrival. In helping the exposition staff
design a basic site plan for the fair, Olmsted initially hoped that the grounds could be
converted to permanent park use after the show was over. But in the minds of
Portland's business leadership—including the exposition's board of director's—such
notions were not worth serious attention. The primary purpose of the extravaganza
was to present an idealized self-portrait of Portland. By advertising the city's most
glorious features throughout America, the economic payoff would be stupendous. The
second major purpose was to promote trade with the Far East. Only in third place did
the exposition developers rank the "City Beautiful" dimension, such as aesthetic
considerations and better civic design. Humanitarian or social planning elements
were barely considered, and only then in terms of increased employment and general
economic benefits to the region. As Rydell has observed:

> The Portland exposition did more than build self-esteem. It also built Portland's economy
> and several fortunes. ... Theodore Wilcox, a prominent Portland grain and flour exporter,
> noted that the 'the exposition at Portland increased his fortune two million dollars,'[17]

The Portland Consolidated Railway Company

Abbot Mills and John Ainsworth hoped—even expected—that the Lewis and Clark
Exposition would greatly increase the revenues of their respective street railway
companies. Taking the lead, Mills spent most of two years creating the legal and
financial package to form the giant Portland Consolidated Railway Company in
October, 1904. (Rarely have records ever revealed so fully how big Portland deals were
conceived and managed.) While earnings of both the City & Suburban and Portland
railways were generally healthy, Mills realized that the companies needed to
strengthen their net assets before a successful merger could be consummated. Stock
dividend rates also had to be increased to attract the necessary financing from New
York investment firms. As 1903 was not a good year to sell railway bonds in the East,
Mills felt obliged to issue $2 million in additional City & Suburban stock. He would use
the proceeds for purchasing new equipment and even for constructing a new electric
generating plant to meet the expected traffic growth ensuing from the exposition. His
major problem was to devise a scheme "to bail out" the Portland Railway Company
mortgage bondholders, William Crocker and Darius Mills.[18]

The negotiations were ticklish. Mills was in almost daily correspondence with his
cousin, the New York investment counselor and banker, Augustus White. Mills discovered that the Portland Railway Company was actually more profitable than the
statements of earnings indicated. For several years the company had been deducting as
operating expenses charges usually listed as fixed by normal accounting procedures.

By reducing its listed earnings in this fashion, the company attempted to justify a minimum franchise charge of only $150 a month for use of the Burnside Bridge. When revised operating income figures were published in 1904, the rate was increased to $1,000 a month, the same rate that the City & Suburban would be forced to pay for use of the new Morrison Bridge. After nearly 20 years, the public treasury was to receive a reasonable income from its bridge franchises.

Mills wanted to keep all the negotiations secret until the final arrangements were settled. He specifically did not want the firm of Moffat and White in New York to issue any circulars showing the current balance sheet and earnings. He was able to convince White that he had the City & Suburban part of the deal well under control, including Charles F. Swigert, who favored issuing more stock, while the nominal president, Tyler Woodward, was opposed. The tentative merger arrangement in March, 1904, called for the City & Suburban to acquire the Portland Railway Company through an exchange of one-third of the existing C & S stock shares for the outstanding Portland Railway mortgage bonds held by W. H. Crocker and D. O. Mills. The newly incorporated Portland Consolidated Railway Company would then acquire all of the C & S stock, through exchange or purchase if necessary.

Also in March, plans were being drafted to build a dam, reservoir and generator on the Little White Salmon River, 55 miles away in Washington. Any surplus power generated could always be sold to the Portland General Electric Company whose expanding needs were rapidly exceeding its generating capacity in 1904. To complete such a project, Mills was aware that the Oregon Legislature had to enact a law to permit power-line transmission from Washington to Oregon. He was prepared to attend the 1905 session for that purpose.

As final negotiations for the merger began to take shape, Augustus White wrote to his cousin Abbot Mills: "Business is wonderfully facilitated when people have confidence in each other." But Mills's confidence in the Portland Railway outfit was shaken when the California investors revealed that they wanted more than one-third of the outstanding City & Suburban stock, including any new issue. Mills was prepared to offer no more than 40 percent; if they did not accept, they would be the losers, as the City & Suburban could survive and operate its own system as well. Mills became discouraged. He was tired and unhappy with both boards of directors "and their carping criticisms, as if I had been proposing some criminal act." Swigert's uncle, Charles Gorrill of San Francisco, the owner of the Pacific Construction Company, and a large stockholder in the City & Suburban, even suggested selling as much as $6 million in stock if it would make Crocker and D. O. Mills happier to own considerably more shares. This idea was "repugnant" to Abbot Mills; it would result in too small a dividend per share.[19]

To facilitate the merger and at the same time make it easier for the new company to be sold to eastern investors at some future date, White and his associates began buying up some of the City & Suburban stock at $80 per share from the minority stockholders. The majority stockholders were the Failing Estate, the First National Bank (of which Mills was now president), the Corbett Estate, Mrs. C. H. Lewis, Henry L. Corbett, Swigert, and Gorrill. It was agreed that the Portland Railway bonds would be exchanged for 40 percent of the existing City & Suburban stock plus 40 percent of a new $600,000 offering to be issued at $80 per share. Also contemplated was the sale of an undetermined amount of additional bonds. When White, who was to handle all transactions, wrote Mills inquiring about the prospects for selling bonds in Portland, Mills replied that although Portland had a reputation for wealth, to his knowledge "the wealthiest families have little or no ready money at any time, employing every dollar they possess actively."[20]

The Portland Consolidated Railway Company was incorporated on October 18, 1904, with $5 million of authorized capital stock. Mills was named president, Ainsworth treasurer, and Cyrus A. Dolph and Swigert vice-presidents. Named as general counsel was Osian F. Paxton, prominent attorney, former partner of Judge McGinn, original receiver of the former Markle properties, and successor to Ainsworth as president of the Portland Railway Company. In recognition of the vested interest of Portland's two largest banks, the company was to split its banking business between the First National and the U.S. National. One month later, the company was awarded its 30-year exclusive franchise by the city council. No further consideration was apparently given to the construction of the White Salmon River electric plant, as the Portland Railway Company already held a contract with Portland General Electric that promised to supply adequate power to the Consolidated system for at least two years. By that date, PGE would be merged with the street-railway properties to form the Portland Railway Light and Power monopoly.

Mills had one important task to perform before he could take the next step toward completing the long and arduous assignment he had undertaken two years previously — to liquidate at maximum profit the street-railway investments of the First National and U.S. National banks, and those of the Corbett, Failing, and Lewis families. The previous June he had won election to the state House of Representatives, with the strong support of Jack Matthews and Charles H. Carey. Mills went to Salem solely to ensure the passage of a law that would benefit the Portland Consolidated Railway Company. Moreover, he went with the understanding that he would be selected Speaker of the House, an honor that would duly recognize his position as the state's leading banker.

The laws of Oregon stated that a franchise could not be transferred from one company to another without the consent of the legislature or of the government body that had granted the franchise. Mills realized that the existence of such a legal restriction could severely jeopardize the eventual sale of the Portland Consolidated Railway Company to eastern investors. The properties would not be worth much without a guaranteed 30-year exclusive franchise.

Senate Bill 255 was introduced into the session of February, 1905, by Senator Herbert Holman, a fellow member with Mills of the Waverly Country Club Executive Board. A brief bill, it was passed within three days by the Senate, 19-7, and six days later by the House, 50-10, under the floor leadership of Mills's fellow Arlington Club member, lawyer William T. Muir. Speaker Mills affixed his signature, appropriately, on February 17, and Governor Chamberlain approved it on February 21. In essence, the bill stipulated that a franchise of an Oregon corporation could be transferred to another corporation with the consent of the stockholders holding two-thirds of the issued capital stock of the franchised corporation, at a regular or special meeting of the said corporation.[21]

The path was now cleared for Augustus White in New York to find a suitable purchaser for the assets of the Portland Consolidated Railway Company. The importance to the company of the Lewis and Clark Exposition's location soon became apparent. In the period from November, 1904 to July, 1905, the monthly passenger revenues increased 120 percent, from $99,200 to $217,000. The railway properties were looking more attractive every day. To the utility financier, the real profit was to be made in the manipulation of security prices. The amount of passenger revenue generated obviously had a direct bearing on the utility stock value. White found an interested New York underwriter by the name of Seligman and Company which in turn found an interested majority stock purchaser by the name of Percy Clark of Philadelphia.[22]

Against the wishes of the Swigert and Gorrill interests, who opposed the sale to eastern investors because they wanted to keep local control, a new Portland Railway Company was incorporated under the new laws of Oregon on October 13, 1905. The next day, the new company bought all the assets of the Portland Consolidated Railway Company for $6 million. For tax purposes, it was assessed at only $850,000. With 20,000 shares of stock outstanding, and with about $2.5 million in bonded debt, each share realized a sale value of about $160, twice its worth a year previously. Some handsome profits resulted. Had Oregon had a franchise tax like that of New York, the company would have been taxed the difference between the total market value of its stocks and bonds and its assessed valuation.

Shortly after its incorporation, Portland Railway issued $3 million in preferred and $4 million in common stock. The whole process was to be repeated, leading to the final merger negotiations that would be inaugurated in 1906 and completed in 1907, resulting in the formation of the $15 million Portland Railway Light and Power Company. Abbot Mills was not directly involved in the venture, his major task having been completed in October, 1905. He had fulfilled his private fiduciary responsibilities with extraordinary skill. The First National Bank's annual dividend rate of more than 30 percent was an adequate testament to his success.[23]

Dirty Politics Again: The Election of 1904

The election of June, 1904, which sent Abbot Mills to the Oregon House of Representatives, was as bitter as any that had been held in the previous decade. The Simon regular Republicans and the Mitchell independent Republicans were engaged "in a knockdown, dragout fight," reported the *Oregonian,* with each faction accusing the other of supporting vice and corruption. Five months earlier, Oregon Water Power & Railway executive William P. Keady had written Jonathan Bourne, Jr.: "Matthews is in full swing here, and you know what that means...Carey and Matthews are to run the machine...You cannot expect good faith in anything controlled by Matthews." According to Keady, Judge Carey was "firmly in Mitchell's camp." Carey would "present his smiling front to the public" while Matthews did the dirty work. In March, the *Oregon Journal* reported that County Clerk Frank S. Fields and Matthews had set an early date for the primary election in an attempt "to harm the Simon faction." According to the *Journal,* the prisoners in the county jail were being registered to vote, using as their address the block on which the jail stood.[24]

All of the Matthews-Carey candidates won with a notable exception: honest Tom Word defeated incumbent Sheriff William A. Storey. Together with District Attorney John Manning, who had been appointed by Governor Chamberlain in 1903, Word created increasing difficulty for the Matthews-Carey machine, and even for Mayor Williams's administration, which later in the year was charged by the grand jury with malfeasance in office. The jury's efforts were impeded by the county judges, who were part of the machine.

The most significant statewide outcome of the election, was the overwhelming approval of the direct primary amendment to the state constitution, by a vote of 56,285 to 16,354. Following Wisconsin's lead by one year, Oregon joined a national trend in which two-thirds of the states enacted direct primary laws within a decade.

Because the U.S. Constitution still prevented the direct election of U.S. Senators, the primary amendment had no legal validity. Senators would still be elected by the legislature. A scheme was devised to make every candidate for the legislature, at the primaries, declare himself on this particular point—to say whether, as a member of the legislature, he would accept the popular choice for U.S. Senator. The new primary law, therefore, provided that every candidate, in advance of the primary election, should have the privilege of subscribing to one of two pledges: "Statement No. 1," that he would support the popular choice, or "Statement No. 2," that he would consider the popular choice "nothing more than a recommendation." The candidate could also remain silent and refuse to sign either pledge. It was thought that public pressure was going to force the great majority of legislative candidates to sign "Statement No. 1" without regard to individual preference.[25]

Jonathan Bourne, Jr. worked hard for this change, which he felt would help secure his election to the U.S. Senate in 1906. Some years later, Judge Henry McGinn declared, "...the Direct Primary law came to us as the result of the most corrupt politics any state has ever known." The direct primary encouraged the people to speak out against the excesses of corruption that had plagued Oregon political life for over 40 years. Men like Governor George E. Chamberlain and his young state land agent, future governor Oswald West, hoped that the "Oregon System" would stimulate the voters to maintain an enduring interest in public affairs.[26]

Questionable Practices

Efforts to increase direct participation in government had little restraining effect on business and corporate wealth when profits were to be made through governmental channels, especially in Portland during the last two years of Mayor George H. Williams's administration. Charges of fraud and scandal became commonplace. When the bottom was left out of the huge Tanner creek sewer, the *Oregon Journal* editorialized:

> Throughout the Tanner creek sewer investigation Mayor Williams uniformly took the side of the contractors against the taxpayers. 'Kickers, knockers, faultfinders' was his designation of the property owners who had the audacity to protest against the acceptance of the sewer. Every possible obstacle was interposed by him to prevent examination of the job, and it was with utmost reluctance that he finally consented to the removal of the city engineer. Finally, when the reports of two investigating committees and admissions of the

engineer himself no longer left any room to dispute that glaring defects existed in the work, Mayor Williams attempted to have the cost of the repairs advanced by the city, rather than compel the contractor's bondsmen to pay for them. The cost of these repairs was estimated at nearly $5,000, though it has far exceeded that sum, and Mayor Williams caused an ordinance to be introduced in the council appropriating the amount from the general fund. Only the opposition of a majority of the councilmen prevented this crowning iniquity to the Tanner creek scandal.[27]

Other charges levelled by the Portland Municipal Association included: $52,000 of extra costs approved for the new Morrison Bridge without bids; the Front Street fill job awarded to the next-lowest bidder after the lowest bidder had supposedly been bribed to withdraw; and municipal supply contracts let to a small clique of political insiders. The resulting public indignation did not seem to bother the principal actors, who remained hidden while the audience saw only the shifting of dummies. The Pacific Bridge Company bore the brunt of many of the accusations directed at the city's public-improvement program. It was by far the largest contractor for bridge, landfill and sewer projects, although the Tanner creek fiasco was not its responsibility. The company was seldom held to its contract requirements. Bid limits were often exceeded because of specification changes, and official completion dates were extended without penalty.[28]

Citizens aroused themselves when for the first time in the city's history the workings of the system were exposed to public view, particularly by the *Oregon Journal*. Collusion was suspected. The owners of Pacific Bridge were closely tied to the major banking and street-railway interests that were well represented on the Executive Board whose task was to approve all contracts, revisions and extensions. Apart from building bridges, the company contracted with the city to execute an enormous landfill that stretched from Sullivan's Gulch in the north to the Hawthorne Bridge in the south, and from the river to east Ninth Avenue. Over a period of two years, four million cubic yards of sand and gravel were dredged from the river and spread over portions of 27 streets. Much of the area had been a frog pond and swamp over which bridges had been built to carry the through traffic. In some sections, the fill depth was 29 feet.

During the depression of 1893, the company had to seek business in other regions of the Northwest, mostly in the state of Washington. Two projects in the Puget Sound area resulted in near bankruptcy. Forced to reorganize in September, 1901, the company borrowed heavily from the First National Bank and George W. Bates. It also borrowed extensively from a new company established by Charles Gorrill in San Francisco, the Pacific Construction Company. As collateral for the initial bank notes, Swigert put up $45,000 in City & Suburban Railway stock.

From 1895 to 1905 the financial affairs of Pacific Bridge and City & Suburban were completely intermingled. Funds were continually shifted from one bank account to another. Swigert enjoyed a full line of credit with the First National Bank, which was a major stockholder in the City & Suburban and the chief source of loans for Pacific Bridge. To make matters more confusing, all of the 20 large projects (excluding the east-side land fill) undertaken by Swigert from 1901 to 1906, totalling over $350,000, were bid by Pacific Construction of San Francisco. Pacific Bridge ended up performing the work and sending half the profits to Pacific Construction. Needless to say the local press had a difficult time reporting accurately on who got what from whom and where, when Pacific Bridge was involved.

Pacific Bridge benefited from the city performance bond requirements. For larger projects over $10,000, the bond amount was $5,000 plus 25 percent of the improvement cost. As in the past, small contractors were automatically excluded. Furthermore, Pacific Bridge always bid for more projects than it could handle, and was thus never able to complete a job by the stipulated date. This procedure allowed the company to use its large backlog of signed city contracts as collateral for its bank loans. All the expenses for a given project were covered by a loan, to be repaid upon completion of the job. The company could undertake an unlimited number of projects with minimal capital reserves. The City & Suburban tracks were used to transport equipment and supplies to the various construction sites at no additional cost to the traction company and at great saving to the construction company. No competitor could bid successfully against such a set-up. To Mills's First National Bank, each transaction meant additional profits. The new Morrison Bridge contract was apparently standard procedure. The Portland voters approved the sale of $400,000 of bridge bonds in June, 1903. The 15 submitted bids ranged from $277,000 to $410,000. Pacific Construction's plan #1 was chosen, for $331,343. The Executive Board considered it the best plan for the type of construction desired by the city engineer. On January 8, 1904, one month after the contract was signed, the company was authorized to substitute steel stringers for wooden ones, at an additional cost of $37,170. On Executive Board member Rodney Glisan's motion, the plan was approved without mention of any bid. In November, 1904, waiting rooms were added, for $7,985, again without bid. In January, 1905, the council hired W. C. Elliott as the Morrison Bridge inspector, for $150 a month. He had just been fired as city engineer for incompetence and suspected fraud in the Tanner creek sewer episode. In February, 1905, Pacific Construction submitted a claim to the Executive Board for $66,626, to cover the design changes and additional construction. The board agreed to pay $58,000 and to keep the remainder in reserve until the bridge was completed. The whole bidding procedure was a farce. Knowing that it could secure subsequent approval for steel stringers, the company could well afford to run the risk of submitting a low bid. When a council member requested an opinion from City Attorney L. A. McNary as to the legality of the practice, the council was informed that the legislative act authorizing the Executive Board to build the bridge, with subsequent voter approval, granted the board very broad powers, independent of ordinary charter provisions. There was no need, said McNary, for the Executive Board to solicit bids for amounts over $250.[29]

Such raids on the public treasury did not seem to bother the city fathers. No specific laws were actually being broken as long as the ordinances were not applied literally. Politics, after all, provided the machinery for promoting private economic interest; using political influence was part of the game. The railroads were never refused requests for street easements in order to construct side tracks, although the city continually petitioned them to repair the streets on which their existing tracks were built. Mayor Williams recognized no conflict in the city's awarding an insurance contract to a company in which he was financially involved. Councilman John P. Sharkey, one of Portland's largest realtors, who lived on the east side, approved the award of the city hall's fire insurance coverage to the Orient Insurance Company of which he was resident agent.

Timber Fraud and the Fall of John H. Mitchell

The zeal for private profits that characterized much of Portland's early history was dramatically illustrated by the disclosures of the federal timber-fraud trials, which began in Portland on November 21, 1904. They involved a large number of prominent Oregonians, and exposed to the nation the code of individual exploitation that dominated much of Portland's business and political life.

Special U.S. prosecutor Francis J. Heney secured 33 convictions out of 34 indictments. Included in the long list were Senator John H. Mitchell, Congressman John N. Williamson from eastern Oregon, U.S. Attorney John Hall, former U.S. attorney and state Senator Franklin Pierce Mays, state Senator Robert A. Booth of the Booth-Kelly Lumber Company, former U.S. Deputy Surveyor Henry Meldrum, and Stephen A. D. Puter, "The King of the Oregon Land Fraud Ring." Congressman Binger Hermann from southern Oregon was indicted, but escaped conviction on a technicality. Thomas B. Walker and Charles A. Smith, wealthy Minnesota lumbermen, were not indictable due to the expiration of the statue of limitations. Numerous others won their freedom in exchange for turning state's evidence. Hundreds more from Oregon would have been indicted had the government used its resources fully. The convicted Puter wrote:

> Thousands upon thousands of acres, which included the very cream of timber claims in Oregon and Washington, were secured by Eastern lumberman and capitalists, the majority of whom came from Wisconsin, Michigan and Minnesota, and nearly all of the claims, to my certain knowledge, were fraudulently obtained.[30]

In the March, 1905, *Bulletin* of the Portland Chamber of Commerce, President William D. Wheelwright declared sadly: "We are ... witness [to] a spectacle of public and private rottenness that is almost without precedent in the annals of the country." The president of the Pacific Export Lumber Company believed that the disclosures constituted "a moral indictment" of Oregon's voters. He went on to state that "one of the remarkable features of the present situation is the absence of a general sense of humiliation. ... We go about our business, we talk of the increasing prosperity of our state and city" as if nothing at all had happened. (This was three months before the opening of the Lewis and Clark Exposition). According to William G. Robbins, the trials were a surprise, not "in the evils they exposed, but rather in the magnitude and scope of the investigations."[31]

To Portland attorneys William D. Fenton and Charles H. Carey, the chief defense counsels during the trials, nothing had really happened that merited prosecution. The U.S. Timber and Stone Act (1878) was designed to save the federal public lands, not for the large operators, but for small people who wanted small holdings. Most of Portland's successful corporate lawyers, however, believed the act to be a bad law, because, if honestly applied, it would prevent the amassing of large timber tracts by the operators. Shortly after arriving in Oregon, Heney had the system explained to him by railroad attorney Fenton at a small dinner party: "So you see, Mr. Heney, it is bad laws that make men — hum, well, let us say, that make such irregularities necessary."

According to Heney, Carey nodded his approval. Heney exploded: "You men corrupt all you touch."[32]

Carey had had long experience with how things were done. He was chief Portland counsel for the Northern Pacific Railroads, which received over 57 million acres of land from the public domain. After the company came under the control of the James J. Hill interests of St. Paul, Minnesota in 1894, it set the pattern of speculative greed that was to be copied by lesser folk like Carey's law partner, Pierce Mays, who was convicted of fraud and perjury. It would be naive to assume that Carey knew nothing of his colleague's shady dealings, as Pierce was reputed to have been the actual head of the Oregon Ring (although Puter was publicly called the "King"). William D. Fenton was the chief Portland counsel of the Southern Pacific Railroad, probably the biggest briber in western American history. The S.P. was reputed to own over 70 billion feet of standing timber in Oregon, most of it legally acquired, but not to be used for the purposes for which it was granted.

The federal government had not been as generous to individual settlers as it was to the railroads. The Homestead Act of 1862 had granted free to each settler a one-quarter section of 160 acres after the grantee lived on the land for five years. After 14 months, however, the settler could purchase the land for $1.25 an acre. The Timber and Stone Act of 1878 raised the price to $2.50 and modified the residence requirements.

Within the American tradition of massive land speculation, aspiring lumber barons sensed the profits to be realized by securing and combining individual claims into large contiguous tracts. If one had to resort to fraud and bribery, those were the rules of the game. From Portland and Albina, carloads of "settlers" were transported to the various land offices, where the dummy applications were filed for sections that had been carefully chosen by Puter and his friends with the connivance of the federal and state surveyors.

The land-fraud ring did not confine its activities to the federal domain. Oregon's school reserve lands were also plundered. According to Robbins, the Oregon land law of 1887 "removed virtually any restraint from the sale of state lands.... It actually urged fraud.... Between 1893 and 1905, 1,381,327 acres of state grant lands were sold"—one-third of the state's grant lands. Bogus applications were filed and approved, and settlers were paid from $200 to $300 for copies of the deeds. Agents like Puter and Mays then sold the fraudulent claims to the timber companies and took their commissions. The federal and state land office officials were bribed to process the dummy applications quickly, before they handled the bona fide ones. While Binger Hermann was commissioner of the U.S. Land Office in Washington, D.C. from 1897 to 1903, he was reputed to have approved thousands of these bogus claims for a price. Mitchell was convicted of accepting $2,000 from Puter to grease the bureaucratic machinery in Washington.[33]

As early as 1903, Secretary of the Interior Ethan Allen Hitchcock had begun to receive tips from Oregon, from the governor's office and from disgruntled bribers who had not been dealt a fair hand. Ordering a quiet investigation, he borrowed the famous Secret Service agent William J. Burns from the Treasury Department. Burns soon had enough evidence to move the Roosevelt administration to take action. From the very moment that special prosecutor Heney's appointment was announced, Oregon's leading politicians and lawyers put every possible obstacle in his path. Senators Charles Fulton and John Mitchell made speeches of protest on the U.S. Senate floor, but to no avail. President Roosevelt announced that he strongly supported the appointment.

Heney and Burns arrived in Portland together, Heney to work the upper and Burns the lower regions of the business-political world. It took almost a year of relentless investigation before the first indictments were brought, but once the trials started on November 21, 1904, the machinery of justice moved swiftly and devastatingly. As William P. Keady wrote to Jonathan Bourne, Jr., on January 3, 1905: "The two grand juries in operation are shaking up the political bed rockers and the local machine is gone — with a big 'G'."[34]

Senator Mitchell had been summoned from Washington to testify before the grand jury. On his return to the Senate on January 6, his colleague Senator Fulton, one of the most skillful influence peddlers in Oregon's history, conveyed the confidence and sympathy of his fellow senators. "Mitchell is being outrageously persecuted," he declared vehemently. A few days later, Keady again wrote Bourne: "The machine is done." Mitchell made the mistake of attacking Puter openly, whereupon Puter, who had already been convicted but not sentenced, went to Heney with the damaging evidence. On February 1, Senator John H. Mitchell was indicted for bribery and perjury. Bourne, Keady and Simon were gleeful. Keady wanted Bourne to return from Massachusetts "to help push the downfall of the Matthews machine." According to Keady, Abbot Mills was being mentioned by the "Matthews people...who claim that Mills will run as their candidate."[35]

Unknown to Keady, Matthews was about to get the official ax as U.S Marshal. It did not take Heney long to realize that if he were going to obtain convictions, he would have to cleanse the federal courthouse thoroughly. He had forced the removal of U.S. Attorney John Hall a few months after his arrival. Heney himself was appointed Acting U.S. Attorney in addition to his special prosecutor's role. Hall was indicted four days after Mitchell. The next major obstacle was U.S Marshall W. F. "Jack" Matthews, the Republican boss of Oregon. In order to be assured of honest, "unfixed" juries, Matthews would have to be dismissed because impanelling juries and serving sub-poenas were his major responsibilities. Fulton had been engaged in a full-scale intrigue in Washington to undermine Heney in support of Matthews. Heney was forced to carry his fight to a meeting of lawyers in Roosevelt's cabinet and then right up to the President himself. After winning this battle, Heney had to exert similar pressure within the Roosevelt administration to force the transfer of recently appointed Oregon Federal Judge, William Cotton. An able lawyer, Cotton had been the chief Portland counsel for the Union Pacific Railroad. Heney did not trust his impartiality.

To replace Matthews, Heney considered a fellow member of the Bohemian Club of San Francisco, one Charles Jerome Reed, or "C.J." as he was known to his friends. Heney's wife and Mrs. Reed had already formed a close friendship. An insurance agent by trade, Reed was the son-in-law of the late Heney Green, the founder of the Portland Gas Company and owner of the luxurious Cedar Hill Estate. He had never been involved in partisan politics although he had always been an independent member of the Establishment. Known as a wit with a sarcastic tongue, he was nevertheless well accepted in Portland society and had maintained a long-time membership in the Arlington Club. When Reed accepted Heney's offer in May, 1905, he was denounced as a traitor to his class and ostracized socially and financially. He did not set foot in the club again for several years, when he took the famous journalist Lincoln Steffens on a personally guided tour and showed him "the crowd that got the timber" sitting around the dining-room table.

Reed's courage in the face of his treatment by the Portland Establishment made an indelible mark on his young son, John, who was to become one of the first American journalists to support the Russian Revolution, and the second American to be buried within the Kremlin walls. In the two-year period following his removal from office by the Taft Administration, C. J. Reed's financial and physical health deteriorated rapidly. John was meanwhile making a reputation for himself as a non-conformist, the antithesis of the worthy Portlander. When John (called "Jack" by his family and friends) wrote Roderick Macleay to thank him for paying his father's delinquent Arlington Club bill, Macleay noted on the letter that Jack was "a radical of the worst sort." The Portland Establishment had pronounced final judgement.[36]

The Election of Harry Lane: The People's Mayor

In the spring of 1905, Portland was caught in the swirl of two opposing currents. One, involving energy, confidence and hope, was generated by the city's boosters in preparation for the June 1 opening of the Lewis and Clark Exposition. The other, combining elements of fear, anger and despair, was a direct consequence of the timber-fraud trials. Facing an uncertain future, the timber buccaneers were predicting the end of the era when forests were cheap and the fast-growing West was crying for more and more lumber; when lumbermen had only to set up their mills, slash down the forests, and bank the proceeds. To make matters worse, the Republican party machinery, which the timber industry had helped subsidize for many years, had broken down.

The survivors of the Mitchell-Carey-Matthews forces were searching desperately for viable candidates. At the municipal level, 82-year-old Mayor George H. Williams was persuaded to run again, in Keady's words, "as a candidate of what is left of the machine." Referring to federal and state offices, Andrew C. Smith, a wealthy physician, active in Republican politics, reported: "Carey, Matthews and the machine crowd join the multitude in rolling up their eyes in surprise and horror at the developments in regard to Mitchell, and at the same time to be veneering themselves with such thin films of decency at Mills, Linthicum, Ayer (hot air at that) and at the same time holding out bouquets to Wilcox, Fenton and Scott."[37]

The Democrats, with the support of a splinter group of Republicans, nominated Dr. Harry Lane for mayor. Lane, a prominent local physician and grandson of Oregon pioneer General Joseph Lane, pledged, "integrity in office." Delivering the keynote speech to 600 listeners, 400 of them Republicans, lawyer John Gearin foreswore any words of personal abuse that might be directed against Williams. "George Williams is an old friend of mine of 30 years standing," declared Gearin, "a man of winning personality, guileless as a child, but he's a foxy old grandpa just the same. ... He has not been a bad mayor, he's not been a mayor at all." He repeated charges that the Williams administration had used $80,000 in gambling and vice fines "to beautify the city," and asserted: "Hear it! This $80,000, stolen by the gamblers from the homes of foolish men in Portland, or perhaps wrung from the earnings of the poor unfortunate girls who were compelled to pay to their masters the price of their shame—this money Mayor Williams and his executive board took to beautify the city."[38]

The newspapers took predictable positions. In supporting Lane, the Democratic *Journal* saw the major issue of the campaign as one of good versus indifferent government, of right and decency versus that of special privileges. Two days before the election, the *Oregonian* castigated the *Journal* as "the organ of plutocracy. ... The plutocratic magnates,...professional Republicans...placed their paper in the hands of a couple of Bryan Democrats." Harvey Scott scorned "the group of Republicans bankers, politicians and monopolists who are running a Democratic newspaper." He could never bring himself to accept Republicans who supported Democrats: "The Democrats are a minority party here and can't elect a Mayor except on false pretenses. ...The most important political office in the state is the office of Mayor of Portland.... The allegations against the administration of Mayor Williams are mostly of a trifling nature. Such as are serious, alleged by the grand jury in its published report, in no way or degree affect him. ... Williams has had to carry the odium of the Matthews machine."[39]

In a predominantly Republican city, Democrat Harry Lane won election on June 5, 1905, by 1,217 votes. Despite the aura of community excitement and confidence generated by the newly opened Lewis and Clark Exposition, the exposes of Williams's administration and timber-fraud trials rebounded in Lane's favor; the voters had had enough. They now had an honest mayor, and, in George E. Chamberlain, an honest governor. Six months later they acquired at least one honest U.S. Senator in John Gearin, whom Chamberlain appointed to succeed the recently deceased Mitchell. On December 8, 1905, Mitchell died of a diabetic coma following dental surgery. Half-way into his 71st year, he was facing a six-months sentence in the county jail.[40]

Lane's election ended a period in Portland's history that Establishment leader Charles F. Beebe proudly eulogized as one of "close" and "intimate relations" between "the chief and the cabinet," (referring to his membership on the Executive Board). The old days had come to an end—a period in Portland's history when business and politics were usually close, intimate activities connected by long-established family and social ties. In the minds of Beebe and his friends, the city would never be quite the same again. Harry Lane was the first east-side resident to be elected mayor. The demographic center was shifting. Between 1905 and 1910, the city's population east of the Willamette river would expand five-fold, while that on the west side increased by barely 40 percent.[41]

18.1 U.S. National Bank of Oregon staff, turn-of-the-century

18.2 Bird's eye view of Lewis and Clark Exposition

18.3 Portion of Lewis and Clark Exposition, 1905

18.4 John C. Ainsworth (1870-1943)

18.5 Francis J. Heney (1859-1937)

18.6 Charles H. Carey (1857-1941)

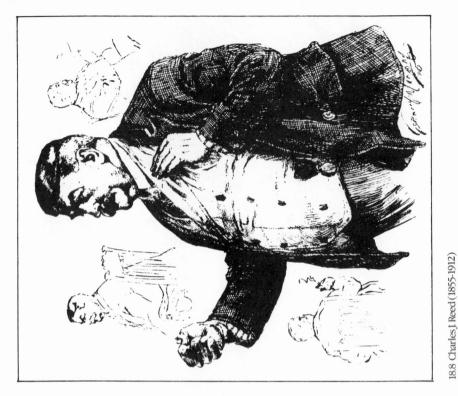

18.8 Charles J. Reed (1855-1912)

18.7 Timber Fraud cartoon: "Uncle Sam As He May Appear Twenty Years from Now"

18.9 View over Willamette River toward Albina and East Portland, 1903. Railroad
bridge (central left) and trestles across Sullivan's Gulch (center).

18.10 S.W. Fifth and Morrison, ca. 1902. Through the rain, Meier and Frank Co.
(right), Pioneer Post Office (left), Portland Hotel (background).

18.11 Mayor's race cartoon, 1905

18.12 Charles F. Beebe (1845-1922)

19

LANE CHAMPIONS
A SQUARE DEAL:
1905-1907

Dr. Harry Lane

B orn in Marysville (Corvallis) in 1855, Harry Lane received his undergraduate and medical degrees from Williamette University in Salem. During his last year of study, he was charged by a member of the university's board of trustees with having used curse words when discussing a question before a group of young people. Although he denied the allegations and was supported by witnesses, he was called before the board to answer the charge, which he again denied. Accused of being a liar, Lane challenged the trustee to meet him outside. As Oswald West later remembered:

> The trustee...slapped the young man's face; but a quick uppercut, catching the trustee on the face, floored him—Harry landing atop. In the 'slug fest,' the combatants rolled off the sidewalk—landing in a sea of mud—Harry still atop. When time was called, the trustee bore a peach of a black eye. When morning came, the impress of the trustee's body still showed plainly in the mud; and many were the curious spectators who gathered to look, smile and praise the prowess of old Joe Lane's grandson.

No one ever called Harry Lane a liar and escaped the wrathful consequences.[1]

After doing post-graduate work at the College of Physicians and Surgeons in New York City and practicing briefly in San Francisco, Lane returned to Oregon and became superintendent of the Oregon State Asylum from 1887 to 1891. This experience marked him for life. According to West, it "caused him to become embittered and suspicious — even to despise — most politicians with whom he came in contact." Within months, Lane discovered the existence of a racket involving state employees, politicians and suppliers, who were substituting inferior goods and food for the better grades called for in their bids and contracts. Lane, outraged, "shouted the story from the house tops. Many rallied to the defense of the crooked merchants—calling Lane a liar—but few came to his defense." As a result of the charges and counter -charges, he was ultimately forced to resign.[2]

Short of funds—he was "always a poor man," according to West—Lane was rescued by Asahel Bush, his grandfather's old political enemy. The aged Salem banker advanced him enough money to buy a modest home in Southeast Portland and to equip a small office in the Worcester Building, where he could practice his profession.

He later undertook further post-graduate study in Europe and joined the staff of the locally prominent Coffey Sanitarium on Northwest 20th Street.[2]

Dr. Lane became increasingly distressed by the municipal corruption, rampant vice, and poor public health conditions that he encountered—the same kind of dirty politics that he had come across in Salem 15 years earlier. For instance, Portland was the only large city in the country with no meat-inspection code. Through friends in city government, Lane promoted an ordinance to regulate the slaughtering of animals by providing for an official meat inspector. Mayor George Williams's announced opposition to the measure may have been what compelled the doctor to run for mayor in 1905. The business most adversely affected would have been the Union Meat Company, owned by council president and long-time Williams crony Louis Zimmerman. Although the council overrode the mayor's veto a few days before the election, Lane had already become convinced that Portland's city government was beholden to private greed at public expense.[3]

A New Breed of Mayor

Harry Lane's mayorship merits scrutiny, because it was during his administration that Portland made its first serious attempt to confront long-ignored municipal problems. His election was part of a broader national reform movement that by 1905 and 1906 stirred people to "consciousness of wrongdoing," in Richard L. McCormick's judgment. "Political and governmental changes ... followed upon the discovery that business corrupts politics." Large numbers felt themselves frustrated by government's failure to deal with the rapid expansion of the private economic sector. Overwhelming public demands were placed on limited municipal services, while fiscal resources were inadequate to meet growing social needs. Everywhere, self-styled progressives were on the rise. According to McCormick, "the progressive concept of corruption regarded the monied interests not as tools of a designing administration but as independent agents. ... In a curious way, ... the old republican view that commerce inherently threatened the people's virtue still persisted." Lane held such views, and furthermore agreed with his friend C. E. S. Wood that "the great issue of the party..fights" was not between Republicans and Democrats per se, but over "privilege, privilege, privilege." In a letter to a constituent several years later, he was unequivocal: "I am opposed to special privileges or favors being granted or continued to any one, as I believe that all our troubles as a nation arise in one way or another from that single fundamental cause. As a public official I have always stood squarely in opposition to such grants."[4]

With no political experience, Lane came into the mayoralty, backed by a mixture of mid-level business and professional men, many crossing party lines to support the first Democratic mayor since 1898. According to Samuel P. Hays, "almost half (48 percent) of the reformers [nationally] were ... doctors, lawyers, ministers, directors of libraries and museums, engineers, architects, school teachers and college professors." Mainly, Hays reasoned, "their interest in reform stemmed from the inherent dynamics of their professions rather than from their class connections." They were generally younger than nonprogressives and in the "vanguard of professional life, actively seeking to apply expertise more widely to public affairs." What little Establishment support Lane received came from attorneys John Gearin, C. E. S. Wood, Richard W. Montague, and Robert L. Sabin; and from *Oregon Journal* publisher C. S. Jackson, all Democrats. It was rumored that Republican banker William M. Ladd also supported Lane.[5]

Distrusting professional "politicians," Lane had "few close political friends," as West remembered. He also strongly disliked the ward system of city government, which he thought decentralized political life, diffused the process of decision making, and obscured accountability. In 1905 the council system had a representative from each of 10 wards and 5 elected at large. In theory, the system appeared to be democratic, but in practice the small ward constituencies made it relatively easy for the railroads and the liquor interests to secure the election of a council majority, or at least enough votes to override a mayor's veto. As Dean Collins observed, Lane faced an uphill battle. He held "a burning and bitter enmity against the folk of Babylon, for both the gambling and the red light district struck blows to his naked heart....[A] vigorous, eccentric character, he pounced upon his enemies...picturesquely and petrifically." Like many reformers of limited political experience, the idealistic Lane wanted to replace "bad men with good," who according to Hays, aimed to "concentrate the political power by sharply centralizing the process of decision-making rather than distribute it through more popular participation in public affairs."[6]

Of the four city councilmen in 1905 who were lawyers, one represented the Harriman railroad interests professionally, one was a Mitchell-Williams crony, and another was deeply involved in real-estate speculation. The largest realtor on the Republican dominated council was east-side resident J. P. Sharkey, who was closely identified with the Southern Pacific-Harriman real-property interests. The other businessmen were a druggist, an undertaker, a farm-implement executive, a transfer-company owner, a jeweler, and a brick manufacturer. East-side plumbing contractor Allan G. Rushlight, an independent Republican, would provide some support to Lane and be elected mayor in 1911. The council's only Democrat, east-side grocer Dan Kellaher, would strongly back Lane's efforts to regulate the public utilities and railroads. The most influential councilman and the mayor's chief antagonist was council president (1905-1906) John Annand, Portland manager of the Postal Telegraph Company and an ally of the railroads. All but J. P. Sharkey were newly elected.

Railroad influence was clearly responsible for some of the new faces. In general, the council came from the emerging stratum of business and professional men directly involved in Portland's burgeoning economic and residential growth resulting from the Lewis and Clark Centennial Exposition. For the first time in over 20 years, not one of them belonged to the Arlington Club. And not one was a professional person given elsewhere to supporting progressives like Lane.

A Profitable Fair — For Some

Few could deny that Portland derived immense financial benefits from the exposition. Nearly $8 million was pumped into the local stream of commerce. According to Carl Abbott's figures, "The Fair attracted 540,000 visitors from Portland, 640,000 from elsewhere in Oregon and Washington, and 408,000 from the rest of the United States and Canada. ...Portland's workshops and factories paid roughly $7,000,000 in salaries and wages to their 9,000 employees in 1905." Out of a total work force of 65,000, nearly

5,000 extra jobs were created during the four-month extravaganza. As Robert Rydell has observed: "The Portland exposition did more than build self-esteem. It also built Portland's economy and several private fortunes." Identifying their economic interests with the city's, "the rich got richer." Abbott further noted, "They gained profit from anything that stimulated urban growth."[7]

In June, 1906, *Sunset* magazine writer Donald Macdonald presented a "vision of a greater Portland" that exceeded the hopes of even the exposition's backers, who had speculated so heavily in the city's future. He projected "a city of towering business blocks, of miles of wharves and adjoining industries, of homes filling the Willamette-Columbia peninsula and covering Council Crest and all the lower ridges." To Macdonald, "the revolution in the lumber trade" was the chief factor in Portland's "marvelous prosperity." Portland was the number one lumber manufacturing city in the United States, the *Oregonian* had reported on June 4, 1905. That year the city's sawmills cut 541,320,000 board feet, an average of 30 percent over 1904. For 1906, sawmill income was projected to produce revenues in excess of $9 million.[8]

Next in importance for Portland's burgeoning commercial growth, reported Macdonald, was "the awakening of the value to the farmer of Oregon's cheap and fertile lands." Fifty thousand square miles of the heart of Oregon territory were being opened up by the extended lines of the Harriman system. The supply and equipment purchases of the Harriman empire, America's largest rail network, exceeded $100,000 a month in Portland alone. From July 1, 1905, to May 1, 1906, almost ten million bushels of wheat and over one million barrels of flour were exported from Portland, much of it having been brought to the city by the Harriman system. Oregon was the leading state in hop production, and its fruit industry was "making amazing strides." Macdonald noted that "Oregon apples command the highest prices in New York; last season they sold f.o.b. shipping point at $2.50 per box of fifty pounds. The car of pears bringing the highest price on record in the New York Market came last fall from Southern Oregon."[9]

The gold at the end of this agricultural rainbow did not escape the notice of eastern investors. Somewhat belatedly, the Hill interests (comprising the Great Northern and Northern Pacific railroads) began to pay more attention to Portland. In 1902, the Northern Pacific had announced plans to bridge the Columbia and to dig a tunnel under North Portland's Peninsula district, at a total cost of over $3 million. In 1906, after forming the Spokane, Portland and Seattle Railroad (a joint venture of his Northern Pacific and Great Northern companies), Hill changed his mind about a tunnel. The SP&S gained city council approval to cut a less costly gap through the peninsula. Hill was also instrumental in the purchase by the United Railways Company of 250 acres in the Guild's Lake former exposition site, for over $250,000. Ostensibly formed by Los Angeles investors but secretly controlled by Hill, United Railways expected to spend upward of $1 million for additional terminal and industrial real estate in the Guild's Lake area. Its primary goal in 1906 was to secure valuable city street franchises for a rail line to connect downtown Portland with 50 miles of electric lines under construction to Forest Grove and Salem.

All this economic growth and commercial activity generated jobs, many of which were filled by recent immigrants to Portland. While the city had over 2,500 manufacturing plants in 1905, employing 26,000 wage earners, manufacturing was still in an embryonic stage. Portland remained primarily a commercial entrepot. In 1910, it would rank twenty-third among American cities for its number of merchants and wholesale dealers, just behind Seattle and Denver. (San Francisco would rank seventh).[10]

Dun & Company's 1907 report of corporate financial worth clearly revealed the extent of Portland's economic growth and its commercial diversity. More than 55 out-of-state companies, each worth over $1 million, had offices or plants in the city. They included two major Chicago meat packers, Armour and Cudahy. Also doing a thriving business were American Can, General Electric, Goodyear Rubber, Fairbanks Morse Machinery, National Biscuit, Marshall-Wells Hardware, Sherwin Williams Paint, American Steel Wire, and the farm machinery corporations J. I. Case and John Deere. The presence of the major oil companies began to be felt as Union, Standard of California and Valvoline built storage tank farms along the Willamette River. Only four locally owned companies were rated as worth over $1 million: Benson Logging and Lumber, Meier & Frank, Portland Flouring, and H. Weinhard Brewers. M. Seller & Company, dealers in glassware and cookery, listed its worth at over $750,000. In the $500,000-$750,000 range were Allen & Lewis (showing a marked decrease in assets since Lewis's death); Eastern and Western Lumber Company; the Olds, Wortman & King department store; and the Corbett owned Portland Hotel Company. Twenty businesses were listed at between $200,000-$500,000. Among some larger corporations not rated were the street railways and the utilities (Portland Gas and Portland General Electric).[11]

Subscriptions to build a new Commercial Club building in May, 1906, indicated reasonably accurately the local private wealth in the post-exposition economic boom. Henry L. Pittock and his son-in-law Frederick W. Leadbetter pledged a total of $37,500. Their major holdings, apart from the *Oregonian,* included the Portland Trust Company; the Camas (Washington), Crown and Williamette paper mills; and the Willamette Valley Lumber Company. Pledging $10,000 were John C. Ainsworth, Henry W. Goode (who died shortly thereafter), Meier & Frank, Herman C. Leonard, Charles F. Swigert (through Pacific Bridge), Harvey W. Scott, William M. Ladd, and Theodore B. Wilcox. Nineteen others, including Simon Benson, the Corbett Estate, the Failing sisters, the Henry Weinhard Estate, and John B. Yeon pledged $5,000 apiece.[12]

Simon Benson and his close friend John Yeon had both made fortunes as loggers and sawmill operators before and after the exposition. The Norwegian-born Benson, Portland's wealthiest lumberman in 1907, would sell his timber holdings in 1910 for nearly $4.5 million. He had spent his early years unsuccessfully farming and logging before be began to accumulate timberlands in the St. Helens, Oregon, area. Designing and building his own donkey engines and logging rail lines, he saved considerable harvesting time and labor costs. Early in the century, Benson decided to ship to the prosperous Southern California market. Objecting to exorbitant railroad and coastal freight rates, he designed gigantic 835-foot rafts, each carrying about 4.5 million feet of logs, and had them towed 1,100 miles to San Diego, to be cut by his own sawmill. Through such resourcefulness, he saved over $150,00 a year.[13]

Yeon, who would later be associated with Benson in the hotel business, sold his large timber holdings in 1906. Shortly afterward, he bought the first of several major downtown properties for $125,000, the future site of the Imperial Hotel. Eight years earlier, the property had sold for $14,000. Another of his purchases became the site of Benson's $1 million hotel in 1913. In one year, Yeon bought three parcels of downtown property for slightly over $400,000. Many friends thought him foolish, but he knew his history and was thoroughly versed in current population trends. Within 20 years, his downtown holdings were worth over $1.5 million.[14]

In 1907, two years after his arrival as a poor young architect, the future president of the First National Bank Ernest Boyd MacNaughton cited the "fever of speculation," calling it "a riot." He borrowed $5,000 on his honest looks, made a down payment on a $20,000 lot and sold it two weeks later for $25,000. He repeated the performance the next month. Overall, from 1900 to 1910, Multnomah County's property assessments increased by over 500 percent, and the value of the city's real-estate transactions by 900 percent.[15]

Large residential developments were equally profitable for those like Theodore B. Wilcox who possessed the resources to undertake them. The president of the Portland Flouring Mills, who had made over $2 million from the exposition, had previously joined Charles E. Ladd in 1897 to form the Equitable Savings & Loan Association. An outgrowth of the Oregon Building & Loan Association, the Equitable was established in 1890. Besides Ladd and Wilcox, the directors were lumberman Winslow B. Ayer, attorney Harold M. Cake, cordage manufacturer Samuel B. Mears, and attorney Edward Cookingham, vice-president of Ladd & Tilton. By late 1903, assets totalled $1.1 million, and doubled in three years as the company made hundreds of private residential home loans throughout the Northwest. Equitable banked with Ladd & Tilton, which held a major block of its stock, and with the Dexter Horton National Bank of Seattle, in which the Ladds held a large interest.[16]

Wilcox played a key role in several post-exposition real-estate developments. In association with downtown businessmen and bankers Walter F. Burrell, John L. Hartman and Edward L. Thompson, he formed the Rose City Park Association of East Portland, along the Northeast Sandy Boulevard street railway line, from 45th to 62nd avenues. Equitable Savings & Loan and Hartman & Thompson provided the mortgage financing for the houses, each of which could cost no less than $1,500. Investor Burrell, son of the founder of Knapp, Burrell & Company, and Hartman, a former banking associate of George B. Markle, Jr., did well by their association with the shrewd Wilcox. Together, the investors realized an 800 percent profit from the venture.[17]

The Embattled Mayor

Despite the rapid growth and new construction following the exposition, the city, under Lane's administrative direction, faced numerous municipal problems that required attention. With the center of the retail trade moving west to Sixth Street, the older buildings closer to the waterfront began to exhibit signs of blight. Broken sidewalks and poorly maintained streets were harmful to Portland's business community, according to the Chamber of Commerce. As its *Bulletin* writer Cecil T. Barker observed:

We mercenary sons of Portland have a beautiful city.. [but] it needs a bath and a new dress ...[to] make her in all things a fitting bride for the wealth that comes to woo... Truly, we sons of Portland are mercenary, for we would sell the beauty of our city at a profit. But we can sell it and keep it, too, and that is good business.[18]

Lane could agree with such sentiments. As an early environmentalist, he would expend much effort during his four years in office attempting to achieve similar though less pretentious goals. More than merely a beautiful city, Lane wanted a liveable, workable place that would benefit everyone, not only the rich and powerful. He feared that the natural environment might be sacrificed to excessive physical growth if private interests, in the pursuit of profits, were allowed the free reign accorded them during the Williams administration. In assuming the role of chief protector of the "public domain" (a term he never clearly defined), Lane became embroiled in many political skirmishes; the battleground was the city council chamber.

During his first year in office, 21 of his 32 vetoes were overridden by a two-thirds vote of the council, and over the span of four years, about half of his record 169 vetoes were overridden. Those that were sustained tended to involve minor procedural or housekeeping matters. The ordinances supporting major interests were almost always passed. The Executive Board, composed of ten Democrats and three Republicans appointed by Mayor Lane, enjoyed only recommendatory powers; the council's decisions were final. The early council meetings were fairly subdued. The mayor drafted a new committee structure, creating 13 in place of the previous 10. For the first time in 36 years, the First National Bank was not made a depository for city funds, although it regained depository status in August, 1906. John C. Ainsworth's U.S. National Bank held the lion's share of deposits, followed by the Merchants National and the Bank of California. The Ladd & Tilton and Portland Trust banks held the city's interest-bearing certificates of deposit.

On August 16, 1905, Mayor Lane submitted his second veto of the session, relative to an ordinance amendment allowing saloons and restaurants to operate closed rooms, or "boxes." Such an amendment, said Lane, would permit combination houses ... productive of evil, ... dives and hiding places for criminals." Portlanders did not want such a condition to exist, he declared. Turning a deaf ear to such notions, the council overrode his veto, 12-3. This was the first of many battles that Lane would lose at the hands of the saloon and liquor interests. The awarding of lucrative liquor licenses and the regulation of saloons produced the largest split in the council for four years. Hours of official time were consumed in heated debate.[19]

The second divisive issue that arose at almost every meeting related to requests for granting street vacations, variances and easements for special construction not in compliance with existing ordinances. Lane vetoed practically every one, and was usually overridden 13-2. He was particularly outspoken 18 months later, when he denounced the council "for the wholesale giving away of street" and property that represented "lots of public money if the land were to be bought on the open market." In this particular instance, he was referring to an ordinance that granted the vacation of a portion of tiny Northwest Hull Street to the Willamette Iron Works. The city did not own even enough dock space for its new fireboat, yet it was giving away public streets to a private company free of charge.[20]

Neither the council nor the county commission paid much heed to the Executive Board, which was considered to be the "mouthpiece" of Mayor Lane. On October 20, 1905, the board filed a formal protest with the county over the commissioners granting the right to use the draw nests of the bridges on the east side of the river for commercial advertising purposes, i.e., the painting and erection of large signs. The board reminded the county that the city had paid for the bridges even though the county was charged with operating and maintaining them. "The use of any part thereof for commercial advertising purposes is offensive to good taste, civic pride and public decency. The county refused to order the signs removed and the council took no action. Two years later, the council did vote to place some height limits on billboards, against the strong opposition of the Foster-Kleiser Company.[21]

In December, 1905, Lane challenged the city's business leaders by vetoing an ordinance authorizing the franchise transfer of the Portland Consolidated Railway properties to the recently incorporated Portland Railway Company. In his message to the council, he said: "It is evident to all that the favors and privileges that have been bestowed in the past as franchises to the several street railways named in this ordinance now have a market value of millions of dollars, all granted without adequate benefit to the City, and it would seem that this excessive generosity with the property of the public should not be continued." Had the Portland Consolidated Railway been charged at a rate of 2 percent of gross earnings in 1905 (San Francisco charged 3 percent), it would have paid the public treasury $30,000 instead of $4,500 exclusive of bridge fees, which amounted to only $10,000. After long debate, the veto was overridden 13-1. In 1906, the Portland Railway Company would pay a total compensation of $20,000 to the city, equal to about a 1 percent gross revenue charge.[22]

This was the first time that any mayor of Portland had ever expressed such contrary opinions, at least publicly. Abbot Mills and his friends were dismayed, but probably not surprised. They knew that Lane and the Executive Board had been studying franchise compensation and comparing Portland's rates with those of other cities. Portland exacted the least compensation of any of the major West Coast cities. Lane had good reason to feel that Portland was being swindled, as it long had been, by the street-railway companies. As a consequence, the city was denied funds that could have been used for capital improvements and park acquisition. When the council was approached in December, 1905, and asked to purchase certain federal buildings at the recently closed exposition site, the city lacked the resources to give the matter more than casual consideration. Had it been able to execute a deal with the federal government and to purchase some of the property below Willamette Heights for a park, as recommended by John Olmsted, Portland today might well possess a lasting commemorative monument to Lewis and Clark, instead of a seedy industrial wasteland. In April, 1906, the city did find enough money to purchase the Forestry Building and two surrounding acres of land. Three years earlier, at the time of Olmsted's visit to Portland, the park commissioners had predicted the conversion of the exposition site to commercial and industrial uses. In their annual report, they noted that, "Although the site...is from many points of view an admirable one [for a park], it is to be regretted that the ground is almost entirely leased territory, and that most of the improvements will either disappear or revert to private use."[23]

When all the bills were paid, the exposition had netted the Lewis and Clark Centennial Exposition Association $111,456. The city made no formal request for any of the profits, but the state did secure the return of $50,000 from its unspent $500,000 appropriation. The exposition association refused to disperse any of the profits for public or community purposes. Under the leadership of Harvey Scott and Abbot Mills, it distributed a 21½ percent dividend on an original stock investment that had held no promise of future redemption at any percentage. Henry W. Corbett's $30,000 "patriotic" contribution was returned to his estate many times over, through the vastly improved fortunes of the First National Bank and the windfall profits derived from the Consolidated Railway Company sale.

Lane's Program

As Mayor Lane prepared his annual address to the council in early January, 1906, he was well aware of the financial stringency facing Portland, with a projected budget imbalance of $64,000. Thus Lane felt strongly that the expanding private industrial and utility sector of the economy should pay a larger share of the growing cost of government. The 53 percent increase in the fire department's budget directly reflected the boom in commercial and residential construction. Existing or contemplated revenues could not be expected to cover spiralling public costs resulting from private development. Furthermore, the city legislators refused to establish a sinking fund for capital improvements or for amortizing past bonded indebtedness.

Lane's speech of January 17, 1906, set the tone and direction of his administration. Most of the specific recommendations related to improving the quality of city services and equal execution of the laws. As his highest priority, the mayor advocated the reorganization of the health department. Portland had the second-lowest death rate of any major city in the country. There was no reason why it could not be rated as America's healthiest city. With this goal in mind, Lane decided that the health officer should be a physician, to be assisted by the medical profession. He subsequently appointed Dr. Esther Pohl Lovejoy, the first woman health officer in Portland's history and one of the first such appointments in the United States.[24]

A related issue was that of garbage. The garbagemen were private operators and their wagons were not watertight; spillage was a serious consequence. According to the mayor, the existing system of garbage collection and disposal provided "great inducement to dump at some more convenient place than the city crematorium. ... I advise that the city take charge of handling the garbage, procure properly built garbage wagons, horses and equipment," and give better service to the public—and, it was hoped, profits to the city. The existing inefficient and costly, crematorium needed to be replaced, but its relocation presented problems. The Northwest residents wanted the site removed from their neighborhood near Guild's Lake at 25th Street. A downtown site along Front Street was more central but too costly. Lane suggested an island in the river, but no one took him seriously. Because the existing plant could handle only about half the garbage collected, much of it continued being "dumped alongside roadways, behind hedges, and in convenient gulches and ravines."[25]

A subject of longstanding interest to Lane was that of city planning. Great benefit would accrue to Portland, said the mayor "if a plan were devised to terrace the hills, by employing a system of contour approaches...in place of the frightfully ugly and costly method now pursued of cutting them up into square blocks and deep cuts, called streets, which are not only expensive but leave the land in many instances almost unapproachable." For the flatter residential districts on the east side, platted on a grid of 200-square-foot blocks, Lane proposed that the city vacate every other street. Except for a 10-foot paved strip in the center, the streets could become park areas with "shade trees and rose vines." Only light delivery vehicles would be allowed on the strips. Such a plan, declared the mayor, "would make Portland the most beautiful city in the world."[26]

Turning to the riverfront, Lane strongly recommended the replacement of the "unsightly and straggly row of wooden docks." The decaying timbers and open sewers presented a health hazard. The docks should be built of stone and concrete. The following year, he commented: "The whole riverfront should be reorganized along lines looking to the betterment of conditions for this city. ... If necessary, the city should take over possession of the waterfront to itself by condemnation proceedings.[27]

The municipal water system also interested Lane. Portland's daily per capita consumption was 30 percent higher than that of 104 other large U.S. cities. The flat fee of $1.50 per month, with reductions to large commercial consumers, encouraged water waste and discriminated against small households and poorer families. The mayor recommended the installation of a meter system combined with a decrease in the minimum use fee. He also wanted the heavy commercial and industrial users to pay their fair share. More revenue needed to be generated, on a more equitable basis, to pay off the staggering $3.1 million bonded indebtedness, which was costing the system $160,000 a year in interest payments.[28]

Lane reserved his strongest and most pointed comments for the end. The city government must execute the laws equally, to rich and poor alike, "without fear or favor." Too many times he had heard people say, "Oh, what's the use. We go down to city hall and are treated like drunks or tramps." Many people in government were "playing politics or taking graft." The public welfare and the public interest at all times had to be considered "of greater importance than the gain of the private individual." Public franchises or public streets should never be parted with, "without full and proper compensation to the public." Referring to the practice of allowing time extensions for the completion of city improvement projects, Lane declared that the government must demand "the exact enforcement of all contracts with the city."[29]

The speech received wide publicity, and led to the formation two months later of the "Committee of One Hundred." Established by the Board of Trade, with encouragement from the mayor, the committee was composed of representatives from each city precinct and was made up almost entirely of business and professional men. Under the leadership of Portland realtor Francis I. McKenna, it proposed a variety of improvement projects, ranging from a belt line railroad along the waterfront to the building of public docks and a system of parks and boulevards recommended by Olmsted in 1904. The committee also favored municipal ownership of gas and light plants.[30]

McKenna represented a new breed of east-side Portland business leader with little direct attachment to the predominantly west-side Establishment. He lived in the Portsmouth section of St. Johns, and with his wife operated a real-estate venture called

The Hub Land Company. During the development boom following the exposition, McKenna showed an evangelical faith in Portland's future, to which his own financial future was closely tied. Evidently he admired Lane's willingness to challenge the downtown Establishment, which had never paid much attention to his far-out northern section of the city. A publicly owned dock on the St. Johns waterfront championed by McKenna, would immensely benefit the area's economy.[31]

The Board of Trade, resurrected by Albina resident William N. Killingsworth in 1899, drew much of its membership from the east side of the Willamette, Lane's base of popular support. Few of the committee's recommendations, including public docks, won favor from the Portland Chamber of Commerce, which represented the Establishment interests of the large private dock owners like the Oregon Railway & Navigation Company. Advocating municipal ownership of gas and light plants also threatened the city's most powerful private concerns, led by banker Abbot Mills. The Committee of 100 nevertheless encouraged Lane to advance his own program in the face of entrenched Establishment opposition.

Lane Challenges the Special Interests

The year 1906 found Mayor Harry Lane embroiled in simultaneous battle against a number of special-interest groups: the vice crowd, the "blanket" franchise beneficiaries, and the Hill and Harriman empires. Governor George Chamberlain (elected to the U.S. Senate in 1909) remembered that Lane "was quick to sense the harmonious relation between powerful figures and the vice ring. With equal celerity he comprehended the inside hold that big institutions maintained in the city and out of which they profited at the expense of the public and the masses." As someone else commented, "Grafters were his sport." The witty pipe-smoking doctor, with his "gray eyes, Gladstonian nose and gladiatorial chin" was fearless in combat. He hunted grafters "as other men hunt leopards and bobcats."[32]

Ineffective vice raids had been conducted spasmodically for over a decade. Lane recommended that the council cancel the licenses of the places where such illegal activities were discovered, as most of them were housed in combined saloon or restaurant facilities. The trial of Thomas Richards brought the issue to a head in January, 1906. Richards Place, a restaurant at the corner of Southwest Park and Alder streets (across from the Arlington Club), was charged with being a front for a prostitution house. When a police investigator asked for female company, Richards was quoted as replying: "No problem. Bring your own lady or I can furnish the goods."[33]

According to the *Journal*, the trial was a farce. Municipal Judge George J. Cameron and Court Clerk Frank Hennessy openly sympathized with liquor interests. Subpoenas were stolen and false ones issued in order to embarrass the prosecutor. The judge allowed the defendant's lawyer to employ questionable obstructionist tactics. Needless to say, Richards was acquitted. The *Journal* charged that the case was "jobbed." During the trial, the paper had revealed that the building was owned by Lauritz W. Therkelson, president of the North Pacific Lumber Company, one of the city's most prominent business leaders, an Arlington Club member, and a 17-year veteran of the Water

Committee. Mayor Lane was furious at the acquittal. When he recommended that the council remove Richards' license, he was rebuffed 8-6.[34]

Over the next year Police Chief Carl Gritzmacher tightened the lid by increasing the number of raids. But in September, 1906, Lane was so incensed by the lack of arrests that he ordered the chief to replace the entire detective force. Success came early in 1907 when the Paris House was closed for good. Opened in late 1904 to entertain visitors to the exposition, Portland's largest bordello occupied two floors of a rambling building on Northwest Davis between Third and Fourth. Each of the more than 100 women rented her own crib and retained her own earnings and liquor receipts.[35]

Lane's efforts were criticized by former councilman Fred Merrill and future Mayor George Baker. The mayor was "misguided," said Merrill. The city "could not put down prostitution and gambling;" the sporting element would end up all over town. Regulation by licensing was the only answer. On numerous occasions Lane received petitions from North End and downtown businessmen to remove the red-light activities to another district: "Get them away from the business center," they demanded. Lane would reply that the same policy should be applied unilaterally throughout the city. "Whether we like it or not, the law forbids bawdy houses. ... I will close up every house in town quite regardless of the consequences." But Merrill's prediction proved accurate. The crusade did little more than scatter the women throughout the wealthier Irvington and West Hills neighborhoods.[36]

Throughout most of 1906, Lane fought one losing battle after another with the electric railway companies and the railroads controlled by out-of-state interests like the firm of Moffat & White of New York. Investment bankers George B. Moffat and W. Augustus White, a Mills relative, were behind much of the early interurban electric railway development. With Abbot Mills and young Henry L. Corbett, they organized the Oregon Electric and Willamette Valley Traction companies in March that year. Three months later, the Oregon Electric absorbed Willamette Valley Traction and planned to begin limited operations from Portland in 1907. The financing for the huge undertaking came from three of America's largest corporations: Standard Oil of New Jersey, General Electric of Boston, and Electric Bond & Share of New York. In negotiating the financial arrangements, Mills played the key local role as he would in later negotiations with the Hill interests, through his Harvard classmate, Northern Pacific President Howard Elliott.[37]

The company attracting Lane's closest attention during the first half of 1906 was United Railways of Los Angeles, which would acquire Oregon Electric in 1910. Secretly controlled by James J. Hill, United Railways played a crucial role in Hill's attempt to outflank Edward H. Harriman's growing interests in Oregon. (To strengthen his local standing, Harriman joined the Arlington Club in 1907.) Over five months of council time was spent on the United Railways' franchise application before it gained final council approval. Considerable opposition arose from Harriman's Southern Pacific, which had been trying for several years to secure a franchise to run a line down Front Street to the Northern Pacific Terminal Depot. The award of the Front Street franchise to United Railways represented a clear defeat for the Harriman interests.

Lane's opposition was confined to three provisions: the franchise payment of $1,000 a year was much too low; the 25-year term was too long a commitment; and the city's right to future acquisition was not clearly established. At least Lane succeeded in getting the council to write in the provision that the city could purchase any portion of the line, rather than the entire system, if future needs should dictate such a decision.[38]

Another major force for railway expansion in Portland was the effort to create a unified belt-line system of freight movement, not passenger traffic. As early as January, 1906, the Northern Pacific was buying large tracts of land along the Columbian Slough for freight yards. Property had shot up to $1,000 an acre, ten times its 1905 value. According to the *Oregon Journal*, Hill was trying to contain Harriman with support from the Weyerhaeusers and some Portland investors, including the First National Bank. The Northern Pacific also received several franchise awards for laying side and switching tracks on public streets north of the depot-terminal area. Lane vetoed each of the ordinances because there was no provision for splitting the switching fees with the city, nor any compensation for the use of public property.[39]

In September and early October, 1906, Lane fought both the Hill and Harriman interests. He lost two battles, but won the third by sheer ingenuity. For years the city had tried at various times to persuade the Southern Pacific to remove its tracks from Southwest Fourth Street. (The legislature had granted the franchise to the Oregon Central Railroad in 1868.) Originally designed for general rail traffic, the track was then used only for freight, but the noise and pollution angered residents in South Portland. When an ordinance was introduced to repeal the franchise, attorney William D. Fenton defended the railroad's interests. He cited the track's economic benefits to the city's commercial life. Moreover, he claimed that the railroad had no other provision for moving freight through the city on the west side, and that cancelling a legally ordained perpetual franchise and forcing the company to abandon its investment would be tantamount to expropriation of private property without due process of law. With typical arrogance, he reminded the councilmen that most of them enjoyed free Southern Pacific rail passes.

On September 19, the council unabashedly failed to support the ordinance by a vote of 10-4. A week later, the mayor transmitted a strong letter to the city legislators to the effect that the old franchise was unconstitutional, that it was in conflict with the current city charter, and that the Southern Pacific had not been the original grantee. Furthermore, the Southern Pacific had a history of not maintaining the streets on which its tracks were laid. This fact alone provided ample legal grounds for cancellation of the franchise, Lane declared. Seven months later, the council adopted a resolution, 6-5, stipulating that the Southern Pacific terminate the use of freight cars and steam locomotives on Fourth Street within 18 months. The railroad had finally decided to build a bridge at Oswego, to connect the west-side traffic with its main line on the east side.[40]

On September 22, 1906, Mayor Lane discovered that the Northern Pacific Terminal Company, owned largely by Harriman and Hill interests, was occupying portions of Northwest Irving and Kearny streets without a franchise. For years the city had been negotiating with the NPT over a suitable location for a new fire station near the terminal. The previous February, the company had proposed leasing space, but not deeding ownership to the city. The offer was declined. Now, with this startling information on his desk, Lane called the manager of the Terminal Company and informed him that all the tracks from the depot to the Steel Bridge passed illegally over two city streets. He reported that he had 20 patrolmen with proper tools prepared to dig up the tracks if a deed to the firehouse site was not granted "post haste." No train could enter or leave the terminal grounds if the mayor were to carry out his threat. On September 26, the mayor informed the council that he had his deed for the station, properly executed by the NPT Company. He had chosen the location at Northwest Third and Glisan streets. He suggested to the council that in exchange for the building site, a "properly guarded franchise" be enacted to legalize the Terminal Company's use of the streets. This was to be Lane's only substantial victory over the entrenched railroad interests in his two terms of office.[41]

Five days later, Lane vetoed an ordinance granting permission to the Spokane, Portland and Seattle Railroad, a joint Northern Pacific-Great Northern enterprise, to excavate a deep cut across North Portland's Peninsula district. Hill had secretly organized the SP&S in 1905 to construct a rail line from Spokane to Portland along the north bank of the Columbia River. The SP&S would also assume control of all freight and passenger operations between Seattle and Portland, using new bridges under construction across both the Columbia and Willamette Rivers. Hill wanted more direct access to the Northern Pacific Terminal grounds and refused to consider a common user arrangement with the Union Pacific, which was planning to build a tunnel under the peninsula, for which it was to receive a franchise in July, 1907.

Among Lane's numerous objections to the ordinance, the most significant was the railroad's authorization to pay nothing beyond the cost of its own land investment and that of four steel bridges to be constructed across the cut. Fourteen existing streets would be closed by the excavation. Calling the whole deal an out-and-out "give-away," Lane said it would be both a "defacement of property and a visual blight." But Portland business leaders were so excited by James J. Hill's recognition of Portland as a major terminus, they felt that any request by Hill should be favored. The council overrode Lane's veto 11-1. The previous week, Lane had suffered a similar defeat over a franchise ordinance granted to the SP&S, authorizing the company to lay tracks on several major cross streets in Northwest Portland for freight terminal development with no compensation to the city.[42]

In July, 1907, Mayor Lane vetoed the Union Pacific's request to build its tunnel under the Peninsula district. Citing some of the same reasons he gave in the SP&S case, he said that, although the franchise contained a common user clause, there was no right-of-way provision for another user to get into or out of the tunnel, and the franchise was perpetual. He deplored the lack of an overall plan for the area: "The interests of the people are greater than those of any corporation." The council overrode the veto 10-4.[43]

Lane's Personal Crusades

Lane seemed to enjoy personally confronting those private interests that he thought were purposely fleecing the public, and to delight in taking remedial action. After several months of reviewing street repair and paving bids, he suspected that contracts had "been submitted in the name of persons of whose existence no evidence can be obtained." He singled out the paving contractors, whose work he personally investigated.[44]

One episode that he later recounted involved an inspection that he made of some recently paved streets in the Irvington district. In the course of his walk he would stop and bang the curb with a rock. Some neighborhood boys asked him what he was up to. Lane informed them that he was the mayor and would like them to help with a project. He gave them some chalk and asked them to proceed up and down the street and hammer the curbs with rocks. Whenever they heard a hollow sound they were to mark the spot with a large "X." Lane then went over to his vehicle and took out a pick and a sledgehammer. He proceeded to hammer the curb spots himself, leaving the pieces in the gutter. The next morning the contractor stormed into city hall and demanded to know why the mayor was destroying his concrete curbing. Lane informed him that if he did not immediately rebuild all the curbs within a specific time period he would have the man thrown in jail and the contract cancelled without any payment for the work completed. A subsequent investigation brought full restitution to the city.[45]

In March, 1907, Lane embarked on another personal crusade against a fraudulent contractor, Lafe Pence. In the waning months of the Williams administration, Pence had sought permission from the city to construct water conduits across portions of Macleay Park. With the support of the Board of Trade, he planned to sluice dirt off the hills behind Willamette Heights and transport it through wooden flumes to the Guild's Lake area as fill for a projected industrial site. Pence was only one of many hungry land developers who could not wait to get their hands on the soon to be vacated exposition grounds. Within two years, he had constructed over 14 miles of sluices, some going way back into the hills of Washington County. Much of the land from which he was dredging dirt was in the town of Linnton (an area that would be annexed to the city in 1915). Using "hydraulic giants," Pence was sluicing as much as 2,000 yards a day, and was ruining the approaches to Macleay Park. During the winter months he used rainfall runoff for most of his water needs, but during the summer he tapped the creeks so that the Balch Creek channel was practically dry at the foot of Willamette Heights. He also had plans to build an electric rail loop through the hills to Linnton and back to Portland on the west side of the exposition grounds. He also planned to terrace the hills adjacent to the rail loop and prepare sites for residential development.

When Lane discovered that Pence had never received official permission to run flumes over city property, he ordered the operation terminated. After a period of non-compliance, the mayor, in company with a couple of policemen, hiked up to the scene with pick and shovel and destroyed the largest of the flumes. But he could not prevent Pence from continuing his rape of the land outside the city limits. The private landowners, who were receiving the dirt, welcomed the development, which promised to increase their property values.[46]

Lane appeared less combative when, a week later, an ad hoc coalition of reformers — progressive Republicans and others, under leadership of state Representative John B. Coffey called for a graft investigation. The group was reportedly raising a fund of $50,000 and negotiating for the return of prosecutor Francis Heney to direct the investigation. "We believe," said the announcement, "that there has been as much graft in Portland as in San Francisco. ... Corporations and trusts must be dealt a blow for their practice of illegally influencing legislation."[47]

Lane's response to the accusations seems puzzling for one who had spent much of his term making similar charges against corporate behavior, the "concrete pool," and fraudulent city contractors. To the *Oregonian,* he expressed doubts that extensive graft existed in Portland. "It is more a case of careless business records and lack of intelligence" characteristic of "past city administrations." Said Lane, "franchises have been blundered away, not grafted away." Lane's ego may have been wounded. He enjoyed his reputation as a crusading leader and may have felt upstaged by Coffey's group.[48]

By March, 1907, Lane expected to run for reelection in June. He may have feared that a public investigation of graft might be used by his opponents to cast discredit on his administration. He also may have been wary of frightening away what little support he enjoyed from the downtown business community. U.S. Bank President John C. Ainsworth, for one, was more supportive of Lane than his counterpart at the First National Bank, Abbot Mills. Lane was helping Ainsworth in his efforts to pass a $1 million park bond levy at the June election. Other measures that Lane supported, with strong local business backing, included $500,000 for municipal dock-land purchase; $450,000 for a new Madison Street Bridge; $3 million for a new Bull Run pipeline; and $275,000 for a new fireboat, fire hydrants and water mains. By embracing the park bonds, Lane risked the disfavor of many of his east-side supporters who wanted more funding for streets and sewers.[49]

Lane Wins Reelection

Lane easily secured the Democratic renomination despite the unhappiness of party leaders with his independence. He announced that he wanted the freedom — "unfettered hands" — to find and install in city management the best people "regardless of party." His opponent was city auditor, Republican Thomas C. Devlin, who built his campaign on the theme that "the reformer ultimately fails." He favored applying the soundest business principles to city affairs. Efficiency would breed honestly and such a government would improve morality.[50]

In two years, Harry Lane had antagonized most of the traditional business and political party leadership. Although he looked upon his years in office as "joyful times," he felt frustrated by the weak mayor-council form of government. The main ill of American cities, he said on many occasions, was "decentralized power and authority." Why? Because "nobody is to blame. ... The public can't put its finger on the guilty man." Everyone sidesteps and "the culprit remains unseen and therefore unwhipped." Like many businessmen and professionals, Lane believed that only a strong mayor could be held accountable. "The eye of the people would be on a single spot. ... Nobody can watch a dozen ratholes simultaneously." His disdain for the traditional ward system of council government was expressed throughout the campaign. He held to his naive view that bad people could be replaced with good; if not, a strong honest mayor, with concentrated power, could save the people from their elected representatives who were submissive to special interests. He knew what was good for the people; it was not difficult for him to play God. At times, he could exhibit a degree of audacity (some called it arrogance) that led to strong disagreement with even his closest friends.[51]

As the election date approached, the *Oregon Journal* reported that the liquor interests were backing Devlin and the reelection of city Judge George J. Cameron. They had also formed a new political society to repeal the initiative and referendum, called "The Patriotic Brotherhood of Liberty Defenders." In no previous municipal campaign of memory had the liquor question created such acrimony. Responding to all the hoopla, the *Journal* declared that "decency and morality" were the only real issues. "There is a solid phalanx of vice, fronting the social order. ... Is Portland to surrender once more to the audacity of the north end cohorts?" On the morning of the election, the *Oregonian* confessed to its readers that "in the present municipal contest" it had "not participated with its customary energy." It was discouraged by the attitude of many regular Republicans, who had publicly broken ranks in support of a Democrat. "They have failed to cooperate."[52]

On June 3, 1907, Harry Lane won reelection by 1,500 votes. He lost in all of the six wards on the west side. The downtown, North End and Portland Heights residents gave Devlin a surplus of 1,000 votes. Lane picked up his surplus on the east side, winning handily in all four wards, especially his own Ward 7 in the Southeast. The only council support he enjoyed came from the east side of the river.[53]

The voters approved a record 11 of 16 amendments to the city charter, (some proposed by initiative), including bond authorizations for the major capital improvements favored by Lane and business leaders like Ainsworth. Also approved were the establishment of a free public employment bureau; an increase in the liquor-store license fee to $800 a year; further regulations on the hours for saloon operations; a stricter 25-year franchise for the Portland Gas Company; and a franchise renewal for the newly incorporated Portland Railway Light & Power Company, which increased its annual compensation payment to $15,000. The only defeated amendment that Lane had strongly supported provided for salary increases to all major city departments.[54]

Reflecting the general tone of discouragement shared by many of Portland's west-side Establishment, financier Augustus White, who followed Portland events closely, wrote his cousin Abbot Mills on June 4: "I see by the evening papers that Lane has been reelected by 1500 — I am sorry."[55]

Undaunted by his failure to attract the support of Portland's business leadership, Harry Lane called for general public interest in the work and decisions of the city council. At the opening of the new council session, he declared:

> The day in which the servants of the people can play "ducks and drakes" with the people's interests or pay off personal or political debts or other obligations at the expense of the people has gone by, let us hope never to return. ... The people are now awake. ... [They] ... expect and demand of their agents ... true and just service. ... I have no enemies to punish or friends to reward in the administration of the City's affairs. ... [My only] desire is to accomplish as much good for the benefit of the people as is possible.[56]

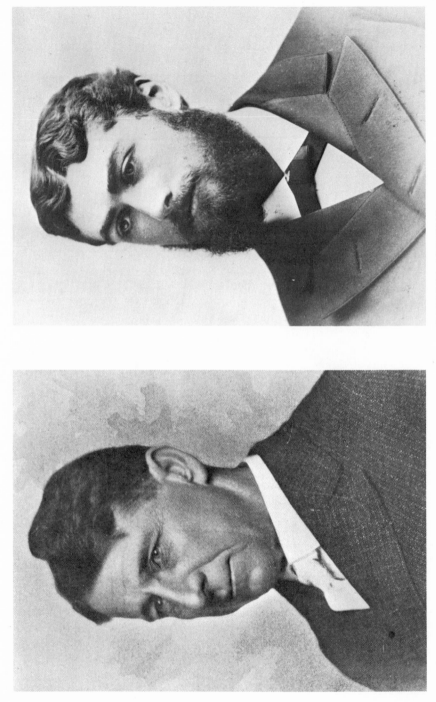

19.2 C.E.S. Wood (1852-1944)

19.1 Harry Lane (1855-1917)

19.3 An interurban train from Portland, c. 1900

19.4 Simon Benson (1851-1942) beside a Benson fountain, Portland

19.5 John B. Yeon (1865-1928) and, to right, William M. Killingsworth (1850-1933)

19.6 Grain Department, Portland Board of Trade, after 1899

19.7 Street and curb work, S.E. Caruthers and Eighth, early 1900s

19.8 Swift and Co. meatpacker

19.9 Cartoon on Portland City Council conflicts

20

CORPORATE INTERESTS AND POWER POLITICS: 1907-1909

Early Moves Toward Corporate Regulation

Early in 1906, following revelations of political and business corruption, the weight of public opinion in Oregon began to accept limited government regulation of public utilities and banks. For years, opposition to such governmental authority had conferred countless privileges on corporations, at great expense to the public treasury. Oregon's experience confirms Richard L. McCormick's conclusion that "The middle years of the twentieth century unmistakably mark[ed] a turning point...when the direction shifted. ...The creation of effective regulatory boards [was] progressivism's most distinctive governmental achievement." Mayor Harry Lane and Governor George Chamberlain pressed for reforms that would serve the best interests of the public and the just economic requirements of private companies.[1]

As early as 1886, gubernatorial candidate Sylvester Pennoyer had campaigned on a platform calling for railroad rate regulation in order to prevent price discrimination and ensure that rates were fair and reasonable. Once elected, he had recommended that all utilities be placed under municipal regulation. Responding cautiously to such requests, the 1887 legislature had created the Board of Railroad Commissioners, only to abolish it in 1898 at the behest of Senate President Joseph Simon, Oregon's leading railroad attorney. No further regulatory efforts were seriously pursued until after the *Oregonian* launched a lengthy attack on the gas company and street-railway franchises during the winter and spring of 1906.

The newspaper accused the gas company of paying taxes on less than half the value of its property: dodging $20,000 in taxes was "one of the thrifty methods of the Portland Gas Co." In June, Judge Henry McGinn charged that Abbot Mills and Charles F. Adams had paid nothing for the company in 1892, "not a solitary dollar." In an accompanying editorial, the *Oregonian* declared that "the organization of the Portland Gas Co. was the most astounding illustration of high finance in the entire history of Portland." The company claimed McGinn was "over capitalized,...the bonds were over-valued and the stocks watered." Four months later, the paper bannered the headline: "Big Grab Plan on River Front." It accused the gas company of making a deal with the Port of Portland to receive dredgings at minimal cost, thereby extending the utility's land into the river, changing the harbor line, and narrowing the river in the process.

The Oregon Railway & Navigation Company and Allen & Lewis Company were in on the deal. Gasco President Adams was treasurer of the port, and the port president was Captain A.L. Pease, an employee of the OR&N. According to the *Oregonian*, the "maneuver" added over $500,000 in value to the gas company's property.[2]

The *Oregonian*'s attack on the street-railway franchises was equally vitriolic. Many readers must have been perplexed—even astounded—by Harvey Scott's charge of June 20, 1906, that the paper had been duped in 1902-3 when it supported the awarding of the new franchises to the City and Suburban and the old Portland Railway companies. The event that ostensibly produced this new outburst was the announcement of the incorporation of the Portland Railway Light & Power Company. The *Oregonian* claimed that the sale to eastern financiers was "political jobbery, costing the city millions of dollars." Citing figures to show that the company expected to earn over $200,000 in 1906 and that the city would receive only $13,380 in compensation, the paper charged "fraud." Wrote Scott, "The tricks of the franchise gang of Portland are coming to light."[3]

The *Oregon Journal* accused the *Oregonian* of hypocrisy. The *Journal* had printed all the facts in November, 1902. It had advised the council to wait until the new charter had taken effect, when higher compensation rates and the 25-year limit would be in effect. The *Journal* charged the *Oregonian* with "newspaper treachery. ...The *Oregonian* has sold itself habitually to the highest bidder for many years." The *Journal* had previously claimed that Scott's attacks on the gas and railway company franchises were really aimed at its chief rival, the *Journal* itself, some of whose stockholders, like Mills and John C. Ainsworth, were utility executives as well as the city's leading bankers.[4]

Before the election of June, 1906, the *Oregonian* had presented legislative candidates with a series of questions regarding utility franchises and regulation. Those who responded favorably received enthusiastic support. Although the paper's efforts were not particularly successful (few of the candidates espousing utility regulation were elected), the *Oregonian*'s so-called campaign at least aroused sufficient public interest to put the issue on the 1907 legislative agenda. Railroad regulation emerged as the first priority after the *Journal* joined the cause in October, 1906. The impetus for its action was the economic distress caused by a railroad boxcar shortage in Oregon and a sudden increase in freight rates, which bankrupted a Portland lumber company.[5]

Railroad Regulation: A First Step

During the period from 1905 to 1909, the Southern Pacific and Union Pacific railroads, controlled by Edward H. Harriman, invested more than $10 million in Oregon. By 1913, when the federal courts decreed their separation, they held a total of 56 franchises within Portland, all received without payment of compensation. Early in 1907, the implications of such powerful growth worried the Portland Chamber of Commerce. Particularly disturbing was the arrogance of Harriman's regional manager, John P. O'Brien, who denied responsibility for the boxcar shortage.[6]

The Transportation Committee of the chamber drafted a bill to re-establish the Railroad Commission of Oregon, consisting of three members to be appointed by the governor, the secretary of state and the state treasurer. Governor Chamberlain warned the legislature that if it failed to take action, the public, by initiative, might produce an instrument that was even more restrictive. Mills appeared relatively unconcerned by the growing mood of the legislature (prodded by the governor) to regulate corporations in which he had a major interest. Writing to Augustus White in New York on January 10, 1907, he commented: "We have many friends in the body and I do not believe that much damage will be wrought by the Legislature to the Gas Company and other Portland corporations."[7]

Established by legislative enactment on February 18, 1907, the railroad commission received only limited powers. It could revise intra-state rates but not formulate complete rate schedules. Its most effective role was to be a collector and publisher of corporate information. For the first time, intra-state railroad books would be opened to public scrutiny. In 1908, the commission's first annual report revealed the astonishing profitability of the Harriman lines: a combined net profit of $22.2 million from their western operations in 1906 and 1907.[8]

A Frightened Portland Gas Company

As Abbot Mills had predicted, his "many friends" in the legislature blocked any attempt to regulate Portland-based public utilities. It was to take four more years of strenuous effort to achieve that goal. Lane was disappointed by Salem's inaction. He had transmitted to the legislature a critical report by a city council committee that he had appointed to investigate the *Oregonian's* charges against Mills's Portland Gas Company. The three major conclusions were that the gas was of poor quality, the public was being grossly overcharged, and the company's dealings with the public were unsatisfactory. The committee recommended that the legislature revoke the company's perpetual franchise. While no legislative action resulted, the threat bothered Mills continually. Almost immediately, he and Adams took steps that led to the sale of the company in 1910. Augustus White responded from New York, "I understand perfectly how disagreeable the present slanders of the *Oregonian* must be and do not wish you to stay in the Gas Co. any longer than is necessary to effect a reasonably satisfactory sale of the Co."[9]

Two weeks later, White again wrote Mills: "We do not want to have you tied up in the Gas Co. a day longer than you wish." Mills encouraged White to push ahead with negotiations, but advised his cousin to work through a third party. The purchaser had to be "considered an entirely independent concern," because of the unpopularity in Portland of any "consolidation of interests." The White cousins and other Mills relatives owned substantial blocks of Gas Company securities, and Mills did not want this to become public knowledge in the course of the negotiations. The Brooklyn and Franklin Trust companies, in which the Mills relatives had interests, had just purchased $100,000 in Gas Company notes.[10]

State Bank Regulation and James Steel

Abbot Mills favored the only other major regulatory action of the 1907 session: the passage of the Oregon Banking Act, which created the State Board of Banking Commissioners. To Mills, the major cause of bank failure was "the improper use of funds of a bank in the pet enterprises of its officers and stockholders." Other pitfalls included putting "too many eggs in one basket," and granting excess bank credits to one borrower. Until the law went into effect on May 25, 1907, Oregon had had no state banking regulations. Henceforth, private and new state banks were to incorporate, but existing state banks were exempted until 1925. The law also provided for the appointment of a state bank examiner, stricter loan regulations, and prohibitions against the conversion of funds to private use by banks or their officers.[11]

The man chosen to be Oregon's first bank examiner was the well-known former Portland banker and street-railway executive James Steel. Few of his contemporaries had been involved in a wider variety of business careers. Since going bankrupt in 1894, he had eked out a living as a partner in his brother's insurance agency and as a promoter of speculative new business ventures. By 1907, at the age of 72, he needed the assured income of a prestigious job. No record exists of how he secured the appointment; it can only be assumed that Governor Chamberlain opposed it, particularly after Steel admitted publicly that his old Metropolitan Railway Company had kept three sets of books. The other two state officers must have chosen him; the state treasurer was his younger brother George.[12]

Although he did not take office until May 25, James Steel began using his official stationery in late February, as he actively promoted the products of a new company he had organized with William H. Adams, the former general manager of Ladd's Oregon Furniture Company. Incorporated as the Oregon Gas Manufacturing Company, the enterprise peddled a system that used carburated water to manufacture clean gas "from all sorts of fuels." In soliciting investment capital from the wealthy Portland attorney Fred W. Mulkey, then serving out the U.S. Senate term of John Mitchell and John Gearin, Steel wrote of the money to be made from clean gas. He and Adams, the inventor of the machinery, planned to "install plants in at least twenty towns and cities" in Oregon to furnish gas at rates 30 percent below those charged by Portland Gas and other local gas companies. His position as bank examiner would give him leverage in securing bank loans and gas contracts in the municipalities he visited while pursuing his official duties. He expected to get the key financing from the Ladd-controlled Title Guarantee & Trust Company of Portland.[13]

Within three weeks of Steel's proposal to Senator Mulkey, the New York stock market began dropping. By June it was in sharper decline. The Panic of 1907 hit Portland earlier than New York. On August 21, the Oregon Trust & Savings Bank closed its doors and entered receivership. The business boom that had swept the country during the previous three years, built upon optimism and extended credit, had ended. Oregon Trust & Savings, a product of the accompanying bank boom, had been organized by Lonner O. Ralston and attorney P. L. Willis in 1904. By 1907 the president was W.H. Moore while the cashier was W.C. Morris, two gentlemen who thoroughly misunderstand the techniques of sound banking. More than most other banks in Portland, Oregon Trust & Savings carried many small savings accounts that it had actively solicited from working-class women and widows. Hundreds of these unfortunate depositors lost all their savings. District Attorney Manning discovered that a large portion of the bank's assets — $320,000 worth — was in bonds of newly organized independent telephone systems in Omaha and Tacoma that had not even begun to operate. The bank's officers had shared in the profits of the bond sales to the bank, and had kept $20,000 in bank commissions for their own use. When depositors sought to withdraw their funds, the bank had insufficient liquidity to meet the demand. Both officers were indicted and convicted and eventually sent to jail.[14]

The Oregon Trust & Savings collapse probably could not have been prevented by bank examiner Steel, who was prohibited by law from making any official examinations until after May 25, 1908. He spent his first year in office travelling widely, acquainting himself with over 100 banking operations, and promoting his clean-gas enterprise. He received assurance from Portland's banking community that there was no need to worry. The Oregon Trust & Savings failure was an exceptional case. "The banks in Portland have never been in better condition than today," declared J. Thorburn Ross, president of the Title Guarantee & Trust Company. Generally speaking, Ross was correct. Business was good in Portland. What Ross did not reveal was that a couple of the savings and trust banks in Portland "had been skyrocketing with other people's money in telephone bonds, irrigation bonds and timber land speculations," according to Joseph Gaston. Ross's bank was one of them.[15]

The following fall, six banks in Manhattan and Brooklyn went into receivership, including the Brooklyn Trust Company of which Abbot Mills's father had been an officer. The most spectacular New York failure was that of the old-line Knickerbocker Trust Company on October 22, 1907. The scare was short-lived, as the U.S. Treasury Department and J.P. Morgan & Company each loaned $25 million to the New York Bank Clearing House Association to support any banks in temporary distress. By December stability had been restored.

In Portland, however, there was more to come. On November 6, Thorburn Ross's Title Guarantee & Trust Company collapsed. Writing from New York to Mills three days later, White commented: "This looks like the gradual weeding out of the weak points in your local situation. ... Most of our banks here would envy your having such a large amount of gold in your vaults." On November 10, the *Journal* reported that Title Guarantee & Trust's total liabilities of $2.6 million made it the largest bank failure in Portland's history. Over $600,000 was owed to the Ladd & Tilton Bank and over $400,000 to the State of Oregon, funds that had been deposited by treasurer George Steel. The *Journal* accused Ross of looting the bank and Steel of incompetence, saying that the state treasurer had put public funds in the bank that was the poorest risk in the state. As a subsequent investigation discovered, Title Guarantee had never been solvent.[16]

Title Guarantee's failure posed many complications for Portland's Establishment, including State Bank Examiner James A. Steel. Forced to borrow $12,500 from his nephew Charles E. Ladd, and to pledge the Oregon Gas Manufacturing Company patents as collateral, he had expected to repay the loan from funds provided by the bank out of proceeds from a bond sale. After the bank's closure, Steel wrote his Corvallis business agent on bank examiner stationery that he "was up against it hard." To his Albany agent he reported that there was "no possibility of getting money out of any of the banks." (The Merchants National Bank had also closed.) On November 21, he informed a friend in Iowa that "those of us who were caught...had to hustle for bread in quick time. I got down to less than $5 before the aid came from New York. ...Most of us have lived through other troubles of this character and are still in the ring, with the same old billious feelings."[17]

Undaunted by defeat, Steel travelled over 8,000, miles during the latter half of 1908, examining each of the 135 banks under his jurisdiction. When the 1909 session of the legislature rejected his request for a deputy examiner, he resigned, and returned to private life in an attempt to restore some financial security. A widower with four married children, the once-prominent brother-in-law of William S. Ladd died at the age of 78 in April, 1913. His estate consisted of one Albina lot worth $1,000, a gold watch, and a diamond ring.[18]

The Legacy of J. Thorburn Ross

Title Guarantee's failure also created severe problems for the Ladd family. Until July, 1906, its president had been William M. Ladd, the oldest son and designated successor of his father. The company was an outgrowth of the Real Estate Title & Trust Company, which had been established in 1888 to fulfill a role for the Ladd & Tilton Bank similar to that later played by the Security Savings & Trust Company for the First National Bank. Much of its business was in real estate mortgages; J. Thorburn Ross had been employed for several years as its secretary and manager.

Before Ross's time, Title Guarantee was known for ruthless adherence to payment schedules, looking for any excuse to take control of property whenever payments were in default. One notorious case involved the prominent Portlander Judge Philip A. Marquam, who lost his large downtown building and 80 acres of farmland on Sandy Road to the bank in July, 1906, following a State Supreme Court ruling. Under Ross, Title Guarantee went in for more speculative ventures. In the Marquam case, Ross was accused of unethical conduct. The bank was both trustee for the family and Marquam's creditor. The bank acquired the building for one-third of its value and the Oregon Supreme Court upheld the bank.

Little in Ross's record commended him for a position of fiscal responsibility. From the mid-1890s he had been a political crony of Joe Simon and former Mayor Henry S. Rowe; running on legislative tickets with George W. Bates and Donald MacKay, he had won election to the 1898 and 1899 sessions of the House. Simon viewed him as an eager and loyal worker who was valuable to his many causes. For a number of years he was known to be close to the liquor interests fighting Harry Lane in 1907. As an agent of William M. Ladd, he had become involved with insurance as well as mortgage banking, but until mid-1906 he had never exercised top administrative responsibility.

A contemporary of Ross's called him "incompetent and extravagant." Former U.S. National Bank President Edward C. Sammons, who had known Ross in his later years, remembered that he was "stupid." He was also dishonest. He was later indicted and convicted for misuse of public funds and for unrelated land fraud. After a short jail sentence, he lapsed into obscurity, to be remembered only for two city streets bearing his middle and last names.[19]

Ross's incompetence was matched by that of State Treasurer George Steel. As the *Journal* was to report, "Steel's relations with the Title Guarantee Boys were very close and they were grabbing everything in sight." Steel was the brother of William M. Ladd's uncle James and had worked closely with old William S. The relationship was so cozy that George never bothered to find out in what accounts the state funds were placed, nor did he bother with such basic essentials as security that was required by statute. He further violated the law by putting the entire state school fund in one bank. Upon investigation it was found that certain state funds went into the bank's active account, making them available for loans. According to the *Journal*, there were "many indications that on some of the bank's loans…heavy rakeoffs were received by individuals connected with the bank."[20]

To make matters worse, when the state's bonding company, American Surety, paid over the sum of $34,009 to reimburse the state for losses incurred in the Oregon Trust and Savings failure, George Steel "promptly plunked the money into the coffers of the Title Guarantee." American Surety was forced to pay double. With revelations of this sort, Governor Chamberlain called for Steel's resignation. The state treasurer had invested $443,819 in the three Portland banks that had failed, three-quarters of it in Ladd and Ross's Title Guarantee & Trust Company.[21]

On December 31, 1907, William M. Ladd publicly offered to assume all credit obligations of the Title Guarantee & Trust Company. As owner of 30 percent of the bank's stock, he had initially announced that he would guarantee payment to cover savings accounts up to a total of $400,000 and that Ladd & Tilton would relinquish the security it held for a claim of $607,000. But, when charged in the press that he must have known of some of Ross's fraudulent transactions and that Ladd & Tilton must have profited from them, he offered to cover everything. His decision cost him not only more than $2.5 million, but control of the Ladd & Tilton Bank.

A Miscast William M. Ladd

William Mead Ladd's life deserves scrutiny. In 1907 he was the ranking leader of Portland's Establishment. Although not a power player by inclination, he had close ties to the power structure within the Portland business-political Establishment. After his graduation from Amherst College, in Massachusetts, he had returned to Portland to help his father manage the family's extensive business enterprises. His first independent venture was as an investor, along with his brother Charles, in several of Jonathan Bourne's mining operations. When W.S. organized the Real Estate Title & Trust Company in 1888, he installed William M. as president. Fulfilling a duty that was incumbent upon a Ladd son, William M. won a seat in the Oregon House in 1889. He had officially launched his career in state Republican politics.

William S. Ladd probably doubted the business abilities of his three sons. Charles had some talent, but liked to fish and hunt. He represented the family on the Port of Portland Commission for many years. The youngest son, John Wesley, was a bit of a scatterbrain who chose to chase women and enliven social gatherings. As a shrewd businessman, William S. Ladd had not been blinded by family loyalty. He knew that the preservation and enhancement of his sizeable holdings depended on the quality of their management, and therefore chose young Theodore B. Wilcox to be his executive assistant and general manager of the extremely profitable Portland Flouring Mills.

When William S. Ladd died in the winter of 1893, William M. became president of Ladd & Tilton, the second-largest bank in Portland, still privately controlled by the Ladd family. He was also to become president of the family-owned Oregon Iron & Steel Company. According to Martin Winch, Wilcox was cut off from everything but Portland Flouring. Apparently Mrs. Ladd and her three sons were jealous of Wilcox, who was a hard-driving and very able administrator. The family considered him an outsider and a threat to their control. At the same time, however, his counsel was required, so that he remained a director of the bank. As Winch wrote to Simeon Reed in June, 1893, William M. Ladd "is not very bright but he needs to rely on Wilcox for advice."[22]

In subsequent years, William M. dedicated himself to some of the worthy causes of Portland life: president of the YMCA, 1895-1922; president of the Art Museum, 1903-1926; treasurer of the Free Bridge Committee, 1891; member of the City Hall Commission, 1896; treasurer of Riverview Cemetery; president of the board of Portland Academy; and trustee of Reed College, 1910-1931. He also served briefly on the Board of Police Commissioners by appointment of Mayor Williams, and as a member of the Water Committee from 1897 until he resigned hastily in October 1905.

On August 30, 1905, William Ladd was accused in court of mishandling the estate of A.H. Johnson, the late owner of the Union Meat Company. At the time of death in 1894, Johnson's estate was valued at $792,000. But he had accumulated debts of $266,000, of which $189,000 was owed to the Ladd & Tilton Bank. Some time before he died, Mr. Johnson had executed a trust deed, turning over to William M. Ladd his property, which, at the time of death, was worth $440,000. Ladd was instructed to sell whatever property was necessary to pay off any existing debts and then to reconvey the remaining property to Johnson's estate for distribution to Johnson's widow and heirs. As it turned out, Johnson's wife predeceased him, and thus the heirs became the sole beneficiaries. All of them were distant relatives, quite poor and widely scattered throughout the country; none lived in or near Portland. In eleven years Ladd had done absolutely nothing to liquidate Johnson's debts. The interest payments to Ladd & Tilton, together with Ladd's executor and trustee fees, had devoured most of the estate. The court ruled that Ladd had "violated the conditions of trust deed." He had allowed his trustee responsibilities to conflict with his personal interest in the business of the bank. A settlement was arranged out of court and the charges were dropped.[23]

By the fall of 1905, William M. Ladd had become a favorite target of the *Oregonian*, in the same way that Mills, Adams and the Gas Company would be singled out the next years. Ladd was a member of the "plutocracy," according to Harvey Scott's unique definition. The "plutocrats" were wealthy Republicans who had provided support for the founding of the *Oregon Journal* in 1902, who had assisted in the sale of the street-railways to eastern bankers, and who dared to vote for a Democrat for public office. Rumor had it that Ladd had endorsed Lane for his first term as mayor.

With glee, on October 18, 1905, the *Oregonian* charged that the Water Committee had accepted an illegal bid of $152,888 from the Oregon Iron and Steel Company because Ladd was both the president of the company and a member of that agency. Oregon Iron and Steel had received over $500,000 in business from the Water Committee since 1894. The company manufactured the only reliable cast-iron pipe in the Northwest. It was more costly than steel pipe but, according to the engineers, it had "better durability." The losing bidders were furious. As one of them remarked, "You might as well look for a snowball in hell as for a square deal here." The next day Ladd resigned from the Water Committee, which, three days later, cancelled all previously submitted bids and readvertised for new ones. The *Oregonian* was jubilant, especially in noting that Mayor Lane, with whom it differed "in almost everything else," gave the paper credit for exposing the apparent conflict of interest.[24]

Ladd's alleged conflicts of interest did not end with the cast-iron pipe episode. In November, 1905, councilman Allan G. Rushlight (who became mayor in 1911) accused Ladd of using his influence with the Water Committee to provide service for his real-estate tracts, to the exclusion of others on the east side that were more deserving in terms of residents' needs. The main Bull Run water conduit ran adjacent to Ladd 's Addition. Rushlight represented Mayor Lane's Ward 7, which included the eastern part of Portland south of Hawthorne Road. As a plumbing contractor, he knew the require-ments of the trade. He singled out Ladd's Addition, which had almost no houses on it and which had been provided with full water-main service before it was platted for sale. He also cited Holladay's Addition, which was being developed by Title Guarantee & Trust. "Hundreds of requests for service have been denied but not these," said Rushlight.[25]

In September, 1906, the *Oregonian* continued its attacks when it headlined: "Ladds are smoked out by exposure." The article related to tax-assessment practices. The previous year, the paper had charged that the Ladd family had enjoyed favored tax treatment for years. The 1906 assessments revealed a sharp increase of more than 220 percent in the total worth of the family's real-estate holdings, to over $1.7 million. Portland Flouring likewise went up, from $150,000 to $1 million, and Security Savings & Trust from $375,150 to $702,000. Public pressure had obviously been effective, and the *Oregonian* received deserved credit for raising the issue initially, even if it did so for Scott's personal reasons rather than public ones.[26]

William M. Ladd was a prototype of the well-educated man of inherited wealth who enjoyed his station in life and fulfilled community responsibilities thrust upon him by virtue of his position in society. Unfortunately he was expected to function successfully in the world of competitive business, which required talents that he did not possess. Unlike Wilcox, he was not concerned with personal power, and rarely exercised directly the resources at his command. Described by his friend William L. Brewster as "a thoughtful, kindly and generous man," the son, like his father, "had a weakness for his own judgment." Some confused his reserve for stuffiness, a characteristic not applicable to his father.[27]

Ladd lived in a world remote from most Portlanders of lesser status. His sister Helen married Henry J. Corbett; his other sister Caroline, married Frederick B. Pratt of Brooklyn, New York, a classmate from Amherst, whose father, Charles Pratt, had been an early associate of John D. Rockefeller in the Standard Oil Company and was the founder of Pratt Institute. Ladd lived comfortably and was one of the first to develop property in the exclusive Rivera (now Dunthorpe) area south of Portland along the Willamette River. It was part of the large tract of wooded land owned by his family's Oregon Iron and Steel Company, the site of the present Tryon Creek State Park.

His influence on important public decisions is hard to evaluate. He could not help but be a force of some significance, because the Ladd & Tilton Bank, with assets of $14.7 million, exerted a major influence on the development of Portland. For years the bank had been the largest purchaser of municipal improvement bonds. By January, 1910, it held over $300,000 worth of Portland Railway Light & Power Company bonds. Ladd & Tilton had a definite interest in the welfare of the company. For a brief spell, at least, Ladd had been a member of Mayor George H. Williams's team. Then he apparently supported Harry Lane, but had broken with the mayor by June, 1906, when Lane fired both him and Wilcox as members of the local San Francisco Relief Committee. A man of genuinely good intentions but of somewhat limited perceptions, William M. Ladd was a symbol of Portland's genteel, respectable and cultured Establishment. As with most of the other members of that body, the major problems facing Portland in 1907 escaped his comprehension.

Major Changes at Ladd & Tilton

For some years, Ladd & Tilton had played a less prominent public role than either the First National or U.S. National banks. As a private institution, it tended to avoid the limelight. Under William S. Ladd's firm hand, it fulfilled one major purpose: to invest its bank resources in and gain control of potentially profitable business enterprises. In 50 years its assets had grown 30,000 percent. With the passage of the Oregon Banking Act in 1907, it was forced, as a private bank, to incorporate and to make its books available to public scrutiny. Beginning with 1908, the corporation records are revealing. Aside from the three Ladd sons and their mother, the major local stockholders were Theodore B. Wilcox; Henry L. Corbett; his mother, Helen Ladd Corbett; and Edward Cookingham, the bank's attorney and vice-president. By 1909 the Pratt family of Brooklyn had gained control by acquiring 5,000 of the 9,000 capital stock shares. For bailing out William M. Ladd to cover his Title Guarantee & Trust losses, the Pratts took possession of his controlling block of stock. At the behest of the Pratts, Cookingham was installed as the chief administrative officer, although his title was only that of vice-president.[28]

The bank's largest single investments were in the Portland Flouring Mills ($2 million) and the Dexter Horton National Bank of Seattle ($1 million). The Portland Flouring Mills holding constituted one-half of the bank's total stock investment. In October, 1910, Ladd & Tilton reduced its holding of $300,000 in Portland Railway Light & Power bonds to $50,000, and bought $338,000 of Portland city improvement bonds. Ladd & Tilton was indeed a profitable institution. The 1908 statement showed a cash surplus of $250,000 and undivided profits for the year of $285,000. In 1910, the combined total was $670,000.

The Ladd & Tilton records reveal how easy it was for insiders like Wilcox to profit richly from confidential information and practically unlimited bank credit. One episode of September, 1911, was probably indicative of practices he had followed for many years. The Portland Flouring Mills and two other Wilcox milling enterprises borrowed $300,000, a sum equal to about 5 percent of the bank's outstanding commercial loans. Wilcox of course was a bank director and a major bank stockholder. And, as noted above, one-half of the bank's own investments were in Portland Flouring. In November, 1914, when wheat prices were escalating worldwide, Wilcox borrowed $800,000, or 10 percent of the bank's commercial loans. There was nothing illegal about these transactions, although they would be expressly prohibited today. On a much smaller scale, Ladd & Tilton was pursuing investment and banking policies similar to those of the New York private banks like J.P. Morgan & Company.

Thus, while William M. Ladd was suffering a decline in fortune, his father's protege, using his father's bank and other resources, was enjoying rapidly increasing wealth. Wilcox was admirably suited to making the most of such opportunities. Following the example of his mentor, he invested his profits in a variety of real-estate packages, including the Rose City Park development. He bought the quarter-block at the southeast corner of Sixth and Washington, on which the Wilcox building was constructed in 1911, for $250,000 in 1908; it was appraised at $675,000 in 1928. He also bought two other downtown parcels in 1908 for $300,000. At a dinner in 1909, railroad magnate James J. Hill praised Wilcox as the one who had "done more than any other man in Portland ... to develop the commerce of the Columbia River." While no doubt exaggerating Wilcox's contribution, Hill had strong reasons for eulogizing his friend, with whom he maintained close business relations for years. Portland Flouring Mills was one of Hill's best Northwest customers, an arrangement that allowed Wilcox to demand and receive illegal rebates on all flour and grain shipments over the Great Northern and Northern Pacific railroads.[29]

The PRL&P Monopoly

The great economic power of a Theodore Wilcox or an Abbot Mills engendered comparable privileges not enjoyed by lesser Portland business leaders. Both were deeply involved in public-utility financing: Mills through majority control of the Portland Gas Company, and Wilcox through Ladd & Tilton's ownership of Portland Railway Company bonds. Both were well aware that utilities, as Carl Harris has noted from Birmingham's experience, "had special vulnerabilities which forced them to engage in continual regulation skirmishes." The immensity of their economic power permitted them to resist such unwanted intrusions. When governmental restrictions seemed burdensome, as Wilcox and Hill viewed federal proscription of rebates, ways were found to skirt the barriers. By their very nature, large public utilities, especially the railroads, exhibited a "public-be-damned" attitude most often associated with the Harriman empire. After the Portland Railway Light & Power Company incorporated on June 29, 1906, it more than matched the Harrimans and Hills in its arrogance toward public authority.[30]

Capitalized as a $15 million holding company, PRL&P took over all Portland Railway properties and those of the Oregon Water Power and Railway Company that had been shifted to Portland Railway a month earlier. The new company's 43 franchises controlled 28 separate street-railway lines covering the entire city. By the end of December, 1907, when it had completed its merger with Portland General Electric, the monopoly comprised 19 companies in control of 161 miles of railway, 431 passenger cars and six power plants. In two years, Abbot Mills's $6 million package had been inflated 250 percent in value. By 1910, the year in which it was cited as a monopoly by the *American Banker*, the company carried 16,712,500 passengers and 5,701,000 ton miles of freight.[31]

In keeping with its eastern ownership, new top management was brought in from Baltimore. Benage Stockwell Josselyn ("B.S.") proved an effective president of the company, at least for his bosses, although toward the City of Portland he recognized few obligations. For the six years that he held sway, he fought the city on every franchise award, bridge-construction project, and street-repair claim. His sole concern as head of a giant public-service corporation was the generation of maximum profits.

Privately, Josselyn lived in a style like some grand nizam of Portland corporate life. For his home, he purchased the former Massachusetts State Building of the Lewis & Clark Exposition, which had been moved section by section to a large tract near Mt. Tabor. By one account, it was an "imposing" and "pretentious residence," with "porticoes" and formal gardens. Being an avid club man, he joined the Arlington and Waverly Golf clubs.[32]

In interest and temperament, two more different people could not be found than B.S. Josselyn and Mayor Harry Lane. For two years Lane was to battle Josselyn and his giant monopoly, but with little success. With Portland banking, business and social leaders like Abbot Mills, Theodore B. Wilcox, Fred V. Holman and Charles F. Swigert, and with a majority of the council lined up in supporting Portland Railway Light & Power, the mayor's chances were limited.

Within a month of its incorporation, the company showed itself a tough negotiator. It refused to meet with the Amalgramated Association of Street and Electric Railway Employees, and a strike was narrowly averted only after the company unilaterally raised wages. In September, 1908, it refused to renegotiate its 30-year Madison Street (Hawthorne) Bridge lease with the city. In previously approving the sale of bonds for a new bridge, the voters had authorized the city to charge the PRL&P a fee of $15,000 a year for use of the new structure. The company referred to the 1891 bridge franchise granted to the Mt. Tabor Street Railway for a $1,200 annual payment. "We insist that our present franchise be not changed," Josselyn declared in a letter to the Executive Board. He admitted that the current payment was low, and indicated a willingness to have it increased "to some extent." But the city could not condemn its tracks; that would amount to "confiscation." The city had no right, he asserted, "to sell bonds before the matter was resolved."[33]

All of Mayor Lane's previously expressed reservations about Portland's "give-away" franchises were clearly illustrated by the case of the 1891 award, in which banker William M. Ladd had played a prominent role as treasurer of the Free Bridge Committee. The franchise ordinance had given the city no authority to change the provisions, and the 30-year limit was ridiculously excessive in terms of unforeseen future requirements. The current city charter, however, did empower the city to renegotiate franchise awards and to take legal action if necessary. Lane's Executive Board ruled that the 1907 charter superseded all previous charter provisions. But the council, under intense pressure from Portland's financial leaders, refused to file suit. A majority of councilmen preferred out-of-court arbitration as a last resort to the uncertainty of trial by a jury of average citizens who might support the interests of the general public. The council finally voted to resubmit the issue to the electorate in June, 1909, and to proceed to consider a new general franchise excluding bridge use.[34]

The company's electric light service was then examined. In the fall of 1906, Mayor Lane had vetoed two franchise awards to Portland General Electric as being excessively generous. He was particularly vexed by the provision that the city had no right to regulate or modify the terms for 25 years. A maximum 2 percent gross revenue tax was fixed in the franchise. He declared: "Irreparable loss has already been suffered by the city for want of such precautions in granting valuable rights to holders of franchises in past times. ... The public is ... groaning under the burdens of excessive charges and inadequate service."[35]

In January, 1909, the mayor again cited the excessive PRL&P's charges for municipal lighting services: "The city is paying more than the service is worth." He refused to pay some of the bills, complaining, "the company is difficult to deal with. ... [It is] an arrogant ... monopoly." Furthermore, the company was demanding higher rates for underground wires, a requirement the council had voted the previous year. Lane suggested that the city consider a municipal plant to provide its public lighting. Although he would prefer to buy power from a competitive private source, none existed in Portland.[36]

The matter of Portland Railway Light & Power Company's new franchise came to a final vote in April, 1909. A number of legal issues had been raised; one related to the use of the company's tracks by Swigert's Pacific Bridge Company. "By what authority," asked councilman Rushlight, "can Portland Railway Light & Power transport freight over the street railways of the city? ... By what authority has the Pacific Bridge Company received exclusive privileges to use the street railways of the city in the performance of public contracts?" No one bothered to answer him.[37]

The council also refused to require a common-user clause as stipulated in the charter. Furthermore, it approved an extremely low rate of compensation payments, beginning with $500 a year. Excluding bridge charges, all the city could expect to receive from a $15 million company over the next 25 years was a total of $20,000.

On April 28, Harry Lane laid down the heaviest barrage of his four years in office. Likening the ordinance to the 1902 "blanket franchise" that Mills had wangled, he declared: "I do not remember ever before having heard of a case where an incorporated municipality so far lost its self-respect as to voluntarily consent to being assessed and taxed by a private corporation which was its own creature." Apart from the provisions already mentioned, the mayor took issue with the company's "guaranteed right to abandon any one of or all 40 streets" any time it wished, "to maroon any line... regardless of the effect of its action on the dependent public." The city had relinquished any authority to prevent such an eventuality. Furthermore, the city was to be required to keep in repair and good condition all switches for PRL&P's use and all elevated roadways and bridges, and to pay 75 percent of the cost. A city that acted in such a fashion, said Lane, that "surrenders its sovereign rights ... is unfit to exist." The council overrode the veto 13-2.[38]

Joe Simon Elected Mayor

In April of 1909, the voters of Portland confronted an approaching mayoralty election. A discouraged Harry Lane had already indicated that he was tired and did not feel up to the physical requirements of running again. The Democratic leadership had decided not to support him even if he changed his mind — which he did at the last moment, running as an Independent Democrat.

Portland business leaders, with the notable exceptions of William M. Ladd and lumberman Winslow B. Ayer, regarded Joseph Simon as someone who could be trusted and who was an integral part of the major corporate complex. Who better than the experienced veteran of many political battles? Since retiring from the U.S. Senate in 1903, Simon had concentrated on his law practice and his downtown investments. As the *Oregon Journal* reported in May, "Every public service corporation president, director, officer and agent is for Simon." Portland, said the *Journal* editorially, "will be scuttled if Simon is elected Mayor."[39]

The *Oregonian* supported Simon in his primary campaign against councilman Allan G. Rushlight, running as an Independent Republican. Simon was picked by the regular Republicans in a party convention that, according to the *Journal*, "was appointed by a handful of manipulators." During the ensuing week, the *Journal* pulled out all of the stops; it printed old editorials and articles from the June, 1886, issues of the *Oregonian* which attacked Simon with a degree of savagery rarely encountered in American journalism. The Journal headlined its May 7 editions, "Boss Rule or Rule by the People—Which?" Two days later Simon defeated Rushlight in a light primary vote that saw an overwhelming turnout from the west side and the North End. Judge M.G. Munly secured the Democratic nomination.[40]

Banker Abbot Mills was a strong supporter of Joe Simon. The Dolph, Simon firm was handling the legal affairs of the Gas Company, particularly those that related to the forthcoming sale of the company to eastern investors. In fact, the election entered subtly into some of the pre-conditions of sale. Throughout the spring, Augustus White wrote Mills that the company's current earnings were not attractive for the price being asked. "New York can't understand why, with the growth of the gas system, the company does not show better earnings." Mills replied that no price change could be contemplated before the election. "We hope that Simon will be elected. ... We can't afford to embarrass Simon."[41]

Mills had little to fear. Simon easily won his return to political office. In a light turnout, the Republicans swept to victory on June 7, 1909, carrying all the municipal offices. Over 20,000 voters had chosen no to go to the polls. The Establishment was back in command after a four-year exile. As the conservative *Spectator* gleefully commented, "The city's affairs [would now be] conducted in a businesslike way." The election result was a "protest against the skyrocketing, fussy-wussy administration that Portland has had for a few years."[42]

Simon's election was less a protest against the Lane administration than a result of other local political circumstances. Simon possessed strong name familiarity, near unanimous support from local Republicans, and strong financial backing from the Portland Establishment (with some exceptions). The local Democratic forces were now split, in part because of Lane's disregard of partisan organization and the importance of loyal party workers at the precinct levels. Lack of support from party leadership, which ran the relatively unknown Judge Munly, severely hampered Lane's belated reelection bid. That nearly 20,000 fewer voters turned out than in 1907, indicated little enthusiasm for either candidate.

Portland's experience did not follow the national trend of resurging conservatism at the local level in 1909, as reported by Richard L. McCormick. The passions of the earlier years (1905-1906), resulting from the discovery that business corrupts politics, reached new heights in the 1909 municipal election. Thirty-two measures were placed on the ballot by initiative; among those receiving overwhelming approval were several regulating public utilities. New franchises were to be subject to popular vote; no territorial or side-track franchises could be issued to a railroad extending the term of the company's original franchise; the articles of every public-utility franchise application were to be specifically set forth and to include a 25-year maximum term and fair compensation to the city; quarterly reports were to be submitted to the auditor with a $500 fine for failure to comply; and franchised property was to be subject to county property taxes. Lane could well take credit for many of these proposals, which he had advocated for four years. The popular will had spoken through the initiative, and the mayor's bitter struggle against city councils dominated by well-financed special interests had been vindicated.[43]

The popular will had also prevailed four months earlier, when the legislature was faced with selecting a new U.S. senator to replace Charles W. Fulton, whose reputation had been tarnished by the timber fraud trials and his strong support of Senator Mitchell.

George E. Chamberlain, the popular Democratic governor, opposed the Republican candidate Harold M. Cake, a prominent Portland attorney and officer of the Equitable Savings & Loan Association. Cake's campaign suffered from a split state party, wounded by the stigma of the trials, although Cake himself was not in any way identified with the lumber interests. Following the requirements of "Statement No. 1," by which legislative candidates agreed to support the popular choice in the 1908 preferential primary, the heavily Republican legislature reluctantly elected Chamberlain by a solid majority.

A number of other significant measures were approved in June, 1909. A new Broadway Bridge was authorized; a 7 percent limitation was placed on bonded indebtedness and a 6 percent limit on taxes; authority was granted to levy a 1 percent tax for a special bridge fund and a one-half percent tax for a much needed sinking fund; bonds were authorized for parks and boulevards ($1 million), docks ($500,000), and the Broadway Bridge ($450,000). These efforts won general support from business leaders, led by John C. Ainsworth. Such capital improvements were deemed essential for an orderly growth of the expanding city. The Broadway Bridge was expected to stimulate economic development in Northwest and Northeast Portland and to provide easier access to the downtown for the burgeoning east-side population.[44]

Lane Bows Out

When Harry Lane left office on June 30, 1909, he received predictably contrary evaluations. The *Oregonian* blistered him, while the *Journal* praised him for leaving Portland "a clean city." Lane, wrote the *Journal*, was a man "of great integrity" who had no political machine ties whatsoever. He did not accomplish much in a material sense, nor was he a great builder of brick and mortar structures. In some ways he was a failure in tangible political and administrative terms. But he was a positive leader, who was not afraid to tell the people the truth as he saw it. He did not flinch from trying to lead the people in directions that he believed were important and necessary for the city's future survival. He was more concerned with human than material values, with "software" rather than hardware. In George Chamberlain's judgment, "He opened the closed eyes of the public to what was going on. ...Without a Lane, Portland might still be in the mire of those rotten times."[45]

The Lane-Simon differences in 1909 were deeply pronounced. They were men with antithetical backgrounds, professions, temperaments and interests. Simon's appointments to the Water and Executive boards were entirely from the Establishment, leaders of the Portland business-financial-social community. U.S. Bank President John C. Ainsworth and Theodore B. Wilcox were named to the Water Board with Wilcox as chairman, and Henry L. (Harry) Corbett, the 26-year-old manager of the Corbett Estate, was appointed to the Executive Board, which was composed entirely of businessmen.

The four newly elected members of the council were a wealthy realtor-contractor, a lawyer, a wealthy grain executive and Thomas C. Devlin the former auditor. Pacific Grain President Gay Lombard was the only councilman to be a member of an exclusive club, in this case Waverly. On the Executive Board, however, were four Waverly Club members, two of whom were also members of the Arlington. Abbot Mills was offered a position on the Executive Board, but declined in favor of his young associate Harry Corbett, who at the time was vice-president of the First National Bank among his many other varied commitments. The Port of Portland Commission, whose members were appointed by the legislature, was the blue ribbon business panel of 1909. Headed by Charles F. Swigert, with Gasco's Charles F. Adams as treasurer, the group included John C. Ainsworth and former Chamber President William D. Wheelwright.

Mayor Joseph Simon's term of office would be safe for the Portland business community. Downtown Portland was back in control. In his first major message to the council in October, Simon reassured his supporters when he stated: "The functions of city government relate almost wholly to business and little to politics. Modern business methods should be applied to their execution," and the departments of government "kept within appropriate limits."[46]

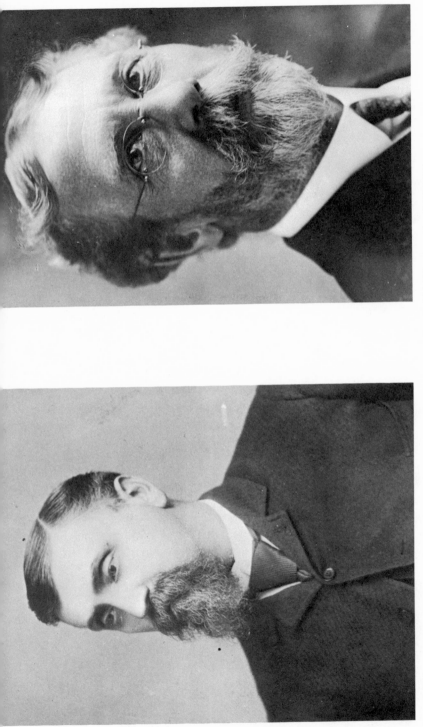

20.2 J. Thorburn Ross (1858-1957)

20.1 George A. Steel (1846-1918)

20.4 Theodore B. Wilcox (1856-1918)

20.3 William M. Ladd (1856-1931)

20.5 Portland Railway Light and Power Co. streetcar, S.W. Washington, east from Sixth

20.6 S.W. Third and Oak streets, 1910, including Lewis Building

20.7 *Oregonian* anti-gas company cartoon, 1906

20.8 *Oregonian* anti-franchise cartoon, 1906

21

THE PORTLAND ESTABLISHMENT AND PROGRESSIVE REFORM: 1910-1913

Mayor Simon's Program

The new mayor was the most experienced political professional in Oregon. A master of the art of compromise, Joe Simon was thoroughly versed in the techniques of self-promotion and public relations. After only six months in office, he was given a glowing evaluation by the *Oregonian* and the heartiest of congratulations from Portland's business leadership.[1]

Simon later boasted of five accomplishments for which he particularly wanted to be remembered: the establishment of a "hard surface" street paving policy (concrete over asphalt); the decision to build a new garbage incinerator at the old Guild's Lake site; the promotion of underground utility wires; the expansion of the Bull Run pipeline; and the purchase and location of parks for additional children's playgrounds. The *Oregonian* praised his efforts to clean up the waterfront, his initiative in lowering the property-tax levy, his promotion of a City Beautiful fund, his sponsorship of a huge new reservoir and park at Mt. Tabor, and his success in abolishing the red-light district in Northwest Portland by eliminating restricted sections for such activities. A few months after its earlier accolade, the *Oregonian* noted, "Vice can never be extirpated, but at Portland it is held now under closest possible restraint."[2]

Except for sponsoring the City Beautiful fund and moving to reduce the tax rate (an action that did not really lower the dollar amount paid because of rapidly increasing assessment values), by and large Simon was simply carrying out programs already approved by the voters. The park-acquisition program had, in fact, moved slowly. Two hundred acres in six months seemed a huge amount compared with the city's previous park acreage, but the voters had authorized a much larger increase to be effected rapidly before the available sites were gobbled up by speculators. With the Park Board, Simon negotiated donations of park property, which included enough parcels of land to begin the Hillside Parkway, a 200-to-400 foot wide strip from Fulton Park on the south to the base of Marquam Hill on the north — part of the current Terwilliger Boulevard. Beginning in January, 1911, the council authorized the mayor to negotiate further with the Oregon Railway & Navigation Company to acquire an additional 65 acres, which would connect South Portland to the Hillside Parkway. This parcel of land near the present Duniway Park, was part of a much larger tract acquired by Henry

Villard in the early 1880s. The construction of a three-mile stretch of the parkway constituted a first step toward fulfilling one of the many recommendations made by John Olmsted in 1903. The project won hearty approval from the mayor, who observed that it showed his "friendly attitude toward the beautifying of our already beautiful city."[3]

The City Beautiful

When Simon and Jonathan Bourne, Jr., successfully created a City Beautiful fund in November, 1909, Portland belatedly embraced the national movement ensuing from the 1893 Columbian Exhibition in Chicago. As Carl Abbott has noted: "The City Beautiful impulse...was an effort to make cities impressive, inspiring and imperial." Portland's movement had been launched by the *Oregon Journal*, John C. Ainsworth, and Park Board Chairman Thomas Lamb Eliot in 1906, to bring he city "into step with the themes of city planning that were transforming major cities from coast to coast." It was a natural undertaking for the mayor and U.S. Senator Bourne (elected in 1907), both veteran political warriors and Establishment members. Like American urban park policy generally, the City Beautiful movement was "a top-down matter," according to Galen Cranz. It appealed to "a social and economic elite, men with considerable power and influence. ... When businessmen...promoted the economic, political, and moral welfare of the city as a whole, their actions had a philanthropic cast. ... The City Beautiful movement embraced economic relationales in order to legitimate many of its goals."[4]

The City Beautiful fund was first proposed at an early organizational meeting of the Civic Improvement League in October, 1909. Within a month, well over half the $20,000 goal had been raised by private subscription, and at its formal organization in December, held at the Commercial Club, the league assumed responsibility for the rest. Simon and Bourne gave full support to the effort, aimed at hiring a leading city planner "to build on the Olmsted report" by "making a comprehensive plan for the building of a civic center and making Portland a ideal city." Included among the $500 contributors were Bourne, Charles F. Adams, Ainsworth, Rodney L. Glisan, Mrs. George F. Lewis, Henry L. Corbett, Walter F. Burrell, Charles F. Swigert, William Killingsworth, the Portland Lumber Company, the Portland Railway Light & Power Company, and Theodore B. Wilcox. Among the $250 contributors were brewer Paul Wessinger, architect Ellis Lawrence and grain broker Gay Lombard. Additional support came from the *Oregon Journal* and the *Oregonian*. The 100 or so contributors constituted Portland's more prominent bankers, shippers, realtors, architects, and publishers, and executives of lumber, construction and utility companies.[5]

Bourne wanted to hire Daniel Burnham of Chicago, the architect of the Columbian Exposition, who had recently been redesigning Washington, D.C., where Bourne had come to know him. When Burnham was unable to accept the commission, the league hired his associate Edward H. Bennett, who was instructed to submit his final proposal by the spring of 1911. Bennett's approach was to give primary attention to the Willamette River frontage and harbor facilities.[6]

Public Docks and Rights-of-Way

When voters approved the sale of $500,000 in dock bonds in June, 1909, they were responding to the dilapidated conditions of the central waterfront. Shippers were beginning to move down river to expanded space and rail connections. What concerned the *Oregon Journal* and other proponents of public docks was that the new private docks and other profitable operating facilities were largely controlled by the railroads. To Simon, who had opposed the dock initiative, it was one thing to clean out old private docks at public expense, but quite another to build public docks that would compete with the new privately owned ones. On May 25, 1910, he vetoed a council ordinance that would have authorized the bond sale, and the council sustained his action. While the *Oregon Journal* was incensed, the *Oregonian* applauded: "Every city should leave to private enterprise the active industries, on which development depends," otherwise "waste, corruption and politics will result." The veteran OR&N lawyer and mayor had no intention of threatening the status quo. The railroad, after all, owned six miles of waterfront, split almost evenly between the west and east sides of the Willamette.[7]

The veto unexpectedly provoked both the chamber of commerce and the Taxpayers League to study waterfront ownership. They were aided by evidence in a widely publicized Federal Commissioner of Corporations report that the railroads largely controlled the nation's water terminals to the disadvantage of water traffic generally. Of the 50 foremost ports, there were 21 "in which railroad ownership and occupancy" covered over 50 percent of the active frontage. The only ports where considerable public control existed were New Orleans, San Francisco, Baltimore, and New York. The commissioner found Portland to have adequate wharf space in fair condition, but no public city dock. All of Portland's frontage was privately owned, almost entirely by the railroads. Attorney Joseph N. Teal, the wealthy son-in-law of former Mayor David P. Thompson and a strong advocate of public docks, also submitted a report to the chamber showing that all the docks in working order were owned by the railroads, including dock space used by large industry.[8]

Teal rallied a variety of interest groups, including the chamber of commerce, to sponsor an initiative charter amendment on the ballot of November, 1910. Aimed at increasing water traffic, the measure provided for the establishment of the Portland Commission of Public Docks. It authorized the commission, not the council, to levy taxes and execute the sale of $2.5 million worth of bonds, five times the original authorization opposed by Simon. The funds were to be used for dock construction, a belt-line railway, and the repurchase of portions of the original levee. The public overwhelmingly voiced its approval.[9]

When Simon vetoed the dock bond sale, the mayor proudly announced a tentative agreement negotiated with the OR&N and Northern Pacific Terminal companies over the eastern approach ramps for the Broadway and new Steel bridges. He had engineered a trade whereby the Harriman lines would give up some existing trackage in exchange for 14 street vacancies that the railroad had long wanted. He also indicated that the OR&N would probably be willing to sell some of its South Portland land to the city for the Hillside Parkway at one-half the appraised value. The council approved the arrangements, as well as additional street vacancies for Harriman's Oregon & California line on East First and Second streets.

Over the next month the public reacted strongly against what the *Oregon Journal* called "this blunder." The *Journal* charged that the railroad was going ahead "with the Steel Bridge ramp foundation on the east side before completion of a formal agreement and in spite of the protests of thousands for an initiative election." Petitions were already circulating that would place the issue on the ballot of June, 1911, but the city attorney refused to issue a formal complaint against the company. Oregon and Adams streets had already been vacated to the railroad by June 14. Five days later, the *Journal* editorialized: "The city affairs of Portland are becoming badly muddled. The stormiest days of Mayor Lane did not approximate the controversies and disturbances of the government in these days of Simon."[10]

The paper's strong dislike of the mayor often inflamed its editorials. The "controversies and disturbances" of Lane's administration were clearly unlike those of Simon's, especially in the degree of bitterness expressed. Lane fought the council on behalf of the public interest (as he defined it), while Simon, with council support, was accused of thwarting the public will. The increasing resort to the initiative process reflected a growing distrust of established governmental institutions at both state and local levels. In November, 1910, for example, Oregon's voters were deluged with 32 initiated and referred measures. *Journal* Publisher C.S. Jackson expressed concern at the number when he warned, "The way to make direct legislation enduring is to employ it with discretion."[11]

The *Journal*, which endorsed most local initiatives despite Jackson's caveat, repeatedly charged that Simon's dealings would harm the city's public dock potential. "The railroads control North Portland. ... The Oregon Railway and Navigation Co. gets the best of the deal by far." The city had agreed to vacate the ends of 14 valuable streets to the OR&N for both its new Steel Bridge ramps and some additional freight-yard space, while the company in turn had only to move a small section of double track to make room for the city's Broadway Bridge ramps. "Condemnation is the preferred route," said the *Journal*, "not exchange."[12]

The *Journal* reported that the east side was angry with Simon over his negotiations and compromises, which were viewed as devices for exchanging east-side rights for benefits to west-side residents. The east-side riverfront was being traded away for west-side park land. The reaction "paid-off" in June, 1911, when voters, by almost 2-1, approved an initiative charter amendment that prohibited future street vacations within 2,000 feet of the waterfront and 1,000 feet of a terminal yard. City approval of any other vacations would require a three-fourths vote of the council and the signature of the mayor. In commenting on the fact that the city had already given away much of the property named in the amendment, one prominent political scientist labeled the action "belated — locking the door after the cow's left."[13]

Oswald West Becomes Governor

Simon's troubles, augmented by his growing unpopularity, injured the local Republican party. Statewide, the party machine was "virtually shipwrecked" by 1910, as *McClure's Magazine* reporter Burton J. Hendrick later commented. "The whole state

was strewn with political cadavers." There were still some smoldering fires of opposition to the Oregon System — those who still believed that the old order could be
restored. "Not inappropriately, Harvey Scott came forth as the spokesman" of the
malcontents. "The Republicans of Oregon," said his *Oregonian*, "intend to repudiate
'Statement No. 1'" (whereby the legislative candidate was expected to support the
popular choice of a primary vote). Scott's group supposedly proposed a long-range
campaign to convene a state constitutional convention to abolish the direct primary,
the initiative and the referendum. Direct democracy had corroded effective party
unity, with the Republicans suffering the most damage.[14]

Reportedly joining Scott were the Harriman and Hill interests, the Portland Railway
Light & Power Company, and the Gas Company. That Abbot Mills acquiesced in Scott's
effort less than three years after the *Oregonian*'s editor had viciously attacked his gas
company, revealed the overriding importance Mills attached to traditional Republican
party principles and loyalties. Joining Mills were former Mayor Henry S. Rowe,
Franklin T. Griffith (who would become president of the PRL&P in 1913), and Judge
M.C. George, a veteran conservative party stalwart and former congressman. Mayor
Simon, a close ally of Mills through his directorship of the Security Savings & Trust
Company, gave tacit support.[15]

The strategy called for the convening of local assemblies all over the state at which
the various legislative candidates could be chosen. They would still have to run in the
direct primary, but would carry the strong support of the party's high command.
According to Hendrick, just before the meeting of the Multnomah County Republican
Assembly, "one of the public-utility law offices of Portland held a meeting, where the
local slate was fixed and 'slipped' to the bosses in control."[16]

The State Assembly that followed in Portland was, in Hendrick's words, "a museum
of political antiquities. ... All the old political war-horses whom the voters had
repudiated ... occupied the front benches on the stage. The legislative agents of the
corporations had favored positions and regularly led the applause." The enthusiasm
reached its highest pitch when the candidate for governor, Jay Bowerman, was
escorted to the platform where he accepted his role to lead Oregon's "return to
representative government."[17]

As the assembly disbanded and proceeded into the street for a parade, one of the
most interested spectators was "a tall, boyish figure, leaning in the darkness against a
telegraph pole." Thirty-seven-year-old Oswald West was bemused by what he saw.
Many of the faces were familiar. As a teller in the Ladd & Bush Bank in Salem in 1897, he
had deposited much of the cash that changed hands between the bosses, the lobbyists
and the legislators. As a respected member of the state railroad commission, West
dreamed of following his mentor, George Chamberlain, into the governor's office.
Later, he reminisced, "I decided to become a candidate myself." After ascertaining that
his friend Harry Lane would not run, West caught an early train for Salem, "borrowed
the required filing fee ... , and thus became a Democratic candidate for Governor."[18]

Without money, influential friends, or a political machine, and as a Democrat in an
overwhelmingly Republican state, West's chances appeared slim. In what turned out to
be a stroke of genius, he sent a personal letter to 15,000 of the 20,000 registered
Oregon Democrats. From the responses, he put together groups of enthusiastic
workers from throughout the state. This was the West machine. Easily obtaining the

Democratic nomination, he spent the next few months travelling to the far corners of the state. He was already fairly well known in many of the rural sections from driving cattle and sheep down the valley and through Eastern Oregon as a young man. His four years as state land agent (1903-1907) had further extended his circle of friendships. He concentrated on meeting people, limiting himself to only a few formal speeches. To win, he obviously had to count on the cross-over vote of a number of Republicans. Senator Jonathan Bourne, Jr., returned from Washington, D.C., to help rally the progressive Republicans to West's support. The old guard leadership never forgave him. (Two years later, with help from Bowerman and his old crony Joe Simon, the party regulars defeated Bourne's effort to gain renomination.)

Early in August, 1910, Harvey W. Scott died halfway through his 72nd year. This event was an omen for the Republican cause, which fell into further disarray. West received an overwhelming popular mandate — a victory that cost him less than $3,000. While the Democrats relished their success, West knew he had won because of his personal, nonpartisan appeal to voters, in a campaign that relied little on the traditional party machinery. His nomination and subsequent election were a result of the direct primary system, which Mills and the conservative Republicans had rightly feared. When West entered the governor's office in January, 1911, progressive reform became firmly implanted at Salem.

Simon: Defender of Private Interests

Mayor Simon appeared in good spirits early in January as he delivered his annual report to the council. He was not only the sole survivor of the old rough-and-ready school of Republican party politics, but he was the mayor of a city enjoying vigorous economic growth. Nearing the age of 60, he was beginning to mellow, less driven than he had been a decade earlier. He no longer thrived on controversy. Compromise was preferable to litigation. As the grand old man of the state Republican party, he preferred the patriarch's role. He not only knew how things should be done, but *what* should be done.

Simon presented the council with a glowing report on the state of the city, which, he claimed, was experiencing a "period of great prosperity and health." In many ways he was right. The city's population of 212,290 had grown an encouraging 8 percent since he entered office. Economically, Portland was the second-ranked American city in wheat exports after New York. Within two years, it would achieve fourth ranking in total exports. Lumber manufacturing and shipping was its largest wealth producer in revenues generated by one industry. In 1910, one-third of the more than 700 million board feet cut in the region went by ship to foreign markets, one-third by rail to California and the east, and one-third to the local market. Of the city's more than 2,200 manufacturing establishments, 713 were related to wood products. Most large lumber shippers, like the Eastern and Western's Winslow B. Ayer, expected to benefit from the construction of public docks, even though he and some others owned their own facilities. Certainly for the general economy, and for some companies, public docks were to prove a blessing. In continuing to oppose their construction (as a perceived threat to railroad interests), Simon always justified his public position by repeating his aversion to excessive pubic debt.[19]

This theme constituted the second part of Simon's council address. While extolling the growth of Portland's private economy, he warned of the "need to economize in public expenditures." The city's accumulated bonded indebtedness (largely for bridges, parks and streets) totalled $8,875,000. (Revenue producing improvement bonds, like those for sewers and the water system, were not included.) While professing concern for the size of the bonded indebtedness, he overlooked the fact that it constituted only 3 percent of the assessed value of property in 1910, well below the city charter limitation of 7 percent. Like Mills and most other Portland business leaders, he opposed increasing taxes either to pay the full cost of some of the projects initially or to accelerate the rate of amortization of the existing debts. Meanwhile, the banks and investment houses made handsome profits from city bond issues, and Portland was soon forced to economize on basic city services. Such were to be the consequences of Simon's application of "modern business methods...to the depart- ments of government."[20]

Generally when the mayor was empowered by the council to resolve a conflict between a private corporation and the city, Simon favored the private interests as the "businesslike" approach. One such transaction involved the Portland Railway Light & Power Company and the old Madison Street Bridge franchise granted to James Steel's Mt. Tabor Street Railway Company. When the PRL&P acquired the railway properties, it argued that the terms of the old franchise—$100 per month—should be transferred to its replacement, the new Hawthorne Bridge. Reflecting its increasing arrogance, the company refused to negotiate a new contract, despite an initiated ordinance requiring an annual fee of $15,000. Authorized by the council to make a deal, Simon allowed Portland Railway Light & Power to continue paying the old rate of $1,200 a year. The council ordinance approving the arrangement allowed the city, at its own expense, to sue the company for the additional $13,800, an action that took two years to consummate.[21]

Another example of Simon's compromising of the city's interests involved a lighting contract that called for certain unmet requirements. Mayor Lane had withheld a $29,000 payment until the terms were fulfilled. Simon instructed the city to pay the utility $20,000 before any of the changes were made. In another case, involving the ill- fated Brooklyn sewer in Southeast Portland, Lane had refused to accept the completed job, as the stone bottom had been laid in dirt rather than concrete. Simon accepted the project on grounds of pubic necessity, and Charles Swigert's Pacific Bridge Company was promptly paid. The city was to endure years of costly repairs as the bottom washed away with regularity.[22]

The Portland Municipal Association, largely composed of younger professionals who monitored public behavior closely, leveled equally serious charges against prevailing vice activities. It cited 98 houses of prostitution that were doing a booming business. After his indictment by the grand jury for malfeasance in office, Chief of Police A.M. Cox denied any responsibility. He said he was "a victim of circumstances," that the decision was made "higher up." The association blamed Simon for knowingly appointing a man with a record of ignoring vice.[23]

By mid-May, 1911, Simon decided to seek reelection as an Independent Republican. Veteran Councilman Allan G. Rushlight had already been assured support from the regular Republicans, and won the primary easily. The remnants of the old Harvey Scott group, west-siders like Mills, Charles F. Beebe, and Henry S. Rowe came out for Simon. The *Oregonian* strongly endorsed him, citing Rushlight as the "minority candidate without business support." In the elections of June 5, Simon was retired for good, by almost 2-1. The Democratic candidate ran a poor third.[24]

The election was significant apart from Simon's forced departure from public life after 34 years. The voters approved a number of long-debated measures, including a charter amendment prohibiting street vacations on the waterfront, the establishment of a municipal garbage-collection system, the construction of both a new city jail (at Southwest Second and Oak streets) and the city's first public auditorium, the regulation of billboards, and the application of a 3 percent tax on the gross receipts from the sale of gas and electricity. The voters rejected the purchase of Council Crest for a city park, a municipal paving plant, and the establishment of a municipal public-service commission to regulate utilities.[25]

When given the opportunity, through the initiative, to vote on specific issues, each with its own price tag, the electorate showed discerning judgment. The weight of public opinion now recognized, ahead of Portland's elected officials, that a larger degree of "centralization, bureaucratization, and government actions," in the words of Richard McCormick, were legitimate ways to "adjust" interest-group differences and meet the needs of an expanding city. Young business and professional reform-minded leaders, increasingly supported by the chamber of commerce, tended to identify their concerns with the whole city, or with a public interest that they defined. The need for functional centralization began to override geographic loyalties and neighborhood ties — the traditional bases of support of ward-elected city councils, which generally opposed such moves. In rejecting the purchase of Council Crest for a city park (supported by west-side resident Mayor Simon), the majority of voters, living on the east side, most likely questioned an acquisition designed primarily to benefit wealthier West Hills neighborhoods.[26]

Rejection of the city public service commission initiative was more complicated. At the legislative session four months earlier, the Malarkey bill to place all public service companies under the regulation of the Railroad Commission had carried by large majorities. Portland supporters of a city public service commission attacked the bill, which they charged as weakened by the omission of key portions of both the Wisconsin and New York laws upon which it was supposedly modeled. East-side proponents wanted "home rule" over all local utility operations, especially since the gas company had been sold in 1910 to American Power & Light, a subsidiary of the giant New York-based Electric Bond & Share Company. Like the railroads, Portland's two largest utilities were controlled by eastern investors and bankers. After putting the Portland measure on the ballot, proponents unexpectedly drew the combined opposition of the *Oregonian* and the *Journal* — one of the rare occasions when the rivals agreed. The *Oregonian* wrote, "It will give them a commission that will not have sufficient scope of jurisdiction to correct the evils of excessive rates and inferior service."[27]

In 1911 nine new members were elected to the city council, but it varied little in composition and character from its predecessors, except that it included four realtors — twice as many as previously. The dominant figure was Republican theater owner-manager George L. Baker, who retained the position of council president. The appointments to the Executive Board were from the same mid-level stratum of business and commercial interests as the mayor, with no representatives of the Portland Establishment. For the first time, two representatives of organized labor — the longshoremen and railway workers — were invited to participate in the higher levels of city government. The loss of official political and social contact with City Hall gravely concerned business leaders like Ainsworth, who began to question the viability of the mayor-council form of government.

Mayor Rushlight's Tribulations

As during previous administrations, the divisive saloon issue continued to plague City Hall. Mayor Rushlight, a bland but dedicated public servant, opened his message to the council with a call for harmony and cooperation. "We must," he said "gauge all our acts by what is best for the city." Unfortunately for the mayor, within a month of assuming office he faced demands for an official vice investigation. Under the editorship of Edgar Piper, Harvey Scott's more moderate successor, the *Oregonian* complained: "The trains are loaded with gamblers, macquereaux, touts, pimps, confidence men, common women ... who have heard that the town is wide open, the pastures are green, and the feeding good." On August 23, 1911, the council passed an ordinance authorizing the mayor to appoint a commission of inquiry. Within hours, Rushlight created the 15-member Vice Commission of the City of Portland, headed by the Reverend Henry R. Talbott of St. David's Episcopal Church and including three other ministers and four doctors. Almost immediately the good citizens, armed with badges of authority, as distinct from earlier privately conducted investigations, proceeded about their work, block by bock, building by building, in quest of evidence.[28]

Not much was heard about the quiet activities of the Reverend Talbott and his cohorts until they presented the council with their first report the following January. It was the briefest of the three that they would make over the period of a year, and its initial findings related largely to the incidence of venereal disease — 21 percent of the total reported diseases in the city. There were 1,360 new cases in October alone. The commission believed the figures to be low as only one-third of the doctors had responded. The commission noted that the city had no public facility to handle the problem. Since neither the mayor nor the council felt any need for urgent action, the report was filed away.[29]

On August 20, 1912, Governor Oswald West announced from Salem, "I am going to clean up Portland next." He had just concluded successful anti-vice campaigns in Redmond and Huntington. Mayor Rushlight responded, "I have no knowledge of any conditions in Portland that require cleaning up by the Governor ... but I will assist him." Two days later, the vice commission published its second report and the police raided 13 establishments in the downtown and North End. The following day West swept into Portland "to wage relentless war upon vice," as the *Journal* proclaimed. The Portland *Daily News* gave the action big play: "Maybe you thought this a clean town; say, read this."[30]

Restirring the popular "consciousness of wrongdoing," West exclaimed on August 24, "I will clean the city or quit my job." He appointed young attorney Walter H. Evans as special prosecutor and all candidates for the 1912 sheriff's election as special agents.

He said: "There is a great deal of property held by people of means that is rented for houses of prostitution. ... That property is held by corporations organized for the purpose of covering up the real ownership. ...I am going to take steps to take away the charters and dissolve such corporations at once." The *Journal* editorialized: "The secret and silent gentlemen who buy automobiles and mansions from the tainted profits of the underworld...are the ramparts of the system." The profits were indeed great, as the commission discovered. The owners of properties given over to vice could count on investment returns of between 84 and 540 percent. One owner invested $10,000 and made $5,400 the first year. A $250 fine was no deterrence.[31]

The *Oregonian* counseled readers to "face the facts—reality:...Social vice is a large and powerful business, and that it exists and spreads is because it pays heavy profits." Anti-vice laws prove little, said Editor Edgar Piper; all they lead to "is the propagation of more vice by increasing its profits. ... Bad as we are, we are no worse than our neighbors." The *Oregonian* seemed to take delight in one of the Report's observations "that a person might stand on the roof of one of the principal churches of the city and throw a stone into any one of 14 places, 10 of which are wholly immoral." Neither amused nor excited, Mayor Rushlight suggested that perhaps the best solution might be for the city to establish "a restricted district for prostitution activities." This pronouncement did little to endear the mayor to the governor.[32]

Report of the Vice Commission

The vice commission's final *Report*, concluding a nine month examination, cited 431 properties "wholly given up to immorality." The commission drew a map and located each establishment with an appropriate circle or square to designate the type of activity. In an attempt to protect the names and reputations of the property owners, the map did not identify the streets. The commission later destroyed its files so that no one could ever be certain who had owned what. According to Fred Merrill, the map caused apoplexy in some and a good deal of mirth in others. One eager observer was pleased to see from his calculations that the Union Station did not appear. Another was relieved to know that none of the girls had taken up residence on the river bridges.[33]

The property owners came from the highest stratum of the Portland Establishment, with Waverly, Arlington and Concordia club members well represented. To the *Oregon Journal*, an examination of the police records revealed the ineffectiveness of raids and arrests; the entrenched power was too strong. The business-political leadership had closed its eyes to the problem, collected its profits and prevented any effective reform. As Governor West declared, "The real prostitutes I am after in Portland are the prostitutes in office" — referring not only to political but corporate office. He blamed the investors, whose sole concern was with money. Greed and vice went hand in hand, he asserted, even for those who attended church regularly on Sunday mornings.

The *Oregon Journal* wrote, perhaps over-simplistically, that the real issue "is the struggle between two systems of government. It is a contest which has been in every city since the beginning. ...One system holds that the law means what it says and says what it means, the other system holds that the law is only to be enforced sometimes."

The same double standard that was applied to matters of private and public interest in business and political affairs was also applied to matters of private and public morality.[34]

PARTIAL LIST OF PROPERTY OWNERS FROM THE 1912
VICE REPORT
(Identified from a reconstructed map in
The Shaping of a City, by E. Kimbark MacColl)

BANKS OWNING OR MANAGING PROPERTY IN THEIR NAMES:
Security Savings & Trust, C.F. Adams, Pres., Mills and Simon, directors.
Hibernia Savings Bank, Dr. A.C. Smith, Lansing Stout, officers.

ESTATES MANAGED BY BANKS:

FAILING	)
CORBETT	)
REED, S.G.	) FIRST NATIONAL BANK
DOLPH, J.N.	)
THOMPSON, R.R.	)

KAMM	)
THOMPSON, D.P.	) U.S. NATIONAL BANK
WEINHARD	)

SMALL TRUST AND INVESTMENT COMPANIES:
Union Trust Investment Co. Wm. MacMaster
General Investment
Beaver Investment
Beck Investment Co.
Nichols Investment Co.
J.C. Ainsworth Co.

REALTY FIRMS:
Fliedner, Morgan & Boyce
Columbia Realty, W.L. Morgan

PROMINENT FAMILY NAMES:

Alisky	Cardwell	Woodward, T.
Cardinell	Harrington	Hawkins, W.J.
Durkheimer	Nicolai	Dolph, C.A.
Hirsch, J.	Fried	Blyth
Warren, F.M.	Blumauer	Spencer
Therkelson	Wemme	Wilson, C.C.
Leadbetter	Watson, J.F.	Ainsworth
Cook, J.W.	Bates	Glisan
Holman, J.	Holbrook	Teal
Ralston	Seller	Henry
	Mayer	Sinnott

West also took aim at the breweries supplying the saloons that served prostitutes and their clients on the floors above them. Liquor was brought to the rooms and sold to customers at a tidy profit. Beer was especially popular, at $1 a bottle. Breweries like Weinhard's, which owned a number of saloons, were charged as accessories and promoters of vice. The governor accused the breweries of running the city. At least, he declared, "Weinhard's brewery won't rule the state of Oregon. ...There isn't a brick in the brewery down here that doesn't represent a broken heart." As the son of an alcoholic father, West's strong aversion to liquor was rooted in painful episodes from his youth. "The Governor may not be able to rid Portland of her jungle," the *Journal* editorialized, "but Oregon will for a time have more officials on the jump than in many a long year." On his return to Salem, West vowed to seek a statewide prostitution-abatement law from the 1913 legislature.[35]

Early in October the council began heated debate on two ordinances that had been strongly recommended by the vice commission. The "Tin-Plate Law" would require owners of hotel, rooming and lodging houses and saloons to maintain a conspicuous plate or sign with the owner's name and address. For non-compliance, a fine of up to $100 a day could be assessed. The second ordinance was designed to regulate hotels, rooming and lodging houses, by requiring a business permit and the posting of a $1,000 performance bond. Apartment houses were deleted from coverage early in the discussion. Both measures passed on October 23 with large majorities. Council president George Baker, the future mayor, led the futile opposition. He used the same argument that Merrill had voiced a decade earlier, that the low-class women would be dispersed either into high-class neighborhoods or into the cheapest of accommodations. Baker raised the question that no one could or would try to answer: Where should the sporting women go?[36]

During the five-week interval before the laws went into effect, some of the owners devised ingenious tactics to protect their reputations. Properties suddenly became owned by groups of mysteriously formed companies. Some plates went up in Arabic, Hebrew or French, although the city subsequently ruled that they had to be in English. By the end of November over 40 indictments had been handed down and the papers reported that most of the property owners were in compliance. Some had even forced the occupants to move and were remodelling their buildings. And the Weinhard Brewery had canceled contracts with five major saloon outlets.

Other Major Urban Issues: 1912-1913

As the council expended much time on franchise applications during the second year of Rushlight's administration, many of the same companies and problems reappeared on the agenda. However, for the first time in the council's history, strong support began to develop for policies advocated by former Mayor Harry Lane. The east-siders led the attack, particularly against the Portland Railway Light & Power Company for bad service. A giant, with over 250 miles of lines (175 miles in Portland proper), 600 cars, 4,000 employees (cut back by a thousand in the winter), and an annual payroll of almost $3 million, the company stated that since 1907 it had spent nearly $5 million on updating services, financed by stock and bond sales. Considering that the city's boundaries had expanded by almost 40 percent since the end of the exposition and that the population had doubled, this was not a large capital investment. The five-year earnings record, since the time that Abbot Mills sold out to the

Clark interests of Philadelphia, showed substantial profits. As reported to the city council, net operating earnings were $12.2 million. Dividends of 6 percent, on capital stock worth $16.25 million, were nearly $1 million.[37]

Several questions were raised in council about these figures during a session in February, 1913. No income was shown for interest on funded debt owed by the company, estimated at $5 million. The $16.2 million value of capital stock was probably not worth that much, as the company had issued increasing amounts of new stock, thus diluting its value per share—or "watering it," to quote the critics. Except for the early years, most private municipal transportation companies, like the PRL&P, never really netted much on passenger revenue if their service was adequate. The largest return to owner-investors came from the manipulation of security prices. The companies always borrowed against anticipated future revenues derived from expansion.

On February 20, 1913, a formal complaint was filed with the council and the Oregon Public Service Commission (established by a referendum vote in November, 1912) against the PRL&P by some 30 organizations, including the Sunnyside and Laurelhurst Improvement clubs. The document cited the need for cross town lines, 33 miles in length. "The trouble with the Railway Co. is that they want it all velvet—all income and no outlay; they want valuable franchises, without money and without price; upon the strength of which they can water, and float their stocks and bonds; with the least possible public accommodation and service." The complaint was particularly aimed at a recent franchise grant, covering 22 miles but with no cross-town line provided. The document further stated that in the 1902-1913 period, more than 35,000 residences had been built on the east side, as opposed to only 4,100 on the west side. The east-side population was 235,000, compared with 41,000 on the west side. Also mentioned was the lack of any service to the new Reed College site in Eastmoreland.[38]

The previous month the council had received a petition from the Portsmouth Commercial Club in North Portland about the company's "poor service." Several months earlier councilman Ralph Clyde had made a strong speech in chamber in favor of the city's taking over the company but he received little support beyond that of councilman Maguire who felt the service to be "rotten."

Beginning to emerge was a general, widespread criticism of Portland's monopolistic public utilities, all controlled out of state. Even the Oregon Public Service Commission was not above reproach. As one commissioner noted in 1919, the companies were only required to present "statements of revenues and expenses, while the value of the service to the patron, his ability to pay, and the service afforded for the rate received or requested" were "apparently of very minor importance." Lack of competition gave private and public customers no choice. State regulation had not produced the consumer benefits promised at the time of its enactment.[39]

By an odd quirk of fate, Abbot Mills found himself joining one phase of the battle in October, 1912. For one who had been instrumental in creating the gas and street railway monopolies to criticize the Bell telephone system, "America's greatest monopoly," must have provoked astonishment and even amusement. At issue was the survival of the independent Home Telegraph Company of Portland, part of a network of Home telephone systems, scattered from San Francisco to Seattle and Spokane. When Home first introduced the automatic telephone in 1905, Mills and other Portland investors had incorporated a Portland exchange. In 1909, Sam Hill, the Seattle investor and son-in-law of James J. Hill, bought majority control of the Portland operation from Mills, who became vice-president, and from directors Theodore B. Wilcox, William M. Ladd, Edward Cookingham, and Henry L. and Elliott R. Corbett, who remained minority stockholders. By any definition, this was an Establishment enterprise.[40]

In October, 1912, Home Telephone's existence was threatened by the Bell System, which was "on the march in the Northwest," acquiring every independent phone company it could find. Mills said that the consequences for Seattle users were "disastrous": rates had increased and service had deteriorated. In a publicly released letter to the "Citizens of Portland," he complained bitterly about the tactics of the Bell System and those of its subsidiary, the Pacific Telephone and Telegraph Company, of which John C. Ainsworth was an Oregon director. "The Home Company is your company, you voted for its existence (by approving its franchise), its stockholders live here, its money is spent here; monopoly and tyranny are synonymous terms. What the American people are entitled to have is competition in quality of service rendered." Even the most dedicated populist-progressive could not have been more succinct. "The Bell telephone monopoly says the people who patronize the Home phone are freaks. ... Read our list of Directors at the top of this letter; are these people freaks?"[41]

Separating reality from rhetoric, Mills was hardly ready to join progressive critics in condemning monopolies like the Portland Railway Light and Power Company or the Electric Bond & Share Company. He and his associates had profitably sold them their investments in the Portland Railway and Portland Gas companies. With Home Telephone, however, they faced losing their investments if the company were forced into bankruptcy, as happened five years later.

The Dock Commission Goes to Work

In its dealings with the Northern Pacific Terminal Company, the commission of Public Docks encountered the same arrogance as the Home Telephone Company faced in competing against the Bell System, or the city in its dealings with the Portland Railway Light & Power Company. A battle ensued between two conservative forces, one local and the other from outside. Both were well represented within the Portland Establishment and the ranks of the Arlington, Concordia and Waverly clubs. The struggle became a lesson for the first commissioners as they attempted to delineate and define private and public functions and responsibilities. As a group they were forced to make decisions that each, individually, might not have approved three years earlier.

Mayor Simon's appointments to the first Commission of Public Docks, drawn from the top ranks of the Portland Establishment, included banker Henry L. Corbett; attorney Fred W. Mulkey, former U.S. senator (for six months in 1907) and Arlington Club resident; businessman Charles B. Moores; investor William MacMaster; and Ben Selling, Portland's leading merchant. Mulkey and Selling were to play the major roles in determining the commission's policy, Selling being the dominant member through his 10 years of commission service. A moderate Republican, he served in the state senate from 1909 to 1911, was president of the senate in 1911, and speaker of the house in 1915. He was defeated for the U.S. Senate in 1912 by Harry Lane.

The commission's *Second Annual Report* of 1912 revealed some of the "essential principles" needing recognition and consideration:

A port should be developed not as an aggregation of individual piers or wharves, indiscriminately constructed to serve various kinds of shipping as the immediate needs demand, but rather a port should be developed as a terminal, each pier or wharf should have some logical relation to those already constructed, to the upland immediately adjacent, and should be but a definite step forward in a well defined plan.

In a port partially developed, especially by private interests, it is exceedingly difficult to follow this principle. The expense is often seemingly prohibitive and leads to makeshift policies on the part of public harbor commissions. In the long run, the larger expenditures for these improvements under a logical plan are the more economic, and therefore should be insisted upon, even if it is necessary to undertake the difficult task of educating the public opinion to such an extent that it will demand the larger expenditures. The economic justification of this assertion is shown by the attitude and accomplishments of the great ports of North Europe and this country.[42]

As one of its first tasks, the commission wanted to get the Northern Pacific Terminal Company's track on North Front Street removed or opened to common use. North Front furnished the best access between the heart of the city and Public Dock No. 1, which was shortly to be constructed. The commission was either going to build its own belt freight line or rent the use of the NPT track. The commission contended that the NPT had no franchise for the track, and City Attorney Frank S. Grant supported this position before the council in October, 1912. He said, "The Northern Pacific Terminal Co. has played fast and loose with its original franchise," which did not extend beyond the city limits at the time of its approval. The company argued that the later extension of the boundary northward automatically extended the franchise northward. The original franchise, like the ones granted to Charles F. Swigert's Willamette Bridge Railway Company in Albina, was a general ordinance—a blanket grant—containing the words "may be extended to the city limits." To the company this wording implied automatic extension. The matter was resolved through compromise in 1914, when the first dock opened. Adding to the commission's problems, the NPT proceeded to lay a second track on North Front Street after the commission had first approached it.[43]

A major purpose of the dock commission was to create a locally controlled public agency to foster maritime commerce. Joseph Teal, regarded as the father of the public-dock ideal in Portland, had long considered that wheat and lumber were not enough to make the city a great commercial port. Only foreign cargo would generate a thriving Portland trade. In 1912 Portland still had no Oriental steamship line providing regular service. Pacific Mail, with its home port in San Francisco, was owned by the Harriman interests, and James J. Hill owned the major steamship service out of Seattle and Tacoma.

Late that year, Teal and other Portland business leaders interested in promoting maritime trade worried about the extent of railroad control over shipping activities. The Port of Portland, which viewed itself as the major proponent of maritime commerce, was suspected of favoring the railroads and was accused of being indifferent to the promotion of the city's maritime trade. Also of concern was an apparent overlap of authority between the two commissions. Which agency would exercise responsibility for straightening the harbor line? Who would decide ownership of the waterfront tidelands between low and high water? Was the land public or private? Overriding all of these questions: Who would tackle the railroads, which continually created obstacles for any public body they could not control?[44]

The Bennett Plan

The joint comprehensive planning needed to guide the dock and port commissions, as advocated by Teal, received detailed attention in Edward H. Bennett's plan submitted to the city in the spring of 1911. Central to the impressive scheme was a rebuilding of harbor facilities on the Willamette River. Of next importance, Bennett focused on street and railroad traffic, and on the need to separate economic functions "for greater efficiency." The result, according to the Chicago designer, would be "the union of the City Practical with the City Beautiful at a minimum cost because of unity of effort." Responding enthusiastically, the Civic Improvement League, Mayor Rushlight and business leaders from the chamber of commerce created a new Greater Portland Plan Association. They aimed to seek formal recognition and voter approval of the Bennett Plan at the election of November, 1912.[45]

Specific recommendations included placing dock and harbor facilities down river as far as St. Johns, restoring public ownership of the downtown waterfront, building elevated bridge ramps, extending the Park Blocks, constructing wide diagonal boulevards as radial arteries with large traffic circles to handle Portland's growing motor vehicle traffic, and creating neighborhood parks in addition to "great woodland or forest reserve areas." The park proposals were reinforced in August, 1912, by a report from L.H. Weir, a prominent park consultant. Portland had fewer neighborhood parks for families than either Seattle or Tacoma, according to Weir. Public school sites were "bare and unlovely, poorly located and unfamiliarly designed." Portland's recreational facilities, furthermore, were too commercialized."[46]

To whip up enthusiasm for the Bennett Plan, members of the Greater Portland Plan Association sponsored public addresses, parades and rallies. One large gathering was held on October 29, 1912, at the Gypsy Smith Tabernacle, a temporary structure erected in the vicinity of Multnomah Field to accommodate a visiting evangelist. Frank Branch Riley, Portland's unofficial "ambassador of good will," boosted Bennett's street plan in his usual florid style. Portland was living in "the age of the highway, not the railroad; the motor car, not the locomotive," he declared. "Connecting up the empire that lies at our back door is just as important as developing our commerce upon the ocean that lies at our front door."[47]

Although the voters of Portland approved the concept of the Bennett Plan by the overwhelming margin of 16,202 to 7,996 in November, 1912, nothing substantial resulted from all the energy and funding that had gone into the preparation of the grand scheme. As one writer was to comment in 1945, "Portland ended up with little more than some beautiful illustrations now almost forgotten, and a sense of frustration." As with the "Boston — 1915" movement, "known as a noble experiment," its "specific accomplishments were few, disappointments many," according to Mel Scott. Some Portland critics, including architect Ellis Lawrence, thought that the plan was out of scale with Portland; it was too massive. Bennett had planned a downtown of great density, as official predictions indicated that Portland's growth would continue to be explosive. From 1900 to 1910, the city's population had grown 129 percent, the third fastest of major American cities after Los Angeles and Seattle. In 1912 the dock commission predicted an increase from approximately 220,000 to 1.5 million by 1950. Bennett had assumed 2 million as his guiding premise.[48]

Voters who approved the Bennett Plan defeated a $2 million park-bonds issue closely associated with it. A major casualty of the defeat, which had long-term consequences for the city, was the 400-acre Ross Island, in the mid-Willamette River at the south edge of the city, which Mayor Rushlight had advocated purchasing for a public park. Many Portlanders considered its cost of $300,000, together with that of other designated park properties, an unnecessary expense. To the *Labor Press,* the park bonds could become a "mother of real estate graft. ... The workingman has to pay all taxes directly or indirectly and will have to pay for this." The Central Labor Council advocated the bonds' defeat. As Mansel G. Blackford has observed:

> The simultaneous approval of the Bennett Plan and the defeat of the park bonds should have forewarned Portland's city planning advocates. The Bennett Plan was passed, because Portlanders viewed it as a general guide that would aid the private business development of their city. The park bonds lost, for they were seen as a specific issue that would cost, not save, money.[49]

In 1945, City Planning Director Arthur D. McVoy put the park-bonds defeat within the context of a chaotic real-estate boom in 1912, placing Portland 13th in the country in new construction. It created forces "in direct conflict with the plan...since land values had grown very high." In a more recent study, Carl Abbott has cited another reason for the city's "failure to implement" the Bennett Plan: "The lack of a niche or a sponsor within the municipal government. Influential businessmen could force council decisions on specific projects, but there had to be clear direction within city hall." While Simon, Rushlight and Council President Baker had participated in the promotional activities, none was a strong advocate of the plan. As with city government, no Establishment businessman or banker assumed a commanding role in implementing the plan. According to Abbot, "the only halting steps toward the vision of a Greater Portland between 1910 and 1920 were taken by the Commission of Public Docks." A further "problem" affecting the plan's fulfillment was that it appeared just as the great boom was collapsing, creating a depression that lasted from 1913 until after World War I.[50]

Women Speak Out for a Minimum Wage

Just as the Oregon economic boom crested in 1912, the state's reform movement levelled off in 1913 after reaching "a summit in 1912," according to Warren M. Blankenship. Yet "some of the reforms enacted in 1913 ... were among the most important...adopted during the Progressive Era." Members of the Portland Establishment played key roles in those developments.[51]

The most significant legislation passed during the 1913 session was the Oregon Minimum Wage Law, patterned after the Massachusetts law of 1912. The 1910 census figures showed that 40,473 females over the age of 10 were employed in Oregon. Of this number, 19,547 were in Portland: 6,636 in domestic and personal employment and

12,911 in all other occupations. The Catholic Women's League and the Oregon Consumers' League lobbied statewide against what they charged was the industrial "exploitation" of underpaid women and minors. Women earning $5 a week could not be expected to survive decently when it cost them $9 a week to live. The Reverend Edwin V. O'Hara, of Portland's Roman Catholic Diocese, who worked closely with both leagues, pounded away at industries "subsidized by the poor." Two members of the consumers' league, who became active proponents of reform, were Mrs. Winslow B. Ayer and Mrs. Henry Ladd Corbett, a staunch Unitarian. Both had worked tirelessly for the successful passage of the Woman's Suffrage Amendment in the election of November, 1912.[52]

Dan J. Malarkey, president of the state senate in 1913, assumed sponsorship of the bill, drafted jointly by both leagues. His leadership became crucial as employers bitterly attacked the measure. A Catholic himself, he knew and respected Father O'Hara and Caroline Gleason, the dynamic field director of the Catholic Women's League. As a member of the Portland Establishment, he was friendly with the Corbetts and Ayers. One of Oregon's most prominent Republicans and an oft-mentioned candidate for the U.S. Senate, he devised the strategy for the legislative hearings. At one meeting, when the employers heatedly denied Caroline Gleason's charges, he asked her if she had anything further to say. She replied quietly: "'If you would like the names and addresses of the firms where these conditions prevail, I shall be glad to give them to you.'" When no one asked for them, Malarkey had won the day. According to a later account, one angry German employer, "as big around as his pickle barrels," said of Caroline Gleason: "'She is a terrible voman. She is vorse than a lawyer.'"[53]

The minimum-wage law passed the senate unanimously and the house with only three negative votes. Taking effect on June 3, it established the Industrial Welfare Commission, which was authorized to set maximum hours and minimum wages for women and girls. Malarkey had wisely recommended deletion of specific wage and hour requirements so as not to encourage opposition. Governor West appointed Father O'Hara as commission chairman, representing the public. Mrs. Bertha Moores, sister-in-law of dock commission member C.B. Moores, represented labor, and Mrs. Amadee M. Smith, wife of a prominent Republican business associate of Charles F. Swigert, represented employers. Caroline Gleason was chosen secretary. For the first time in Oregon's history, women constituted a majority of a major state regulatory agency. Oregon joined California and Washington among eight states enacting minimum-wage legislation for women in 1913; Oregon and California were two of only four states that had commissions with power to regulate working hours for women and children. The Pacific states were among nine employing the commission method of fixing minimum wage rates for women and children.[54]

Dan Malarkey and Ben Selling

Malarkey had also been instrumental in passing the Oregon Public Utilities Commission Act in 1911, in conjunction with senate President Ben Selling. A corollary law established the Oregon State Tax Commission. Its first report, in 1911, revealed a new program for assessing the property of public-service corporations. They would henceforth be assessed by the state, as units. The old county system, which had functioned unevenly and inconsistently, was thus abolished. Malarkey's final public accomplishment in 1913 was in establishing the office of the Oregon State Corporations Commissioner, a landmark in Oregon history. The legislation compelled investment companies and corporations to file a full description of their business and prohibited their selling of securities until authorized by the commissioner of corporations. For years, misrepresentation had been widely practiced. Companies were deliberately over-capitalized, often with as much as 90 percent of the stock "in water."[55]

While Governor West received much credit for the package of reform legislation enacted in 1911 and 1913, without the strong and shrewd leadership of Portland Republicans Selling and Malarkey the record might have been quite different. (West always considered Malarkey the brightest person he ever knew.) Through their close association with Portland's business community, they exploited unique opportunities to affect progressive legislation. With their keen political foresight, they sensed trends that would inevitably bring about regulation of business. Operating from political self-interest as well as conviction, they had the strategic and organizational skills to produce what they considered constructive regulations that would actually aid business. As Robert H. Wiebe has observed, nationally "the business community was the most important single factor — or set of factors — in the development of economic regulation. And a significant portion of this influence supported reform."[56]

Political realists who lacked a grand social vision, Selling and Malarkey were at least partially motivated in the minimum-wage and-hour issue by humane and religious considerations. Selling, the elder of the two, was known for his fair treatment of employees. A generous person, he was a champion of suffering humanity anywhere. He raised over $100,000 for Armenian Relief work, and during the depressions of 1893 and 1907 established kitchens for the unemployed. For this he was named the founder of "The Workingman's Club." He was also a major supporter of the Waverly Baby Home and the Jewish Neighborhood House in South Portland. Although influenced by the growing progressive spirit, he always remained a party regular, winning the Republican nomination in 1912 to succeed the discredited U.S. Senator Jonathan Bourne who had endorsed Oswald West in 1910. (The Republican-dominated 1913 legislature, responding to the preference vote of the 1912 primary election, swallowed hard and selected the ever-popular Harry Lane.)

Malarkey, considered one of the most skillful trial lawyers in the West, was a product of the early Mitchell-Carey machine. In promoting the reform of working conditions for women, he was influenced by Father O'Hara, and by his "strong-minded" wife, Laurie. According to their son, Thomas B. Malarkey, the latter was not averse to using "boudoir sabotage." The younger Malarkey thinks his father was more "liberal" than the "stand-patter" reputation accorded him by such staunch progressive Republicans as George W. Joseph. In early 1913, when rumors began spreading that Senator Chamberlain might win a post in President Woodrow Wilson's cabinet, Republican Party leaders began to propose Malarkey to succeed him. Not only was the incumbent uninterested, but Laurie Malarkey said no. If her husband went to Washington, she declared, he went alone. On this note, Malarkey retired from public office at the age of 43.[57]

Municipal Reform: Commission Government

The progressive movement that encouraged business and political leaders like Selling and Malarkey "to define more carefully what they wanted" (as Wiebe puts it) also encouraged *Oregon Journal* publisher C.S. Jackson to look hard at Portland's mayor-council form of government. He headed a committee of prominent citizens interested in establishing a bureau of municipal research, similar to that of New York City's. Founded in 1906 and financed largely through the efforts of Andrew Carnegie and John D. Rockefeller, New York's example offered "the model of the efficient business enterprise…, rather than the New England town meeting… as the positive inspiration for the municipal reformer," according to Samuel P. Hays. Joining Jackson were lumberman Winslow Ayer and attorneys James B. Kerr, Richard W. Montague and Kingman Brewster. Kerr (a partner of railroad attorney Charles H. Carey) and Ayer were Arlington Club members. Montague was C.E.S. Wood's partner; Brewster (who would father a future president of Yale University) practiced in Portland only briefly before joining the Wilson administration during World War I.[58]

To show their Portland friends the value of such an institution, the committee contracted with the New York bureau for a general survey of the city's governmental organization and business methods. Jackson hoped that the resulting report would generate more enthusiasm for both a new city charter and a new form of city government. As published in April, 1913, the report was a shocker. Exceeding Jackson's expectations, the impact was immediate and decisive. The survey's findings clearly revealed that Portland was "operating by the seat of its pants." With $3 million in general-fund income and $15 million in total receipts, the city was managing its municipal affairs much as at the time of consolidation in 1891, when the population and the municipal funds were less than one-quarter of those in 1913.[59]

City council President George Baker, who favored reform and who served as mayor from 1917 to 1933, declared that the government was so fragmented with excessive overlap of authority that it took "30 men to kill a fly." Governmental services needed simplification and efficiency. Like many east-side residents, he was also unhappy with the representational imbalance of the 15-member council. With over 60 percent of the city's population living east of the Willamette River, the west side held a council advantage of nine to six. Baker and other reform-minded east-siders believed that electing all commissioners at-large offered the best chance to effect a more equitable geographic representation.[60]

This was a key feature of the so-called Galveston Plan, which commission propo-nents, through the initiative, placed on the ballot in May, 1913. It would replace the 15 part-time councilmen with four full-time commissioners, each assigned a major department of city government by a full-time mayor who would also administer at least one department, usually the police. The commissioners and the mayor, each elected for four-year terms, would have equal votes in legislative matters, with the veto abolished. City elections would be conducted on a non-partisan basis. The mayor and the commissioners would assume both legislative and administrative responsibilities, with all citizen boards also abolished except for civil service.

To those who yearned primarily for more governmental efficiency, or "profes-sionalism," as some called it, the need for functional centralization overrode geo-graphic loyalties and neighborhood ties. Many business and professional reform leaders, supported by the chamber of commerce, tended to identify their concerns with the whole city, or with the public interest, a favorite progressive term. Others, like B.S. Josselyn, the president of Portland's giant utility monopoly and largest private property owner, wanted city-wide decision making organized along corporate lines so as to promote a smoother and more efficiently administered urban economy over which they hoped to exercise a greater degree of control than in the past.

Josselyn and Simon Benson were unhappy with the caliber of the existing council, which contained few notables by their definition. Mayor A.G. Rushlight was a plumbing contractor and council president George Baker a theater owner and impresario. The other members of the last ward council in 1913 included two relatively obscure lawyers, three realtor-developers, an undertaker and furniture-store owner, two printers, an insurance executive who was to be elected chamber of commerce president in 1915, the manager of a boiler works, and the owner of a stove works. In the minds of many of the city's leading bankers, businessmen, lawyers, and ministers, most of these councilmen were not fit to lead Portland through the next stage of its promising growth. The problem was to convince the voters — not an easy task considering the large number of new residents, a weakened political party structure, barely lukewarm support for change from the *Oregonian*, and the opposition of organized labor as well as many other public and private wage earners.

The New York survey was injected forcefully into a two-phased political struggle, one involving consideration of the new charter, and the other relating to the partisan race for mayor, which would proceed along traditional lines even if the new charter were adopted. The charter and primary votes were set for May 3 and the election of city officers for June 2. Councilman Gay Lombard, millionaire president of the Pacific Grain Company, was both the chief opponent of the new charter and the leading Republican mayoralty candidate. An ally of Joseph Simon and Abbot Mills, Lombard charged that the new charter was "compiled largely by men who have increased taxation, [and] failed to make good in the conduct of the city's business." The existing charter was not to blame for the city's problems, he said. He accused seven members of the Rushlight administration of failure to perform their duties. The chief evil was not government itself, but popular apathy.[61]

By late April the political fray had become more personal. Opposing Lombard in the Republican primary, Rushlight accused the businessman of favoring such large corporations as the PRL&P. George Baker, an articulate orator, supported both Rushlight and the new charter, citing examples of a city that had long outgrown its old charter. He mentioned a $238,000 water department deficiency that Water Board chairman, Theodore B. Wilcox, could not explain. Baker insisted that elected city officials, not a wealthy businessman with no responsibility to the voters, should have control over such important city services.[62]

White-collar Democrats, led by C.E.S. Wood, were active charter proponents, while the blue-collar Democratic *Labor Press* was not satisfied: "Let's wait and get a better one." Abigail Scott Duniway strongly opposed the measure, which had been drafted by an all-male charter commission. The more conservative Republican business elements were also against it, whereas liberal Republicans of the stamp of Winslow B. Ayer, William M. Ladd, Joseph N. Teal, William L. Brewster and James B. Kerr joined *Journal* Publisher C.S. Jackson in a strong endorsement. The Roosevelt Progressives, the Portland Municipal Association, the Greater Portland Plan Association, and members of the educational-religious community led by Dr. Thomas Lamb Eliot provided active assistance. Even the opening of the Broadway Bridge with great fanfare did not diminish the political acrobatics.[63]

The *Oregonian* alone remained unexcited. Although the idea of a commission government appealed to Editor Piper, "Beware," he said, "of creating a fetish over governmental forms." Wood, although generally supportive of the commission concept, clearly foresaw some inherent deficiencies in it, fearing that it would further erode political party organization and discipline and reduce governmental participation by the working classes.[64]

He also foresaw a problem that would only increase with the passage of time. By eliminating political parties as primary recipients and dispensers of campaign funds, the mayor and commissioners would be burdened with raising their own funds, and would thus become even more personally indebted to their contributors than if political parties had been involved. This partnership arrangement became the primary mechanism for dominance by special interests. Influence was to be wielded more than in the past through private negotiations, often conducted within the confines of city hall offices or private clubs.

Barely 12 percent of the registered voters were responsible for the passage of the commission plan by a margin of 722 votes — hardly an outpouring of reformist enthusiasm. The east side carried the election with a majority of 2,004 votes, while the west side voted it down by a margin of 1,281. West-side opposition reflected a divided Portland Establishment with few dedicated Progressives in its ranks. The city's business leaders who favored commission government "in no sense" accepted the proposition "that all segments of society should be involved equally in municipal decision-making," as Samuel P. Hays has observed. "They meant that their concept of the city's welfare would be best achieved if the business community controlled city government.[65]

Commission Government and the Establishment

Immediately after the election, the predicted scramble for new offices caused bedlam. A self-appointed Committee of 100, organized by leaders of the business-professional Establishment to secure the most qualified candidates, included Abbot Mills, Theodore Wilcox, and others who opposed commission government. Also involved were Selling, Rodney Glisan, William Wheelwright, Teal, Ayer, Wood, Thomas Strong, and numerous ministers and educators. Before a week had passed, 84 prospects had surfaced. The election of June 3, 1913, turned out 9,000 more voters than the previous month, and the forces of "better government" seemed pleased.

The mayor-elect, H. Russell Albee, had joined the Progressive Party when it organized in 1912. The 43-year-old native of Illinois had come to Oregon in 1897 as Portland manager of the Northwestern Mutual Life Insurance Company. Committed to public service, he was a Democratic member of the city council from 1902 to 1905 and served in the state senate in 1909 and 1911, where he heartily supported progressive legislation. As an east-side resident from the exclusive Laurelhurst district, he was joined on the commission council by Progressive Will H. Daly, manager of the Portland Monotype Company, a former councilman-at-large and friend of organized labor; and by Charles A. Bigelow, a Republican department-store manager who had just completed two years on the Executive Board. Elected from the west side were 37-year-old Robert G. Dieck, a civil-engineering graduate of the University of Pennsylvania, and 47-year-old William L. Brewster, a graduate of Wesleyan University and Columbia Law School. Both were East Coast natives and progressive Republicans. A member of the law firm of Cotton, Teal and Minor, Brewster had solid Establishment credentials and a commitment to public office shared by his partner Joseph N. Teal. He had served on the civil service board since 1905 and was active in the library and art associations. Membership in the Arlington and Waverly Golf clubs solidified his social connections.[66]

Setting a pattern that prevailed for over 40 years, east-siders constituted a commission majority. In theory, the commission plan was expected by many of its supporters to shift power from the working class to the upper-income and professional classes. For its first four years, these expectations were realized. However, after 1917 the socio-economic composition of the commission councils varied little from that of the older ward councils, with three exceptions: commissioners increasingly tended to represent functional activities, such as labor unions and trade associations, and realtor-developers and attorneys were noticeably absent, although not lacking in influence. (For nearly 60 years no attorney would be elected from the east side.) By 1917, the entire council, including the mayor, were all east-siders, with the west-side Establishment unrepresented for nearly three decades.

Portland's early Progressive Era experience differed from that of Des Moines and Pittsburgh, as described by Hays and certain other scholars. The business and financial Establishment, centered largely on the west side, did not capture city government through Portland's creation of commission government. It achieved little more power than it had enjoyed under the old mayor-council system. By centralizing decision-making in fewer hands, however, commission government made it easier for business to influence the council. Only three of five commissioners, including the mayor, had to be convinced, rather than eight of 15 councilmen (as in the old system). As Wood had predicted, non-partisan commissioners became more accessible than the old councilmen to contributors — and more indebted to them. Although administrative responsibilities were divided (each commissioner administered at least one governmental bureau), the mayor's powers were increased, even without the veto. By allocating bureau assignments to the other commissioners — the mayor usually kept that of the police — he could exercise a degree of control not enjoyed by previous mayors. Under the old council system, the mayors had appointed bureau chiefs and members of boards and commissions, but only with council approval. While the old councils could create their own committees, none had exercised any administrative responsibilities.[67]

No one fulfilled the new mayor's role more effectively than George L. Baker, who held the office for 16 years. In Baker, business had a loyal friend, who could normally be relied upon to support its interests. Onto new advisory commissions and boards went such of Baker's Establishment friends as banker John C. Ainsworth, scion of the old Establishment family. As a theater owner, with a family insurance business on the side, Baker had a local merchant's approach to government: actively encourage business growth and discourage regulation and governmental costs.

An even cozier relationship developed between Baker and Franklin T. Griffith, president of the Portland Railway Light & Power Company after June 1, 1913. Eight years later, Griffith and some business friends quietly paid off Mayor Baker's $7,100 home mortgage. Unable to live on his salary, Baker had contemplated leaving office. When it later learned of the action, the conservative *Oregon Voter* justified the gift, asserting that had the public known the truth about Baker's financial hardship, thousands of dollars would have flowed into the coffers to help a mayor "whom we all love."[68]

And Still the Establishment

The growth of a Portland Establishment from 1851 to 1913 clearly showed that money and power were the basic sources of elite status. Establishment political power generally reflected its economic power, but it was not always united politically, as the battle over commission government revealed. Through the years the Establishment had often split over parties, personalities and various political and economic issues. As G. William Domhoff has shown, "the great amount of conflict manifest in American public life" was "not incompatible with a ruling class perspective. Conflict within the special-interest process" was "over narrow issues" that did not challenge Establishment power; in fact, many of these conflicts were often between segments of the business community. With the "candidate-selection process," the bitter contention was primarily personal in nature, rarely embodying any disparagement of the Establishment itself.[69]

By 1913, the political power of the Establishment had changed, as the city had grown larger, economically more diverse, and socially more heterogeneous. Power was increasingly exercised through secondary spheres of community life: private relationships, voluntary organizations, and philanthropic and cultural organizations. As Frederic Cople Jaher concluded from his national study of *The Urban Establishment*:

> Civic welfare activities legitimized leadership claims by giving renown to the establishment and providing the means to indoctrinate the urban masses and control dependent groups. ...Group cohesion was enhanced when the establishment fulfilled expectations of leadership roles and distributed rewards of wealth, influence, and fame to its members.[70]

Portland's urban elite survived, united by traditions and inter-generational kinship networks. Jacob Kamm's death in December, 1912, at the age of 89, left only John McCraken from Portland's first Establishment, until his death in 1915. Henry Pittock, who died four years later, did not achieve Establishment stature until he bought the *Oregonian* in 1860, and even then he played only a quiet role, never joining the Arlington Club or other social and community organizations. In 1913, the Establishment was led largely, but not exclusively, by the sons, grandsons, and relatives of the city's pioneer merchants, and by the newer rich among such incipient entrepreneurs as architect-investor E.B. MacNaughton and the corporate executive Franklin T. Griffith. Although some women had achieved a degree of local prominence through suffrage and groups like the Oregon Consumers' League, the Establishment was still, and would remain, male dominated. It was a conglomerate of interests and outlooks, cemented together by intermarriage and membership in exclusive men's clubs.

Between the 1890s and 1913, the Establishment reluctantly accepted a limited role for government in promoting certain political, economic, and social reforms which recognized legitimate public interests. By compromise and adaptation to the absentee-ownership of the city's largest corporations, it had retained its power and perpetuated its cherished allegiance to that private enterprise system which had so richly rewarded it. The underfinanced city government, with its authority weak and diffused, remained the handmaiden of Portland's Establishment.

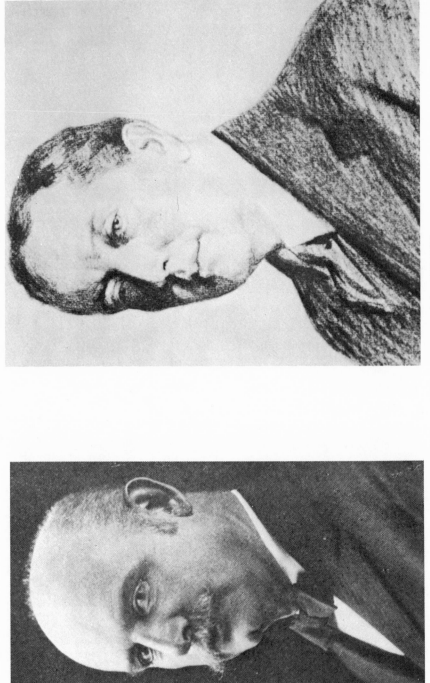

21.2 Dan J. Malarkey (1870-1939)

21.1 Ben Selling (1852-1931)

21.4 Oswald West (1875-1960)

21.3 Joseph N. Teal (1858-1929), c. 1929

21.5 1912 Bennett Plan proposal for intersection of West Burnside St., North Park
Blocks, and extended Park Blocks looking north to a new railway station
and bridge.

21.6 Pier A, Municipal Dock No. 1, opened March 28, 1914

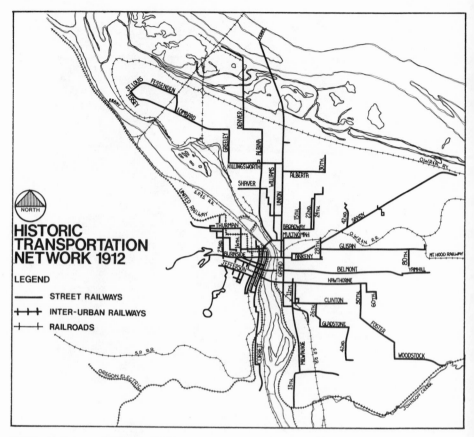

21.7 Historic Transportation Network 1912

21.8 Downtown Portland, looking east toward Mt. Hood, c. 1912

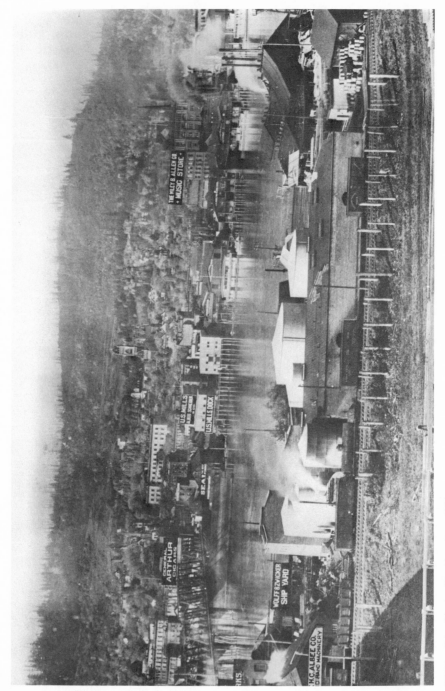

21.9 East Side of Portland, looking west, c. 1912

21.10 1912 Bennett Plan for center of city

NOTES

Note: *Oregon Historical Quarterly* appears as *OHQ*; Oregon Historical Society Library collections are cited as OHS; OHS scrapbooks are cited as S.B.; Hubert H. Bancroft Papers at the Bancroft Library, University of California, Berkeley, are cited as BL; Manuscript and Special Collections Libraries at the University of Oregon are cited as UO. Citation of Portland City Hall Archives refers to documents stored at City Hall; citation of City of Portland Archives refers to documents stored at the Portland Archives and Record Center.

INTRODUCTION

[1]See particularly: David C. Hammack, "Problems in the Historical Study of Power in the Cities and Towns of the United States, 1800-1960," *American Historical Review*, 83 (April, 1978), 323-49; Frederic Cople Jaher, *The Urban Establishment* (Urbana, 1982); Carl V. Harris, *Political Power in Birmingham, 1871-1921* (Knoxville, 1977); Samuel P. Hays, *American Political History as Social Analysis* (Knoxville, 1980).

[2]Henry Steele Commager, "America's Heritage of Bigness," *Saturday Review* (4 July, 1970), 11.

[3]Sam B. Warner, Jr., *Streetcar Suburbs* (New York, 1969), 155.

[4]David C. Hammack, "Elite Perceptions of Power in the Cities of the United States, 1880-1900, The Evidence of James Bryce, Moisei Ostrogorski, and their American Informants," *Journal of Urban History*, 4 (August, 1978), 365.

[5]Paul G. Merriam, "Urban Elite in the Far West, Portland, Oregon, 1870-1890," *Arizona and The West* 18 (Spring, 1976), 41.

CHAPTER 1 FOOTNOTES

[1]Arthur L. Throckmorton, *Oregon Argonauts* (Portland, 1961), 113-114; Elsie Y. Brown, comp., *United States Census of Oregon Territory* (Salem, 1970); United States Census Office, *Census of Oregon* (Washington, 1860); Jesse S. Douglas, "Origins of the Population of Oregon in 1850," *Pacific Northwest Quarterly* 41 (January, 1950), 95-108.

[2]Hubert H. Bancroft, *Chronicles of the Builders of the Commonwealth*, (San Francisco, 1891), 1:602-3.

[3]William A. Bowen, *The Willamette Valley* (Seattle, 1978), 53.

[4]Malcolm Clark, Jr., *Eden Seekers* (Boston, 1981), 237; Bowen, *Willamette Valley*, 22; Oscar O. Winther, *The Old Oregon Country* (Lincoln, 1969), 6.

[5]Throckmorton, *Argonauts*, 29, 30, 32, 39, 40; Samuel Eliot Morison, *The Maritime History of Massachusetts, 1783-1860* (Boston, 1921), 66; John N. Cushing to Caleb Cushing, January, 1837, and February, 1851, in Claude M. Fuess, *The Life of Caleb Cushing* (New York, 1923), 1:247, 2:21.

[6]Throckmorton, *Argonauts*, ch. 3; Bancroft, *Chronicles*, 1:603; Richard A. Bartlett, *The New Country* (New York, 1974), 101-2; Ray Allen Billington, *The Far Western Frontier, 1830-1860* (New York, 1956), 70-73; Robert G. Albion, *The Rise of New York Port, 1815-1860* (New York, 1939), ch. 13; James E. Hendrickson, *Joe Lane of Oregon* (New Haven, 1967), 41.

[7]Bancroft, *Chronicles*, 1:602.

[8]Bowen, *Willamette Valley*, 23; Bancroft, *Chronicles*, 1:602.

[9]Bowen, *Willamette Valley*, 17-21; Elizabeth McLagan, *A Peculiar Paradise* (Portland, 1980), 29.

[10]Peter H. Burnett, *Recollections and Opinions of an Old Pioneer* (New York, 1880), 181.

[11]Burnett, *Recollections*, 138, also see James W. Hurst, *Law and the Conditions of Freedom in the Nineteenth Century United States* (Madison, 1956), 13; Deady quoted in Walter C. Woodward, *Rise and Early History of Political Parties in Oregon, 1843-1868* (Portland, 1913), 4, 10.

[12]Bowen, *Willamette Valley*, 18; Dorothy O. Johansen, "The Role of Land Laws in the Settlement of Oregon," in *Genealogical Material in Oregon Donation Land Claims*(Portland, 1957);Applegate quoted in S.B.271,p.75.

[13]Eugene E. Snyder, *Early Portland* (Portland, 1970), 16-17.

[14]Irena Narell, *Our City* (San Diego, 1981), 34-37; John Reps, *Cities of the American West* (Princeton, 1979), 164; Barnaby Conrad, *San Francisco* (New York, 1959), 16-17; Bartlett, *New Country*, 411-14.

[15]Peter R. Decker, *Fortunes and Failures* (Cambridge, 1978), 44-45, 90-91, ch. 3; William Issel and Robert W. Cherny, *San Francisco, 1865-1932* (Berkeley, 1986), ch. 1.

[16]Throckmorton, *Argonauts*, 102-5.

[17]Bancroft, *Chronicles*, 1:603.

[18]Bancroft, *Chronicles*, 1:603; Daniel Webster, "On Agriculture," 13 January, 1840, quoted in John Bartlett, *Familiar Quotations* (Boston, 1968), 548. Ladd had met Webster while working as a railroad passenger agent.

[19]Lewis Mumford, *The City in History* (New York, 1961), 426.

[20]Asa Lovejoy, "Lovejoy's Pioneer Narrative, 1842-1848," ed. Henry E. Reed, *OHQ* 31 (September, 1930), 253-54. Asa Lawrence Lovejoy was a nephew of wealthy Boston capitalist Abbott Lawrence, who founded Lawrence, Massachusetts, in 1845. The Lawrences, one of Boston's first families, also gave birth to Lawrence College and Lawrence, Kansas.

[21]*Oregon Spectator*, 30 September, 1847.

[22]David Logan to Mary Logan, 3 January, 1851, in "22 Letters of David Logan, Pioneer Oregon Lawyer," ed. Harry E. Pratt, *OHQ* 44 (September, 1943) 258-59; Johansen, "Role of Land Laws."

[23]John Mack Faragher, *Women and Men on the Overland Trail* (New Haven, 1979), 34-35.

[24]Lovejoy, "Lovejoy's Pioneer Narrative," 254.

[25]Lovejoy, "Lovejoy's Pioneer Narrative," 255; F. W. Pettygrove, "Oregon in 1843," *Oregonian*, 28 June, 1880; Thomas R. Cox, *Mills and Markets* (Seattle, 1974), 30.

[26]John Minto, "What I Know of Dr. McLoughlin and How I Know It," *OHQ* 11 (June, 1910), 193.

[27]Minto, "What I Know," 193; Earl Pomeroy, *The Pacific Slope* (New York, 1965), 120-21.

[28]Lovejoy,"Lovejoy's Pioneer Narrative,"252;*Oregonian*,28 June,1882; A. A. Lovejoy,"Founding of Portland," BL.

[29]Reps, *Cities*, x; Michel J. Doucet, "Urban Land Development in Nineteenth-Century North America," *Journal of Urban History* 8 (May, 1982), 310.

[30]Reps,*Cities*, ch. 8; Charles H. Chapman, "Oregon: A Slighted Beauty," *The Nation* 1, (7 February, 1923), 142. Block dimensions of cities in California were: San Jose (1847), 500 by 225 feet; San Diego (1849), 300 by 200 feet; San Francisco (1847), 800 by 400 feet.

[31]Lovejoy, "Lovejoy's Pioneer Narrative," 256; Lovejoy, "Founding of Portland"; Washington County Deed Book B, 7, Daniel H. Lownsdale Papers, OHS. Eugene Snyder estimates that half the 110 head of cattle sold for two-thirds of the gold Stark paid Lovejoy. A half-interest in the claim netted Lovejoy about $390 in gold. Snyder, *Early Portland*, p. 34; Lovejoy deposition in *Stark v. Starr*, in *Photostatic Copies of Depositions and Transfer of Titles, City of Portland, 1845-50*, 11, Port of Portland Papers, OHS.

[32]Stark's travels and intentions may be traced in the Benjamin Stark Papers and their guide, OHS. See Decker, *Fortunes and Failures*, 15, for comments on supercargoes.

[33]Snyder, *Early Portland*, 33, 41; Cox, *Mills and Markets*, 30.

[34]F. W. Pettygrove, "Oregon in 1843," 9, BL.

[35]Pettygrove, "Oregon in 1843," 9-10; Snyder, *Early Portland*, 33-41.

[36]Throckmorton, *Argonauts*, 58; Clark, *Eden*, 190.

[37]*Oregon Spectator*, 15 April and 13 May, 1847, quoted in Cox, *Mills and Markets*, 31.

[38]Bowen, *Willamette Valley*, 13; Snyder,*Early Portland*, 42; S.B. 112, p. 140; *Oregon Spectator*, 30 September, 1847.

[39]*Oregon Journal*, 5 September, 1928; Howard M. Corning, *Willamette Landings* (Portland, 1973), 20-21.

[40]Throckmorton, *Argonauts*, 61-62, 67; Neil M. Howison, "Report of Lieutenant Neil M. Howison on Oregon, 1846," *OHQ* 14 (March, 1913), 42; Pettygrove, "Oregon in 1843," 10, 24; Dorothy O. Johansen, "Capitalism on the Far Western Frontier: The Oregon Steam Navigation Company," (Ph.D. diss., University of Washington, 1941), 51.

[41]S. J. McCormick, comp., *The Portland Directory for the Year 1863* (Portland, 1863), 7; Fred Lockley,*History of the Columbia River Valley From The Dalles to the Sea* (Chicago, 1928), 1:415.

[42]"Brief and Argument for appellants by W. W. and J. C. Chapman," *William P. Burke et al. v. Heirs of D. H. Lownsdale, Patrick O'Neil, J. C. Morrison, and F. W. Pettygrove* (Portland, 1873), 4, 7, in Uncataloged

Manuscripts, OHS; Pettygrove, "Oregon in 1843," 1, 10; copy of sale by Pettygrove to Lownsdale in Washington County Deed Book B, 756, Lownsdale Papers, OHS; "Printed Land Claim Papers etc.," Lownsdale Papers, OHS. Compare Pettygrove's capital with a skilled worker's expectation of earning $1,000 to $1,500 for the entire year of 1850 in Portland. William S. Ladd's one-story brick building reputedly cost $7,500 to erect in 1853.

[43]Thomas L. Cole, *Historic Towns of the Western States* (New York, 1901), 557.

[44]Percy Maddux, *City on the Willamette* (Portland, 1952), 22.

[45]*Burke v. Heirs*, 6-7, 9, 12. Pettygrove refused to admit that he had sold any Stark property. "I did not ignore Stark's interest," he claimed, in Pettygrove deposition in *Lamb v. Vaughn* (1870), in *Photostatic Copies*, 39. Both Peter Burnett and Lovejoy had been appointed by Stark in 1846 to watch over his legal interests, but were in California when Pettygrove sold to Lownsdale and thus could not question that sale, according to the Lovejoy deposition in *Stark v. Starr* (1876), in *Photostatic Copies*, 11.

[46]*Burke v. Heirs*, 6-7; *Starr v. Stark*, 22 Federal Case 13317 (1874), 1116-17. Clark, *Eden*, 241, offers another interpretation of what Lownsdale knew.

[47]Lovejoy, "Founding of Portland," Pettygrove deposition in *Lamb v. Vaughn* (1870), in *Photostatic Copies*, 11.

[48]Benjamin Stark deposition in *Stark v. Starr* (1876), in *Photostatic Copies*, 52.

[49]A copy of the 1848 Plan of Portland is in the Multnomah County Library.

[50]*Burke v. Heirs*, 54; Washington County Deed Book B, 7, Lownsdale Papers.

[51]S.B. 112, p. 140.

[52]Sidney Teiser, "First Associate Justice of the Oregon Territory: Orville C. Pratt," *OHQ* 49 (September, 1948), 177; Clark, *Eden*, 228.

[53]Guide to Stark Papers; *Oregon Spectator*, 4 October, 1849.

[54]Guide to Stark Papers; *Weekly Oregonian*, 4 December, 1850; Clark, *Eden*, 190. *Stark v. Starr*, 481-82.

[55]There is contradictory evidence in the records. Instead of selling Coffin a half-interest in the townsite, Lownsdale sold him the entire townsite and then repurchased half of it. The difference represented $6,000 to Lownsdale. Coffin agreed to split the costs and profits with Lownsdale. The two men concluded a trust agreement in which Coffin retained all property in his name—possibly a device to protect Lownsdale from Stark's litigation.

[56]*Autobiography of Samuel L. Campbell, 1824-1902: Frontiersman and Oregon Pioneer* (Mannford, Oklahoma, 1986), 140-41.

[57]*Burke v. Heirs*, 54.

[58]*Oregonian*, 4 December, 1900; C. H. Lewis, "Draft of Biographical Sketch," 8, BL; Matthew P. Deady, "Portland-on-Wallamet," *The Overland Monthly* 1 (July, 1868), 370.

[59]Charles Stevens to brother Levi and sister Emma Kelsey and the girls, 31 October, 1852, in "Letters of Charles Stevens," ed. G. Ruth Rockwood, *OHQ* 37 (June, 1936), 146-47. *Stark v. Starr*, 473-80.

[60]*Stark v. Starr*, 473-80; copy of indenture between Stark (signed by Couch) and Lownsdale, 1 March, 1850, in Thorne's Numerical System, "Title of Abstracts, Portland, 1877," 129-30, OHS.

[61]*Stark v. Starr*, 473-80.

[62]S.B. 259, pp. 40-41.

[63]Couch sale to Flanders, 30 June, 1850, Glisan-Minott Papers, OHS; Reps, *Cities of the American West*, 351.

[64]Lownsdale, generous about parks, fought to hold riverbank properties he believed were exclusively his. *The Weekly Oregonian* of 1 April, 1851, printed his advertisement warning trespassers against despoiling his riverbank properties and against building structures on his land. W. W. Page to Asahel Bush, 24 August, 1858, in Asahel Bush Papers, Bush House. Reps, *Cities of the American West*, 351 and n. 19, speculates that Lownsdale, a Kentucky native, might have borrowed the park-strip idea from Louisville. Also see City of Portland, *Park Commission Report, 1901* (Portland, 1902), 5, and Eileen Fitzsimons, "South Park Blocks Historical Study," Portland Historical Landmarks Commission draft, 1979, OHS. Fitzsimons speculates on the influence of Lownsdale's two years of European travels.

[65]Terence O'Donnell, "Oregon History," in *Oregon Blue Book, 1985-1986* (Salem, 1985), 441; *Weekly Oregonian*, 4 December, 1850; *Oregonian*, 4 December, 1900; S.B. 259, p. 21.

[66]E. W. Conyers, "Diary of E. W. Conyers, A Pioneer of 1852," *Transactions of the Thirty-Third Annual Reunion of the Oregon Pioneer Association* (Portland, 1906), 508; S.B. 259, p. 21, OHS. The mud, dust, haze, and general street conditions are depicted in Harry H. Stein, Kathleen Ryan and Mark Beach, *Portland* (Virginia Beach, Va., 1980), ch. 1.

[67]Mrs. Elinor Smith, Barrell's grand-daughter, related many family stories to E. Kimbark MacColl through the years. See also Ladd family and W. S. Ladd & Co. Papers, 1.

[68]*Oregon Spectator*, 13 March, 1851; Lockley, *History*, 1:415.

[69]Lockley, *History*, 1:661-91.

[70]Paul G. Merriam, "Portland, Oregon, 1840-1890: A Social and Economic History" (Ph.D. diss., University of Oregon, 1971), 29; Dean Collins, "Portland: A Pilgrim's Progress," in *The Taming of the Frontier*, ed. Duncan Aikman (New York, 1925): 29, 163; Clark, *Eden*, 248; Richard L. Hale, *The Log of a Forty-Niner*, ed. Caroline H. Russ (Boston, 1923), 72, 78. Peter Loudine, cook at the California House, was married to a Spokane Indian.

[71]4 March, 1877, entry in "Autobiographical Account," John C. Ainsworth Papers, OHS; *Oregonian*, 4 December, 1900.

[72]"Portland's First Census, 1850," Henry E. Reed Papers, OHS.

[73]Eugene E. Snyder, *Skidmore's Portland* (Portland, 1973), 16; Hale, *Log*, 72; David Newsom, *David Newsom* (Portland, 1972), 38.

[74]Merriam, "Portland, Oregon," 24-25; advertisements in various issues of the *Weekly Oregonian* for 1851; newspaper advertisements in Snyder, *Portland*, and Snyder, *Skidmore*.

[75]Ladd-Reed and Co. Papers, 1; Bancroft, *Builders* 1:604-5; William S. Ladd, "Dictation," 10, BL.

[76]Ladd-Reed and Co. Papers, 1.

[77]The Failings and Cicero H. Lewis arrived in Portland on 9 June, 1851, not in May, 1851, as many published sources state. They sailed from New York on 15 April, 1851. "Draft of Biographical Sketch of J. Failing, with Notes on H. Failing," BL.

CHAPTER 2 FOOTNOTES

[1]Henry Failing, "Draft of Biographical Sketch of J. Failing, with Notes on H. Failing," 2-3, BL.

[2]C. H. Lewis, "Dictation," 2-3, BL; Alfred De Witt to Mrs. C. H. Lewis, 12 January, 1897, C. H. Lewis Papers, OHS.

[3]Harvey W. Scott, ed., *History of Portland, Oregon* (Syracuse, 1890), 140-41; William Toll, *The Making of an Ethnic Middle Class* (Albany, 1982), 9-11; R. Scott Cline, "Community Structure on the Urban Frontier: The Jews of Portland, Oregon, 1849-1887" (M.A. thesis, Portland State University, 1981), 10; Peter R. Decker, *Fortunes and Failures* (Cambridge, 1978), 82.

[4]Decker, *Fortunes and Failures*, 34, 90-91.

[5]Arthur L. Throckmorton, *Oregon Argonauts* (Portland, 1961), 132, 136; Robert G. Albion, *The Rise of New York Port, 1815-1860* (New York, 1939), 284; Decker, *Fortunes and Failures*, 17. Many of the practices Decker describes as occurring in San Francisco apply to Portland and its ties to New York.

[6]Henry W. Corbett to Charles Lanman, 16 January, 1867, Charles Lanman Papers, OHS; Hubert H. Bancroft, *Chronicles of the Builders of the Commonwealth* (San Francisco, 1891), 2:572-93; Day Book of H. W. Corbett Company, Corbett-Failing Papers, UO; Scott, *Portland*, 485; Throckmorton, *Argonauts*, 129-30.

[7]Throckmorton, *Argonauts*, 132-33; Day Book of H. W. Corbett Company; Bancroft, *Builders*, 2:572-93; Failing, "Biographical Sketch of J. Failing," 3.

[8]Throckmorton, *Argonauts*, 132; Richard L. Hale, *The Log of a Forty-Niner*, ed. Caroline H. Russ (Boston, 1923), 84; C. H. Lewis, "Dictation," 18. On 13 October, 1852, "Everything seems plenty and money is not behind. Business is brisk and lively" in Portland. John T. Kerns, "Journal of Crossing the Plains in 1852," in *Transactions of the Forty-Second Annual Reunion of the Oregon Pioneer Association* (Portland, 1977), 192.

[9]Albion, *New York Port*, 283.

¹⁰Unidentified Portland newspaper clipping (obituary), ca. 31 March, 1903, in Henry W. Corbett Papers, OHS; Richard Marlitt, ed., *The Corbett Tree, 1827-1982* (Portland, 1982); Throckmorton, *Argonauts*, 133.

¹¹Mrs. Zachariah Norton, in a letter of 7 March, 1850, wrote of Portland, "In this little town the Sabbath is more regarded than in any country I have found while rounding the mighty continent," in "Voyage of the *Seguin*, 1849," *OHQ* 34 (September, 1933), 257. Throckmorton, *Argonauts*, 175, 233, 239; *Weekly Oregonian*, 6 May, 1854; United States Census Office, *Census of Oregon* (Washington, 1860).

¹²Throckmorton, *Argonauts*, 133.

¹³Joseph Gaston, *The Centennial History of Oregon, 1811-1912*, (Chicago, 1912), 2:18.

¹⁴"Biographical Sketch of J. Failing," 4; Gaston, *Oregon* 2:18; Throckmorton, *Argonauts*, 135. The Portland Wells Fargo office opened in October, 1852; "Slowly, but surely, transportation and communication facilities radiated out of Portland." W. Turrentine Jackson, "Wells Fargo &Co.: Into the Inland Empire and Idaho Territory," *Idaho Yesterdays* 25 (Winter, 1982), 2.

¹⁵Throckmorton, *Argonauts*, 135-38.

¹⁶"Biographical Sketch of J. Failing," 5-6.

¹⁷Throckmorton, *Argonauts*, 241; United States Census Office, *Census of Oregon* (Washington, 1860).

¹⁸C. H. Lewis, "Dictation," 2-3; Alfred De Witt to Mrs. C. H. Lewis, 12 January, 1897, Lewis Papers.

¹⁹C. H. Lewis, "Dictation," 7, 36-46; C. H. Lewis, "Draft of Biographical Sketch," 8, BL.

²⁰C. H. Lewis, "Dictation," 7; Cicero H. Lewis to David C. Lewis, 4 April, 1853, Lewis Papers.

²¹C. H. Lewis, "Dictation," 7; "Biographical Sketch," 7.

²²C. H. Lewis, "Dictation," 7; "Biographical Sketch," 7; Henry E. Reed, *Cavalcade of Front Street, 1866-1941* (Portland, 1941), 2. For a thorough study of merchant credit practices nationally, see James E. Vance, *The Merchant's World* (Englewood Cliffs, N.J., 1970), esp. 75-76, 83.

²³S.B. 34, p. 54; Vance, *Merchant's World*, 75-76; Decker, *Fortunes and Failures*, 87.

²⁴S.B. 122, p. 163.

²⁵William S. Ladd, "Dictation," 12-15, BL; Account Book, August, 1851 to 1853, Ladd Family and W. S. Ladd & Co. Papers, OHS.

²⁶William S. Ladd, "Dictation," 13-14; *Oregon Statesman*, 9 April, 1853. The "& Co." indicated one or more silent partners.

²⁷William S. Ladd, "Dictation," 16; Extract of letter by the Rev. St. M. Fackler, "Immigration of 1852," Works Progress Administration, Oregon Historical Records Survey, 1936, Oregon State Library; Throckmorton, *Argonauts*, 167. See W. Turrentine Jackson, "Portland: Wells Fargo's Hub for the Pacific Northwest," *OHQ* 86 (Fall, 1985), 229-66.

²⁸William S. Ladd, "Dictation," 15.

²⁹Orin K. Burrell, *Gold in the Woodpile* (Eugene, 1967), 42, 49; Thorne's Numerical System, "Title of Abstracts, Portland, 1887," 141, OHS.

³⁰Harvey W. Scott, ed., *History of Portland, Oregon* (Syracuse, 1890), 141.

³¹Dorothy O. Johansen, "Early History of Reed College," 1-2, work in progress in the possession of the author; Dorothy O. Johansen, "The Oregon Steam Navigation Company: An Example of Capitalism on the Frontier," *Pacific Historical Review* 10 (June, 1941): 179-188 (hereafter cited as "OSN"); Johansen, "Capitalism on the Far-Western Frontier: The Oregon Steam Navigation Company" (Ph.D. diss., University of Washington, 1941), 163-64 (hereafter cited as "Capitalism").

³²Simeon G. Reed, "Biographical Sketch," BL.

³³Throckmorton, *Argonauts*, 177-78; Snyder, *Early Portland*, 168-73.

³⁴John Reps, *Cities of the American West* (Princeton, 1979), 356; Richard C. Wade, *The Urban Frontier* (Chicago, 1959), 66; Early Pomeroy, *The Pacific Slope* (New York, 1965), 6; Joseph Gaston, *Portland, Oregon, Its History and Builders* (Portland, 1911), 2:442. David R. Goldfield, "The Urban South: A Regional Framework," *American Historical Review* 86 (December, 1981), 1012 n. 12 defines a "town" as having fewer than 1,500 inhabitants in 1850.

35Most of the biographical information on Wilson comes from John Wilson, "Chapter of Autobiography," typed in 1921 from the 1899 original, in the possession of his great-grandson James B. Robertson, Ashland, Oregon. Other information comes from the John Wilson Papers in the possession of his great-grand-daughter Susan Wilson Gallagher, Portland.

36John Wilson, "Chapter of Autobiography," John Wilson Papers.

37Wade, *Urban Frontier*, 70.

3818 February, 1877, entry in John C. Ainsworth, "Account of My Life," UO (hereafter cited as "Diary").

39Ainsworth "Diary," 18 February, 1877; Snyder, *Early Portland*, ch. 13. Several accounts, including Ainsworth's diary, note that Samuel Clemens (Mark Twain) was one of Ainsworth's river pilots. Clemens was only 14 in 1849, and would not have been a regular pilot; however, he may have ridden or worked on Ainsworth's riverboat.

40Ainsworth "Diary," 18 February, 1877; *Oregon Spectator*, 4 October, 1851; Throckmorton, *Argonauts*, 119-20.

41Ainsworth "Diary," 18 February, 1877; Eugene Synder, *Portland Names and Neighborhoods* (Portland, 1979), 77.

42Throckmorton, *Argonauts*, 206; Oscar O. Winther, *The Oregon Country* (Lincoln, 1969), 169; Randall V. Mills, *Stern-Wheelers Up Columbia* (Lincoln, 1977), ch. 3.

43Throckmorton, *Argonauts*, 206; F. J. Smith, comp., "Marine Records of Oregon, 1850-1917," Columbia River Maritime Museum (on exhibit); *United States Census of Oregon Territory, 1850*, OHS.

44*United States Census of Oregon Territory, 1850*, OHS.

45S.B. 259, 18; Snyder, *Portland Names*, 150-51.

46H. K. Hines, *An Illustrated History of the State of Oregon* (Chicago, 1893), 1074; Gaston, *Centennial History*, 2: 54-62; Harvey W. Scott, *History of Oregon Country*, comp. Leslie M. Scott (Portland, 1924) 2:274.

47Gaston, *Centennial History*, 2:56-57.

48Throckmorton, *Argonauts*, 171.

49Gaston, *Centennial History*, 2:57. Leonard's detailed account of his life is an excellent though disorganized description of the early merchant-shipping business.

50Gaston, *Centennial History*, 2:56, 60; Herman C. Leonard, "A Letter of Certification," 16 March, 1907, in the possession of Lady James McDonald, Portland.

51E. Kimbark MacColl, *The Shaping of a City* (Portland, 1976), 162-63. The gas and water enterprises are treated in a later chapter.

52*United States Census of Oregon Territory, 1850*, OHS.

CHAPTER 3 FOOTNOTES

1Robert G. Albion, *The Rise of New York Port, 1815-1860* (New York, 1939), 323; Malcolm Clark, Jr., *Eden Seekers* (Boston, 1981), 242; Arthur L. Throckmorton, *Oregon Argonauts* (Portland, 1961), 113.

2Eugene E. Snyder, *Early Portland* (Portland, 1970), 76-77, 80-81; Clark, *Eden*, 243; Robert C. Notson, *Making the Day Begin* (Portland, 1976), 5; *Oregonian*, 19 October, 1892.

3Snyder, *Early Portland*, 85-86; Clark, *Eden*, 242; Percy Maddux, *City on the Willamette* (Portland, 1952), 25; Edgar W. Wright, ed., *Lewis and Dryden's Marine History of the Pacific Northwest* (Portland, 1895), 51.

4Snyder, *Early Portland*, 83-84.

5Philip A. Marquam, "Dictation," 7, BL; Snyder, *Early Portland*, 89-90. According to Marquam, the block was worth $250,000 in 1889.

6Snyder, *Early Portland*, 89; Clark, *Eden*, 248-49.

7Waymire, as quoted in Throckmorton, *Argonauts*, 224; Snyder, *Early Portland*, 150-55; Harvey W. Scott, *History of the Oregon Country*, comp. Leslie M. Scott (Portland, 1924), 2:278.

[8]*Weekly Oregonian*, 4 December, 1850; D. H. Lownsdale to William M. King, 13 January, 1850, William M. King Papers, OHS; Deady's opinion of Chapman in Matthew P. Deady, *Pharisee Among Philistines, The Diary of Matthew P. Deady, 1871-1892*, ed. Malcolm Clark, Jr. (Portland, 1975), 1:xix; Snyder, *Early Portland*, 148.

[9]Oscar O. Winther, *The Old Oregon Country* (Lincoln, Neb., 1969), 124; Scott, *Oregon Country* 2:278; *Oregonian* quoted in Snyder, *Early Portland*, 150.

[10]"Plank Road," Works Progress Administration, Oregon Historical Records Survey, 1936, Oregon State Library; Scott, *Oregon Country*, 2:278.

[11]*Oregon Statesman*, 20 January, 1852, 17 February, 1852, 3 February, 1852; list of property transactions, King Papers; *Oregonian*, 14 August, 1902.

[12]From 13 August, 1850, until 20 June, 1851, Lownsdale sold King 25 lots; the two exchanged other lots. Lot 107 was partially for the new state penitentiary. List of property transactions, King Papers.

[13]*Oregon Weekly Times*, 2 October, 1851, as quoted in Winther, *Old Oregon*, 124; Terence O'Donnell and Thomas Vaughan, *Portland* (Portland, 1984), 14-15.

[14]"Plank Road"; Scott, *Oregon Country*, 2:278; Waymire, as quoted in Throckmorton, *Argonauts*, 224; *Weekly Oregonian*, 19 May, 1855.

[15]Scott, *Oregon Country*, 2:87; Winther, *Old Oregon*, 124; No. 7170, Provisional and Territorial Government Papers, OHS.

[16]*Lamb v. Davenport* Federal Case 8015 (1871); 85 U.S. 307 (1873). See also *Photostatic Copies of Depositions and Transfer of Titles, City of Portland, 1845-50*, 166-69, Port of Portland Papers, OHS.

[17]*Oregon Statesman*, 6 February, 1855, 6 March, 1855.

[18]*Oregon Spectator*, 11 November, 1851; *Oregon Weekly Times*, 15 November, 1851; George M. Belknap, *Oregon Imprints, 1845-1870* (Eugene, 1968), 50; Charles A. Tracy III, "Police Function in Portland, 1851-1874 Part 1," *OHQ* 80 (Spring, 1979), 12; David Logan to Mary Logan, 20 February, 1852, in "22 Letters of David Logan, Pioneer Oregon Lawyer," ed. Harry E. Pratt, *OHQ* 44 (September, 1943), 261; Clark, *Eden*, 251-52; Sidney Teiser, "First Associate Justice of the Oregon Territory: O. C. Pratt," *OHQ* 49 (September, 1948), 174. See chapters 4 and 5 for the politics behind the two-to-one supreme court decision in favor of Chapman.

[19]Notice of 28 August, 1856, Daniel H. Lownsdale Papers, OHS. *Oregon Statesman*, 6 March, 1855.

[20]Coffin deposition in *Photostatic Copies*, 142; City "Claims" in Oregon, Bureau of Land Management Papers, Federal Records Center, Seattle; Daniel H. Lownsdale to the *Oregon Statesman*, 18 October, 1858.

[21]*Oregon Statesman*, 2 August, 1853, Leslie M. Scott, ed., "Grand Lodge of Oregon, 1851-1861," in *Masonic Papers* 2 (Portland, 1938), 335-63.

[22]*Oregon Statesman*, 6 March, 1855.

[23]*Oregon Statesman*, 6 March, 1855.

[24]*Oregon Statesman*, 6 February, 1855; John Reps, *Cities of the American West* (Princeton, 1979), 10, 697. "An Act for the Relief of the Citizens of Towns upon the Lands of the United States," 23 May, 1844, was the official title of the Townsite Act.

[25]*Oregon Statesman*, 6 February, 1855.

[26]"Commissioner, General Land Office, Oct. 18, 1858, "City Claims" in Oregon, Bureau of Land Management Papers.

[27]*Stark v. Starr*, 94 U.S. 477: 483-84; *Starr v. Stark*, 22 Federal Case 13317 (1874). For Deady's reaction, see Ralph James Mooney, "Formalism and Fairness: Matthew P. Deady and Federal Public Land Law in the Early West," work in progress in the possession of the author, Eugene, Oregon.

[28]United States Census Office, *Census of Oregon* (Washington, 1860); Thorne's Numerical System, "Title of Abstracts, Portland, 1887," 146; Lownsdale Estate Papers, 1852-1872, Multnomah County Records Management File, OHS.

[29]Lownsdale Estate Papers, 1852-1872. Deady could never afford to build on the property.

[30]Lownsdale Estate Papers; Mooney, "Formalism and Fairness," 38-39; Sawyer quoted in Harvey W. Scott, ed., *History of Portland, Oregon* (Syracuse, 1890), 123.

[31]*Weekly Oregonian*, 20 August, 1859. In 1868, Deady ruled that Daniel Lownsdale had been entitled to only a one-fifth interest in Nancy's claim.

[32]United States Census Office, *Census of Oregon* (Washington, 1870); *Oregonian*, 19 October, 1892; Park Bureau Files, 1870-1871, Box 17, City of Portland Archives.

[33]*Weekly Oregonian*, 4 February, 1854; Clark, *Eden*, 245. Records in the William King Papers verify King's purchase of 21 lots on block 107 for $98.00.

[34]*Weekly Oregonian*, 4 February, 1854.

[35]*Oregonian*, 15, 22 September, 1862, 5, 6 December, 1862.

[36]Joseph Gaston, *Portland, Oregon, Its History and Builders* (Portland, 1911), 3:496-498; Howard M. Corning, ed., *Dictionary of Oregon History* (Portland, 1956), 57.

[37]*Oregonian*, 5 March, 1882; Park Bureau Files, 1870-1871, Box 17, City of Portland Archives.

[38]Scott, *History of Portland*, 136-37; Deady, *Pharisee*, Appendix A, 112-113; Eugene E. Snyder, *Portland Names and Neighborhoods* (Portland, 1979), 214-15.

[39]City of Portland, *Water* (Portland, 1983), 2-3.

[40]Scott, *Portland*, 137. The same story will be told in a later chapter.

[41]*William P. Burke et al. vs. Heirs of D. H. Lownsdale, Patrick O'Neil, J. C. Morrison, and F. W. Pettygrove* (Portland, 1873), 72-83; Corning, *Dictionary*, 240; Lownsdale Estate Papers, 1852-1872.

[42]Lownsdale Estate Papers, 1852-1872.

[43]S.B. 259, pp. 120-21.

[44]*Oregon Statesman*, 12 August, 1851.

[45]S.B. 259, pp. 120-21; Corning, *Dictionary*, 244.

[46]Corning, *Dictionary*, 234; "Portland, Oregon: Its Founding and Early Businessmen," *The Oregon Native Son* 2 (December, 1900), 338-39.

[47]"Portland, Oregon," 338-39; Scott, *Oregon Country*, 2:88, 279; S.B. 259, p. 65.

[48]Lownsdale Estate Papers, 1852-1872; Corning, *Dictionary*, 234; United States Census Office, *Census of Oregon* (Washington, 1870).

[49]*Oregon Statesman*, 25 October, 1859; W. W. Page to Asahel Bush, 24 August, 1859, Asahel Bush Papers, Bush House.

[50]Matthew P. Deady to Asahel Bush, 18 February, 1863, Asahel Bush Papers, OHS.

[51]"The Descendants of Captain and Mrs. John H. Couch, 1811-1948," mimeographed, OHS; United States Census Office, *Census of Oregon* (Washington, 1870); Gaston, *Portland*, 2:375; S.B. 112, pp. 138-140; "Inventory of the Estate of John H. Couch," Personal Business Files of W. S. Caldwell, Auditor's Office, City of Portland, Archives; "Petition's Folder — Miscellaneous," City of Portland Archives.

CHAPTER 4 FOOTNOTES

[1]Quoted in James R. Robertson, "Social Evolution of Oregon," *OHQ* 3 (March, 1902), 32; James W. Hurst, *Law and the Conditions of Freedom in the Nineteenth Century United States* (Madison, 1956), 13; Terence O'Donnell, "Oregon History," in *Oregon Blue Book, 1985-1986* (Salem, 1985), 441.

[2]For early *Oregonian* coverage, see George S. Turnbull, *History of Oregon Newspapers* (Portland, 1939), 61-85. For general comments, see Richard L. McCormick, "The Party Period and Public Policy: An Exploratory Hypothesis," *Journal of American History* 66 (September, 1979), 279-98.

[3]For an analysis of community political power structure pertinent to the 1850s, see Prologue of David Fasenfast, "Community Politics and Urban Redevelopment," *Urban Affairs Quarterly* 22 (September, 1986), 101.

[4]W. S. Ladd to Asahel Bush, 18 May, 1855, Asahel Bush Papers, Bush House.

[5]Rush Welter, *The Mind of America, 1820-1860* (New York, 1975), 129, 133; Edward F. Failing, "Dictation of Edward F. Failing Relating to His Father, Josiah Failing," BL; Robert Johannsen, *Frontier Politics and the Sectional Crisis* (Seattle, 1955), 14.

[6]Welter, *Mind of America*, 165.

[7]Sam Bass Warner, Jr., *The Private City* (Philadelphia, 1968), 99; Welter, *Mind of America*, 165; Kenneth Fox, *Better City Government* (Philadelphia, 1977), xiv.

[8]Minutes of the Proceedings of the City Council, City of Portland, vol. 1, Portland City Hall Archives (hereafter cited as Council Proceedings).

[9]Kenneth N. Owens, "Patterns and Structures in Western Territorial Politics," *Western Historical Quarterly* 1 (October, 1970), 377.

[10]Beatrice Decker, city archivist, to Editor, *OHQ* 56 (December, 1955), 354-56. The exact date of the election in April, 1851, is disputed; it was not reported in the press. April 6 has become the generally accepted date for Portland's birthday. As April 6, 1851, was a Sunday, April 7 appears to have been the election day, since elections were never held on Sundays.

[11]Decker to Editor, 354; Charles A. Tracy III, "Police Functions in Portland, 1851-1874," Part 1, *OHQ* 80 (Spring, 1979), 9-10.

[12]Decker to Editor, 355; S.B. 259, pp. 21-22; Council Proceedings, 1.

[13]Decker to Editor, 356. After leaving office, the restless O'Bryant moved to Douglas County, Oregon, then to Walla Walla, Washington, and finally to California.

[14]Numbers 4512, 4509 and 4510, Provisional and Territorial Government Papers, OHS; *Oregon Statesman*, 9 April, 1853; *Weekly Oregonian*, 5 November, 1853.

[15]*Weekly Oregonian*, 15 October, 1853, 5 November, 1853.

[16]*Weekly Oregonian*, 11, 18 March, 1853; *Oregonian*, 5 June, 1904.

[17]Decker to Editor, 356; Council Proceedings, 1; E. Kimbark MacColl, *The Shaping of a City* (Portland, 1976), 24.

[18]Ads in *Weekly Oregonian* for June, 1855; *Oregon Statesman*, 25 October, 1859; United States Census Office, *Census of Oregon* (Washington, 1870); Eugene Snyder, *Portland Names and Neighborhoods* (Portland, 1979), 222.

[19]Dorothy O. Johansen, "Capitalism on the Far-Western Frontier: The Oregon Steam Navigation Company" (Ph.D. diss., University of Washington, 1941), 62; Cayuse, Yakima and Rogue River War Papers, folder 2, University of Oregon Library; Harvey W. Scott, ed., *History of Portland, Oregon* (Syracuse, 1890), 142.

[20]Tracy, "Police Function," 24; George Vaughn to Governor Curry, 2 October, 1855, Cayuse, Yakima and Rogue River War Papers; "Indian Wars, October, 1855-June, 1856," Port of Portland Papers, OHS.

[21]The Holmes-Norris conflict recorded in S.B. 259, pp. 10-11, and in Council Proceedings, vol. 1. For an uncritical sketch of Holmes, see Scott, *Portland*, 557-58.

[22]The estimated worth of Holmes's estate is based on the tripling of real-estate values between 1858 and the 1860 U.S. Census, which reported his total worth as $85,000. S.B. 259, pp. 10-11.

[23]Tracy, "Police Function," 25.

[24]Leslie M. Scott, ed., "Grand Lodge of Oregon, 1851-61," in *Masonic Papers* 2 (Portland, 1938), 335-63.

[25]Tracy, "Police Function," 26. Council date is taken from Council Proceedings, vol. 1.

[26]*Oregonian*, 1 May, 1891; Charles A. Tracy III, "Police Functions in Portland, 1851-1874," Part 2, *OHQ* (Summer, 1979), 134, 137.

[27]"Facts for the People of Portland relating to the Levee Case," Portland, 1860, No. 588 in George N. Belknap, *Oregon Imprints, 1845-1870* (Eugene, 1968); Scott, *Portland*, 136.

[28]"Facts for the People."

[29]Scott, *Portland*, 134; "Facts for the People."

[30]Scott, *Portland*, 134.

[31]Ralph James Mooney, "Formalism and Fairness: Matthew Deady and Federal Public Land Law in the West," work in progress in the possession of the author, Eugene, Oregon; *Olney* decision, 1 Oregon 69 (1853); *Williams* decision quoted in *Oregonian*, 23 April, 1940.

[32]"Facts for the People"; Council Proceedings, vol. 1, 7 June, 1856; No. 9803, Provisional and Territorial Government Papers, OHS.

[33]Council Proceedings, vol. 1, 29 October, 1858, and 7 January, 1859; *Weekly Oregonian*, 23, 24, March, 1860.

[34]*Weekly Oregonian*, 24, 31 March, 1860. Mayor Harry Lane became involved in three similar episodes in 1906-1907.

[35]Portland Council Documents, Box 4, City of Portland Archives; Council Proceedings, vol. 2, 25 July, 1860.

[36]Scott, *Portland*, 134-135; Council Proceedings, vol. 2, 7 and 14 June, 1861.

[37]Scott, *Portland*, 135; *Lownsdale vs. Portland*, 1 Oregon 398; Moody, "Deady," 26-28.

[38]W. S. Ladd to James W. Nesmith, 11 January, 1862, James W. Nesmith Papers, OHS.

[39]Michael H. Frisch, "The Community Elite and the Emergence of Urban Politics: Springfield, Massachusetts, 1840-1880," in *Nineteenth-Century Cities*, ed. Stephen Thernstrom and Richard Sennett (New Haven, 1969), 281. See also Carl V. Harris, *Political Power in Birmingham, 1871-1921* (Knoxville, 1977), 64.

[40]*Weekly Oregonian*, 9 April, 1859.

[41]David A. Johnson, "Political Generations in American History: The Far Western States, 1840-1860," paper presented at the Annual Convention, American Historical Association, 30 December, 1984, 18; Richard Hofstadter, *The American Political Tradition and the Men Who Made It* (New York, 1968), 59.

[42]On New York, see David C. Hammack, *Power and Society* (New York, 1982), 131; on San Francisco, see William Issel and Robert W. Cherny, *San Francisco, 1865-1932* (Berkeley, 1986), 21-22.

[43]*Portland Commercial*, 24 March, 1853; Tracy, "Police Function," 2, 135-36.

[44]Sam Bass Warner, Jr., *The Private City* (Philadelphia, 1968), xi, 4.

CHAPTER 5 FOOTNOTES

[1]See Robert E. Burton, *Democrats of Oregon* (Eugene, 1970), 3.

[2]William S. Ladd, "Dictation," 4 November, 1889, BL. On the Bush-Ladd relation, see the Ladd correspondence in "Political Correspondence," Asahel Bush Papers, Bush House.

[3]Richard Hofstadter, *The American Political Tradition and the Men Who Made It* (New York, 1968), 56; Gene M. Gressley, "The West: Past, Present and Future," *Western Historical Quarterly* 17 (January, 1986), 5-25.

[4]*Oregon Spectator*, 22 February, 1849; Malcolm Clark, *Eden Seekers* (Boston, 1981), 232; James E. Hendrickson, *Joe Lane of Oregon* (New Haven, 1967), 17-18; Arthur L. Throckmorton, *Oregon Argonauts* (Portland, 1961), 28.

[5]Robert R. Thompson, "Account of My Life," BL; Joseph Lane to James W. Nesmith, 15 November, 1849, James W. Nesmith Papers, OHS.

[6]Hendrickson, *Joe Lane*, 18; *Oregonian*, 5 October, 1888; John McCraken, "Dictation," BL.

[7]McCraken, "Dictation"; Kenneth M. Owens, "Pattern and Structure in Western Territorial Politics," *Western Historical Quarterly* 1 (October, 1970): 375-76.

[8]John McCraken to Asahel Bush, 28 October, 1855, Bush Papers. See also David A. Johnson, "Confronting a New World: Oregon's Founding Fathers and the Political Economy of Development, 1855-1885," paper presented at the Pacific Coast Branch, American Historical Association, 19 August, 1981, 3.

[9]Clark, *Eden*, 239, 246; Hendrickson, *Joe Lane*, 27.

[10]Robert R. Thompson to Joseph Lane, 1852, quoted in Thompson, "Account"; Hendrickson, *Joe Lane*, 58; Matthew P. Deady to James W. Nesmith, 8 November, 1852, Nesmith Papers.

[11]Donald C. Johnson, "Politics, Personalities and Policies of the Oregon Territorial Supreme Court, 1849-1859," *Environmental Law* 4 (Fall, 1973), 45-46; Hendrickson, *Joe Lane*, 46-47. On the Chapman-Pratt incident, see the previous chapter.

[12]Hendrickson, *Joe Lane*, 74; Clark, *Eden*, 265-66.

[13]Thompson, "Account." The Dalles received its current name in 1860. Founded as a Methodist mission, the townsite was laid out as Fort Dalles in 1854, when lots were being sold at about the time of Thompson's arrival.

[14]Thompson, "Account."

[15]Hendrickson, *Joe Lane*, 46, 93; Johnson, "Confronting," 3: *Oregonian*, 18 June, 1853; Robert H. Wiebe, *The Opening of American Society* (New York, 1984), 365.

[16]*Oregon Statesman*, 4 July, 1853.

[17]David Logan to his sister, 28 November, 1855, in David Logan, "22 Letters of David Logan, Pioneer Oregon Lawyer," ed. Harry E. Pratt, *OHQ* 44 (September, 1943), 269; Clark, *Eden*, 270.

[18]Hendrickson, *Joe Lane*, 113-14; Clark, *Eden*, 272-74; William S. Ladd to Asahel Bush, 18 May, 1855, Asahel Bush Papers. See also Priscilla Knuth, "Oregon Know Nothing Pamphlet Illustrates Early Politics," *OHQ* 54 (March, 1953), 45-52.

[19]David A. Johnson, "Political Generations in American History: The Far Western United States, 1840-1880," paper presented at the Annual Convention, American Historical Association, 30 December, 1984; Hendrickson, *Joe Lane*, 140.

[20]William S. Ladd to Asahel Bush, 9 March, 1857, Asahel Bush Papers.

[21]*Oregon Statesman*, 3 March, 1857, 28 July, 1857, 4 August, 1857; Hendrickson, *Joe Lane*, 140; Clark, *Eden*, 290; Elizabeth McLagan, *A Peculiar Paradise* (Portland, 1980), 50-51. Ladd's attitude toward free blacks is not clear, either in his surviving letters or in Hubert Bancroft's *Chronicles of the Builders of the Commonwealth*. His attitudes toward public education in the 1860s are implied from these sources. See Ladd, "Dictation."

[22]Johnson, "Political Generations," 12-14; Clark, *Eden*, 290; Robert W. Johannsen, "Spectators of Disunion: The Pacific Northwest and the Civil War," *Pacific Northwest Quarterly* 44 (July, 1953), 108.

[23]As quoted in Gordon B. Dodds, *Oregon* (New York, 1977), 101.

[24]Waymire quoted in Throckmorton, *Argonauts*, 224; Clark, *Eden*, 291.

[25]Johnson, "Political Generations," 6-9; Clark, *Eden*, 291; Hofstadter, *Political Tradition*, 58; Richard L. McCormick, "The Party Period and Public Policy: An Exploratory Hypothesis," *Journal of American History* 66 (September, 1979), 287; Oregon Constitution, Article 11.

[26]Clark, *Eden*, 290; *Oregon Statesman*, 22 December, 1857, quoted in Hendrickson, *Joe Lane*. Ladd voted for the Democrat Stephen A. Douglas against Lincoln in 1860. Bush and Douglas supported popular sovereignty. Ladd, "Dictation."

[27]Harry C. Blair and Rebecca Tarshis, *Colonel Edward D. Baker* (Portland, 1960), 92; Clark, *Eden,* 300.

[28]*Weekly Oregonian*, 2 and 9 April, 1859.

[29]Blair and Tarshis, *Colonel Baker*, 98; T. W. Davenport, "Slavery in Oregon," *OHQ* 9 (December, 1908), 347-48. Davenport actually observed Baker's Oregon campaigning. Also from a participant is George H. Williams, "Political History of Oregon from 1853 to 1865," *OHQ* 2 (March, 1901), 24.

[30]Blair and Tarshis, *Colonel Baker*, 101-102; Williams, "Political History," 24.

[31]*Oregon Statesman*, 3 October, 1860.

[32]Williams, "Political History," 28-31. The Union Party movement among Democrats (in contrast to the regular Democrats nationally) supported the war and the suppression of southern rebellion. It "inured to the benefit of the Republicans, whose postwar attitude involved little of gratitude to the Democrats for wartime support." J. G. Randall and David Donald, *The Civil War and Reconstruction* (Boston, 1961), 457.

[33]Clark, *Eden*, 301; Owens, "Patterns and Structure," 380-81.

[34]*Weekly Oregonian*, 10 November, 1860.

[35]Robert C. Notson, *Making the Day Begin* (Portland, 1976), 6-7; *Oregonian*, 4 December, 1900. Henry Pittock II, of Cannon Beach, Oregon, has copies of Dryer's debts, as of April 1, 1860. For Dryer's later debts, see the Daniel Lownsdale Papers, OHS: To Thomas J. Carter, June, 1862, as trustee for Lownsdale, $586.10, and to James Terwilliger, February, 1864, $1,084.

[36]Blair and Tarshis, *Colonel Baker*, 129.

[37]Martha Anderson, *Black Pioneers of the Northwest, 1800-1918* (Portland, 1980), 64. Anderson mistakenly identified The Dalles, rather than Dallas, Oregon, as the site of the effigy. Also see Blair and Tarshis, *Colonel Baker*, 115.

[38]Clark, *Eden*, 302; Anderson, *Black Pioneers*, 64.

[39]Blair and Tarshis, *Colonel Baker*, ch. 15.

[40]See G. Thomas Edwards, "Benjamin Stark, the United States Senate, and 1862 Membership Issues," Part 1, *OHQ* 72 (December, 1971), 315-38. The Asahel Bush Papers of Bush House contain many references to Stark's notes held by Bush during the 1850s. John McCraken's letter to Bush of 31 January, 1859, mentions Bush's mortgages on buildings and lots in Portland blocks 40 and 41.

[41]Davenport, "Slavery in Oregon," 352.

CHAPTER 6 FOOTNOTES

[1]Arthur L. Throckmorton, *Oregon Argonauts* (Portland, 1961), 183-89. Citations for repayment authorizations are in *U.S. Statutes at Large*, v. 12 (1861) 198, v. 15 (1867), 24, v. 18 (1875) 417, v. 19 (1877) 374, v. 20 (1878) 127, v. 20 (1879) 423, v. 21 (1881) 431, v. 22 (1882) 280, v. 24 (1886) 195, 300, 305.

[2]Throckmorton, *Argonauts*, 189, 235; Malcolm Clark, *Eden Seekers* (Boston, 1981), 285; "Claims Against the United States for Horses Lost in the Indian Wars, 1855-56," James Steel Papers in the possession of the Great Northwest Bookstore, Portland; "Letter to the Secretary of the Treasury, Treasury Department, Third Auditor's Office," 14 November, 1871, 42nd Congress, 2nd. session, Senate, Ex. Doc. No. 1, 1-2.

[3]Among the 14 are branches of two San Francisco firms. Real-estate speculation is excluded from the multiplier of 20, which in 1988 seems the best approximate equation for 1855 dollars. For general reference, see Lee Soltow, *Men and Wealth in the United States, 1850-1870* (New Haven, 1975), 52-85, and Edward Pessen, *Riches, Class and Power Before the Civil War* (Lexington, Mass., 1973), 29.

[4]David Logan to his sister, 27 January, 1856, and 27 January (1857?), in David Logan, "22 Letters of David Logan, Pioneer Oregon Lawyer," ed. Harry E. Pratt, *OHQ* 44 (September, 1943), 270-71, 273-74; Throckmorton, *Argonauts*, 233-34.

[5]Throckmorton, *Argonauts*, 203; Oscar O. Winther, *The Old Oregon Country* (Lincoln, 1969), 175; Percy Maddux, *City on the Willamette* (Portland, 1952), 6; Jean-Nicolas Perlot, *Gold Seeker*, ed. Howard R. Lamar (New Haven, 1985), 359.

[6]Throckmorton, *Argonauts*, 229, 241.

[7]Throckmorton, *Argonauts*, 212; W. S. Ladd to Asahel Bush, 15 September, 1856, Asahel Bush Papers, Bush House.

[8]Throckmorton, *Argonauts*, 206; Dorothy D. Hirsch, "Study of the Foreign Wheat Trade of Oregon, 1869-1887," *Reed College Bulletin* 31 (August, 1953), 51.

[9]Robert G. Albion, *The Rise of New York Port, 1815-1860* (New York, 1939), 284; Bray Hammond, *Banks and Politics in America* (Princeton, 1957), 626.

[10]W. S. Ladd, "Dictation," 4 November, 1889, BL.

[11]W. S. Ladd, "Dictation," 4 November, 1889; Hubert H. Bancroft, *Chronicles of the Builders of the Commonwealth* (San Francisco, 1891), 1:610.

[12]W. S. Ladd, "Dictation," 4 November, 1889. The *Oregonian* now occupies the site of the Ladd home.

[13]Glen Porter and Harold C. Livesay, *Merchants and Manufacturers* (Baltimore, 1971), 69-72, 128; Orin K. Burrell, *Gold in the Woodpile* (Eugene, 1967), 43; E. Digby Baltzell, *Puritan Boston and Quaker Philadelphia* (New York, 1979), 230-31.

[14]Porter and Livesay, *Merchants and Manufacturers*, 129; W. Turrentine Jackson, "Portland: Wells Fargo's Hub for the Pacific Northwest," *OHQ* 86 (Fall, 1985), 233.

[15]Albert R. Gutowsky, "History of Commercial Banking in Oregon," *Oregon Business Review* 24 (August, 1965), 1-6. See also Hammond, *Banks and Politics*, 605, 606, 617, and the Oregon Supreme Court ruling in *Oregon v. Hibernian Savings and Loan Association*, 8 Bellinger 399-402. The National Banking Act of 3 June, 1864, completely revised the banking system first enacted by the National Currency Act of 25 February, 1863; the revised law essentially launched the national banking system.

[16]W. S. Ladd to Asahel Bush, 23 March, 1859, Bush Papers; W. W. Page to Asahel Bush, 24 August, 1858, Bush Papers; Throckmorton, *Argonauts*, 243.

[17]W. S. Ladd to Howland & Aspinwell, 20 June, 1859, quoted in Burrell, *Gold in the Woodpile*, 45.

[18]Throckmorton, *Argonauts*, 271; Philip A. Marquam, "Dictation," 22 November, 1889, BL; James E. Vance, Jr., *The Merchant's World* (Englewood Cliffs, N.J., 1970), 75-76. For Ladd's correspondence (which also shows his active management and approach to customers), see Ladd Family and W. S. Ladd and Co. Papers, OHS.

[19]S.B. 71, p. 182, *Sixty Milestones of Progress, 1859-1919*, ed. Martin E. Fitzgerland (Portland, 1919), 19.

[20]Throckmorton, *Argonauts*, ch. 10; Paul G. Merriam, "Portland, Oregon, 1840-1890: A Social and Economic History" (Ph.D. diss., University of Oregon, 1971), 215; Michael P. Conzen, "The Maturing Urban System in the United States, 1840-1910," *Annals of the American Association of Geographers* 67 (No. 3, 1977), 90; Dorothy O. Johansen, "Capitalism on the Far Western Frontier: The Oregon Steam Navigation Company" (Ph.D. diss., University of Washington, 1941), 166.

[21]Sam Bass Warner, Jr., *The Private City* (Philadelphia, 1968), 4; Samuel P. Hays, *American Political History as Social Analysis* (Knoxville, 1980), 191; Hammond, *Banks and Politics*, 630.

[22]Hammond, *Banks and Politics*, 630; *Weekly Oregonian*, 15 October, 1859.

[23]"First Congregational Church" (Portland, 1984); Maddux, *City*, 42.

[24]S.B. 62, p. 86, Arthur C. Spencer III, "Trinity Episcopal Church in Northwest Portland ... An Informal History," *Old Portland Today*, 1 June, 1975; Arthur C. Spencer III, "Historical Notes, Trinity Episcopal Church Archives," OHS; Glenn Chesney Quiett, *They Built the West* (New York, 1934), 350.

[25]Dean Collins, "Portland: A Pilgrim's Progress," in The *Taming of the Frontier*, ed. Duncan Aikman (New York, 1925), 160.

[26]Leslie M. Scott, "Grand Lodge of Oregon, 1851-61," in *Masonic Papers* (Portland, 1938), 2: 353; "Historical Sketch for the First 50 Years, 1850-1900 (Portland, c. 1900)" in "Willamette Lodge No. 2, A.F. & A.M., 1850-1950, Portland, Oregon (Portland, 1950)"; Fred Lockley, *History of the Columbia River Valley From The Dalles to the Sea* (Chicago, 1928), 662-64, 669.

[27]Harvey W. Scott, ed., *History of Portland, Oregon* (Syracuse, 1890), 160; S.B. 259, p. 12; *Oregonian*, 1 May, 1891. See John E. Caswell, "The Prohibition Movement in Oregon. Part I, 1836-1904," *OHQ* 39 (September, 1939), 234-61.

[28]See John M. Swarthout and Kenneth Gervais, "Oregon: Political Experiment State," in Frank S. Jones, ed., *Politics and the American West* (Salt Lake, 1969). Quiett, *They Built the West*, 350; *Oregonian*, 15 November, 1903; Collins, "Portland," 169; S.B. 25, p. 1. The Oregon Historical Society Museum displays the copper penny.

[29]Quiett, *They Built the West*, 350-51.

[30]On the supposed New England heritage, see for instance Carl Abbott, "On Portland," *The Business Journal*, 27 October, 1986. Collins, "Portland," 157; Scott, *Portland*, 452; Oswald West to Dorothy Johansen, 15 March, 1960, Oswald West Papers, OHS.

[31]"Historical Sketch" in *Inventory of the County Archives of Oregon, No. 26. Multnomah County* (Portland, June, 1940), 1: 34; Thomas L. Cole, "Portland," in *Historic Towns of the Western States*, ed. Lynn P. Powell (New York, 1901), 562; Matthew P. Deady, "Portland-on-Wallamet," *The Overland Monthly* 1 (July, 1868) 37; *Samuel's Directory of Portland and East Portland for 1873* (Portland, 1873), 29.

[32]*Photostatic Copies of Depositions and Transfer of Titles, City of Portland, 1845-50*, Port of Portland Papers, 202-210, OHS; Deady, "Portland," 36.

[33]"Pioneer Seat of Learning," *The Oregon Native Son* 2 (November, 1990), 286-94.

[34]"Pioneer Seat of Learning," 286-94; Page Smith, *As A City Upon A Hill* (New York, 1968), 222.

[35]Dryer quoted in Carl Abbott, *Portland: Gateway to the Northwest* (Northridge, Calif., 1985), 30; Stark quoted in Thomas K. Worcester, *Bunco Kelly and Other Yarns of Portland and Northwest Oregon* (Beaverton, Ore., 1983), 22.

[36]Howard Corning, ed., *Dictionary of Oregon History* (Portland, 1956), 194-95; *Weekly Oregonian*, 9 December, 1854; "Historical Sketch," 35; Joseph Gaston, *The Centennial History of Oregon, 1811-1912* (Chicago, 1912), 1:409.

[37]Scott, Portland, 384-85; Gaston, *Centennial History*, 1:409.

[38]Scott, *Portland*, 183; S.B. 259, pp. 31-32.

[39]Eugene E. Snyder, *Skidmore's Portland* (Portland, 1973), 28.

[40]Paul G. Merriam, "Urban Elite in the Far West: Portland, Oregon, 1870-1890," *Arizona and the West* 18 (Spring, 1976), 41.

[41]Failing quoted in Charles H. Lewis, "Draft of Biographical Statement," BL.

[42]Deady, "Portland," 40; Quiett, *They Built the West*, 353; Oregonian, 15 November, 1903.

[43]*Oregonian*, 16 November 1903.

[44]Pittock published the account of his life before 4 February, 1911, in the *Oregonian*, 30 January, 1919.

[45]Information on Pittock comes from family and personal documents in the possession of Henry Pittock II of Cannon Beach, Oregon; the *Oregonian*, 30 January, 1919; Robert C. Notson, *Making the Day Begin* (Portland, 1973); and various sections of E. Kimbark MacColl, *The Shaping of a City* (Portland, 1976) and *The Growth of a City* (Portland, 1979).

[46]Notson, *Making the Day Begin*, 7.

[47]*Oregonian*, 4 February, 1861.

[48]Notson, *Making the Day Begin*, 7; *Oregonian*, 6 and 7 February, 1861, 9 March, 1861, 18 and 23 April, 1861.

CHAPTER 7 FOOTNOTES

[1]Robert R. Thompson, "Account of My Life," BL; Randall V. Mills, *Stern-Wheelers Up Columbia* (Lincoln, 1977), 130-31.

[2]Thompson, "Account."

[3]Oscar O. Winther, *The Old Oregon Country* (Lincoln, 1969), 170; Dorothy O. Johansen, "Capitalism on the Far-Western Frontier: The Oregon Steam Navigation Company" (Ph.D. diss., University of Washington, 1941), 69; Earle K. Stewart, "Steamboats on the Columbia: The Pioneer Period," in *Steamboat Days on the River* (Portland, 1969), 84-85.

[4]Jacob Kamm quoted in *Oregonian*, 27 November, 1910; Thompson, "Account"; entry, 29 April, 1877, John C. Ainsworth Diary, John C. Ainsworth Papers, UO; Reed quoted in Winther, *Old Oregon*, 234.

[5]Thompson "Account"; entry, 29 April, 1877, Ainsworth Diary; Mills, *Stern-Wheelers*, ch. 4; T. C. Elliott, "The Dalles-Celilo Portage: Its History and Influence," *OHQ* 16 (June, 1915), 159.

[6]Johansen, "Capitalism," 76-78; Stock subscription of Oregon Steam Navigation Company, 1860, BL; Thompson, "Account"; Elliott, "Portage," 162.

[7]Johansen, "Capitalism," 76-78; Stock subscription of Oregon Steam Navigation Company, 1860, BL; Thompson, "Account." The Multnomah Hotel, built on Thompson property, yielded sizeable family income for years.

[8]R. R. Thompson File and OSN File, Ainsworth Papers, UO; Johansen, "Capitalism," 76, 163.

[9]Ralston made money in San Francisco trade and banking and later founded the Bank of California. He and Ainsworth were born near one another on the Ohio River. They left together for California in 1850 but Ralston remained in Panama for four years.

[10]Jean-Nicolas Perlot, *Gold Seeker*, ed. Howard R. Lamar (New Haven, 1985), 359.

[11]Johansen, "Capitalism," 82-91; Arthur L. Throckmorton, *Oregon Argonauts* (Portland, 1961), 260; Simeon G. Reed, "Biographical Sketch," BL; Matthew P. Deady to Benjamin Stark, 22 October, 1861, Benjamin Stark Papers, OHS.

[12]Johansen, "Capitalism," 82-91; entry, 29 April, 1877, Ainsworth Diary, Ainsworth Papers, UO.

[13]Irene Lincoln Poppleton, "Oregon's First Monopoly: The O.S.N. Company," *OHQ* 9 (September, 1908), 284, with corrected Ladd & Tilton figures.

[14]Mills, *Stern-Wheelers*, 68-69; Elliott, "Portage," 159.

[15]Throckmorton, *Argonauts*, 253-54; Mills, *Stern-Wheelers*, 54-59; Johansen, "Capitalism," 113; *Oregonian*, 5 and 6 December, 1862, 9 January, 1863 (editorial).

[16]Throckmorton, *Argonauts*, 253-54; Johansen, "Capitalism," 118.

[17]Johansen, "Capitalism," 100, 115-18.

[18]Johansen, "Capitalism," 91, 100; Mills, *Stern-Wheelers*, 42; OSN File, Ainsworth Papers, UO; "Annual Gold Fever," VIc, Works Progress Administration, Oregon Historical Records Survey, 1936, Oregon State Library.

[19]William J. Hawkins III, *The Grand Era of Cast-Iron Architecture in Portland* (Portland, 1976), 38-39; R. R. Thompson to D. F. Bradford, 15 June, 1866 (reviewing the history of the OSN) in Robert R. Thompson File, Ainsworth Papers. "Empire of the Columbia" is the title of the book by Dorothy Johansen and Charles Gates.

[20]Johansen, "Capitalism," 140, 166; entry, 6 May, 1877, Ainsworth Diary, Ainsworth Papers, UO.

[21]Johansen, "Capitalism," 150; entry, 6 May, 1877, Ainsworth Diary, Ainsworth Papers, UO.

[22]Johansen, "Capitalism," 152-54.

[23]Johansen, "Capitalism," 152-54.

[24]Johansen, "Capitalism," 154-55; Matthew P. Deady, *Pharisee Among Philistines*, ed. Malcolm Clark, Jr. (Portland, 1975), 1:58-59.

[25]Deady, *Pharisee*, 1: 58-59; Johansen, "Capitalism," 167. See Dorothy O. Johansen and Frank B. Gill, "A Chapter in the History of the Oregon Steam Navigation Company: The Ocean Steamships *Oregonian*," *OHQ* 38 (March, September, December, 1937), 1-43, 300-322, 398-410.

[26]Johansen, "Capitalism," 171.

[27]Johansen, "Capitalism," 187.

[28]John C. Ainsworth to Alvinza Hayward, 18 October, 1866, 1 November, 1866, and entry, 6 May, 1877, Ainsworth Diary, Ainsworth Papers.

[29]Robert R. Thompson to D. F. Bradford, 6 June, 1877, Thompson File, Ainsworth Papers, UO; *Oregonian*, 7 December, 1866, 9 June, 1866, and "Stark Financial Records," Stark Papers.

[30]Johansen, "Capitalism," 141, 181.

[31]Deady, *Pharisee*, 1: 58-59; Johansen, "Capitalism," 180.

[32]Johansen, "Capitalism," 181; Deady, *Pharisee*, 1: 58-59, 65-66.

[33]Entry, 6 May, 1877, Ainsworth Diary, Ainsworth Papers.

[34]Entry, 6 May, 1877, Ainsworth Diary, Ainsworth Papers.

[35]Deady, *Pharisee*, II: 451, 459.

[36]Winther, *Old Oregon*, 234, 240; Reed quoted in Dorothy O. Johansen, "The Oregon Steam Navigation Company: An Example of Capitalism on the Frontier," *Pacific Historical Review* 10 (June, 1941), 185.

[37]Johansen, "Capitalism," 138; Simeon Reed to John C. Ainsworth, 7 May, 1866, and 19 March, 1866, quoted in Johansen, "Capitalism," 228, 133.

[38]Simeon G. Reed to John C. Ainsworth, 16 May, 1866, quoted in Johansen, "Capitalism," 169-70.

[39]Simeon G. Reed to John C. Ainsworth, 16 May, 1866, quoted in Johansen, "Capitalism," 169-70.

[40]*Oregonian*, 3 February, 1866; Johansen, "Capitalism," 198.

[41]Simeon G. Reed to John C. Ainsworth, 29 March, 1866, quoted in Johansen, "Capitalism," 200.

[42]E. Digby Baltzell, *Puritan Boston and Quaker Philadelphia* (New York, 1979), 233; Sam Bass Warner, Jr., *The Private City* (Philadelphia, 1968), 83.

[43]Glenn Chesney Quiett, *They Built the West* (New York, 1934), 407-8. See Alex Groner, *The History of American Business and Industry* (New York, 1972), 165.

[44]Ellis Lucia, *The Saga of Ben Holladay* (New York, 1959), 217, 225; "Disposition of David G. Elliott," in the Circuit Court of Oregon, *Benjamin Holladay & C. Temple Emmett vs. Simon G. Elliott* (Portland, 1871), 7. See also James V. Frederick, *Ben Holladay, The Stagecoach King* (Glendale, Calif., 1940), 243-62. The Overland Mail Co.'s sale price has usually been reported as $1.5 million. J. V. Frederick adds an inventory worth of $800,000, raising the total to $2.3 million. That seems to be the full value Holladay received in the transaction. See Dietrich G. Buss, "Henry Villard: A Study in Transatlantic Investment Interests, 1870-1895" (Ph.D. diss., Claremont Graduate School, 1976, published by Arno Press, 1977), 37 ff.

[45]Arthur M. Johnson and Barry Supple, *Boston Capitalists and Western Railroads* (Cambridge, 1967), 195.

[46]Johansen, "Capitalism," 203-5.

⁴⁷23 April, 1867, notation in Railroad File, Ainsworth Papers.

⁴⁸Percy Maddux, *City on the Willamette* (Portland, 1952), 58; Johansen, "Capitalism," 206; Deady, *Pharisee*, 1: 46.

⁴⁹Simeon G. Reed to Henry W. Corbett and George H. Williams, 9 December, 1867, quoted in Johansen, "Capitalism," 207-8.

⁵⁰*The Arlington Club and the Men Who Built It* (Portland, 1968), 1, 7.

⁵¹Lucia, *The Saga*, 237; *Holladay and Emmett vs. Elliott*.

⁵²*Holladay and Emmett vs. Elliott*, 7; Deady, *Pharisee*, 1: 46.

⁵³Quiett, *They Built the West*, 357.

⁵⁴Railroad File, Ainsworth Papers, UO.

⁵⁵Railroad File, Ainsworth Papers, UO; Johansen, "Capitalism," 182.

⁵⁶E. Kimbark MacColl, *The Shaping of a City* (Portland, 1976), 40-41.

⁵⁷Quiett, *They Built the West*, 353.

⁵⁸Harvey W. Scott, *History of the Oregon Country*, comp. Leslie M. Scott (Portland, 1924), 4: 352; David M. Ellis, "The Oregon and California Railroad Land Grant, 1866-1945," *Pacific Northwest Quarterly* 39 (October, 1948), 255-56.

⁵⁹Railroad File, Ainsworth Papers, UO.

⁶⁰Johansen, "Capitalism," 214, 228. The surviving OSN figures were refigured as of 1 June, 1870.

⁶¹Thompson, "Account," BL.

⁶²Thompson, "Account"; Scott, *Oregon Country*, 4: 353.

⁶³*Oregonian*, 5 June, 1870 (editorial); Ladd quoted in Quiett, *They Built the West*, 359.

⁶⁴"An Ugly Record for Old Ben," undated handwritten copy in Thompson File, Ainsworth Papers, UO; Scott, *Oregon Country*, 4: 352-53.

⁶⁵Scott, *Oregon Country*, 4: 354; *Arlington Club*, 5-6.

⁶⁶Johansen, "Capitalism," 76, and "The Oregon Steam Navigation Company," 179-88.

⁶⁷*Oregonian*, 22 May, 1869.

CHAPTER 8 FOOTNOTES

¹United States Census Office, *Census of Oregon* (Washington, 1870).

²Jean-Nicolas Perlot, *Gold Seeker*, ed. Howard R. Lamar (New Haven, 1985), 372.

³Perlot, *Gold Seeker*, 318; Matthew P. Deady, "Portland-on-Wallamet, *The Overland Monthly* 1 (July, 1868), 38-39; Dorothy D. Hirsch, "Study of the Foreign Wheat Trade of Oregon, 1869-1887," *Reed College Bulletin* 31 (August, 1953), 60; *Oregon and Washington Almanac for the Year 1862* (Portland, 1862), 30-31; *Oregonian*, 25 and 28 December, 1869, 28 January, 1870.

⁴Deady, "Portland-on-Wallamet," 42-43.

⁵*Portland Directory for 1863* (Portland, 1863).

⁶W. Turrentine Jackson, "Portland: Wells Fargo's Hub for the Pacific Northwest," *OHQ* 86 (Fall, 1985), 245. On Ladd's relationships to new enterprises, see generally Ladd Family and W. S. Ladd and Co. Papers, OHS.

⁷Orin K. Burrell, *Gold in the Woodpile* (Eugene, 1967), 44-53; Arthur L. Throckmorton, *Oregon Argonauts* (Portland, 1961), 313.

⁸William L. Brewster, *William M. Ladd of Portland, Oregon* (Portland, 1933), 19-20, 26.

⁹"Abstract of Title," lots 2 and 3, Block 11, Tilton's Addition, Title Guarantee & Trust Co., Portland, 1926, in possession of Thomas O. Smith, Portland.

¹⁰Throckmorton, *Argonauts*, 242-48, 277-78.

¹¹Gordon B. Dodds, *Oregon* (New York, 1977), 76; Glen Porter and Harold C. Livesay, *Merchants and Manufacturers* (Baltimore, 1971), 10, 125; "Value of the Greenback," Works Progress Administration, Oregon

Historical Records Survey, 1936, Oregon State Library; Morton Keller, *Affairs of State* (Cambridge, 1977), 23; Throckmorton, *Argonauts*, 281.

[12]Throckmorton, *Argonauts*, 280-81; Matthew P. Deady to Benjamin Stark, 21 April, 1864, Benjamin Stark Papers, OHS; William S. Ladd to Matthew P. Deady, 7 October, 1864, Matthew P. Deady Letters, OHS.

[13]"Benjamin Stark's Financial Records with Ladd & Tilton" and Benjamin Stark to William S. Ladd, 6 October, 1863, Stark Papers. Also see Benjamin Stark to William S. Ladd, 9 June, 1866, and 31 July, 1868, Stark Papers.

[14]Throckmorton, *Argonauts*, 289.

[15]Throckmorton, *Argonauts*, 291-93.

[16]While the merger date is usually listed as 1871, a WPA researcher recorded it from an original document as 2 January, 1870, "General History," Works Progress Administration, Oregon Historical Records Survey, 1936, Oregon State Library.

[17]*First National Bank of Oregon: Our First One Hundred Years, 1865-1965* (Portland, 1965). The bank changed its name from "Portland" to "Oregon" in 1964. Lewis M. Starr, "Dictation," 1883, BL; *Oregonian*, 2 May, 1892.

[18]Charles A. Tracy III, "Police Function in Portland, 1851-1874," Part 2, *OHQ* 80 (Summer, 1979), 142.

[19]L. M. Starr, "Dictation"; *First National Bank*; National Banking Act, 3 June, 1864; William J. Hawkins III, *Portland's Historic New Market Theater* (Portland, 1984), 5; Perlot, *Gold Seeker*, 328; Burt B. Barker, "Early History: First National Bank of Portland, Oregon," 1941, 1, OHS.

[20]L. M. Starr, "Dictation"; *First National Bank*; Barker, "Early History," 5-6.

[21]Barker, "Early History," 31, 35-36, 47; Harvey W. Scott, *History of the Oregon Country*, comp. Leslie M. Scott (Portland, 1924), 5: 185.

[22]Barker, "Early History," 57-60; Throckmorton, *Argonauts*, 312.

[23]Much of the material on James A. Steel is in his Papers, spanning 50 years, in the possession of the Great Northwest Bookstore, Portland.

[24]Steel Papers. The "Horse Claims" were against the U.S. Government for horses it had obtained but lost in the Indian Wars of 1855-56. By 1867, Congress had not appropriated the funds to pay most of these claims. Steel and his partners secured lists of the claimants and offered them an average $45 per claim. When Congress eventually paid the claims, they brought as much as $200 each. Senator Henry W. Corbett, who had two claims, accelerated the process in February, 1871, by Senate Resolution. Letter to the Secretary of the Treasury, Treasury Department, Third Auditor's Office, 14 November, 1871, 42d Congress, 2d session, Senate, Executive Documents, No. 1; Glenn C. Quiett, *They Built the West* (New York, 1934), 401.

[25]Paul C. Merriam, "Portland, Oregon, 1840-1890: A Social and Economic History" (Ph.D. diss., University of Oregon, 1971), 215; Throckmorton, *Argonauts*, 309-11; Deady, "Portland-on-Wallamet," 38-39.

[26]Dodds, *Oregon*, 76; Throckmorton, *Argonauts*, 309-10; Howard M. Corning, ed., *Dictionary of Oregon History* (Portland, 1956), 227, 274. See Scott Cline, "The Jews of Portland, Oregon: A Statistical Dimension, 1860-1880," *OHQ* 88 (Spring, 1987), 4-25.

[27]Corning, *Dictionary*, 274.

[28]Rodman W. Paul, "After the Gold Rush: San Francisco and Portland," *Pacific Historical Review* 51 (February, 1982), 17.

[29]Barker, "Early History," 42; Throckmorton, *Argonauts*, 299; Charles H. Carey, *A General History of Oregon* (Portland, 1935), 2: 751; *Oregon Journal*, 11 December, 1932.

[30]Jackson, "Portland," 238-41.

[31]Quiett, *They Built the West*, 351-52; Jackson, "Portland," 254-55; H. K. Hines, *An Illustrated History of the State of Oregon* (Chicago, 1893), 691; Oscar O. Winther, *The Old Oregon Country* (Lincoln, 1969), 256-57.

[32]"Portland Macadamized Road Records," Personal Business Files of W. S. Caldwell, Auditor's Office, City of Portland Archives; *Oregonian*, 10 April, 1865; Margaret Pietsch, *Riverwood* (Portland, 1980), 5-6.

[33]Herbert L. Hegert, "Early Iron Industry in Oregon," *Reed College Bulletin* 26 (January, 1948), 2-12.

[34]Hegert, "Early Iron," 2-12.

35Investment File and entry, 6 May, 1877, John C. Ainsworth, "Diary," UO; *Oregonian*, 2 April, 1864; S.B. 112, p. 75.

36Dorothy O. Johansen, "Capitalism on the Far-Western Frontier: The Oregon Steam Navigation Company" (Ph.D. diss., University of Washington, 1941), 169; *Oregonian*, 27 June, 1864, 18 July, 1864.

37Henry Failing to John Hatt, 28 March, 1865, and 1 June, 1865, quoted in Throckmorton, *Argonauts*, 265-66; Harrison Olmsted to Ladd & Tilton, 19 January, 1866, quoted in Johansen, "Capitalism," 169. Failing's vote for Robbins is in Portland City Council Documents, Box 4, City of Portland Archives.

38*Oregonian*, 20 February, 1865; S.B. 112, p. 131, "Value of the Greenback."

39Bernard Goldsmith "Dictation," 1889, BL; *Oregonian*, 22 May, 1869; William Toll, *The Making of an Ethnic Middle Class* (Albany, N.Y., 1982), 10, 15, 80-83. Goldsmith gained no profit from his brief investment in the First National Bank.

40Hirsch, "Foreign Wheat Trade," 53; Merriam, "Portland," 228-30.

41Hirsch, "Foreign Wheat Trade," 55-57; Merriam, "Portland," 229; Scott Cline, "Community Structure on the Urban Frontier: The Jews of Portland, Oregon, 1849-1887" (M.A. thesis, Portland State University, 1981), 91; Goldsmith "Dictation"; Throckmorton, *Argonauts*, 308. Corbett & Macleay was established in September, 1866. *Oregonian*, 16 September, 1866.

42William F. Willingham, *Army Engineers and the Development of Oregon* (Washington, 1983), 10-11; Goldsmith, "Dictation."

43Scott, *Oregon Country*, 3: 217; Willingham, *Army Engineers*, 11.

44Hirsch, "Foreign Wheat Trade," 63; Merriam, "Portland," 230.

45Scott, *Oregon Country*, 3: 104, 169-70; Randall V. Mills, *Stern-Wheelers Up Columbia* (Lincoln, 1977), 60, 102, 142-43; Corning, *Dictionary*, 266; Johansen, "Capitalism," 249.

46Mills, *Stern-Wheelers* 103; Corning, *Dictionary*, 266.

47Johansen, "Capitalism," 251; Goldsmith, "Dictation."

48Burrell, *Gold*, 47.

49Burrell, *Gold*, 47.

50Burrell, *Gold*, 47-48; William J. Hawkins, *The Grand Era of Cast-Iron Architecture in Portland* (Portland, 1976), 44; *Oregonian*, 12 January, 1869; *70 Years, Ladd & Bush Bankers* (Salem, 1939).

51Merriam, "Portland," 229; *Oregonian*, 17 August, 1869; Throckmorton, *Argonauts*, 315.

52Hirsch, "Foreign Wheat Trade," 60, 66; Deady, "Portland-on-Wallamet," 38; Merriam, "Portland," 284.

CHAPTER 9 FOOTNOTES

1Matthew P. Deady, *Pharisee Among Philistines*, ed. Malcolm Clark, Jr. (Portland, 1975), 1: 257; Matthew P. Deady to San Francisco *Bulletin*, 3 October, 1866, quoted in Walter C. Woodward, "Rise and Early History of Political Parties in Oregon," *OHQ* 13 (March, 1912), 58-59.

2David C. Hammack, "Small Business and Urban Power: Some Notes on the History of Economic Policy in Nineteenth-Century American Cities," in *Small Business in American Life*, ed. Stuart W. Bruchey (New York, 1980), 327.

3Matthew P. Deady to James W. Nesmith, 1 February, 1865, James W. Nesmith Papers, OHS. For a comparative study, see Richard A. Bartlett, *The New Century* (New York, 1974), 421-22.

4Paul G. Merriam, "The Other Portland: A Statistical Note on Foreign-Born, 1860-1910," *OHQ* 80 (Fall, 1979), 258-68.

5Henry Villard, *Early Transportation in Oregon*, ed. Oswald G. Villard (Eugene, 1944), 43-44; Jesse Applegate to John C. Ainsworth, 3 September, 1869, John C. Ainsworth Papers, UO; Lawrence H. Larsen, *The Urban West at the End of the Frontier* (Lawrence, 1978), 47.

6Matthew P. Deady, "Portland-on-Wallamet," *The Overland Monthly* 1 (July, 1868), 47.

7Charter Amendments-Charter Summaries, City of Portland Archives.

8Charles A. Tracy, "Police Function in Portland, 1851-1874," Part 2, *OHQ* 80 (Summer, 1979), 147.

⁹Tracy, "Police Function," 151-52; Portland City Council Proceedings, 3 (28 June, 1866), Portland City Hall.

¹⁰*Oregonian*, 16 August, 1866.

¹¹Tracy, "Police Function," 153-56.

¹²Merriam, "The 'Other Portland,'" 266-67; *Oregonian*, 14 May, 1868; Charles A. Tracy, *Arrest and Crime Data, Portland, Oregon, 1868-1885* (Portland, 1970), 2: 17-19; Robert S. Cline, "The Jews of Portland, Oregon: A Statistical Dimension, 1860-1880" (M.A. thesis, Portland State University, 1982), 86.

¹³Tracy, *Arrest and Crime Data*, 2: 9-10.

¹⁴*Oregonian*, 13 June, 1873.

¹⁵William Toll, *The Making of an Ethnic Middle Class* (Albany, N.Y., 1982), 83.

¹⁶Toll, *Ethnic Middle Class*, 81-82; Cline, "Community Structure," 86.

¹⁷Toll, *Ethnic Middle Class*, 81; Tracy, "Police Function," 168-69.

¹⁸Tracy, "Police Function in Portland, 1851-1874," Part 3, *OHQ* 80 (Fall, 1979), 288, 299.

¹⁹Portland City Council Documents, Box 20, and Portland Park Bureau Files, 1870-71, Box 17, City of Portland Archives. The Portland Park Commission *Report*, 1901, "listing all park property acquired through Dec. 31, 1901," is inaccurate, according to City Council documents. No titles could have been transferred until after 15 January, 1865, the date of federal patent issues. Purchase prices are not accurate. Coffin, not Chapman, conveyed the seven South Park Blocks in July, 1871, not December, 1867.

²⁰Portland City Council Documents, Box 20; Park Commission *Report*, 1901, 18.

²¹Park Commission *Report*, 1901, 18; *A Guide to Portland's Historic Parks and Gardens* (Portland, 1985); Portland Park Bureau Files, 1870-71, boxes 15 and 20; *Oregonian*, 16 June, 1878.

²²Portland City Council Documents, Box 20; Park Bureau Files, 1870-71, Box 15.

²³Jon C. Teaford, *The Unheralded Triumph* (Baltimore, 1984), 8-9.

²⁴For a detailed account, see Deady, *Pharisee*, 1: 151-52, and E. Kimbark MacColl, *The Shaping of a City* (Portland, 1976), 201-203. *Oregonian*, 16 June, 1873.

²⁵Burton J. Hendrick, "Initiative and Referendum and How Oregon Got Them," *McClure's Magazine* 37 (July, 1911), 243.

²⁶MacColl, *Shaping*, 202-203; Hendrick, "Initiative," 243; Woodward, "Political Parties," 58.

²⁷Harvey W. Scott, ed., *History of Portland, Oregon* (Syracuse, 1890), 137; Eugene Snyder, *Portland Names and Neighborhoods* (Portland, 1979), 215.

²⁸Deady, *Pharisee*, 1: 113-14, 102.

²⁹Deady, *Pharisee*, 1: 106, 154-55.

³⁰Deady, *Pharisee*, 1: 79, 154-55; Fred Lockley, *Conversations with Bullwhackers and Muleskinners, Pioneers, Prospectors, '49ers, Indian Fighters, Trappers, ex-Barkeepers, Authors, Preachers, Poets and Near-Poets & All Sorts and Conditions of Men*, comp. and ed. Mike Helm (Eugene, 1981), 212.

³¹Deady, *Pharisee*, 1: 154-55.

³²Deady, *Pharisee*, 1: 76, 102. On 23 December, 1872, William S. Ladd reported to Deady that Mitchell's net assets were $50,000, involving "1/15 of the Caruthers Land Co. stock," placing him within the top 50 of Portland's most affluent residents—well ahead of *Oregonian* Publisher Henry Pittock, for example. William S. Ladd to Matthew P. Deady, 23 December, 1872, quoted in *Pharisee*, 1: 102.

³³Deady, *Pharisee*, 1: 208.

³⁴*Oregonian*, 16 June, 1873.

³⁵*Oregonian*, 16 June, 1873.

³⁶Toll, *Ethnic Middle Class*, 80-81; Tracy, "Police Function," Part 3, 307; *Oregonian*, 16 June, 1873.

³⁷Deady, *Pharisee*, 1: 104, 132.

³⁸Deady, *Pharisee*, 1: 104, 132, 153.

[39]For the fire and its aftermath, see Box 4 of Henry Failing Papers, OHS, and S.B. 38, p. 181. Percy Maddux, *City on the Willamette*, 72; *Oregonian*, 4 August, 1873; Eugene E. Snyder, *Skidmore's Portland* (Portland, 1973), 62; John M. Tess, *Uphill Downhill Yamhill* (Portland, 1977), 65-70.

[40]Hubert H. Bancroft, *Chronicles of the Builders of the Commonwealth* (San Francisco, 1891), 1: 615.

[41]Tracy, "Police Function," Part 3, 309-310.

[42]Tracy, "Police Function," Part 3, 310.

[43]Tracy, "Police Function," Part 3, 319.

[44]"Our Illustrations," *The West Shore* 1 (March, 1876), 5.

[45]*Oregonian*, 22 June, 1875.

[46]Arthur W. Hawn, "The Henry Failing House," *OHQ* 82 (Winter, 1981), 363.

CHAPTER 10 FOOTNOTES

[1]Dorothy O. Johansen and Charles M. Gates, *Empire of the Columbia* (New York, 1957), 347-48; Dorothy O. Johansen, "Capitalism on the Far-Western Frontier: The Oregon Steam Navigation Company" (Ph.D. diss., University of Washington, 1941), 216-17; Earl Pomeroy, *The Pacific Slope* (New York, 1956), 136-37; Rush Welter, "The American Money Mentality After the Civil War" (Paper delivered at the Annual Meeting of the Organization of American Historians, 1985).

[2]William S. Ladd, "Dictation," BL.

[3]*Oregonian*, 22 May, 1869; United States Census Office, *Census of Oregon* (Washington, 1870); *The Arlington Club and the Men Who Built It* (Portland, 1968), 2.

[4]John Reps, *The Making of Urban America* (Princeton, 1965), 412; Simeon G. Reed to David Smith, 6 May, 1871, "Letters," vol. 2, Simeon G. Reed Papers, Reed College Library; William J. Hawkins III, *The Grand Era of Cast-Iron Architecture in Portland* (Portland, 1976).

[5]Simeon G. Reed to David Smith, 6 May, 1871, Reed Papers; Harvey W. Scott, ed., *History of Portland, Oregon* (Syracuse, 1890), 144-63; S.B. 259, p. 21; Matthew P. Deady, "Portland-on-Wallamet," *The Overland Monthly* 1 (July, 1868), 38.

[6]Simeon G. Reed to Benjamin Stark, 14 April, 1871, quoted in Johansen, "Capitalism," 216; "In the matter of the Estate of John Couch. Statement of Administrator as to the disposition of the property named in the Inventory," Petitions Folder, Personal Files of W. S. Caldwell, Auditor's Office, City of Portland Archives.

[7]*Samuel's Directory of Portland and East Portland for 1873* (Portland, 1873), 25-26; Portland, Multnomah County and Oregon listings in R. G. Dun and Company, *Mercantile Reference Book and Key for the Pacific Coast* (San Francisco, 1878). For the commercial buildings, see Hawkins, *Grand Era*, and Portland Friends of Cast-Iron Architecture, *Newsletter* (April, 1982, January, 1983).

[8]*Oregonian*, 27 July, 1868, and 22 May, 1869.

[9]S.B. 21, p. 21; Scott, *Portland*, 545-46; H. K. Hines, *An Illustrated History of the State of Oregon* (Chicago, 1893), 1032; *Early Oregon Wills: Multnomah County, Oregon*, 6: 6, OHS; Joseph Gaston, *Portland, Oregon, Its History and Builders* (Chicago, 1911), 2: 308.

[10]Wallis Nash, *Two Years in Oregon* (New York, 1882), 256-63.

[11]Nash, *Two Years*, 259; Hawkins, *Grand Era*, 204-5; E. Kimbark MacColl, *The Shaping of a City* (Portland, 1976), 11.

[12]Barbara B. Hartwell, *Sprigs of Rosemary* (Portland, 1975), 4, 11; Mary Cable, *Top Drawer* (New York, 1984), 92.

[13]William S. Ladd to Benjamin Stark, 6 November, 1868, Benjamin Stark Papers, OHS; John W. Ladd to Simeon G. Reed, 27 December, 1869, Correspondence to Reed, vol. 31, Reed Papers; Matthew P. Deady, *Pharisee Among Philistines*, ed. Malcolm Clark (Portland, 1975), 1: 58.

[14]Arthur W. Hawn, "The Henry Failing House," *OHQ* 82 (Winter, 1981), 354-55; Wallace Kay Huntington, "Victorian Architecture," in *Space, Style and Structure*, ed. Thomas Vaughan and Virginia G. Ferriday (Portland, 1974), 1: 280-82.

[15]Richard Marlitt, *Nineteenth Street* (Portland, 1968), 58-59; Huntington, "Victorian Architecture," 276-77.

[16]Johansen and Gates, *Empire*, 351; Dorothy O. Johansen, "Early History of Reed College"; Paul G. Merriam, "Urban Elite in the Far West: Portland, Oregon, 1870-1890," *Arizona and the West* 18 (Spring, 1976), 47.

[17]Merriam, "Urban Elite," 47.

[18]Simeon G. Reed to David Smith, 6 May, 1871, Reed Papers; Morton T. Rosenbloom," Simeon Gannett Reed, Gentleman Farmer," *Reed College Bulletin* 27 (June, 1949), 115, 117.

[19]Rosenbloom, "Reed," 115-35; Simeon G. Reed to L.C. White, 9 November, 1893, quoted in Richard J. Peterson, "Pacific Northwest Entrepreneur: The Social and Political Behavior of Simeon Gannett Reed," *Idaho Yesterdays* 24 (Fall, 1980), 32.

[20]Hubert H. Bancroft, *Chronicles of the Builders of the Commonwealth* (San Francisco, 1891), 2: 614-15; MacColl, *Shaping*, 25.

[21]Frances F. Victor, *All Over Oregon and Washington* (San Francisco, 1872), 152; William J. Hawkins III, *Portland's Historic New Market Theater* (Portland, 1984), 18; Deady, "Portland," 40.

[22]Deady, *Pharisee*, 1: 201, 210; Victor, "All Over Oregon," 152.

[23]Victor, "All Over Oregon," 152; Deady, "Portland," 41; Margaret Pietsch, *Riverwood* (Portland, 1980), 6-8.

[24]William Toll, *The Making of an Ethnic Middle Class* (Albany, N.Y., 1982), 25-26.

[25]Toll, *Ethnic Middle Class*, 49.

[26]Toll, *Ethnic Middle Class*, 33-34.

[27]*Samuel's Directory*, 26; Deady, *Pharisee*, 1: 138, 160, 2: 418.

[28]Earl M. Wilbur and Evadne Hilands, *A Time to Build* (Portland, 1966), 12, 18, 149.

[29]Stuart M. Blumin, "The Hypothesis of Middle-Class Formation in Nineteenth-Century America: A Critique and Some Proposals," *American Historical Review* 90 (April, 1985), 335.

[30]E. Kimbark MacColl, "The Women to the Rescue," Address to the Annual Meeting of the Parry Center, Portland, December, 1980; *A Selection of Wills*, comp. Albert L. Grutze (Portland, 1925), 32-37.

[31]Paula Baker, "The Domestication of Politics: Women and American Political Society, 1780-1920," *American Historical Review* 89 (June, 1984), 623-33; Marilyn Gittel and Teresa Shtob, "Changing Women's Roles in Political Volunteerism and Reform of the City," in *Women and the American City*, ed. Catharine R. Stimson et al. (Chicago, 1981), 64.

[32]Wilbur and Hilands, *A Time to Build*, 15; John F. Scheck, "Thomas Lamb Eliot and His Vision of an Enlightened Community," in *The Western Shore*, ed. Thomas Vaughan (Portland, 1975), 246-47.

[33]Helen K. Smith, *The Presumptuous Dreamers* (Lake Oswego, Oregon, 1974), 1: 152-53.

[34]Smith, *Presumptuous Dreamers*, 152-53. Smith acknowledges that neither Duniway nor Scott recorded this precise information, "but the sentiment was expressed and re-expressed in various ways for more than twenty years." Smith, *Presumptuous Dreamers*, 255.

[35]Ruth B. Moynihan, *Rebel for Rights* (New Haven, 1983), 113-14.

[36]Moynihan, *Rebel*, 174; Robert C. Clark, *History of the Willamette Valley* (Chicago, 1927), 1: 710.

[37]Moynihan, *Rebel*, 138; *New Northwest*, 17 April, 1874.

[38]Malcolm H. Clark, Jr., "The War on the Webfoot Saloon," in *The War on the Webfoot Saloon & Other Tales of Feminine Adventures* (Portland, 1969), 5-6; Dun and Company, *Mercantile Reference Book*; Dean Collins, "Portland: A Pilgrim's Progress," in *The Taming of the Frontier*, ed. Duncan Aikman (New York, 1925), 171; Scott, *History of Portland*, 452; Scheck, "Eliot," 252.

[39]Clark, "War," 9-10.

[40]Clark, "War," 19; Charles A. Tracy III, "Police Function in Portland, 1851-1874," Part 3, *OHQ* 80 (Fall, 1979), 19; Scheck, "Eliot," 252-53. Also see Barnett Singer, "Oregon's Nineteenth-Century Notables: Simeon Gannett Reed and Thomas Lamb Eliot," in *Northwest Perspectives*, ed. Edwin R. Bingham and Glen A. Love (Seattle, 1979).

[41]*New Northwest*, 17 July, 1874.

[42]List of School Board members, Records of Portland School District No. 1, Multnomah County, Portland School District Archives; Frederic C. Jaher, *The Urban Establishment* (Urbana, 1982), 503-4.

[43]Helen M. Casey, *Portland's Compromise: The Colored School, 1867-1872* (Portland, 1980); MacColl, *Shaping* 24; Schools File, John C. Ainsworth Papers, UO.

[44]Elizabeth McLagan, *A Peculiar Paradise* (Portland, 1980), 72; Casey, *Portland's Compromise*; *Oregonian*, 29 May, 1867. For a study of anti-black sentiment, see K. Keith Richard, "Unwelcome Settlers: Black and Mulatto Oregon Pioneers," Part 1, *OHQ* 84 (Spring, 1983), 29-55, and Part 2 (Summer, 1983), 173-205.

[45]Casey, *Portland's Compromise*.

[46]Bancroft, *Chronicles*, 2: 630; Casey, *Portland's Compromise*.

[47]"Libraries," in *Encyclopedia Britannica* (Chicago, 1960), 14: 22-24.

[48]Percy Maddux, *City on the Willamette* (Portland, 1952), 52-53; City Club of Portland, *Report on the Future of Multnomah County Library* 67 (28 August, 1986), 68; Earl M. Wilbur, *Thomas Lamb Eliot* (Portland, 1937), 85.

[49]Maddux, *City*, 52-53; Bancroft, *Chronicles*, 2: 623.

[50]Deady, *Pharisee*, 1: 185, 201, 212, and 2: 420, 531.

[51]S.B. 259, pp. 133-34; Katherine Anderson, *Historical Sketch of the Library Association of Portland, 1864-1964* (Portland, 1964), 37.

[52]Bancroft, *Chronicles*, 2: 623.

CHAPTER 11 FOOTNOTES

[1]Dietrich G. Buss, "Henry Villard: A Study in Transatlantic Investment Interests, 1870-1895" (Ph.D. diss., Claremont Graduate School, 1976, published by Arno Press, 1977), 85; Paul G. Merriam, "Portland, Oregon, 1840-1890: A Social and Economic History" (Ph.D. diss., University of Oregon, 1971), 327.

[2]Quoted in Dorothy O. Johansen, "Capitalism on the Far-Western Frontier: The Oregon Steam Navigation Company" (Ph.D. diss., University of Washington, 1941), 258.

[3]*Oregonian*, 26 August, 1873; quoted in Johansen, "Capitalism," 259; J. W. Hayes, "Looking Backward at Portland."

[4]Johansen, "Capitalism," 231.

[5]Barnett Singer, "Oregon's Nineteenth-Century Notables: Simeon Gannett Reed and Thomas Lamb Eliot," in *Northwest Perspectives, Essays on the Culture of the Pacific Northwest*, comp. and ed. Edwin R. Bingham and Glen A. Love (Seattle, 1979), 64-65.

[6]Singer, "Notables," 66-67; Dorothy O. Johansen, "Early History of Reed College," 4.

[7]Singer, "Notables," 66; Merriam, "Portland," 168-69; Johansen, "Reed," 4.

[8]Johansen, "Capitalism," 223, 246, 221.

[9]Buss, "Villard," 34.

[10]Glenn Chesney Quiett, *They Built the West* (New York, 1934), 360.

[11]Robert H. Wiebe, *The Search for Order, 1877-1920* (New York, 1967), 1; Ben B. Seligman, *The Potentates* (New York, 1971), 135; Buss, "Villard," 4; Albro Martin, *James J. Hill and the Opening of the Northwest* (New York, 1976), 119; Johansen, "Capitalism," 220. For similar problems affecting the Union Pacific, see Arthur M. Johnson and Barry E. Supple, *Boston Capitalism and Western Railroads* (Cambridge, Mass., 1967), 195, and Alfred D. Chandler, Jr., *The Visible Hand* (Cambridge, Mass., 1977), ch. 5.

[12]Johansen, "Capitalism," 223; Quiett, *They Built the West*, 413.

[13]Johansen, "Capitalism," 223; Robert R. Thompson, "Account of My Life," BL.

[14]Johansen, "Capitalism," 223-24.

[15]Buss, "Villard," 43-45.

[16]Quiett, *They Built the West*, 361; Buss, "Villard," 48. On 17 November, 1884, Deady referred in his diary to a copy of a letter from Holladay to his associate Rufus Ingalls, admitting that he "had spent $250,000 on Oregon politics." Matthew P. Deady, *Pharisee Among Philistines*, ed. Malcolm Clark, Jr. (Portland, 1975), 1: 189.

[17]Quiett, *They Built the West*, 361; Buss, "Villard," 49.

[18]Buss, "Villard," 51-55; Deady, *Pharisee*, 2: 533.

[19]*Oregonian*, 13 April, 1876.

[20]*Oregonian*, 11 May, 1876.

[21]Buss, "Villard," 56.

[22]Johansen, "Capitalism," 270; Quiett, *They Built the West*, 363.

[23]Buss, "Villard," 89; Seligman, *The Potentates*, 139-41; Chandler, *The Visible Hand*, 148.

[24]Buss, "Villard," 88.

[25]Johansen, "Capitalism," 268-72; Quiett, *They Built the West*, 365.

[26]Johansen, "Capitalism," 273; Thompson, "Account of My Life." Quiett's account in *They Built the West* is inaccurate.

[27]Johansen, "Capitalism," 273-75, 277; Thompson, "Account of My Life." For conversion to current currency values, a multiple of 20 was chosen for 1866. Between 1866 and 1880 the basic commodity price dropped 34 percent, reducing the multiple to 13, used to convert OSN sale profits to approximate current values. These data are from works in which two scholars use the words "Consumer Price Index" for those years: Lee Soltow, *Men and Wealth in the United States, 1850-1870* (New Haven, 1975), 52, 64-65, and Benjamin J. Wattenberg, Introduction and User's Guide to *The Statistical History of the United States From Colonial Times to the Present*, United States Bureau of the Census (New York, 1976), 212, 702. See also National Bureau of Economic Resources, *Trends in the American Economy in the Nineteenth Century* (Princeton, 1960), 24: 462, and *Oregonian*, 3 April, 1880.

[28]National Bureau, *Trends*, 24: 275; Oregon Steam Navigation File, John C. Ainsworth Papers, UO. Failing's and Lewis's combined OR&N shares were worth $190,000 upon their deaths. The value of Corbett's OR&N shares, exchanged for Union Pacific stock in 1889 when the OR&N was sold, exceeded $127,000 in 1903. Files of the Probate Department, Multnomah County Clerk's Office.

[29]OSN File and Building and House Records, Ainsworth Papers, UO; Johansen, "Capitalism," 278-79; Henry Villard, *Early Transportation in Oregon*, ed. Oswald G. Villard (Eugene, 1944), 91; *Samuel's Directory for Portland and East Portland for 1880* (Portland, 1880), 19.

[30]Villard, *Early Transportation*, 91.

[31]R. G. Dun and Company, *Mercantile Reference Book and Key for the Pacific Coast* (San Francisco, 1878); United States Census Office, *Census of Oregon* (Washington, 1880).

[32]Dun and Company, *Mercantile Reference*; entry for 19 January, 1881, "Record of the Proceedings of the Common Council of the City of Portland, abbrev. form.," vol. 7, Portland City Hall Archives.

[33]Weidler's grandson, William Jewett, told E. K. MacColl about Burns's advice to Weidler. Dun and Company, *Mercantile Reference*; Dorothy D. Hirsch, "Study of the Foreign Wheat Trade of Oregon, 1869-1887," *Reed College Bulletin* 31 (August, 1951), 60.

[34]James B. Montgomery, "Dictation," BL.

[35]E. Kimbark MacColl, *The Shaping of a City* (Portland, 1976), 54; Howard M. Corning, ed., *Dictionary of Oregon History* (Portland, 1956), 173-74; W. Turrentine Jackson, *Investors in the American West After 1873* (Edinburgh, 1968), 30-32; Donald Macleay to John C. Ainsworth, 14 April, 1874, Ainsworth Papers, UO; Reid "ad" quoted in "Speech by Robin Angus at the Ivory and Sime, International Investment Seminar," Gullane, Scotland, 15 October, 1984.

[36]MacColl, *Shaping*, 69; Montgomery, "Dictation"; Malcolm Clark, Jr., in Deady, *Pharisee*, 1: 296.

[37]Corning, *Dictionary*, 43, 155; Thomas R. Cox, *Mills and Markets* (Seattle, 1974), 140-41.

[38]Cox, *Mills and Markets*, 141-43, 149.

[39]Cox, *Mills and Markets*, 141-43, 149.

[40]Estate Records, Ainsworth Papers, UO; Corning, *Dictionary*, 109.

[41]William J. Hawkins III, *The Grand Era of Cast-Iron Architecture in Portland* (Portland, 1976), 112.

[42]Fred Lockley, *History of the Columbia River Valley From The Dalles to the Sea* (Chicago, 1928), 3: 93; S.B. 217, p. 43; *Samuel's Directory of Portland and East Portland for 1878* (Portland, 1878); *Oregonian*, 14 December, 1911.

⁴³See footnote 42; L. F. Cartee to Governor Curry, 19 February, 1859, Miscellaneous Documents File, David P. Thompson Papers, OHS.

⁴⁴Deady, *Pharisee*, 1: 17; entry for 15 December, 1880, Council Proceedings, vol. 7; "Parrish Abstract #502, Abstract of Title 1, Block 33, City of Portland," 46-48, Thompson Papers.

⁴⁵Hawkins, *Grand Era*, 120, 144. See footnote 42.

⁴⁶Entry for 19 January, 1881, Council Proceedings, vol. 7.

⁴⁷Thomas Oaks to Henry Villard, 5 December, 1881, quoted in THomas C. Cochran, *Railroad Leaders, 1845-1890* (Cambridge, Mass., 1953), 205-206.

⁴⁸"Diary," 4 January, 1882, 135, John C. Ainsworth Papers, OHS.

⁴⁹MacColl, *Shaping*, 60; Joseph Simon, "Dictation," BL.

⁵⁰MacColl, *Shaping*, 69; entry for 19 January, 1881, Council Proceedings, vol. 7.

⁵¹Entry for 19 January, 1881, Council Proceedings, vol. 7.

⁵²"Earliest Authorities in Oregon," *Oregon Blue Book, 1987-1988* (Salem, 1987), 409-422.

⁵³*Oregonian*, 13, 18, 20, 21, and 22 June, 1881.

⁵⁴Entries for 6 July and 3 August, 1881, Council Proceedings, vol. 7; *Oregonian*, 4 August and 2 December, 1881.

⁵⁵*Oregonian*, 18, 19, and 20 June, 1881.

⁵⁶*Oregonian*, 27 September, 3 October, 22 November, 1883, 3 and 9 February, 1884; Lockley, *History*, 1: 455; *Probated Intestate Estates: Multnomah County, Oregon*, Part 4, 4: 77, OHS.

⁵⁷See footnote 42; *The Arlington Club and the Men Who Built It* (Portland, 1968), 105.

⁵⁸Villard, *Early Transportation*, 91; Thomas Cochran, "Henry Villard: Entrepreneur," in *Understanding the American Past*, ed. Edward N. Saveth (Boston, 1965), 359.

⁵⁹Buss, "Villard," 122-23; Maury Klein, *Union Pacific* (New York, 1987), 437.

⁶⁰Cochran, "Villard," 359-60; Chandler, *The Visible Hand*, 166-67, 170.

⁶¹MacColl, *Shaping*, 69-70; 4 January, 1882, "Diary," 114, Ainsworth Papers, OHS; Jackson, *Investors*, 32.

⁶²MacColl, *Shaping*, 70.

⁶³Villard, *Early Transportation*, 94; Edward W. Nolan, *Northern Pacific Views* (Helena, 1983), 38, 81-82.

⁶⁴Villard, *Early Transportation*, 94; Oscar O. Winther, *The Old Oregon Country* (Lincoln, 1969), 241-42; O. B. Coldwell, "Early Days of Electricity in Portland," *OHQ* 42 (December, 1941), 281-83.

⁶⁵Quiett, *They Built the West*, 366; Cochran, "Villard," 359; Nolan, *Northern Pacific*, 44; Buss, "Villard," 129-31.

⁶⁶William S. Ladd to Matthew P. Deady, 17 November, 1881, quoted in Orin K. Burrell, *Gold in the Woodpile* (Eugene, 1967), 54.

⁶⁷4 January, 1882, "Diary," 134, Ainsworth Papers, OHS.

⁶⁸Dorothy Johansen, "Organization and Finance of the Oregon Iron & Steel Company, 1880-1895," *Pacific Northwest Quarterly* 31 (April, 1940), 129.

⁶⁹Johansen, "Oregon Iron & Steel," 129; Herbert L. Hegert, "Early Iron Industry in Oregon," *Reed College Bulletin* 26 (January, 1948), 18-19.

⁷⁰*Oregonian*, 14 June, 1882.

⁷¹Johansen, "Oregon Iron & Steel," 130-33.

⁷²Thomas Oaks to C. H. Prescott, 4 February, 1883, quoted in Cochran, *Railroad*, 206; Deady, *Pharisee*, 2: 413.

⁷³Quiett, *They Built the West*, 368; Villard quoted in Buss, "Villard," 138-39; Nolan, *Northern Pacific*, 68.

⁷⁴*Oregonian*, 9 and 12 September, 1883; Macleay quoted in Henry E. Reed, *Cavalcade of Front Street, 1866-1941* (Portland, 1941), 2.

⁷⁵Quoted in Johansen, "Oregon Iron & Steel," 146.

[76]Buss, "Villard," 160.

[77]Quoted in Johansen, "Oregon Iron & Steel," 146.

[78]Quoted in Johansen, "Oregon Iron & Steel," 146; Deady, *Pharisee*, 2: 486.

[79]"The Metropolis of the Pacific Northwest," *The West Shore* 14 (May, 1888), 239; MacColl, *Shaping*, 46-47.

CHAPTER 12 FOOTNOTES

[1]William J. Hawkins III, *The Grand Era of Cast-Iron Architecture in Portland* (Portland, 1976), 100-137; United States Census Office, *Census of Oregon* (Washington, D.C., 1880); approximate population figure for 1883 from *Portland City Directory, 1884* (Portland, 1884), 27-30.

[2]Marion D. Ross, "Architecture in Oregon, 1845-1895," *OHQ* 57 (March, 1956), 54; Harvey W. Scott, ed., *History of Portland, Oregon* (Syracuse, 1890), 431; *Portland City Directory, 1884*, 27. Also see Richard Marlitt, *Nineteenth Street* (Portland, 1968).

[3]Jean Muir, "The Elegant Eighties," *Oregon Journal*, Sunday Magazine, 14 April, 1940.

[4]Thomas B. Merry, "Portland, the Beautiful Metropolis of the Pacific Northwest," *The Northwest* 3 (November, 1884), 29; *The West Shore* 14 (September, 1888), 459-60.

[5]Dorothy D. Hirsch, "Study of the Foreign Wheat Trade of Oregon, 1869-1887," *Reed College Bulletin* 31 (August, 1953), 60, 79, 82; E. Kimbark MacColl, *The Shaping of a City* (Portland, 1976), 359.

[6]Hawkins, *Grand Era*, 190-91; *R.L. Polk & Co.'s Portland City Directory, 1885* (Portland, 1885), 57-59.

[7]Paul G. Merriam, "Portland, Oregon, 1840-1890: A Social and Economic History" (Ph.D. diss., University of Oregon, 1971), 327; *City Directory, 1885*, 59; Scott, *Portland*, 299.

[8]Richard H. Peterson, "Simeon Gannett Reed and the Bunker Hill and Sullivan: The Frustrations of a Mining Investor," *Idaho Yesterdays* 23 (Fall, 1979), 2-8.

[9]*The Nation* quoted in Samuel Reznick, *Business Depressions and Financial Panics* (New York, 1968), 151, 155; Hirsch, "Wheat," 60; *City Directory, 1885*, 57.

[10]*City Directory, 1885*, 57.

[11]*Oregonian*, 21, 22, 24, 30 December, 1884.

[12]Carlos A. Schwantes, "Protest in a Promised Land: Unemployment, Disinheritance, and the Origin of Labor Militancy in the Pacific Northwest, 1885-1886," *The Western Historical Quarterly* 13 (October, 1982), 374; W. Thomas White, "Race, Ethnicity, and Gender in the Revolutionary Work Force: The Case of the Far Northwest, 1883-1918," *The Western Historical Quarterly* 16 (July, 1965), 267; Paul G. Merriam, "The 'Other Portland': A Statistical Note on Foreign-Born, 1860-1910," *OHQ* 80 (Fall, 1979), 266; Merriam, "Portland," 71.

[13]*Oregonian*, 28 December, 1884; Merriam, "The 'Other Portland,'" 267.

[14]Schwantes, "Protest in a Promised Land," 373-78.

[15]*Oregonian*, 28 January, 1886; Matthew P. Deady, *Pharisee Among Philistines*, ed. Malcolm Clark, Jr. (Portland, 1975), 2: 508.

[16]Malcolm Clark, Jr., "The Bigot Disclosed: 90 Years of Nativism," *OHQ* 75 (June, 1974), 128; Deady, *Pharisee*, 2: 508; Robert E. Wynne, *Reaction to the Chinese in the Pacific Northwest and British Columbia* (New York, 1978), 103-104.

[17]Deady, *Pharisee*, 2: 509; *Oregonian*, 4, 29 January, 23, 26, 27 February, 1 March, 1886; Clark, "The Bigot Disclosed," 129; Wynne, *Reaction to the Chinese*, 103-104.

[18]*Oregonian*, 12 March, 1886; Clark, "The Bigot Disclosed," 130; Deady, *Pharisee*, 2: 509; Nelson Chia-Chi Ho, *Portland's Chinatown* (Portland, 1978), 10; Ben Selling to "Bennie," 23 March, 1886, Ben Selling Papers, OHS.

[19]Clark, "The Bigot Disclosed," 130; *Oregonian*, 4 January, 23 February, 1886; Ruth B. Moynihan, *Rebel For Rights* (New Haven, 1983), 152.

[20]Schwantes, "Protest in a Promised Land," 380, 389; Harvey W. Stone, "The Beginning of the Labor Movement in the Pacific Northwest," *OHQ* 47 (June, 1946), 157-59.

[21]*Oregonian*, 5 May, 1886; Walter M. Pierce, *Oregon Cattleman, Governor, Congressman*, ed. and expanded by Arthur H. Bone (Portland, 1981), 26.

[22]Deady, *Pharisee*, 2: 509, 558; Ralph J. Mooney, "Matthew Deady and the Federal Judicial Response to Racism in the Early West," *Oregon Law Review* 63 (1984), 636-37. See John R. Wunder, "Chinese and the Courts in the Pacific Northwest," *Pacific Historical Review* 52 (May, 1983), 191-211, and E. Digby Baltzell, *Puritan Boston and Quaker Philadelphia* (New York, 1979), 77.

[23]Frederic C. Jaher, *The Urban Establishment* (Urbana, 1982), 8.

[24]"Boys and Girls Aid Society" and "Patton Home," Works Progress Administration, Oregon Historical Records Survey, 1936, Oregon State Library; Earl M. Wilbur and Evadne Hilands, *A Time To Build* (Portland, 1966), 25-32.

[25]*Oregonian*, 7 June and 30 November, 1987; Elizabeth S. Hamilton, "The Portland Woman's Union," in *The Souvenir of Western Women*, ed. Mary O. Douthit (Portland, 1905), 137.

[26]Entry for 15 July, 1885, Portland City Council Proceedings, vol. 8, City of Portland Archives; Tenth and Eleventh *Annual Reports of the Portland Chamber of Commerce*; Clark, "The Bigot Disclosed," 130.

[27]Hawkins, *Grand Era*, 148; *Oregonian*, 28 February, 1886; Merriam, "Portland," 315; MacColl, *Shaping*, 51.

[28]Merriam, "Portland," 314-15.

[29]Claude Singer, *U.S. National Bank of Oregon and U.S. Bancorp, 1891-1984* (Portland, 1984), 3.

[30]"Ledgers," James Steel Papers in the possession of the Great Northwest Bookstore, Portland; MacColl, *Shaping*, 494.

[31]MacColl, *Shaping*, 99, 494.

[32]MacColl, *Shaping*, 493-95.

[33]*Oregon Journal*, 2 May, 1909; MacColl, *Shaping*, 60; John C. Teaford, *The Unheralded Triumph* (Baltimore, 1984), 175-6.

[34]*Oregon Journal*, 2 May, 1909.

[35]Material from the Minutes of the Board of Police Commissioners, City of Portland Archives; Deady, *Pharisee*, 2: 394.

[36]Abraham W. Lafferty to E. B. McNaughton, 12 January, 1949, Abraham W. Lafferty Papers, OHS.

[37]General biographical data from Jonathan Bourne, Jr., Papers, UO; Leonard Schlup, "Republican Insurgent: Jonathan Bourne and The Politics of Progressivism, 1908-1912," *OHQ* (Fall, 1986), 229.

[38]MacColl, *Shaping*, 63-64; Lafferty to McNaughton, 12 January, 1949, Lafferty Papers.

[39]MacColl, *Shaping*, 64; Stuart Galischoff, "Triumph and Failure: The American Response to the Urban Water Supply Problem, 1860-1923," *Pollution and Reform in American Cities, 1870-1930*, ed. Martin V. Melosi (Austin, 1980), 35.

[40]City of Portland, *Water* (Portland, 1983), 11; entry for 18 November, 1885, Portland City Council Proceedings, vol. 8.

[41]Entry for 18 November, 1885, Portland City Council Proceedings, vol. 8.

[42]City Waterworks Scrapbook, p. 4, OHS; Records of the Proceedings of the Water Committee of Portland, 1: 55, City of Portland Archives.

[43]City Waterworks Scrapbook, p. 18.

[44]City Waterworks Scrapbook, p. 18.

[45]Herbert C. Hegert, "Early Iron Industry in Oregon," *Reed College Bulletin* 26 (January, 1948), 26.

[46]MacColl, *Shaping*, 67; City of Portland, *Water*, 20-23.

[47]City of Portland, *Water*, 24.

[48]Martin Shafter, "The Regional Receptivity to Reform: The Legacy of the Progressive Era," *Political Science Quarterly* 98 (Fall, 1983), 469-70; Paul Kleppner, "Voters and Parties in the Western States, 1876-1900," *Western Historical Quarterly* 14 (January, 1983), 66.

[49]MacColl, *Shaping*, 71; Harvey W. Scott, *History of the Oregon Country* (Cambridge, 1924), 4: 309-311.

[50]MacColl, *Shaping*, 71.

[51]*Sixth Annual Report of the OR&N Company* (Boston, 1884).

[52]MacColl, *Shaping*, 72.

[53]MacColl, *Shaping*, 46, 72-73; Scott, *Oregon Country*, 4: 310-11.

[54]MacColl, *Shaping*, 46.

[55]Shafter, "Regional Receptivity," 469; *Fortune* 16 (November, 1937), 98.

[56]Merriam, "Portland," 308; *The West Shore* 14 (December, 1888), 651.

CHAPTER 13 FOOTNOTES

[1]Randall V. Mills, "Development of the Mass Transit Pattern of Portland, Oregon," in *Selections From the Oregon Business Review, 1941-1964*, ed. Catherine Lauris (Eugene, 1963), 8; "The Metropolis of the Pacific Northwest," *West Shore* 14 (May, 1888), 234.

[2]Mills, "Mass Transit Pattern," 8.

[3]Lewis Mumford, *The City in History* (New York, 1961), 425-6.

[4]Mills, "Mass Transit Pattern," 9; E. Kimbark MacColl, *The Shaping of a City* (Portland, 1976), 487.

[5]MacColl, *Shaping*, 487.

[6]MacColl, *Shaping*, 92; S.B. 50, p. 122; *Oregonian*, 23 February, 1914; Joseph Gaston, *Portland* (Portland, 1911),
1: 180; Claude Singer, "History of the U.S. Bank," 6, draft, OHS.

[7]Documentation for these and the ensuing activities are in Portland City Council Proceedings and, by year, under "Franchises," in Portland City Council Papers, City of Portland Archives.

[8]Information on Markle and their uncle's family provided by Alvan Markle, Jr., of Hazleton, and Henry Wilkins Rustin, of New York.

[9]The Lombard Investment Company report, using 1887 figures, was published in June, 1888. For an account of the Portland Stock Exchange, see Marian V. Sears, "Jonathan Bourne, Jr., Capital Market and the Portland Stock Exchange...1887," *OHQ* 69 (September, 1968), 197.

[10]MacColl, *Shaping*, 151, 157-8; Charles E. Sawyer, "Concerning Portland's Bridges," *Portland Chamber of Commerce Bulletin* (12 December, 1912), 36; O. B. Coldwell, "Early Days of Electricity in Portland," *OHQ* 42 (December, 1941), 286. See also R. R. Robley, *Portland Electric Power Company With Its Predecessor Companies, 1860-1935* (Portland, 1935).

[11]MacColl, *Shaping*, 81; Carl Gohs, "There Stood the Portland Hotel," *Oregonian* Northwest Magazine, 25 May, 1975; Portland Hotel Records, OHS.

[12]Sources on DeLashmutt's life are from a variety of newspapers; city directories; the Simeon G. Reed Papers, Reed College; and his obituary, *Oregonian*, 6 October, 1921.

[13]Van B. DeLashmutt, "Dictation," BL.

[14]"As It Looks From Here," *Oregonian* Magazine, 12 September, 1948.

[15]In 1975 the owner of the former Markle home, Robert Autrey, provided documentation of Markle's private financial affairs relating to real estate and mortgage loans in Abstract of Title, Property of F. F. and B. C. Pittock, Block 115, Grover's Addition, Multnomah County, 1926.

[16]Gohs, "Portland Hotel."

[17]*History of Portland, Oregon*, ed. Harvey W. Scott (Syracuse, 1890), 434-5; Matthew P. Deady, *Pharisee Among Philistines*, ed. Malcolm Clark, Jr. (Portland, 1975), 2: 614.

[18]Scott, *Portland*, 630.

[19]Stanley Mallach, "The Origins of the Decline of the Urban Mass Transportation in the United States, 1890-1930," *Urbanism Past and Present* 8 (Summer, 1979), 1.

[20]*West Shore* 14 (August, 1888); 442-3; Philip A. Marquam, "Dictation," BL.

[21]MacColl, *Shaping*, 94.

[22]MacColl, *Shaping*, 483.

[23]Sawyer, "Concerning Portland's Bridges," 306; entry for 11 November, 1891, Portland City Council Proceedings.

²⁴Ordinances of the City of Portland, 1892, pp. 541-4, Portland City Hall Archives; *Oregonian*, 7 April, 1926.

²⁵MacColl, *Shaping*, 124.

²⁶*West Shore* 14 (December, 1888), 651.

²⁷Information on Swigert comes from the Charles F. Swigert Papers, OHS, and the author's many conversations with Swigert's late son, Ernest G. Swigert, including an informative interview of 25 November, 1975. MacColl, *Shaping*, 95-96.

²⁸James T. Covert, *A Point of Pride* (Portland, 1976), 12-15.

²⁹Covert, *A Point of Pride*, 15, 21-2.

³⁰*Oregonian*, 4 June, 1889; Coldwell, "Early Days," 289-90.

³¹MacColl, *Shaping*, 94-95, 487.

³²MacColl, *Shaping*, 95.

³³Claude Singer, *U.S. National Bank of Oregon and U.S. Bancorp, 1891-1984* (Portland, 1984), 3.

³⁴Singer, *U.S. National Bank*, 3-5.

³⁵MacColl, *Shaping*, 99; Martin Winch to Simeon G. Reed, 15 December, 1892, Reed Papers.

³⁶Mallach, "Urban Mass Transportation," 2.

³⁷Coldwell, "Early Days," 292.

³⁸Coldwell, "Early Days," 292; MacColl, *Shaping*, 158.

³⁹MacColl, *Shaping*, 158; "Portland Gas & Coke Co., History," provided the author by Northwest Natural Gas Company; "Origin, Growth and Development of the Northwest Natural Gas Co.," statement issued by the company, 13 November, 1972.

⁴⁰"Origin, Growth, and Development"; MacColl, *Shaping*, 164.

⁴¹Charles F. Adams, Jr., in conversation with the author, 27 January, 1976.

⁴²"Stock Registration for the Security Savings and Trust Company," in custody of the First Interstate Bank, Portland.

CHAPTER 14 FOOTNOTES

¹Michael J. Doucet, "Urban Land Development in Nineteenth-Century North America: Themes in the Literature," *Journal of Urban History* 8 (May, 1982), 299.

²On Ladd's holdings, see Ladd Family and W. S. Ladd and Co. Papers, OHS; his probated estate, Files of the Probate Department, Multnomah County Clerk's Office; and title abstracts for his properties, Land, Miscellaneous File, OHS: Lot 7 Block 112 (Laurelhurst) and Block 44, East Portland (Ladd's Addition). See also Assessment Role, 1895, vol. 11, Multnomah County Clerk's Office, and S.B. 259, pp. 150-51.

³"Eastside History," *Sunday Oregonian*, 9 July, 1893.

⁴East Portland City Council Minutes, City of Portland Archives.

⁵"Eastside History."

⁶*Oregon Journal*, 18 September, 1922.

⁷*Oregonian*, 2 April, 1887.

⁸*Oregonian*, 6 March, 1888.

⁹*History of Portland, Oregon*, ed. Harvey W. Scott (Syracuse, 1890), 428-29.

¹⁰Albina City Ordinances, in Laws and Ordinances of the City of Portland, 1892, City of Portland Archives; Fred Lockley, "Impressions and Observations of the Journal Man," *Oregon Journal*, 18 January, 1939.

¹¹Laws and Ordinances of the City of Portland, 1892, pp. 815-54.

¹²E. Kimbark MacColl, *Shaping of a City* (Portland, 1976), 140.

¹³Information on Bates is from news files, official records, interviews, and *The Portrait and Biographical Record, Portland and Vicinity* (Portland, 1903), 172-73.

14Information on Hoffman is from members of his family; from Fred Westerland of the Hoffman Construction Company, who is preparing a corporate history; from Margarey Hoffman Smith Collection, OHS; and from MacColl, *Shaping*, 141.

15Entry, 23 July, 1891, for City Council Proceedings and Ordinances, vol. 12, Portland City Hall Archives; Percy Maddux, *City on the Willamette* (Portland, 1952), 132; the author's discussions with S. Mason Ehrman and Spencer M. Ehrman, Jr., son and grandson of Edward H. Ehrman; Julian Hawthorne, *The Story of Oregon* (New York, 1892), 2: 266.

16Lawrence H. Larsen, *The Urban West at the End of the Frontier* (Lawrence, 1978), 115; MacColl, *Shaping*, 144.

17Entry, 23 July, 1891, for City Council Proceedings and Ordinances, vol. 12.

18*Oregonian*, 1 January, 1891; Minutes of the Board of Police Commissioners, pp. 78, 89, Portland City Hall Archives.

19Entries, 6 August, 1891, 21 November, 1891, and 25 September, 1891 (vol. 12) and 1 March, 1893, entry for City Council Proceedings and Ordinances, vol. 13.

20Entry, 23 July, 1891, for City Council Proceedings and Ordinances; Joseph Gaston to Benjamin Harrison, 8 December, 1891, William Lair Hill Papers, OHS.

21*Oregonian*, 19 June, 1889; "Committee Report...to the Ministerial Association of Portland," n.d., OHS.

22"Committee Report."

23"Committee Report."

24"Committee Report."

25Samuel P. Hays, "The Changing Political Structure of the City in Industrial America," *Journal of Urban History* 1 (November, 1974), 21.

26Hays, "Changing Political Structure," 18.

27Ray Kell, former member of the Portland Dock Commission, in "Policy of the Port," League of Women Voters of Portland, September, 1973, p. 1; Dennis Lindsay, President of the Port of Portland, "75 Years with the Port of Portland," *Greater Portland Commerce* (1 April, 1966), 16; William F. Willingham, *Army Engineers and the Development of Oregon* (Washington, 1983), 54, 71.

28Names of Port commissioners are on file with the Records Office, Port of Portland.

29Willingham, *Army Engineers*, 74; Kell, "Policy of the Port," 1.

CHAPTER 15 FOOTNOTES

1S.B. 5, p. 31; Matthew P. Deady, *Pharisee Among Philistines*, ed. Malcolm Clark, Jr. (Portland, 1975), 2: 623.

2Information on the dinner guests is from R. G. Dun and Co., *The Mercantile Agency Reference Book & Key Concerning Ratings of the Merchants, Manufacturers, and Trades Generally Throughout the Pacific States and Territories* (New York, 1894), and from city directories and scrapbooks at the OHS.

3S.B. 211, p. 126.

4Margaret Pietsch, *Riverwood, Yesterday and Today* (Portland, 1980), 22-24.

5S.B. 5, p. 31.

6S.B. 5, p. 31.

7Michael J. Doucet, "Urban Land Development in Nineteenth-Century North American: Themes in the Literature," *Journal of Urban History* 8 (May, 1982), 326.

8S.B. 21, pp. 86, 88.

9Erskine Wood, *Life of Charles Erskine Scott Wood By His Son* (Portland, 1978), 58; Eugene E. Snyder, *Skidmore's Portland* (Portland, 1973), 123-24.

10Wood, *Charles Erskine Scott Wood*, 51.

11Files of the Probate Department, Multnomah County Clerk's Office; E. Kimbark MacColl, *The Shaping of a City* (Portland, 1976), 25; William M. Ladd to Asahel Bush, 17 November, 1898, in the possession of the author; Peter Kerr to James Dewar, 18 February, 1893, Peter Kerr Letters, OHS.

12"Ghouls of Riverview, An Oregon Mystery," *Oregonian* Magazine, 1 December, 1935, p. 13.

[13]Deady, *Pharisee*, 2: 268; Miscellaneous File, Simeon G. Reed Papers, Reed College Library.

[14]*19th Annual Report of the Portland Chamber of Commerce, 1893*, p. 17; *Pacific Banker & Investor* 1 (March, 1893), 7.

[15]MacColl, *Shaping*, 100.

[16]Peter Kerr to William McGill, 19 May, 1893, Kerr Letters.

[17]Samuel Reznick, *Business Depressions and Financial Panics* (New York, 1968), 177; John W. S. Platt (Kerr's son-in-law) to the author, April, 1988; Peter Kerr to William McKinney, 5 December, 1892, Kerr Letters.

[18]*Pacific Banker & Investor* 1 (November, 1893), 54; *Oregonian*, 4 September, 1898.

[19]Peter Kerr to James Dewar, 18 July, 1893, Kerr Letters.

[20]Peter Kerr to James Dewar, 26 July, 1893, Kerr Letters.

[21]Martin Winch to Simeon G. Reed, 27 July, 1893, Reed Papers.

[22]*Pacific Banker & Investor* 1 (August, 1893), 43.

[23]Martin Winch to Simeon G. Reed, 1 August, 1893, Reed Papers; "Abstract of Title, Property of F. F. and B. C. Pittock," Block 115, Grover's Addition, Multnomah County, 1926, in the possession of Robert Autrey, Portland.

[24]Orin K. Burrell, *Gold in the Woodpile* (Eugene, 1967), 129-67.

[25]Henry W. Rustin (Markle's nephew) to the author, 21 December, 1975.

[26]MacColl, *Shaping*, 104; *Oregonian*, 21 April, 1894.

[27]Joseph Gaston, *Portland, Oregon, Its History and Builders* (Portland, 1911) 1: 610; *Oregonian*, 2 January, 1932; Alfred D. Chandler, Jr., *The Visible Hand* (Cambridge, 1977), 171.

[28]Herman C. Voeltz, "Coxey's Army in Oregon, 1894," *OHQ* 65 (September, 1964), 264, 272, 273; *Oregonian*, 6, 20 and 21 April, 1894.

[29]W. Thomas White, "Race, Ethnicity, and Gender in the Railroad Work Force: The Case of the Far Northwest, 1883-1918," *The Western Historical Quarterly* 16 (July, 1965), 276; *Telegram*, 19 April, 1894, quoted in Voeltz, "Coxey's Army," 276.

[30]*Oregonian*, 27, 29 and 30 April, 1894; Voeltz, "Coxey's Army," 279-91.

[31]Henry L. Pittock to George T. Myers, 17 October, 1893, in the possession of Henry Pittock II, Cannon Beach, Oregon; *The Arlington Club and the Men Who Built It* (Portland, 1968), 81.

[32]*Oregonian*, 22 April, 1894.

[33]S.B. 54, p. 45.

[34]*Oregonian*, 1 January, 1895; Esther C. P. Lovejoy, "My Medical School 1890-1894," Introduction by Bertha Hallam, from an essay "As I Remember," *OHQ* 75 (March, 1974), 28.

[35]Hoffman & Bates file and Julia Lee Hoffman note, Margery Hoffman Smith Collection, OHS; *Oregon Journal*, 20 October, 1917.

[36]Martin Winch to Simeon G. Reed, 1 August, 1894, Reed Papers; Claude Singer, *U.S. National Bank of Oregon and U.S. Bancorp, 1891-1984* (Portland, 1984), 10-11.

[37]"Estate Accounting of C. H. Lewis," *Early Oregon Wills: Multnomah County, Oregon*, 7: 235, OHS.

[38]"Ledgers," James Steel Papers in the possession of the Great Northwest Bookstore, Portland.

[39]MacColl, *Shaping*, 104.

[40]"Articles of Incorporation," 2: 116, Multnomah County Clerk's Office; MacColl, *Shaping*, 181.

CHAPTER 16 FOOTNOTES

[1]On the flood, see "The Flood of 1894 or Venice of the Northwest," *Old Portland Today* 3 (1 March, 1975), *Oregon Journal*, 29 March, 1972, and *Albina Weekly Courier*, 9 June, 1894.

[2]*Albina Weekly Courier*, 9 June, 1894; "Estate Accounting of C. H. Lewis," *Early Oregon Wills: Multnomah County, Oregon*, 7: 235, OHS.

[3]"Flood of 1894"; E. Kimbark MacColl, *The Shaping of a City* (Portland, 1976), 169.

[4]*Albina Weekly Courier*, 9 June, 1894.

⁵*Oregonian*, 16 March, 1896.

⁶MacColl, *Shaping*, 186.

⁷For information on Lotan, see publications also relating to W. F. (Jack) Matthews: S.B. 53, p. 75, S.B. 55, p. 125, S.B. 261, pp. 141-42, various city directories, and *Oregon Journal*, 28 May, 1909.

⁸*Oregonian*, 24 December, 1893; Dean Collins, "Portland: A Pilgrim's Promise," in *The Taming of the Frontier*, ed. Duncan Aikman (New York, 1925), 181.

⁹*Oregonian*, 3 March, 1896.

¹⁰*Oregon Journal*, 28 May, 1909; "Journals," Pacific Bridge Co. Papers, OHS; Estate Inventory of Henry W. Corbett, Files of the Probate Department, Multnomah County Clerk's Office.

¹¹Lincoln Steffens paraphrased in Samuel P. Hays, "The Politics of Reform in Municipal Government in the Progressive Era," in Samuel P. Hays, *American Political History as Social Analysis* (Knoxville, 1979), 206.

¹²*Oregon Journal*, 19 July, 1910; Walter M. Pierce, *Oregon Cattleman, Governor, Congressman*, ed. and expanded by Arthur H. Bone (Portland, 1981), 37, 39, 418. Much of the material on Bourne comes from Bourne's remarks in Washington, D.C., to Cornelia Marvin Pierce, as recorded in her diary; Bourne lived in Washington while Pierce served in Congress. Henry Corbett quoted in *Oregonian*, 15 October, 1896.

¹³Oswald West, "Them Were the Days," unidentified clipping in Oswald West Papers, OHS.

¹⁴*Oregonian*, 20 April, 1894; Percy Maddux, *City on the Willamette* (Portland, 1952) 135, 141.

¹⁵MacColl, *Shaping*, 197-98.

¹⁶Stewart Holbrook, "Portland's Greatest Moral Crusade," *Sunday Oregonian*, 2 August, 1936; Collins, "Portland," 180-81.

¹⁷*Oregonian*, 10 April, 1895.

¹⁸*Oregonian*, 15 March, 1896.

¹⁹*Oregonian*, 8 March, 1896.

²⁰*Oregonian*, 8 March, 1896.

²¹*Oregonian*, 8 March, 1896.

²²Marie Lazenby, "The Conservative Defense in Portland, 1896" (B.A. thesis, Reed College, 1948), 13.

²³Pierce, *Oregon Cattleman*, 39-40.

²⁴*Oregonian*, 27 November, 1896.

²⁵Pierce, *Oregon Cattleman*, 40.

²⁶Pierce, *Oregon Cattleman*, 40-41; *Oregon Journal*, 19 June, 1910.

²⁷S.B. 274, p. 52; Henry Corbett to Editor, *Oregonian*, 10 March, 1898.

²⁸Henry Corbett to William P. Lord, 6 October, 1898, Henry E. Reed Papers, OHS; MacColl, *Shaping*, 210.

²⁹Richard Pintarich, "His Eccentricity," *Oregon Magazine* 12 (November, 1982), 52-56.

³⁰Joseph Simon to Jonathan Bourne, Jr., 11 March, 17 and 30 August, 13 October, and 9 December, 1897, Jonathan Bourne, Jr., Papers, UO.

³¹Joseph Simon to Jonathan Bourne, Jr., 23 December, 1897, Bourne Papers.

³²Amadee Smith to Jonathan Bourne, Jr., 7 and 20 May, 1898, Bourne Papers.

³³*Oregonian*, 7 May, 1898.

³⁴*Oregonian*, 21 July, 1898; Portland City Council Proceedings 18: 32, Portland City Archives.

³⁵*Oregonian*, 9 July, 1898.

³⁶*Biennial Report of the Secretary of State of Oregon, 1898-1900* (Salem, 1900), 37.

³⁷MacColl, *Shaping*, 217; Samuel P. Hays, "The Changing Political Structure of the City in Industrial America," *Journal of Urban History* 1 (November, 1974), 15.

CHAPTER 17 FOOTNOTES

¹Dorothy O. Johansen and Charles M. Gates, *Empire of the Columbia* (New York, 1957), 489.

[2]Fred Lockley, *History of the Columbia River Valley From The Dalles to the Sea* (Chicago, 1928), 1: 678.

[3]Lockley, *History*, 1: 678.

[4]Newspaper clipping, 17 January, 1902, in S.B. 48, pp. 86, 111; Peter Kerr to James Dewar, 3 April, 1897, Peter Kerr Letters, OHS.

[5]*Portland Chamber of Commerce Bulletin* 5 (August, 1906), 10; *Twelfth Census of the United States, 1900, vol. 8. Manufactures, pt. 22* (Washington, 1900), 733; *Financial Redbook* list in *Oregonian*, 14 October, 1903.

[6]Ray Stannard Baker, "The Great Northwest," *Century Magazine* 65 (March, 1903), 658-59; Lewis Mumford, *The City in History* (New York, 1961), 425; Joseph Gaston, *Portland, Oregon, Its History and Builders* (Portland, 1911), 1: 584.

[7]Carl Abbott, *Portland* (Lincoln, 1982), 33-34.

[8]Gaston, *Portland, Oregon, Its History and Builders*, 1: 611; "Minutes of the Executive Committee," 5 July, 1902, cited in Robert W. Rydell, "Expositions in Portland and Seattle: Political Culture in the Making, 1905-1909," p. 1, paper presented at the Pacific Coast Branch, American Historical Association, 19 August, 1981.

[9]Mansel G. Blackford, "The Lost Dream: Businessmen and City Planning in Portland, Oregon, 1903-1914," *The Western Historical Quarterly* 15 (January, 1984), 40.

[10]*Oregonian*, 10 November 1901.

[11]City revenues are from the 1885-1905 issues of the *Mayor's Message and Annual Report*, City of Portland Archives. Comparable municipal revenue problems and solutions are discussed in Carl V. Harris, *Political Power in Birmingham, 1871-1921* (Knoxville, 1977), 96, 112, and William Issel and Robert W. Cherny, *San Francisco, 1865-1932* (Berkeley, 1984), 153.

[12]Newspaper clipping, 20 May, 1902, in S.B. 48, p. 5.

[13]*Oregon Journal*, 27 December 1907.

[14]*Biennial Report of the Secretary of State of Oregon, 1901-1902* (Salem, 1903), lxxvi, xliv, xlv.

[15]*Portland Labor Press*, 10 March, 1905; Rydell, "Expositions," 5; Craig E. Wollner, *The City Builders* (work in progress), 44.

[16]Wollner, *City Builders*; Peter Kerr to David McLaren, 17 February, 1893, Kerr Letters.

[17]Gwladys Bowen, "Socially Speaking," *Sunday Oregonian*, 23 February, 1936; Marie Lazenby, "The Conservative Defense in Portland, 1896" (B.A. thesis, Reed College, 1948), 142.

[18]Roderick Macleay Scrapbook, in the possession of Mrs. Richard Phillippi, Portland.

[19]Elizabeth F. Dimon, *Twas Many Years Since* (Milwaukie, 1981), 43-45; C. Edwin Francis, *Waverley Country Club, 1899-1915* (Portland, 1988), 14-15.

[20]Lawrence Pratt, *I Remember Portland, 1899-1915* (Portland, 1965), 28.

[21]Stewart Holbrook, "The Life of Fred T. Merrill," *Sunday Oregonian*, 22 March, 1936.

[22]Holbrook, "Fred T. Merrill."

[23]Holbrook, "Fred T. Merrill."

[24]S.B. 261, p. 104; 30 October, 1899, entry, Minutes of the Board of Police Commissioners, 2: 185-86, Portland City Hall Archives.

[25]D. A. Lund, "'Skidroad' Now Purified," *Oregon Sunday Journal*, undated Works Progress Administration, Oregon Historical Records Survey, 1936, Clippings, Series 1, Box 20, Oregon State Library.

[26]Stephen Wise to Louise Wise, 28 October, 1902, quoted in William Toll, *The Making of an Ethnic Middle Class* (Albany, N.Y., 1982), 95; Stephen Wise, *Challenging Years* (New York, 1949), 7-8; Dean Collins, "Portland: A Pilgrim's Promise," in *The Taming of the Frontier*, ed. Duncan Aikman (New York, 1925), 173.

[27]Newspaper clipping, 16 June, 1902, in S.B. 48, p. 27.

[28]*Oregonian*, 12 December, 1894; Minutes of the Board of Public Works, 1: 364-381, 418, Portland City Hall Archives.

[29]Records of the Proceedings of the Water Committee of Portland, 2: 116, City of Portland Archives; *Oregonian*, 10 October, 1901.

[30]Records of the Proceedings of the Water Committee of Portland, 2: 116; undated clipping in S.B. 48, p. 24.

31Information is from both volumes of the Minutes of the Board of Public Works.

32*Daily Times* 9 December, 1900, in Miscellaneous Politics Papers, OHS.

33Minutes of the Board of Public Works, 1: 733.

34Ellis Hughes to City Council, 4 September, 1901, Miscellaneous Portland City Council Papers, City of Portland Archives.

35See footnote 34.

36*Oregonian*, 19, 20, 23 February, 1901; *Oregon Journal*, 19, June, 1910; Jonathan Bourne, Jr., to B. F. Mulkey, 26 February, 1901, and to T. A. Johnson, 20 March, 1901, Jonathan Bourne, Jr., Papers, UO.

37Charter of the City of Portland, 1902, Portland City Hall Archives.

38William S. U'Ren, "The Initiative and Referendum in Oregon," *Arena* 29 (March, 1903), 270-75; Walter Pierce, *Oregon Cattleman, Governor, Congressman*, ed. and expanded by Arthur H. Bone (Portland, 1981), 42.

39Toney H. Evans, "Oregon Progressive Reform, 1902-1914" (Ph.D. thesis, University of California, Berkeley, 1966), 71-72.

40*Oregonian*, 22 April, 1902.

41*New Age*, 10 and 17 May, 1902; Evans, "Oregon," 71; Pierce, *Oregon Cattleman*, 47.

42Richard Marlitt, *Nineteenth Street* (Portland, 1968), 26-27; Matthew P. Deady, *Pharisee Among Philistines*, ed. Malcolm Clark, Jr. (Portland, 1975), 1: xxv; Henry W. Corbett to Matthew P. Deady, 4 and 8 May, 1870, Matthew P. Deady Letters, OHS.

43Portland City Council Proceedings, 20: 503, City of Portland Archives.

44Minutes of the Board of Police Commissioners, 2: 353; Portland City Council Proceedings, 20: 503.

45Nelson Chia-Chi Ho, *Portland's Chinatown* (Portland Bureau of Planning, December, 1978), 22; Thomas B. Malarkey, Sr., *The Burgess Family and The Malarkey Family* (Portland, 1980), 24.

46Malarkey, *The Burgess Family*, 25.

47*New Age*, 2 February, 1903; Thomas L. Eliot to George H. Williams, 27 August, 1903, quoted in John F. Scheck, "Thomas Lamb Eliot and His Vision of an Enlightened Community," in *The Western Shore*, ed. Thomas Vaughan (Portland, 1975), 264.

48Collins, "A Pilgrim's Promise," 174; undated newspaper account of Turk, (see footnote 25 (WPA).

49Oscar C. Christensen, "The Grand Old Man of Oregon: The Life of George H. Williams" (Ph.D. thesis, University of Oregon, reproduced as University of Oregon Thesis Series No. 5, 1939); Minutes of the Executive Board, 2: 202, Portland City Hall Archives.

50*Arlington Club*, 82.

CHAPTER 18 FOOTNOTES

1Files on Lewis and Clark Exposition financial management, Abbot L. Mills Papers, UO; Carl Abbott, *The Great Extravaganza* (Portland, 1981), 20, 21, 63.

2E. Kimbark MacColl, *The Shaping of a City* (Portland, 1976), 266, Appendix I.

3Claude Singer, *U.S. National Bank of Oregon and U.S. Bancorp, 1891-1984* (Portland, 1984), 14-17; John C. Ainsworth to George B. McLeod, 21 January, 1936, John C. Ainsworth Papers (those of the younger Ainsworth), UO.

4*Revised General Ordinances, City of Portland, 1905*, 66-77, 85-108, Portland City Hall Archives.

5*Revised General Ordinances*, 109-132; Journal of the Pacific Bridge Company, 1901-1909, Box 1, and Records of the City & Suburban Railway Company in Pacific Bridge Company Papers, OHS.

6*Journal of the Senate of the Legislative Assembly of the State of Oregon, 1903 Session*, 3.

7*Journal of the Senate of the Legislative Assembly of the State of Oregon, 1903 Session*, 154.

8Abbott, *Great Extravaganza*, 69; MacColl, *Shaping*, 256-67.

[9]Walter Pierce, *Oregon Cattleman, Governor, Congressman*, ed. and expanded by Arthur H. Bone (Portland, 1981), 54.

[10]Pierce, *Oregon Cattleman*, 54, 56; MacColl, *Shaping*, 250.

[11]Pierce, *Oregon Cattleman*, 59-62; *Muller* v. *Oregon* 208 U.S. 412 (1908).

[12]*Oregonian*, 1 April, 1903; *Oregon Journal*, 1 April, 1903; *Oregon Statesman*, 1 April, 1903.

[13]Information on Corbett is from the H. W. Corbett Papers and Corbett Investment Company Papers, OHS, from the author's numerous conversations with many members of the Corbett family, and from an interview with Mrs. Henry L. Corbett, 29 March, 1975. *A Selection of Wills*, comp. Albert L. Grutze (Portland, 1925), 1: 32-37.

[14]Inventory of Henry W. Corbett Estate, Files of the Probate Department, Multnomah County Clerk's Office; Corbett Investment Company Papers.

[15]Robert W. Rydell, "Expositions in Portland and Seattle: Political Culture in the Making, 1905-1909," 3-4, paper presented at the Pacific Coast Branch, American Historical Association, 19 August, 1981.

[16]Abbott, *Great Extravaganza*, 21; MacColl, *Shaping*, 268-69; City of Portland, *Park Commission Report, 1901* (Portland, 1901); City of Portland, *Report of Park Board, 1903* (Portland, 1903).

[17]Wilcox interview with *San Diego Union*, in Rydell, "Expositions," p. 29.

[18]City & Suburban Folder, and Abbot L. Mills to William A. White, 10 August, 1903, Mills Papers.

[19]Mills to White, 17 May, 12 June, 13 July, 1904, Mills Papers.

[20]Mills to White, 14 July, 1904, Mills Papers.

[21]*Journal of the House of the Legislative Assembly of the State of Oregon, 1905 Session*, p. 1383; *Journal of the Senate of the State of Oregon, 1905 Session*, p. 765.

[22]Pacific Bridge Company Papers, Box 1, 1904, 1905, OHS.

[23]Information is from Pacific Bridge Company Papers and from City & Suburban and Portland Consolidated Folders, Mills Papers.

[24]*Oregonian*, 16 March, 1904; William P. Keady to Jonathan Bourne, Jr., 18 and 19 January, 1904, Jonathan Bourne, Jr., Papers, UO; *Oregon Journal*, 5 and 7 March, 1904.

[25]Burton J. Hendrick, "'Statement No. 1,' How the Oregon Democracy, Working under the Direct Primary, has destroyed the political machine," *McClure's Magazine* 37 (September, 1911), 506-507; Samuel Eliot Morrison, Henry Steel Commager and William E. Leuchtenberg, *The Growth of the American Republic* (New York, 1969), 2: 288.

[26]Quoted in S.B. 275, n.d.

[27]*Oregon Journal*, 22 May, 1905.

[28]Untitled flyer, 2 May, 1905, Portland Municipal Association Folder, Miscellaneous Associations, Institutions, Etc. Papers, OHS.

[29]Minutes of the Executive Board, 1: 342, 380, 2: 46, 48, Portland City Hall Archives.

[30]Stephen A. D. Puter, *Looters of the Public Domain* (Portland, 1908), 21.

[31]William D. Wheelwright, "The Businessman in Politics," *Chamber of Commerce Bulletin* 3 (March, 1905), 4; William G. Robbins, *Land: Its Use and Abuse in Oregon, 1848-1910* (Corvallis, December, 1974), 34.

[32]Lincoln Steffens, "The Taming of the West," *American Magazine* 64 (September and October, 1907), 590.

[33]Robbins, *Land*, 14-16. See also John Messing, "Public Land, Politics, and Progressives: The Oregon Land Fraud Trials, 1903-1910," *Pacific Historical Review* 34 (January, 1966), 35-66.

[34]William P. Keady to Jonathan Bourne, Jr., 3 January, 1905, Bourne Papers.

[35]*Oregonian*, 7 January, 1905; William P. Keady to Jonathan Bourne, Jr., 11 January, 1095, 4 February, 1905, Bourne Papers.

[36]On C. J. Reed and Heney, see footnote 32, and for John Reed, Richard D. O'Connor and D. L. Walker, *The Lost Revolutionary* (New York, 1967), esp. 20-25, and Robert A. Rosenstone, *Romantic Revolutionary* (New York, 1975), chs. 1-3.

[37]William P. Keady to Jonathan Bourne, Jr., 3 March, 1905, and Andrew C. Smith to Bourne, 20 May, 1905, Bourne Papers.

[38]*Oregon Journal*, 23 May, 1905.

[39]*Oregon Journal*, 22 May, 1905; *Oregonian*, 4 and 5 June, 1905.

[40]*Oregonian*, 6 June, 1905.

[41]Minutes of the Executive Board, 2: 202; Abbott, *Great Extravaganza*, 72.

CHAPTER 19 FOOTNOTES

[1]Oswald West, "Reminiscences," *OHQ* 52 (September, 1951), 148-49.

[2]West, "Reminiscences," 150.

[3]June 7, 1905, entry, Minutes of the Executive Board, 2: 198, Portland City Hall Archives; Harry Lane to "Dear Sir," 9 August, 1912, E. Kimbark MacColl Collection.

[4]Richard L. McCormick, "The Discovery That Business Corrupts Politics: A Reappraisal of the Origins of Progressivism," *American Historical Review* 86 (April, 1981), 265, 273; Lane quoted in Erskine Wood, *Life of C. E. S. Wood* (Portland, 1978), 103.

[5]Samuel B. Hays, "The Politics of Reform in Municipal Government in the Progressive Era," *Pacific Northwest Quarterly* 55 (October, 1964), 160.

[6]West, "Reminiscences," 151; Dean Collins, "Portland: A Pilgrim's Progress," in *The Taming of the Frontier*, ed. Duncan Aikman (New York, 1925), 190; Hays, "Politics of Reform," 163.

[7]Carl Abbott, *The Great Extravaganza* (Portland, 1981), 64, 69; Robert W. Rydell, "Expositions in Portland and Seattle: Political Culture in the Making, 1905-1909," p. 29, paper presented at the Pacific Coast Branch, American Historical Association, 19 August, 1981.

[8]Richard M. McCann in *Chamber of Commerce Bulletin* 4 (March, 1906), 8; Donald Macdonald, "Portland Points the Way," *Sunset* 17 (June, 1906), 50.

[9]Macdonald, "Portland Points the Way," 58, 60.

[10]Macdonald, "Portland Points the Way," 65; James E. Vance, Jr., *The Merchant's World* (Englewood Cliffs, 1970), 92.

[11]R. G. Dun and Co., *The Mercantile Agency, Reference Book & Key* (New York, 1907).

[12]*Oregonian*, 13 June, 1907.

[13]For John Yeon, see Fred Lockley's columns in *Oregon Journal*, 3 and 4 December, 1919. Stewart Holbrook, "Simon Benson, the All-Steam Bunyan," *Oregonian*, 1 May, 1935; Simon Benson vertical file, OHS.

[14]Information is from Chester Moore's Papers before they were organized by the OHS.

[15]See footnote 14.

[16]Equitable Savings & Loan Papers, Box 1, OHS; Joseph Gaston, *Portland, Oregon, Its History and Builders* (Portland, 1911), 1: 527-28.

[17]E. Kimbark MacColl, *The Shaping of a City* (Portland, 1976), 311, 365.

[18]Cecil T. Barker in *Chamber of Commerce Bulletin* 4 (December, 1905), 6.

[19]Portland City Council Proceedings, 23: 342, Portland City Hall Archives.

[20]*Oregonian*, 31 December, 1906.

[21]Entry for 20 October, 1905, Minutes of the Executive Board, vol. 2.

[22]Portland City Council Proceedings, 23: 589.

[23]City of Portland, *Report of the Park Board, 1903* (Portland, 1903), 6.

[24]Portland City Council Proceedings, 23: 690ff.

[25]Portland City Council Proceedings, 23: 690ff.

[26]Portland City Council Proceedings, 23: 691-94; *Oregon Journal*, 28 April, 1907.

[27]Portland City Council Proceedings, 27: 1ff.

[28]Portland City Council Proceedings, 23: 692.

[29]*Oregonian*, 21 August, 1914; Portland City Council Proceedings, 23: 694.

[30]*Oregon Journal*, 5, 6, 13, 18, 19 March, 1906.

[31]Eugene Snyder, *Portland Names and Neighborhoods* (Portland, 1979), 124-25, 178.

[32]George E. Chamberlain, "Memorial Address," in "Memorial Addresses on the Life and Character of Harry Lane," *Proceedings in the Senate*, Sixty-fifth Congress, 16 September, 1917 (Washington, 1920), 18-20; *Oregonian*, 21 August, 1914.

[33]*Oregon Journal*, 17 January, 1906.

[34]*Oregon Journal*, 17 January, 1906.

[35]Stewart Holbrook in *Oregonian*, 9 September, 1936.

[36]Fred Merrill quoted in *Oregonian*, 22 March, 1936; Harry Lane to City Council, 24 August, 1908, Harry Lane Papers, OHS.

[37]Guy Talbot, a close friend of Moffat and later president of the Oregon Electric Railway, detailed Moffat's and White's roles in a handwritten account, which Abbot L. Mills, Jr., gave to the author.

[38]Portland City Council Proceedings, 24: 189.

[39]*Oregon Journal*, 20 January, 1906.

[40]Portland City Council Proceedings, 25: 125; miscellaneous documents, Harry Lane Papers.

[41]Portland City Council Proceedings, 25: 127.

[42]Portland City Council Proceedings, 25: 127.

[43]Entry for 13 July, 1907, Portland City Council Proceedings, vol. 26.

[44]Entry for 7 November, 1906, Portland City Council Proceedings, vol. 25.

[45]*Oregon Journal*, 27 May, 1917.

[46]*Oregonian*, 11 and 15 March, 1907.

[47]*Oregonian*, 24 March, 1907.

[48]*Oregonian*, 24 March, 1907; *Oregon Journal*, 1 May, 1907.

[49]*Oregon Journal*, 9 May, 1907.

[50]*Oregonian*, 5 April, 1907.

[51]Morrow in *Oregonian*, 21 August, 1914.

[52]*Oregon Journal*, 1 June, 1907; *Oregonian*, 3 June, 1907.

[53]*Oregonian*, 4 June, 1907.

[54]*Oregonian*, 4 June, 1907; untitled, *Arena Magazine* 30 (August, 1907), 194-95.

[55]Augustus White to Abbot Mills, 4 June, 1907, Abbot L. Mills Papers, UO.

[56]Entry for 3 July, 1907, Portland City Council Proceedings, vol. 26.

CHAPTER 20 FOOTNOTES

[1]Richard L. McCormick, "The Discovery that Business Corrupts Politics: A Reappraisal of the Origins of Progressivism," *American Historical Review* 86 (April, 1981), 268.

[2]*Oregonian*, 19, 20, 24, June, 1906, 13 October, 1906.

[3]*Oregonian*, 20, 23, June, 1906.

[4]*Oregon Journal*, 2 March and 20 July, 1906.

[5]*Oregon Journal*, 7 December, 1906.

[6]*Franchise Reports to the City Auditor* begin in 1913, in Miscellaneous Archives, Portland City Archives.

[7]Abbot Mills to Augustus White, 10 January, 1907, Abbot Mills Papers, UO.

[8]See *First Annual Report of the Railroad Commission of Oregon to the Governor* (Salem, 1908).

[9]Portland City Council Proceedings, 25: 612, Portland City Hall Archives.

[10]Augustus White to Abbot Mills, 22 March, 1907, and Abbot Mills to Augustus White, 11 April, 107, Mills Papers.

[11]1907 Scrapbook, Mills Papers; Orin K. Burrell, *Gold in the Woodpile* (Eugene, 1967), 227.

[12]E. Kimbark MacColl, *The Shaping of a City* (Portland, 1976), 353; Financial Records, James Steel Papers, in possession of the Great Northwest Bookstore, Portland.

[13]James Steel to F. W. Mulkey, 14 February, 1907, Steel Papers. In these uncatalogued papers, beginning in mid-February, 1907, and continuing for the next nine months, are many letters from Steel on Bank Examiner stationery relating to bank loans and municipal gas contracts. Steel sought franchises from Corvallis, Albany, Baker, and St. Johns and the Sellwood district of Portland.

[14]*Oregon Journal*, 21 August, 1907; 1907 Scrapbook, Mills Papers.

[15]*Oregon Journal*, 21 August, 1907; Joseph Gaston, *Portland, Oregon, Its History and Builders* (Portland, 1911), 1: 516.

[16]Augustus White to Abbot Mills, 11 November, 1907, Mills Papers.

[17]James A. Steel to Charles E. Ladd, 2 September, 1907, James A. Steel to E. F. Sox, 20 November, 1907, and James A. Steel to J. F. Yates, 20 November, 1907, Steel Papers.

[18]*Last Will and Testament of James A. Steel*, (Will # 11820), Files of the Probate Department, Multnomah County Clerk's Office; Burrell, *Gold*, 227-29.

[19]E. Kimbark MacColl interview with Edward C. Sammons, 3 April, 1975; unidentified banker in *Telegram*, 2 February, 1908; 1908 scrapbook, Mills Papers.

[20]*Oregon Journal*, 26 December, 1907.

[21]*Oregon Journal*, 26 December, 1907, 22 November, 1907; Burrell, *Gold*, 72-73.

[22]Martin Winch to Simeon G. Reed, 8 June, 1893, Simeon G. Reed Papers, Reed College Library.

[23]*Oregonian*, 30 August, 1905, 21 October, 1905.

[24]*Oregonian*, 22 October, 1905.

[25]*Oregonian*, 5 November, 1905.

[26]*Oregonian*, 23 September, 1906.

[27]Various people who knew William M. Ladd related such comments in conversations with E. Kimbark MacColl. See also William L. Brewster, *William Mead Ladd* (Portland, 1913).

[28]Corporate Records, Ladd & Tilton Papers, 1, OHS.

[29]*Oregonian*, 22 April, 1918; E. Kimbark MacColl, *The Growth of a City* (Portland, 1979), 101. This and earlier paragraphs are also based on the Corporate Records, Ladd & Tilton Papers, 1, OHS.

[30]Carl V. Harris, *Political Power In Birmingham, 1871-1921* (Knoxville, 1977), 269.

[31]R. R. Robley, *Portland Electric Power Company With Its Predecessor Companies, 1860-1935* (Portland, 1935), 119.

[32]MacColl, *Shaping*, 368.

[33]Minutes of the Executive Board, 4: 668, Portland City Hall Archives.

[34]Entry for 13 November, 1908, Minutes of the Executive Board.

[35]Portland City Council Proceedings, 25: 381.

[36]Entries for 9 January, and 13 January, 1909, Portland City Council Proceedings.

[37]Entry for 14 April, 1909, Portland City Council Proceedings, vol. 30.

[38]Portland City Council Proceedings, 30: 379-81.

[39]*Oregon Journal*, 4 May, 1909.

[40]*Oregon Journal*, 1 May, 1909.

[41]Augustus White to Abbot Mills, 6 June, 1909, Gas Company folder, Mills Papers.

[42]Undated *Spectator* clipping in Joseph Simon Papers, OHS.

[43]*Oregonian*, 8 June 1909; Portland City Council Proceedings, 30: 173; McCormick, "Discovery," 272-73.

⁴⁴*Oregonian*, 8 June 1909.

⁴⁵George E. Chamberlain, "Memorial Address," in "Memorial Addresses on the Life and Character of Harry Lane," *Proceedings in the Senate*, Sixty-fifth Congress, 16 September, 1917, (Washington, 1920), 15-16.

⁴⁶Entry for 27 October, 1909, Portland City Council Proceedings, vol. 31.

CHAPTER 21 FOOTNOTES

¹*Oregonian*, 2 January, 1910.

²For Simon's accomplishments, see his scrapbook in Joseph Simon Papers, OHS. *Oregonian*, 2 January, 1910, 26 June, 1910.

³Galen Cranz, *The Politics of Park Design* (Cambridge, 1982), 158, 163; Mansel G. Blackford, "The Lost Dream: Businessmen and City Planning in Portland, Oregon, 1903-1914," *The Western Historical Quarterly* 15 (January, 1984), 46-47; Carl Abbot, *Portland* (Lincoln, 1983), 58. See also William H. Wilson, "J. Horace McFarland and the City Beautiful Movement," *Journal of Urban History* 7 (May, 1981), 316; Mel Scott, *American City Planning Since 1890* (Berkeley, 1969), 45.

⁴*Oregon Journal*, 28 and 29 October, 1909, 7 and 13 November, 1909, 8 December, 1909; *Oregonian*, 13 November, 1909; Abbott, *Portland*, 62; Subscription List to City Beautiful Fund, Mayor's Office Files, 1909, Portland City Archives.

⁵Blackford, "Lost Dream," 47; Abbott, *Portland*, 62.

⁶Entry for 25 May, 1910, Portland City Council Proceedings, 32, Portland City Hall Archives; *Oregonian*, editorial 26 May, 1910; scrapbook, Simon Papers.

⁷See Herbert K. Smith's excerpts from *Report of the Federal Commissioner of Corporations*, in S.B. 50, p. 44.

⁸J. B. Ziegler to Editor, *Oregon Journal*, 6 September, 1912. Ziegler played an active part in promoting the initiative amendment.

⁹*Oregon Journal*, 14 and 19 June, 1910.

¹⁰Waldo Schumacher, "Thirty Years of the People's Rule in Oregon: An Analysis," *Political Science Quarterly* 47 (June, 1932), 243; Warren M. Blankenship, "Progressives and the Progressive Party in Oregon, 1906-1916" (Ph.D. diss., University of Oregon, 1966), 212.

¹¹*Oregon Journal*, 22 June, 1910.

¹²*Oregon Journal*, 22 and 23 June, 1910.

¹³*Oregon Journal*, 22 and 23 June, 1910; George H. Haynes, "People's Rule," *Political Science Quarterly* 26 (September, 1911), 440-41.

¹⁴Burton J. Hendrick, "'Statement No. 1', How the Oregon Democracy, Working under the Direct Primary, Has Destroyed the Political Machine," *McClure's Magazine* 37 (September, 1912), 515.

¹⁵Hendrick, "Statement," 515.

¹⁶Hendrick, "Statement," 516.

¹⁷Hendrick, "Statement," 517-18.

¹⁸Oswald West, "Reminiscences," *OHQ* 52 (September, 1951), 153.

¹⁹*Thirteenth Census of the United States, 1910, Abstract with Supplement for Oregon* (Washington, 1911), 568-87; Joseph Gaston, *Portland, Oregon, Its History and Builders* (Portland, 1911), 1: 614-15; Hendrick, "Statement," 518.

²⁰Entries for 11 January, 1911, and 27 October, 1909, Portland City Council Proceedings, vols. 34 and 31.

²¹*Oregon Journal*, 3 June, 1911.

²²*Oregon Journal*, 3 June, 1911.

²³*Oregonian*, 30 April, 1911.

²⁴*Oregonian*, 8 May, 1911.

²⁵Haynes, "People's Rule," 433.

[26]Richard L. McCormick, "The Discovery that Business Corrupts Politics: A Reappraisal of the Origins of Progressivism," *American Historical Review* 86 (April, 1981), 268.

[27]*Oregon Journal*, 18, 19 and 26 January, 1911; E. Kimbark MacColl, *The Shaping of a City* (Portland, 1976), 164; *Oregonian*, 29 May, 1911.

[28]Entry for July 5, 1911, Portland City Council Proceedings, vol. 36, quoted in Helen Barney, "Sporting Women," *Metropolis*, (Portland State University), March, 1973.

[29]*First Report of the Vice Commission of the City of Portland* (Portland, January, 1912), p. 2, OHS.

[30]*Oregon Journal*, 20 and 23 August, 1912; *Portland Daily News*, 23 August, 1912.

[31]*Oregon Journal*, 24 August, 1912.

[32]*Oregonian*, 23 and 24 August, 1912; *Portland Daily News*, 24 August, 1912.

[33]*Second Report of the Vice Commission of the City of Portland* (Portland, August, 1912); Stewart H. Holbrook, "Portland's Greatest Moral Crusade," *Sunday Oregonian*, 16 August, 1936.

[34]*Oregon Journal*, 26 and 29 August, 1912.

[35]*Oregon Journal*, 3, 4 and 5 September, 1912.

[36]*Oregon Journal*, 7 September, 1912; entries of 9 and 23 October, 1912, Portland City Council Proceedings, vol. 40.

[37]*Oregon Journal*, 31 December, 1910; entry for 20 February, 1913, Portland City Council Proceedings, vol. 42.

[38]Entry for 20 February, 1913, Portland City Council Proceedings, vol. 42.

[39]*Public Service Commission Report, 1919*, "Investigation of Public Utilities," p. 9, Claude R. Lester Papers, UO.

[40]E. Kimbark MacColl, *The Growth of a City* (Portland, 1979), 675; John E. Tuhy, *Sam Hill* (Portland, 1983), 118-21.

[41]Abbot L. Mills to Citizens of Portland, 20 October, 1912, S.B. 56, p. 37.

[42]*Commission of Public Docks — Second Annual Report* (Portland, 1912), 10-11.

[43]Portland City Council Proceedings, 40: 618; *Commission of Public Docks—Third Annual Report* (Portland, 1912), 7-8.

[44]*Oregon Journal*, 6 September and 20 August, 1912.

[45]Abbott, *Portland*, 63; Blackford, "Lost Dreams," 48.

[46]MacColl, *Shaping*, 428; Marshall N. Dana and Ellis Lawrence, eds., *The Greater Portland Plan* (Portland, 1912, reprinted by Portland City Planning Commission, 1976); Paul Pintarich, "Portland Plan of 1912," *Oregonian*, 26 March, 1972.

[47]Frank B. Riley quoted in John Dierdorff, "Backstage with Frank Branch Riley, Regional Troubadour," *OHQ* 74 (September, 1973), 212; Kenneth T. Jackson, *Crabgrass Frontier* (New York, 1985), 159-60.

[48]Arthur D. McVoy, "A History of City Planning in Portland," *OHQ* 46 (March, 1945), 3-21; *Commission of Public Docks — Second Annual Report*, vol. 2; Scott, *American City Planning*, 116. Population comparisons in Robert M. Fogelson, *The Fragmented Metropolis* (Cambridge, 1967), 79.

[49]*Portland Labor Press*, 17 October, 1912.

[50]McVoy, "History of City Planning," 4; Abbott, *Portland*, 66-68.

[51]Blankenship, "Progressives," 277.

[52]Edwin V. O'Hara, *Welfare Legislation for Women and Minors* (Portland, 19 November, 1912); J. G. Shaw, *Edwin Vincent O'Hara, American Prelate* (New York, 1957), 47. See William Graebner, "Federalism in the Progressive Era: A Structural Interpretation of Reform," *Journal of American History* 64 (September, 1977), 341.

[53]Emsie Howard, "She Worked in Sweatshops to Win Oregon Wage Law," *Oregon Labor Press*, 24 July, 1959; Gladys Turley, "Industry and Sister Miriam," *Oregon Journal*, 6 May, 1951.

[54]Graebner, "Federalists," 341; Caroline Gleason, "For Working Women in Oregon," *The Survey* (9 September, 1916), 585.

[55]MacColl, *Shaping*, 465. See *First Annual Report of the Corporations Commissioner to the Governor of the State of Oregon, 30 June, 1914*, (Salem, 1914), 13.

[56]Robert H. Wiebe, *Businessmen and Reform* (Chicago, 1962), 217; Thomas B. Malarkey, Sr., *The Burgess Family and the Malarkey Family, A Reminiscence* (Portland, 1980), 26-28; numerous E. Kimbark MacColl conversations with Dan Malarkey's son, Tom, and with West's daughter, Mrs. Frank McHugh.

[57]Blankenship, "Progressives," 225.

[58]Wiebe, *Businessmen*, 219.

[59]New York Bureau of Municipal Research, *Organization and Business Methods of the City Government of Portland, Oregon* (Portland, April, 1913), 5.

[60]*Oregonian*, 22 April, 1913.

[61]*Oregonian*, 20 April, 1913.

[62]*Oregonian*, 22 April, 1913.

[63]*Oregonian*, 23, 24 and 25 April, 1913; *Oregon Labor Press*, 28 April, 1913.

[64]*Oregonian*, 2 May, 1913.

[65]*Oregonian*, 4 May, 1913; Samuel P. Hays, "The Politics of Reform in Municipal Government in the Progressive Era," *Pacific Northwest Quarterly* 55 (October, 1964), 159, 160, 168.

[66]Blankenship, "Progressives," 234; MacColl, *Shaping*, 446.

[67]Hays, "Politics," 162.

[68]*Oregon Voter*, 25 October, 1924.

[69]G. William Domhoff, *The Powers That Be* (New York, 1979), 199.

[70]Frederic C. Jaher, *The Urban Establishment* (Urbana, 1982), 9-10.

BIBLIOGRAPHY OF
MANUSCRIPTS AND DOCUMENTS

OREGON HISTORICAL SOCIETY, PORTLAND

"The Descendants of Captain and Mrs. John H. Couch, 1811-1948"

Early Oregon Wills: Multnomah County, Oregon

Probated Intestate Estates: Multnomah County, Oregon

John C. Ainsworth Papers

Asahel Bush Papers

City Waterworks Scrapbook

"Committee Report...To The Ministerial Association of Portland"

Henry W. Corbett Papers

Corbett Investment Company Papers

Matthew P. Deady Letters

Equitable Savings and Loan Papers

Henry Failing Papers

First Report of the Vice Commission of the City of Portland (Portland, January, 1912)

Glisan-Minott Family Papers

Franklin P. Griffith Papers

Henry Hazen Papers

William Lair Hill Papers

Ben Holladay Papers

Peter Kerr Letters

William M. King Papers

Harry Lane Papers

William S. Ladd Papers

Ladd Estate Papers

Ladd Family and W.S. Ladd and Company Papers

Ladd & Tilton Bank Papers

Land, Miscellaneous Papers

Charles Lanman Papers

Cicero H. Lewis Papers

Daniel H. Lownsdale Papers

Miscellaneous Associations, Institutions, Etc. Papers

Chester Moores Papers

Multnomah County Records Management File

James W. Nesmith Papers
Pacific Bridge Company Papers

Politics, Miscelleneous Papers

Port of Portland Papers

Portland Hotel Records

Provisional and Territorial Government Papers, Nos. 4509, 4510, 4512, 7170, 9803

Henry E. Reed Papers

Second Report of the Vice Commission of the City of Portland (Portland, August, 1912)

Ben Selling Papers

Joseph Simon Papers

Margery Hoffman Smith Papers

Benjamin Stark Papers

Charles F. Swigert Papers

David P. Thompson Papers

Uncataloged Documents

Oswald West Papers

BANCROFT LIBRARY, UNIVERSITY OF
CALIFORNIA, BERKELEY

Hubert H. Bancroft Papers:

Van B. DeLashmutt, "Dictation"

Edward F. Failing, "Dictation of Edward F. Failing Relating to His Father, Josiah Failing"

Henry Failing, "Draft of Biographical Sketch of J. Failing With Notes on H. Failing"

Bernard Goldsmith, "Dictation"

William S. Ladd, "Dictation"

Cicero H. Lewis, "Dictation"

Cicero H. Lewis, "Draft of Biographical Sketch"
Amos A. Lovejoy, "Founding of Portland"

John McCraken, "Dictation"

Phillip A. Marquam, "Dictation"

James B. Montgomery, "Dictation"

Oregon Steam Navigation Papers

Francis W. Pettigrove, "Oregon in 1843"

Simeon G. Reed, "Biographical Sketch"

Joseph Simon, "Dictation"

Lewis M. Starr, "Dictation"

Robert R. Thompson, "Account of My Life"

PORTLAND ARCHIVES AND RECORD CENTER
(FORMERLY CITY OF PORTLAND ARCHIVES),
PORTLAND

Auditor's Office, Personal Business Files of W.S. Caldwell

Charter Amendments—Charter Summaries, Box 1

Mayor's Correspondence File, 1905

Minutes of the Board of Police Commissioners

Minutes of the Proceedings of the City Council, City of Portland

Miscellaneous Portland City Council Papers

Park Bureau Files, 1870-1871, Boxes 15, 17, 20

PORTLAND CITY HALL ARCHIVES (SOME SINCE MOVED TO PORTLAND ARCHIVES AND RECORD CENTER)

Charter of the City of Portland, 1902 City Council Proceedings and Ordinances

East Portland City Council Minutes

Laws and Ordinances of the City of Portland, 1892

Mayor Message and Annual Report, 1885-1905

Mayor's Office Files, 1909

Minutes of the Executive Board

Minutes of the Board of Police Commissioners

Minutes of the Board of Public Works, vols. 1, 2

Miscellaneous Archives

Petitions Folder — Miscellaneous

Portland City Council Documents, Boxes 4, 20

Portland City Council Papers

Portland City Council Proceedings, vols. 3, 8, 18, 20, 23, 31, 32, 32, 34, 40, 42

Records of the Proceedings of the Common Council of the City of Portland, abbrev. form, vol. 7

Records of the Proceedings of the Water Committee, Portland, vols. 1, 2

Revised General Ordinances, City of Portland, 1905

PRIVATELY HELD MANUSCRIPTS

"Abstract of Titles," Lots 2 and 3, Block 11, Tilton's Addition, Title Guarantee & Trust Company, Portland, 1926, in possession of Thomas O. Smith, Portland

"Abstract of Titles, property of F.F. and B.C. Pittock," Block 115, Grover's Addition, Multnomah County, 1926, in possession of Robert Autrey, Portland

"Speech by Robin Angus at The Ivory and Sime International Investment Seminar," Gallane, Scotland, October 15, 1984, in possession of E. Kimbark MacColl, Portland

Henry L. Pittock to George T. Meyers of Portland Oregon, October 17, 1893 and Thomas Dryer's list of debts as of April 1, 1860, and Henry Pittock Papers, in possession of Henry Pittock II, Cannon Beach, OR

Dorothy O. Johansen, "Early History of Reed College," in possession of Dorothy O. Johansen, Portland

Herman C. Leonard, "A Letter of Certification," March 16, 1907, in possession of Lady James Mac-Donald, Portland

James Steel Papers, in possession of the Great Northwest Bookstore, Portland

John Wilson, "Chapter of Autobiography," 1921, typed ms. from 1889 original, in possession of James B. Robertson, Ashland, John Wilson Papers, in possession of Susan Wilson Gallagher, Portland

UNIVERSITY OF OREGON LIBRARY, EUGENE

John C. Ainsworth Papers

Jonathan Bourne, Jr. Papers

Cayuse, Yakima and Rogue River War Papers

Corbett-Failing Papers

Claude R. Lester Papers

Abbot L. Mills Papers

OREGON STATE LIBRARY, SALEM

W.P.A., Clips, Series 1, Box 20

W.P.A., Oregon Historical Records Survey, 1936

MULTNOMAH COUNTY CLERK'S OFFICE, PORTLAND

Assessment Roll, 1895, vol. 11

Files of the Probate Department

BUSH HOUSE, SALEM

Asahel Bush Papers

REED COLLEGE LIBRARY, PORTLAND

Simeon G. Reed Papers

FEDERAL RECORDS CENTER, SEATTLE

City Claims in Oregon, Box 49

FIRST INTERSTATE BANK, PORTLAND

Stock Registration for the Security Savings and Trust Company

COLUMBIA RIVER MARITIME MUSEUM, ASTORIA

Marine Records of Oregon, 1850-1971, comp. F. J. Smith (1917), on exhibit

INDEX